THE CODE
OF KINGS

*The Language of Seven Sacred Maya
Temples and Tombs*

LINDA SCHELE
AND PETER MATHEWS

PHOTOGRAPHS BY
MacDuff Everton and Justin Kerr

SCRIBNER

SCRIBNER
1230 Avenue of the Americas
New York, NY 10020

DESIGNED BY ERICH HOBBING

Set in Adobe Garamond

Manufactured in the United States of America

10 9 8 7 6 5 4 3 2 1

Library of Congress Cataloging-in-Publication Data
Schele, Linda.
The code of kings: the language of seven sacred Maya temples and tombs / Linda Schele and Peter Mathews;
photographs by MacDuff Everton and Justin Kerr.
p.   cm.
Includes bibliographical references and index.
1. Mayas—Religion. 2. Maya architecture. 3. Maya sculpture. 4. Sacred space—Mexico.
5. Sacred space—Central America. 6. Maya languages—Writing. 7. Names, Maya.
8. Inscriptions, Maya. 9. Mexico—Antiquities. 10. Central America—Antiquities.
I. Mathews, Peter, date. II. Title.
F1435.3.A6S34   1998
972.81'016—dc21   97-36409
CIP

ISBN 0-684-80106-X

Dedicated to
ELIZABETH POLK BENSON
and
JANET MATHEWS
and
BARBARA KERR
and
MARY HEEBNER

Contents

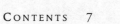

Acknowledgments

We want to express our thanks to the many people who helped us in the process of researching and writing this book. First we acknowledge the very special help that we were given by our fellow scholars who shared their insights with us and most of all provided information to us that only they had. Without their help this book would not have the same shape it now does.

Peter Harrison read the Tikal chapter and corrected erroneous attributions that we had drawn from other sources of information. He shared his understanding of the history of the Central Acropolis freely and in great detail. Federico Fahsen did the same for an early version of the same chapter and broke us free of a strategy of presentation that did not work as well as the present one does. Jeff Kowalski shared his resources on Uxmal with us and most of all the remarkable insights he has gained in long years of work on the site. He also is working on the Nunnery Quadrangle and will eventually publish a far more technical analysis of its history and interpretation. We highly recommend his work on Uxmal and the Puuk to interested readers. Steve Whittington read the chapter on Iximche' and shared his work on the skeletons that had been excavated by George Guillemin. He also corrected several misapprehensions we had derived from the published literature. Gordon Willey shared his insights into Seibal with us and generously made available to us photographs of the plaster sculpture fragments of Structure A-3. We particularly wish to acknowledge the remarkable generosity and openness of these scholars, who shared their ongoing and unpublished work with us without reservation. This spirit is what makes our field work.

Logan Wagner and his students from the School of Architecture at the University of Texas, Austin, provided us with invaluable information and drawings of the buildings of Chich'en Itza and Uxmal. Logan has spent years measuring, photographing, and thinking about architecture throughout Mesoamerica. He enthusiastically shared his expertise and resources with us.

Merle Greene Robertson helped us with photographs and drawings from Palenque, and the CD-ROMs with her rubbings allowed us to make new and more accurate drawings of material from Chich'en Itza, Seibal, Dos Pilas, and other sites

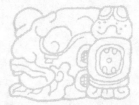

included in this book. George Andrews kindly made both published and unpublished drawings available to us that enriched the chapters on Palenque and Uxmal in very important ways. We also used aerial photographs from the William Ferguson archive at the Department of Art and Art History of the University of Texas.

Tanya Adams, director of the Centro de Investigaciones Regionales de Mesoamerica (CIRMA), gave us access to George Guillemin's archives and photographs stored at CIRMA. Allen Christenson read the manuscript and shared his insights into the K'iche'an histories recorded in the ethnohistorical sources from the Guatemalan highlands. Ruth Krochock, Erik Boot, Linnea Wren, Lynn Foster, and Peter Keeler of the Chich'en study group at the Texas Meetings were participants in and catalysts for many of the new interpretations we present on Chich'en Itza. David Freidel argued with us for many hours over the history of northern Yukatan and Chich'en Itza.

We are particularly grateful to William Fash, Barbara Fash, Ricardo Agurcia, and the Instituto Hondureño de Antropología e Historia for the use of drawings and photographs from Copan. Barbara kindly agreed to let us ink some of her field drawings for this publication. David Sedat, Julie Miller, Robert Sharer, Alfonso Morales, Jeff Stomper, and others in the Copan project have engaged in endless hours of discussion and debate over the history of Copan and Waxaklahun-Ubah-K'awil's career. In similar fashion, we have relied on Matthew Looper's work to understand K'ak'-Tiliw, the rival ruler of Quirigua.

We especially acknowledge Elizabeth Carmichael and John Mack of the British Museum for giving us extensive access to the museum's extraordinary collection of casts made by Alfred P. Maudslay in the late nineteenth century. David Noden spent days with us as we worked to check drawings against this critically important archival record. He was very patient with us in our quest to leave no cast unturned. This collection of casts preserves remarkably important detail and sculptural information that has been lost or diminished on the original objects due to erosion and time.

Sue Giles of the City of Bristol Museums and Art Gallery gave us access to the archives and magnificent paintings of Adela Breton. Adela Breton's work, like Maudslay's, preserves information on paintings and sculptures of Chich'en Itza that have been lost or damaged since she worked there.

Khristaan Villela hunted many of the older resources for us and saved us countless hours retrieving and copying nineteenth-century publications on the buildings we studied. Matthew Looper, Mark Van Stone, John Montgomery, Heather Pierson, Ed Barnhardt, and Julie Acuff have contributed significantly to our field research, and a cadre of students from the School of Architecture of the University of Texas helped us prepare the many drawings included in this volume. The archivist of the drawings collection of the School of Architecture gave us time and cooperation. Armando Anaya also provided help during the research for this book. We thank Helene Jorgenson and Bonnie Meyer for letting us use their photographs. In addition, we would like to thank Annette Morris for her thoughtful suggestions on improving the manuscript.

While in the field, we were also helped by many people. Alfonso Escobedo gave a rest stop and home away from home in Mérida, provided cars and contacts for our field trips, and accompanied us on many adventures as we visited sites in Yukatan. Marco Antonio Tello did the same for us in Guatemala. Both of these people are good friends who helped with their humor and enthusiasm as much as with cars and hotels. Antonio Bustillos, gerente of the Hacienda Uxmal, helped us at both Chich'en Itza and Uxmal, while Antonio Ortíz made our stay at the Jungle Lodge in Tikal both pleasant and successful. Others who offered help at critical times included Frank and Judy Saul, Norman Hammond, Nikolai Grube, Simon Martin, Federico Fahsen, Marion Hatch, Jeff Braswell, Nora England, Mary Dell Lucas and Rebecca Orozco of Far Horizons, and the members of Peter's and Linda's 1995 and 1996 tours.

We want to thank Armstrong Photolab, whose workers developed MacDuff's film, made duplicate slides for all of us at a great discount, and provided a color darkroom rental where MacDuff made all the prints. To Cornell Schorle, who designed the Noblex panoramic camera. The lens barrel actually rotates and provides an approximately 145-degree view which corresponds to what the human eye sees with peripheral vision. The panoramic camera has existed since the 1800s; what Cornell accomplished was designing a camera that could work and also be hand-held in the field and withstand the rigors and elements of shooting in places such as the jungles of Mesoamerica. To Hilario Hiler and Charles Demangate, who have shared ideas, adventures, and dreams with MacDuff for over twenty-five years of working together in Yukatan, and El Circo Magico Modelo, the regional family-owned Yukatekan circus that provided MacDuff access to so many of the small villages throughout the peninsula.

Accugraphics of Austin, Texas, also did miraculous things in reducing our huge drawings of the architecture to small-scale Velox prints without losing quality. We much appreciate their craftsmanship and attention to our specialized requirements.

Linda received support for a semester of research and writing from the University of Texas Research Institute and also did some of the research for this book while serving as the Bernard Visiting Professor at Williams College. She also used the resources of the John D. Murchison Regents Professorship in Art of the University of Texas to pay for travel, field expenses, drawings, and other activities while writing and researching this book. Peter received support during a sabbatical leave and also a Killam Resident Fellowship from the University of Calgary.

Finally and most important was the support and encouragement of Maria Guarnaschelli of Scribner. She gave us the chance to write this book. Scott Moyers became our editor and nursed the book through its editing and production phases. He often surprised us with his suggestions, and his insights added immeasurably to our efforts to make this book accessible to nonspecialists.

CHAPTER 1

Pyramid-Mountains and Plaza-Seas

Maya scholars have participated in a revolution. The past four decades have seen the decipherment of the Maya hieroglyphic writing system and the reading of the history of one of the great civilizations of the world. This decipherment has recovered the names of kings, their families, members of their courts, and artists, artisans, and builders who served them. Growing understanding of Maya imagery has combined with increasingly subtle decipherments of the glyphs to give us new insights into court life, religious ideas, and the politics of the time, as well as the economies and social mechanisms that allowed Maya civilization to flourish. Excavations conducted by archaeologists not only have tested the "truth" of these histories in the ground, but also have sought to understand better the lifeways of the ancient Maya people, from the most exalted to the lowliest members of society.

As epigraphers who have participated in this revolution, we find that our personal relationship to Maya cities has changed forever. We can't now walk among the buildings without thinking about who built them and why. We now consider them not just as objects of beauty, but also as political and religious statements aimed at an audience of nobles and commoners. Maya buildings were instruments of state that registered Maya identity, religion, and history.

How different it is to walk through a ruined city when it has become a historical place—to "read" a building and to know who looks out from a sculpted portrait. The ruins cease to be anonymous places admired only for their beauty and mystery. Instead, they become the works of people who had names and motivations that we can understand, even from our distant points of view. And the buildings and images created by these once-living people become their voices, telling us something about the agendas that guided their decisions, the larger political framework that conditioned those agendas, and the understanding of the world that gave meaning to both.

We have shared our vision of Maya cities as historical places with people who have toured with us over the years and in public lectures. When we were thinking about what to do in this book, we realized that many more people who visit Maya places and who love Maya art and archaeology might be interested in seeing their architecture through the lens of history. We wanted to show people how to "read" Maya political and religious art and architecture.

In designing this book, we deliberately picked some of the most famous buildings in Maya archaeology, partially because, famous though they are, they remain virtually anonymous to the people who visit them. Three are in Mexico, three in Guatemala, and one in Honduras, and we selected seven different kinds of buildings to serve as archetypes. These seven are a palace and family shrine center, a pyramid-temple and tomb, a plaza with stelae (upright, carved monuments), a building designed to celebrate the end of an important Maya cycle of time, a court for playing ball, a conjuring house and war monument, and, finally, a conquest period capital from the Guatemala highlands. Although there are other types of Maya buildings, these seven constitute the elements that the ancient Maya considered necessary to charge a city with religious and political meaning. Most cities had all these types of buildings, although their styles varied widely from place to place.

We have used the nuances of these buildings to explore the way Maya architecture worked and how the Maya generated sacred space within their cities through the use of buildings and the symbolic information contained in them. We have designed the book to operate on multiple levels. On one level, it serves as a guided tour through the buildings. Much of the information necessary to understand the layout and basic contents of each building can be gleaned from the maps and illustrations alone. We have included a map of each building with its components designated by letters or numbers.[1] We have used the same designations as headings in the descriptive sections of the text. Readers can follow our suggested path through the building or they can go to any part of it by finding the section that corresponds to the letter on the building plan.

The texts discuss each building in progressively greater detail, moving from the general to the specific, so that readers can choose the amount of information they wish to consume and skip over the more detailed discussions when they so desire. The notes provide the scholarly background to our interpretations and add more detailed information to our discussions. We have also included a glossary of gods and supernaturals at the end of the book to serve as a quick reference for those who are less familiar with the Maya world.

MAYA SOCIETY IN TIME AND SPACE

The Maya lived in a large cultural area that archaeologists call Mesoamerica (Fig. 1.1). Encompassing the region from the deserts of northern Mexico to the east-

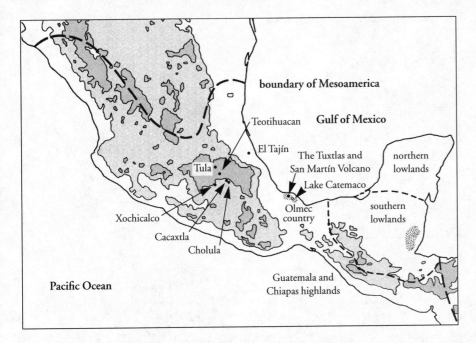

Fig. 1.1. Map of Mesoamerica showing topography over 2,000 and 3,000 feet.

ern third of Honduras and El Salvador, Mesoamerica refers less to geography than to the societies and cultural traditions that occupied this land until the arrival of Europeans. Like the people of Europe, Mesoamericans shared definitions about how to grow and distribute food, what constituted government, and how the world worked, both on the mundane and the cosmological level.

The land of the Maya occupies the eastern third of Mesoamerica, in what is now southern Mexico, Guatemala, Belize, and western Honduras (Fig. 1.2). This area is covered by ruined cities from a cultural tradition that was 2,500 years old when the Spanish conquered the inhabitants and forever changed their world. The descendants of the Maya who built those ruined cities today number in the millions and speak over two dozen related Maya languages. They communicate with the world over the Internet, yet also live in direct contact with the beliefs and understanding of the world that lay at the heart of the cities built by their ancestors millennia before.

The topography of the Maya landscape varies enormously, from the volcanic mountains that form a spine along the Pacific coast to the tropical-forest lowlands that comprise the northern two-thirds of the Yukatan peninsula. Rivers cut through the mountains, draining into the Gulf of Mexico via the Grijalva and Usumacinta Rivers and to the Caribbean by the Motagua and numerous smaller rivers. The swampy southern lowlands receive up to 120 inches of rain a year, while the northern lowlands are drier and have no rivers. There in the north, people get their water from cenotes (*tz'onot* in Maya), sinkholes that dot the limestone terrain of Yukatan. The high-canopy forest that covers the south-

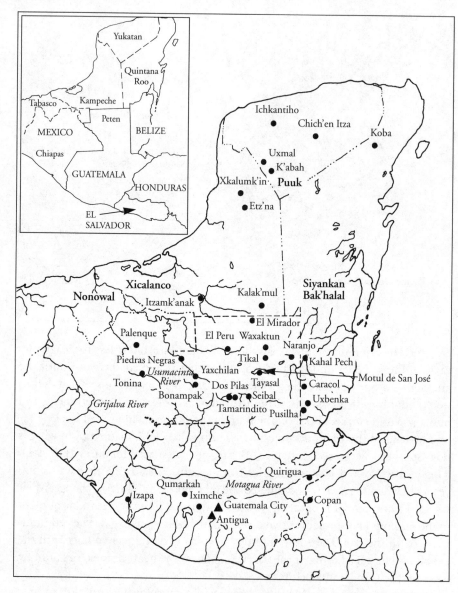

Fig. 1.2.
The Maya region.

ern lowlands transforms into pine forest in the highlands and into low, scrub forest in the north.

Archaeologists divide the later history of Mesoamerica into three great periods—the Preclassic (1500 B.C.–A.D. 200), the Classic (A.D. 200–910), and the Postclassic (A.D. 910–1524). The first of these periods, the **Preclassic,** saw the rise of the Olmec, the first great civilization that modern scholars recognize in Mesoamerica. Occupying the swampy lowlands surrounding the Tuxtla volcanos in southern Veracruz, the Olmec built the first cities in a landscape that can be described as mountains surrounded by swamps. This extraordinary people created the first kingdoms and developed the templates of worldview and political symbolism that formed the basis of all subsequent societies in Mesoamerica. In a real sense, they invented civilized life in this region of the world.

By 1000 B.C., the Maya had begun to build villages in the mountainous highlands and lowland forests of eastern Mesoamerica. These early villagers built houses that were much like those still used by their descendants today. They used pole frames and thatched roofs to construct houses with a single room. In some regions, villagers favored houses with oval floor plans, while in others they preferred rectangular forms. The center of the house was always a hearth made of three stones set in a triangle to allow wood to be fed into the fire while cooking. The hearth was the center of family life, where women prepared food and did the work of the household. Men worked in agricultural fields called *kol,* where they planted maize, beans, squash, and chile. They planted fruit trees of many kinds around their houses and near their cornfields.

Households consisted of several related adults, and could include couples with young children, adolescents, young adults, and grandparents. Large families provided the people required for farming, a labor-intensive activity that involved yearly cycles of preparing the fields, planting, cultivating, and harvesting. Moreover, large families could help in other activities, such as the building and refurbishing of houses, kitchens, and storerooms, the collection of firewood, the preparation of food, and the repair and maintenance of tools. More specialized crafts included weaving and decorating cloth, the manufacture of tools and household objects of all sorts, and the making of pottery. The Maya could use these products in their own households or exchange them for other goods and services within their communities. As their families grew, villagers built additional houses around courtyards to form compounds. Four houses around a courtyard became one of the characteristic forms of Maya architecture.

Like other Mesoamerican peoples, the Maya adopted Olmec innovations in symbolic imagery and social institutions. By 500 B.C., the Maya began to build cities in the lowland forests and in the highland mountains. They amplified the traditional layout of the family compound into a square plaza surfaced with plaster and surrounded on three or four sides by pyramids with temples on top. They used tamped earth to build their pyramids in the highlands, and earth and rubble in the lowlands. Some of these very early structures are the largest ever built by the Maya. People flying over them today often think they are natural hills rising above the forest canopy. In fact, the ancients did conceive of their pyramids as mountains rising out of the surrounding swamps and forest. They began to surface them with imagery modeled in plaster to give them meaning and to create sacred environments in which history, politics, and urban life unfolded.

Early kings, called *ahaw,* also began to portray themselves on stone monuments erected in the plazas at the feet of their pyramid-mountains. During the last third of the Preclassic period, the idea of writing developed as a way of describing who was shown on these monuments, as well as when and where the actions occurred. This was the beginning of history for the Maya.

During the **Classic** period (A.D. 200–910), the number of kingdoms grew rapidly, to as many as sixty at the height of lowland Maya civilization in the eighth century. Beginning in the fifth century, these kingdoms organized themselves into great alliances headed by the kingdoms known today as Tikal and Kalak'mul.[2] Some of the great cities of the Preclassic period, such as El Mirador, had collapsed, while others, like Tikal, grew into political and economic dominance. The Maya of Tikal and other cities came into powerful contact with the central Mexican city of Teotihuacan during the early part of the Classic period. The mechanism of this exchange is still a matter of debate, but its effect is not. The Maya adopted imagery and an artistic style from the Teotihuacanos that became intimately associated with warfare and the symbolism of the "Place of Reeds," one of the central elements in myths of origin that dominated Mesoamerican history.

While the Maya kingdoms enjoyed a high degree of sovereignty, their political fortunes often depended on the alliances to which they belonged. From the sixth century onward, this system of alliances and the rivalry between them dominated Maya politics and economics. The old adage "The enemy of my enemy is my friend" is highly applicable to this period of Maya history.

Ancient Maya kings rarely alluded explicitly to economic affairs in their public inscriptions. However, we can surmise much about ancient Maya economy through the archaeological record, the images, and the inscriptions left to us. Tribute was one of the primary means to collect goods and labor for redistribution within communities of all sizes. It was a fact of life, rather like our own taxation system. Lesser nobles and lineage heads paid tribute to their overlords in the form of raw materials, manufactured goods, and labor. Farmers might also pay tribute through goods they produced, but even more likely, they paid by providing labor on building projects in the urban centers, service on the farms of their kings and lords, or in military service. The economy of every kingdom was administered strategically by the king and his court, but even they paid tribute to their overlords within the large system of alliances. At this higher level, tribute could also be paid in the form of raw materials, such as minerals, wood, and sacred stone; manufactured goods, such as cloth and jewelry; labor for regional projects, such as the construction of causeways between sites; and military service.

Victory in battle often resulted in the loser's obligation to pay tribute to the winner. This could include goods and service, but in addition, artists and artisans, as well as laborers and captured soldiers from losing sites, could become commodities that benefited the winners. In some situations, the local elites retained their positions after defeat, but they became tribute vassals of the winners.[3]

The Maya calendar provided dates that were used to time markets and fairs in which the Maya carried out their business transactions. Some of these dates had well-known, widely shared significance from Maya mythology and religion, so that everyone knew about them. Others had importance on a regional or local level, and could involve not only religion, but important dynastic celebrations as well. These festivals were a major part of Maya life throughout history. Nobles from allied kingdoms used them as opportunities to visit one another and to negotiate broader economic arrangements.

Merchants operating beyond the borders of their kingdoms became economic and political extensions of their kings. Their patron was God L, a powerful god who destroyed the previous Creation by flood, sat on the first throne to be set up in the present Creation, and operated as a god of warriors and merchants. Such royal business was so economically vital that the merchants involved in it were high nobles and even members of the royal household. Using the metaphor of pilgrimage and alliance, merchants traveled to the great festivals of neighbors and distant states that controlled strategic goods. Such merchants could function as state ambassadors bearing "gifts" to royal neighbors and allies, or they could spy out the land in preparation for conquest.

The Maya used commodities both in their raw state and as worked objects for money.[4] These currencies included jade and other green stones; flint and obsidian, in both worked and unworked forms; other precious stones and minerals; spondylus (spiny oyster) shells; cacao beans; lengths of cotton cloth, both in plain weave and made into clothes; spices; measures of sea salt; birds and their feathers; animal pelts; forest products such as dyes, resins, incense, and rubber; wood in both worked and unworked form; and ceramics, especially beautifully painted elite wares. People at all levels of society used these currencies within their communities as well as in the markets and fairs. Farmers and villagers could use their crops and handicrafts to barter for or buy other goods for use in their daily lives or in special rituals, such as marriages, funerals, and house dedications.

People throughout Mesoamerica wore these currencies as jewelry and clothing to display the wealth and enterprise of their families. These currencies were in wide demand throughout the Mesoamerican world, so that Maya kingdoms traded the specialties of their area—such as cotton, cacao, tropical birds and their feathers, rubber, special woods, shells, etc.—over long distances to obtain commodities that were not available locally. This access to materials and goods from far-distant places may have been negotiated by local lords, but the alliance structures very probably facilitated these international relations with kingdoms in, for example, the southern highlands of Guatemala. We suspect that Tikal had trade agreements and perhaps a political alliance with Teotihuacan in central Mexico. These long-distance relationships were of crucial importance to the economic well-being of every state. Maya kings gathered prestige through the successful activity of obtaining goods from distant places and distributing them among their vassal lords and allies.[5] These lesser lords in turn distributed the goods to their constituents in the form of gifts or exchanges. A portion of these commodities could filter down into the general everyday transactions of the villagers and farmers.

One result of the competition for territory, resources, and tribute was a cataclysmic series of wars between the competing alliances led by Tikal and Kalak'mul that began in the sixth century. In the archaeology, kingdoms that won wars during these conflicts show enormous growth in population, in wealth at all social levels, in access to foreign goods, and in extensive building programs. Losers usually show the reverse, but being a winner or loser was rarely permanent. Reversals of fortunes and the resulting change in economic status were commonplace.

By A.D. 700, these wars had resulted in the multiple sackings of major cities like Palenque and Tikal. One of the major effects of these wars was a series of migrations, probably consisting in large part of male nobles and soldiers displaced by the wars or seeking their fortunes elsewhere. A series of migrations from the south to the northern lowlands eventually led to the founding of Chich'en Itza. In A.D. 800, these outsiders, who were called the Itza, and the older kingdoms in the north established a confederation. These migrations may also have affected central Mexico and the establishment of kingdoms like Xochicalco and Cacaxtla in the wake of Teotihuacan's destruction in the mid-seventh century.

The Classic period ended with a general political collapse in much of the Maya region, although in some areas, such as northern Belize and Yukatan, many communities survived without a break until modern times. The final phase of precolumbian history—the **Postclassic**—lasted from A.D. 910 until the Spanish conquests of Guatemala in 1524 and Yukatan in 1542. Events during the last decades of the Classic period became the legends of origin for Postclassic kingdoms. In the north after the collapse of Chich'en Itza, the area was dominated by an alliance centered on the city of Mayapan. Although the population of the southern lowlands never again achieved the levels of the Classic period, large alliances centered on Itzamk'anak and Tayasal, the capital of the Itza, endured into the century after the conquest. In the south, the K'iche' Maya forged an empire by conquest and diplomacy that dominated most of the highlands until late in the fifteenth century. Although the capital cities of these empires and kingdoms may seem unimpressive when compared to the great Classic cities, these Postclassic kingdoms exercised political and economic dominance that was at least as effective as that of their predecessors.

MAYA HIEROGLYPHIC WRITING AND HISTORY

During the nineteenth century, travelers began to penetrate the forests that had regrown over the ancient ruins after the Spanish conquest. They brought back intriguing tales of lost cities and ruined temples. These travelers published drawings and photographs (Fig. 1.3) in books, some of which became bestsellers of

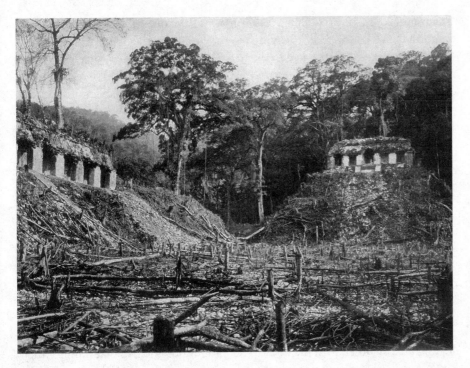

Fig. 1.3. A photograph of the palace and the Temple of Inscriptions at Palenque taken by Alfred Maudslay in 1891. This is what Maya architecture looks like before it is excavated and restored.

their day. By the end of the century, scientific expeditions began to excavate the ancient buildings and restore them to something of their former glory. Today millions of pilgrims from all over the world come to see these restored Maya cities and to understand at least a little about the people who built them.

Palenque, one of the most beautiful of the ancient Maya cities, was a focus of these early explorers from the beginning of modern interest in the Maya. Because its buildings, sculptures, and inscriptions survived remarkably intact, Palenque has played a central role in our thinking about the Maya for the past 150 years.

Peter and Linda also fell under Palenque's spell when we first walked among its plazas and temples. Even though Palenque had been so central to European ideas about the Maya, it was still an anonymous place when we attended the First Palenque Round Table, a now-famous 1973 conference that led to critical breakthroughs in the understanding of the city's history.[6] Before this conference, the ruins were mute, more admired for their mystery than for the greatness of the people who had built them. In less than a week all that changed.

We remember the moment it all happened. We had been working together during the conference, but on the last day we were asked to see if we could find some more history in Palenque's hieroglyphic texts. We were lucky because drawings had been published of the many inscriptions the people of Palenque had put in their buildings. In three hours, we amplified our understanding of the lives of seven kings, so that a real history of Palenque began to emerge. More important, we connected these kings to the buildings they had commissioned and the messages incorporated in them.

In many ways, this conference was a turning point in the field of Maya hieroglyphic studies. Using the work of past scholars, we had available to us knowledge of how the Maya used their glyphs to spell words. We also knew they recorded history as their main subject matter, and we knew they used the writing system to record spoken language, not just as mnemonic devices. Working with many other people,[7] we began to paraphrase whole texts from Palenque and construct an understanding of what the rulers of that city had said to their people in their public monuments.

The rich and expressive script used by the Maya in their writing system could faithfully record every nuance of sound, meaning, and grammatical structure in their language. Scribes could spell words with single signs called *logographs,* with phonetic signs representing syllables, or with combinations of both. For example, *witz,* a Maya word for "mountain," could be written with a picture of a convoluted stone or personified as a mountain monster (Fig. 1.4). However, the Maya had other words meaning "hill" or "mountain," including *puuk, mul, buk'tun,* and *tzuk.* To avoid confusion, Maya scribes attached syllabic signs to logographs in order to indicate how to pronounce them. For example, they could attach the syllabic sign *wi* to the front of the "mountain" logograph, giving the spelling *wi-witz.* Since no other word for "mountain" began with *wi,* people knew that here they should read *witz,* instead of any of the other alternatives. Since these phonetic signs represented the sounds of syllables, the Maya could spell the word using only phonetic signs, thus eliminating the logograph altogether. The system they devised used two syllable signs to spell a word composed of a consonant-vowel-consonant. For example, they spelled *witz* with the sign *wi* combined with *tzi* to form *wi-tz(i).* The final vowel in this kind of spelling was not pronounced.

The unsurpassed calligraphic elegance of this writing system derives from its origins as a painted script. No matter the medium they used—whether limestone, jade, shell, bone, wood, or paper—Maya scribes never lost the original painterly grace of their hieroglyphs. They played with the graphics of the system, always looking for new and innovative ways to write their words. They had many signs to record the same sounds, and each of these could be written in a plain form or personified as a human or animal. Maya scribes used this system to record the history of their leaders, the names and ownership of objects, the names and actions of gods and supernaturals, the rituals that filled their lives, divination and prophecy, and their understanding of the ancestral past and present. Most particularly for this book, they recorded the names of their buildings, as well as who owned them, and the rituals used to dedicate them.

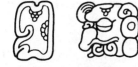

witz as a logograph

wi-witz
syllable sign + logograph

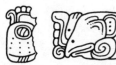

wi-tz(i), syllabic spelling
of *witz*

Fig. 1.4. Different ways of spelling *witz,* the word for "mountain," in the Maya hieroglyphic writing system.

MAYA ARCHITECTURE

Experiencing Maya architecture can be disconcerting for people who grew up with the European tradition all around them. European architecture focuses for the most part on interior space. In Maya public architecture, the operational spaces are the plazas and courtyards that are surrounded by buildings. The small, dark interiors, especially of the temples, were places where the gods, ancestors, and a few authorized lords visited. Even in the palaces, the public stayed in the courtyards, where they were the audience for the dances and processions that were at the heart of Maya rituals and festivals. Maya architects designed their buildings to encompass motion and performance so that they operated like stage sets in which drama and ritual unfolded.

Maya kingdoms consisted of forests, farmlands, hamlets, and towns, all ruled from capital cities. Using settlement surveys, archaeologists have shown that the Maya lived in and around their cities and towns in dense and permanent settlements. Adding the population living in the hinterlands and smaller towns to that of the capitals gives population numbers ranging from twenty thousand up to a hundred thousand, and perhaps more for the largest kingdoms.

Decipherments of the Maya hieroglyphic texts and archaeological investigations at places like Tikal, Copan, Caracol, and Dos Pilas have given us a much better understanding of how Maya political geography worked. In the inscriptions (Fig. 1.5), "emblem" glyphs named the kingdoms that dotted the political landscape, and within these kingdoms there were locations identified by place names.[8] Kingdoms were also subdivided into "provinces," or *tzuk*. For example, Tikal had thirteen *tzuk*, while Naranjo had seven. The geographic size of a kingdom did not necessarily correspond to its importance. Younger kingdoms on the periphery, like Palenque and Copan, were geographically larger than the older central kingdoms, but they certainly were not more powerful.

The towns and hamlets surrounding the capital cities could have different names and were often ruled by secondary nobles obligated to the high kings. For example, the texts call the kingdom of Palenque *Bak*, or "Bone," while the capital city was known as *Lakam Ha*, "Big Water." Tortuguero, a large town to the west of *Lakam Ha*, also used the *Bak* kingdom name, although it had its own rulers who conducted their own wars, probably under the authority of the Palenque king.

All Maya cities, including the towns, had sacred precincts near the center. Sometimes walls surrounded these areas to separate them from adjacent residential zones. Often a causeway, called a *sak beh*, or "white road," led from outlying areas into these centers. At Copan, the Maya erected a special stela to mark the entrance into their sacred precinct. This monument presents a text arranged in the pattern of a mat (*pop* in Maya) to people arriving on the *sak beh*. *Popol*, or "mat," was one of the words used for "a place of assembly," "community," and

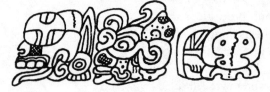

K'ul Mutul Ahaw
"Holy Tikal Lord"

tan kun Mutul
"in the seat of Mutul"

oxlahun tzuk Mutulnal
"13 provinces *Mutul* place"

  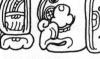

"it happened at the Bearded Jaguar God sky seat"
This is a Tikal toponym.

K'ul Bak Ahaw
"Holy Palenque Lord"

Lakam Ha Kan Kun
"Big Water Sky Seat,"
the capital of *Bak*

Fig. 1.5.
"Emblem" glyphs
and toponyms
from various sites.

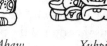

K'ul Xukpi Ahaw
"Holy Copan Lord"

Xukpi Kan Kun
"Copan Sky Seat"

"Holy Seibal Lord"

"governance." To people leaving, this same monument presents a *tzuk,* "province," face to remind them they were reentering a partition or neighborhood.

The sacred centers contain pyramid-mountains with temples on top; groups of buildings arranged on top of platforms to serve as administrative, religious, or residential complexes; ancestral shrines; sculpted monuments to document the history of the ruling dynasty; ballcourts; plazas; and other types of buildings that included space for schools and markets. Some of these building types were duplicated in outlying areas to serve as the sacred centers for nonroyal lineages. However, the capitals functioned for the entire kingdom, not just a single lineage.

The areas around these sacred precincts included compounds of varying size and complexity that housed nonroyal, but often wealthy, lineages. Where these outlying compounds have been excavated, the quality and amount of art varies with the prestige and rank of the lineage. And in the largest of these compounds, the sculptures and monuments bear the same imagery and symbolism as royal art, and are equal in terms of aesthetics and craftsmanship.

Towns within the larger kingdoms had their own rulers who erected historical imagery and ornate public architecture for themselves. Often their art proudly acknowledged their subordination to their ruling lords and the preeminence of the capital, but we cannot always distinguish lords from kings by imagery alone. We have to have written titles and statements of affiliation to be able to distinguish between the various ranks. However, location is often a clue, because these secondary lords mounted their inscriptions in spaces that were accessible only to lineage members. The audience for their art was not the public at large, as it was for royal messages. Archaeologists at Copan have detected at least four different categories of size and complexity among these lineage compounds, while work at Caracol and Tikal has shown that the secondary nobles, even those of very low rank, had access to wealth and exotic goods in times of prosperity.

The buildings that housed the common people are much harder to detect and count for population estimates because archaeologists often cannot find them without excavation. They often have only low surface mounds to mark their position and a good proportion of them are "invisible" until excavated. Nevertheless, such humble dwellings, the nonroyal compounds, and hamlets and small towns have received concentrated attention from archaeologists over the last thirty years. Their work shows us that in many ways this kind of housing has not changed during the last four thousand years.

Xanil nah, "thatched house," is the name that modern Yukatek Maya call the houses used by ordinary villagers and farmers (Fig. 1.6). The Maya built these

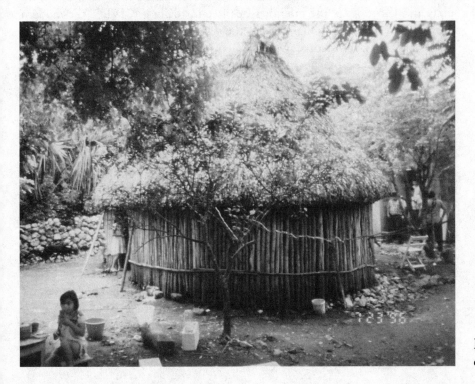

Fig. 1.6. A *xanil nah,* or "thatched house."

houses on platforms raised only slightly above ground level. Four posts carried the roof beams, while stick walls enclosed a single room. Sometimes the Maya used mud and plaster to finish the walls, but they could also leave the walls open for ventilation. The high-pitched roof consisted of palm thatch tied to a framework lashed to the main beams.[9]

The *xanil nah* very probably provided the template from which specialized architecture for political and religious ritual developed, as the Maya evolved more complex social and political organization. The Maya made their royal houses out of stone, but they replicated this basic pattern. Corbeled vaults and interior beams reproduced the triangular interior space of the house frame and thatched roof. People slept and worked on benches built into the sides or backs of rooms, and the interiors remained small and dark. With both royal and commoner houses, the working space with the best light was in the courtyards.

In modern Maya communities, all parts of the house have special terms associated with them, usually likening them to parts of the human body. Houses were and are living beings to the Maya. We do not have the ancient names for house parts, but in their dedication rituals, the Maya of olden times placed offerings under the floors of the houses and temples. These offerings contained materials identified with *k'ulel,* the living soul-force that imbues the universe. Thus, in dedicating a building, the Maya gave it a soul.

Baskets and net bags suspended from the roof beams kept food safe from pests and left most of the interior space free for daily use. While the modern Maya of Yukatan sleep in hammocks, their ancestors appear to have used mats on benches of various sorts. Women prepared maize and other foods for the family at the three-stone hearth and they dug into its center to bury the umbilicuses of their children. Even today, many Maya ask where you are from with the question, "Where is your umbilicus buried?"

The Maya added other thatched structures, *xanil nah,* to form compounds around courtyards in order to accommodate growing families. Throughout postconquest times, family compounds usually had an ancestral shrine or an altar of some kind, although the way these things were arranged varied from town to town. There is good reason to suppose that these shrines and family altars have always been a part of Maya residential architecture from earliest times.

Early villagers used *xanil nah* for public buildings also, but they often made them larger and raised them on higher platforms. In time, this raised building became the terraced, pyramidal platform with a temple on top. The terraces served as a place for dancing and ritual performances of all sorts for audiences located in the courtyards below. Both temple-pyramids and temple groups on top of individual pyramids could be clustered to form groups. The most sacred and ancient of these arrangements was the triangular form that echoed the three stones of the Cosmic Hearth constructed by the gods to center the world. Four-sided arrangements generated the square, the other form that the Maya tied to

Creation. The square, in fact, resulted when the creator gods arranged the *kan tzuk, kan xuk,* "the four sides, the four corners," to give shape and order to the cosmos. The gods then raised the great center tree called the *Wakah-Kan,* the "Raised-up Sky." Maya repeated these world-making activities by placing an altar or a tree in the center of the four-cornered, four-sided plaza. The resulting form with its four corners and a center is called a "quincunx" by modern researchers. This quincunx symbol of the cosmos also appeared in inscriptions as the sign for *beh,* "road."

Several of these courts could be joined together on top of platforms to create residential palaces, administrative compounds, and acropolises of various sorts. The North Acropolis at Tikal consisted of religious buildings and royal shrines, while the Central Acropolis was residential and administrative. Usually religious buildings had between one and three rooms and emphasized the vertical axis with towering roofcombs. Residential and administrative buildings often had multiple courts, many rooms opening onto the courts, and a horizontal axis.

The more important architecture was larger than domestic buildings, built from stone, finished with plaster, and decorated with passages of sculpture and paintings that signaled their function to the people using them or coming into the spaces they addressed. Buildings and spaces also reproduced sacred places that played a role in Creation, so that rituals conducted in them remade the space and time of Creation in elaborate public dramas. The Maya signaled these identities of sacred place and function through sculptural compositions. They controlled access, funneled movement, used architecture as backdrops, and placed close attention to vistas in order to integrate architectural space and to enhance the effect of drama.

Site and Building Planning

If the Maya had "professional" architects, we have not been able to identify their names or titles in the inscriptions. Maya structures were more likely to have been made by master builders, rather than by architects who separated the task of designing a structure from actually building it. Vernacular buildings and perhaps the stone houses of the lower ranks could be designed and supervised by older men who had experience in building, but the construction of more elaborate buildings in the sacred centers and in elite compounds was overseen by specialists in the arts of building construction and decoration. Since building orientation, shape, and proportion reflected the geometry and time of the sacred world, religious and craft specialists were also involved, not only in designing and laying out the building, but also in dedicating it. Some of these specialists were called *ah uxul,* "sculptor," *ah tz'ib,* "scribe," and *ah yul,* "polisher" (Fig. 1.7). The most accomplished of them carried the title *itz'at,* "learned one" or "sage."

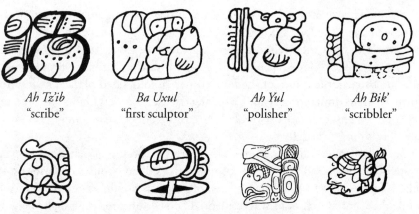

Ah Tz'ib	Ba Uxul	Ah Yul	Ah Bik'
"scribe"	"first sculptor"	"polisher"	"scribbler"

Fig. 1.7. Titles for artists and craftsmen.

Chuwen	Itz'at, "sage"
"artisan"	(in phonetic and head-variant form)

As in other Maya arts, builders valued subtle and refined execution of these sacred activities more than they did individual creativity and novel results. Traditional and conventional definitions of space and form were powerful elements in Maya aesthetics. They provided a language of meaning that oriented the Maya to everything in their world.

No tax or labor records have survived to identify the workmen who labored on the great public buildings. However, we have other hints about how construction projects worked. Archaeologists consistently find thin walls creating "construction pens" inside pyramids, and often neighboring pens have different fill materials. These pens have been found under courts and plazas, so that they may have served as much to organize labor as to provide containing walls inside a construction. A likely system would have been to assign a certain number of pens to different lineages,[10] who would then be responsible for finding the fill and bringing it to the pens. Each lineage would have fed its own people and perhaps contributed additional food and materials to the main construction project. People in these lineages owed labor to their own lords, just as their lords owed labor to their overlords. Presumably every lineage in a kingdom contributed to great public projects in this way.

These public building projects also required specialized labor. Laying out a new building required knowledge of construction techniques and materials, but also of sacred lore needed to orient the building correctly and tie it to its predecessors. Much of the physical labor of construction, like quarrying and shaping the stone, mixing mortar, leveling courses and floors, setting lintels, etc., did not require special training. Knowledgeable supervision would have been enough. But specialists were needed to incorporate decorations and sculptures into buildings. By looking at ancient Maya buildings, we can surmise other kinds of specializations, such as artists to plan the composition and apply the guide drawings; stone carvers to prepare armatures and relief sculptures; wall plasterers and sculptors specialized in plaster modeling; wood sculptors for carved lintels; and finally, painters for the complex polychrome painting of reliefs and for murals of various kinds.

These specialists, including the master builders, must have had other people working for them to help in preparing materials and in executing less critical parts of a work. However, we do not know if these skilled laborers operated within a lineage system or were organized in groups like guilds. We do know that the best of the craftsmen and artists traveled around their kingdoms to work on different projects, because we have their names on artworks from the towns as well as in the capitals. In addition, the Maya gave artworks by master artists as gifts and received them in tribute.

Access to finished buildings was controlled according to the function and meaning of the architecture. People of all ranks and affiliations visited the public plazas to participate in the great festivals, dances, dramas, and public rituals. If those rituals were anything like Maya festivals today, they would have gone on for days, with people coming in, leaving, and rejoining the ritual as their status and roles demanded. Markets would have been associated with these festivals, as well as pilgrimages and visits between both friendly and enemy states.

The courtyards within religious and administrative compounds would have been more restricted, but not by signs saying "no entry." Instead, the Maya controlled access and channeled movement by the use of stairways, constricted or blind entrances, causeways, and other devices that were part of the spatial design of their buildings. People learned from their earliest days where they were allowed to go and where they were not.

A full range of activities took place in residential compounds, including lineage festivals, administrative overseeing, manufacture, gathering of tribute, adjudications, child rearing, food preparation, and a hundred other enterprises. Residential compounds would have been noisy places. At Copan these stone constructions lie side by side, sometimes with only narrow alleyways between. With children, turkeys, many adults, and activities of all kinds, the noise levels must have rivaled those at the modern town of Copan, with its buses and boom boxes. Rooms were small and dark with stone benches for sleeping and working. Weaving and other kinds of activities took place outside in the courtyards, perhaps using awnings to keep off the sun.[11]

The temples would have been the most restricted space of all. The gods and ancestors resided there in special locations called *pib nah,* "underground house," *kunul,* "conjuring place," *kun,* "seat," and *waybil,* "resting place." Only kings, lords, and specialists responsible for the care and feeding of the gods would have mounted the pyramid-mountains to enter these inner sanctums. These places of the gods and ancestors were too dangerous to be entered casually by people who were unprepared.

ARCHITECTURE AND ITS ELEMENTS

As the Maya developed hierarchical social structures, they, like other societies around the world, developed myths and metaphors to explain how the world came to be what it is, and why stratification was the natural order of things. In the process, they began constructing large public buildings that transmitted these myths and legends through sculptural programs and the rituals associated with them. Their symbolism publicly confirmed the divine sanction of their social order and declared the origins of their institutions. This transformation began around 600 B.C., and by 400 B.C. the Maya regularly decorated their great public buildings with programs of sculptural and painted imagery. Very early platforms at sites like Copan and Kahal Pech were built of clay or adobe painted red and with thatched-roofed structures on top. At most sites, buildings with earth and rubble cores replaced these clay platforms by the Early Classic period, but Copan continued to use them in sacred and residential architecture until at least A.D. 550.[12]

Rubble-core buildings became the rule in lowland architecture because clay platforms were difficult to maintain in areas with heavy tropical rainfall. The ratio between earth and stone in the rubble cores varied from site to site and from building to building. However, the stability of these cores depended less on the amount of stone than on the way they were laid. Wet fill made for a compressed and very stable matrix, while dry fill tended to be unstable even in precolumbian times. Today, dry fill poses severe excavation problems for archaeologists.

Masonry walls differed from site to site depending on the local material available to the builders. For example, Palenque's masons used a limestone that came out of the quarries in large natural slabs that required little shaping. They laid these rough stones in courses using a lime mortar, and then smoothed the final wall surfaces by applying thick plaster. Maya buildings also had sculpture modeled in plaster over stone armatures. Builders used this technique throughout most of Chiapas, Peten, and Belize, and in southern Quintana Roo and Kampeche, although the quality of the limestone differed from region to region.

In the early history of Copan, builders also employed these plaster techniques, but they used volcanic tuff and river cobbles instead of limestone inside their rubble cores. Some of the best preserved plaster sculptures from Classic-period architecture lie under the acropolis of Copan. However, sometime during the seventh century, builders in Copan changed to a new technique using well-dressed blocks to lay a smooth wall that required only a thin finishing layer of plaster. They also converted from modeled-plaster sculpture on terraces and entablatures to stone-mosaic sculpture of great refinement. Their problem may have lain in the use of mud without lime for mortar in buildings throughout the valley. This technique and the use of beam and mortar roofs required very thick layers of plaster (up to seven inches) to seal horizontal surfaces against the rain. Copan's buildings required continuous maintenance of these seals, because as water penetrated bearing walls, it dissolved the mud mortar, and the buildings collapsed. Since plaster was the most expensive material used in Maya architecture,[13] Copan's builders apparently developed techniques to conserve as much of it as possible for the sealing layers.

The cost of plaster may or may not have influenced architectural technique in the northern lowlands, including much of the modern states of Kampeche, Quintana Roo, and Yukatan. The limestone there is inferior to the stone found farther south. As in the south, builders used modeled plaster in Preclassic and Early Classic buildings, but changed to rubble core–veneer techniques during the Late Classic period. However, these northern builders surfaced their cores with thin, finely cut veneer stones. In the Ch'enes area in Kampeche, builders developed mosaic-stone sculptures much in the tradition of the Copan style to create gigantic images of mountain and sky monsters that wrapped around the doors of buildings. In the Puuk region and at Chich'en Itza, the Maya brought this mosaic technique to its most refined expression.

Maya builders used several types of plans, including a single room or gallery, double galleries entered either from a single side or from both sides of the center wall, and multiple galleries. Long galleries could be subdivided into rooms by nonbearing curtain walls, although at Palenque they sometimes left these long galleries open. In palace or administrative structures, the Maya created complex patterns of space not by constructing buildings with a great many rooms, but by assembling discrete buildings around open spaces. At Palenque, artists decorated each facade to carry messages to the court space in front of it. The internal coherence of a building was less important than the effectiveness of each facade as a dispenser of political and religious information. Over time, various sites and regions developed their own strategies for presenting this kind of information, as well as conventions of style and preferences for materials for individual and group buildings, so that architectural style became a recognizable ethnic and community marker.

The Maya spanned interior rooms of their buildings in four ways (Fig. 1.8):

1. The corbeled vault was the most elaborate and prestigious way to create interior space. To make it, the masons built vertical bearing walls to a height where they intended to construct the vault. Then they brought successive courses closer together until the gap at the top could be closed with a capstone. It is a simple technique that did not result in a self-supporting structural system. This construction method first appeared in tombs and then expanded to public architecture.

Corbeled vaults can achieve great height, but each wall is independently balanced. If the angle of the corbel becomes too oblique, the vault will fall. As a result, Maya buildings have high but very narrow rooms characterized by the triangular space of the corbeled vault span. Normally each side of the corbeled vault balanced independently, but Palenque's masons learned to angle the outer walls of a double gallery so that they leaned against the central wall. The result-

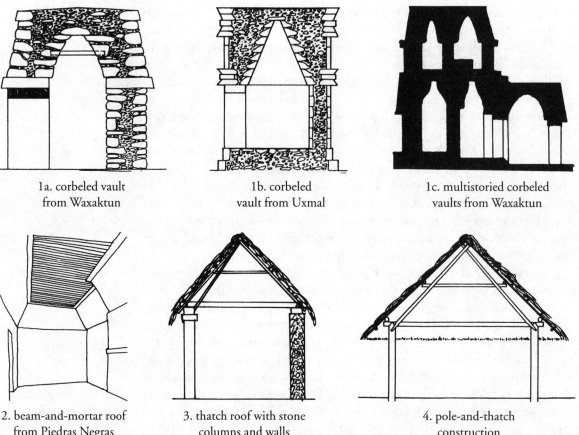

1a. corbeled vault
from Waxaktun

1b. corbeled
vault from Uxmal

1c. multistoried corbeled
vaults from Waxaktun

2. beam-and-mortar roof
from Piedras Negras

3. thatch roof with stone
columns and walls

4. pole-and-thatch
construction

Fig. 1.8. Construction techniques used in ancient Maya buildings.

ing roof contour looks a little like a mansard roof. At other Maya sites, any of the corbeled walls could be left standing when a building collapsed, but at Palenque, only the center walls survived the collapse of a building.

The ratio between vault span and wall thickness varied considerably in the different traditions that developed. In central Peten, the span-to-wall ratio was very low, and in temples it was often negative. In other words, the walls were thicker than the width of the rooms they created. This dominance of wall mass is most extreme in the temples of Tikal, where the doorways provided the largest interior space in the temple buildings.

The builders of Palenque used their leaning corbels and cross-vaulting to achieve one of the highest span-to-wall ratios in Maya architecture. By reducing the outer bearing walls to piers standing between large doors, they let in more light and created airier buildings than any other Maya site. Uxmal's buildings are also famous for their wide spans and thin walls, but they used only one door per room, thus creating dark chambers like the ones in Peten architecture.

2. Beam-and-mortar roofs were made by using wooden beams to span the bearing walls. Thin poles were laid across them, and the entire construction was then filled with a thick layer of plaster. At Copan, we have seen remnants of this kind of beam-and-mortar roof over a foot thick. They were heavy, and if water got inside they could be very dangerous. This kind of roof was used primarily in the Copan Valley and in northern Yukatan.

3. Columns and beams were used as part of roofing and wall systems in the northern lowlands, although one example is known from Tikal. In the past, this system has been taken as a Toltec (central Mexican) trait, but builders in southern Quintana Roo and Kampeche had started using columns to support doorways during the Early Classic period. The builders of Chich'en Itza took the technology far beyond its limited use of earlier times to create huge colonnaded halls covered by thatched roofs or corbeled vaults.

4. Thatched roofs were the preferred form for commoner houses, although thatch was also used to roof many public buildings throughout the Classic period. At first glance, thatch would seem to be the cheapest of all roofing systems, but this may not always have been true. Today dense populations and deforestation make palm thatching an extremely expensive commodity. The same was probably true in the Late Classic period. Burning the towns of enemies may have had far more devastating consequences than we might first imagine.

Builders extended the heights of public buildings, especially temples, by adding parapets and extensions called roofcombs (Fig. 1.9). These differed in structure and style from region to region. At Tikal and other central Peten sites, the roofcombs were massive and often larger than the buildings that supported them. They were vaulted to reduce their enormous weight, and they were built over the thick rear and center bearing walls of the temple. Their backs were usually plain, but the fronts carried deep relief images signaling the meaning of the building. The roofcomb of Tikal Temple 1 displayed a huge image of a seated lord, probably the king Hasaw-Kan-K'awil, who built it. Temple 6 had a long

Fig. 1.9. Roofcombs of various styles.

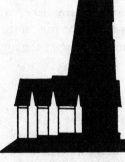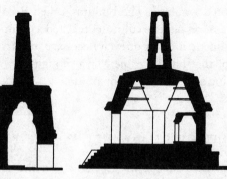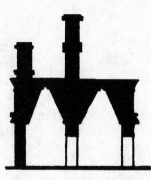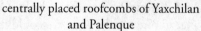

Tikal and central Peten roofcombs

centrally placed roofcombs of Yaxchilan and Palenque

parapets and central roofcomb from Chich'en Itza

inscription discussing Tikal's history and its patron gods all the way back to Olmec times.

The builders of most of the kingdoms along the Usumacinta River and in Chiapas preferred a style using lighter roofcombs. At Palenque, they almost became lattice frameworks of stone that supported larger-than-life-size figures modeled fully in the round using plaster over stone armatures. Yaxchilan and Piedras Negras used more solid forms, and they also centered the roofcomb.

Copan's builders chose yet another alternative. They used silhouetted forms cut from stone and mounted along the edge of the building like a parapet.[14] In addition to edging stones, Temple 22A also had a large stone sculpture representing the king seated on a jaguar throne mounted on top of the roof. Once again, Copan seems to prefigure Puuk-style architecture of northern Yukatan. In that style, builders mounted parapets above the outer edges of the roof to extend the space of the frieze. Roofcombs could also sit along the central axis of the building in some of the Yukatek traditions.

These regional and local styles of architecture developed in part because of the kinds of materials available to builders. But perhaps they were more the result of a Maya worldview that included powerful veneration of ancestors so that builders strove to reproduce the character of ancestral buildings as they physically incorporated them inside their own constructions. Particularly effective, and usually long-lived, rulers often left legacies of art and architecture that were emulated by subsequent generations. Thus, individual rulers could have powerful effects on style through their patronage of the arts. Moreover, Maya builders evoked prestigious styles of neighbors or distant places as statements of origin or affiliation. In Maya art, style could be political.

Maintenance was a problem in all these roofing styles. Thatched roofs last for only ten to fifteen years and they host a lot of pests. All of the stone roofs had to be kept waterproof with plaster seals. The large public buildings, especially those with plaster sculpture, presented constant maintenance problems, as modern archaeologists have found. The plaster surfaces had to be patched, renewed, and repainted regularly. The building called Rosalila at Copan has taught us that maintaining plaster sculptures reached a point of diminishing returns that eventually made it easier or even necessary to start all over again. Apparently in the case of that building, the Maya thought it a better solution to encase the old building and rebuild on top of it.

ARCHITECTURAL SYMMETRY

In our own careers, we learned about the subtleties of Maya architecture by focusing on Palenque. In measuring the buildings we realized that the parts were proportional to one another, but we could not find a consistent pattern to the proportional system or a fundamental measure. Other people after us have observed symmetries in Maya art and tried to explain them, but it took a graduate student named Christopher Powell to figure out how the Maya designed their architecture and controlled its proportions.[15]

The Maya artists' measuring device was a simple cord cut to a multiple of some body measure—such as the distance from the fingertips to the shoulder or from hand to hand across outstretched arms. Today the Maya count multiples—say, twenty or forty—of this fundamental measure to get the overall length of their measuring cords. Using the cord, they first lay out a square of predetermined size, such as 3 x 3 or 5 x 5, depending on the size of what they want to build. Then they use the cord to square up the angles by making sure that both diagonals are equal. This measuring of the square with a cord was the first action of the gods when they created the cosmos. The square gave four sides, four corners, and the center. As Powell says, it is the fundamental shape of Maya geometry—the module from which all Creation was generated.

Once they form a square, the builders halve the cord to find the center of a side, then stretch the cord up to a corner, swinging down to create the baseline of a rectangle (Fig. 1.10). This rectangle has the famous proportion known as the "golden mean," which is found in art around the world and throughout history. It permeates nature in the growth patterns of creatures like the nautilus shell. Powell told us that his Yukatek teachers told him that using the cord makes their houses like flowers because of the inherent relationship of their proportions.

Architecture from thatched-roof houses of farmers to the most exalted temples and palaces used the cord to generate a harmonious whole. Sculptors and weavers used the device to proportion their compositions, and corn farmers used it to lay out their fields. The gods used it to lay out the cosmos:

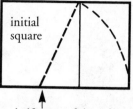

half point of the side rectangle with the golden mean proportion

Fig. 1.10. How Maya artists made the "golden mean" using cords to lay out buildings and organize artistic compositions.

Its four sides (or sections)	*U kaj tzuquxiik*
Its four cornerings	*U kaj xukuutaxiik*
Its measurings	*Retaxiik*
Its four stakings	*U kaj chee'xiik*
Its doubling-over cord measurement	*U mej k'amaxiik*
Its stretching cord measurement	*U yuq k'amaxiik*
Its womb sky	*U paa kaaj*
Its womb earth	*U paa uleew*
Four sides	*Kaj tzuq*
Four corners as it is said	*Kaj xukuut chuch'axiik*[16]

As Powell says, the center four lines in this passage describe the way the Maya created a "golden-mean" rectangle. To us the most revealing thing about Powell's discoveries is that this way of measuring things and the proportionality it naturally generates does not require special knowledge, like abstract geometry, to use it. The cord gave a harmonious proportionality to everything the Maya did in their art and architecture, and it joined their human-made art to the symmetries that permeate the natural world. To create the harmonies of the cosmos, the gods used the same method of measure as a weaver, house builder, and cornfield maker. But cord measuring also revealed the innate symmetries of nature, so that in reality, Maya art and daily life harmonized with cosmic symmetry without the necessity of conscious design.

MYTHS OF CREATION AND ORIGIN

The Maya and other Mesoamericans often designed their sacred centers to reproduce the structures from the myths that were central to their ideology. For the Maya, two of these myths were of particular importance: the story of Creation, which explained how the world came to have its present form, and the story of the origin of civilized life and the birth of their patron gods. Since these myths are so central to the physical forms that Maya cities took, we will give a brief synopsis of them here.

Our knowledge of the Maya story of Creation comes from two sources: the Popol Vuh, a seventeenth-century book recording the history of the K'iche' Maya, and inscriptions and imagery from the Classic period. The story involves the activities of the Twin Maize Gods and their family in the Third Creation. When playing ball one day, the Maize Gods disturbed the lords of Xibalba, the Maya underworld. The Xibalbans summoned the Maize Gods to the underworld to answer for their misbehavior, subjected them to a series of trials, and killed them when they failed. The Xibalbans buried the Maize Gods in the Ballcourt of Xibalba, after taking the head of the older twin and hanging it in a gourd tree next to the ballcourt, as a lesson to anyone who might tempt the wrath of the Lords of Xibalba. Ignoring the warning, the daughter of a Xibalban lord went to visit the skull, which spoke to her. The skull spat in her hand and made her pregnant. After escaping from Xibalba, she gave birth to a second set of boys, called the Hero Twins, who were themselves summoned to Xibalba after they found their fathers' ballplaying equipment. They also had made too much noise with their exuberant play, but unlike their forebears, they were not fooled by the Xibalbans' tricks.

After a long series of confrontations through ballgames, the Hero Twins, called Hun-Ahaw and Yax-Balam in the Classic period, defeated the Lords of Death and resurrected their fathers from the ballcourt. Reborn as infants, the Maize Gods grew quickly into adulthood to be dressed in their full glory by goddesses. With dwarf helpers, they woke up three old gods. We call two of them the Paddler Gods, because they paddled the Maize Gods to the place of Creation. The third oldster, God L, the patron of merchants and warriors, destroyed the Third Creation by a great flood.

When the Maize Gods arrived at the place of the new Creation, they sprang up from a crack in the back of a Cosmic Turtle. The Maya saw this turtle as the three stars that we call Orion's Belt, and they also saw the crack in the turtle's back as the ballcourt. Once reborn, the Maize Gods directed four old gods to set up the first Hearth of Creation to center the new order. This hearth consisted of three throne stones—one in the form of a jaguar that was set up by the Paddlers at a place called *Na-Ho-Kan,* "First-Five-Sky" or "House-Five-Sky"; the second in the form of a snake that was set up on the earth by an unknown god; and the third, a crocodile or shark monster that was set up in the sea by Itzamna, the First Sorcerer. The Maya saw this hearth as the triangle of stars below Orion's Belt, with the Orion Nebula as the fire. Today we call these stars Alnitak, Saiph, and Rigel. The gods set up this hearth on 13.0.0.0.0 4 Ahaw 8 Kumk'u, or August 13, 3114 B.C.

Five hundred and forty-two days later, the Maize Gods completed the structure of this, the Fourth Creation, by setting up the four sides and corners of the cosmos and erecting the center tree. The Maya called this tree *Wakah-Kan,* or "Raised-up Sky." They visualized it as a great ceiba tree in flower, because February 5, the day when it was erected, falls into the flowering season of that great sacred tree. But they also saw the tree as the Milky Way arching across the sky with its roots on the southern horizon and its branches to the north.[17]

The raising of this tree created the space in which we all live in this, the Fourth Creation. But the gods were not done. On the same day, the Maize Gods spun the heart of the sky in the motion used by weavers spinning thread. This spinning corresponds to the motion of the constellations around the north pivot of the sky. This motion is the basis of all time perception for human beings, so that the gods gave symmetry and order to both space and time by their action in erecting the tree and setting out the four corners and four sides of the cosmos.

The second myth, concerning the beginning of civilized life, comes to us primarily from Aztec sources, although the myth was known in various forms throughout Mesoamerica. This myth involves Snake Mountain and the Place of Reeds, or *Coatepec* and *Tollan,* as the Aztec called them. There are several versions of these stories in central Mexican sources.[18] The myth concerns the migrations of the Aztec to the place where they would establish their state and capital city. Along the way, they came to Coatepec (Snake Mountain), near Tollan (Place of Cattail Reeds). In one version of the story, the Aztec built a temple on top of Snake Mountain for their patron god Huitzilopochtli. Huitzilopochtli then built a ballcourt at the base of the mountain, and in the center he placed a hole, called an *Itzompan,* or "Skull Place." Under his directions, the Aztec partially dammed up the hole to create what was called the "Well of Water." They cultivated plants in and around the hole, which was filled with freshwater creatures of all sorts. From this well, sweet water formed a lake and made the surrounding landscape fertile.

In one version of the myth,[19] a faction of the migrants, the Four-Hundred Southerners (*Centzon Huitznahuatl*), decided they wanted to stay in this fine new home to create Mexico, instead of continuing in their migrations. This angered Huitzilopochtli, who came down from his mountain armed for war. He surrounded the Four-Hundred Southerners and their older sister, a goddess named Coyolxauhcihuatl, who is identified in this version of the myth as the mother of Huitzilopochtli. The Four-Hundred were his uncles. In the ballcourt, he killed Coyolxauhcihuatl by decapitation, then destroyed the Four-Hundred and ate their hearts. He destroyed the dam in the Well of Water and it dried up, forcing the terrified Aztec to resume their journey.

In an alternative version, the Aztec found Coatlicue, the mother of Huitzilopochtli, living on Coatepec. When she became miraculously pregnant, her other children, Coyolxauhqui and the Four-Hundred Southerners, decided to kill their mother for her presumed transgression. Coatlicue gave birth to a fully adult Huitzilopochtli armed with his shield and spears. After hacking up Coyolxauhqui and throwing her down the mountain, he destroyed the Four-Hundred Southerners and forced the Aztec out of Coatepec.

The Aztec generated important archetypes from this myth: the deaths of Coyolxauhqui and the Four-Hundred Southerners provided the archetype for war and sacrifice, and Coatepec provided the archetype for how to create the sacred precinct of a city. However, the Aztec did not invent this myth. They reworked it from far older stories of origin. We have Snake Mountains at Teotihuacan, Xochicalco, Tula, El Tajín, Chich'en Itza, Tikal, Waxaktun, Cerros, and other sites beginning as early as 100 B.C. Many of these Snake Mountains have ballcourts adjacent to them. The particular gods of the Aztec myth—Huitzilopochtli, Coatlicue, and Coyolxauhqui—were particular to their version of the story, but all Mesoamerican cities had their own gods who were born at their version of this place of origin. And while the names of the gods and the details of the myth changed through time and space, the core function of the myth to create archetypes for building sacred centers and for conducting war was valid for everyone.

The other myth of origin concerns the Place of Cattail Reeds—Tollan to the Aztec. In their migration story, the Aztec also stopped at Tollan, which was near Coatepec. The Aztec described the Toltecs, the inhabitants of Tollan, as great sages who had invented the calendar, divination, astronomy, the arts, writing, medicine, monumental architecture, the institutions of government, agriculture, money, and all things civilized. They discovered jade and obsidian, and they found turquoise. They were especially pious and they were rich.[20] According to the Aztec, they were the ancestors of all the people who spoke properly. For the Aztec that meant speakers of Nahua languages. In the rest of Mesoamerica, the "proper" language was locally defined.

The Aztec used *Tollan* not only as a reference to this legendary place of origin, but also as a general term for "city." They used Tollan to refer to their own capital, Tenochtitlan, to Tula in Hidalgo, to Teotihuacan, and to Cholula. Moreover, they used the term *Toltec* to refer to the original inhabitants of the legendary Tollan, but also to artisans and artists.

For many years, Mesoamerican scholars argued fiercely over the identification of Tollan or Tula. By the 1950s, the majority had come to the consensus that it corresponded to the archaeological site of Tula, Hidalgo.[21] David Stuart has offered an alternative identification by showing that the Maya of the Classic period referred to Teotihuacan as *Puh,* the Maya word for "Cattail Reed."[22] Moreover, the Pyramid of the Feathered Serpent at Teotihuacan is a powerful image of Snake Mountain. It has multiple images of feathered snakes emerging from the Primordial Sea carrying the headdress, eyerings, and nose ornament of kings. This building became the equivalent of the Parthenon or Pantheon to Mesoamericans as they reproduced it over and over again for the next twelve centuries. The people of Teotihuacan may have been the "Toltecs" of postconquest legends. To us, Stuart's discovery represents primary written evidence from the Classic period that Teotihuacan was a Tollan, "Place of Reeds." However, we do not think it was the only one, nor the first one.[23]

We know that during the Preclassic period, the Maya at several sites, such as Cerros and Waxaktun, built pyramids that carried the image of mountain monsters with snakes emerging from their mouths or penetrating their heads from side to side. The famous Temple E-VII-sub at Waxaktun has snake heads emerging from the stair balustrades on all four sides.[24] The Maya built all of these Snake Mountains before the Teotihuacanos constructed their great temples and pyramids.

If both the early Maya and the people of Teotihuacan built their cities to be replicas of the Place of Reeds and Snake Mountain, who were the people they saw as the inventors of civilized life? Was there a great civilization older than both? In fact, there was—the Olmec.

Olmec country fits the description of the Place of Cattail Reeds and Snake Mountain perfectly. The Olmec built their cities on high areas in the swampy landscapes of the Gulf Coast of Veracruz and Tabasco. They built pyramid-mountains in the core of their towns, and at sites like La Venta, they placed a pair of parallel buildings at the base of their artificial mountain. Kent Reilly has suggested that these parallel buildings were ballcourts, and certainly the discovery of rubber balls at El Manatí[25] shows beyond a doubt that the Olmec played the ballgame. All Olmec sites have channeled water and many sites have sunken courts with associated water iconography. At La Venta, this channeling and the sunken court are next to the ballcourt.

Moreover, the Tuxtla Mountains with their volcanoes and Lake Catemaco are the perfect natural model for the Place of Reeds and Snake Mountain. These volcanic mountains rise precipitously from the encircling swamps and the three highest volcanoes surround a huge crater lake called Catemaco. In a crevice leading into the crater of the tallest volcano, San Martín Pajapan, explorers found an Olmec statue of a deity raising a tree, and on Tenaspi Island in Lake Catemaco, there was a sculpture of an egg with a human face emerging from its side.[26] The statues depict the Olmec equivalents of raising the World Tree and the birth of humanity. The Olmec clearly thought of this mountain and the lake at its base as places of Creation.

The Olmec invented many of the symbols and institutions that remained at the heart of political and religious authority for the rest of Mesoamerican history. Most specifically, the symbolism of the ruler for both the Teotihuacanos and the Maya derived directly from royal imagery of the Olmec. If civilized life really was invented in the Gulf Coast swamps, then that topography was the model for the Place of Reeds, and the Tuxtlas were the first Snake Mountains. Thus, *Puh/Tollan* as a city in a reed-laden swamp and the *Ah Puh/Toltec* as the people who invented the arts and institutions of the state were very ancient concepts indeed.

These two myths provided archetypal symbolism that the Maya and other Mesoamerican peoples used to create the sacred centers of their cities and to charge their buildings with the energy and symmetry generated during these mythic times. For Mesoamericans, history, ritual, and governance unfolded within these charged environments.

SYMBOLISM OF ARCHITECTURE AND ITS SCULPTURE

Unlike the European tradition of architecture, the Maya did not build their structures with the primary aim of creating interior space. Instead public architecture functioned like a gigantic stage set to serve as the backdrop for huge processional rituals, dances, and public dramas. The small interior spaces held gods and ancestral images housed in special places called *pib nah,* "underground structure," *kun,* "seat," or *waybil,* "resting place" (Fig. 1.11). At Palenque, the *pib nah* are small buildings inside larger temples. They are also marked as *Itzam Nah,* "sorcery house," by stucco *Itzam-Ye* birds modeled across their entablatures.

Maya builders placed modeled-plaster or carved-stone sculpture on pyramid terraces, stairways, stair balustrades, building platforms, vertical bearing walls, doorjambs, door lintels, various moldings, the entablatures, and finally the roofcomb (Fig. 1.12). Different kingdoms favored different areas for displaying sculpture, so that distinct stylistic traditions developed in local and regional ways. Moreover, the design of the building also determined where and how the Maya presented their imagery. When they built frontal buildings, they usually concentrated on the surfaces facing inward to the audience. In these buildings the designs on the entablature often addressed all four sides, while all other imagery, such as on the roofcomb or terraces, faced the court.

Radial buildings, on the other hand, had stairways ascending all four sides of

waybil
"sleeping" or
"dreaming
place"

pib nah
"underground
house," "sweat
bath"

u kunul
"his conjuring
place"

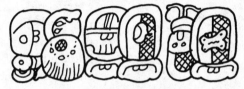

utiy Lakam Ha Kan Kun tu Kun,
"it happened at Lakam Ha Sky
Seat at his seat"

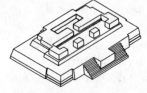

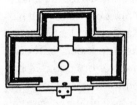

buildings with inner
sanctums from Piedras
Negras and Iximche'

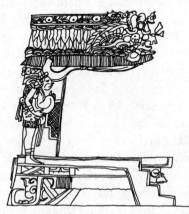

an *Itzam Nah* from a pot

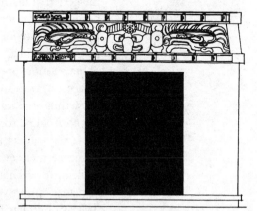

a *pib nah* from Palenque with
Itzam-Ye on the entablature

**Fig. 1.11. Conjuring
houses and inner
sanctums.**

Fig. 1.12. A hypothetical temple-pyramid
with the potential
areas for sculptural
decoration marked.
No single temple used
all of them, but all
these areas carried
sculpture in one exam-
ple or another. Tem-
ples at Palenque could
also contain a smaller
interior temple that
also carried sculpture.

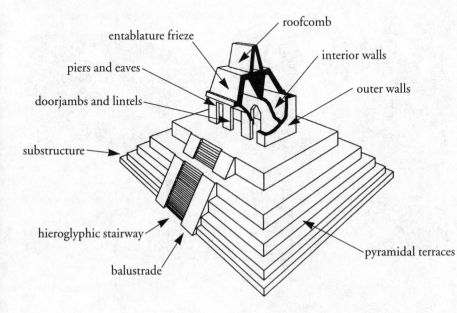

roofcomb

entablature frieze

interior walls

piers and eaves

doorjambs and lintels

outer walls

substructure

hieroglyphic stairway

balustrade

pyramidal terraces

the pyramid. Many of these radial pyramids, especially the early ones, like Structure E-VII-sub of Waxaktun and the Lost World Pyramid of Tikal, have sculpture facing outward in all four directions. In "E-groups," the radial pyramid sits in the middle of a plaza, with three buildings lined up on a platform to the east, and far more rarely to the west. In "twin-pyramid complexes," two radial pyramids sit across from each other on an east-west axis, with other smaller buildings in the north and south. Known examples of twin-pyramid complexes do not have temples on top of the pyramids nor any kind of architectural sculpture.

Architectural sculpture usually falls into one of the following categories: (1) imagery that defined the building as a particular sacred space in order to create a performance-oriented environment; (2) narratives displaying historical information in both imagery and texts; (3) narratives that showed stories and myths in progress; (4) imagery that froze ritual performance in progress; (5) combinations of one or more of these types. By and large, stela compositions fall into these same categories, with special emphasis on historical narrative and sacred context. The Maya thus used architectural sculpture to create sacred environments for the unfolding of ritual performance and to freeze the ephemeral actions of rituals into narrative sequences that locked history into the center of sacred space. Creation and its reenactment evoked cyclical time and the myths of origin and social authority, while historical narratives placed linear time into the context of ritual so that performance operated in both the cosmic and historical environments at the same time.

Maya builders had a language of metaphor and image available to create this charged environment. The entire society shared this language of symbols, which endured for thousands of years. Some of the key metaphors are as follows:

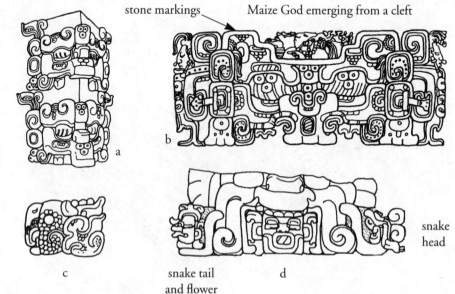

stone markings

Maize God emerging from a cleft

Fig. 1.13. Mountain images from (a) Copan Temple 22, (b) a *Yax-Hal-Witz* from Bonampak' Stela 1, (c) *Mo'-Witz* from Copan, and (d) a Snake Mountain from Waxaktun.

a

b

c

snake tail and flower

d

snake head

1. The pyramid was a **mountain,** or *witz* in the Maya languages (Fig. 1.13). Since the Maya conceived of mountains as living beings, they represented them as zoomorphic creatures, complete with eyes, muzzle, mouth, and ear ornaments. Mountain monsters, identified by a combination of *tun* ("stone") markings and a cleft in their forehead, occur on the corners of buildings, on terraces, and around the doorways. There were two principal mountains of particular importance in Maya cosmology and political symbolism: Sustenance Mountain, also called *Yax-Hal-Witz,* "First True Mountain," which was shown as a split mountain with the Maize God emerging from the cleft, and Snake Mountain, called *Kan-Witz,* which they showed as a mountain monster with snakes emerging from its mouth, or penetrating it from side to side, or with snakes around the base of a pyramid.

2. The **cave** inside the pyramid-mountain provided a path to the Otherworld (Fig. 1.14). Buildings were sometimes constructed over caves, as at Dos Pilas and the High Priest's Grave at Chich'en Itza, or next to them, as at Mayapan. The Maya also symbolized the cave by wrapping a *witz* monster around the door of the temple so that the door, or "mouth of the house," became the "mouth of the mountain."

3. Public buildings could also represent themselves as stone effigies of *xanil nah,* "thatched house." Sometimes sculptors incorporated the imagery of a thatched-roof house into the entablatures, as in the Nunnery Quadrangle at Uxmal, or they could model the plaster on the medial molding to look like thatch, as in House E at Palenque. Maya languages have two words for "house." *Otot* and its cognates refer to a house with the sense that it is inalienably possessed, much like the English word "home." *Otot* always occurs with a possessive pronoun, as in *yotot,* "his house." *Nah* is "house," simply as an unpossessed building. Often the proper names included the *nah* word, but the structure was the *yotot* of the king or a lord (Fig. 1.15).

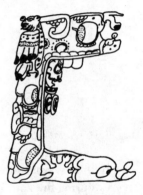

Fig. 1.14. The cave was the mouth of the mountain.

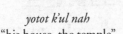

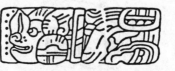

yotot
"his house"

yotot k'ul nah
"his house, the temple"

k'ul xulpi nah yotot
"Holy Copan building, his house"

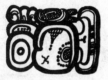

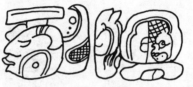

wi te nah
"root tree building"

sak nuk nah
"white big building"

nah u muknal
"building, his tomb"

Fig. 1.15. Glyphs for houses and buildings.

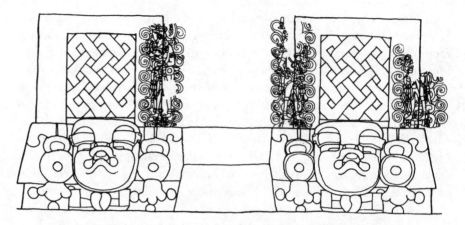

Fig. 1.16. A *popol nah,* or "mat house," built at Waxaktun during the Late Preclassic period.

4. There were special kinds of **council houses** called *popol nah,* "mat house" (Fig. 1.16), *nikte'il nah,* "flower house," or *sak nah,* "white house." These were community houses in which councils of lords met, where dancing and feasting took place, and where the regalia of ritual and dance were kept. The community houses could function at the level of the state, but lineage groups and small towns also had their community houses.

5. The **Cosmic Hearth** consisted of three "throne stones"—a jaguar, a snake, and a shark or crocodile—set in a triangle (Fig. 1.17). In the sky, this hearth is found in the constellation of Orion, but in architecture, the Maya reproduced it by arranging their buildings in the same triangular form. The imagery of buildings could also refer to the hearth.

6. *Na-Ho-Kan,* "**First-Five-Sky,**" was the location of the first stone of the

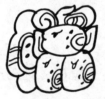

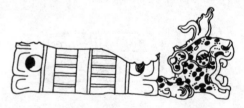

Fig. 1.17. The Cosmic Hearth and its three throne stones.

Yax Ox-Tunal
"First" or "Green Three Stone Place"

Jaguar Throne Stone

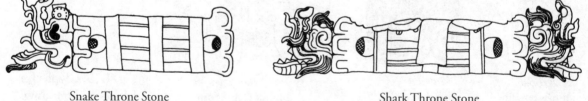

Snake Throne Stone

Shark Throne Stone

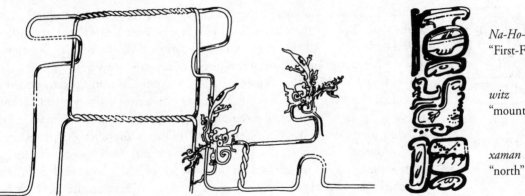

Na-Ho-Kan
"First-Five-Sky"

witz
"mountain"

xaman
"north"

Cosmic Hearth, the Jaguar Throne Stone. A snake umbilicus also emerged from this place in the form of entwined snakes (Fig. 1.18).

7. There were several kinds of **portals** called by different names. With a pedigree beginning in Olmec times, the quatrefoil shape represents the most ancient portal. The Maya called it *ol*, meaning "the heart of," or *hol*, "door" or "portal." Another image presents the jaws of the *Sak-Bak-Na-Kan*, the "White-Bone-Snake." The image of this skeletal portal could appear in a recognizable snake form, but there was also a more abstract form that depicted cenotes, caves, and other openings into the earth. This portal was the *Ek' Waynal*, the "Black Transformation Place," or the "Black Dreaming Place" (Fig. 1.19).

8. The glyph for **"plaza"** combines the *ol* quatrefoil with stone signs and waterlilies (Fig. 1.20). The Maya saw plazas as portals opening onto the Primor-

Fig. 1.18. The intertwined snakes that symbolize the Sky Umbilicus and the glyph for *Na-Ho-Kan*, the place where the gods set up the Jaguar Throne Stone.

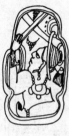

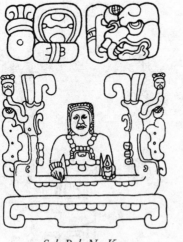

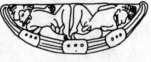

yol
"his portal"

Sak-Bak-Na-Kan
"White-Bone-Snake"

Ek'Waynal
"Black Dreaming Place"

Fig. 1.19. Passageways to the Otherworld.

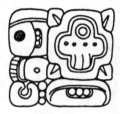

Fig. 1.20. The glyphs for "It happened in the plaza."

dial Sea. This association may have come from Maya experience in tropical rainstorms that filled up the plaster-lined plazas with water. At Copan and other sites, they built special drainage systems to carry off the rainwater.[27] At many sites, the Maya captured this runoff water in cisterns or reservoirs.

9. Maya scholars have identified the ubiquitous **long-nosed god** of Yukatekan architecture as Chak since the late nineteenth century.[28] In fact, the long-nosed gods of architectural sculpture can represent several different gods, including the *witz* monster, a crocodile sky monster, umbilicus serpents, and most commonly, the sacred bird named *Itzam-Ye* and *Mut Itzamna*. This last identification is a new one based on the presence of a headband with a flower, the signal that marks both the old god Itzamna and his avatar, the great supernatural bird that sat on top of the World Tree. This bird held an ancient place in

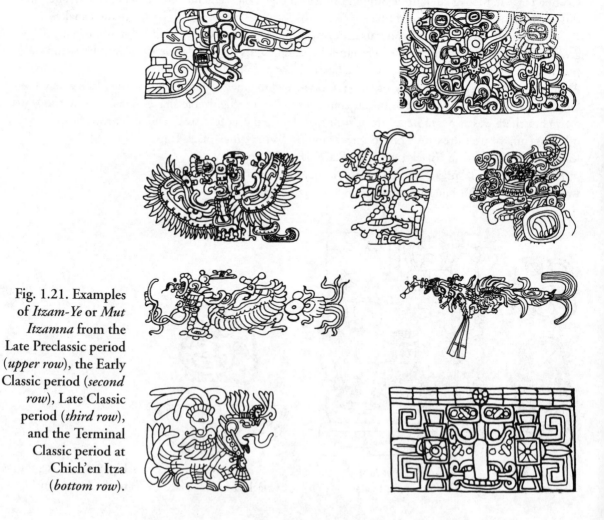

Fig. 1.21. Examples of *Itzam-Ye* or *Mut Itzamna* from the Late Preclassic period (*upper row*), the Early Classic period (*second row*), Late Classic period (*third row*), and the Terminal Classic period at Chich'en Itza (*bottom row*).

Maya imagery, with the earliest known versions dating to the Late Preclassic period (400 B.C.–A.D. 100). The presence of the bird on Maya architecture, either as an image spreading out across a terrace or entablature or as a stack of long-beaked masks on the corner of a building, designated that the associated structure was an *Itzam Nah,* "conjuring house." We have included illustrations that diagram the development of the *Itzam-Ye* bird over time and show how it became the Puuk-style long-nosed mask (Fig. 1.21).

10. **Feathered serpents** and other kinds of snakes played a crucial role in Maya imagery of all types. In general, they symbolized the transition between one state and another or one world and another. Vision Serpents could take many different forms, but one of the most important was entwined serpents that represented the umbilicus that connected Maya lords to their source of power. From the Late Preclassic period on, Maya sculpture placed the sky umbilicus in frames around architectural terraces to define context. The heads of these snakes were often fused with the glyph for "white" or "white flower" to show that they were conduits for human souls (Fig. 1.22).

Artists also depicted Vision Serpents rearing in front of people deep in trance states, or undulating across building facades or up corners to emit beings they had brought from the Otherworld. Among the many varieties were feathered

Fig. 1.22. Vision Serpents of various kinds from monuments and pottery scenes. Serpents a and b have "white flowers" on their tails, while serpent f carries the flower on the ends of its noses. Serpent d has a flint knife, and serpent e has a K'awil on its tail.

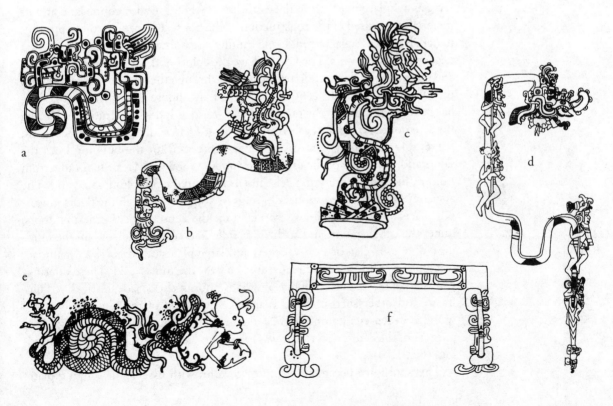

serpents, but to some degree, feathers were an attribute that could be added to any Vision Serpent. For example, the War Serpent called *Waxaklahun-Ubah-Kan* wore feather fans attached to its head and body. Copan particularly favored feathered serpents, and as far as we know, Copan artists were the first to put legs on their feathered serpents. The earliest legged serpent known in Mesoamerica appears on Rosalila, a buried temple built at Copan in the late sixth century. This legged serpent with feathers became central to the art of Chich'en Itza and other Terminal Classic and Early Postclassic traditions in Mesoamerica. We have included illustrations that detail the development of the feathered serpent in Olmec and Maya art (Fig. 1.23).

THE DEDICATION OF MAYA BUILDINGS AND THEIR PROPER NAMES

Maya lords conducted special rituals of dedication to bring life into their buildings and to make them ready for the use of the human and spiritual beings who resided in them. Today, Maya still dedicate their houses in complex rituals that vary from community to community with a core of meaning common to all. For example, many Maya present a live offering, such as a chicken or a sheep, to serve as a replacement gift to the earth spirits who have allowed the land and its materials to be used in the construction of the house. Incense and other precious materials such as sugar, alcohol, and candles, are burned in a plate or on an altar decorated with flowers. The flowers have the colors of the four world directions, and often the ritual incorporates movement through the four directions and into the four corners and the center. And very often a house altar carries a cross that has its roots as much in the precolumbian world as it does in Jerusalem. During the ceremonies, the priest, called an *Ah Q'ih* or *H'Men,* depending on the region, recites a long litany of prayers invoking protection for the building from the saints and the spirits of the earth. The *santos* of modern Maya ritual came from Europe, but almost everything else has its roots in the precolumbian world. The ancient Maya deposited special offerings in holes cut through the floors in various places in their buildings, especially on the central axis, inside the doors, under the center point, and at the four sides and corners. To contain the offerings, they used clay or stone buckets and large plates called *sak-lak,* "manufactured plate," with a second plate inverted over the top as a lid. These offerings consisted of severed heads, flints, obsidians, thorns, shells, jade, mirrors, red pigment, and other such precious material. Almost all of these materials corresponded to representations of *k'ulel,* the living force that imbues all things. One purpose of the dedication rituals was to put the *k'ulel,* or "soul-force," into buildings (Fig. 1.24).

This soul-force became ever more powerful with usage. The offering plates

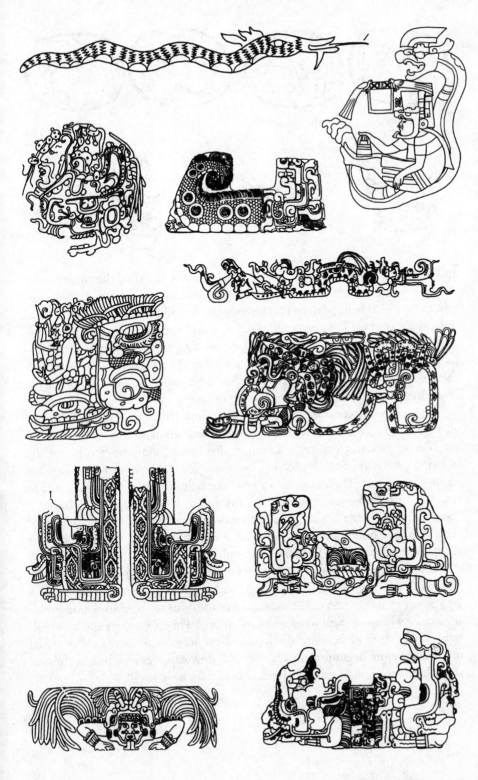

Fig. 1.23. Feathered serpents from Olmec and Maya imagery of the Preclassic (*upper two*); Early Classic and Late Classic periods (*middle five*); legged serpents from Copan and Chich'en Itza (*bottom four*).

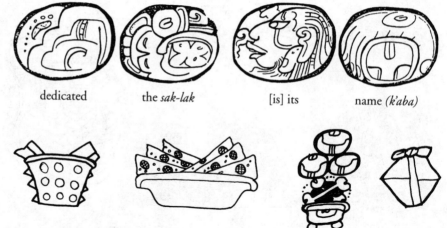

dedicated   the *sak-lak*   [is] its   name *(k'aba)*

Fig. 1.24. A dedication phrase from a *sak-lak* and pictures of various offering plates and buckets from Maya art.

and buckets opened an *ol,* or "portal," that allowed access to the supernatural world. When the Maya materialized their gods and ancestors through these portals, the spiritual beings left residual energy in the buildings and the objects that opened the portals. Thus, very old buildings, very sacred rituals, and very powerful people affected this energy in proportionally greater ways, so that the oldest portals contained the most intense *k'ulel* of all. The Maya kept building over these portals for hundreds of years, so that their buildings were like onions— layer after layer accumulating over the sacred core.

The inscriptions recorded these dedication rituals for objects and buildings of all types.[29] The conventional structure of a dedication statement (Fig. 1.25) includes an introductory verb, a verb of dedication, the proper name of the object, a phrase reading "its name," the word for the type of object, and the name of its owner. These statements give us a rich inventory of actions used to dedicate things, the terms for various categories of objects, such as "house," "bowl," "plate," "stela," "altar," etc., and most interestingly, the proper names of the objects and buildings being dedicated. Finally, these texts sometimes include the names[30] of the painters, scribes, and sculptors who made the objects.

These dedication rituals are as important to archaeologists as they are to art historians and epigraphers. The offerings sealed under floors and inside terraces and plazas contain some of the most important evidence used in dating buildings and developing chronologies of various sites. For epigraphers and archaeologists alike, these dedication offerings and the termination rituals that ended one phase before beginning another are like time capsules that bear witness to the beliefs, economics, and social practices of ancient Maya life.

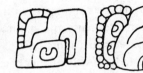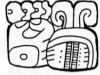

made sacred   *t'ab,*   *och k'ak'*
"ascend, finish the surface"   "entered fire"

el   *u k'aba*
"burn"   "its name"

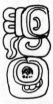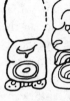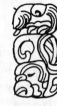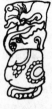

erected   (proper name)   was the   the stela
name of

entered   (proper name)   was the holy   his house
fire into   name of

Fig. 1.25. Glyphic expressions for the dedication of houses, stelae, and other objects.

MAYA HISTORY AND CHRONOLOGY

The great archaeological periods we discussed at the beginning of this chapter give us the framework into which we place Maya history and contemplate its meaning. Archaeologists derived these periods—the Preclassic (1500 B.C.–A.D. 200), the Classic (A.D. 200–910), and the Postclassic (A.D. 910–1524)—and their subdivisions from the material record that they have recovered from archaeology. The features they observe include the style and materials used in pottery, architecture and lithic technology, the appearance of writing and imagery and their style and development, the association of dated monuments with other archaeological material, burial practices, and the contents and methods of placing offerings. Radiocarbon dates from organic remains and a host of newer dating methods, some of which are still being tested, provide further data.

The other major method of dating Maya history comes from the chronologies the Maya themselves recorded on their monuments. The Maya used a complex set of calendars that kept track of many different cycles to date events in their public inscriptions. The most sacred of these cycles was a count of 260 days we call the *tzolk'in*. Consisting of thirteen numbers combined with twenty days, this calendar was used for divination and as a fundamental cycle of time throughout Mesoamerica. The Maya combined this cycle with the *haab*, a count of 365 days divided into eighteen months of twenty days. To bring the count to the full 365 days, they added a five-day period called *Wayeb* ("resting days") at the end of the year. It took fifty-two years or a Calendar Round for the same combination of days in the *tzolk'in* and *haab* to recur. The Maya combined these three calendar cycles with an era-based calendar called the Long Count. The base date in this Long Count, written 13.0.0.0.0 4 Ahaw 8 Kumk'u in the Maya system, corresponded to August 13, 3114 B.C., in the modern calendar. The Long-Count calendar recorded accumulated years of 360 days consisting of eighteen months of twenty days. The Maya numerical system was base-twenty, so they counted in groups of twenty years instead of ten as we do. The year was called a "tun"; twenty tuns made a "k'atun," and twenty k'atuns made a "bak'-tun." We have examples of numbers written with twenty places above the bak'-tun. Since each bak'tun was four hundred years long, they paid far more attention to the k'atun. For example, they also used a shorter cycle of thirteen k'atuns that ran through all the possible names of the k'atuns. They named each k'atun for the day on which it ended, and they celebrated k'atuns when they were completed, just as we celebrate babies' first birthday after they have lived for a year. Most of the history recorded in the inscriptions took place in bak'tuns 8, 9, and 10. We are living today in the last k'atun of bak'tun 13.

A summary of the history of the sites in this book is as follows:

EARLY PRECLASSIC

1000 B.C.   Florescence of Gulf Coast Olmec; early villagers and beginnings of hierarchical social organization in the Pacific zone and Peten; permanent settlements in the Copan Valley

MIDDLE PRECLASSIC

900 B.C.   Rich tombs in the Copan Valley

600 B.C.   Tikal settled by early villagers

500 B.C.   Large towns and long-distance trading appear in Peten, Guatemala

400 B.C.		Late Preclassic period begins; construction of large temples with plaster masks flourishes at Nak'be, El Mirador, and other early Maya sites; formulation of the institution of kingship
200 B.C.		Early Izapa monuments with Popol Vuh mythology in the south; sculpted temples begin to appear throughout the northern lowlands; carved and dated monuments and large towns in the southern highlands; early settlements at Teotihuacan
100 B.C.		Appearance of writing in the Maya zone; Snake Mountains appear in the architecture of Waxaktun and Cerros
50 B.C.		Structure 5C-2nd at Cerros; North Acropolis and stelae at Tikal; Group H at Waxaktun; El Mirador the dominant lowland center; green obsidian from Teotihuacan region at Nohmul
A.D. 100		El Mirador and other Late Preclassic centers abandoned
	8.3.0.0.0	First date with a king found in Loltun Cave, Yukatan
120	8.4.0.0.0	Date recorded with an inscription and royal imagery on a broken jade plaque in the Dumbarton Oaks Collection
160	8.6.0.0.0	The kingdom of Copan established

EARLY CLASSIC

219	8.9.0.0.0	Approximate time of the reign of Yax-Moch-Xok and founding of the Tikal dynasty
292	8.12.14.8.15	Stela 29, earliest dated monument at Tikal
317	8.14.0.0.0	Toh-Chak-Ich'ak celebrated the end of the k'atun at Tikal
376	8.17.0.0.0	Toh-Chak-Ich'ak ended the k'atun at Tikal
378	8.17.1.4.12	Tikal conquered Waxaktun; first appearance of Tlaloc-war complex in Maya imagery; Toh-Chak-Ich'ak died from wounds
379	8.17.2.16.17	Yax-Ain acceded at Tikal under K'ak'-Sih
396	8.18.0.0.0	K'ak'-Sih ended the k'atun at Waxaktun; Yax-Ain ended it at Tikal
411	8.18.15.11.0	Sian-Kan-K'awil became the Ahaw of Tikal
426	8.19.10.0.0	Sian-Kan-K'awil closed the headband and became the Kolomte of Tikal
426	8.19.10.11.17	Yax-K'uk'-Mo' of Copan took the K'awil of the Ch'okte-Nah and established the dynasty at Copan

431	8.19.15.3.4	K'uk'-Balam acceded and founded the dynasty of Palenque
439	9.0.3.9.18	Last event recorded on Stela 31 at Tikal
475	9.2.0.0.0	K'an-Ak ruled at Tikal
537	9.5.3.19.15	Double-Bird, the twenty-first king of Tikal, acceded (?)
553	9.5.19.1.2	Yahaw-Te of Caracol acceded by the action of the king of Tikal
556	9.6.2.1.11	Tikal attacked and sacked Caracol
557	9.6.3.9.15	Last date at Tikal before they lost to Caracol
562	9.6.8.4.2	Caracol defeated Tikal in a "starwar"

LATE CLASSIC

603	9.8.9.13.0	Hanab-Pakal the Great was born at Palenque during the reign of Ah-Ne-Ol-Mat
	9.8.9.15.11	A Bonampak' lord threw down the "Flint-Shield" of a lord of Palenque
612	9.8.19.7.18	Lady Sak-K'uk', Hanab-Pakal's mother, acceded at Palenque
615	9.9.2.4.8	Hanab-Pakal of Palenque acceded
625	9.9.12.11.2	Balah-Kan-K'awil, son of Animal-Skull of Tikal, acceded at Dos Pilas
628	9.9.14.17.5	K'ak'-Nab-K'awil (Smoke-Imix-God K) of Copan acceded
	9.9.15.0.0	Animal-Skull of Tikal named on a monument at Altar de Sacrificios
633	9.10.0.0.0	Hanab-Pakal of Palenque ended the first k'atun of his reign
635	9.10.2.6.6	Kan-Balam, son of Hanab-Pakal of Palenque, was born
640	9.10.7.13.5	Lady Sak-K'uk', Hanab-Pakal's mother, died at Palenque
641	9.10.8.9.3	Kan-Balam of Palenque was designated heir to the throne
643	9.10.10.1.6	K'an-Mo'-Balam, Hanab-Pakal's father, died at Palenque
644	9.10.11.17.0	K'an-Hok'-Chitam, brother of Kan-Balam, was born at Palenque; Balam-Ahaw of Tortuguero conducted a series of wars along Palenque's western frontier
647	9.10.14.5.10	Hanab-Pakal dedicated his first temple at Palenque
649	9.10.16.16.19	Yich'ak-K'ak' of Kalak'mul born
650		Teotihuacan was sacked around this time

652	9.11.0.0.0	K'ak'-Nab-K'awil of Copan celebrated the k'atun at Quirigua and in the Copan Valley; Hanab-Pakal celebrated the k'atun-ending at Palenque
657	9.11.4.5.14	Nun-Bak-Chak of Tikal was driven into exile
659	9.11.6.16.17	Nun-Bak-Chak of Tikal arrived in Palenque
672	9.12.0.8.3	Nun-Bak-Chak of Tikal attacked Dos Pilas and forced Balah-Kan-K'awil into exile
675	9.12.3.6.6	Hanab-Pakal begins construction of the Temple of Inscriptions at Palenque
675		Nun-Bak-Chak may have dedicated the ballcourt in the East Plaza at Tikal around this time
677	9.12.5.10.1	Balah-Kan-K'awil of Dos Pilas and the Yukun-Kun of Kalak'mul forced Nun-Bak-Chak of Tikal out of Dos Pilas
679	9.12.6.16.17	Balah-Kan-K'awil of Dos Pilas threw down the "Flint-Shield" of Nun-Bak-Chak of Tikal and sacrificed him
682	9.12.9.17.16	Hasaw-Kan-K'awil of Tikal acceded as king
	9.12.10.5.12	Lady Wak-Kan-Ahaw, daughter of Balah-Kan-K'awil of Dos Pilas, arrived at Naranjo and reestablished its royal house
683	9.12.11.5.18	Hanab-Pakal of Palenque died and was buried soon after
684	9.12.11.12.10	Kan-Balam of Palenque acceded in a ten-day-long ceremony
686	9.12.13.17.7	Ich'ak-K'ak' of Kalak'mul acceded with Balah-Kan-K'awil of Dos Pilas witnessing the ritual
690	9.12.18.5.16+	Kan-Balam of Palenque dedicated the Group of the Cross in a three-day-long ceremony
692	9.13.0.0.0	Hasaw-Kan-K'awil planted his first stela and built a twin-pyramid complex
		During the twenty years before this date, the Tutul Xiw leave Nonowal and begin their migrations; at the same time, the Itza arrived at Siyan Kan Bak'halal and began sixty years of reign
693	9.13.1.3.19	K'ak'-Tiliw of Naranjo, grandson of Balah-Kan-K'awil of Dos Pilas, acceded at age five, and Naranjo attacked a series of sites over the next year
695	9.13.3.6.8	Waxaklahun-Ubah-K'awil of Copan acceded
	9.13.3.7.18	Hasaw-Kan-K'awil of Tikal captured Ich'ak-K'ak' of Kalak'mul

	9.13.3.8.11	Hasaw-Kan-K'awil displayed his captive
	9.13.3.9.18	Hasaw-Kan-K'awil undertook a conjuring rite and displayed the palanquin he captured from Kalak'mul; this took place 260 tuns (13 k'atuns) after the last date on Stela 31, the stela celebrating Tikal's conquest of Waxaktun
702	9.13.10.0.0	Waxaklahun-Ubah-K'awil dedicated his first stela at Copan
	9.13.10.1.5	Kan-Balam of Palenque died
	9.13.10.6.8	K'an-Hok'-Chitam, the younger brother of Kan-Balam, acceded to the throne of Palenque
711	9.14.0.0.0	Waxaklahun-Ubah-K'awil of Copan erected his first stela in the Great Plaza
715	9.14.3.6.8	Waxaklahun-Ubah-K'awil of Copan dedicated Temple 22 to celebrate the first k'atun-anniversary of his accession
721	9.14.10.0.0	Waxaklahun-Ubah-K'awil erected Stela F
726	9.14.15.0.0	Waxaklahun-Ubah-K'awil erected Stela 4
731	9.14.19.5.0	Waxaklahun-Ubah-K'awil erected Stela H and completed a ritual with the bones of an ancestor
	9.14.19.8.0	Waxaklahun-Ubah-K'awil erected Stela A
	9.15.0.0.0	Waxaklahun-Ubah-K'awil erected Stela B
		During this k'atun, Ah-Kuy-Tok' established himself at Uxmal; at the same time, Holol-Chan-Tepew and Ah-Mek'at-Tutul-Xiw arrived at Chaknabiton and began a ninety-nine-year stay
734	9.15.3.6.8	Yik'in-Kan-K'awil, son of Hasaw-Kan-K'awil, became the king of Tikal
736	9.15.5.0.0	Waxaklahun-Ubah-K'awil erected Stela D at Copan; K'ak'-Tiliw of Quirigua erected a monument and was visited by a lord of Kalak'mul
738	9.15.6.8.13	Waxaklahun-Ubah-K'awil dedicated Ballcourt IIIA at Copan
	9.15.6.14.0	K'ak'-Tiliw of Quirigua burned the gods of Waxaklahun-Ubah-K'awil
	9.15.6.14.6	K'ak'-Tiliw of Quirigua took Waxaklahun-Ubah-K'awil of Copan captive and sacrificed him
	9.15.6.16.5	Smoke-Monkey of Copan acceded
743	9.15.12.2.2	Yik'in-Kan-K'awil of Tikal attacked El Peru and captured a palanquin

744	9.15.12.11.13	Yik'in-Kan-K'awil of Tikal attacked Naranjo and captured Yax-May-Kan-Chak and his palanquin god, K'in-Hix-Ek'-Way
746	9.15.15.2.3	Yik'in-Kan-K'awil of Tikal paraded in his captured palanquin
749	9.15.17.12.16	Smoke-Monkey of Copan died
	9.15.17.12.10	Smoke-Shell, the son of Smoke-Monkey of Copan, acceded
763	9.16.12.5.17	Yax-Pasah of Copan, son of a woman of Palenque, acceded
766	9.16.15.0.0	Yax-Pasah of Copan set up Altar G2 in the Great Plaza
768	9.16.17.16.4	Yax-Ain (Ruler C) of Tikal acceded
769	9.16.18.0.0	Yax-Pasah of Copan began remodeling Temple 11
773	9.17.2.12.16	Yax-Pasah dedicated the upper temple of Structure 11
775	9.17.4.7.12	A date recorded in the House of the Seven Dolls at Tz'ibilchaltun
	9.17.5.0.0	Yax-Pasah dedicated Altar Q
790	9.18.0.0.0	During the twenty years before this k'atun-ending, the Itza held an assembly at Ichkantiho (Tz'ibilchaltun) to establish the Itza confederacy
795	9.18.5.0.0	Last date at Bonampak'; Yax-Pasah placed an altar in the Temple 22A council house
799	9.18.9.4.4	Accession of 6-Kimi-Hanab-Pakal at Palenque; the last date at Palenque
800	9.18.10.0.0	Yax-Pasah erected Altar G in the Great Plaza
807	9.18.17.1.13	Ballgame event on La Amelia Stela 1; last date associated with the Petexbatun state
808	9.18.17.13.4	Last date at Yaxchilan

TERMINAL CLASSIC

810	9.19.0.0.0	Yax-Pasah goes to Quiriguá to celebrate the k'atun-ending
		Last date at Piedras Negras
		Last monument erected at Chink'ultik
		Last date at Kalak'mul
		Last date at Naranjo
		Last date at Quirigua
820	9.19.10.0.0	Yax-K'uk'-Mo's dynasty ended at Copan

822	9.19.11.14.5	U-Kit-Tok' of Copan acceded and within ten years the central government collapsed
830	9.19.19.17.19	Wat'ul arrived at Seibal because of the king of Ucanal
	10.0.0.0.0	The bak'tun-ending celebrated at Oxpemul and Waxaktun
832	10.0.2.7.13	The Temple of the Hieroglyphic Jambs dedicated at Chich'en Itza
841	10.0.10.17.15	Last date at Machaquila
842	10.0.12.8.0	The High Priest's Grave was dedicated at Chich'en Itza
849	10.1.0.0.0	Wat'ul of Seibal dedicated Temple A-3 and his stelae
		Last date at Altar de Sacrificios, Xunantunich, and Ucanal
859	10.1.10.0.0	Last date at Caracol
864	10.1.15.3.6	The Great Ballcourt of Chich'en Itza was dedicated
869	10.2.0.0.0	Hasaw-Kan-K'awil, the last ruler of Tikal, scattered; last date at Tikal
	10.2.0.1.9	Fire ceremonies for K'ak'upakal and Hun-Pik-Tok' in the Casa Colorado at Chich'en Itza
	10.2.0.11.8	The Halak'al Lintel mentioned Hun-Pik-Tok' at Chich'en Itza
870	10.2.1.0.0	The Ak'ab Tz'ib Lintel was dedicated by a Kokom lord at Chich'en Itza
873	10.2.3.12.1, 10.2.4.8.4	K'ak'upakal did fire rituals at Chich'en Itza (Yula lintels)
877	10.2.8.10.4	Temple of Owls capstone was dedicated at Chich'en Itza
878	10.2.9.1.9	The Temple of the Initial Series was dedicated at Chich'en Itza
879	10.2.10.0.0	Monuments dedicated at Ixlu, Jimbal, Sacchana, and Chich'en Itza
880	10.2.10.11.17	The Monjas lintels were dedicated at Chich'en Itza
881	10.2.12.1.8	Members of the Multepal dedicated the Temple of the Four Lintels at Chich'en Itza
883	10.2.13.13.1	Monjas capstones were dedicated at Chich'en Itza
	10.2.13.15.11	Chan or Tan died (probably in battle) at K'abah
		The Tutul Xiw would have arrived at Uxmal during this k'atun if they had stayed in Chaknabiton for ninety-nine years
		K'ak'upakal mentioned in the inscriptions of Uxmal (The text includes a *ch'ak* destruction event that may

refer to the creation by conquest of a regional state by the Tutul Xiw in concert with Chich'en Itza. The date 11 Ahaw occurs in the text, but it cannot be placed in the Long Count.)

889	10.3.0.0.0	Last date at Waxaktun enacted by the local lord under the authority of Hasaw-Kan-K'awil of Tikal; monuments dedicated at La Muñeca, Xultun, Jimbal, Seibal, and Sayil
901	10.3.11.15.14	The Ballcourt Marker at Uxmal was dedicated by Chan-Chak-K'ak'nal-Ahaw
907	10.3.17.12.1	Chan-Chak-K'ak'nal-Ahaw dedicated one of the buildings in the Nunnery Quadrangle at Uxmal
908	10.3.18.9.2	Chan-Chak-K'ak'nal-Ahaw dedicated another building in the Nunnery Quadrangle
909	10.4.0.0.0	Stelae were dedicated at Uxmal, Tonina, and Chich'en Itza
910	10.4.1.0.0	Itzimte Stela 5 recorded that a ruler scattered; this is the latest known date in the inscriptions

POSTCLASSIC

948	10.6.0.0.0	Chich'en Itza was abandoned for the first time during this k'atun, and the Itza established themselves at Chak'anputun, which they ruled for thirteen k'atuns
1185	10.18.0.0.0	10 Ahaw recorded on Stela 1 of Mayapan The Itza left Chak'anputun
1194	10.18.10.0.0	The Hunak-Kel incident where Chak-Xib-Chak was forced out of Chich'en Itza for the second time; Itza retreated to Tan Xuluk Mul, reigned a second time in Chak'anputun; K'ak'upakal and Tekuylu conquered Chak'anputun
1224	11.0.0.0.0	During this k'atun, K'inich K'ak'-Mo and Popolchan of Itzamal were driven out by Hunak-Kel; the Itza, in concert with the men of Ulil of Itzamal, attacked Mayapan 4 Ahaw recorded on Stela 4 of Mayapan
1263	11.2.0.0.0	During this k'atun, the Itza defeated Mayapan, established a new confederacy, and became known as Maya 2 Ahaw recorded on Stela 13 of Mayapan
1382	11.8.0.0.0	Mayapan was abandoned

1384	11.8.1.0.0	The Tutul Xiw left Mayapan
1441	11.11.0.0.0	Mayapan was finally abandoned, and the Maya were scattered in the region
1470		Around this time, the K'iche' under K'iq'ab were establishing an empire in highland Guatemala
1485		Around this time, the Kaqchikels separated from the K'iche' and established their capital at Iximche'
1493	11.13.12.15.13	The Akahals and the Tukuches rebelled against the Iximche' Kaqchikels and their kings Oxlahuh-Tz'i' and Kablahuh-Tihax
1500	11.14.0.0.0	The first epidemic of smallpox or some other European disease raged in Yukatan during the years just before this k'atun-ending
1502	11.14.2.0.0	A Maya trading canoe was contacted in the Bay of Honduras during the fourth voyage of Columbus
1508	11.14.8.4.12	Oxlahuh-T'zi' of Iximche' died
1511	11.14.11.0.0	Aguilar and Guerrero shipwrecked on the coast of Yukatan
1519	11.14.18.17.16	Cortés landed on Cozumel Island
1521	11.15.1.8.13	Tenochtitlan, the Aztec capital, fell
1524	11.15.4.1.8	Alvarado and the Spaniards defeated the K'iche' in the battle of Xelahuh
	11.15.4.2.4	Alvarado burned the K'iche' kings at the stake and destroyed their capital, Q'umarkah
	11.15.4.4.0	The Spaniards entered Iximche' and were welcomed by the Kaqchikel kings
	11.15.4.9.4	Alvarado declared Iximche' to be *Santiago de los Caballeros de Guatemala* and capital of the new territories he intended to conquer
	11.15.4.10.16	The outraged Kaqchikels abandoned Iximche' and began a war against the Spanish invaders
1525	11.15.5.2.1	Cortés met King Kan-Ek' at the Itza capital of Tayasal during his trip across Maya country to Honduras
1526	11.15.6.1.6	Spanish deserters burned Iximche'
1530	11.15.10.6.17	The Kaqchikel kings and their lords surrendered
1540	11.16.0.10.8	Alvarado hanged the Kaqchikel kings who had surrendered
1541	11.16.1.12.10	Alvarado died
	11.16.1.15.18	Torrential rains caused a landslide on Agua Volcano

		and destroyed the Spaniards' new capital at Ciudad Vieja
1542	11.16.2.3.14	The Spaniards founded the city of Mérida over the ruins of Tiho
1546	11.16.7.2.6	The Maya of eastern Yukatan rose up against the Spaniards
1697	12.3.19.11.6	The Spaniards defeated the Itza of Tayasal and the last independent Maya kingdom fell

CHAPTER 2

Tikal: Toh-Chak-Ich'ak's Palace

Flying into Flores, the gateway to Tikal, takes one over some of the remaining forest that once covered the southern Maya lowlands. The plane lands next to Lake Peten Itza, the heart of the original lands of the Itza. In fact, the Itza people probably took their name from that of the lake; *Itz-a* means "Enchanted Waters." The modern road from Flores leads around the southern shore of the lake, turning north at its east end to rise slowly through the national forest into the archaeological park. You can feel the temperature drop as you drive through the surviving forest. Animals and birds of all sorts appear along the fringes of the road because this is one of the few refuges where they still survive. The park is full of ocellated turkeys, macaws, parrots, toucans, and spider monkeys that have lost their fear of people because of their protection. But watch out about standing under monkeys—what you feel may not be rain.

Tikal is famous for its towering pyramids that stand above the sea of trees that surround them (Fig. 2.1). The forest still edges up to the cleared areas of the city as if it would claim the old buildings back from the tourists if they blinked for a moment. Walking in the forest around Tikal is one of the true joys of being at the site.

Tikal is an old city, with its earliest levels dating back to at least 900 B.C. In fact, Tikal existed for over a thousand years before its surviving written history began. The earliest surviving monument in that history is Stela 29, dated to A.D. 292.[1] The dynasty of Tikal recorded their history on similar monuments for the next six hundred years and documented the deeds of one of the longest-lived dynasties ever to rule a Maya kingdom. Founded by a king modern scholars call Yax-Moch-Xok (or, more likely, Yax-Ch'akte-Xok),[2] Tikal's dynasty ruled one of the most powerful and populous of all Maya kingdoms. Its dynasty played a role in Maya history that equaled the size and magnificence of its capital city.

The modern name given to the ruins of that capital city is Tikal, but that is not what its original inhabitants called their kingdom. To them, it was *Mutul*. Found in "emblem glyph" titles, the glyph for Tikal depicts the rear view of a human head with a knot tied across it (Fig. 2.2). We are lucky to have examples

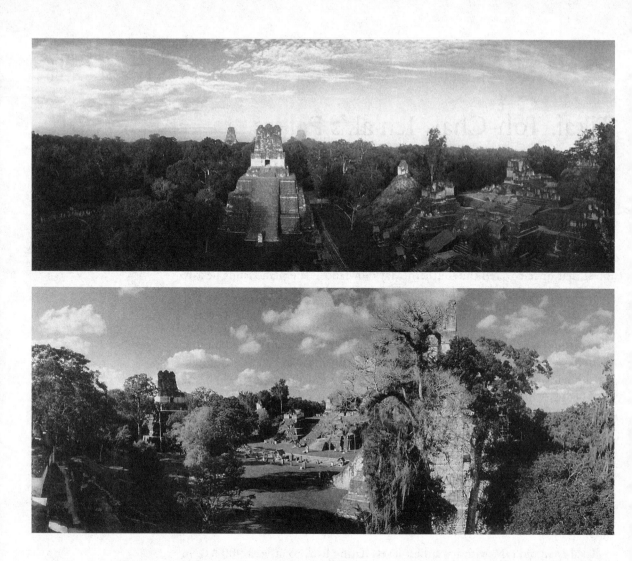

Fig. 2.1.
Tikal in the forest.

with phonetic complements showing that this hair knot reads *mu-t(u)* and *mu-tu-l(a)*.[3] *Mut* means "bird" and "prognostication" in both Chol and Yukatek, while *mutul* is the Yukatek word for a "knot of hair." Sometimes the scribes of *Mutul* called it *Yax Mutul,* "First Mutul,"[4] perhaps because at least one other kingdom, Dos Pilas, used the same name. The rulers of the great capital wanted all to know that it was the first kingdom of that name.

A—THE CITY AND ITS HISTORY

Mutul sprawls over many square kilometers. Much of it is still buried in the ground under the thick tropical forest that survives in the national park. Past

K'ul Mutul Ahaw
"Holy Mutul Lord"

tan kun Mutul
"in the seat of
Mutul"

Ah mu-mutul   *mut-tu*
(phonetic complements
attached to the logograph
mutul)

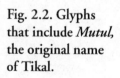

Fig. 2.2. Glyphs
that include *Mutul,*
the original name
of Tikal.

archaeological investigations have concentrated, for the most part, on the huge complexes in the center of the city, although excavators have also investigated outlying groups that housed high-ranking but nonroyal lineages. Compared to most other Maya cities, a lot has been learned about Mutul and its archaeology over the last forty years.[5]

The long inscriptional history of Mutul opened in A.D. 292 with the erection of Stela 29, a monument celebrating a ruler nicknamed Foliated-Jaguar (Fig. 2.3). He wrote a date on the rear of the stela in the Maya Long-Count calendar, but the event he recorded did not survive. Thus, we know the date of the event, but not the action. He was not the first ruler, nor was his stela the first one set up by a Mutul king, but by historical accident his is the first written record we have. Unfortunately, monuments from the next eighty-six years of Tikal's history are missing, but we can reconstruct some of the missing events from a retrospective account carved into the back of Stela 31 at the behest of a later ruler, Sian-Kan-K'awil.[6]

     (ruler glyph)

Yax-Moch-
Xok

Foliated-
Jaguar

K'ak'-Sih

Toh-Chak-
Ich'ak

Yax-Ain

Sian-Kan-
K'awil

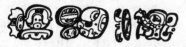 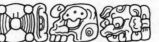

Animal-Skull, Ete

Nun-Bak-Chak

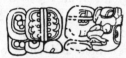

Hasaw-Kan-K'awil

Yik'in-Kan-K'awil

Yax-Ain

Fig. 2.3. Names
of the dramatis
personae from Mutul.

According to the Stela 31 chronicle, a successor of Foliated-Jaguar ruled Mutul when the k'atun (twenty-year period) ended in A.D. 317 (8.14.0.0.0). Named *Toh-Chak-Ich'ak*, "True-Great-Jaguar-Claw," this ruler was one of the greatest and most influential in Mutul's history. Although we do not know his accession date, he held office for at least sixty-one years,[7] so that he must have been an old man when he led Mutul into war in the last great act of his life. The war was against the nearby rival kingdom of Waxaktun, known as *Sian-Kan*, "Heaven-Born," in the inscriptions. We deduce[8] that Mutul had been at war with Sian-Kan for many years before this final battle, although we do not know for how long nor do we have details of the conflict. However, the inscriptions of both cities record Mutul's victory in 378, and Stela 31 acknowledged Toh-Chak-Ich'ak's death from wounds on that very day.[9]

He was succeeded by two people. K'ak'-Sih ("Fire-Born," also known as "Smoking-Frog" in the literature), who had actually led the Mutul army against Waxaktun, became the ruler of the new combined kingdom, while Yax-Ain I ("Green or First Crocodile," also known as Curl-Snout) became the *ahaw* of the old capital of Mutul, and in time of the entire kingdom. Toh-Chak-Ich'ak, Yax-Ain I, and his son, Sian-Kan-K'awil,[10] expanded Mutul through alliances and conquest until it dominated central Peten and affected the early histories of distant sites like Uxbenka in Belize, Copan in Honduras, and Palenque in Chiapas. The tombs and texts of these three lords constitute one of the great heritages we have from the Classic period.

Nothing lasts forever, including Mutul's good fortune. In time, its great wealth and influence drew other rivals, the principal one of which was Kalak'-mul, a kingdom located to the north of Tikal in modern Kampeche. Known to the ancient world as *Kan*, "Snake," that northern kingdom established a hegemony that opposed Mutul in war and economics until at least A.D. 906. In fact, much of Classic-period Maya history, especially the wars, can be seen as resulting from the rivalry between these two great hegemonies.[11]

Yet as the future unfolded for good and bad, the people of Mutul never forgot the conquest of Waxaktun, the heroes involved in it, or the ruler who had led them to victory. They celebrated their great ancestor, Toh-Chak-Ich'ak, for the rest of Mutul's history. Interestingly, very few public works from his long reign survive. Most of the major monuments from Toh-Chak-Ich'ak's reign have been subsumed by the buildings of later rulers, or perhaps they were destroyed in the war.[12] However, one building—the palace he built in the Central Acropolis (Fig. 2.4)—became a shrine that was preserved until the final destruction of Mutul in the tenth century. That palace and the buildings around it are the focus of this chapter.[13]

Toh-Chak-Ich'ak built his palace to the east and south of the North Acropolis, where Tikal's early kings had been building their temples and tombs for hundreds of years. As his successors built their own palaces near his shrine, the

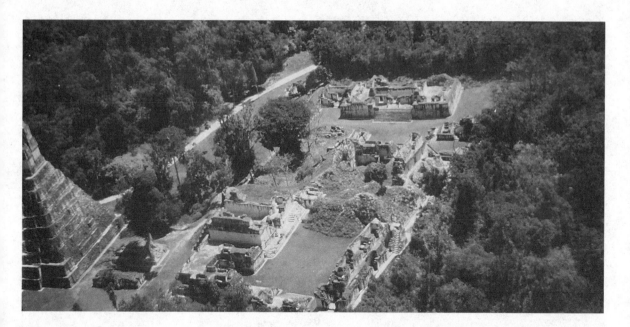

Central Acropolis grew upward and westward to form the southern boundary of the Great Plaza and the East Plaza. Today, visitors can enter the Central Acropolis from either place, but at the time Toh-Chak-Ich'ak constructed his palace, it rose above the East Plaza in isolated splendor.

Fig. 2.4. Aerial view of the Central Acropolis, with Toh-Chak-Ich'ak's Palace at the top.

Three trails (Fig. 2.5a) lead into the East Plaza today: one proceeds through twin-pyramid complexes to the Maler Causeway, which enters from the north; another leads through Group F and around the East Acropolis and a Late-Classic group thought to be a market; and the third leads through the forest to the Mendez Causeway and the southeast corner of the East Plaza.

B—THE EAST PLAZA BALLCOURT AND STRUCTURE 5D-43

The East Plaza has a long and interesting history, although most of it is buried under later renovations. When Toh-Chak-Ich'ak built his palace, the East Plaza was a large open space, but his successors turned it into a vital ceremonial space by building Mutul's first twin-pyramid complex. His successors conducted the important ceremonies that closed the twenty-year period called a k'atun in this complex, probably beginning in 9.2.0.0.0 (A.D. 475). During this time, huge acropolis platforms closed the eastern and western ends of the plaza, while paired radial pyramids sat in the center of the space.[14] Nothing of this twin-pyramid complex remains visible today, although the East Acropolis still sits in the forest next to Group F.

This East Plaza changed its character forever in the wake of a momentous change in Mutul's history.[15] In A.D. 553, the king of Tikal installed a new ruler in

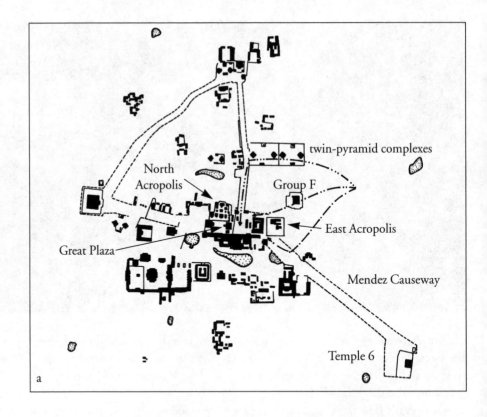

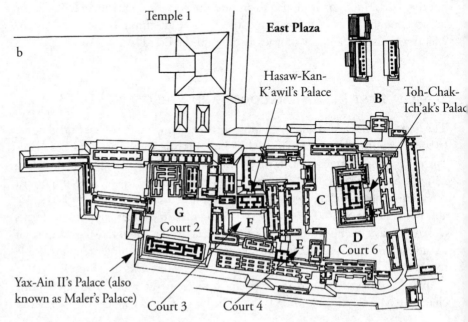

twin-pyramid complexes

North Acropolis

Group F

East Acropolis

Great Plaza

Mendez Causeway

Temple 6

a

Temple 1

East Plaza

b

Hasaw-Kan-K'awil's Palace

B

Toh-Chak-Ich'ak's Palac

G

Court 2

F

C

E

D

Court 6

Fig. 2.5. (a) Map of the center of Tikal, with the trails shown, and (b) a detail of the Central Acropolis.

Yax-Ain II's Palace (also known as Maler's Palace)

Court 3

Court 4

the allied kingdom of Caracol, located to the southeast in modern Belize. Shortly thereafter, in 556, Tikal attacked Caracol apparently because its new king had switched his allegiance to Tikal's great rival, Kalak'mul. In 562, Caracol, in concert with Kalak'mul, attacked and defeated Tikal and killed its king. We suspect that the victors sacked the sacred center of Mutul during this period, and surely Tikal found itself paying tribute to the winners for at least a time.

After the disastrous defeat, a new ruler, the twenty-second in the dynasty of Yax-Moch-Xok, took office at Mutul. We do not know much about his reign because no monuments survive from that period. Known as Animal-Skull (probably *Ete* in the original spelling), this ruler apparently countered the Caracol victory by establishing a new bellicose satellite kingdom in the Petexbatun to the southwest of Tikal. The lords of Altar de Sacrificios referred to him on 9.9.15.0.0 (February 15, 628), only two years after his son, a man named *Balah-Kan-K'awil* (also known as Flint-Sky-God K), became the king of Dos Pilas.[16] If we presume that Animal-Skull acceded soon after the twenty-first king died at the hands of Caracol's ruler, he would have been on the throne for sixty-five years by the time of the Altar de Sacrificios date. He very likely died soon thereafter, for he would have been in his late seventies or early eighties by the time of these events.

Animal-Skull was a long-lived and successful ruler. His successor laid him to rest in a rich tomb[17] adjacent to the buildings that held the tombs of the great Sian-Kan-K'awil and Yax-Ain I. Afterward they built a huge new temple (5D-32-1st) over his grave and initiated a major renovation of the North Acropolis, the North Terrace, and the Great Plaza (Fig. 2.6).

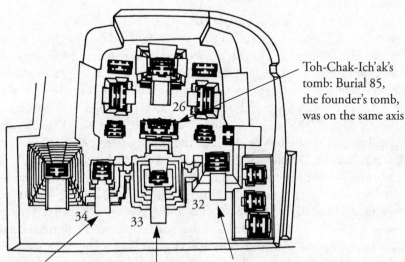

Toh-Chak-Ich'ak's tomb: Burial 85, the founder's tomb, was on the same axis

Yax-Ain's tomb and the caching of Stela 26

Sian-Kan-K'awil's tomb, Burials 23 and 24, and the caching of Stela 31

Animal-Skull's tomb

Fig. 2.6. The North Acropolis and the burial sites of the great Early Classic kings.

The newly installed ruler of Dos Pilas soon defected to the other side, although we do not know whether this occurred before or after his father died. This change of allegiance must have been devastating to Tikal because it cut them off from access to the southwest as they had already been contained to the southeast. Kalak'mul had also established alliances to the east and west of Tikal at the sites of Naranjo and El Peru.

We know nothing about the twenty-third and twenty-fourth rulers of Tikal, but they must have had short reigns. They were succeeded by the twenty-fifth king of Tikal,[18] *Nun-Bak-Chak* (also known as Shield-Skull), who was either the son or grandson of Animal-Skull. It fell to him to repair the damage done by his kinsman's defection. The confrontation began in 657, when a war with Kalak'-mul forced Nun-Bak-Chak into exile. He found refuge at Palenque in 659, gathered his strength, and returned in 672 to begin a second war. After having regained his own kingdom, he forced his traitorous kinsman into exile from Dos Pilas. The triumph was short-lived because five years later, Balah-Kan-K'awil, in concert with his overlord, the king of Kalak'mul, returned with a vengeance, defeated the Tikal king, and sacrificed him on May 3, 679.[19]

The texts from Dos Pilas say that the victors buried bones from the thirteen provinces of Tikal, implying that the battle left many dead. They may even have forced their way into Tikal's center, killing people as they went and sacking the city. We know from the archaeological records that many historical monuments from the previous two hundred years, especially those that recorded Tikal's ancient victory over Waxaktun, were smashed. Twice within a twenty-year period, Tikal lost wars (in 657 and 672), which probably resulted in a sacking of the central zone of the city.

During the aftermath of one of these losses,[20] either Nun-Bak-Chak or his son Hasaw-Kan-K'awil began a campaign to rebuild the devastated capital and recover the honor of the kingdom. Whichever king it was, he repaired damage done to the North Acropolis and the monuments in front of the buildings holding the tombs of the most important of his ancestors—Toh-Chak-Ich'ak,[21] Yax-Ain I, Sian-Kan-K'awil, and Animal-Skull. He inserted a tomb deep inside Temple 33-2nd, the Snake Mountain that covered Sian-Kan-K'awil's tomb. He installed the shattered Stela 26 inside the bench of Temple 34, the temple that covered Yax-Ain I's tomb. With even more ceremony, he put the broken Stela 31 and pieces of shattered altar inside Temple 33-2nd, and after extensive rituals that included constructing a scaffold and burning major fires,[22] he built a huge new temple over the old Snake Mountain. If Hasaw-Kan-K'awil was the instigator of all this, he probably dedicated the new temple exactly thirteen k'atuns, or 260 years, after the last date on the buried stela. The text on that stela commemorates the k'atun-endings of Toh-Chak-Ich'ak's reign, his victory over Waxaktun, and the history of the subsequent fifty years.

During this huge renovation episode, the people of Mutul built a new ballcourt and an extraordinary radial building in the East Plaza over the floor that had buried the twin-pyramid complex.[23] They placed this ballcourt near the palace of Toh-Chak-Ich'ak, the man who had led them to glory centuries earlier. Today the forest at the edge of the East Plaza shrouds the playing alley, leaving the strange little end temple (5D-43) to stand in lonely isolation against the eastern end of the Central Acropolis.

The new set of buildings presented exotic features that were appropriate to the context of war and ancestral revival. The ballcourt had flanking buildings with round columns in the doors that are unique in the architecture of Tikal (Fig. 2.7). However, the people of Tz'ibanche and other sites in southern Quintana Roo used round columns from the Early Classic period onwards. Perhaps the Tikal king used this style to evoke his great enemy—Kalak'mul, the major site in that region.

Archaeologists found fragments of glyphic inscriptions in the panels that once graced the top of the angled benches. These give some fragmentary but important information. The western text had a glyph reading *och k'ak'*, "entered fire," a well-known expression used in dedicatory rites. Glyphs from the eastern panel included a period-ending expression[24] and an important phrase suggesting a time frame centered on 9.11.15.0.0 (A.D. 667), during the period after Nun-Bak-Chak returned from exile and before he attacked Dos Pilas.[25]

The end structure of the ballcourt with its *talud-tablero* platform is a unique building in Tikal, but its close juxtaposition to Toh-Chak-Ich'ak's Palace is a clue to its meaning. It was a radial building in its original form, with four entry doorways and three stairways (Fig. 2.8). The south side was too close to the Central Acropolis for a stairway. Eventually, three of the doors were walled in and the single square room became two chambers.

The most important feature of the building is the profile of the platform,

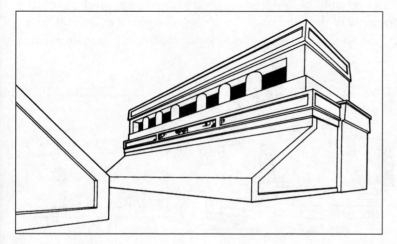

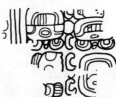

Fig. 2.7. The East Plaza ballcourt and text fragments recording a date and a dedication verb located in the panels above the sloping benches.

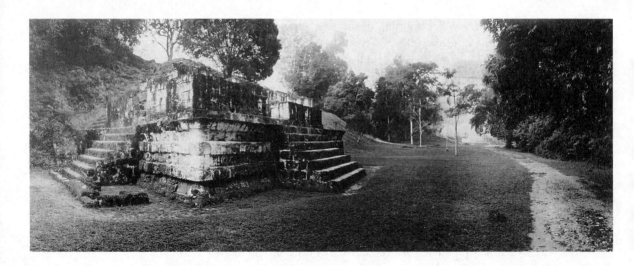

Fig. 2.8. Structure 5D-43, the East Plaza, and Temple 1.

which has a style called *talud-tablero* by archaeologists. Traditionally, scholars have associated this platform style with architecture at the site of Teotihuacan in central Mexico. However, the Tikal version has an angled panel, called a *talud,* both above and below an enframed panel called a *tablero* (Fig. 2.9), while Teotihuacan architecture has the *tablero* and a lower *talud.* Christopher Jones, who excavated this building, commented[26] that its three-part profile has more affinities with buildings at El Tajín and Xochicalco,[27] than with those at Teotihuacan. The Tikal builders placed paired disks inside the *tableros,* and set large flowers resembling the Maya glyph for "zero" into the angled panels. This second design is related to the "star" and "Venus" symbols used at Teotihuacan and other western Mesoamerican sites.

Today, visitors see the final two-chambered form of the temple sitting on top of the platform against the Central Acropolis. The stairway at the rear of the building was a later addition, but it gives a good position from which to view the surviving fragment of the entablature frieze that once graced the roof of Structure 5D-43. The surviving imagery shows a giant monster face, perhaps a jaguar,

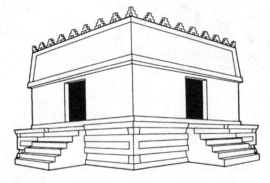

Fig. 2.9. B: Structure 5D-43 and the double rings and flowers on the *talud-tablero.*

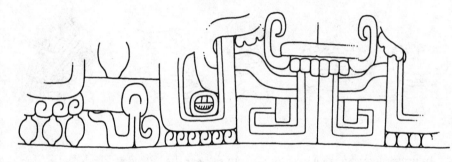

Fig. 2.10. Surviving parts of the frieze from the entablature of Structure 5D-43.

with another toothy head emerging from its mouth (Fig. 2.10). The emerging creature has a huge bifurcated tongue, but its teeth suggest it was not a snake. Whatever the species, it was a great Vision Beast emerging from the throat of another supernatural creature. These images suggest that the building was used to call out ancestors like Toh-Chak-Ich'ak in the context of the ballgame.

In Mesoamerica, the ballgame had a sacred function related directly to the myths of Creation and Origin. The Maize God died and was reborn in the ballcourt. The Maya defined the ballcourt as a crack in the top of a mountain or in the carapace of the Cosmic Turtle, because these were also conceived as rebirth places of the Maize God. People went down this crack to contact their ancestors and consult oracular deities. The Maya and other Mesoamericans negotiated and sealed alliances in the ballcourt, and captured kings died by sacrifice in the ballcourt.

Snake Mountain, the place where civilization was invented, also had a ballcourt at its base. In mythology, water from the ballcourt irrigated the land around Snake Mountain and gave abundant harvests to the people. The people of Mutul constructed their Snake Mountain as Temple 33-2nd in the front of the North Acropolis. They identified it by covering its terraces with plaster masks of mountain monsters with snakes emerging from their mouths (Fig. 2.11).[28]

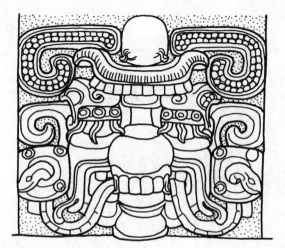

Fig. 2.11. Snake Mountain from Temple 33-2nd.

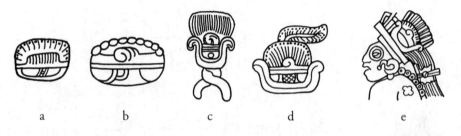

Fig. 2.12. (a–b) Glyphs for *Puh,* (c–d) examples of cattail reeds from Tikal and Akank'e, and (e) the Teotihuacan version of *ahaw,* with a *Puh* sign in its headdress from the inscription of Temple 26 at Copan.

a   b   c   d   e

In mythology, Snake Mountain was in or near the "Place of Reeds," also identified as the home of the people who invented civilized life. To the Maya and the rest of Mesoamerica, Teotihuacan was a "Place of Reeds."[29] The Maya called it *Puh,* "Cattail Reed" (Fig. 2.12), while to the peoples of the period, it was *Tollan.* The Maya of Tikal used the *talud-tablero* style to mark this building as one associated with *Puh,* "Cattail Reed." Its placement in this out-of-the-way location instead of in the Great Plaza may seem strange, until we realize that its builders placed it near the ancestral shrine of Toh-Chak-Ich'ak, the king who brought the symbolism of Teotihuacan to Tikal. We think that the king who commissioned this ballcourt used this strategy to confirm that he and his dynasty were also *Ah Puh,* or "People of the Reed."

B1—THE GRAFFITI

Incised graffiti that once graced the inside of Temple 43 gave witness to the kinds of activities that people saw around it. Now all are gone because of water erosion, but fortunately they were drawn and published before they disappeared.[30] For example, one depicted a ballgame in progress with one player throwing himself on the ground opposite his elaborately dressed opponent (Fig. 2.13). Other

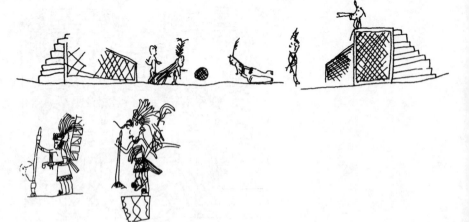

Fig. 2.13. Graffiti showing a ballgame and two warriors with war banners.

images included warriors with banners in the back of their belts, a spear-bearing warrior, dancers, and animals that appear to be deer. From these pictures, we can surmise that ballgame rituals and dances took place around this building and that processions very likely moved from the East Plaza up past the ballcourt and into Court 6, where the ancestral shrine of the royal family was carefully preserved.

C—THE PALACE OF TOH-CHAK-ICH'AK (TRUE-GREAT-JAGUAR-CLAW)

Court 6 is a complicated set of spaces and buildings that radiates around an ancient palace sitting in the center of the lowest end of the Central Acropolis (Fig. 2.14; Fig. 2.5b). Although changed by the buildings and platforms built around it, the old palace originally sat on a high platform mounted by stairs on the east and west sides. In later times, its east stairs were buried under new construction that created a tiny private court on that side of the building. Later kings also added other rooms and court spaces to the north, south, and west sides of the palace to accommodate the festivals and other rituals held to commemorate the illustrious ancestor, Toh-Chak-Ich'ak.

Originally, the palace had three doorways penetrating through its eastern and western outer walls and leading to three interior galleries. Toh-Chak-Ich'ak's builders divided the western gallery into two rooms and put a bench across the end of the northernmost room. They used a different plan in the two eastern gal-

Fig. 2.14. C: Aerial view with Toh-Chak-Ich'ak's Palace and Court 6 (D) on the left and Maler's Palace and Court 2 (G) on the right.

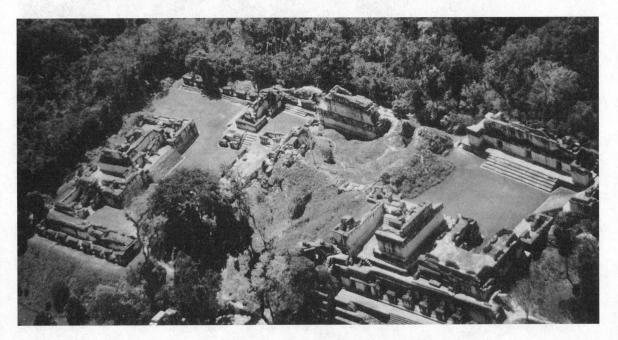

leries that cut off small chambers on both ends. In the northern chamber, they constructed a stairway that spiraled up to the second story (Fig. 2.15). Today, visitors can climb up to the mostly destroyed second story to get a better view of Court 6 and its surrounding buildings.

The eastern side of the building was most likely the front when Toh-Chak-Ich'ak used the palace. Its three doors enter an outer chamber that leads to an inner throne room. This inner room has a central bench where the king sat to conduct business and hold rituals. Flanking benches on either end of the throne room provided areas where various officials, scribes, and other members of the court could attend their lord.

C1—THE LORD'S BENCH

A Maya depiction of just such a palace ritual helps us to visualize what the palace looked like when Toh-Chak-Ich'ak was in residence. The scene (Fig. 2.16) shows a lord leaning back against a large pillow under a rolled-up curtain, as atten-

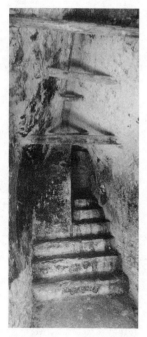

Fig. 2.15. Stairway in the north end of Toh-Chak-Ich'ak's Palace.

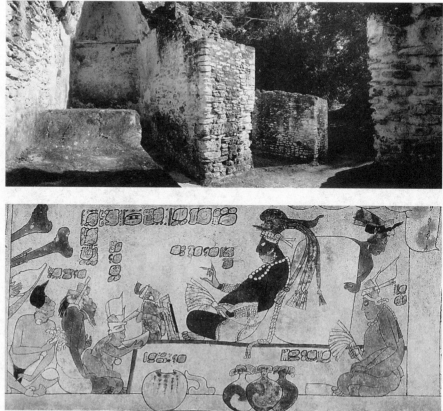

Fig. 2.16. C1: The bench in the eastern chamber of Toh-Chak-Ich'ak's Palace compared to a pottery scene showing a lord seated on a similar bench attended by his court. The musicians play in the part of the room behind the outer wall.

dant lords see to his needs. A little chubby from his good life, the lord admires himself in a mirror held by a dwarf. Two other dwarves sit beside the bench with one drinking from a bowl. The Maya saw dwarves as *mas*, "hobgoblin," who became servants of the king because they could tap into the supernatural.

A courtier sits behind them with the flowers he has brought for his lord, and the wooden trumpets and conch shell of court musicians peek out from behind the wall. The musicians are sitting at the end of a long throne room exactly like the one in Toh-Chak-Ich'ak's Palace. Another *itz'at*, or sage, sits on the opposite side of the lord's bench holding an object that appears to be made from cut paper.

Such palace rituals require drink and food, which are held in the vessels lying on the floor. One is a large round gourd with its lid next to it. The gourd is called *kuch ti utz*, "container for goodies." In fact, the other small text above the middle dwarf records *tos utz*, "powdered good." *Utz* is the Maya word for "good," both as a value and as taste. "Good"-tasting drinks were made from honey, chocolate, sweet atole, and other delicacies of Maya cuisine.

C2—THE STAIRWAY CACHES AND TOH-CHAK-ICH'AK

The stairways on both the east and west sides contained caches placed when the first building and subsequent renovations were dedicated. Each of the three caches on the east included burials, with the earliest of these probably placed by Toh-Chak-Ich'ak himself.[31]

The dedicatory cache under the west stairs contained the most important offering, making possible the identification of the core building as the Toh-Chak-Ich'ak's Palace. The offering (Fig. 2.17) included flint blades and shells arranged next to a beautifully carved cache vessel that contained a figurine, jade medallions, shell, pyrite, and obsidian mosaics.[32]

Fig. 2.17. C2: The cache under the west stairs of Toh-Chak-Ich'ak's Palace. Note the flint blades in the dirt around the pot.

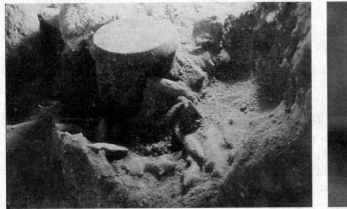

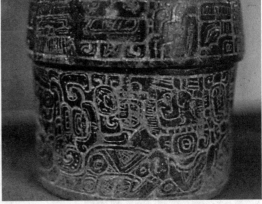

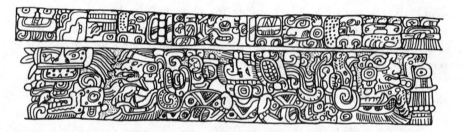

Fig. 2.18. The cache pot shows the Maize God holding the ecliptic serpent, from whose mouths the Paddler Gods emerge. The text records the dedication of the palace, while the owner's name, Toh-Chak-Ich'ak Mutul Ahaw, occurs in the last two glyphs.

The scene on this extraordinary pot sets the context for the dedication rituals. The image (Fig. 2.18) depicts the Maize God at the moment of Creation spreading out the ecliptic snake with the Paddler Gods emerging from each end. Next to the Maize God sits the Quadripartite God, who is the personified offering plate that opens a portal to the Otherworld. The Maize God used this sacred plate in a later act of Creation to raise the World Tree, called *Wakah-Kan*.

The text on this pot reads *ali t'ab yotot k'ul nal, bolon tz'akabil ahaw Ch'akte-Xok, Wak Kan Ak K'ul Na, Toh-Chak-Ich'ak, Mutul Ahaw*, "They say he ascended to his house, the Holy Place, the ninth successor lord of Ch'akte-Xok, Six-Sky-Turtle Holy Building, True-Great-Jaguar-Claw, Mutul Lord."[33] This dedication text identifies the owner of the building as Toh-Chak-Ich'ak. He was the ninth king of Mutul and the man who led Mutul to victory over Waxaktun, although he died on the day of final victory. His descendants and his vassals greatly honored him by recalling the victory in several texts, by naming at least two later kings after him, and most of all by preserving his palace as the most important lineage shrine in the city.

C3—RENOVATIONS BY LATER KINGS

Sometime in the mid eighth century, Yik'in-Kan-K'awil, the twenty-seventh king of Tikal and son of Hasaw-Kan-K'awil, initiated a major renovation project that began around Toh-Chak-Ich'ak's Palace.[34] Builders extended its platform to the north and south and constructed new patios surrounded by several rooms (Fig. 2.19). The north patio has a small corner platform that may have served for holding pots or statues. These patios provided space for ancestral rituals conducted in relationship to the old palace they encased. They were probably used for feasting and for the trance-vision rituals that materialized ancestors like Toh-Chak-Ich'ak for their descendants. Taking place over days, these rituals featured dancing and the drawing of blood from the penis and tongue. Using the motion of the dance, exhaustion, sleep deprivation, driving music—especially from drums—and psychoactive plants, the Maya went into deep trance states, which allowed them to communicate with beings in the Otherworld. They encoded these trance experiences as serpents rearing up through clouds of incense smoke to belch out the ancestor or god whom they wished to contact.

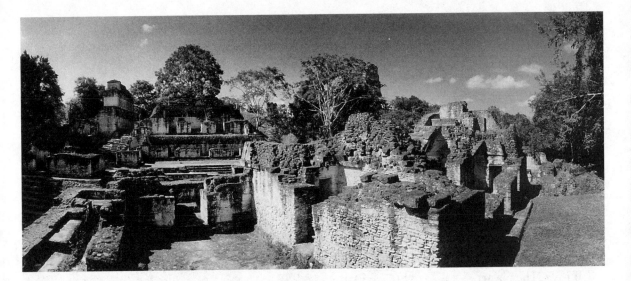

Ancestral shrines like this survive today among many Maya groups. The K'iche' Maya of the Guatemalan highlands conduct ceremonies at their shrines for their dead ancestors, while the Awakatek Maya unchain their ancestral dead by dancing near their graves on the Day of the Dead. These ideas that the dead affect the living and that the living can call out the dead are very ancient concepts among the Maya.[35]

Fig. 2.19. The south annex to Toh-Chak-Ich'ak's Palace. This addition and its twin on the north side were probably built by Yax-Ain II, also known as Ruler C.

C4—AN OLD STUCCO BURIED

Yik'in-Kan-K'awil's new north building leaned against the structure designated 5D-141 and obscured an inscription and relief image of a seated lord. Visitors cannot see this panel today because it was sealed in by consolidation work, but its text (Fig. 2.20) gives us information about Toh-Chak-Ich'ak's Palace. Although the inscription is difficult to read, we know it mentions a place called *Wi-Na*, "Root Structure" or "Origin Structure."

Stela 31 twice records events that occurred at a building called *Wi-Te-Na*, "Root Structure" or "Origin Tree Structure." We suspect that the *Wi-Na* and the *Wi-Te-Na* are the same and that both names refer to Toh-Chak-Ich'ak's Palace. One of the events reads *t'ab Wi-Te-Na*, "he ascended the Origin Tree House," while the other says that Yax-Ain II's accession happened at the *Wi-Te-Na*. If we are correct in our identification, then Yax-Ain II became the king in the house where his predecessor, perhaps his father, resided during his life.

Wi-Te-Na

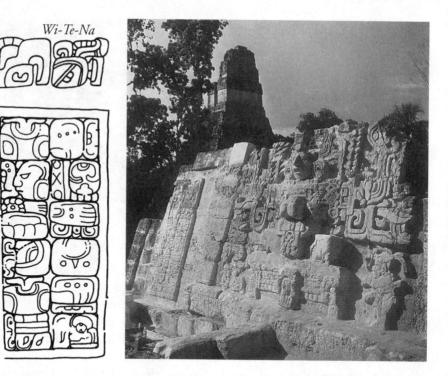

Wi-Na

Fig. 2.20. The texts from Stela 31 and Structure 5D-141 mentioning *Wi-Te-Na* and *Wi-Na*. The plaster scene showing a lord seated on a throne with a dwarf on his right is now covered by a wall.

D—COURT 6

Yax-Ain II, who was the twenty-ninth ruler of Tikal and the grandson of Hasaw-Kan-K'awil, also contributed to the final form of the spaces around Toh-Chak-Ich'ak's Palace.[36] As his predecessors had before him, he added buildings to the court and remodeled those that were already there. These additions reduced the open space to two small court areas, bordered by galleried buildings that provided many small rooms around the courts. Most likely participants in lineage rituals, visitors from other areas of the kingdom, and caretakers used these many rooms while they participated in ancestral rituals. Some of these surrounding buildings may also have housed permanent caretakers, whose responsibilities very likely included regular rituals for the ancestors, much like those of the *cofradistas* of the communities of modern Guatemala and Chiapas. Such responsibilities for modern ritual specialists endure throughout the year as well as during the rituals themselves, and we assume the same was true for their ancient forebears.

The builders maintained larger spaces on the west and south sides of the palace, but they enclosed the eastern side with a small restricted court that must have housed more private rituals. Across the court from the west facade, the accumulated renovations from several kings resulted in an unusual stepped configuration with the roof of one building providing a wide patio for the level above (Fig. 2.21). These patios were used for dancing in the celebrations honor-

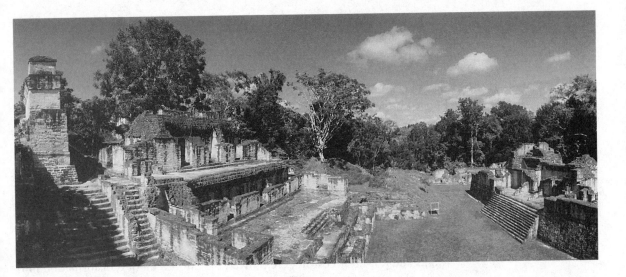

ing Toh-Chak-Ich'ak and his lineage. Feasting and other celebratory rituals could well have occurred throughout the spaces of Court 6.

Fig. 2.21. Structures 53 and 54 with the stairway leading up to Court 3. Toh-Chak-Ich'ak's Palace is on the right

D1—More Graffiti

The Maya left images that help us imagine the splendor and pageantry of their ancestral rituals. Once again, the drawings cannot be seen today, but they once decorated the walls of Toh-Chak-Ich'ak's throne room. One depicted a procession of befeathered lords in a ritual taking place on a series of wide terraces (Fig. 2.22). In this image, some lords carry or wear branches of a plant, while others, including a couple of women, stand among huge banners.

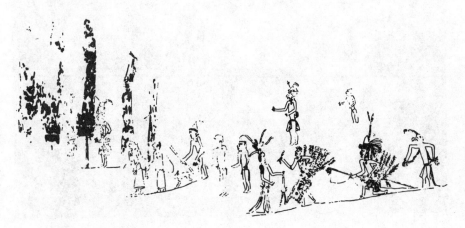

Fig. 2.22. D1: Painting of a ritual with banners on a series of terraces. This was found inside Toh-Chak-Ich'ak's Palace.

Dances and processional rituals were frequent subjects for Maya artists. In fact, the ancient Maya used dance as a major part of their rituals throughout their history. Kings, lords, and commoners danced, dressed in masked costumes that represented the gods, spirits, and ancestors into whom they transformed as they performed. Painters and sculptors depicted dances like these on pots, stelae, lintels, and many other media. Texts recorded not only who was shown, but also what kind of dance they were doing. The glyph for dance reads *ak'ot*[37] and the kind of dance is usually identified by the objects carried or worn by the dancer. Some of the scenes on Maya pottery will help us visualize how such dances appeared.

D2A—DANCE OF THE JAGUAR

Masks and full-body costumes reinforced the impression of transformation into spiritual and animal forms (Fig. 2.23). The "dance of the carrier jaguar" (*ak'ot ti kuchol balam*) depicts a masked transformation dance. The scene centers on a lord from Motul de San José affectionately known as the "Fat Cacique." He rides the shoulders of an acrobatic jaguar doing a handstand. At his side, a kneeling attendant holds a bowl with bloodletters for his chubby lord, who wears a human mask (perhaps representing an ancestor) and jaguar mittens. In front of the Fat Cacique, a dancer cavorts, wearing the mask of an "insect" monster associated with the ballgame. Behind him, another dancer impersonating an anthropomorphic Jaguar God gracefully moves through his steps in front of yet another masked dancer, who carries a banner apparently made of flowers. Dances like this would have taken place in Court 6 and other plazas throughout the city.

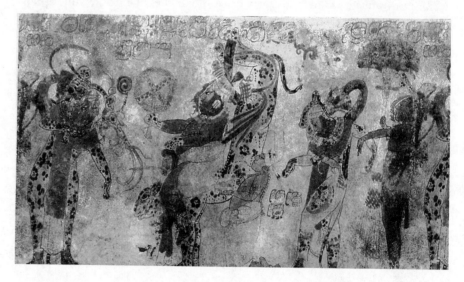

Fig. 2.23. Pot D2A: Spectacles like this Dance of the Jaguar took place in Court 6 around Toh-Chak-Ich'ak's Palace.

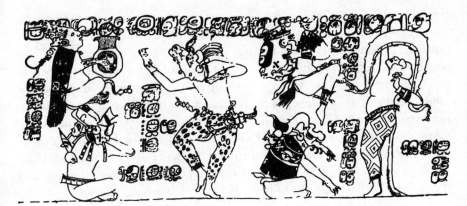

Fig. 2.24. Pot D2B: *Wayob,* or "spirit companions," dancing on a pot from Altar de Sacrificios.

D2B AND D2C—*Wayob*

Masked dances also involved transformations of humans into their *wayob*[38] (singular *way*), or "spirit companions" (Fig. 2.24). According to Maya belief, all human beings have spirit companions with whom they share their souls. Adepts using the dance and trancing transformed into their spirit companions to access the power of the supernatural world. Archaeologists found this pot in the tomb of a noblewoman of Altar de Sacrificios. The dancer holding the snake aloft is *Buchte Kan,* while the dancer with the jaguar pants is *Chak-Balam,* "Red-Jaguar." Other *wayob* hover between the dancers, including *Nupul Balam,* "War-Jaguar" (upper left); "Decapitating God A" (lower left); "Grasping or Conjuring God A" (upper right); and finally a monster (lower right) not unlike the insect being we saw dancing in front of the acrobatic jaguar (D2A). By wearing masks and full-bodied costuming, the Maya aided the transformation, which was at least for the dancer a real one.

The ritual on Pot D2C occurs in and around a conjuring house marked by the bird on its roof as an *Itzam Nah* "Sorcery House" (Fig. 2.25). People who have transformed into their *wayob* dance as they carry great flint-headed staves, eccentric lightning stones, battle axes, seed bags, or skull rattles. With one excep-

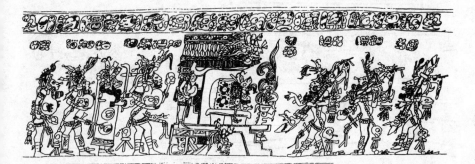

Fig. 2.25. Pot D2C: *Wayob* dance in a house ritual.

tion, they are all scantily dressed in chest belts, foot gear, garters on their thighs, and ornate headdresses. Huge bone awls held in place by paper bindings perforate their penises as they dance through their steps. Inside the *Itzam Nah* "Sorcery House," a huge bundle and a very large ornate headdress sit on a bench, while another headdress rests on the ground next to the temple. In front of the house, great billows of smoke rise from a brazier, containing an infant sacrifice of the type known as *k'ex,* or "substitution." The sacrifice may not be an infant, but rather a gift given to the denizens of Xibalba in exchange for the birth of a child. Many Maya believe that a newborn baby receives the soul of a dead ancestor. This sort of ancestral ceremony involving penis perforation, trance dancing, and the calling of beings from the Otherworld surely happened in Court 6.

E—Court 4

Yax-Ain II included Court 4 in his renovations to the buildings surrounding Toh-Chak-Ich'ak's Palace. This little court is of interest in itself. Structure 49 on the east side allows passage through the building to a stairway that drops down into the south side of Court 6, while across the court, another stairway leads up past Structure 51 into Court 3. From the stairs, the plaster sculpture on the side of Structure 51's roof is visible. It represents the front view of the *Itzam-Ye* or *Mut Itzamna* bird (Fig. 2.26), who earmarks the building as an *Itzam Nah,* or "Sorcery House," just like the building depicted on Pot D2C.

Peter Harrison,[39] the archaeologist who excavated the Central Acropolis, found that Structure 51 played a role in the last, tragic days of Mutul. During the city's last years, sometime after part of the interior had collapsed, someone cut holes in the doorjambs so that wooden bars could be placed across the door. They had changed the inner rooms of a conjuring house into a captive pen, per-

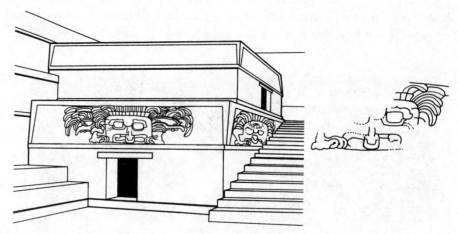

Fig. 2.26. E: A hypothetical reconstruction of Structure 51 with *Itzam-Ye* birds. The bird on the right was drawn from slides and field drawings.

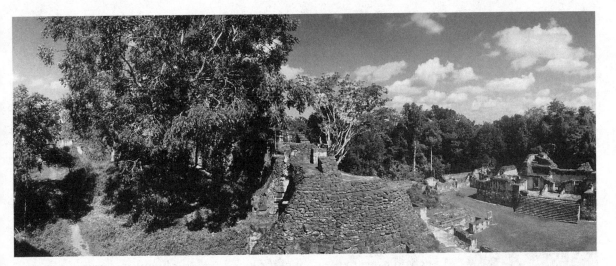

haps to hold some of the last members of the Mutul royal line. The feces and food left by the captives as they waited to die were sealed in when the rest of the building collapsed. We do not know who their killers were, but the location of the captive pen is probably no accident. It was near the ancestral shrine of the most revered king in Mutul's history. Perhaps the prisoners contemplated that history before they died.

Fig. 2.27. F: Vista with Court 3 on the left, Structure 54 in the center, and Toh-Chak-Ich'ak's Palace and Court 6 on the right.

F—Court 3 and Structure 5D-57

The steps next to the *Itzam Nah* lead into Court 3, where Hasaw-Kan-K'awil, the twenty-sixth king in the Mutul dynasty, built his palace. Taking advantage of the honored position near the shrine of his illustrious ancestor, he dedicated a new palace (5D-57) and Court 3 to war and a victory of his own that rivaled that of his ancestor. At first glance Court 3 does not look like much, because it has not been restored like some of the other courts (Fig. 2.27). Nevertheless, it has details of great interest. The back of Structure 52, a later addition by Yik'in-Kan-K'awil (Ruler B), closes the court's southern side and obscures the view once enjoyed by Hasaw-Kan-K'awil's Palace. Structure 54, the eastern building in the court, has some of the most interesting vault beams from the Central Acropolis. The artists carved them to look as if they were bound by cloth in the center (Fig. 2.28). Similar detailing appears on stone columns in the Osario Group at Chich'en Itza.

Today, the most important building in the court is a fallen remnant of its former glory, but when the University of Pennsylvania originally investigated it, they found a plaster relief of enormous importance to our understanding of the political history of Mutul and the Central Acropolis. Mutul artists modeled the plaster relief over stone armatures in the entablature of Structure 5D-57 so that all who entered the court could read the imagery in this prominent location.

F1—HASAW-KAN-K'AWIL'S VICTORY

In the image (Fig. 2.29a), Hasaw-Kan-K'awil stands over a bound prisoner who sits on the ground at his feet. He wears a costume associated with the Venus-Tlaloc war, the same type of conquest warfare that was introduced into Maya imagery with the conquest of Waxaktun by his ancestor Toh-Chak-Ich'ak. The square shield he holds, the owl that penetrates his headdress, and the mosaiclike costume he wears all occur with this war complex both in Maya imagery and at Teotihuacan. Thus, Hasaw-Kan-K'awil wrapped himself in the imagery associated with one of the most glorious and celebrated moments in Mutul's history. The glyph panel to the right of the king names the humiliated captive sitting at his feet as *Yich'ak-K'ak'* (Fire-Claw), the king of Kalak'mul.

We have already discussed the history leading up to the moment recorded in this image. Remember that the king of Dos Pilas in concert with his Kalak'mul overlord captured and sacrificed Nun-Bak-Chak, Hasaw's father. A little over thirteen years after he acceded, Hasaw-Kan-K'awil went to war against the arch-enemy Kalak'mul and took its king captive just as his father had been taken sixteen years earlier. During his victorious battle on 9.13.3.8.18 (August 8, 695), he also captured a great palanquin bearing one of the patron gods of Kalak'mul. He pictured himself proudly sitting in that palanquin on Lintel 3 of Temple 1, and on Lintel 2 he depicted himself in what may have been the palanquin of Waxaktun taken centuries before (Fig. 2.29 c and b).[40]

Hasaw-Kan-K'awil paraded his doomed captive before his people thirteen days after the battle and depicted this moment of triumph on his palace. This image dominated the space where he conducted the business of the court and sat close to the ancient house of the king who had defeated Waxaktun. But the captive held more importance than just his rank. He was the successor, and probably the son, of the Kalak'mul king who had killed Hasaw-Kan-K'awil's father. Twenty-seven days after humiliating his hapless captive, he paraded through the city on the palanquin he had captured from Yich'ak-K'ak'.

G—COURT 2 AND MALER'S PALACE (STRUCTURE 5D-65)

Moving past Hasaw-Kan-K'awil's Palace between Structures 58 and 59 leads into Court 2, the last great space to be constructed in the Central Acropolis. It is dominated by Maler's Palace[41] (Structure 5D-65), one of the most elegant and well-preserved buildings in the Central Acropolis (Fig. 2.30). Across the court

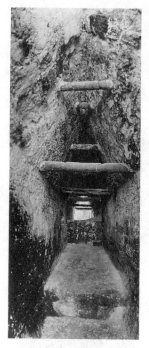

Fig. 2.28. Interior of Structure 54 with the original beams in place.

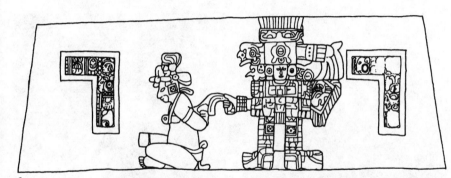

Hasaw-Kan-K'awil standing over Yich'ak-K'ak' of Kalak'mul

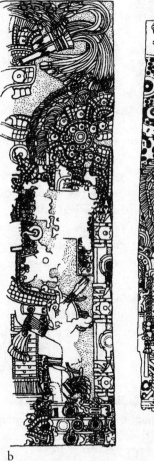

This palanquin shows the Waxaklahun-Ubah Snake captured from Waxaktun centuries earlier.

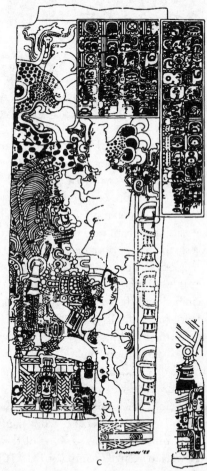

The text records the downing of the "flint-shield" of Yich'ak-K'ak' from Kalak'mul and conjuring rituals forty days later. The palanquin was captured from Yich'ak-K'ak'.

Fig. 2.29. F1: (a) The stucco frieze from Structure 5D-57, (b) Temple 1, Lintel 2, and (c) Temple 1, Lintel 3.

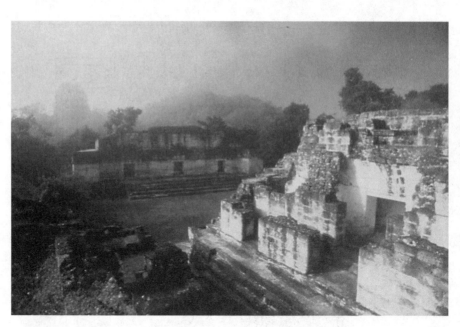

Fig. 2.30. G: Maler's
Palace and Court 2.

sit three buildings filled with small rooms that do not open into the larger court
in a formal way. They were probably residential and perhaps housed members of
the king's family or functionaries of the court. Structure 118 on the west side of
the court is a presentation building where lords sat on benches in the inner
room, and others stood in the outer gallery. The very wide door allowed them to
be easily seen from the court. Structure 66 is a temple and may have functioned
as a shrine or to house religious regalia and statues used in court rituals.

Maler's Palace was the administrative center for one of the later kings of the
city. It has not been precisely dated, but a calendar round date, 7 Etz'nab 6 Ch'en,
scratched into the wall of an interior room gives us a time when it was in use. The
calendar round falls on 9.18.9.15.18 (July 4, 800). Using archaeology and the
style of the building, Peter Harrison has attributed it to Yax-Ain II (Ruler C).[42]

The center room of Maler's Palace is the heart of this court. It has a bench
around three sides so that the king could sit in the center with attendants and
court functionaries at his sides. The stairs leading up to this room are tall and
served both for climbing up to the building and to provide seating for court
functionaries. Palace scenes from painted pots help us in imagining how these
palaces must have looked. One of the most interesting scenes is on a pot from
Hasaw-Kan-K'awil's tomb (Burial 116).

In the scene depicted on Pot G1 (Fig. 2.31), large steps like those in front of
Maler's Palace lead up to a bench where a lord sits in elegant grace. Two of his
subordinates or perhaps visiting lords present him with gifts or, more likely, with
tribute. On the lowest level, seven men stand or kneel as they observe the presentation of the gifts. They all wear long cotton robes and necklaces with three

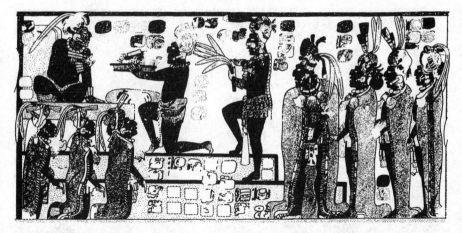

Fig. 2.31. Pot G1:
A vessel from Hasaw-
Kan-K'awil's tomb
shows this scene of
tribute. The men
wearing the capes are
secondary nobles
called *sahal* who
commonly appear
in the imagery from
the Usumacinta zone.
Perhaps they came
from an allied state in
that region to pay
their tribute to the
ruler of Tikal.

large spondylus shells, attributes that mark each of them as a *sahal,* a subsidiary office found in the inscriptions of many sites in the western zone of the Maya area. Sculptures and paintings at Yaxchilan and Bonampak'[43] show lords dressed exactly as these attending the king and helping him in ritual. *Sahalob* also ruled towns for their overlords and served as war leaders and court officials.[44] The people shown on this pot could be visiting lords from the Usumacinta zone, but just as likely they are the Mutul king's subordinate lords. Their spangled headdresses mark them as *itz'at,* or "sages." In other words, they are the lords who ran the city for him, bringing their lord tribute from areas of his kingdom. Whether they are local vassals or foreign visitors, they meet in a structure like Maler's Palace.

Another pot, G2, shows lords of all ranks receiving tribute from their subordinates in palaces like these (Fig. 2.32). Often, the lord shared his bench with attendants and members of his family and court. In this scene, the lord sniffs a bundle of flowers as he sits with a cylindrical vase and a mirror arranged in front of him. His "first lord," *ba ahaw,* sits across the bench from him with another

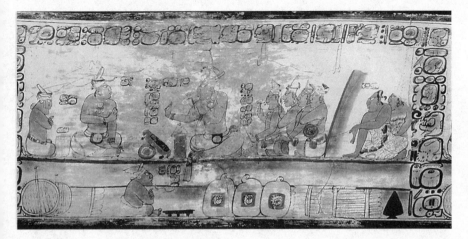

Fig. 2.32. Pot G2: A tribute scene showing bags of beans, piles of cloth, fans, rubber, and other items.

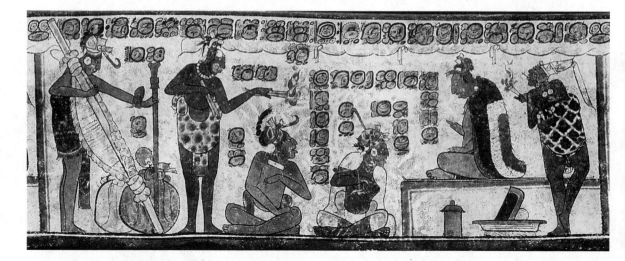

Fig. 2.33. Pot G3: A tribute scene showing the presentation of cloth and other objects by lords holding the title *Ah K'ul Hun,* "Keeper of the Holy Books."

lord. They have a *chach,* or "strainer," between them. Four more lords are lined up behind the ruler, sniffing flowers or holding fans as they watch him converse with his first lord. The women of the court sit to the far right under the rolled curtains hanging in the upper part of the palace door.

The large steps in front of the palace hold tribute of several types watched over by an attendant. He has a trifooted plate called a *hawate* on the floor in front of him and behind him lie woven fans and bound folds of tribute cloth. To his front rest three large bundles reading *ka bul, ka bul,* and *ox ka bul,* "our beans, our beans, three [bundles] of our beans." The tribute piles continue with more bundled cloth, and a large black object that may be rubber.

Because it was made by hand on backstrap looms, cloth was also a valuable commodity collected in tribute. Another scene, depicted on Pot G3 (Fig. 2.33),

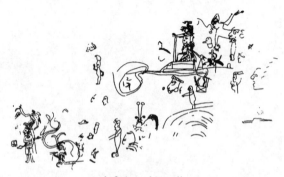

left (north) wall

shows the presentation of large bundles, a feathered cloth rolled up on a pole, and a tall staff that may be a wooden trumpet. The text identifies some of the tribute as *yub,* a Yukatekan word for "curtain" or "canopy." The next man in the scene holds a burning torch over a seated man who carries the title *Ah K'ul Hun,* "He of the Holy Books." His seated companion has the headdress of a scribe. The text in front of him mentions *yubte,* the word for tribute cloth, and *u tohol,* "he paid." Similar tribute payments by subordinate lords likely occurred in Maler's Palace. Perhaps the many rooms to the south side of the building and on its second story held some of the tribute until it could be redistributed.

The arts, visits by subordinates and foreigners, and tribute collection and distribution were not the only activities to take place in Maler's Palace. Looking at G4, we see that Room 9 to the west of the central room has very special graffiti depicting rituals that once took place within view of Court 2 (Fig. 2.34). Surrounding the bench in the east end of the room, Maya scratched drawings on all three walls showing pyramids, palanquins, and sacrificial rituals of various sorts. Some of these palanquins look like small houses with tiny people inside. But others are the great war litters that carried huge images of the protector gods, the *wayob,* into battle. The anonymous witness twice depicted the palanquin Hasaw-Kan-K'awil captured from Kalak'mul. Another palanquin captured from Naranjo by Hasaw-Kan-K'awil's son appears on these walls at least three times.

This is interesting because Maler's Palace was likely built by Yax-Ain II, the grandson of Hasaw-Kan-K'awil. If these drawings were scratched into the wall by

Fig. 2.34. G4: The graffiti images from the west end of Room 9 in Maler's Palace. Palanquins captured in the wars of Hasaw-Kan-K'awil and Yik'in-Kan-K'awil appear in various parts of the imagery, along with pyramids and platforms.

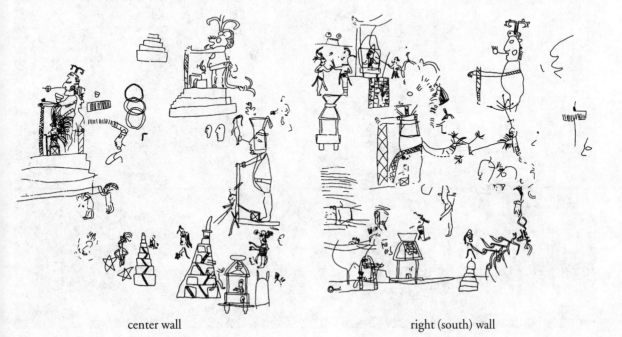

center wall   right (south) wall

people who observed such parades, then the display of captured palanquins must have continued for generations after battle victories. Other graffiti show war banners standing in front of buildings just as they must have once been erected in front of Maler's Palace, as well as processions and dancers transforming into gods. Pottery scenes augment these scratched depictions of victory celebrations. Palanquins and the disposition of captives also appeared in pottery scenes.

In the scene depicted on G5, a palanquin, mounted by its rather strange war beast, sits on the floor below the terrace of a palace (Fig. 2.35). A courtier seems to be arranging a jaguar pelt on its floor, as a sublord sits inside a palace high above him. In front, four warriors stand around three seated figures. Two appear to be captives and the other an official who is counting the booty laid out on the stairs. The principal lord sits on a large throne inside his curtained palace. Attendant lords surround him as he converses with a kneeling warrior. Thus, the parading of palanquins involved the presentation of captives and display of tribute and booty as well as the commemoration of great victories. Maler's Palace must have been the site of this kind of ritual, with the palanquin in the court below the king.

Fig. 2.35. Pot G5: A presentation of captives and a captured palanquin.

As the scene depicted on Pot G6 shows, palanquins also brought lords, in this case our friend the Fat Cacique, to locations where rituals took place (Fig. 2.36). He and all the lords with him wear anthropomorphic masks, perhaps represent-

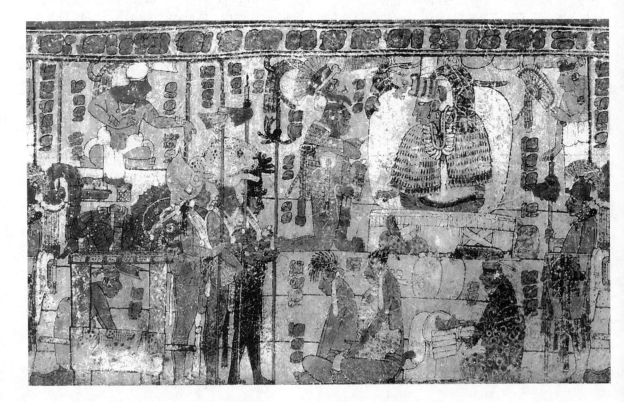

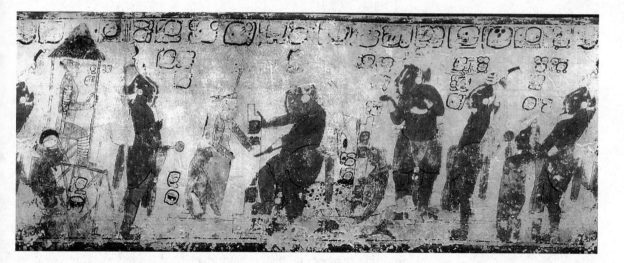

ing ancestors. Two bearers kneel in place after they have lowered the palanquin for their lord before a high scaffold holding a trussed-up, naked sacrificial victim. Similar scaffolds appear on stelae at Piedras Negras, where the sacrificed person lies dead across an altar at the bottom of the scaffold. In these accession scenes, the new king has replaced the sacrificed lord, who was his *k'ex,* or "substitution." Many of the altars of Mutul show captives bound to these scaffolds ready for sacrifice. Thus, we know that the Maya used scaffolds in rituals of both sacrifice and accession. Interestingly, postholes for just such a scaffold structure were found in front of Structure 33-2nd,[45] the temple that carried images of Snake Mountain, until it was buried. Thus, palanquin rituals took place in Court 2 and the lords of Mutul erected scaffold structures in the Great Plaza in front of the most important building in the North Acropolis.

Fig. 2.36. Pot G6: A sacrificial victim sits tied in a scaffold like the one that once stood in front of Structure 33. Lords wear masks as they stand near the ruler, who has arrived on a palanquin.

H—PUTTING PEOPLE BACK IN THE PALACES OF TIKAL

In our early visits to Tikal, we were like most visitors. We found ourselves blown away by the towering great temples and the dark mystery of the forest all around us. We remember wending our way through the labyrinthine corridors and courts of the Central Acropolis in utter confusion. We knew it was a palace, but we had no way of imagining how it was used.

Even after we learned about the history of Tikal's dynasty, the Central Acropolis was still confusing. We could imagine people in it then, but only through the imagery on the pots. We had no names and could associate no history or personality with its silent chambers.

Our confusion vanished following a funny incident with our colleague Peter Harrison, the archaeologist who excavated the Central Acropolis. Linda read the text from the dedication pot we discussed earlier at a meeting attended by Peter Harrison. She identified the owner of the pot as Jaguar-Paw, or Toh-Chak-Ich'ak. Later, we heard him give a paper in which he identified Structure 5D-46 as Jaguar-Paw's (Toh-Chak-Ich'ak's) Palace. Surprised, Linda asked how he knew that.

He answered, "You told me."

"I told you?"

"Yeah . . . when you said the pot belonged to Jaguar-Paw."

"Why's that important?"

"Because it was in the dedication offering under the stair of the palace."

Although feeling a bit of a fool, Linda went through an epiphany at that moment. The Central Acropolis ceased to be anonymous and became one of the most interesting buildings from the entire history of the Maya.

Think of it! Toh-Chak-Ich'ak was a man like Alexander the Great or George Washington. He marked the history and identity of his city for the rest of its existence. His descendants preserved his house unchanged for over five hundred years—and that for a Maya building is an eternity. They built their own palaces around the enshrined house of their great ancestor, making it the most important and revered place in the entire kingdom.[46]

CHAPTER 3

Palenque: Hanab-Pakal's Tomb

Palenque sits like a jewel against the Chiapas Mountains overlooking the broad coastal plain that came to be known as Nonowal and Xicalanco to later peoples in Mesoamerica. The ancient Palenque people constructed their palaces, temples, and houses on natural and manufactured terraces that rise up the northern side of the first ridge of these forest-covered limestone mountains (Fig. 3.1). They called their city *Lakam Ha,* "Big Water," and their kingdom *Bak,* "Bone."[1]

Crystalline waters laden with dissolved limestone tumble down the rocky creeks that divide the city into natural sections. Palenque's builders incorporated these streams into their city by channeling the water through aqueducts and containing walls, and by building bridges that crossed them. The most important of these streams, today called the Otolum, flows out of a valley called *Toktan,* "Cloud-center," to cut through the center of the ceremonial precinct. The biggest aqueduct takes the Otolum (Fig. 3.2) on the eastern side of the palace, which served as the administrative heart of the kingdom. The valley of *Toktan* and the wide plazas next to it held the oldest and most important buildings in the city. K'uk'-Balam, the founder of the dynasty of Bak, came from this province and was called a "holy *Toktan* lord."

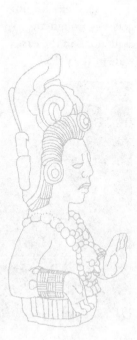

One of the most famous buildings ever built by the Maya stands against the ridge that rises above the large plaza on the western edge of *Toktan.* Between 1949 and 1952, excavations by the great Mexican archaeologist Alberto Ruz culminated in the discovery of a spectacular tomb deep inside the pyramid. The imagery and inscriptions associated with this temple and tomb constitute one of the greatest historical legacies in the Americas.

The creator of this magnificent building was Hanab-Pakal, son of Lady Sak-K'uk' and her consort, K'an-Mo'-Balam. Born on March 26, 603, he replaced his mother as ruler of Bak on July 29, 615, when he had reached the age of twelve. During the first thirty-five years of his reign, he led several wars aimed at stabilizing a kingdom that had been twice savaged by Kalak'mul and once by Bonampak' in the twenty years before his accession. The second half of his reign began with the visit of Nun-Bak-Chak, the exiled king of Mutul (Tikal), who

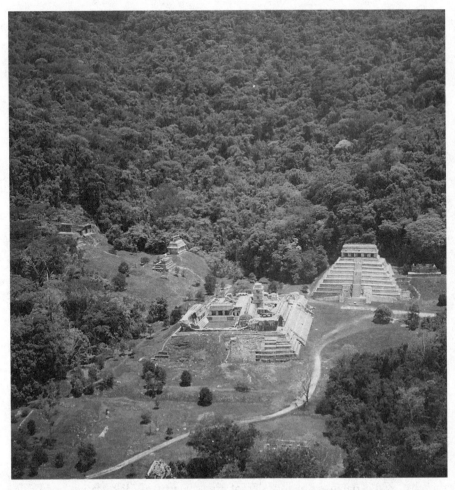

Fig. 3.1. Palenque lies on the first terrace of the forest-covered Chiapas Mountains. The Group of the Cross is on the left, the palace in the center, and the Temple of the Inscriptions on the right.

Fig. 3.2. The Otolum passes through an aqueduct on the east side of the palace.

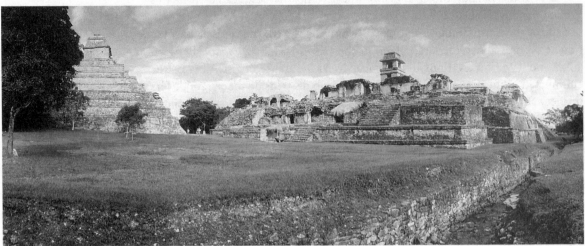

had been defeated by Kalak'mul. The Mutul king arrived in Palenque on August 16, 659. Pakal apparently considered that visit to be the highlight of his reign because he recorded it in detail in two of the most important buildings he commissioned. Only his birth and accession dates received more attention in his public inscriptions.

During his middle age, Hanab-Pakal turned his hand from war to guide his people through a renaissance of building that remade the face of his city. His career as a great patron of the arts climaxed around 675, when at seventy-two he began preparing his own tomb. He chose a site lying against the base of a mountain (Fig. 3.3) looking north toward the Gulf of Mexico, and then spent the remaining eight years of his life overseeing the construction of the temple, the contents of the inscriptions, and the symbolism of the imagery that was to carry his memory into the future and his soul into the afterlife. In many ways, he fulfilled his ambition because he remained the most revered king in Palenque's history and one of the best-known Maya kings to the modern world.

A—THE SUBSTRUCTURE AND ITS HISTORY

The original plan for the huge pyramidal base apparently called for eight terraces to rise up to the platform of the temple on the summit, but the intentions of the builders went astray when the interior fill became unstable. To compensate for slumping that began at the time of the original construction, they added great buttress walls to the sides of the substructure, changing the eight terraces into three with inset corners.[2] A steep, narrow stairway led upward from a wider section at the base of the pyramid. Today, another path leads to the back, where the

Fig. 3.3. The Temple of the Inscriptions and its companion temples.

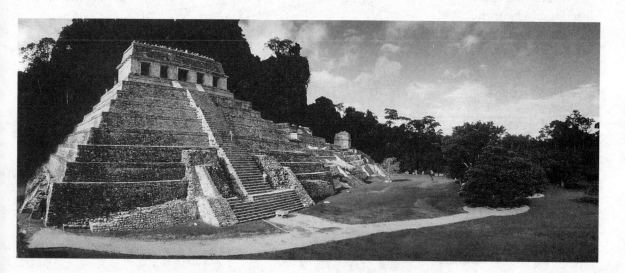

pyramid merged with the mountain behind it. Stairs built into the southwest corner of the rear terraces give access to the top of the pyramid (Fig. 3.4).

Excavations of the substructure removed the remains of the great buttress walls so that the slumping begun during Pakal's life caused the entire northern side to collapse during excavations. Archaeologists reconstructed most of the terraces that are visible today, although stubs of the buttress walls remain visible.

B—THE TEMPLE

Built on its own platform atop the pyramidal base, the temple faced north with five doorways breaking its front wall (Fig. 3.5). A roofcomb once graced the top of the

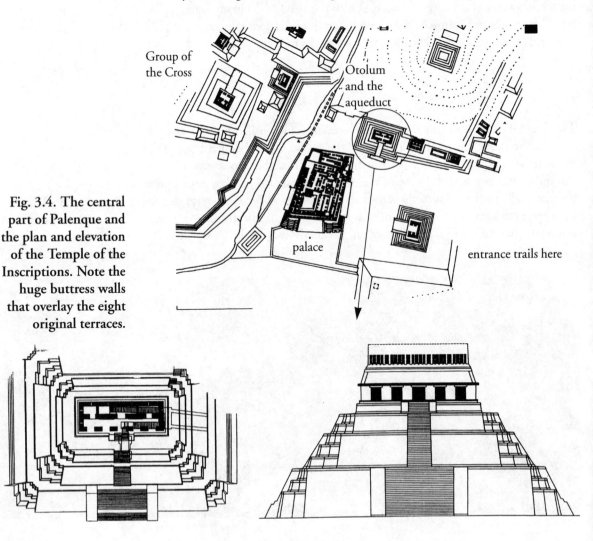

Fig. 3.4. The central part of Palenque and the plan and elevation of the Temple of the Inscriptions. Note the huge buttress walls that overlay the eight original terraces.

Group of the Cross

Otolum and the aqueduct

palace

entrance trails here

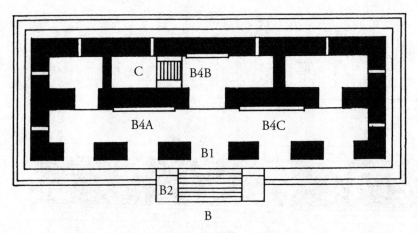

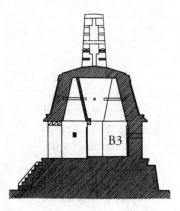

temple and elaborate plaster sculpture adorned the entablature and the roofcomb. Only a few lonely fragments of these reliefs survived into modern times.

Fig. 3.5. The plan and section of the temple structure.

B1—THE PIERS

We will never know what Pakal intended for the six piers of his temple, because his son, Kan-Balam, took this very public location to show the ritual in which he became the heir and proved his divine nature. His artists used the four inner piers to depict ancestors presenting the six-year-old heir from the front of the pyramid. The image confirmed Kan-Balam's divinity by showing the ax of K'awil penetrating his forehead and one of his legs transforming into a serpent. He is both the child heir (the *ba ch'ok*, or "first sprout," of the lineage) and the embodiment of the divinity personified in K'awil.

A skyband enframes each presentation scene to affirm the divine aspect of the event. This sky frame emanates from a monster head under the feet of the presenting adults (Fig. 3.6). On the two outer piers (b and e), the sky comes from the personified sacrificial bowl known to modern researchers as the Quadripartite Badge. On the inner pair (c and d), the sky rises from the Nine-God and the Seven-Black-Yellow God that designate sacred locations in the Otherworld.[3] The figures on the four middle piers represent ancestors standing in the Otherworld as they present the child to the people of Palenque, but which ancestors are they? On pier b, the quetzal bird and jaguar muzzle in the headdress name K'uk'-Balam (Quetzal-Jaguar), the founder of Palenque's dynasty. On pier e, a jaguar head with snake teeth designates Kan-Balam I, the great-great-grandfather and namesake of the child. The two center figures cannot be identified with certainty, but since they wear the net skirts of First Father and First Mother, we suspect they are the parents of the child, Hanab-Pakal and Lady Tz'ak-Ahaw. These figures, then, represent the child's most significant ancestors—his parents,

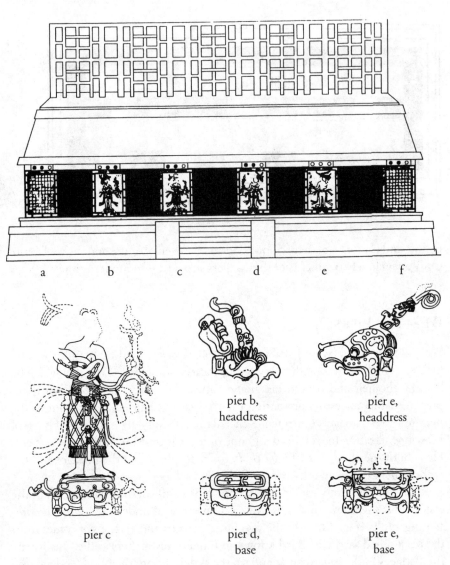

Fig. 3.6. B1: The piers of the temple show the presentation of Kan-Balam as heir to the throne by the founder of the lineage (pier b), his mother (pier c), his father (pier d), and his great-great-grandfather and namesake (pier e).

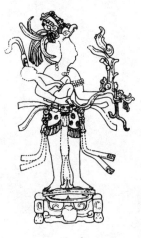

pier b

pier c

pier b, headdress

pier e, headdress

pier d, base

pier e, base

his namesake, and the dynasty founder—materialized at the heir-designation so that they could present the child Kan-Balam to the public. These rituals began on June 17, 641, and culminated four days later on the summer solstice.

Kan-Balam's names and titles appear among the few surviving glyphs from the texts that once graced the outer piers. Circular cartouches on the eaves above the piers displayed yet another text. We have been able to reconstruct two dates from the remnants,[4] May 28, 678, and May 25, 690. We suspect that these two dates corresponded to dedication rituals for different phases of the building. We think Kan-Balam conducted the later ritual, perhaps to dedicate the sculptures on these very piers.

B2—THE BALUSTRADES

The balustrades on both sides of the stairs leading up into the temple depict kneeling figures whose faces turn toward the stairs (Fig. 3.7). They wear bar pectorals on their chests, fancy loincloths, ornate earflares and nose pieces, and one has a zoomorphic headdress. They are almost identical in style and iconography to the figures on the balustrades that flank the Hieroglyphic Stairs of House C in the palace, where, fortunately, the context is clearer. The surviving House C figure wears a pectoral with an eroded day sign and the number seven. The Hieroglyphic Stairway records the sacrifice of six captives on the day 7 Chuwen. The kneeling figures on the substructure of House C represent these six sacrificed lords. The day worn by the balustrade figure on the Hieroglyphic Stairs surely refers to this 7 Chuwen sacrifice.

One balustrade figure on the Temple of the Inscriptions wears the number six over a day sign, while the other has thirteen and a day sign. It happens that the sacrifice mentioned in House C was followed six days later by the arrival of Nun-Bak-Chak, the king of Tikal who had recently been forced into exile by Kalak'-mul. This memorable visit fell on 13 Kaban. We think that the figures on the balustrades of the Temple of the Inscriptions and House C commemorate these momentous days on their pectorals, so that all who entered the temple would remember Pakal's finest hour.

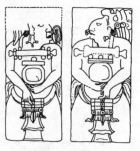

Fig. 3.7. B2: The balustrades from the upper section of the stairs.

B3—THE TEMPLE INTERIOR

The builders created two long, high galleries on the interior of the temple (Fig. 3.8). A corbeled vault spans both of them, but the masons used curtain walls to

Fig. 3.8. B3: The front gallery of the temple with the text panels to the right.

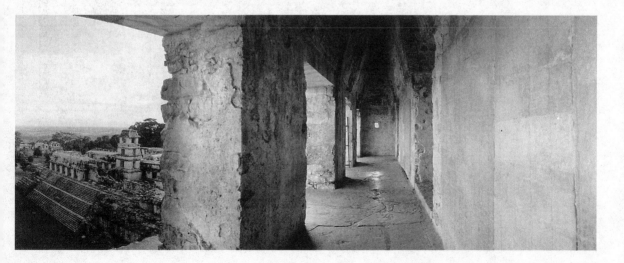

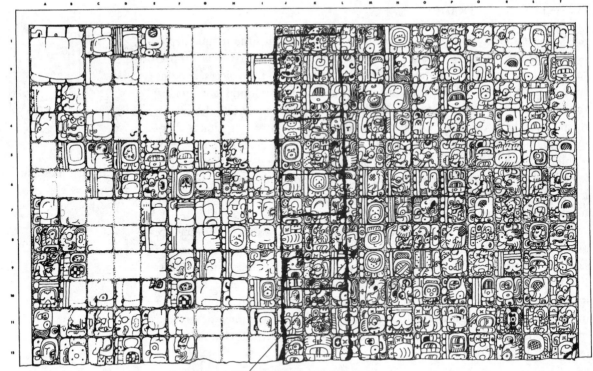

the sacking of Lakam-Ha by Kalak'mul

B4A: Panel 1 ties the accessions of eight lords to the k'atun-endings beginning with 9.4.0.0.0 and running to 9.10.0.0.0.

B4B: Panel 2 records the rituals for 9.11.0.0.0 and 9.12.0.0.0, especially concentrating on the costumes of the patron gods that were removed from bundles and shown during the ceremonies.

Fig. 3.9. B4:
The inscriptions
from the temple.

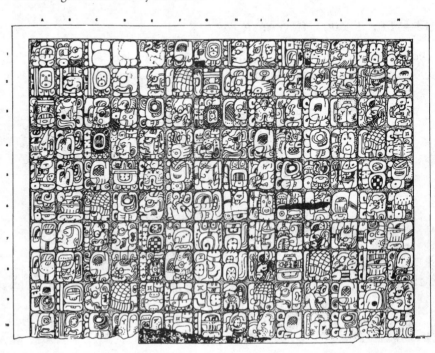

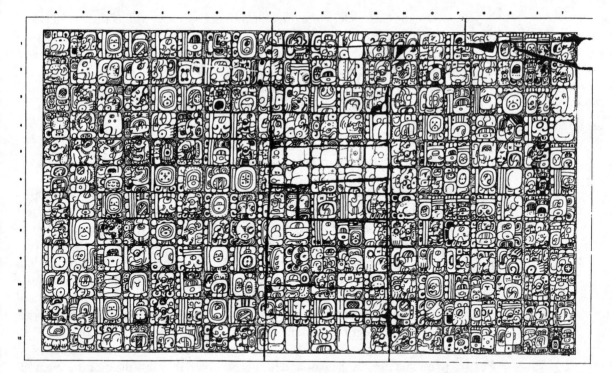

The first section concludes by taking the period-ending dates up to the end of the first piktun, or 8,000-year period.

Section 2 casts Pakal's birth and accession far into the past and into the future.

Pakal concentrated on important events in his reign in the last section, including a visit by the exiled Nun-Bak-Chak of Tikal and the death of his wife. His son, Kan-Balam, recorded Pakal's death and his own accession, and ended the text by saying that he gave special care to the tomb of Pakal.

B4C: The third panel completes the first section, then ties Pakal to events in the remote past and future, and finally turns to the significant events in Pakal's last two k'atuns of reign.

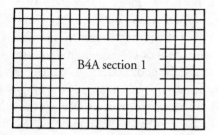

B4A section 1

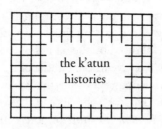

the k'atun histories

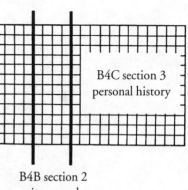

B4C section 3
personal history

B4B section 2
time travel

divide the back gallery into three chambers. Doorways with corbeled vaults lead through the central wall into the three chambers, which are all a step higher than the front gallery. The Maya mounted huge hieroglyphic panels in the center wall between the doorways and on the back wall of the middle chamber. These panels not only gave the temple its modern name, but they form the longest continuous text from the Classic period to survive intact.

B4—THE INSCRIPTION PANELS

It is doubtful that members of the public ever entered into the inner sanctum to be in the presence of these inscriptions, but scribes and *itz'at* surely read the text aloud so that crowds below could hear the history of their dynasty and most revered king. The reader would have begun with the east panel, moved to the center, and then ended with the west (Fig. 3.9). The scribes divided the long text into three sections like chapters, in order to highlight the different aspects of history that Pakal wanted his people to remember. Section 1 includes all of the first and second panels and the first four columns of the third panel. It is a dynastic history tying the seatings of Palenque's kings to the endings of the nine k'atuns (180 years) that culminated in Pakal's life. Section 2 connects his birth and accession to mythic time in the past and future. Section 3 recounts the most momentous events in his life, concluding with his death and the accession of his son.

B4A—SECTION 1: THE K'ATUN HISTORY

The focus of this section is the sequence of nine k'atun-endings, but the scribes presented the accessions of Palenque's kings as the background to these period-ending rituals (Fig. 3.10). The text opens with the anchor date and the first of the nine k'atuns—9.4.0.0.0, or October 18, 514. Then a distance number of 13.10.3 links the k'atun-ending to the seating as king of Akul-Anab I on 9.3.6.7.17 (June 5, 501). The k'atun-ending ritual in this and the subsequent passages read *yak'wa u pih u k'ul,* followed by the names of the patron gods of Palenque. This passage translates as "he gave it, the bundle of the souls of the gods." The gods named or implied in these passages were the Palenque Triad, the patron gods of the kingdom and the dynasty. Scholars call them GI, who was a form of the Maize God; GII or *Nen K'awil,* the "mirror god"; and GIII, who had a plethora of names, including *Yahaw K'in* (the Lord Sun) and *K'inich Tah Way* (Sun-faced Torch Nawal). At every k'atun-ending, the reigning king gave offerings to the holy bundles of these gods.

Sometimes more than one king acceded within a k'atun. In these exceptional cases, the scribes used the thirteenth tun (Maya year) in the k'atun (twenty Maya

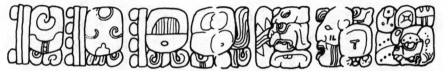

| 12 days | 14 winals | 9 tuns | *chumwan,* "she was seated" | *ta hun* "with the crown" | Lady Olnal | *K'ul Bak Ahaw,* "Holy Palenque Lord" |

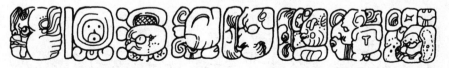

| *u k'al k'atun* "she ended the tun" | 5 Ahaw 3 Ch'en (9.8.0.0.0) | *yak'wa* "she gave it" | *u pih* "their bundle" | *u k'ul* "the gods of" | Lady Olnal | *K'ul Bak Ahaw,* "Holy Palenque Lord" |

Fig. 3.10. The formula for the period-ending phrases in Section 1.

years) as a second anchor. The thirteenth tun always has the same *ahaw*[5] name as the previous k'atun-ending. Here is a summary of the k'atun history:

Akul-Anab I was seated in k'atun 13 Ahaw ending on 9.4.0.0.0.
K'an-Hok'-Chitam I was seated in k'atun 11 Ahaw ending on 9.5.0.0.0.
    He also celebrated k'atun 9 Ahaw ending on 9.6.0.0.0.
Akul-Anab II's accession was linked to 9.6.13.0.0.
Kan-Balam I was seated in k'atun 7 Ahaw ending on 9.7.0.0.0.
    He also celebrated 9.7.5.0.0.
Lady Olnal was seated in k'atun 5 Ahaw ending on 9.8.0.0.0.
Ah-Ne-Ol-Mat's accession was linked to 9.8.13.0.0.
Lady Sak-K'uk' was seated in k'atun 3 Ahaw ending on 9.9.0.0.0.
Hanab-Pakal was seated in k'atun 1 Ahaw ending on 9.10.0.0.0.
    He also celebrated k'atun 12 Ahaw ending on 9.11.0.0.0.
    He also celebrated k'atun 10 Ahaw ending on 9.12.0.0.0.

The text also mentions that Ah-Ne-Ol-Mat's reign saw the destruction of Lakam-Ha by an attack from Kalak'mul (Fig. 3.11). When the scribes came to Pakal's mother, Lady Sak-K'uk', they expanded the formula to give us more information. They told us what the sky was like on the last four k'atun-endings in the list. 9.9.0.0.0 and 9.12.0.0.0 were maximum elongations of the Eveningstar; 9.11.0.0.0 was the heliacal rising of the Eveningstar; and 9.10.0.0.0 had nothing significant. 9.9.0.0.0 was also a k'atun in which *satay ahaw, satay k'ul,* "the lords died, the gods died," from the attacks—two of them—by Kalak'mul (Fig. 3.11).[6]

The scribes also recorded that Pakal's mother did not do some of the critical

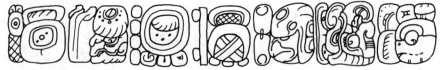

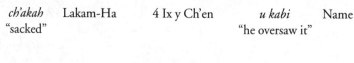

ch'akah   Lakam-Ha   4 Ix y Ch'en   *u kabi*   Name   *K'ul Kan*
"sacked"   "he oversaw it"   *Ahaw,* "Holy
                                                      Kalak'mul Lord"

Fig. 3.11. The passage recording Kalak'mul's attack against Palenque and the resulting k'atun "prophecy."

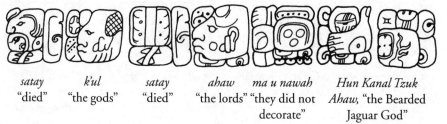

satay   *k'ul*   *satay*   *ahaw*   *ma u nawah*   *Hun Kanal Tzuk*
"died"   "the gods"   "died"   "the lords" "they did not   *Ahaw,* "the Bearded
                                        decorate"   Jaguar God"

rituals that her son performed during his lifetime. That the scribes specifically recorded that she did not perform certain rituals suggests that the patron gods had been damaged or destroyed by the attacks.

For his own k'atun-ending, Pakal expanded information about what was inside the *pi* bundles (Fig. 3.12). Each patron god had a bundle with his specific earflares (*tup*), necklace (*uh*), head cover (*pixom*), headband (*sak hunal*), and headdress (*kohaw*). Presumably *itz'at* opened these bundles to show their contents to the gathered lords, and perhaps dancers wore these accouterments in ritual that materialized the gods from the Otherworld for the k'atun-ending rituals.

This section concludes by casting time and the k'atun-endings into the future to anticipate the endings of 9.13.0.0.0 (March 18, 692), 10.0.0.0.0 (March 15, 830), and 1.0.0.0.0.0 (October 15, A.D. 4772).

B4B—SECTION 2: TIME TRAVEL

In the second section of the text, the scribes first locked Pakal's birth and accession to the k'atun-ending 9.9.0.0.0.[7] Then they recorded a huge distance number linking his accession to that of a remote ancestral god 1,246,826 years and 270 days in the past. This same god appears in the inscriptions of Naranjo where he operates like a supernatural anchoring ancestor for that city's royal lineage. He may have fulfilled the same role at Palenque, although no other rulers evoked his name. Pakal intended this very remote accession to give scale to his own enthronement. To give modern readers a sense of this scale, *Homo erectus* walked the plains of east Africa when that ancient god became an *ahaw*.

Not satisfied with this chronological feat, Pakal started from his birth date to

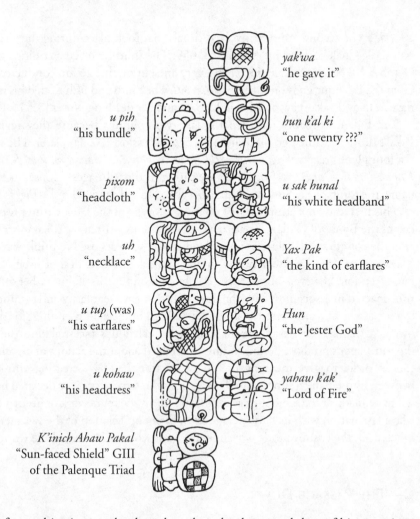

yak'wa
"he gave it"

u pih
"his bundle"

hun k'al ki
"one twenty ???"

pixom
"headcloth"

u sak hunal
"his white headband"

uh
"necklace"

Yax Pak
"the kind of earflares"

u tup (was)
"his earflares"

Hun
"the Jester God"

u kohaw
"his headdress"

yahaw k'ak'
"Lord of Fire"

K'inich Ahaw Pakal
"Sun-faced Shield" GIII
of the Palenque Triad

Fig. 3.12. The action of giving an offering to the bundle holding the costume of the patron god GIII.

cast forward in time to the day when the calendar-round date of his accession, 5 Lamat 1 Mol, would repeat for the eightieth time, which, it so happens, will occur only eight days after the end of the first 8,000-year period (*piktun*) after the Creation day, 4 Ahaw 8 Kumk'u. This anniversary has yet to occur. We will have to wait until October 23, A.D. 4772, to confirm his prophecy. Obviously, Pakal and his *itz'at* did not believe that the world would end on 13.0.0.0.0 in A.D. 2012, as modern myth would have it.[8]

B4C—SECTION 3: MOMENTOUS EVENTS IN THE REIGN OF PAKAL

In this section, the scribes recorded five major episodes in Pakal's life. The first is the least understood, but it involved a complex ritual dance that took place on April

19, 653. The second episode involved rituals that took place during the visit of Nun-Bak-Chak of Tikal on August 16, 659. The third involved a conjuring on October 20, 675, in association with a very ancient mythic action conducted by GI of the Palenque gods on June 23, 3023 B.C. The fouth and fifth related his marriage to Lady Tz'ak-Ahaw on March 22, 626, and her death on November 16, 672.

Kan-Balam probably recorded the last two columns because they register Pakal's death, but then go on to note his own accession 132 days later. The very last four glyphs read *yak'wa huntan, Bolon-Et-Nah, u k'ul k'aba, u muknal K'inich Hanab-Pakal, K'ul Bak Ahaw,* "He gave caring to the 9-Images[9]-House, its holy name, the tomb of the Sun-faced Hanab-Pakal, Holy Palenque Lord" (Fig. 3.13).

This first known k'atun history was the prototype of the later k'atun prophecies of the Books of Chilam Balam, the famous books written by Yukatan scribes after the conquest.[10] Because of texts like this one, scholars used to think that the Maya had an obsessive fascination with time, almost a worship of time itself. With rare exception, however, Maya scribes focused not on time itself, but rather on the rites enacted in association with the timeposts that gave regularity and symmetry to the passage of time. Here Pakal is less interested in the k'atun-endings for their own sake than he is in describing the actions that Palenque's ancestral kings did for the patron gods on those period endings. He talked about the actions of his ancestors in order to give meaning to his own actions, and by creating affinities between himself and a supernatural being from the remote past, he declared himself to be made of the same stuff as the gods. Time is the framework of history, and Maya fascination with its nature came from their appreciation of the symmetries inherent in the cosmic fabric woven by the gods when they created the world.

C—THE PASSAGE DOWN

When Alberto Ruz[11] examined the center, rear chamber of the temple, he found a slab with pairs of drill holes set into the floor. When workmen lifted the slab, they found hard-packed rubble and earth. Excavating straight down in the cen-

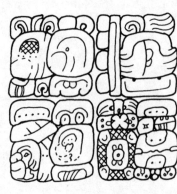

yak'wa huntan,
"he gave caring,"

Bolon-Et-Nah
"9-Images-House"

Fig. 3.13. The final phrase from the inscription panels.

u k'ul k'aba u muknal
"(was) the holy name of the tomb of"

K'inich Hanab-Pakal, K'ul Bak Ahaw
"Sun-faced Hanab-Pakal, Holy Palenque Lord"

ter of the opening, they eventually found a step, and then another and another. Gradually they revealed a corbeled-vaulted staircase plunging down into the depths of the pyramid (Fig. 3.14). As they dug, they kept finding little offerings deposited in the fill by the people who had originally sealed the passageway. So packed was the rubble and so deep the stairs that it took Ruz and his crew four long, hot seasons to clear the passage.

Halfway down, the passageway made a turn, and Ruz found tunnels leading off through the pyramid to exit on the western side. At first, he thought his workmen had found secret passages that allowed priests to appear magically in the temple above, but it turned out that the stairs made a U-turn and kept going down. The little tunnels were ventilation ducts. The workmen continued digging until they reached ground level and a little below. There they found two steps and a small platform with a stone box resting on top. When they opened the box, they found the remains of five or six slaughtered and dismembered human sacrifices. A stone pipe, today called a psychoduct, ran down the stairs all the way from the slab above to a huge triangular door that stood on the northern side of this platform. The idea of the psychoduct is that the psyche or soul could move up and down the duct to communicate with the living people in the temple above.

D—The Tomb

After the excavators documented and removed the box with the sacrificed people, Ruz[12] turned his attention to the huge triangular slab that formed the north

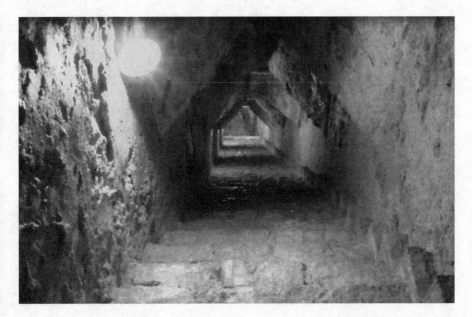

Fig. 3.14. C: Looking up the passage leading down to the tomb. The psychoduct is on the right.

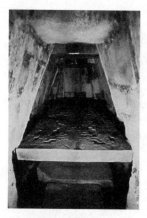

Fig. 3.15. D:
The tomb chamber.

wall of the corridor. There was a gap between the slab and the wall. He set his workmen to clearing the hard mortar and stones that blocked the gap until one of the workmen broke through the seal with a crowbar and found vacant space behind. Using an electric light, Ruz and his colleagues peered through the gap to see a huge chamber lined with plaster sculpture and an enormous sculptured stone monument almost filling up the room. Imagine the emotion of that moment! After four years of hard work, they needed two more days to free up the door and work it open. On June 15, 1952, human beings gazed upon Pakal's tomb and came into his presence for the first time in over twelve centuries.

E—THE SARCOPHAGUS

When Ruz stepped through the open door for the first time, he saw a huge limestone block running south to north that filled the vaulted chamber (Fig. 3.15). Calcium deposits reflected the light in a magical way that is evident even in black-and-white photographs taken on that day. Ruz stood on the threshold of a unique and unparalleled example of Maya art. In terms of pottery or jade, richer tombs have since been found, but nothing to equal the sarcophagus in size or imagery is known in all the Americas. Relief carvings adorn the top and edges of the lid, the sides of the sarcophagus, and the blocks on which it stands. Together the images and text give us the most detailed and elegant exposition on Maya concepts of death, resurrection, and the afterlife.

E1—THE LID

Measuring 3.8 meters by 2.2 meters, the lid (Fig. 3.16) is visible from the door, albeit from an angled point of view. The artists oriented both the sarcophagus and the tomb crypt to the cardinal directions with the long axis running south to north. In the imagery on the lid, north corresponds to up and south to down. The elegant, articulate imagery details what happened to Pakal at the moment of his death. We will take this image apart and explain it in detail.

E1A—THE FRAME

A band encircles the entire image on the lid like the frame of a picture (Fig. 3.17). Segmented skybands line the long sides, with the center segment on the east side reading *k'in,* "sun" or "day," and on the west reading *uh,* "moon." *K'in* also repeats in the northeast corner, where the artists opposed it with an *ak'bal,* "darkness" and "night," symbol in the northwest corner. Thus, the two skybands

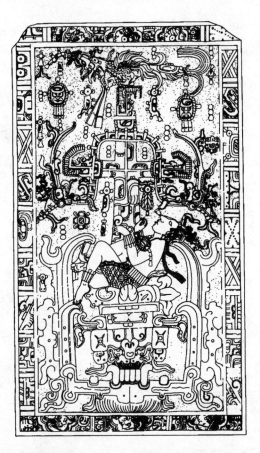

Fig. 3.16. E1:
The sarcophagus lid.

resonate with their east and west positions by evoking symbols of the day and night. We do not understand the other partitions in the skyband very well, but we can identify Venus, crossed bands representing the crossings points of the ecliptic and the Milky Way, and a head that reads *tzuk,* "partition," as a reference to constellation divisions (Fig. 3.17).

On the north and south ends, three individuals emerge from quatrefoil shapes. The same three people reappear on the limestone legs of the sarcophagus. Glyph texts name all three and give their ranks (Fig. 3.17). A lord named Chak-Kan appears in the center of both ends and on the northwest leg. Yuk-Sahal occupies the western sides and the northeast leg, and Mut looks out from the eastern sides and southeast leg. Chak-Kan and Mut were *Ah K'ul Hun,* "Keeper of the Holy Books," while Yuk had the rank of *sahal,* a kind of court official. These men were secondary lords who served Pakal as administrators and court officials.

The question is, Why would secondary lords be represented on the sarcophagus of a king? We have contemplated what these men might have done to deserve such an honor from Pakal, and we suspect they were the architect and administrators who oversaw the construction and decoration of the temple and tomb.

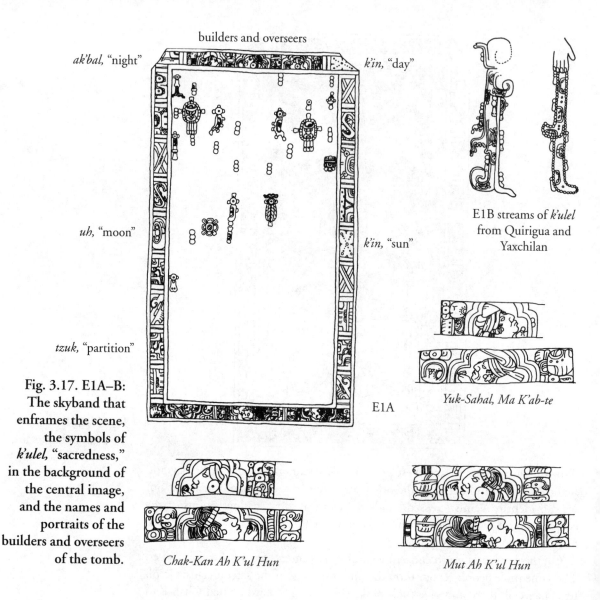

builders and overseers

ak'bal, "night"

k'in, "day"

uh, "moon"

k'in, "sun"

tzuk, "partition"

E1B streams of *k'ulel*
from Quirigua and
Yaxchilan

**Fig. 3.17. E1A–B:
The skyband that
enframes the scene,
the symbols of
k'ulel, "sacredness,"
in the background of
the central image,
and the names and
portraits of the
builders and overseers
of the tomb.**

E1A

Yuk-Sahal, Ma K'ab-te

Chak-Kan Ah K'ul Hun

Mut Ah K'ul Hun

E1B—THE BACKGROUND

Various symbols, including flowers, shells, jade beads, "zero" signs, bones, and feathered ornaments, float in the background behind the depicted objects (Fig. 3.17). These materials all embody *k'ul* or *k'ulel,* the indestructible, living force that imbues all things. *K'ul* resides in the blood of humans and animals, and in the sap of plants, and it permeates mountains, valleys, rivers, houses, objects of office, and all things that connect with the sacred world. Here *k'ulel* denotes that the event took place in ambient sacredness.

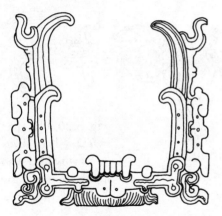

The White-Bone-Snake opening into
the Otherworld

The Quadripartite God, who
symbolizes a personified offering plate

Fig. 3.18. E1C:
The maw of the
Otherworld and the
offering plate.

E1C—THE PORTAL

At the base of the lid sits the split image of a giant skeletal snake known to the Maya as the *Sak-Bak-Nakan,* "White-Bone-Snake" (Fig. 3.18). Since this snake connects the world of the living to the world of ancestors, it often appears at the corners of mirrors depicting the arrival of ancestors from the Otherworld. Here it represents the portal through which Pakal passed in death.

In the open maw of the snake sits another kind of portal—a sacred sacrificial plate personified into the image of an incense burner. The sign of the sun, *k'in,* marks the plate, *lak,* which holds another of the symbols called the Quadripartite Badge. It consists of a spondylus shell, a stingray spine, and a vegetal image with a *kimi,* "death," in the center. The shell symbolizes *k'ulel;* the stingray spine draws the blood of sacrifice; and the vegetal sign reads *way,* meaning "to dream," "to sleep," and "to transform into a nawal." Shortly after the last Creation, this bowl of sacrifice generated the World Tree, called *Wakah-Kan,* "Raised-up Sky."[13] Here it opens the portal in the mouth of the White-Bone-Snake.

E1D—THE WORLD TREE

A great tree (Fig. 3.19) emerges from the bowl of sacrifice and rises behind the body of the dying king. The trunk carries a *tzuk* head to mark it as the center partition. Mirror signs define its substance as something "shiny," while *te',* "tree," signs assure us that it is a tree. The branches terminate in beaded flowers with square-nosed, bejeweled serpents emerging from their centers. These are the personified stamens of the blossom. Ceiba trees flower in late January and early February, just at the time Maya myth says First Father raised this tree.

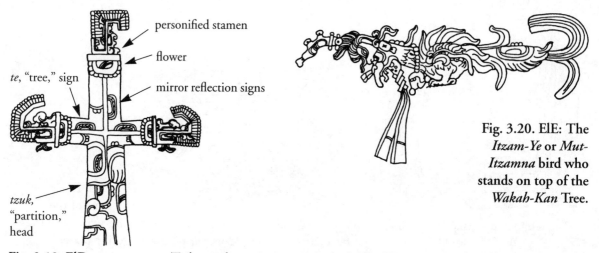

te, "tree," sign

personified stamen

flower

mirror reflection signs

tzuk, "partition," head

Fig. 3.19. ElD: The *Wakah-Kan,* "Raised-up Sky," or World Tree.

Fig. 3.20. ElE: The *Itzam-Ye* or *Mut-Itzamna* bird who stands on top of the *Wakah-Kan* Tree.

Today we know it represents the Milky Way as it stretches across the sky from the southern horizon to the north. The White-Bone-Snake at the base of this image represents the hole in the southern horizon that is the passageway of souls and ancestors who have been reborn. The Maya name for the Milky Way was *Sak Beh,* the "White Road."

E1E—THE BIRD

A supernatural bird (Fig. 3.20) perches atop the tallest flower of the tree, resplendent with his long tail and personified wings. He grasps a ribboned symbol in his latch-beaked mouth and wears a necklace like a human lord. The cut-shell head ornament marks him as the nawal (animal spirit companion) of Itzamna, the first sorcerer of this creation. The Maya called this bird *Itzam-Ye, Itzam-Kah,* and *Mut-Itzamna.* The presence of the bird declares the capacity to make magic and to engage in the shamanistic journey of the trance. He makes this tree and the tomb an *Itzam Nah,* or "Sorcery House."

E1F—THE DOUBLE-HEADED SERPENT

A double-headed snake (Fig. 3.21) with a body made of jade flower segments intertwines through the branches of the tree. Since the words for "sky" and "snake" are both *kan,* the Maya associated snakes with the sky and the umbilical cord that connected Maya lords to the sky realm. They symbolized this umbilical cord in several ways: as a rope ending in a *sak-nik,* "white-flower," sign; as two serpents entwining to evoke the twisted form of an umbilical cord; and as arching serpents carrying the white flowers on their snouts. The snake umbilicus

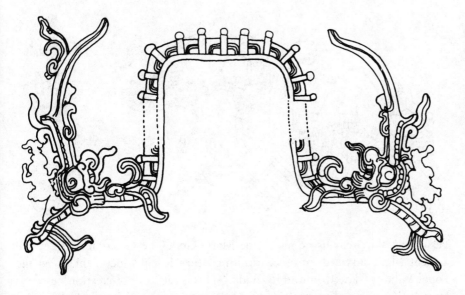

Fig. 3.21. E1F: The double-headed serpent (*left*) that represents the ecliptic in the sky and the umbilicus that connected Maya rulers to the sky and the Milky Way.

also symbolized the ecliptic so that the planets traveled along the snake's body. The king held the double-headed snake to show he controlled this conduit to the source of power and ancestral wisdom. Here the double-headed snake is both the ecliptic and the symbol of Pakal's connection to sacred authority.

E1G—The Emerging Gods

Two small gods emerge from the open mouths of the double-headed serpent (Fig. 3.22). *Sak Hunal,* the embodiment of the sacred headband of kings, comes forth from the right (east) head, while the left (west) head emits *K'awil,* a god invoking the concept of sustenance, deity statues, and the divine spirit contained in such statues. *K'awil* is also the embodiment of the Vision Serpent. Together the two gods evoke the ideas of kingship and divinity.

E1H—Pakal as the Maize God

Hanab-Pakal's impossibly awkward position declares that this is the moment of greatest transformation in his life (Fig. 3.23). His upturned loincloth and akimbo jewelry rise as he falls into the maw of the White-Bone-Snake. As he falls, he travels down the tree that had its analog as the Milky Way, or *Sak Beh.* The verb describing the event of death reads *och beh,* "he entered the road." Death is a journey down the Milky Way tree-road into the Otherworld.

This journey carried with it the promise of rebirth and resurrection. Hanab-

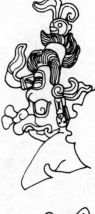

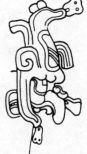

Fig. 3.22. E1G: The deities who emerge from the serpent, *K'awil* (*top*) and *Sak Hunal.*

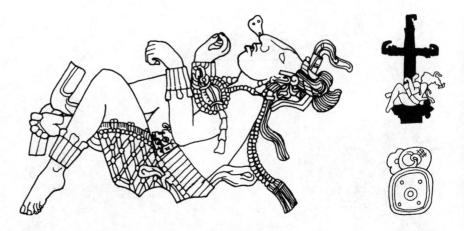

Fig. 3.23. E1H: At the moment of his death, Pakal falls down the Milky Way to *och beh*, "enter the road," into the Otherworld.

Pakal's net skirt tells us he fell as the Maize God. The Creation myth of the ancient Maya survived in a seventeenth-century K'iche' document called the Popol Vuh, or "The Community Book." This great story of creation descends from the Classic-period myth that told the story of the Maize Gods, beautiful young ballplayers who disturbed the Lords of Death with their play. They were summoned to Xibalba, the Maya name for the Otherworld, and after losing a series of trials, the Lords of Death killed and buried them in the Ballcourt of Sacrifice. To warn others who contemplated similar misbehavior, they hung the head of Hun Nal, the Maize God, in a gourd tree.

Ignoring the prohibition of her father to go near the skull, the daughter of a Xibalba lord went to the ballcourt and spoke to the head, which promptly spat into her hand and made her pregnant. After escaping from her angry father, she went to Middleworld and found shelter with the grandmother of her unborn children. There she gave birth to a second set of twins named Hun-Ahaw and Yax-Balam, who grew up to be summoned to Xibalba in their turn. They, however, outsmarted and then defeated the Lords of Death through a dance of sacrifice. They then went to the ballcourt to resurrect their fathers.

Once the Maize Gods were reborn, beautiful women dressed them, dwarves helped them to wake up old gods who would help them in creating the world, and old gods called the Paddlers took them in a canoe to the place of rebirth. There they emerged from a crack in the back of the Cosmic Turtle that we know today as Orion's Belt, and they directed their helper gods to build the first hearth and kindle the first fire. When the new cosmos was properly centered, they raised the *Wakah-Kan* and stretched out the ecliptic as the sky umbilicus. Once the gods finished making human beings, we were connected to the sky by that same umbilicus.

On the sarcophagus, Hanab-Pakal falls as the Maize God,[14] but on his chest, he carries the Cosmic Turtle (Fig. 3.24), where he will be reborn as a hedge against the possibility that he might not survive the trials of Xibalba. His son

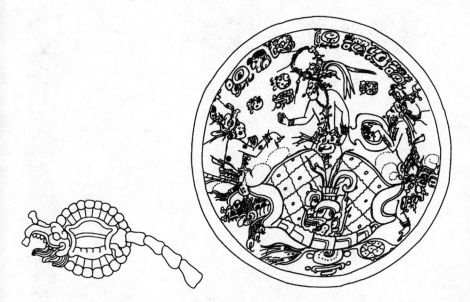

Fig. 3.24. E1I: The turtle pectoral that Pakal wears evokes the Maize God's rebirth from the Cosmic Turtle.

Kan-Balam represented the generation of the Hero Twins. Like them, he played the ballgame as a way of bringing his father back to life as a revered ancestor.

The symbolism also acknowledged this eventuality. The flaming ax of K'awil emerges from Pakal's forehead to mark him as divine. Living rulers can hold K'awil as an object or wear it as part of their headdresses, but only dead kings and the child on the piers above wear the K'awil ax through their own foreheads.[15]

E2—The Texts

The inscriptions on the sarcophagus lid (Fig. 3.25) begin on the east side with a phrase reading "they closed the lid, the sarcophagus of the Maize God [Pakal]."[16] The text continues by recording the deaths of the same kings whose accession and k'atun rituals fill the panels in the temple above. The scribe used the same formula for every passage: first comes the date, then the verb *och beh*, "he entered the road," and finally the name. In order to anchor the chronology, the scribes divided the same nine k'atuns registered in the history above (9.4.0.0.0 to 9.13.0.0.0) into thirds by inserting the dates 9.7.0.0.0 and 9.10.0.0.0 into the sequence of deaths.

This death sequence gives us the names of eight generations of kings before Hanab-Pakal:

Akul-Anab I died on 9.4.10.4.17 (December 1, 524).
K'an-Hok'-Chitam I died on 9.6.11.0.16 (February 8, 565).
Akul-Anab II died on 9.6.16.10.7 (July 23, 570).

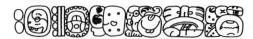

death of Ah-Ne-Ol-Mat

death of Lady Olnal

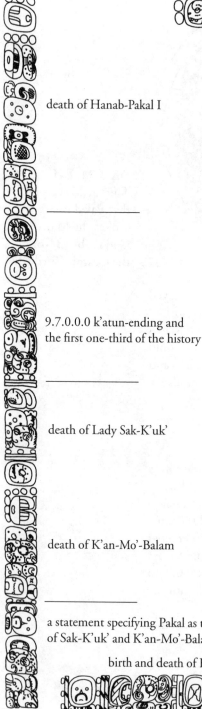

death of Hanab-Pakal I

———————

death of Kan-Balam I

Fig. 3.25. E2:
The inscriptions around the
edge of the sarcophagus lid.

———————

9.10.0.0.0 k'atun-ending and
the second one-third of the history

9.7.0.0.0 k'atun-ending and
the first one-third of the history

———————

death of Akul-Anab II

———————

death of Lady Sak-K'uk'

death of K'an-Hok'-Chitam

———————

death of K'an-Mo'-Balam

death of Akul-Anab I

closed the coffin of the Maize God

ancestral Vision Serpent

———————

a statement specifying Pakal as the child
of Sak-K'uk' and K'an-Mo'-Balam

birth and death of Hanab-Pakal

Kan-Balam I celebrated the k'atun-ending 9.7.0.0.0 (December 7, 573).
   He died on 9.7.9.5.5 (February 3, 583).
Lady Olnal died on 9.8.11.6.12 (November 7, 604).
Ah-Ne-Ol-Mat died on 9.8.19.4.6 (August 11, 612).
Hanab-Pakal I died on 9.8.18.14.11 (March 9, 612).
Lady Sak-K'uk' celebrated the k'atun-ending 9.10.0.0.0 (January 27, 633).
   She died on 9.10.7.13.5 (September 12, 640).
K'an-Mo'-Balam died on 9.10.10.1.6 (January 1, 643).

The last four glyphs on the west side record "the child of" Lady Sak-K'uk' and K'an-Mo'-Balam, the people on the north and south ends of the sarcophagus. While the child is not named, the context is clear—Hanab-Pakal was the protagonist of the text and his birth and death dates are just around the corner facing the entry door. He was the child intended in this parentage statement. The text goes on: "8 Ahaw 13 Pop, he was born; 6 Etz'nab 11 Yax, four were his tun seatings and then he entered the road, Sun-faced Hanab-Pakal, Holy Lord."[17]

   The final three glyphs (Fig. 3.33) in the text read *u tz'akabi u kabi u mam Tz'at ? ? Na Kan,* "they succeeded, they oversaw it, the grandfathers [i.e., ancestors] of the *Tz'at* Snake." *Tz'at* is one of the variants of *itz'at,* the Maya term for nobles as knowledgeable, wise, and literate people.[18] Here the text implies that there was a special Vision Serpent called the *Tz'at Na Kan* that acted as the conduit for noble ancestors who enabled the succession of the dynasty. Moreover, the *Tz'at Na Kan* may also have been a real object embodied in the psychoduct that connects the inside of the tomb to the temple above.

F—THE SARCOPHAGUS SIDES

The ancestors mentioned in the last clause of the text line the sides of the sarcophagus, surrounding their descendant who lies in the center. The artists presented each figure in the same way—emerging from a crack in the earth along with a tree. The overall composition was a marvel of subtlety and detail. The costumes and other elements consist of a set of constants and variables that the artists arranged around the center pivot of Pakal's body. The system they used was simple in its application, but it resulted in a marvelously rich and complicated pattern that reveals a lot about how the Maya thought about the world.

F1—THE IDENTITIES

We know who the ten figures are (Fig. 3.26) because they are named by the glyphs next to them and in their headdresses.[19] The earliest king, Akul-Anab I, appears on the south end of the east side. He is the first king that Pakal included in the Temple of the Inscriptions, although he was the fourth king in the succession of the dynasty. His headdress has a toothed frog and a macaw beak to represent the *anab* part of his name. The beak is the *a* in *anab*, while the frog is the *nab*. His "ik'" pectoral reads *nal* and he emerges from the earth with a *patah*, "guayaba" (*Psidium guajaba L.*), tree.

K'an-Hok'-Chitam I, the son of Akul-Anab I, sits across the sarcophagus in the south position on the west side. He wears a *chitam*, "peccary," head with a *k'an* sign in its eye in his headdress to embody his name. His pectoral reads *bi*, "road," and his tree is the *on*, "avocado" (*Persea americana*).

K'an-Hok'-Chitam I had two sons who became king, but only the younger one, Kan-Balam I, appears on the sarcophagus sides. He appears in the center of the east side with his name on the left and the emblem glyph of Palenque on the right. His headdress displays the jaguar, *balam*, part of his name, and his tree is *ha'as*, "zapote" (*Calocarpum mammosum Pierre*).

His daughter, the powerful Lady Olnal, appears across from him in the center of the west side and in the north position of the east side. She wears a *nal* ("ik'") pectoral in both locations, while she has an avocado tree (*on*) on the east side and a zapote (*ha'as*) on the west. Her headdress is difficult to interpret because the quetzal bird she wears does not appear related to her name. However, *k'uk'*, the Maya word for quetzal, also means "sprouts" and "new growth," and by extension, "descendant." She may be so marked for two reasons: to reinforce that she sprouted from Kan-Balam I, the prior king, and to acknowledge that she represented "new growth." As a woman, she belonged to the patriline descended from the founder, K'uk'-Balam, but her children did not. Because they belonged to the lineage of their father, her accession caused a break in the descent line from the founder. It was a matter of concern for her children and their descendants, including Pakal, to legitimize this lineage shift.

Lady Olnal apparently had two children—Ah-Ne-Ol-Mat and Hanab-Pakal I. The deaths of both appear in the text, but only Ah-Ne-Ol-Mat became king. His younger brother died before he could accede, yet the artist chose to portray him, instead of his kingly brother. Why? We think the portraits on the sarcophagus side record a lineal descent, not a succession. Only those people whose children inherited the throne were depicted. If this is true, the next ruler was the child of the younger brother, Hanab-Pakal.[20]

Hanab-Pakal, the grandfather of the Hanab-Pakal who built the tomb, appears in the north position of the west side without a pectoral, apparently because he never ruled. The scribes spelled his name phonetically as *ha-na-bi pa-ka-la*, but they did not include an emblem glyph. His name appears in his headdress as an owl, the head variant substitution for the *hanab* part of his name. His tree is the guayaba (*patah*).

The pairs of figures on the north and south ends of the sarcophagus both

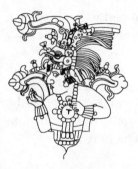

Generation 1
Akul-Anab I
East 1

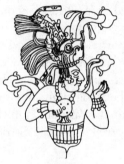

Generation 2
K'an-Hok'-Chitam
West 3

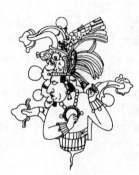

Generation 3
Kan-Balam I
East 2

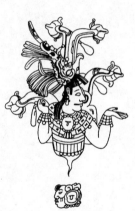

Generation 4
Lady Olnal
East 3

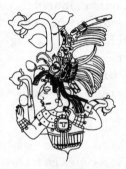

Generation 4
Lady Olnal
West 2

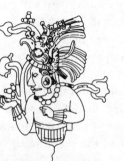

Generation 5
Hanab-Pakal I
West 1

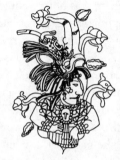

Generation 6
Lady Sak-K'uk', the mother
North 1

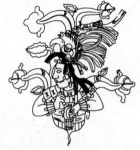

Generation 6
Lady Sak-K'uk', the mother
South 2

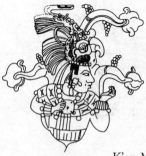

Generation 6
K'an-Mo'-Balam, Choh
Ahaw, the father
North 2

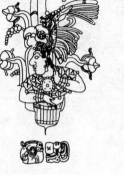

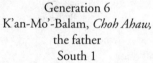

Generation 6
K'an-Mo'-Balam, *Choh Ahaw*,
the father
South 1

Fig. 3.26. F1:
The ancestors on
the sarcophagus sides.
Here they are
presented in chrono-
logical order.

repeat the parents of the dead king. Wearing a quetzal bird in her headdress, Lady Sak-K'uk', the mother, sits always on the eastern side of the ends. She wears a *nal* ("ik'") pectoral in both portraits and emerges with a cacao (*kakaw*) tree.

Her husband, K'an-Mo'-Balam wears a macaw with a jaguar eye in his headdress, while he emerges with a nancé (*chi'*) tree. His name contains a title that reads *Choh Ahaw,* in lieu of the emblem glyph. However, his name on the edge of the sarcophagus does contain the Palenque emblem glyph, so that we know he was not a foreigner. *Choh* may well record the district of his birth.[21]

F2—AN ORCHARD OF ANCESTORS

The figures on the sarcophagus constitute a forest growing around the coffin of the king, but it is not a wild forest. Instead the ancestors emerge with fruit trees that the Maya grew and tended around their houses. This metaphor of the ancestral orchard was not invented by Pakal's artists just for his sarcophagus. Instead they amplified an idea that had been in Maya art for far longer. One of the most informative examples occurs on a pot now in Berlin's Museum für Völkerkunde (Fig. 3.27). The scene depicts a Maya funeral and the rebirth of the deceased lord as a cacao tree. The bundled corpse of the recently dead man lies on a bench inside a tomb built into a flower mountain called *Hok'al Witz,* "Leaving Mountain" or "Departure Mountain."[22] The bench sits in a water band to signify that death leads to the Watery Underworld, and figuratively, to the Primordial Sea.

**Fig. 3.27.
Dead ancestors are
reborn as trees.**

The glyph on the left leg of the bench reads *och beh,* "he entered the road." Above his waist, another glyph reads *k'a',* "finished," with the *sak-nik* sign for his

The dead man, now reduced to bones, lies in his grave, but his soul has been reborn as the central cacao tree above the grave. His bones lie in the Primordial Sea.

The deceased wrapped in a burial bundle lies on a bench in his grave inside *Hok'al Witz.* A monkey and jaguar, his nawals sit on the mountain flanking a moon sign and the glyph for the white-flower soul. Mourners dressed as the Maize God lament his death.

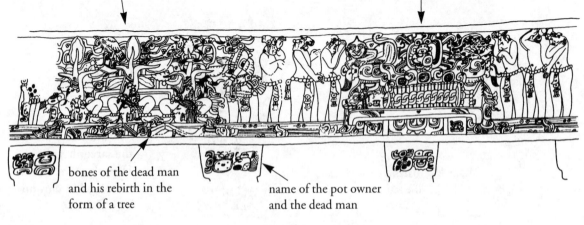

bones of the dead man
and his rebirth in the
form of a tree

name of the pot owner
and the dead man

soul floating in the cartouche above. The glyph on the right leg depicts the turtle carapace from whence he will be reborn. His body is bundled in wrappings with his feet and head sticking out. A spider monkey and jaguar, probably his nawals, crouch on top of the mountain, flanking an ancestor cartouche with his *sak-nik* soul inside. Mourners dressed as the Maize God wail their lamentations in dramatic expressions of their grief.

The opposite side of the pot details resurrection and rebirth. We are still at Hok'al Mountain, but now the tomb is sealed, and the corpse has turned to bone. Three tree people rise above the tomb, their heads down and their fingers elongated like roots gripping the stone. The center tree is cacao. An owl grasping a snake in its talons perches in the left tree, which has spiky fruit. An iguana sits in the right tree, which is identified only by a vine, perhaps a strangler fig, climbing its trunk. Two of the three tree people wear *itz* headbands, and all three have name glyphs on top of their heads. The two flankers we cannot identify, but the name of the central tree corresponds to the owner of the pot. His name includes information of great interest—he was *yune Itza Ahaw,* "the child of the Itza lord." The "child" is the man in the tomb, who has been reborn as a cacao tree.

We do not know if the Maya conceived of the relationship between ancestors and trees as simply metaphorical, but if it operated on a literal level, then the living were surrounded by ancestors reborn as the fruit trees that inevitably surround Maya houses. This is exactly the point expressed by the Palenque sarcophagus imagery.

F3—THE DISTRIBUTION OF ELEMENTS

The most subtle aspect of the sarcophagus composition lies in the way the artists distributed the costume elements among the ten figures (Fig. 3.28). Some elements remained constant. Everybody wears personified wings and three panaches of feathers in their headdresses. All have a stuffed jaguar tail and jade flower with ribbons emerging from the top of their headdresses. They all have jade-cylinder belts tied over their cotton undergarments. All of them wear jade headbands fastened over stepped haircuts, although the women wear their hair much longer than the men. And as we have seen, all carry their names in their headdresses.

The variables include the capes, wristlets, pectorals, and effigy gods worn by the figures, their gestures, the directions they face, the fruit on their trees, and of course their position in the Palenque dynasty. Some distributions are obvious. For example, both the women and Hanab-Pakal's father wear capes; everyone else is bare chested. Other distributions are more subtle and treat Pakal's body as a pivotal center around which various elements were arranged. The artists treated the long sides and the short sides as separate units of six and four figures, respectively. They then distributed all of the variables evenly within each of these

the constants

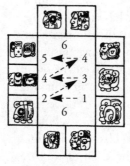

generations
and identities

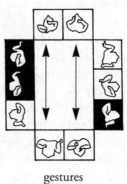

gestures

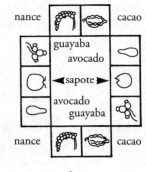

facedness

capes

wrist cuffs

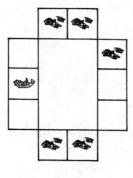

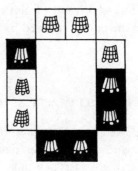

nance   cacao

guayaba
avocado

sapote

avocado
guayaba

nance   cacao

fruits

Ahaw-te'

headdress gods

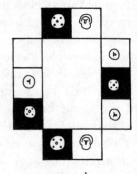

pectorals

**Fig. 3.28. F3:
The distribution
of elements among
the ten figures on
the sarcophagus sides.**

units, but since they never repeated the same distributional pattern, every figure on the sarcophagus sides appears to be unique.

This compositional device tells us something about the way they were thinking. Since they knew no one would ever be able to walk around the sarcophagus, even when the tomb was open, they ignored reading order as an organizational principle, except in the text on the lid. Writing, after all, requires reading order to be intelligible. In the imagery, they were free to choose other ways of creating meaningful patterns. They elected to use Hanab-Pakal's body as the central pivot around which they arranged all the elements that constituted the imagery of the ancestors. But they did it in a way that evoked the inherent symmetry of the cosmos as well as the infinite variability that resulted from the work of the divine *itz'at* who had created the world.

The Maya still adhere to these principles. We learned this from a wonderful story that Gene Stuart told us when she was writing her part of *The Mysterious Maya*.[23] She had been working with Chip Morris, a specialist on weaving in the Chiapas highlands, about the tradition of weaving and the work of master Tzotzil weavers. In her article, she quoted Chip's description of a very special huipil: "The weaver has created a huipil which describes the whole universe in a way so subtle that even fellow weavers won't notice, but so repetitious that the gods cannot help but see. She has described the complex relationship of time and space, and placed the gods of fertility in positions of power in order that all life may flourish."

Later when she was talking to us about the sarcophagus, she made a leap of understanding that linked the seventh-century tomb to the twentieth-century huipil. With excitement alight in her voice, she described the huipil to us and then said that Chip had asked the weaver why she had made the design so complicated, especially since no one could see the whole design when the huipil was worn and folded into her waistband. "Ah ha!" the woman said. "God can see the pattern." In astonishment, Gene realized that the woman placed herself at the center of the cosmos when she pulled the huipil over her head, just as Pakal put himself in the center of his orchard of ancestors. Both artists created messages with a complexity that exceeds casual comprehension. Both generated art works that were never meant to be seen fully or at all—because their audiences were not human. Yet both put a person at the center of the cosmos, as if human comprehension of the subtle symmetry of the cosmos honored the gods who had created it.

G—The Coffin and the Body

The coffin is a two-meter-long, body-shaped cavity in the center of the sarcophagus (Fig. 3.29). A thin stone cover with stone plugs in its four corners sealed the cavity. Red paint covered all the interior walls of the coffin as well as the bones. Pakal's body[24] lay extended on its back, head to the north, arms at his sides. His

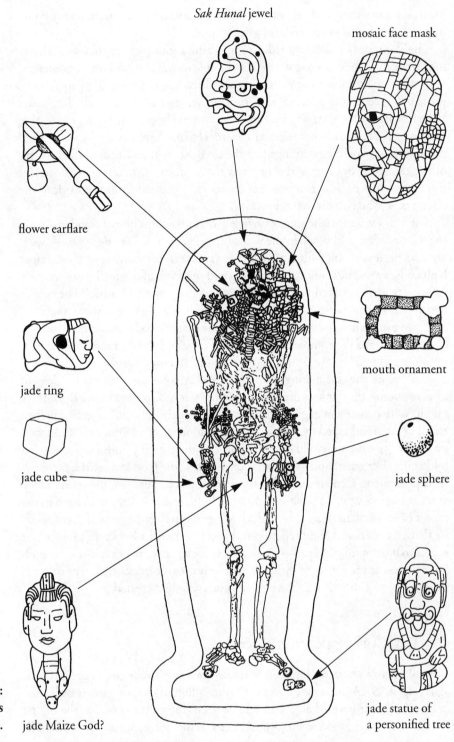

Sak Hunal jewel

mosaic face mask

flower earflare

jade ring

mouth ornament

jade cube

jade sphere

Fig. 3.29. G:
The body and its
accouterments.

jade Maize God?

jade statue of
a personified tree

body was encrusted with jewelry, including a huge collar composed of hundreds of jade cylinders and beads. The jade artist had cut some of the beads to resemble squash, a plant grown with maize and brought into the world by the Maize God. His wrists were encased with jade bead cuffs, and he wore a jade ring on every finger. The carving on one of them represents a human figure crouched down on his knees and elbows.

A jade-mosaic portrait mask covered his face, but he also wore a jade headband with the royal *hunal* jewel over his forehead. His square earflares carry inscriptions marking them as the property of the Chak gods. Jade cylinders and carved beads created the stamen for the flowers carved on the front of the earflares. A large counterweight assembled from mother-of-pearl pieces to resemble a large pearl balanced the weight of the jade stamen so that it stood out from his face. These earflares represented the flowers of the great ceiba tree.

Over his mouth, Hanab-Pakal wore a thin open rectangle made of pyrite (or hematite) and shell mosaic covered with a fine layer of red-painted plaster (Fig. 3.30). Alberto Ruz[25] knew of no other archaeological examples of this object, but he pointed out the representation of one on Naranjo Stela 13. Since his publication, a second example has appeared on Dos Pilas Stela 17, but this time the artist depicted the king in profile view so that we can identify more of his costume. The Maize God wore this backrack when he danced just before he began to create the cosmos. In fact, he carries the cosmos in his backrack, as symbolized by a skyband rising up from a waterlily monster to provide a perch to the *Itzam-Ye* bird. The tiny jaguar he transports in the backrack symbolizes the first throne stone of the Cosmic Hearth he set up in Orion. Thus, the Dos Pilas king assumed the role of the Maize God for the celebration of the world-creating ritual of the k'atun-ending. The people of Palenque put the Maize God's mouth ornament over Hanab-Pakal's mouth so that he would go to his grave as First Father, with the promise of rebirth.

This identity with the Maize God may explain why the plan of the tomb with its niches evokes the I-shaped pattern of a ballcourt.[26] The Maya saw a connection between the ballcourt and tombs. Not only were the Maize Gods buried in a ballcourt, but in K'iche' *hom* was the word for both "ballcourt" and "tomb." In the Classic period, *hom* meant "crack" or "chasm," and it referred to the ballcourt as a crack in the top of Sustenance Mountain and the Cosmic Turtle. Thus, the subtle reference to the shape of the ballcourt in the tomb created a perfect environment for the burial of a king who had become the Maize God.

A tiny jade figurine lay over Pakal's groin, but we are not sure who it represents. A larger jade figurine at his feet depicts the patron god of the month Pax. Glyphically, this god records *te'*, the word for "tree." They may have put this personification of "tree" at Hanab-Pakal's feet as a promise that he would become a tree just like his illustrious ancestors.

The most provocative contents of the tomb are the jade cube in his right hand and the jade sphere in his left. The cube and the sphere are a natural opposition

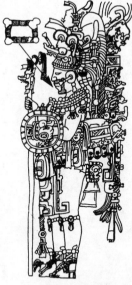

Fig. 3.30. Pakal's mouth ornament and the Maize God as dancer from Dos Pilas Stela 17.

that must have been meaningful to the Maya. Unfortunately they left us no information about what they meant by the opposition.

Finally, the red paint that covered the interior walls of the coffin also covered Hanab-Pakal's bones. After studying burial practices throughout Mesoamerica, Ruz concluded that "the corpses were painted with cinnabar before their inhumation, probably in order to give them the appearance of living bodies, and . . . in many cases they were wrapped in a cotton shroud also painted red."[27] Recent excavations in Copan offer new information. There, the bones from all royal tombs were painted red, while those from elite tombs were not.[28] Moreover, cinnabar appears to have been painted on the bones after the flesh was gone. In some early Copan tombs, cinnabar covers everything, so that it presents a danger to archaeologists, because its base element, mercury, is highly toxic. Glyphic descriptions of death rituals also speak of "staining with red paint" (*nab*).[29] Furthermore, archaeologists throughout the Maya region have found evidence for tomb reentry both in the way tombs have been resealed and in the architectural features built into them.[30] Thus, Hanab-Pakal's bones may have been painted red after his flesh had disappeared.

H—THE NINE WALL FIGURES

Nine life-size figures modeled in stucco graced the walls of the crypt (Fig. 3.31). Two appear seated in cross-legged position on both sides of the stairs into the tomb (Fig. 3.32a) and another seated figure sits above the platform on the north wall. The niches in the side wall carry the other six, with one figure in each of the south niches and a pair of figures in each of the north niches.

The most common interpretation of these figures has been that they represent the Nine Lords of the Night, but we find no real evidence supporting this interpretation. The nine figures present the same image with subtle variation. They have ornate headdresses with a quetzal-like bird, feather capes, high-backed sandals and crossed-leg ornates, and various pectorals. Each of them holds out a K'awil-serpent scepter and wears a Bearded Jaguar God shield on their wrists. All of them wear the rectangular mouthpiece of the Maize God, perhaps to show that they are in the same state as the man in the coffin they guard.

The most telling information comes from the distribution of their skirts: eight wear short jaguar kilts and one wears a long knee-length net skirt. Moreover, the figure with the skirt has *Ahaw Na Ol* in its headdress (Fig. 3.32b). This glyphic sign is part of the name of Lady Olnal, the only woman to rule Palenque in her own right. In addition, the headdress animal of the ninth figure (on the east side of the entry stairway) has the same lizard ear and teeth that we see in Akul-Anab's headdress on the sarcophagus sides. Thus, we deduce one of these figures is Lady Olnal and the other is Akul-Anab. Who, then, are the other figures?

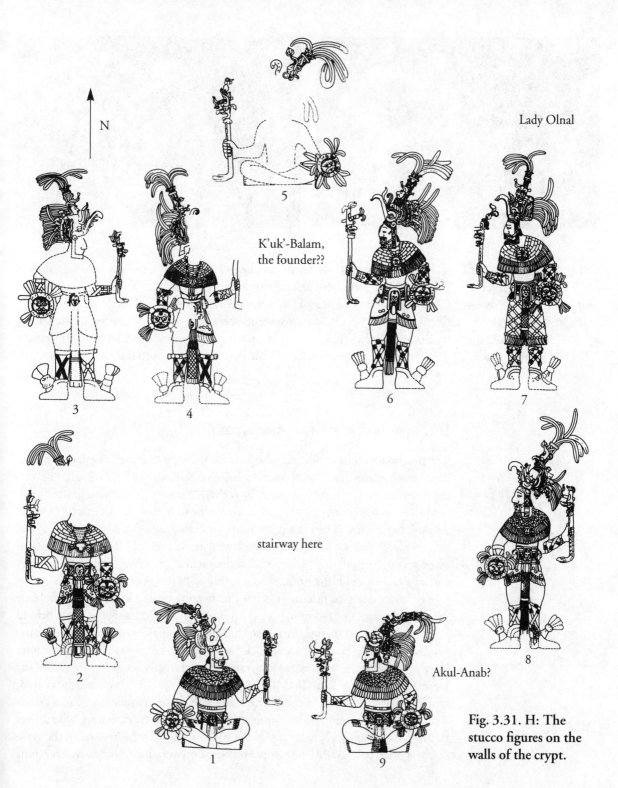

N

Lady Olnal

K'uk'-Balam, the founder??

5

3

4

6

7

stairway here

2

8

Akul-Anab?

1

9

Fig. 3.31. H: The stucco figures on the walls of the crypt.

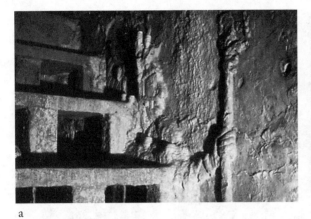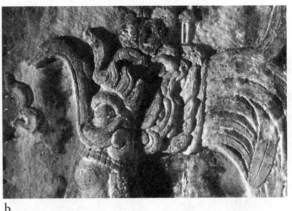

a   b

Fig. 3.32. (a) One of the stucco figures behind the entry stairway, and (b) the headdress with Lady Olnal's name.

If we consider his mother to have been a regent, then there were nine rulers of Palenque before Hanab-Pakal: the founder K'uk'-Balam, "Casper," Butz'ah-Sak-Chik, Akul-Anab I, K'an-Hok'-Chitam I, Akul-Anab II, Kan-Balam I, Lady Olnal, and Ah-Ne-Ol-Mat. We think these rulers are represented in the stucco figures so that these portraits represent the full dynastic succession, in contrast to the sarcophagus sides that depict the direct descent from father to son through seven generations.

I—Speaking with the Ancestors

The pyschoduct tube connecting the tomb to the temple above materialized a conduit between the dead Pakal and his living descendants (Fig. 3.33a). The sarcophagus named this conduit the *Tz'at Nakan*, "Serpent of the Wise Ones"[31] (Fig. 3.33b). A lip-to-lip offering plate of unknown provenience tells us exactly how the *Tz'at Nakan* worked. The inscription reads *ayal t'ab u sak lak, u cha k'aba ???*, "it was that he ascended up his made-plate, [was] its name, ???" The text speaks of ascending up the offering plate, which is designated by the very sun plate sign that carries Pakal through the portal. In fact, this plate is one of those portals.

The image depicts a field of *k'ulel* like that floating behind Pakal. We see the *Tz'at Nakan* the instant its head breaches the surface. The jeweled leaf hangs down behind its head with the *tz'a-to* signs visible to the right. The snake yawns wide to emit the head of a smoking death god known as God A. A stinking bone serves as the god's headband, while a sprouting maize symbol rides above the bone. The name of the famous Tikal king Toh-Chak-Ich'ak, whose palace we have already visited, replaced the kernels in the corn cartouche. This contradictory image of a boney death god and sprouting maize signals the resurrection of the dead king, who arrives from his harrowing of Xibalba inside the gullet of the *Tz'at Nakan* and in the guise of the god.[32] Just as this image portrays the materialization of an illustrious

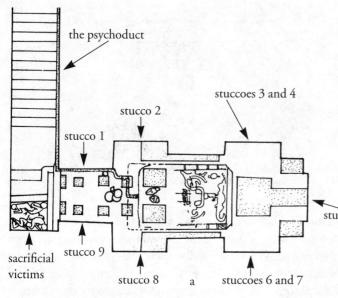

the psychoduct

stucco 2

stucco 1

stuccoes 3 and 4

sacrificial
victims

stucco 9

stucco 8   a   stuccoes 6 and 7

stucco 5

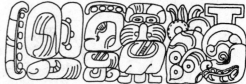

u tz'akabhi   u kabi u mam   Tz'at??? Nakan
"they   "they oversaw it,   "the Snake of
succeeded"   the ancestors of"   the Sages"

b

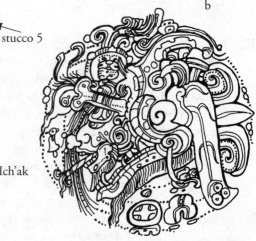

The *Tz'at Nakan* emits a god of the Otherworld
who wears the name of the Tikal king Toh-Chak-Ich'ak
in his headdress.

ancestor as he resurrects, so the descendants of Pakal expected to contact their ancestors arriving through the conduit they had built into his funerary temple.

In a visit to Santiago Atitlan, Linda saw a startling connection between the *Tz'at
Nakan* and the imagery of the sarcophagus to modern Maya symbolism of birth
and death. She and Nikolai Grube had gone there to participate in a ceremony in
the *cofradia* of San Juan with their friend Vicente, an anthropologist who lives there
and who had been a member of the *cofradia*. During the long ritual, Linda
became curious about a box hanging from the ceiling by wires. It was near the altar
and adjacent to the place where the women of the *cofradia* sat during the ritual.

During a lull in the ceremony, Linda asked Vicente about the strange box. He
explained that the people of Santiago believe that fetuses are connected to their
mother by a Rainbow Serpent that delivers heat and sustenance to the child
while it is in the womb. Birth severs the child from the Rainbow Serpent, so that
sick babies, they believe, have lost too much heat and must be reconnected to
the serpent. Healing ceremonies conducted in the *cofradia* house place the baby
back in a prebirth condition. The babies are put back in the womb (the box) so
that the Rainbow Serpent (the wires) can reconnect them to the sky (the ceiling
of the *cofradia* house).

Fig. 3.33. I: The psy-
choduct that connects
the dead Hanab-Pakal
to his successors.

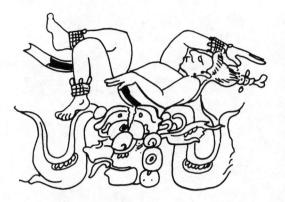

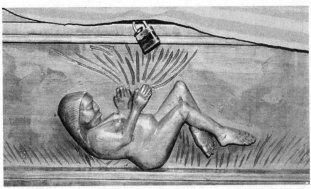

Fig. 3.34. The Maize
God reborn from
a flower and the
cofradia box from
San Juan at
Santiago Atitlan.

Although Vicente told Linda that an Atiteco sculptor had carved the image of a pregnant woman on the box, it was not until the following year that she got a really good look at the carving. When she finally saw it, she could not believe the image. Carved in the center of the side, a pregnant woman floats (Fig. 3.34) in a mirror image of Pakal's position on the sarcophagus. Of course, we do not know if the Atiteco sculptor had seen an image of Pakal's sarcophagus, but if he had, he certainly would not have been told about the modern interpretation of the image. The question for Linda was, Why had he used an image to signify birth that was so close to the most famous image of death from the precolumbian world?

It happens that the ancient Maya associated this posture with birth, just as their descendants do. We have pottery imagery from the Classic period that shows the Maize God and other deities being born in exactly this position, so that the connection between birth and death is a very ancient one. Pakal falls in death, but his very position also signaled birth—his birth into the Otherworld and his eventual rebirth as the Maize God and revered ancestor.

CHAPTER 4

Copan: The Great Plaza
of Waxaklahun-Ubah-K'awil

In every civilization of the ancient world, there are art works and monuments that stand out among their fellows as objects of special character. The great portrait sculptures that stand in silent rows down the center of the Great Plaza of Copan created one of these special places. They constitute one of the great masterpieces of the Maya legacy. Although the artists who made them did not sign their works and leave us their names, the patron of these great works did. He was Waxaklahun-Ubah-K'awil (commonly known as 18 Rabbit),[1] the thirteenth king of the Copan dynasty.

Waxaklahun-Ubah-K'awil and his fellow lords did not call their kingdom Copan, as modern archaeologists do. It had a name that could be written in three different ways (Fig. 4.1): *xuk,* meaning "corner"; *xukpi,* meaning "corner bundle"; and *xukup,* meaning "motmot," which is a kind of bird.[2] These names reflected Copan's position in the southeast corner of the area occupied by Maya-speaking peoples. The valleys beyond Copan in both Honduras and El Salvador were occupied by non-Maya ethnic groups.

Xukpi lies in a beautiful valley drained by the Copan River, a tributary of the great Motagua. Today, the way into Xukpi, from both the Honduras and Guatemala sides, winds through mountains and valleys filled with cornfields and cattle ranches. Most of the people who live on the Guatemala side of the approach are Chorti Maya, the descendants of the people of Xukpi. In their hamlets away from the road, they still live much as they did during the Classic period. Crosses covered with plants sit in small shrines along the road to protect the maize fields beyond. The floor of the Copan Valley sits at about 3,000 feet, just at the altitude where pine trees begin to grow. The floor of the valley has tropical forest and fruit trees, but the roads entering the valley from either end rise up through pine trees in a scenery very different from that of the Peten sites. Today the land owners rotate crops of maize and tobacco in the valley bottom, while poorer people work their cornfields on the steep slopes of the surrounding

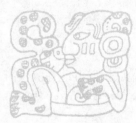

k'ul xuk ahaw   *xuk ahaw*   *k'ul xukpi ahaw*   *xukpi ahaw*   *xukup ahaw*   *k'ul xukup nah*   *xukpip ahaw*

Fig. 4.1. Variants of the Copan emblem glyph.

mountains. The modern town of Copan Ruinas lies about a kilometer from the archaeological park. New hotels and restaurants are changing its face very rapidly, but its center plaza was designed by the great Tatiana Proskouriakoff, who worked there in the 1930s. In fact, archaeology and archaeologists have been part of the life of this town since the 1890s.

The history of Xukpi is long and rich, and the heritage left by Copan's kings is one of the most beautiful and elegant collections of architecture and sculpture in the Maya world.[3] Although people began living in the Copan Valley as early as 900 B.C., the dynasty that ruled Xukpi throughout the Classic period did not start until 8.19.10.11.0 8 Ahaw 18 Yaxk'in (September 9, 426). Its founder, Yax-K'uk'-Mo' (Fig. 4.2), established a dynasty that endured for 384 years until it ended on another 8 Ahaw (May 6, 820, 9.19.10.0.0). The founder and his son, the second ruler in the dynasty, had affiliations with Tikal and Kaminaljuyu, and perhaps with far-distant Teotihuacan, or *Puh,* "Cattail Reed," as the Maya called it.[4]

The founder and his immediate successors were energetic builders who raised an enormous number of buildings very quickly, thus establishing the template that their descendants followed as they built over the earlier architecture, eventually to create a huge complex now called the Acropolis. Moreover, some of these early buildings and burials show affiliations with imagery and building styles associated with Teotihuacan, a practice that continued for the rest of Copan's history.[5] By using these types of images, Yax-K'uk'-Mo' and his successors declared themselves to be a lineage descended from the *Ah Puh,* the ancient people from the Place of Cattail Reeds who invented civilized life, the arts, writing, and war. Several early buildings also show affiliations with Tikal, another kingdom that declared itself to be a "Place of Cattails."

Named after the great War Serpent of the Maya, Waxaklahun-Ubah-K'awil took over the throne on July 19, 695, from his father, K'ak'-Nab-K'awil (also known as Smoke-Imix-God K), the longest-ruling king in Copan's history. He inherited the kingdom at its strongest and wealthiest moment. During his father's sixty-seven-year reign (February 8, 628–June 18, 695), Xukpi dominated Quirigua, a town on the Motagua River to the north, and its influence was felt as far as Pusilha and Nimli Punit in southern Belize.[6] The father also had commissioned an ambitious program of monuments, including the erection of a set of stelae at various places around the valley, to declare the entire area a sacred

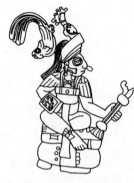

Fig. 4.2. The founder Yax-K'uk'-Mo' from Altar Q.

seat of Xukpi's protector gods. Identifying specific architectural projects with K'ak'-Nab-K'awil has been difficult, but likely candidates include Temple 22-2nd and earlier versions of Temples 16 and 26.

When Waxaklahun-Ubah-K'awil became king, he turned his attention to the downtown part of the kingdom—that is, the Acropolis and its nearby courts. His early works included the final version of Temple 22, which commemorated the first k'atun anniversary of his accession. He also remodeled the ballcourt by putting in a new floor and capping the old markers with new, thinner ones. These are the famous ballcourt markers of Copan. He also began the famous Hieroglyphic Stairs[7] during his work on Temple 26.

1—STRUCTURE 4

While those building projects proceeded, Waxaklahun-Ubah-K'awil also began to erect a magnificent stelae program in the large plazas to the north of the Acropolis (Fig. 4.3). He chose the space next to a radial pyramid (Structure 4) that had been constructed during the founder's time. Alfred Maudslay, one of the early explorers who photographed the site and published drawings of its monuments, excavated this little pyramid during his visit over a century ago. At plaza level, he found an offering pot (Fig. 4.4) containing a necklace made of pearls and jade beads, small figures cut from shell, several large pieces of jade, cinnabar, and several ounces of mercury.[8] Three meters below that he found the remains of a jaguar buried under a layer of charcoal. The founder or his son probably commissioned the first version of this pyramid. Interestingly, the last king in this dynasty placed the bodies of fifteen jaguars in a pit next to the altar

Fig. 4.3. A perspective drawing of Copan, showing the Great Plaza, the ballcourt, the Acropolis, and the Royal Residence.

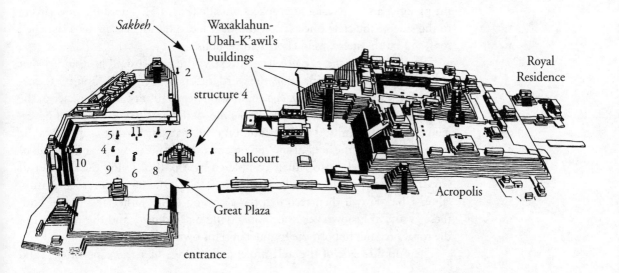

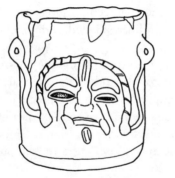

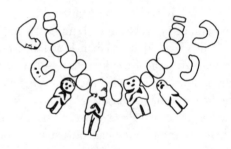

Fig. 4.4. 1: The cache pot and necklace from the offering inside Structure 4.

celebrating the founder and all of his successors in the dynasty. Perhaps these two jaguar offerings were related.

After rebuilding this sacred mountain, Waxaklahun-Ubah-K'awil began to erect the stelae that portray him confronting the supernatural on every major period-ending date during his first thirty-five years of reign. His program captured an unequaled view of Maya ritual and belief, while at the same time creating one of the great artistic legacies from the precolumbian world.

2—Stela J and the East Plaza

Stela J, the first installation in this new program, went into the East Plaza to celebrate the first major period ending of Waxaklahun-Ubah-K'awil's reign, 9.13.10.0.0 (January 26, 702). He set it up where a *sak beh* that leads from residential zones to the east passes into the sacred center. The imagery his artists carved into this stela defined the boundary between the hallowed spaces inside the precinct and the residential spaces outside (Fig. 4.5). The stone now sitting to the side of the stela once sat on top of it like a hat. It represents a thatched roof, so that the stela was in effect a stone house.

The side facing the *sak beh* has its text written on a double-stranded mat design. The Maya combined *pop,* the word for "mat," with *nah,* "house," to designate the idea of community. *Pop* could also refer to royalty. The presence of the *pop* design on this boundary stela marks the sacred precinct as a place of governance and community. The inscription on the mat side further emphasizes the royal character of the area inside the precinct. It connects the period ending of the stela, 9.13.10.0.0, to rituals completed by Yax-K'uk'-Mo', the founder of Copan's dynasty, on the end of the bak'tun (9.0.0.0.0), 266 years earlier. Waxaklahun-Ubah-K'awil then recorded the accession of his father and linked both these events to his own accession, thus tying his authority and the character of the royal precinct to both the founder and his own father.

The opposite side of the stela presents the image of a *tzuk,* "partition," and

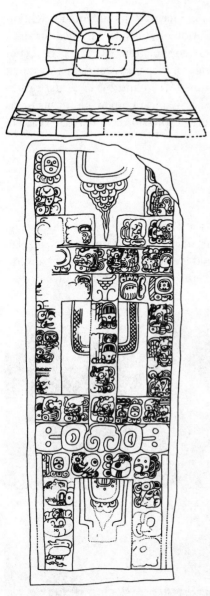

west

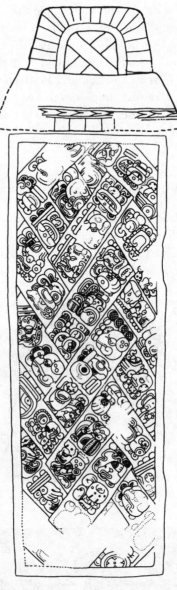

east

Fig. 4.5. 2: Stela J. The west side shows a *tzuk,* "partition," design (the face covered by hieroglyphs) and a *nah,* "house" motif (represented by the thatched rooftop). The east side contains an inscription arranged in the pattern of a mat, a symbol used to mark the royal precinct.

nah, "house," to remind people that they were reentering residential neighborhoods as they left the East Plaza. The inscription on this side is more difficult. It records the conjuring of the Paddler Gods in conjunction with the period ending, but it also links an early date in the reign of Copan's second king to supernatural events thirteen and fourteen bak'tuns (5,125 and 5,519 years) earlier. Evoking the distant past in this way created a mythical framework for historical events. The sides register special period-ending expressions connected to each of the twenty tuns within a k'atun.

3—THE GREAT PLAZA

Waxaklahun-Ubah-K'awil next turned his attention to the Great Plaza (Fig. 4.6). Earlier rulers had already left their marks on this space. Balam-Nan (aka Waterlily-Jaguar), the seventh king, had erected Stela E in front of a mini-acropolis on the western side of the Great Plaza, while K'ak'-Nab-K'awil had set

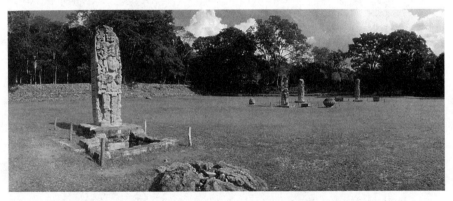

View looking northwest with Stelae A, 4, B, and C, left to right.

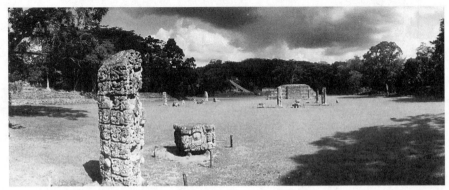

Fig. 4.6. 3: Views of the Great Plaza.

View looking south with Stelae D, F, H, C, A, 4, and B, left to right.

up Stela I in the southeastern corner. Both stelae depict these rulers in the traditional pose of Copan kings—holding a Ceremonial Bar as they stand in the guise of a god they have materialized.

The inscriptions on both stelae are also similar. They record the date of dedication and the formal names of each stela. Balam-Nan mentioned Yax-K'uk'-Mo' and another lord named K'ak'-K'awil. K'ak'-Nab-K'awil chose an eclipse station, 9.12.3.14.0 (March 22, 676), to dedicate his stela. He discussed the period-ending rituals and linked them to a very early date, 8.6.0.0.0 (December 19, 159), and an event that involved Xukpi as a geographical location. Stela 17, a broken Early Classic stela that was found in the rubble at the north end of the Great Plaza, recorded this same date. As we shall see, the people of Copan may have associated this day with their patron gods and perhaps with the establishment of their kingdom.

When Waxaklahun-Ubah-K'awil began his own opus in the Great Plaza, he set his first stela to the north and east of the center point (Fig. 4.7), for reasons we have yet to discern. Moreover, as he brought his plan for the plaza to fruition, he continued to favor its eastern half for setting up his stelae. He positioned the stelae so that each has a clear view of the rising or setting sun.[9]

The styles of the six stelae in the Great Plaza display considerable variation in the way they are carved. Herbert Spinden,[10] the first archaeologist to look at them as a coherent group, suggested that this variation derived from an evolution of artistic accomplishment that took place over a period of seventy years. But the inscriptions now show us that Waxaklahun-Ubah-K'awil commissioned the entire sequence of monuments in an order that does not correspond to their stylistic seriation. What, then, accounts for the differences in style between the stelae? Our personal interpretation is that two master artists or two workshops—one conservative (A, B, H, and C), and the other innovative (F, 4, and D)—worked on the Great Plaza stelae.

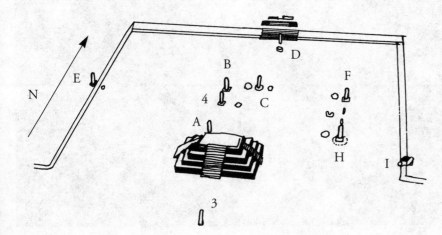

Fig. 4.7. Diagram of the Great Plaza and the placement of the stelae.

The principal innovation that we see is the remarkable volumetric nature of the sculpture,[11] especially in Stelae F, 4, and D. The anatomy and accouterments of these figures were almost entirely cut free of the stone mass, while the more conservative group of sculptors maintained the core mass of the stelae and limited volumetric rendering to details. Of course, all of these stelae remain frontal when compared to the Greek and Roman sculptural traditions. To us, this is not a useful comparison because the Maya were not interested in casual poses or the spontaneity of a moment. Rulers wanted to be presented in the kind of dignified, formal postures that are naturally frontal, just as the human body is naturally frontal. Nevertheless, the sculptors of Stelae F and 4 achieved a powerful volumetric modeling that was only equaled at Copan by the sculptor of Temple 22 and Stela M. We suspect that the sculptors of those monuments were, in fact, the same person or workshop. However, since the Copan sculptors did not sign their works as did their colleagues at other sites, we cannot confirm our speculation on this point.

Each stela stands over a cruciform chamber whose axes are oriented to the cardinal directions. Today only the chamber under Stela A remains open (Fig. 4.8). These chambers held offerings placed during the rituals that brought the stelae to life and vested power in the space they occupied. In the discussions of the stelae that follow, we will comment only on those offerings that are particularly interesting.

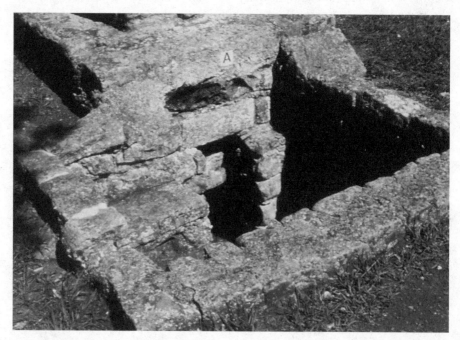

Fig. 4.8. Cruciform vault under Stela A.

4—Stela C

To commemorate 9.14.0.0.0 (December 5, 711), the first k'atun-ending after his accession, Waxaklahun-Ubah-K'awil commissioned a magnificent, larger-than-life-size statue of himself frozen in the midst of materializing beings from the Otherworld (Fig. 4.9). In fact, he depicted himself twice on opposite sides of this stela so that he could face both the rising and the setting sun. On both sides he holds the most important royal scepter, a Double-headed Serpent Bar, against his chest, but the details of his costume and accouterments reflect the direction he faces and the patterns in the sky on the night the k'atun ended. He copied this double-portrait format from his father, who had erected images of himself facing north and south to celebrate 9.11.0.0.0, the k'atun-ending sixty years earlier. Both of these k'atun-endings fell on the day Venus was first seen in the evening sky.

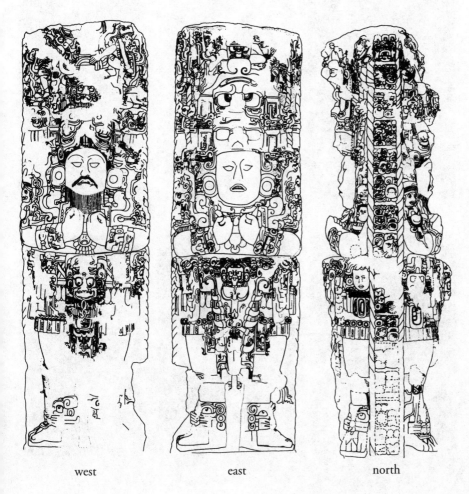

west   east   north   **Fig. 4.9. 4: Stela C.**

THE EAST SIDE

Waxaklahun-Ubah-K'awil's high-cheeked visage gazes out of the center of the east side, its red paint still lending a sense of immediacy to the portrait (Fig. 4.10e). The heads of his Serpent Bar frame his face, emitting ancestral beings wearing ornate, stacked headdresses (Fig. 4.10f). Waxaklahun-Ubah-K'awil's headdress supports three stacked heads, culminating with the Jester God, who was known as *Sak Hunal.*

Another ancestral figure sits cross-legged behind *Sak Hunal* holding his own Serpent Bar, out of which emerge yet other figures holding their Serpent Bars. Unfortunately, this uppermost figure was badly broken when the stela fell in earlier times, but the figures coming out of these Serpent Bars are a visual joy. The artist depicted only one of their arms and legs as they lean out of the open maws of the

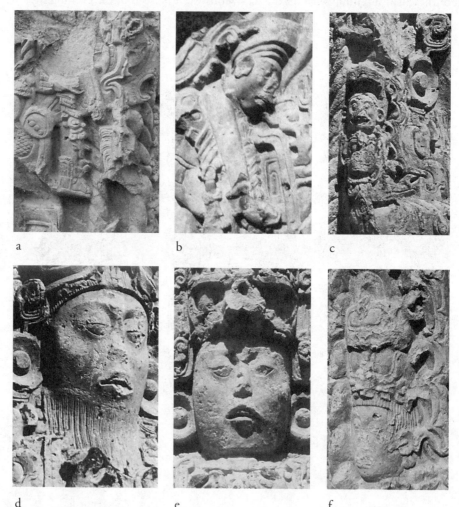

Fig. 4.10. Details from Stela C: (a) a nawal emerging from the upper east side; (b) a nawal emerging from the upper west side; (c) the deity emerging from the Serpent Bar on the west side; (d) the main face from the west side; (e) the main face from the east side; (f) the deity emerging from the Serpent Bar on the east side.

a   b   c

d   e   f

snakes. The Serpent Bars they hold spit out flint blades of war and sacrifice (Fig. 4.10a). Twisted ropes emerge beside the flints to drop downward on either side of Waxaklahun-Ubah-K'awil's headdress. The ropes have three knots and a bat head, probably reading *xu*, tied to it. These ropes are the umbilical cord, called the *kuxan sum* by the Yukateks, that connected Maya lords to the sky and their source of power and authority. Here they connect Waxaklahun-Ubah-K'awil to that sacred realm.

The lower half of the stela shows Waxaklahun-Ubah-K'awil as a crocodile tree emerging from a crack in a mountain. The tree appears in two forms. His loin apron is the *Wakah-Kan* or World Tree with its square-nosed serpent branches ending in leaf forms (Fig. 4.11a). The crocodile head that overlaps his apron represents another form of the World Tree—one that ended in a crocodile head where its roots would be (Fig. 4.11b). The crocodile muzzle points downward, with huge teeth splayed out on both sides, and the front feet of the crocodile hang down from the king's waist.

Two mountain monsters hang mouth-up just inside the crocodile's feet. Waxaklahun-Ubah-K'awil's entire waist represents the open maw of the mountain, with the crocodile tree emerging in the form of the king. Moreover, this crocodile tree was the home of the great cosmic bird *Itzam-Ye*.[12] In the myth of Creation, the Hero Twins shot this bird out of the tree to prepare for the Fourth Creation. The Maya saw this crocodile head as the dark cleft in the Milky Way, and the tree as the Milky Way itself, arching across the sky from the southwest to the northeast.

However, this stela was more than just a realization of the myth—it recorded the pattern of the sky after sunset on the night of December 5, 711. On this night, Venus made its first appearance as Eveningstar, becoming visible at sunset in the constellation of Sagittarius at the base of the Milky Way crocodile tree (Fig. 4.12a). Thus the stela replicates symbolically what Waxaklahun-Ubah-K'awil and his people saw on that important night.

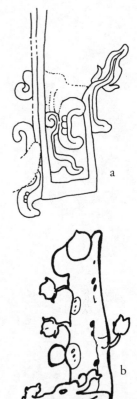

Fig. 4.11. The loin-cloth tree with its leaf and a crocodile tree from a pottery scene.

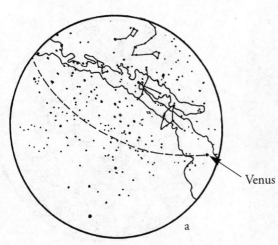

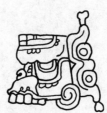

Fig. 4.12. The sky at sunset on 9.14.0.0.0, or December 5, 711, and the god of the Eveningstar worn by Hasaw-Kan-K'awil at Tikal.

This correspondence with Venus was important to the Maya, because the Eveningstar was a powerful god associated with death and war. Waxaklahun-Ubah-K'awil's father, K'ak'-Nab-K'awil, and his contemporary, Hanab-Pakal of Palenque, had both recorded the first appearance of the Eveningstar as a crucial feature of the k'atun-ending 9.11.0.0.0. For K'ak'-Nab-K'awil, it was an especially powerful association, because he encircled the Copan Valley with stelae celebrating the stations of Venus leading up to its arrival as the Eveningstar on the night of the k'atun-ending. Sixty years later on 9.14.0.0.0, Hasaw-Kan-K'awil of Tikal acknowledged the first appearance of the Eveningstar on his Stela 16, by having his artists depict him wearing a mosaic image of the skeletal god of the Eveningstar (Fig. 4.12b).[13] Waxaklahun-Ubah-K'awil also connected himself to the Eveningstar on this same k'atun-ending, but he did it in a different way, as we have seen. He pictured himself as the image of the Milky Way when Venus became visible at its base.

THE WEST SIDE

The west side of Stela C continues to play on the themes of Creation and the sky on the night of the k'atun-ending. The key is the giant turtle altar set in front of Waxaklahun-Ubah-K'awil's feet. To see the stela across the altar re-creates the image of the Maize God being reborn from a cleft in the Cosmic Turtle's back.[14] At the end of the Third Creation in Maya mythology, the Hero Twins defeated the Lords of Death and then went to the Ballcourt of Xibalba to resurrect the Maize Gods, who were their fathers (Fig. 4.13). In the imagery of the times, these gods were reborn from a crack in the carapace of this Cosmic Turtle. Like the crocodile tree, the Cosmic Turtle occurred in the sky. It corresponded to the

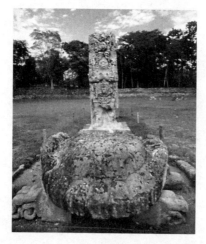

Fig. 4.13. The turtle altar of Stela C and the resurrection of the Maize God.

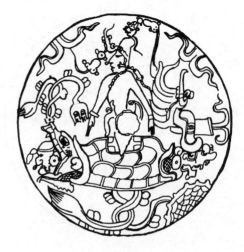

belt of Orion, a constellation that happened to be directly overhead at midnight on this k'atun-ending.[15]

Waxaklahun-Ubah-K'awil's features appear to be relatively young, but he wears a long beard, a rare feature among Maya men. We suspect the beard was false, but its meaning is not entirely clear. As he did on the east side, Waxaklahun-Ubah-K'awil wears a skirt with the *Wakah-Kan* apron, but here a waterlily transforms the *tzuk* head on the tree trunk into a reference to the Primordial Sea, in which the Cosmic Turtle floats. The belt heads represent the cruller-eyed Jaguar God who is sometimes the sun and at other times Venus. As we shall see, this Jaguar God played a role in the myth of Copan's patron gods. The side heads are the patron gods of the month Pax. In actuality, they personify the glyphic sign *te'*, or "tree."

In his arms, Waxaklahun-Ubah-K'awil carries a Ceremonial Serpent Bar with turbaned old men emerging from the mouths of the snakes (Fig. 4.10c). These little figures, who may represent aged ancestors or gods wearing Copan attire, contrast with the young deities on the east side. They hold severed heads of zoomorphic Maize Gods in their hands.

Waxaklahun-Ubah-K'awil's headdress displays a single zoomorphic deity who wears a jade headband surmounted by three heads. The central head is a *Hunal* Jester God, while the side heads combine an *ahaw* face reading *nik*, "flower," with the stem and leaf of a tree (Fig. 4.14). These personified flower-trees mark him as a *yahaw-te'*, "tree lord," while the front head declares him to be a king.

The summit of the headdress mirrors the east side. A now-damaged figure sits cross-legged on top of the headdress holding a Serpent Bar that emits yet other turbaned figures holding their own Serpent Bars (Fig. 4.10b). Twisted cords representing the umbilicus descend to medallions with *xok*, "shark" fishes. Two tiny gods sit atop the medallions holding the umbilicus.

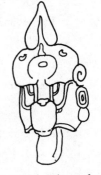

Fig. 4.14. The *yahaw-te'* title from the head-band on the west side of Stela C.

THE ALTARS

The turtle altar on the west side of Stela C balances an uncarved rectangular altar on the east. The turtle altar has two heads that match the images of the Cosmic Turtle as it was represented on pottery (Fig. 4.15). Glyphic texts elsewhere make

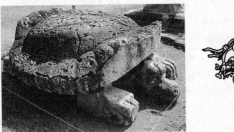

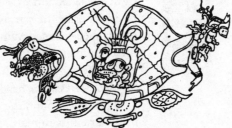

Fig. 4.15.
The Cosmic Turtle.

The Moon Goddess counted the year

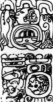

13 kalabtuns, 6 Ahaw

13 K'ayab, he ended the tun

Hanal Ek'-Hun Wi Ha

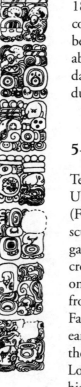

no [days], 1 winal, 5 tuns

14 k'atuns, 11 bak'tuns

after it happened, 6 Ahaw

13 K'ayab after it happened

6 Ahaw 13 Muwan

he erected . . . *chal*

tunil, was its holy name

the *lakamtun* ("big stone") . . .
tzahan . . .

Fig. 4.16. The inscription from the south side of Stela C.

clear that this turtle was *ak* and the cleft in its carapace was an *ol,* or "portal." He is the Cosmic Turtle that floated in the Primordial Sea and sat in Orion.

THE INSCRIPTION

The text (Fig. 4.16) confirms the association of Venus with the k'atun-ending and with a series of mythological events that took place in sacred places located in the Otherworld.

The south text links the tying of a stone 4,617 years earlier to the erection of the stela. The verb reading *tz'apah,* "it was set in the ground," precedes the proper name of the stela, but it is too damaged to decipher fully. The text includes the word for "stela" as a *lakamtun,* or a "big stone."[16]

The north text is far more difficult to read. It has a series of calendar rounds, 5 Ahaw 8 Kumk'u, 4 Ahaw 18 Wo, and 5 Ahaw 18 Wo, with tun-ending events. One of these, 4 Ahaw 18 Wo, corresponds to the end of thirteen kalabtuns (2,050,146.46 years) before the creation date 4 Ahaw 8 Kumk'u, but no one has been able to place the other dates in the Long-Count calendar. Each date is associated with a tun-ending (*u k'al tun*) event conducted by a supernatural at a sacred location.

5—STELA F

Ten years after the 9.14.0.0.0 k'atun-ending, Waxaklahun-Ubah-K'awil erected another stela just to the east of Stela C (Fig. 4.17). Cut by a master sculptor using a new fully round sculptural style, Waxaklahun-Ubah-K'awil stands in full elegant costume with a feathered backrack that runs from the crown of his headdress to his ankles. So deep is the relief that one can see the back of his knees and the curve of his buttocks from the side, and his feet ride at a natural 45-degree angle. Facing toward the setting sun, he wears the guise of a jaguar-eared, shell-bearded Venus God, who is named on the rear of the monument as *Hun-Kanal-Tzuk-Ahaw,* "One-Sky Bearded Lord." He has ropes on his knees, a mat over his loincloth, and his belt carries *ahaw* heads and pouches for stingray spines.

Wrapping around the sides of the stela, his Ceremonial Serpent Bar emits miniature K'awil gods whose foreheads trans-

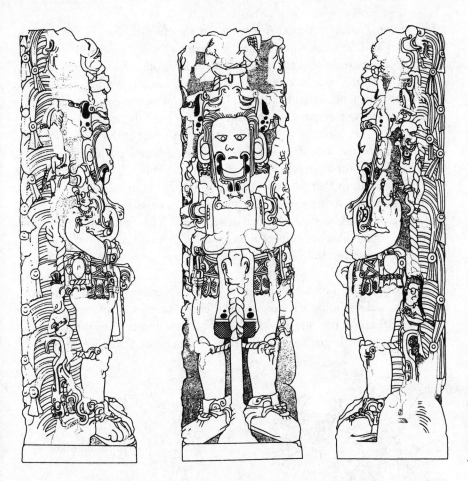

Fig. 4. 17. 5: Stela F showing Waxaklahun-Ubah-K'awil in the guise of the Bearded Jaguar God.

form into flint blades. A second set of serpents can be seen behind his ankles, where they also belch up huge personified flints, and a now-destroyed figure held yet another serpent on top of his headdress. The *kuxan sum* descends from its mouth, giving access to a set of *wayob,* or spirit companions, the king has materialized into our world. They climb down the rope, peeking out of the feathers of Waxaklahun-Ubah-K'awil's backrack.

This beautiful stela sets Waxaklahun-Ubah-K'awil into the story of the two patron gods of Copan—Kan-Te-Ahaw and Bolon-K'awil.[17] Unfortunately, this story, unlike the mythic sagas in the Popol Vuh, did not survive to be recorded in the postconquest literature of the Maya, but it was so popular as a myth that episodes from it were painted many times on funerary pottery of the Classic period. By comparing scenes on these pots, Nikolai Grube has reconstructed a series of events that include some of the following episodes.

Chak and a skeletal death god throw a Baby Jaguar down a mountain into the Otherworld. The mountain, which can have a snake emerging from its eye, has a tree growing on its summit. A serpent emerges from a knot in the tree and belches up an Old God, who fondles the breast of a beautiful young woman. The tail of the snake also transforms into K'awil, one of the patron gods of Copan. The young woman cares for two mummy bundles holding the remains of gods, and she tends a dying old man. In other episodes, she rides a deer, in the presence of young men who may be aspects of the Hero Twins.

Stela 35 of Naranjo (Fig. 4.18) leads into another part of the story. The scene on the front of the stela depicts a ruler wearing a headdress made of stacked mats, holding a burning torch, and standing on waterlilies. The text on the back of this stela[18] tells us that the event occurs on the day Ix in the month Kumk'u, but the numbers are destroyed. The glyphs go on to say that the "First Baby Jaguar, Black Headdress" was burned at *Na-Ho-Kan* (the place where the gods set up the Jaguar Throne Stone of the Cosmic Hearth on the day of Creation). According to the text, this burning happened because of Kan-Te-Ahaw, the god who is also a patron deity of Copan.

Two pots link this Naranjo episode to Stela F. Both of them have dates with the day Ix and the month Kumk'u, but their numbers are different. One pot shows an episode in the saga in which Kan-Te-Ahaw throws a huge stone tied up with rope onto the Jaguar God's belly. The other one shows Kan-Te-Ahaw hold-

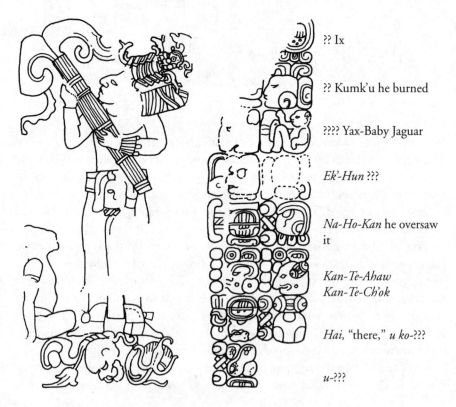

?? Ix

?? Kumk'u he burned

???? Yax-Baby Jaguar

Ek'-Hun ???

Na-Ho-Kan he oversaw it

Kan-Te-Ahaw
Kan-Te-Ch'ok

Hai, "there," *u ko-*???

u-???

Fig. 4.18. Naranjo Stela 35 shows a lord holding a torch, while the text records the burning of the Baby Jaguar at the hands of Kan-Te-Ahaw, who was also the patron god of Copan.

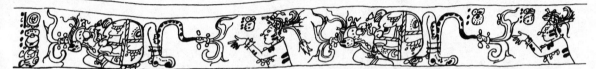

Kan-Te-Ahaw throws a tied stone onto the Bearded Jaguar God, here named *Ox-Te-Ha*, "Three Water."

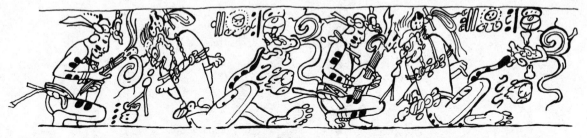

Kan-Te-Ahaw holds a torch, ready to burn the Bearded Jaguar God, here named *K'ak'-K'in*, "Fire-Sun."

ing a torch, ready to burn the adult form of the Baby Jaguar (Fig. 4.19). The poor Jaguar God is tied up like a captive.

This adult form of the Baby Jaguar often wears a shell beard on his chin, a twisted cord between his eyes, and jaguar ears above his human ones. He has many names in the inscriptions, including *Hun-Kanal-Tzuk-Ahaw* (One-Sky-Bearded-Lord), *K'in-Hix* (Sun-Jaguar), *K'inich-Tah-Way* (Sun-Faced-Torch-Nawal), and *K'inich-Ahaw-Pakal* (Sun-Faced-Lord-Shield). On one of these pots, he is *K'ak'-K'in* (Fire-Sun). Both Tikal and Palenque also claimed this god as their patron deity. Stela F portrays Waxaklahun-Ubah-K'awil as this Bearded Jaguar God, and as we will see, the altar depicts the Baby Jaguar tumbling down the mountain.

Fig. 4.19. The Patron God of Copan confronts the Bearded Jaguar God.

THE INSCRIPTION

The sculptors placed the text (Fig. 4.20) on the back of Stela F inside twisted rope circles flanked by arching feathers, as if the glyphs are part of Waxaklahun-Ubah-K'awil's backrack. A rope twists around every group of four glyphs until it falls to the ground to terminate in *ak'bal*, "night," deities. The text specified the date of the action as 9.14.10.0.0 (October 13, 721) and gives the stela two proper names. One evokes the personified flints that materialize in the Vision Serpents that surround the king, while the other refers to the Bearded Jaguar God whom the king impersonates. In fact, the scribe completed the text by specifying that Waxaklahun-Ubah-K'awil conjured *Hun-Wi-Kanal Tzuk-Ahaw*, which was the god's personal name.

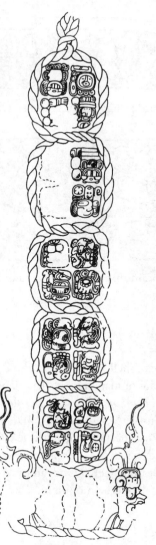

The patron of Mak counted the year
5 Ahaw
3 Mak
in the center of

...
on 15 k'atuns
...
k'inil . . . tok'

is its holy name
Bearded Jaguar God
First Cleft Sky
is its name

the *lakamtun*
...
he forced it out
Waxaklahun

Ubah-K'awil
??? harvested ??
Hun Wi Kanal Ah-Tzuk Ahaw

Fig. 4.20.
The text of Stela F.

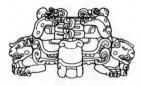

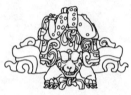

Fig. 4.21. The altar
of Stela F with the
tumbling jaguars.

THE ALTAR

The altar that sits in front of Waxaklahun-Ubah-K'awil's wide-open eyes represents a huge mountain monster (Fig. 4.21). The knots tied across its forehead may refer to the bound stone that Kan-Te-Ahaw threw onto the belly of the Jaguar God. Today the mountain sits alone, but early photographs show jaguars descending the sides of its head. These are Baby Jaguars in their animal form tumbling down the mountain into the earth. At some time in the early part of the twentieth century, they were broken and the fragments were scattered around the Great Plaza. They are now protected in the storerooms at Copan.

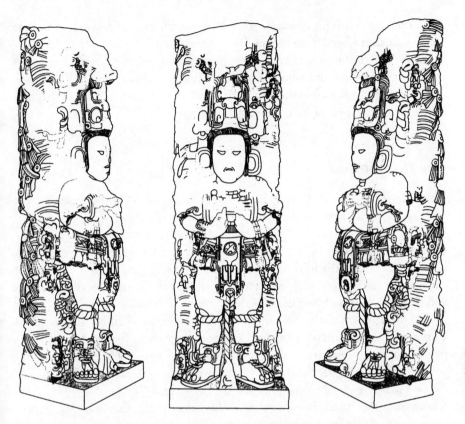

Fig. 4.22. 6: Stela 4, a portrait of Waxak-lahun-Ubah-K'awil in the guise of Bolon-K'awil.

6—STELA 4

This monument appears to have been carved by the same innovative artist who carved Stela F (Fig. 4.22). Both stelae present a fully round portrait of Waxak-lahun-Ubah-K'awil wearing a body-length backrack, but on Stela 4, the sculptor completely freed the back of his knees from the mass of the stone. The details of the costume differ also, but this stela probably continues the story of the patron god. Waxaklahun-Ubah-K'awil is wearing the attributes of Bolon-K'awil, the other patron god in the story.

He wears rope around his knees and more rope emerges from the mouth of the *tzuk*, "partition," head on his apron. His belt carries *ahaw*, "lord," heads at the sides, stingray spine pouches in the front, and oliva shells along the bottom edge. The shells must have made music when he moved. His Serpent Bar originally emitted beings from the Otherworld, but almost no details have survived.

As on Stela F, serpents emerge from behind Waxaklahun-Ubah-K'awil's ankles. The legs of the small being that once sat on top of his headdress remain visible, but the rest of him has been destroyed over time. He held yet another Serpent Bar, of which only small details remain. His headdress god is K'awil, but the flaming ax that is his characteristic feature has broken off, leaving only a scar where it once emerged from the middle of the mirror.

Instead of the umbilical rope, this stela has looped and knotted serpents stacked between the king's body and the arching feathers of his backrack. The snake bodies bear K'awil heads. In this ritual, Waxaklahun-Ubah-K'awil became K'awil in every aspect of his conjuring.

THE INSCRIPTION

This text[19] links very early events that took place on 8.6.0.0.0 (December 19, 159) to a reenactment of those same events by Waxaklahun-Ubah-K'awil on 9.14.15.0.0 (September 17, 726) (Fig. 4.23). The ancestral events involved the receiving or grasping of a flower and a black headdress. Flowers were holy objects that carried the spiritual power to the Maya. Today, the Tzotzil Maya of Zinacantan use flowers, *nichim,* interchangeably with the concept of sacredness and they use them to bring life into their crosses. The black headdress is harder to explain. It refers to the ubiquitous turban headdress worn by the royalty of Copan as a distinct marker of their kingdom. However, the myth of Copan's patron gods also refers to a black headdress in the name of one of its participants—the Baby Jaguar that is thrown down a mountain. Kan-Te-Ahaw, one of the two patron gods of Copan, burned the Baby Jaguar in that story. Thus, this reference to the "black headdress" (*Ek'-Hun*) may evoke that story in the legendary past of Copan's beginning as a kingdom.

The text also identifies the stela as an image of Waxaklahun-Ubah-K'awil as a *Kuy Nik Ahaw,* "Ceiba Flower Bird." This was an important title for Copan's kings.

THE ALTARS AND OFFERINGS

The principal altar for Stela 4 depicts a flattened sphere bound by a twisted cord (Fig. 4.24). Similar objects appear on the markers from Ballcourt IIb, where we can identify them as rubber balls still hanging from a binding rope tied to the rafters of a house. The Maya apparently stored their rubber balls in this way to keep them round. The presence of the ball associates Stela 4 with the myths of Creation as recounted in the Popol Vuh and the ballcourt, because Waxaklahun-Ubah-K'awil also commissioned the ballcourt markers showing the ball. By placing the stone ball in the Great Plaza, he linked the symbolism of these two important locations.

A rectangular stone wrapped up like a Christmas present lies on the ground between the stone ball and the stela. Archaeologists found this little altar in the

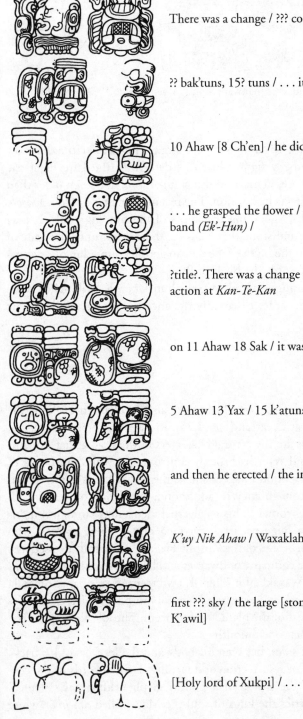

There was a change / ??? counted the year

?? bak'tuns, 15? tuns / . . . it happened on

10 Ahaw [8 Ch'en] / he did something at *Kan-Te-Kan*

. . . he grasped the flower / he grasped the black head-band *(Ek'-Hun)* /

?title?. There was a change / and then he did the same action at *Kan-Te-Kan*

on 11 Ahaw 18 Sak / it was 5 tuns behind

5 Ahaw 13 Yax / 15 k'atuns ended

and then he erected / the image of

K'uy Nik Ahaw / Waxaklahun-Ubah-K'awil

first ??? sky / the large [stone] of Waxaklahun-[Ubah-K'awil]

[Holy lord of Xukpi] / . . .

**Fig. 4.23.
The inscription on the rear of Stela 4 records a very early event involving the patron gods of the city.**

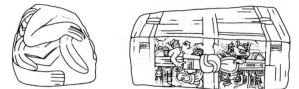
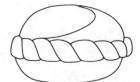

Fig. 4.24. The altars
associated with Stela 4.

the potbelly figure and bound altar that were found in
the substela cache (not to scale)

the public altar

east foundation under Stela 4,[20] along with the strange potbelly statue that now
sits behind the stela. Potbelly figures like this date from the Late Preclassic
period in the highlands of Guatemala, so this statue is probably even older than
the 8.6.0.0.0 date in the stela's inscription. The rectangular altar has four *wayob,*
"animal-spirit companions," guarding the knots of the binding cloth. It may
very well represent the bound stone that Kan-Te-Ahaw threw onto the belly of
the Bearded Jaguar God in the myth of the patron gods recounted in our discussion of Stela F. The text records the birth of Butz'-Chan,[21] the eleventh king of
the dynasty, and his conjuring of a god. Waxaklahun-Ubah-K'awil cached these
heirlooms under Stela 4 in order to sanctify the ancestral events recalled in its
inscription.

7—STELA H

This magnificent stela[22] depicts Waxaklahun-Ubah-K'awil in the role of the
Maize God as he danced at Creation (Fig. 4.25). In the Classic-period story of
Creation, the Maize Gods are the central characters in the drama that explains
the processes of death and rebirth through confrontation with the Lords of
Death in Xibalba. Classic-period imagery shows the Maize Gods being reborn
from a snake, growing from infancy to adulthood, and being dressed in full
regalia by beautiful young women. This regalia included a net skirt, a fish monster–and-shell belt, and a huge backrack carrying one of three animals who
would become the Throne Stones of the Cosmic Hearth. Once fully dressed, the
Maize Gods danced in the company of dwarves and began the activities that led
to the Fourth Creation.[23] Waxaklahun-Ubah-K'awil reenacts this dance on Stela
H, and to reinforce his identity, he wears a huge zoomorphic Maize God headdress with the leaves and ear of the plant arching over his head. His Serpent Bar
emits K'awil gods from their open mouths.

The imagery along the sides, between his body and the feathers of his backrack, reiterate the themes of resurrection and fertility. Twisted cords of the cosmic umbilicus rise from the inside of a hollow glyph reading *sak,* "white,"
because the umbilicus carries the kind of soul the Maya called *sak nik,* "white

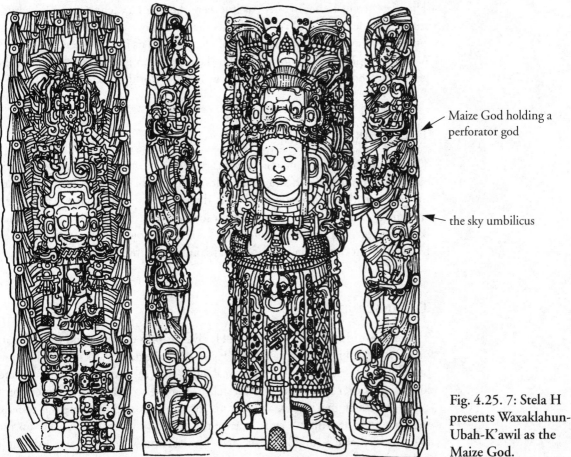

Maize God holding a perforator god

the sky umbilicus

Fig. 4.25. 7: Stela H presents Waxaklahun-Ubah-K'awil as the Maize God.

flower." The white signs hold *wayob,* "animal-spirit companions," conjured from the Otherworld. Square-nosed serpents with glyphs for "white flower" attached to their noses terminate the twisted cords. These "white flower" signs refer both to the flowers that grow on the branches of the *Wakah-Kan* World Tree and to the human soul, because we humans are like the flowers of this tree. Clinging to the twisted cords like monkeys are four Maize Gods, one of whom carries a bloodletter in personified form. Personal bloodletting was the ritual sacred to the Maize Gods and to the process of rebirth.

The back of Stela H shows the Maize God's backrack in all its glory. The normal version of this backrack has the sacred bird *Itzam-Ye* perching on a skyband that rises above a mountain monster. One of the animals connected with the first three stones of Creation usually sits on the mountain inside the sky frame. Here we have a variation. The sacrificial plate (*lak*) and its personified base replaces the mountain and the throne animal that usually occupied the center.

The plate seems to be inverted, as if it were the lid of a cache vessel.[24] The huge stingray spine, shell, and crossed bands that rise above the plate typically occur with this image as symbols of the act of sacrifice and its transformational effect.[25] A *way*, or "spirit companion," rides in the rear apron just below a mat and the personified bowl. The apron itself represents the World Tree.

THE ALTAR

The great stone in front of Stela H was carved into the form of square-eyed deities emerging from the north and south sides. A throne band circles the top edge of the altar, identifying it as a *tz'am tun*, or "throne stone." Not enough details of the emerging gods survive to identify them securely, but they have long hair pulled back from their faces and tied into a top knot. They hold their arms up with their hands in front of their faces as if they are pulling themselves out of the stone.

THE INSCRIPTION

The text records the erection of Stela H, gives its proper name, and identifies its owner as Waxaklahun-Ubah-K'awil (Fig. 4.26). The date, 9.14.19.5.0 (December 5, 731), is exactly nineteen tropical years after the erection of Stela C, and four k'atuns after Stela 3, the pivotal stela in K'ak'-Nab-K'awil's monument program. Waxaklahun-Ubah-K'awil's motivation in choosing this date was to have the stars and the Milky Way in exactly the same positions as they were on the dates when Stelae 3 and C were erected. The last phrase is badly damaged, but it appears to refer to four gourd trees in the royal precinct. Spelled *makom*,[26] these gourd trees evoke the one in which the Lords of Death hung the head of the Maize God after his death.

In an unusual repetition, the scribes also recorded the Stela H events on the back of Stela A across the plaza. From that text, we learn that these events involved the recalling of ancestors from the Otherworld. Although many parts of this passage on Stela A remain obscure, we can recognize references to the erection of Stela H, to ancestral events conducted for Butz'-Chan (the eleventh king in the dynasty), and to the cutting of bones associated with death and burial. The Maya used ancestral bones as sacred relics, and this text appears to refer to the retrieval of sacred bones from the grave of an earlier king.[27]

Once again the chronology interlocks with the text of Stela 3. Four k'atuns earlier, K'ak'-Nab-K'awil had also recalled Butz'-Chan through ancestral rituals,[28] although we have more detail about the later ritual. According to Stela A, Waxaklahun-Ubah-K'awil personified a Vision Serpent called the "Fire-Sun-Shield," and he conducted rituals with the cut-bone relics.

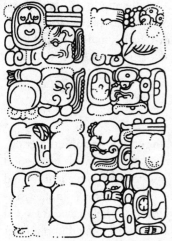

4 Ahaw 18 Muwan / it happened, divinity

it was erected, the stood-up thing / K'an ????

was its name / the *lakam* / *tun* of Waxaklahun-Ubah-K'awil

/[Holy Copan Lord] . . . / four gourd trees at the royal precinct

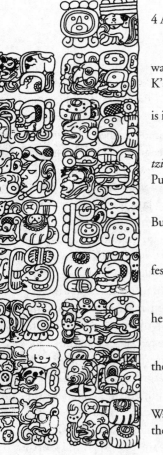

4 Ahaw 18 Muwan

was erected, the *lakamtun* / the stood-up thing, K'an ???

is its name; he died / *tzi-pi-k'a*, Scatterer

tzi-pi-k'a, Nun (intermediary) / Three Monkey, Pu-wi Ahaw

Butz'-Chan, *Ma Ahaw* / *bolon iplah*, bone . . .

festival, they cut / the bones, of the dead one

he entered the road, he set up / the *lakamtun*

the image of "Fire-Sun-Shield" Snake / ??? ???

Waxaklahun-Ubah-K'awil / Holy Copan Lord, the Representative

Fig. 4.26. The inscription from Stela H (*top*) and its elaboration on Stela A.

The myth of the Maize God being resurrected by digging up his bones and using them to generate his rebirth may have served as the archetype for this ritual with relic bones. If this is correct, Waxaklahun-Ubah-K'awil depicted himself as the Maize God on Stela H to evoke the myth of ancestral rebirth.

THE SUBSTELA OFFERING

Hard-packed earth and tree roots completely filled the cruciform vault under this stela. Nevertheless, archaeologists found many fragments of beads made of jade and other material, bits of jade plaques, two shells, and most important, a pair of gold legs, one broken below and the other above the knee. Analysis of the gold suggested its origin was Panamanian or Colombian. This find in the substela cache at Copan represents the earliest known appearance of gold in the Maya area, and implies that trade connections with lower Central America were in place by A.D. 730.[29]

8—STELA A

Waxaklahun-Ubah-K'awil erected this monument three winals, or just sixty days, after Stela H (Fig. 4.27). As with all his other stelae, he depicted himself standing in formal pose holding a Ceremonial Serpent Bar. At his shoulders, snakes emit Sun God flints, while at his ankles, another double-headed serpent belches out *ha winik,* or "water persons." On either side of his headdress perch a pair of tiny *wayob,* who hold flower-tailed snakes rearing up between their legs. The snakes belch up a plant element that may be related to the *lakam* sign for "banner" and "big."

Waxaklahun-Ubah-K'awil's belt carries three *ahaw* heads and small lancet or perforator bags that hang between them. The Maya used these lancets for drawing their blood in various rituals. The shells hanging from his belt and stone celts dangling below the *ahaw* heads would have made tinkling sounds as he moved, especially in dance. Serpent branches of the World Tree decorate his apron, but a pair of disks replace the center head we would normally see. Staffs bearing shields and paper decorations fill the space behind his legs and arms.

His headdress consists of intricately woven mats forming a cylinder, surmounted by a skeletalized personification of the *sak nik,* or "white flower." Snaggle-toothed heads personify the ends of the mat strands in the headdress. The headdress is an important one, but we are not sure of its full meaning.[30] One important association is with Kan-Te-Ahaw. On Naranjo Stela 35 (Fig. 4.18), where part of the myth is told, the front shows a lord wielding the torch just like the one that Kan-Te-Ahaw used to burn the Bearded Jaguar God. The lord wears this same headdress. If the stela depicts the myth, then the lord impersonates Kan-Te-Ahaw. Could Stela A represent Waxaklahun-Ubah-K'awil as the patron god of Copan?

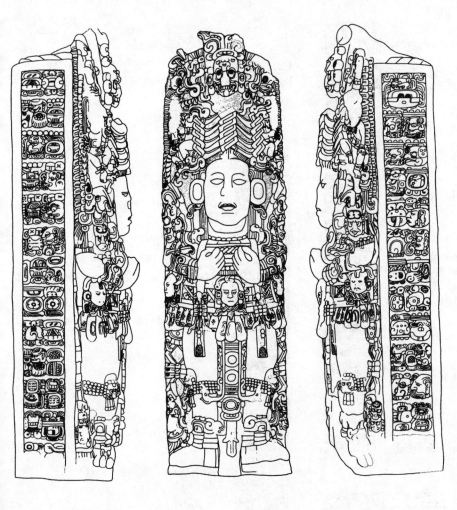

Fig. 4.27. 8: Stela A depicts Waxaklahun-Ubah-K'awil as Kan-Te-Ahaw.

THE INSCRIPTION

The first passage records the erection of Stela A and gives the date in its most ornate form (Fig. 4.28). We also learn that the name of the monument is "Standing Blue White Straight . . . Sun Lord." The inclusion of the sun in this name apparently refers to the sun-faced flints in the open snake mouths of Waxaklahun-Ubah-K'awil's Ceremonial Bar, but we are not sure of the meaning of the remaining part of the name.

We have already discussed the middle passage concerning the dedication of Stela H, so we will not repeat the information here. However, the final passage in the text talks about rituals in which the Maya placed offerings in the cruciform chamber under the stela base. This is a very famous passage because it has been interpreted as a reference to four regional capitals and to an overarching Maya political organization.[31] As we shall see, another reference to foreign emblem

The patron of Kumk'u counted the year

9 bak'tuns, 14 k'atuns

19 tuns, 8 winals

no k'ins, 12 Ahaw

G4 closed the headband

on Nen-K'awil

15 days after the moon arrived,
6 moons had ended

K'an ahaw was the name of

the twenty-nine, 8 Kumk'u

it happened, the erection of the stone

standing

Yax Sak Tobah

Wuk ??? K'in Ahaw / his
holy lakamtun

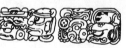

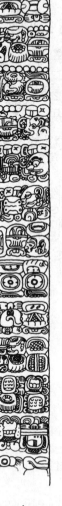

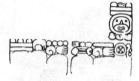

12 Ahaw / 13 . . . [Mak] / they
witnessed it, four . . . / gourd
trees / five . . . , . . .

north (xaman) gourd tree

Hao Ha, four te skies

four na skies, four ni skies

four "deerhoof" skies, Holy Copan Lord

Holy Tikal Lord, Holy Kalak'mul Lord

Holy Palenque Lord, he did something

??? sky, ??? earth

lak'in (east), ochk'in (west)

nohol (south), xaman (north)

Hao Ha, it was opened

the ??? hole, it was closed

the ??? hole, at the middle of

???, ???

first phrase   last phrase

**Fig. 4.28. The first
and last phrases of
the inscription
from Stela A.**

glyphs occurs at Seibal. These texts appear to record the participation of visitors from other sites in the various kinds of rituals.

The destroyed verb at the beginning of the passage may well have been *yilah*, "to see" or "to witness." If this is correct, the passage proceeds with a series of sacred objects, including four gourd trees, five unknown objects, a north gourd tree, and a location called *Hao Ha*, or *Hao* "Water." We think this is the name of the Great Plaza. At the time Waxaklahun-Ubah-K'awil erected this monument, four stelae in his program (C, F, 4, and H) were already in place. Stela A became the fifth, so that these references may be to the five stelae he had erected.

The passage continues with a series of references to four skies, each using a different numerical classifier, including *te, na, ni,* and a deer hoof that we do not know how to read. Numerical classifiers are special elements used in the counting of things, such as "five *head of* cattle." Since the scribe of Stela A used four different numerical classifiers, he seems to be referring to four contrasting kinds of heavens that are themselves arranged in groups of four.

Next the text mentions four witnesses—unnamed holy lords from Copan, Tikal, Kalak'mul, and Palenque. At other sites, texts include the proper names and titles of such visitors, so that we know they were distinguished lords who had come as representatives of their kings. We presume the Copan scribe referred to the same kind of visitors in this passage.

The second part of this text begins with another verb, but we have not yet deciphered it. Then, a pair of glyphs contrasting sky and earth (i.e., "up" and "down") introduce additional glyphs contrasting east to west and south to north. These three contrasts correspond to the three axes of the cruciform vault: up-down, east-west, and south-north. This "directional" passage closes by giving the general location of the action as the Great Plaza. Finally, we learn that the cruciform chamber was opened (probably for the deposition of the substela offering) and then closed.

In summary, the text of Stela A records its own dedication rituals, ancestral ceremonies connected to the dedication of Stela H, and finally, the deposition of the offering in the cruciform chamber some 260 days after the erection of the stela. Unfortunately, only a couple of sherds survived from that offering.

9—STELA B

Waxaklahun-Ubah-K'awil closed the k'atun by erecting Stela B adjacent to Stela C, the monument that had begun the series (Fig. 4.29). Like the 9.14.0.0.0 k'atun-ending, 9.15.0.0.0 (August 22, 731) found Venus at an important station as the Eveningstar: it was at its maximum elongation in Virgo, a constellation that the ancient Maya saw as the god Chak. Waxaklahun-Ubah-K'awil wears the diadem of Chak over his turban headdress and he materializes Chak out of his Ceremonial Serpent Bar in honor of the Eveningstar and its host constellation.

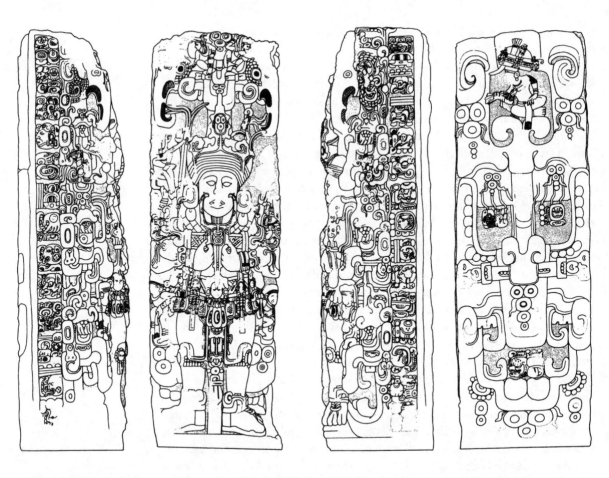

Fig. 4.29. 9: Stela B showing Waxaklahun-Ubah-K'awil at Macaw Mountain.

The appearance of Chak as the king's guise on Stela B may also evoke the myth of the patron gods again. Across the Great Plaza on Stela F, Waxaklahun-Ubah-K'awil wears the guise of the Bearded Jaguar God while the altar in front of his feet shows the Baby Jaguars tumbling down the mountain monster. Chak is the god who threw the Baby Jaguar down the mountain in the myth of Copan's patron gods.

The rest of his costume is fairly conventional, with its royal belt, *ahaw* heads, and perforator bags riding over the World Tree apron. A wide collar made of jade or shell mosaic appears behind his Serpent Bar. Clusters of feathers and foliation sporting the head of the Maize God rise from the top of his turban. Finally he wears a shell face ornament like that on Stela F, perhaps because he enacts one of the episodes in the Kan-Te-Ahaw myth. The Bearded Jaguar God in that myth wears an identical beard, as does Waxaklahun-Ubah-K'awil on Stela F.

It is the background of this stela that is so unusual. On Stelae F, 4, and H, the sculptors presented Waxaklahun-Ubah-K'awil as if he were standing in the plaza wearing his ornate clothing and a full-length backrack. On Stela A, they replaced the backrack with a long inscription on the sides and back of the monument. On Stela B, Waxaklahun-Ubah-K'awil stands inside a great mountain structure that surrounds him on three sides. Above his head, we can see the muzzle, eyes, and forehead of the mountain monster with small ancestral Chak figures sitting in its eyes. The huge macaw heads that emerge from the corners of the mountain mark it as *Mo'-Witz*, "Macaw Mountain." The lower jaw and teeth of this Macaw Mountain curve up behind Waxaklahun-Ubah-K'awil's ankles. A stack of three smaller mountain monsters rises up the sides of the stela to the level of the macaw heads. A *way* wearing the Copan turban rides the muzzle of the lowermost mountain on each side.

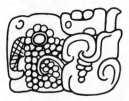

Mo'-Witz
Macaw Mountain

The entire rear surface also represents a mountain, with glyphs in its eyes and an ancestral figure sitting inside its forehead cavity. The ancestor wears a huge domed headdress decorated with anthropomorphic god heads and an upright jaguar paw.

The glyphs (Fig. 4.30) in the shuttered eyes of this great Mountain Monster declare its proper name and associate it with sacred space. The eye on the left reads *Mo'-Witz*, "Macaw Mountain," while the other reads *Kan Na Kan*, "four *na* skies," one of the sky locations on Stela A. Below the eyes, huge tube ornaments emerge from the nostrils, while the muzzle drops down over the open mouth. There, another glyph names a critical location for the dynasty of Yax-K'uk'-Mo'—*Baknal Ox Witik*. *Ox Witik*, "Three Sources," was the ancient location where Yax-K'uk'-Mo' founded his dynasty. Inscriptions referred to it throughout the history of the dynasty, until it became *Kan Witik*, "Four Sources," during the lifetime of the last king. Thus, both the front and back of Stela B identify Waxaklahun-Ubah-K'awil's location as Macaw Mountain, and on the back we learn that the people of Copan associated the mountain with *Kan Na Kan* and *Ox Witik*.

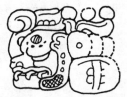

Kan Na Kan
four *na* skies

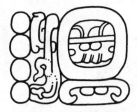

Baknal Ox Witik
Bone Place Three Sources

Fig. 4.30.
The glyphs in the eyes and mouth of the mountain monster.

THE INSCRIPTION

The inscription (Fig. 4.31) begins on the north side of the stela[32] with the Long-Count date of the events, 9.15.0.0.0 4 Ahaw 13 Yax. Three related phrases follow the date: a sky god, an earth god, and Hun-Kanal-Tzuk-Ahaw, the name of the Bearded Jaguar God on Stela F. This god may reflect that Venus was at its maximum elongation on this night.[33]

The text jumps to the other side where the first phrase records the erection of the stela, with its proper name "Great Partition of the Sky." Then the text says that Waxaklahun-Ubah-K'awil is in the persona[34] of the Macaw Mountain Lord, a reference to the mountain imagery all around him. It goes on to record the k'atun-ending and the scattering ritual that he performed. Finally, the personification expression occurs again in front of a jaguar-eared old god who has fire in front of his face combined with a name ending in *Nen-K'awil*, "Mirror-K'awil."

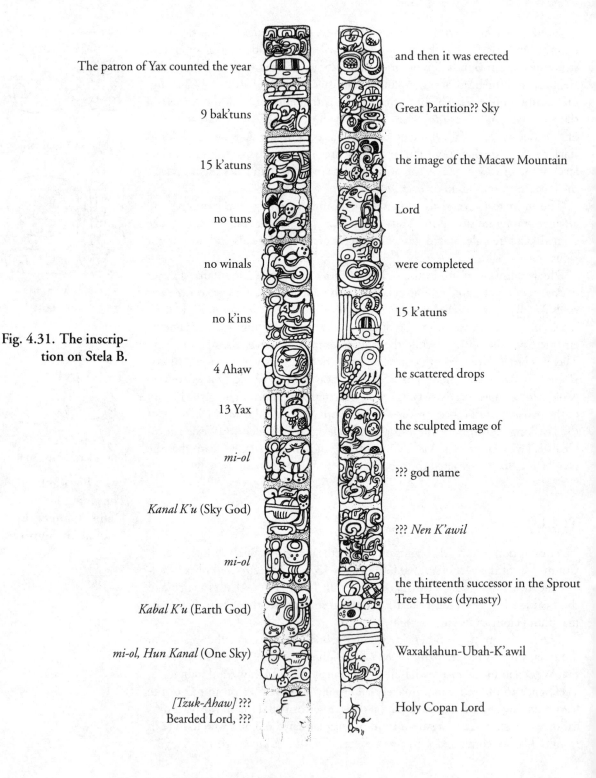

The patron of Yax counted the year

9 bak'tuns

15 k'atuns

no tuns

no winals

no k'ins

Fig. 4.31. The inscription on Stela B.

4 Ahaw

13 Yax

mi-ol

Kanal K'u (Sky God)

mi-ol

Kabal K'u (Earth God)

mi-ol, Hun Kanal (One Sky)

[Tzuk-Ahaw] ???
Bearded Lord, ???

and then it was erected

Great Partition?? Sky

the image of the Macaw Mountain

Lord

were completed

15 k'atuns

he scattered drops

the sculpted image of

??? god name

??? *Nen K'awil*

the thirteenth successor in the Sprout Tree House (dynasty)

Waxaklahun-Ubah-K'awil

Holy Copan Lord

The phrase may name the ancestral figure emerging from the mountain cleft on the other side of the stela. This little fellow holds a bundle that may contain the mirror. Finally, the text ends by recording Waxaklahun-Ubah-K'awil with his title as the thirteenth king in the dynasty of Copan. The word for "dynasty" or "lineage" is *Ch'ok-Te-Nah,* "Sprout-Tree-House."

10—Stela D

With his k'atun program finished, Waxaklahun-Ubah-K'awil waited for another five years to initiate the program intended to embrace the next k'atun in his reign. The bloodletting imagery he evoked seems oddly prophetic in retrospect, because he was captured and sacrificed by K'ak'-Tiliw of Quirigua a little over a year after he erected this magnificent stela (Fig. 4.32). The personified perforator gods sit-

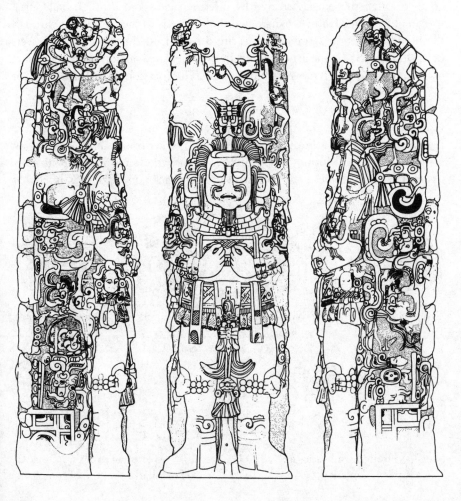

4.32. 10:
Stela D showing Wax-aklahun-Ubah-K'awil at *Wak-Kan.*

ting on top of his head and hanging over his loincloth signal the bloodletting theme.

Waxaklahun-Ubah-K'awil holds a Ceremonial Serpent Bar with emerging K'awils and he wears the mask of the god who has materialized in his body. His human eyes and mouth are visible through holes in the mask. Unfortunately, the mask does not have the kind of distinguishing features we need to identify the god, but the chin beard that hangs under it is a new feature in the Great Plaza portraits. Interestingly, Yax-Pasah, one of Waxaklahun-Ubah-K'awil's successors at Copan, wore an identical beard, but more important, K'ak'-Tiliw, the man who killed Waxaklahun-Ubah-K'awil, featured exactly this kind of beard in his late portraits at Quirigua, perhaps in imitation of the man he conquered.

As he trances, Waxaklahun-Ubah-K'awil stands in front of skybands that step up to support two sacred locations, known as the Nine-God Place and the Seven-Black-Yellow Place[35] to modern researchers. These sacred locations are in the Otherworld where the gods and ancestors lived. The Maya reached them by going through the portals created by offering plates and through ballcourts. Presumably, Waxaklahun-Ubah-K'awil took himself to these locations through the bloodletting and a trance-vision rite depicted on this stela. On the west (left) side of Stela D, the artists added an intermediate location inside a concavity left after they had removed a flint nodule. This location reads *Waxak Lok'*, or "Eight Coming Out."

Recent discoveries (Fig. 4.33) have shown how these "nine" and "seven" locations were associated with the great ancestor Yax-K'uk'-Mo', who founded the dynasty, and to his firstborn son. On a round marker found in the floor of an early temple called Motmot by the archaeologists who found it, Yax-K'uk'-Mo' has his feet on the Nine-God Place, while his son, nicknamed Popol-K'inich, has

| Seven-Black-Yel-low from Stela D | Nine-God from Stela D | Seven-Black-Yellow from Tikal | Nine-God from a looted cache plate |

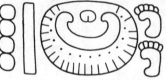

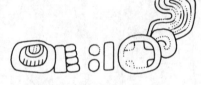

Fig. 4.33. The Seven-Black-Yellow and Nine-God locations.

Nine-God from the substructure called Margarita

the paired locations from the floor marker in front of Motmot his on the Seven-Black-Yellow Place. An even earlier temple called Margarita has the Nine-God Place under the talons of huge entwined quetzal and macaw birds. They are emblematic renditions of Yax-K'uk'-Mo'. Waxaklahun-Ubah-K'awil was using trance to take himself to the places particularly associated with the founder of his dynasty.

The "Eight Coming out" glyph may very well refer to what "comes out" of the two sacred locations. Six huge Vision Serpents loop across the sides and top to intertwine around Waxaklahun-Ubah-K'awil's body. We have found six heads and four tails in this very complex imagery (Fig. 4.34). All six heads belch out K'awil gods who carry plant sprigs of various types. These snakes very probably manifest *Wakah-Kan,* a cosmic term for the World Tree. *Wakah-Kan* normally means "Raised-up Sky" or "Six Sky," but here the sculptors played with the concept by representing it as six snakes, which is also *Wak-Kan.*

It is very difficult to resolve exactly how these serpents work. Rearing upward from the skybands, two of them belch out their K'awils at hip level. Their bod-

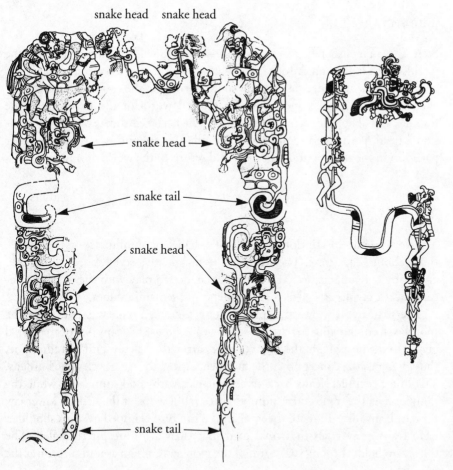

Fig. 4.34. The six snakes that constitute the *Wak-Kan* framework on Stela D (left) and the *Wak-Kan* snake from the Hauberg Stela.

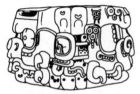

Fig. 4.35. The altar of Stela D, with a sun-death head on the north side (left), a stone partition head on the south side (right), and a half-fleshed, half-skeletal jaguar leg between them.

ies apparently disappear into the sky. Curving tails of two other serpents end at Waxaklahun-Ubah-K'awil's waist in symbols reading *sak nik,* "white flower." "White flower" is a metaphor for the human soul so that these snakes also represent the sky umbilicus that emerged from the center of the sky where the gods set up the great Cosmic Hearth at the time of Creation.

The sculptors either hid the tails of the other two snakes behind Waxaklahun-Ubah-K'awil's headdress or they meant them to be read as a double-headed serpent. In either case, *wayob* materialized from the Otherworld cavort among the serpent bodies in a replay of one of the oldest images of conjuring surviving from Maya art—the Hauberg Stela. That very early monument[36] shows a young man soon to be king also wearing a mask as he holds up a rearing *Wak-Kan* that supports four *wayob* representing constellations. This is the prototype of the image Waxaklahun-Ubah-K'awil used to show himself in *Wakah-Kan* at the places where the founder went in death.[37]

THE ALTAR

Stela D's altar also reflects Waxaklahun-Ubah-K'awil's location between the worlds of the living and the dead (Fig. 4.35). The visage of a skeletal jaguar being with sun-signs in his eyes faces south so that people in the court would see Waxaklahun-Ubah-K'awil standing in the skeletal world of the dead where the founder was. The side facing Waxaklahun-Ubah-K'awil shows the *tzuk,* "partition," head, perhaps to remind him that the Otherworld was simply another partition in the cosmos and that he would return to the world of humans.

THE INSCRIPTION

This very famous inscription (Fig. 4.36) has had a lot of influence on the way we think about Maya time. The wonderfully imaginative style, called full-figured glyphs by epigraphers, gave the scribes a chance to play with the graphic concepts of the glyphs as well as their phonetic and semantic values.

The first glyph shows the lovely Moon Goddess, who was patron of the month Ch'en, hanging her arm over the year sign as she leans out of the initial glyph. In the next glyph, the number nine carries the bak'tun bird in a tumpline, thus giving us the concept that the numbers carried the time cycles like burdens. The number fifteen leans back as he struggles with the k'atun bird, while the number five (the same god as number fifteen, but without the skeletal lower jaw for ten) leans forward, with the wing of the tun bird clamped over his shoulder. Zero leans away from the winal toad, but their arms are intermingled. The other zero holds the long snake arm of the monkey-*k'in* sign as if in surprise at the

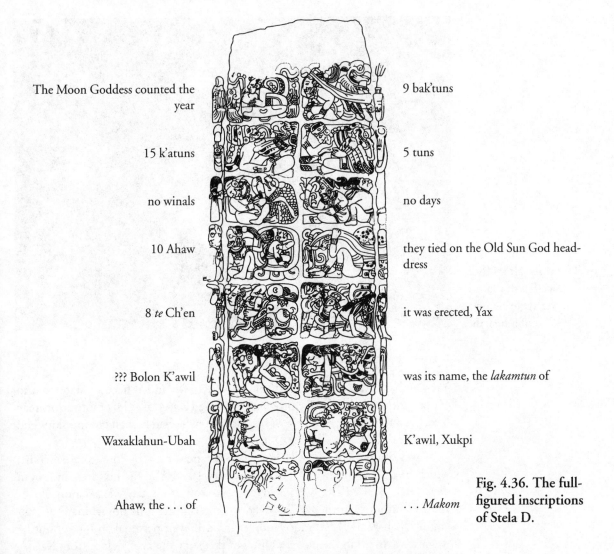

The Moon Goddess counted the year

15 k'atuns

no winals

10 Ahaw

8 *te* Ch'en

??? Bolon K'awil

Waxaklahun-Ubah

Ahaw, the . . . of

9 bak'tuns

5 tuns

no days

they tied on the Old Sun God head-dress

it was erected, Yax

was its name, the *lakamtun* of

K'awil, Xukpi

. . . *Makom*

Fig. 4.36. The full-figured inscriptions of Stela D.

anatomical transformation of his catch. The number ten precedes the day sign cartouche containing a seated lord to give 10 Ahaw. And the final part of the date depicts the number eight as the Maize God holding *te* (a numerical classifier) in his arms as he leans against the month glyph Ch'en.

The remainder of the text records the erection of the stela, its proper name (although we cannot read all of it), and its owner, Waxaklahun-Ubah-K'awil. The sculptors had a bit of bad luck with his name, because another flint ball lay just under the surface. They left it in place and wrapped the number eighteen around it. One of the most delightful signs is the bat of the Copan emblem glyph who leans back, his head looking up, and his leathery wings spread wide.

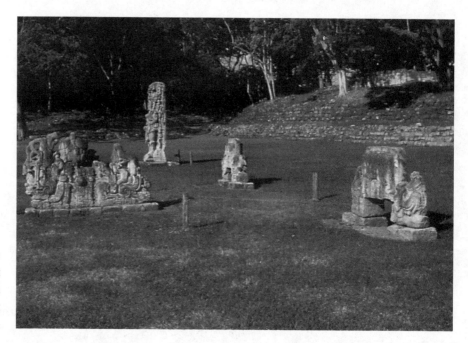

Fig. 4.37. 11:
The three altars that
Yax-Pasah placed
in the arrangement
of a hearth.

11—THE SNAKE ALTARS

Yax-Pasah, the last king of Yax-K'uk'-Mo's dynasty, added his own statement to Waxaklahun-Ubah-K'awil's program of stelae (Fig. 4.37). His motivation may have been to recoup the honor of his ancestor, who had met an ignominious end at the hands of K'ak'-Tiliw of Quirigua.

Waxaklahun-Ubah-K'awil's last year was spent on rebuilding the ballcourt, which he dedicated on 9.15.6.8.13 (January 10, 738). One hundred and seven days later, K'ak'-Tiliw, who had come to office under Waxaklahun-Ubah-K'awil's authority, turned on his overlord and captured the unfortunate Waxaklahun-Ubah-K'awil. His motivation may have been personal ambition, but he was also involved in the power politics of the great alliances. A lord from Kalak'-mul, Tikal's great enemy, celebrated a period ending at Quirigua a year before this war.[38] The Quirigua rebellion signaled Kalak'mul's intervention into the politics of the southeastern zone and perhaps a bid for control of the Motagua drainage and the trade in jade and obsidian. In any case, we think that Waxaklahun-Ubah-K'awil moved against his vassal to prevent him from or to punish him for changing sides. But the Quirigua king prevailed. Perhaps a factor in his victory was that he was a young king in his prime facing a man who had been ruling for close to forty-three years. Waxaklahun-Ubah-K'awil was well past his prime as a warrior at the time of the battle.

K'ak'-Tiliw not only captured his overlord, but according to the inscriptions, he also chopped up and burned the statues of Copan's patron gods. Destroying your enemies' gods robbed them of their supernatural protection. Six days after destroying the gods, he decapitated Waxaklahun-Ubah-K'awil, on 9.15.6.14.6 (May 3, 738).

K'ak'-Tiliw may have wanted to become the ruler of the larger kingdom of Xukpi, but it never happened. A new ruler, the fourteenth in the dynasty of Copan, acceded thirty-nine days after Waxaklahun-Ubah-K'awil died. The Quirigua king lived a long and prosperous life, and oversaw the creation of a sculpture program that equaled Waxaklahun-Ubah-K'awil's in creativity and exceeded it in scale. He outlived the fourteenth king of Copan, who had replaced his enemy. Then he outlived the fifteenth king. He was still in office twenty years after the sixteenth king and last ruler acceded at Copan.

That sixteenth ruler, Yax-Pasah, seemed obsessed by his hapless ancestor, because he repeatedly incorporated Waxaklahun-Ubah-K'awil into his own inscriptions, especially in Temple 11. Perhaps he was paying homage to his dead ancestor in defiance of K'ak'-Tiliw. In any case, less than three years after his accession, he planted the first of three altars in the middle of Waxaklahun-Ubah-K'awil's stelae. Furthermore, the symbolism of a double-headed feathered snake emphasized his desire to communicate with his dead ancestor through trance ritual. The undulating body of the snake arches over an inscription recording 9.16.15.0.0 (February 19, 766).

Thirty years later, long after the death of K'ak'-Tiliw, Yax-Pasah set up a second feathered serpent, bearing the date 9.18.5.0.0 (September 15, 795). And five years later, on 9.18.10.0.0 (August 19, 800), he completed the triangular arrangement with the largest altar of the three to form his earthly hearth. At dawn on the day of this period ending, the sky hearth in Orion was over the earthly one. In the final altar (Fig. 4.38), his sculptors combined a skeletal snake on the western side with a fleshed one on the east. Both are feathered, but more important, both have front legs. K'awil emerges from the skeletal snake, while a Pawahtun emerges from the fleshed one.

As far as we know, the artists of Copan were the first people in Mesoamerica

Fig. 4.38. Altar G represents a double-headed serpent with legs.

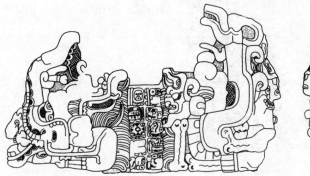
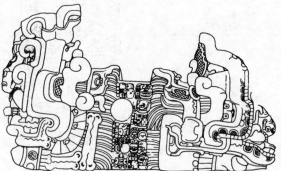

to depict legged serpents. We have examples at Copan on the temple called Ros-alila, which was built during the last third of the sixth century. We think the legged serpents of Chich'en Itza derive from these Copan prototypes, although the artists of Chich'en preferred to show them in front, rather than from the side. This preference led to a representation of a legged serpent with a feathered crest flaring out from the sides of its head and an ancestral warrior emerging from its open mouth.

THE INSCRIPTION

The north side records the making of the "Plaza Snake" under the authority of Yax-Pasah (Fig. 4.39). We do not understand the other side very well at all. It begins with one of the most important locations in the city, Witik, but here the traditional number three has been changed to four. Since Yax-Pasah himself used *Ox Witik* in connection with the founding events as he recorded them on Altar Q, we know that he deliberately changed the number to four on this late monu-ment.[39] Since K'ak'-Tiliw first recorded "four *witik*," perhaps Yax-Pasah was acknowledging some basic change in the political structure created by K'ak'-Tiliw's victory.

Nu-Yahaw-Kan-Ah-Bak, the name of either a subordinate lord or a personal god of the king, follows the *Kan-Witik* glyph. We once thought this person was Yax-Pasah's brother, but new decipherments have made this interpretation less likely.[40] Whether this person was a lord or a personal god, there is no doubt he

Fig. 4.39. The inscrip-tion on Altar G.

10 Ahaw / 8 Sak

was made / the snake

of the plaza / he oversaw it

. . . / Yax-Pasah-Kan

Yoat / Holy Copan Lord

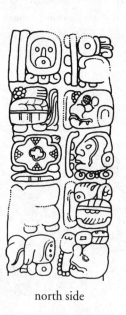

north side

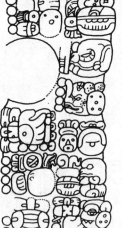

south side

Kan-Witik mab, "Four Sources box" / Nu-Yahaw-Kan

Ah-Bak

kan xuk pib (four corner pits)

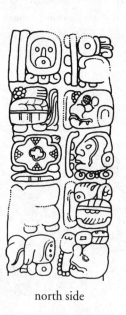

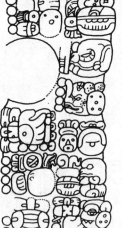

172   LINDA SCHELE AND PETER MATHEWS

was important to Yax-Pasah, because his name appears on Altars T and U as well as on this snake altar. All three occur in important royal spaces usually reserved for royal monuments.

A series of obscure phrases we do not yet understand follows Nu-Yahaw-Kan-Ah-Bak's name. One refers to four corner ovens or pits that could be caches, and another reads four *makom,* or gourd trees. Perhaps the text describes rituals following the Maya custom of arranging objects and offerings in groups of four, oriented either to the cardinal directions or to the corners of a plaza.

12—WAXAKLAHUN-UBAH-K'AWIL'S LEGACY

The Great Plaza of Copan is a unique monument, consisting of seven very large, exquisitely carved stelae commissioned by a single king and executed by a generation of extraordinary artists. In Copan's artistic history, the sculptors of these stelae took the art of portrait representation to a new level of subtlety and volumetric veracity. Moreover, these artists executed this new deeply cut manner of carving without losing the power of symbolic detail. If the Maya wanted their stelae to be portraits of rituals as well as portraits of their lords, this extraordinary group of stelae has succeeded admirably. Waxaklahun-Ubah-K'awil created a heritage that carried his name forward into the future and preserved his conception of the cosmos and his place in it. Even today, visitors feel the special power of his vision.

Waxaklahun-Ubah-K'awil linked himself and his ancestral past by joining them to the imagery and symbolism of Creation[41] and the myths surrounding the patron gods of the kingdom. He enacted moments of these myths in his person as he materialized the gods for the duration of his ritual performance. He created a progression of ritual reenacts beginning with a k'atun-ending and marching forward in time by five- or ten-tun intervals. He focused on the timeposts that allowed the Maya to perceive the symmetry and cosmic rhythms of nature and to associate their lives with cosmic frameworks.

Stelae H and A sit inside the framework he created, but instead of commemorating the timeposts themselves, these monuments evoke ancestral history, locking it to the actions of the gods in creating the cosmos. By choosing such dates to commemorate important ancestral events, he placed his own actions in a larger historical context and asserted divine causality for them. Finally, he clothed himself in costumes that reflected the imagery written in the stars on the nights of the rituals, especially at the moments just after sunset, before dawn, and at midnight.

These stelae represent a pinnacle of Maya aesthetic accomplishment that was much admired during his lifetime and afterward. The power of the place created by Waxaklahun-Ubah-K'awil even overshadowed the memory of his inglorious end at the hands of K'ak'-Tiliw. His first two successors mentioned him only in passing, but Yax-Pasah, the last king of the dynasty, appears to have embraced Waxaklahun-Ubah-K'awil's greatness. He arranged three double-headed feathered serpents in a triangular pattern that evoked the three stones of the first Cosmic Hearth. At dawn on the day he placed the last of these three snakes, the Cosmic Hearth in Orion shone in the sky above the Great Plaza. This earthly hearth of feathered serpents renewed the center of Xukpi, and it prefigured the legged, feathered serpents that became so important at Chich'en Itza during the following century. Waxaklahun-Ubah-K'awil left a legacy of art and beauty that stands among the great works of humanity.

CHAPTER 5

Seibal: A K'atun-ending Commemoration of Ah-Bolon-Abta Wat'ul-Chatel

In the southwestern corner of Peten, the northern department of Guatemala, lies Seibal, a small city built on a bluff above the west side of the Pasión River. Visitors can reach it in two ways, both beginning in the river town of Sayaxche. Launches carry people sixteen kilometers up the Pasión to the base of the bluff, where they must climb up through some of the most beautiful forest left in Peten. There is also a road from Sayaxche, but it can require a four-wheel-drive vehicle, especially in the rainy season.

Seibal got its name from a great stand of ceiba trees, called a *ceibal*. Teobert Maler, who visited the ruins in 1895, used the Germanic form beginning with an "s" in his published report. Thus, "Seibal" has become the usual English version of the name, even though the proper term in Spanish is Ceibal. Maler also reported that the Lakandons living in the area called it *Sakt'ankiki,* the name of a white hawk, although he rejected the name because he thought the local guide just wanted a grander name for the place than Ceibal.

The ancient Maya had yet another name for the city. Maya then and now cook on a hearth made of three stones arranged in a triangle. They sat clay pots on top of the stones and fed wood between them into the fire. Today they consider the hearth to be the center of the home and the family, and often bury the afterbirth of their children under the hearth. Maya Creation also centered the cosmos in a three-stone hearth that lay in the constellation of Orion with the stars we call Alnitak, Saiph, and Rigel. Using this same metaphor, the people of Seibal centered their world by using the image of the three-stone hearth as the name of their kingdom[1] (Fig. 5.1).

When archaeologists[2] mapped Seibal (Fig. 5.2), they found it to be a medium-size site with two major concentrations of public buildings connected by causeways. Group D lies at the edge of the bluff, protected by deep arroyos

THE CODE OF KINGS 175

THE CODE OF KINGS   175

Fig. 5.1. Two exam-
ples of the Seibal
emblem glyph (left)
and two location
glyphs referring to the
place of Seibal. One
has a *mi* phonetic
complement and
the other a *tzi*.

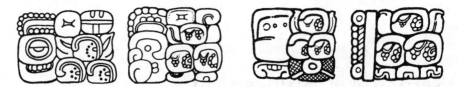

and linked by a *sak beh* to a second concentration of buildings called Group A.
Another leg of this *sak beh* leads to a round platform built on the southern edge
of the site. Both the modern road and the path from the river lead to Group A,
where the people of Seibal erected almost all of their stelae. What we have
learned from these inscriptions explains why they had a mind toward defense.

THE HISTORY

According to the archaeology, settlers first arrived in Seibal around 900 B.C. Population increased gradually for several hundred years, surging to its highest levels
in Seibal's history around 200 B.C. By A.D. 300, something drastic happened because
the site appears to have been abandoned, although we have no idea why. New populations began moving into the area around A.D. 650 to establish a new kingdom.

Fig. 5.2. A map of
Seibal, its barrancas,
and Group A.

The earliest written mention of Seibal appears on Dos Pilas Stela 15 on the
date 9.14.10.0.0 (October 13, 721), in reference to Seibal's becoming embroiled
in the wars that had been raging between Tikal, Dos Pilas, and Kalak'mul for
over fifty years.[3] As discussed in chapter two, the hostilities began during the
mid-sixth century when Tikal (*Mutul*) suffered a major defeat by Caracol

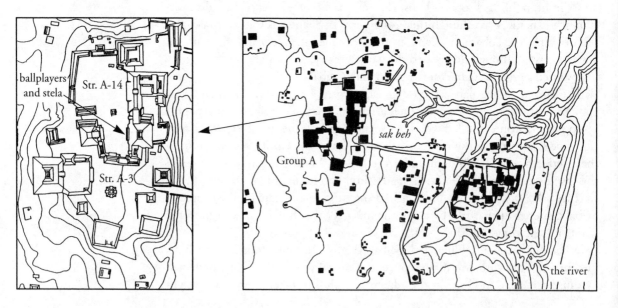

(*K'antumak*) with the help of Kalak'mul (*Kan*), Tikal's longtime antagonist. In response, Animal-Skull, Mutul's new king, set up a branch kingdom on 9.9.12.11.2 (October 18, 625) at Dos Pilas to establish control of the Pasión River region. This new kingdom, like Tikal, bore the name *Mutul*. This strategy did not work, because Kalak'mul quickly subverted the new king, enticing him to change sides. The wars that ensued lasted for thirty years and led to the deaths of the Mutul king, Nun-Bak-Chak, and the Kalak'mul ruler, Yich'ak-K'ak'.

After his victory, the founder of Dos Pilas, Balah-Kan-K'awil, and his two successors forged a regional state that encompassed all of the Pasión region. It was the third king in the dynasty who turned his attention toward Seibal. He defeated Seibal and captured its king, Yich'ak-Balam (also known as Jaguar-Paw), on 9.15.4.6.4 (December 3, 735), and as a result, Seibal became a vassal state within the Dos Pilas hegemony.

The Dos Pilas victors gloated over their defeat of Yich'ak-Balam on stelae at Dos Pilas and Aguateca, and they erected a Hieroglyphic Stairway at Seibal registering its new vassal status. No monuments survive from the Seibal kings who ruled before this great defeat, perhaps because they were destroyed. Both victory monuments at Dos Pilas and Aguateca say specifically that "they destroyed the writing,"[4] but the Dos Pilas stela goes further by recording *ch'ak u tz'ibal pat k'awil*, "they chopped the writing of the statues that were made" (Fig. 5.3). The Seibal dynasty lost its history when it lost the war.

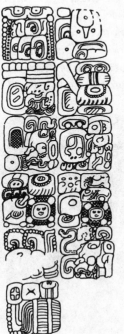

war at Seibal   one day later

on 9 Chikchan 18 Muwan   they chopped the writing of

pat k'awil, the made statue   they oversaw it the good

yax tol ba pakal first ??? first shield   ??? his flint-shield

To-??-n (Ruler 3)   K'awil

Holy Lord of Dos Pilas

Fig. 5.3. The defeat of Seibal by Dos Pilas and the resulting destruction of history at Seibal.

Things went well for Dos Pilas for another twenty years or so, but their former victims, led by the ruler of the nearby site of Tamarindito, exacted vengeance on 9.16.9.15.10 (January 26, 761) by sacking Dos Pilas and forcing its king to retreat to Aguateca. The hegemony fragmented as a result, with at least two kings—one at Aguateca and the other at Seibal and La Amelia—claiming to be the king of Mutul.

Monuments from the time of Seibal's subordination lie in the Central Plaza of Group A. A stairway recording events in the years following Seibal's defeat once decorated Structure A-14, which now lies obscured in the forest covering the north half of the plaza. Pieces of these stairs now line one of the thatch-roofed buildings in the old project camp.

The southern half of the Central Plaza had a ballcourt and another stairway (Fig. 5.4), flanked by two panels showing the later pretender king as a ballplayer. A stela recording his accession stood at the top of the stairs. The lower half is still in situ, while the upper half lies in the grass across the plaza. Archaeologists found it erected upside down in the center of the plaza in front of the stairs. Perhaps the people of Seibal were making their true feelings known about this foreign ruler. The last date in his inscriptions—9.18.10.0.0 (August 19, 800)—began a thirty-year-long silence during which the kingdom of Seibal erected no monuments.

On the day before the end of the tenth bak'tun, a new set of elites, who brought a new pottery style with them, arrived at Seibal and began a resurgence in monument erection and architectural construction in the South Plaza of Group A. The great Tatiana Proskouriakoff first pointed out that these new rulers looked foreign and wore costumes that have affinities with the "Toltec-Maya" of Chich'en Itza. These observations have led to a general assumption that they were foreign invaders, usually presumed to be Mexicanized Maya who came up the Usumacinta from the Gulf Coast. However, this assumption is con-

Fig. 5.4. The Central Plaza of Seibal Group A where the Dos Pilas rulers erected their monuments.

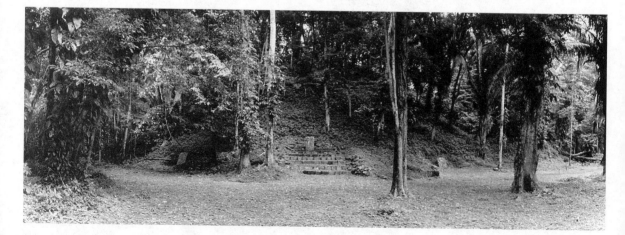

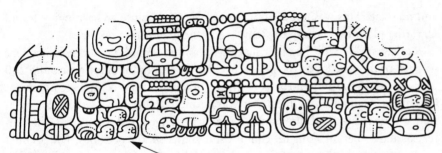

one day? 6 Kawak 17 Sip he arrived in the center of Seibal, Ah-Bolon-Abta; he oversaw it, Kan-Ek', Ho Pet, He of Ucanal

Fig. 5.5. The arrival of foreign lords from Ucanal to reestablish Seibal.

tradicted by the inscriptions that the new king of Seibal erected. On Stela 11, he told us exactly who he was and where he came from (Fig. 5.5). Named Ah-Bolon-Abta Wat'ul-Chatel,[5] the new ruler arrived one day before the end of the tenth bak'tun in 830. He had been sent by the king of Ucanal, a Maya capital in eastern Peten, to reestablish a seat of power in the Pasión region. Wat'ul and his followers were foreigners to Seibal, but not to Peten nor to the Maya region.[6]

A—TEMPLE A-3

Ah-Bolon-Abta Wat'ul-Chatel consolidated his power during the next twenty years and prepared a magnificent and innovative monumental group to celebrate the first k'atun-ending in the new bak'tun (400-year cycle). He selected the area south of the Central Plaza in Group A, where the kings of the earlier Dos Pilas dynasty had placed their history. There he built a temple group (Fig. 5.6) that combined one of the most ancient and sacred temple forms—the radial pyramid—with a new and highly inventive use of stelae placement, imagery,

Fig. 5.6. A: Temple A-3 at Seibal.

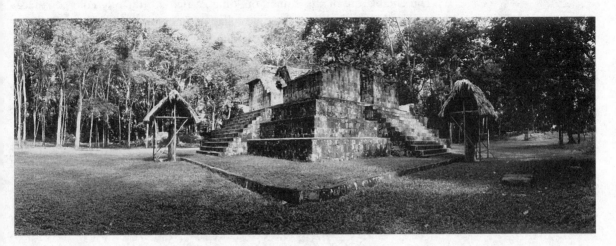

and message. This was not a virgin area of Seibal, because archaeologists found an earlier platform beneath the temple and the final plaza floor level.

Radial temples with their four stairways pointing toward the cardinal directions go back to the Late Preclassic period in the Maya tradition. Starting around 200 B.C., the Maya used the form as the focus of architectural complexes known as "E-groups," named after Group E at Waxaktun. In the archetype, the radial pyramid and its temple had three small buildings arranged to the east, with the center axis and corners marking the equinox and solstice sunrise positions. The pyramid substructure had stucco masks on the balustrades of the four stairways. There the lowest masks are snakes marking the temple as "Snake Mountain" and Waxaktun of the Late Preclassic period as an expression of *Puh,* or "Place of Cattail Reeds." This *Puh/Tollan* symbolism is less clear in other E-groups of the same period, perhaps because very little of the stucco decoration has survived elsewhere.

By A.D. 550, the Maya of Tikal started using radial pyramids in a new way—the "twin-pyramid complex." This arrangement had two radial pyramids without temples facing each other on an east-west axis. To the north inside a walled enclosure, they placed a stela celebrating the end of a k'atun and depicting the current ruler standing over an altar displaying a captive destined for sacrifice. A nine-doored, vaulted, single-roomed structure sat on the opposite side to complete the north-south axis.

Wat'ul combined these two functions—a statement of origin and affiliation, and a k'atun-ending celebration—to create his new masterpiece. His radial platform is low and not very impressive by earlier standards, but what he lacked in scale, he made up for in innovative presentation (Fig. 5.7). Atop his undecorated radial pyramid, his builders constructed a square temple with a doorway above each of the four stairs. The interior has three parallel vaults running north to south with doors placed through the center of the bearing walls to create the east-west axis. Thus, the temple above addresses the four directions, as do the stairs.

The entablature of this square building carried a brilliantly colored stucco frieze that shattered when the temple collapsed in precolumbian times. By carefully plotting where the fragments had fallen, archaeologists were able to reassemble enough to allow Proskouriakoff to make reconstruction drawings of the frieze.[7] Proskouriakoff knew as much about Maya iconography as anyone who has ever worked in the field. Given her expertise and the information available from the archaeology, her reconstruction is an astute conjecture about what was originally there.

Larger-than-life portraits of Wat'ul stood over each of the entry doors dressed in full regalia, brilliantly colored to give the impression that he was actually there. Twelve life-size figures stood at the corners and halfway between the corners and the doors. We do not know who these figures were, but from other Maya narratives, we surmise they may have been ancestors, members of Wat'ul's council, or the Ucanal lords who were the source of his authority.

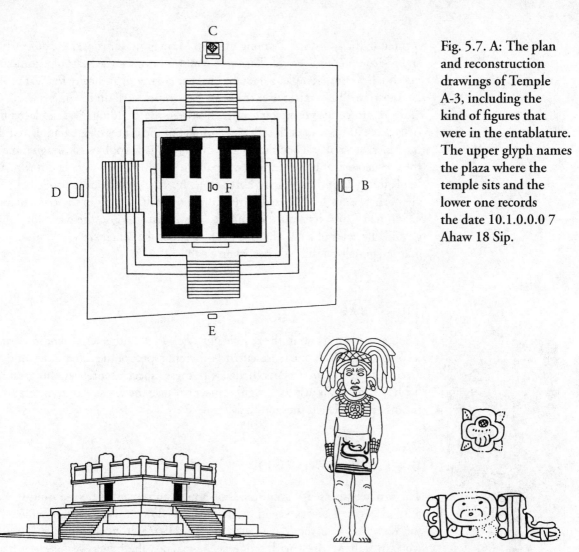

Fig. 5.7. A: The plan
and reconstruction
drawings of Temple
A-3, including the
kind of figures that
were in the entablature.
The upper glyph names
the plaza where the
temple sits and the
lower one records
the date 10.1.0.0.0 7
Ahaw 18 Sip.

reconstruction of the temple

composite reconstruction of a figure
from the entablature and stucco glyphs
from the inscription

The areas between the figures had cross-hatched panels and ornate vegetation filled with animals of several kinds. In the center of these panels sat old gods, probably sixteen in all. They seem to represent different old gods, with at least one Pawahtun and Itzamna among them. Modern Maya connect one of the animals portrayed, a howler monkey, with people left over from the Third Creation in Maya mythology. With the animals juxtaposed with portraits of old gods and growing maize foliation, we suspect Wat'ul and his associates stood in the time and place of Creation. New Year celebrations and the making of god pots documented in the codices and among modern Maya groups involved the destruction and re-creation of the world. The same symbolism was at the heart of k'atun-ending rituals.[8] Thus, Temple A-3 established the charter of authority for Wat'ul and demonstrated his control over the most dangerous forces in the universe.

To reinforce the cosmological significance of his building, Wat'ul placed five stelae, one in front of each stairway and one in the center of the temple. Under the center stela, he cached three large, unworked jade cobbles, although none of the archaeological reports tell us the pattern in which they were laid down. We have already pointed out that "three-stone hearth" was the name of Seibal. The glyph that Maya scribes used to record the Cosmic Hearth in the constellation Orion had *yax* in its name. *Yax* means "first," but it is also the word for "blue-green," the color of jade. The jade cobbles under the center stela of Wat'ul's program materialized this jade hearth on earth.

THE STELAE

The stelae around and in the temple portray Wat'ul in the period-ending rituals he performed. Each one represented a different aspect of the ceremonies, and his costumes and accouterments change with these aspects. Moreover, this great ritual had more than just local significance, because the texts record visitors from the other great Peten sites of the day.

B—THE EAST: STELA 11

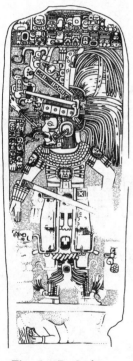

Fig. 5.8 B: Stela 11 records the arrival of Wat'ul at Seibal and shows him standing over a captive.

The ornately dressed Wat'ul stands on top of an unnamed bound captive (Fig. 5.8). He wears a jade cape with suspended jade flowers and an apron rendered as the *Wakah-Kan,* as the Maya called the World Tree. In his left hand, he holds a wooden staff wrapped with twine, as he extends the fingers of his right hand toward the ground in the gesture that signals the "scattering" rite in which lords dropped offerings of many types into flaming braziers.

Wat'ul's befeathered headdress is almost too complicated to read. Huge groups of feathers extend from stylized bird wings at the back of his head, although we can see only one of them from this viewpoint. Another group of feathers rises from the top of his head along with a stuffed jaguar tail and a jade flower ornament. His huge earflare is also a flower, with the hanging square-nosed serpent representing the stamen. His thick hair has been cut long and square in a style that became popular among Terminal Classic Maya lords. The jade headband that holds his hair in place includes the Jester God, whose name was *Sak Hunal,* "white headband," the mark of kings.

His face shows through a mosaic mask identified as the Waterlily Monster by the detail at the top of his head. A huge waterlily blossom nibbled by a fish cantilevers out in front of his face. A skyband ending in a *tzuk,* "partition," symbol carries a shell-winged dragon as it angles upward. This combination of symbols represents the watery landscape of swamps and rivers, agricultural abundance, and Wat'ul's obligation to maintain both.

B1—THE INSCRIPTION

This text records the arrival of the new king Wat'ul with his palanquins and the new patron gods (Fig. 5.9). He arrived under the authority of the king of Ucanal one day before the end of the tenth bak'tun (9.19.19.17.19, March 14, 830). He

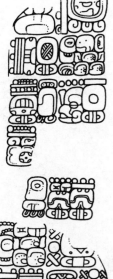
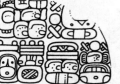
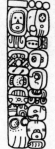

[it was] one day after / 6 Kawak

17 Sip / he arrived at the center of Seibal

Ah-Bolon-Abta; he oversaw it, Kan-Ek', Ho-Pet

He of Ucanal.

They arrived / four palanquin lords, the eight palanquins

the Holy Seibal lords [it was] one day until

7 Ahaw 18 Sip / the tenth *pik* (bak'tun). [It was] / one k'atun [until]

5 Ahaw 3 K'ayab

the first k'atun; he oversaw it

Wat'ul-Chatel. . . .

**Fig. 5.9.
The inscription
of Stela 11.**

did not have time to erect a monument for the end of the bak'tun, so he waited one k'atun until 10.1.0.0.0 (November 3, 849) to commission the great monument program that would preserve his name into the future.

C—THE NORTH: STELA 10

On this stela, Wat'ul portrayed himself in a different ritual that required another set of accouterments and dress (Fig. 5.10). His apron once again represents the *Wakah-Kan* and his belt has the form of a skyband. He has high-back sandals and a kilt made of a jaguar pelt. He still wears his *Sak Hunal* headband, but this time it carries three Jester God heads, of which we can see two. He has the same flower earflare, but his large collar consists of rows of twisted cloth or rope overlaid with mat symbols.

Fig. 5.10. C: Stela 10 depicts Wat'ul holding the Cosmic Monster. Compare his headdress to similar ones worn by (b) K'an-Hok'-Chitam from Palenque, (c) Shield-Jaguar from Yaxchilan, and (d) a moon god from a pot.

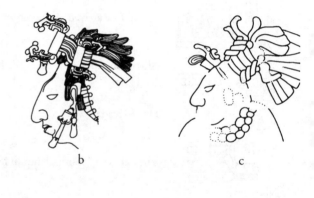

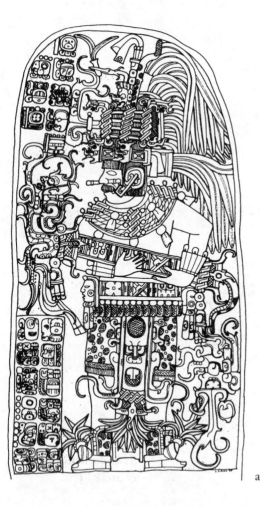

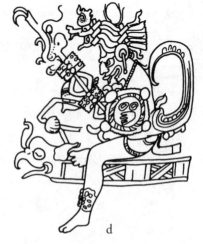

Once again, he wears a very complex headdress heavy with long arching feathers. His hair looks like the beehive style of the 1960s; it may well have been a wig. A multitiered frame made of woven mat sits on his hair like a crown. We saw this same headdress worn by Waxaklahun-Ubah-K'awil on Stela A at Copan. K'an-Hok'-Chitam II of Palenque also wore it in his accession ritual, and Shield-Jaguar of Yaxchilan wore it in the Otherworld. And it is associated with Kan-Te-Ahaw, one of Copan's patron gods, and a jaguar-featured moon god.

On Stela 10 this headdress also seems associated with patron gods, but here with those of Seibal. A strange combination of a heron with a god's head for its breast perches on top of the headdress. The heron holds a small fish in its mouth. This odd image also appears on the summit of Seibal Stela 2 and in several inscriptions recording the patron gods of Seibal. These two gods consist of the heron-GI[9] and K'awil (Fig. 5.11), both of whom were also patron gods of Palenque. The flames emerging from the front of Watul's headdress read *k'a* as the first syllable and symbol of K'awil. Thus, both patron gods are in his headdress, although in stylized form. Wat'ul was declaring these ancient patron gods of Seibal to be his own by incorporating them in his headdress. He may have started as a foreigner, but he ended up embracing the Classic heritage of his new kingdom.

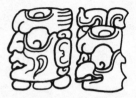
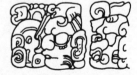

Fig. 5.11. The patron gods of Seibal.

Wat'ul cradles a ceremonial bar in his arms, but the way he uses it represents a real innovation. In the age-old tradition of the Maya, kings held Double-headed Serpent Bars that symbolized the ecliptic path of the sun and royal integration with the larger cosmos. Here, Wat'ul has replaced the snake with the Cosmic Monster that represented the arch of the sky in the form of the Milky Way when it is oriented east to west. However, the Maya usually depicted this Cosmic Monster as a crocodile. Here, Wat'ul's artist gave it a skyband and snake body to merge the two great domains into one. This improvisation is the performance of a virtuoso in Maya symbolism.

C1—THE INSCRIPTION

In this text, Wat'ul recorded the title *Ah-Hun-K'in-K'ak'*, "He of One-Day Fire" (Fig. 5.12). Perhaps this title refers to his arrival in Seibal one day before the end of the bak'tun. He wrote of his ritual scattering of drops. This ritual involved throwing into a brazier offerings that could include incense, blood, rubber, or other burnable materials.

This monument is particularly important for the study of Terminal Classic politics. Wat'ul received noble visitors from other kingdoms who came to witness his period-ending rituals and very probably to reinforce mutual obligations and loyalty between allies. Since the Dos Pilas/Aguateca kingdom was extinct by this time, the Mutul in this text must refer to another realm. Tikal is one candi-

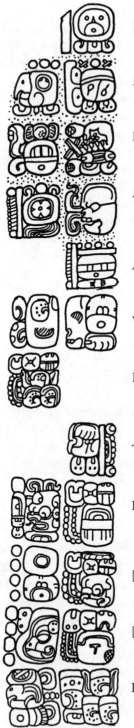

[On] 5 Ahaw

3 K'ayab / [was] the first

k'atun / he scattered drops

Ah-Hun-K'in / K'ak'

Ah-Bolon-Abta

Wat'ul / Chatel

Holy Lord of Seibal

They witnessed it

Hun . . . K'awil / Holy Lord of Mutul (Tikal)

[and] Kan-Pet / Holy Lord of Kan (Kalak'mul)

[and] Kan-Ek'/ Holy Lord of Nal (Motul de San José).

It happened in / the center of Seibal.

Fig. 5.12. The inscrip-
tion of Stela 10.

186   LINDA SCHELE AND PETER MATHEWS

date, but by this time its power was much reduced. Sections of the former kingdom had broken off to become independent. For example, Ixlu, located on the eastern end of Lake Peten Itza, was independent, but also called itself Mutul. Thus, the visiting Mutul lord may have come from Tikal or the splinter kingdom of Ixlu.

The second visitor was Kan-Pet of Kalak'mul, the longtime antagonist of Tikal. We do not know much about the relationship between Tikal and Kalak'mul at this late date. It may be that they had fought each other into exhaustion, or that such period-ending rituals were inviolable occasions when enemies could safely come together. The other possibility is that the splinter Mutul (Ixlu) sent the embassy and, like its predecessor Dos Pilas, it was allied with Kalak'mul against Tikal. In this scenario, the two men would not have been enemies.

The third man carried a very famous name. Kan-Ek' was the name of the Itza king when Cortés crossed Peten in the sixteenth century, and when the Spaniards conquered the Itza in 1697, another Kan-Ek' was the Itza king. Kan-Ek' appears to have been the formal name taken by kings of the Itza. Here is the same name used in the ninth century for a lord who came from Motul de San José, a site on the north shore of Lake Peten Itza in the heart of historical Itza territory.[10] In fact, in the ninth century, Kan-Ek' appears as a name on several pots looted from some Peten site, on a stela from Motul de San José, and in the texts of Chich'en Itza, as well as in this text from Seibal (Fig. 5.13). It was a traditional name in Peten for at least nine hundred years.

D—THE WEST: STELA 9

Stela 9 presents a problem of identification (Fig. 5.14). At first, the person portrayed looks different from Wat'ul as his artists depicted him on Stelae 10 and 11. The man on Stela 9 does not have a mustache, and he shows the flattened forehead characteristic of the head deformation that the Classic Maya used as an ethnic and rank marker. However, the archaeologists say that head deformation did not appear in the Seibal's archaeological record until this period. According to this information, Wat'ul and his compatriots ought to have had deformed skulls. Moreover, the text on Stela 9 identifies its protagonist as Wat'ul.

The alternative explanation is that the man depicted on Stela 9 is the visitor named in the second passage of the text. However, the verb in the first clause says that Wat'ul witnessed the materialization of a Vision Serpent and that "he held or grasped the god." The person in the scene is obviously doing exactly this action. We find this very strong evidence against the interpretation that someone else is portrayed here. Perhaps Wat'ul instructed his artists to represent him emphasizing different features on each monument.

In this ritual, Wat'ul wears a collar, cuffs, and belt made of jade cylinders and

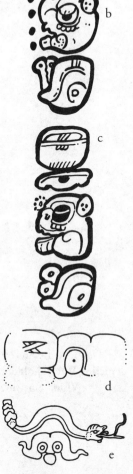

Fig. 5.13. Kan-Ek' names from (a) Seibal, (b–c) pots, and (d–e) Chich'en Itza.

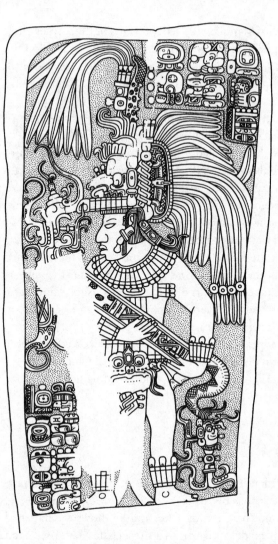

Fig. 5.14. D: Stela 9
depicting Wat'ul holding
a Vision Serpent.

beads. A bar pectoral hangs from his collar and he stands barefooted. The *xok* fish and shell device that hangs from his belt identifies his role as that of the Maize God, First Father of Creation.

His headdress reinforces this Maize God identification. Although zoomorphic in form, the main head has the tonsured hair form and maize leaves characteristic of standard Maize God portraits. The rest of the headdress assemblage is fairly conventional, with the expected feathers, miscellaneous panels, jaguar tail, and jade flowers.

Wat'ul holds a Vision Serpent whose body merges with a skyband in a form that deliberately echoes the Cosmic Monster on Stela 10. A *te* sign emerges from its gaping mouth and a bearded head is attached to its tail.

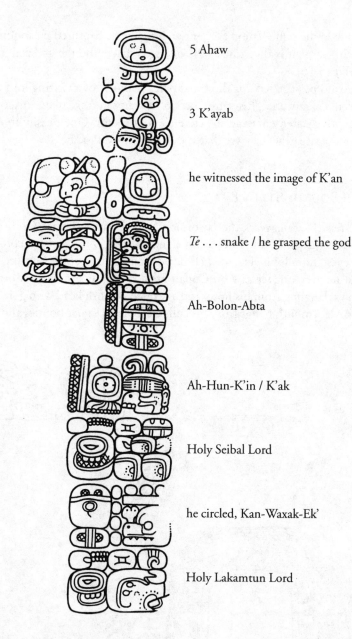

5 Ahaw

3 K'ayab

he witnessed the image of K'an

Te . . . snake / he grasped the god

Ah-Bolon-Abta

Ah-Hun-K'in / K'ak

Holy Seibal Lord

he circled, Kan-Waxak-Ek'

Holy Lakamtun Lord

Fig. 5.15. The inscription from Stela 9.

D1—THE INSCRIPTION

In this text, Wat'ul says he witnessed the appearance of a Vision Serpent (Fig. 5.15). The proper name of this serpent includes a zoomorphic head with a *te* sign emerging from its mouth. The same *te* sign can be seen in the mouth of the serpent bar he holds in his arms, so that there is no doubt that this is the object mentioned in the text. On Lintel 3 of Temple 4, Yik'in-Kan-K'awil (Ruler B) of

Tikal depicted the same Vision Serpent arching over a captured palanquin. The name of this serpent is the same as the one at Seibal, although at Tikal it wears feathers (Fig. 5.16).

The second passage records the ritual participation[11] of a visiting lord from a place called Lakamtun. This same location occurs in Yaxchilan's inscriptions both in captive statements and in reference to a visitor. One possibility is that Lakamtun is a site near the river that is called Lakantun today.

E—THE SOUTH: STELA 8

On this stela, Wat'ul wears the costume of the Bearded Jaguar God, who is sometimes Venus and sometimes a sun jaguar (Fig. 5.17). A twisted cord decorates his eyes and a long elegant shell beard frames his mouth, forming a false beard just like the one we saw on Copan Stela F. Wat'ul also wears a bead and long ribbon dangling from his nose, and a severed *xok*-fish head with gore falling from its jawless mouth hangs from his collar. He wears jaguar booties and gloves

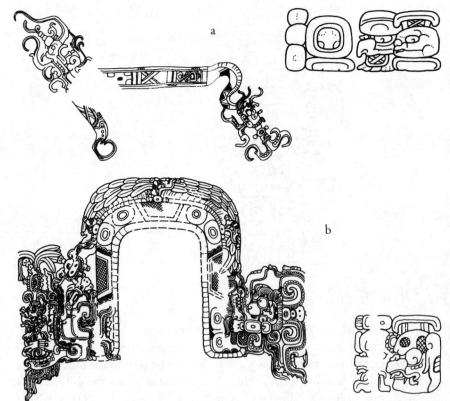

Fig. 5.16. The Vision Serpents and their names from (a) Seibal and (b) Tikal Temple 4, Lintel 3.

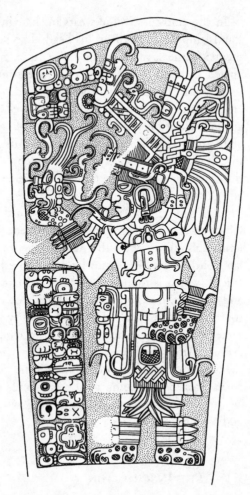

Fig. 5.17. E: Stela 8,
depicting Wat'ul
in the guise of the
Bearded Jaguar God.

as he holds out the head of K'awil. The *Wakah-Kan* apron rides over a skirt made of knee-length strips. Since hand-woven cloth cannot be cut without unraveling, the skirt was probably made of bark paper, leather, or perhaps woven strips. Paper knots signaling bloodletting surround his ankles and wrists.

We have seen this cruller-eyed god at Copan and Tikal, where texts identify him as *Hun-Kanal-Tzuk-Ahaw* and *K'in-Hix Ek'-Hun*. His story is intimately involved in the myth of Copan's patron gods, and since other deities in this story also show up as the patron gods of Tikal, Palenque, and Seibal, perhaps all three sites incorporated the same myth into their political imagery. However, Wat'ul may also have chosen to materialize this god because of the night sky on the k'atun-ending. It happens that Venus was in Capricorn (a jaguar to the Maya) just past its maximum elongation as Eveningstar.[12] If this is correct, then Wat'ul, like his predecessors at Palenque, Copan, and Tikal, used ritual and period-ending ceremonies to connect himself to the larger cosmos.

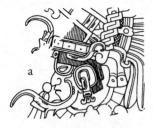

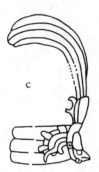

Fig. 5.18. Cotingas on headdresses from (a) Seibal Stela 8, (b) Chich'en Itza Temple of the Warriors, and a quetzal from (c) Tikal Stela 25.

In this portrait, Wat'ul wears his hair in a more traditional cut, but it still stands impossibly high on his head. The headdress includes the expected elements: feathers, mats, jaguar tail, and jade flower and ribbon ornaments. An angled skyband carries the shell-winged dragon, but the waterlily pad usually found with this device has been replaced by a sprouting *tzuk* head. The most crucial part of his headgear is his segmented headband, tied on by a cloth ribbon at the back of his head. The front of the band carries a diving bird whose tail arches up and away from Wat'ul's face. Although its head is broken off, we surmise it is a *yaxun,* or lovely cotinga (Fig. 5.18).[13] This bird of omen was sacred to the Maya, who referred to it in the Dresden Codex, the Books of Chilam Balam, and the Popol Vuh.

At this same time, the diving *yaxun* bird appears on warriors' headdresses at Chich'en Itza. There, scholars have identified this blue bird as a *xiuh tototl* ("turquoise bird") after the Aztec name, but the lovely cotinga is not a highland bird. It lives in the lowland rain forest canopy, in contrast to the quetzal (*k'uk'*), which is found in the highland cloud forest of Guatemala, Honduras, and Chiapas. Both birds occur as a paired opposition in Maya ethnohistorical sources. In the first half of the sixth century, Tikal Stela 25 depicted a *k'uk'* in the same position on the headdress of a woman. Both birds and their feathers were exported from the Maya area into central Mexico during Aztec times. However, the usage of the *yaxun* and the *k'uk'* on the front of a headdress occurs first in the Maya area, before going to the highlands of central Mexico. Here at Seibal, Wat'ul wore this *yaxun* headband along with a very orthodox and ancient Maya god costume.

E1—THE INSCRIPTION

The first part of the text (Fig. 5.19) simply records that Wat'ul, *u k'al wa tun,* "ended the tun." The second half gives us a truly important connection to the Postclassic histories of the K'iche' and Kaqchikel peoples of Guatemala. The passage records a witness, whose emblem glyph comes first, perhaps because of its importance. He is a *K'ul Puh Ahaw,* or a "Holy Cattail-Reed Lord." This visitor was a "Toltec" in the sense that he came from the place of origin identified with cattail reeds. Our problem is to determine which "reed place" the scribe intended. It is unlikely to have been Teotihuacan, because it had been sacked and burned 150 years earlier. More likely, this fellow came from a Maya *Tulan/Puh.* At this time, Chich'en Itza was the principal Maya *Puh,* although Tikal and Copan had also laid claim to that distinction.

The text also gives us the visitor's personal name—*Hakawitzil.*[14] In the Popol Vuh, *Hakawitz* was also the patron god given to the K'iche' progenitor Mahucutah at *Tulan Suywa.* This association with *Tulan* matches the *Puh* reference in

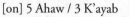
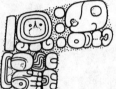

[on] 5 Ahaw / 3 K'ayab

he ended the tun

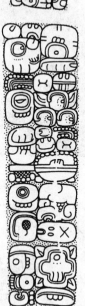

Wat'ul-Chatel

Holy Seibal Lord

He witnessed it / Holy Lord of the Cattails (*Puh*)

Hakawitzil

It happened in / the plaza

Fig. 5.19. The inscription from Stela 8.

the Seibal texts. *Hakawitz* has no meaning in K'iche', but in Cholan it is "Beginning Mountain."[15] We think it possible that this text refers to the historical event that gave rise to the *Hakawitz* legend among the K'iche'[16] so that the Postclassic foundation legends of the K'iche' overlap with Terminal Classic inscriptions at Seibal.

The last phrase names the location of these events as the plaza in which Temple A-3 sits. The glyph for plaza shows a quatrefoil portal called an *ol* by the Maya. This sign merges with the glyph for "ocean" or "water" to signal that plazas were analogs of the Primordial Sea.

F—The Center: Stela 21

The fifth stela in the program stands in the center of the temple above the offering containing the jade hearth (Fig. 5.20). Once again, Wat'ul depicted himself wearing the same eye cruller and shell beard as he did on Stela 8 (Fig. 5.21). However, on this occasion, he did not use the jaguar booties, mitts, and collar. Suspended from his collar is a pendant that is often associated with portrayals of

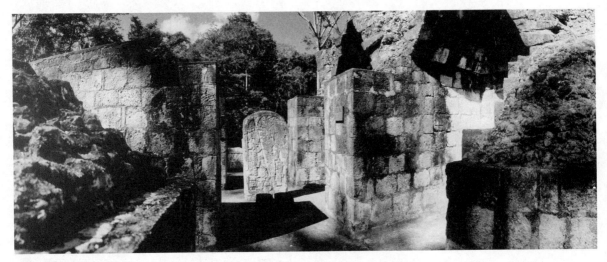

Fig. 5.20. The interior
of Temple A-3, with
Stela 21 in the center.

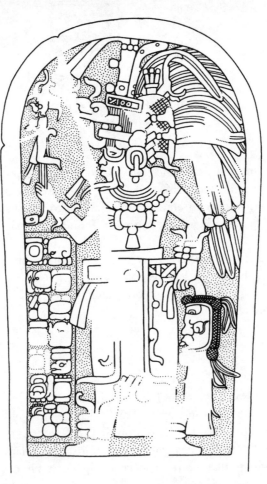

Fig. 5.21. F: Stela 21,
depicting Wat'ul as the
Bearded Jaguar God.

GI, Chak, and other deities. In his right hand, he holds a K'awil scepter that is the *way,* or nawal, of the Vision Serpent.[17] His other hand grasps the handle of a shield carrying the face of the Sun God.

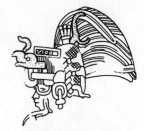

Fig. 5.22. The bird in the wig Wat'ul wore for the period-ending.

The most bizarre element in his costume occurs in his headdress. A large bird dives through his beehive (or perhaps we should say "birdnest") hairdo. Its neck and head emerge from the front hair, while its talons extend upward from the back of Wat'ul's head (Fig. 5.22). This bizarre image evokes a pair of Tikal censers showing the cruller-eyed Bearded Jaguar God with a diving bird appended to his head. There the bird has black-tipped feathers and a large beaked head like the Seibal example. We don't understand the symbolism at the present time, but we suspect that the combination identifies a special aspect of the Bearded Jaguar God we have tracked at Copan and Seibal.

F1—THE INSCRIPTION

The eroded state of Stela 21's inscription prevents us from discussing its message in detail. We can recognize the date 5 Ahaw 3 K'ayab, a verb probably reading *yilah,* "he witnessed it," and the final phrase reading *yitah Bolon-Abta, K'ul* Seibal *Ahaw,* "the companion of Bolon-Abta, Holy Seibal Lord." This *yitah,* "companion," can occur between rulers and their kin, rulers and their lords, and rulers and their patron gods. We do not know which was involved here.

G—THE HISTORICAL AND POLITICAL CONTEXT OF TEMPLE A-3

Seibal played a tragic role in the Late Classic period. The neighboring kingdom of Dos Pilas captured its king and for the next sixty-five years or more, foreign rulers controlled the city. Then there was a thirty-year gap of which we know little, until in A.D. 829 a new ruler arrived on the scene. He was a foreigner, but he came from a kingdom, Ucanal, that had been a player in the power politics of central Peten for hundreds of years. Rather than being "non-Classic Maya invaders" from the outside, as some have argued, this new ruler, Ah-Bolon-Abta Wat'ul-Chatel, represented a continuation of the politics of the Tikal-Kalak'mul hegemonies, although by this time the major players had changed.

Far from being foreign, Wat'ul's construction created a charter for authority derived from the most ancient and orthodox of Maya religious and political thought. Yet at the same time, his elaborations on those themes were virtuoso performances of innovation. He not only captured the past, but he formulated an elegant statement incorporating the new international language of power that swept Mesoamerica after the fall of Teotihuacan.

Moreover, his legacy to the Maya of today is one of incalculable value, because his inscriptions provide written connections from the old political structures of the Classic period to the new lineages that would rule during the Postclassic. The names in his inscriptions, *Kan-Ek'* and *Hakawitzil,* occur in the foundation myths of highland and lowland Maya alike. He gave the Maya an unbroken written history that started before the beginning of the Christian era and continues today.

CHAPTER 6

Chich'en Itza:
The Great Ballcourt

Chich'en Itza has figured prominently in the European imagination since Diego de Landa, the second bishop of Yukatan, first visited it shortly after the Spanish conquest of Yukatan. At the time, the once-great city was mostly abandoned, but his description suggests that Maya people were still going there to throw offerings into the great well, or *tz'onot* (*cenote* in modern Spanish), and to remember the former greatness of its builders. Today tens of thousands of visitors come from the playgrounds of Cancun or the old Spanish capital of Mérida to visit these spectacular ruins as modern pilgrims. Visitors can drive from there using the "superhighway" that crosses the peninsula, but taking the old roads brings contact with the people of Yukatan and their towns and villages. Both ways lead to the new visitor center at the entrance to Chich'en Itza. Gravel paths lead the multitudes of tourists to the ancient buildings, where the portraits of Itza kings and lords look out upon the crowds.

According to the legends of Landa's time, Chich'en Itza had been founded by three brothers, who built all of the great buildings there. We have reason to believe these legends reflected a real history, because the inscriptions of Chich'en Itza name a group of five individuals as its rulers. Texts call all five of these people *yitah*[1] or "companion," while two of them were children of the same woman. Thus, we know that brothers were among the council, or *multepal* ("joined reign"), that ruled the ancient kingdom.

Moreover, people named in the inscriptions of Chich'en also appear in the Books of Chilam Balam, prophetic histories written after the conquest by Maya scribes.[2] Among the names from the Chilam Balams is K'ak'upakal,[3] one of the brothers who ruled in the council of Chich'en; Ah-Holtun-Balam,[4] one of the founding lords of Chich'en; and Hun-Pik-Tok', the conqueror of Itzamal.[5] We also have people called *K'ul Kokom Ahaw*, "Holy Kokom Lords." The ethnohistorical sources say that the Kokom family ruled Chich'en and the surrounding region until the Spanish conquest. Their descendants still live in Yukatan today. This convergence of historical records written both in precolumbian and postconquest times is very rare in Mesoamerica.

These same historical sources record two names for the ancient city. The most famous of the two is *Chich'en Itza,* which means "Mouth of the Well of the Itza." *Itza* is a name that means "sorcerer of water."[6] We now know that the name first appeared around Lake Peten Itza in the Peten region of Guatemala, and that it probably came north with migrants from that area. *Itza Ahaw* also occurs in Chich'en's inscriptions, so we know that the lords of Chich'en called themselves Itza even in ancient times. The other name, *Wuk Yabnal,* also appears in the inscriptions, but in the form both of *Yabnal,* "Abundance Place"; *Ah Abnal,* "He of Abnal"; and *Wak Abil,* "Six Years" or "Six Grandchildren."[7] Thus, the people and places associated with Chich'en Itza in chronicles written after the conquest also occur in the histories commissioned by its ancient rulers.

The history and origin of the people called the Itza is still a matter of great debate. Much of what we know comes from Bishop de Landa's *Relación de las Cosas de Yucatan* and the complex and enigmatic k'atun histories recorded in the Books of Chilam Balam, books of history and mythology recorded by Yukatek Maya scribes in the centuries following the conquest. These sources led early archaeologists to identify two great phases at Chich'en Itza—a "Maya" one corresponding to the inscriptional history, falling between 10.0.2.7.13 (August 4, A.D. 832)[8] and 10.4.0.0.0 (January 20, 909), and a much later "Toltec" phase they placed in the eleventh and twelfth centuries. However, this chronology has come under increasing challenge by archaeologists, art historians, and epigraphers. Carbon-14 dates and new ceramic interpretations have compressed the Toltec phase with the earlier Maya one. All the major public architecture and its subsequent renovations seem to have been constructed during the time of Chich'en's inscriptions (A.D. 800–948). Thus, the myth of the Toltecs and the identity of the Itza become critical questions.

THE QUESTION OF THE TOLTECS

Since the mid-nineteenth century, scholars have associated Chich'en Itza with a central Mexican people called the Toltecs, who according to legend migrated from Tula, a famous precolumbian ruin in the modern Mexican state of Hidalgo, to conquer the peaceful Maya of Yukatan and to teach them the ways of war and sacrifice.[9] At the heart of this interpretation lies the legend of a great Toltec king named "Feathered-Serpent" (*Quetzalcoatl* in Aztec and *K'uk'ulkan* in Maya), who once ruled Tula. The legend says that this famous king led the Toltecs into greatness, but for one reason or another—depending on the particular version of the story—he fell from power and caused the ruin of Tula. In shame, Quetzalcoatl and his loyal friends left Tula and traveled toward the east, saying that one day they would return.

By the late nineteenth century, scholars had associated Quetzalcoatl of the Toltec story with a person called K'uk'ulkan, who appears in Landa's accounts of Maya history as a foreign conqueror.[10] In the modern interpretation of Landa's account, the exiled Toltecs traveled to the east until they entered the Yukatan peninsula. There they conquered the peaceful Maya and set up a great imperium that endured until they were overthrown centuries later.

Proponents of this Toltec interpretation say that Chich'en's architecture can be divided into two distinct phases, using the styles of decoration as the criterion. They see one set of buildings—those that use the fine mosaic relief that was very popular in the cities of the Puuk area, like Uxmal and K'abah—as a pure Maya style. This Maya-Puuk style is famous for its subtle relief entablatures and its very "busy" compositions. Proponents of this view have dated the buildings of Maya-Puuk style at Chich'en Itza to be contemporary with the Puuk cities, circa A.D. 700–1000. Since buildings of this type cluster in the southern zone of the sacred precinct, they call this zone "Old Chich'en." Buildings identified with "Old Chich'en" include the Monjas, the Caracol, the Casa Colorada, and the Ak'ab Tz'ib, among others.

Advocates of this interpretation see the northern half of the sacred precinct, which they call "New Chich'en," in stark contrast to the Puuk-style buildings in the southern zone. The buildings in the north are much larger, have few Maya-style inscriptions, show many figures wearing clothes with affinities to central Mexico, and in general have a very different "feel" about them. In particular, many of the architectural traits in "New Chich'en" also appear in central Mexican sites, especially at Tula. Because of this identification with Tula, the inhabitants of "New Chich'en" have been called "Toltec-Maya." "New Chich'en" includes the Great Ballcourt, the Castillo, and all the buildings associated with the Temple of the Warriors,[11] and is traditionally dated to the eleventh and twelfth centuries.

From the beginning, there were scholars who opposed these interpretations of a dichotomy between "Old Chich'en" and "New Chich'en." Early opponents argued that Tollan was a legendary construct rather than a historical reality that can be identified with the site of Tula, Hidalgo. Other scholars argued that Chich'en was earlier than Tula, and that it was the innovative center that lent much of the symbolism to Tula, rather than the reverse.[12] Today, people who oppose the Toltec-Maya hypothesis accept the existence of Tollan as a geographical place, but contend that it was built many times by many people as a declaration of origin. According to this viewpoint, there was not just one Tollan, but many.

We believe that the archaeological evidence indicates that "Old" and "New" Chich'en were contemporary. For example, all radiocarbon dates associated with the ceramic style that archaeologists use to identify the presence of Toltec-Maya fall before A.D. 1000.[13] Pots made in this "Toltec-Maya" style of ceramics, which archaeologists call Sotuta, have also been found sealed inside buildings at

Uxmal, which is supposed to be contemporary with "Old Chich'en." Moreover, the Great Ballcourt, generally identified as a "Toltec-Maya" building, was dedicated on 10.1.15.3.6 (November 18, 864).[14] This date falls during the Terminal Classic period, so that it must be seen as a Maya building, rather than as one built by invading Toltecs. Moreover, all of the hieroglyphic dates at Chich'en Itza and Uxmal fall before A.D. 909, and while both cities surely continued to be occupied after this time, neither city endured as a major capital for much more than a century afterward.[15] Present archaeological evidence indicates that the Itza constructed all the main ceremonial buildings at Chich'en before A.D. 1000.

This means that Chich'en Itza was earlier than its central Mexican counterpart at Tula, Hidalgo, the Toltec phase of which archaeologists date to A.D. 950–1150. If these chronologies hold, it means that the scenario of the Toltec conquest of Chich'en is highly unlikely because there is so little overlap in time between the two sites.

However, there is also a question of just who the Toltecs were. As we discussed in chapter one, *Tollan* (also known as *Tulan*) comes from the Aztec myth of migration. *Tollan* simply means "Place of Cattail Reeds," and a "Toltec" was an inhabitant of that place. In Mesoamerican legend, "the Place of Cattail Reeds" was a special location of origin, where people first learned the arts, writing, and the ways of civilized life. In the literature of many Postclassic peoples, including the Maya,[16] the Mixtec, and the Aztec, rulers went to the "Place of Reeds" to obtain the patron gods of their lineages and the emblems of office that provided the charter for their authority. The Mixtec codices of the Postclassic period also include cattail reeds in the names of the places where their lords underwent nose-piercing ceremonies. Aztec sources clearly name at least four *Tollans*—Teotihuacan, Tula, Cholula, and Tenochtitlan. In fact, the Aztecs also used *Tollan* simply to mean "metropolis." In other words, there were many "Places of Reeds," with inhabitants from many different ethnic groups.

We also now know that the Classic-period Maya called Teotihuacan *Puh*, the Maya word for "cattail reed," as discussed in chapter one. We also know that they adopted much of Teotihuacan's symbolism as part of their own discourse on origins and warfare.[17] However, the Maya began building cities with the symbolism of "Place of Reeds" (and "Snake Mountain") at least 250 years before Teotihuacan was built. And as we discussed in the first chapter, the "Place of Reeds" is likely to have originated with the Olmecs and the landscape of the southern Gulf Coast.

So, how do these ideas relate to Chich'en Itza? First of all, they provide another, we think better, reason for the "Toltec" iconography at Chich'en and weaken the idea of invaders from Tula, Hidalgo. They identify the most prominent Tollan during the Classic period as Teotihuacan and generalize the idea of "Place of Reeds" as the designation of any city claimed as an ancestral origin place. For the Maya of Chich'en, their *Puh* may have been Teotihuacan, or just as likely it was Tikal or Palenque or Kalak'mul or any other powerful Classic-period city that used the complex of images that the Maya had appropriated from Teotihuacan. All of these Maya cities had declared themselves to be *Puh,* "Cattail Reed," and their ancestors to be *Ah Puh,* "People of Cattail Reeds." The "Toltec" imagery at Chich'en was continuing a Maya tradition that was at least 400 years old when Chich'en was built.[18]

The Maya of Chich'en Itza apparently did intend to declare themselves *Ah Puh* and their city a "Place of Reeds," but this does not imply nor require an invasion of outsiders.[19] Rather, the Itza chose to frame their own claim to legitimacy in the most ancient and honored of all expressions of Mesoamerican political and religious authority—that of the "Place of Reeds." Just as kings of Europe declared themselves to be inheritors of the Holy Roman Empire regardless of their familial and social histories, so the Itza claimed to be descendants of the *Ah Puh* and inhabitants of the new "Place of Reeds." But so did everybody else throughout the Classic and Postclassic periods—*Puh* and the *Ah Puh,* or as the Aztec called them, Tollan and the Toltecs, were the political currency of the times.

WHO WERE THE ITZA?

What we know about the Itza comes from Landa, the Books of Chilam Balam, and the Classic-period inscriptions. These sources tell us that they had a special relationship with the god called Itzamna. The first priest of Chich'en was called *Zamma (Itzamna),*[20] and the Chilam Balam of Chumayel says, "Chich'en Itzam was its name because the Itza went there. Then he removed the stones of the land, the stones of the sowed land, the place of Itzam."[21] Most of the long-snouted masks at Chich'en have a flower headband that identifies them as *Itzam-Ye* or *Mut Itzamna,* the great bird that sat atop the World Tree. It is the most frequent image in the city and may be why Maya of later times called Chich'en the "Place of Itzam."

The various histories in the Books of Chilam Balam chronicle the migration of the Itza into Yukatan and the establishment of their capital at Chich'en Itza, but there is still great debate concerning their origins. One view is that they were Toltecs from central Mexico who conquered the peaceful Maya of northern Yukatan, as we recounted above. A second view identifies them as Mexicanized Maya, called the Putun,[22] who had lived on the Tabasco-Campeche coast before moving into Yukatan as well as up the Usumacinta to Seibal. A more recent interpretation[23] associates the Itza with an ancient port on the northern coast of Yukatan, and suggests that they moved south from there.

However, the k'atun histories of the Chilam Balams point more strongly to migrations from the southern lowlands, beginning in the k'atun named 8 Ahaw

(A.D. 672–692). Comparing the Chilam Balams with the inscriptions from the southern kingdoms suggests that the Itza themselves may have been migrants moving to avoid the wars that were raging between the alliances to the south. We have discussed these wars and their economic effects in chapters one, two, and five.

In many ways, these wars peaked in the k'atun named 8 Ahaw that fell between 672 and 692. In chapter two, we related the story of Dos Pilas and Tikal in which Balah-Kan-K'awil, a member of Tikal's royal house who ruled Dos Pilas, changed his allegiance and accepted the king of Kalak'mul as his overlord. Tikal's answer was war, and after a long series of clashes, the hostilities climaxed in a tragic defeat for Tikal. On 9.12.6.16.17 (May 3, A.D. 679), the Dos Pilas king, in concert with Kalak'mul, captured and killed Nun-Bak-Chak, the king of Tikal.

In the aftermath of this victory, the Dos Pilas king sent his daughter to Naranjo to reestablish that city's royal line, which had been destroyed by Caracol and Kalak'mul forty years earlier. The date of her arrival, 9.12.10.5.12 (August 30, A.D. 682), was recorded not only at Naranjo, but also on a stela at Koba,[24] a kingdom in northeastern Yukatan that was the bitter rival of Chich'en Itza. Was Koba a member of the Kalak'mul hegemony? We think so.

Five years after her arrival, the Dos Pilas princess gave birth to a son she named K'ak'-Tiliw.[25] When he became the king of Naranjo at age five, a series of battles started that culminated on 9.13.2.16.0 (January 22, A.D. 695) with the capture of Sih-K'awil, a noble of Tikal. Once again Tikal suffered at the hands of a member of the Kalak'mul hegemony.

These repeated defeats apparently did not crush Tikal completely, because on 9.13.3.7.18 (August 8, A.D. 695), Hasaw-Kan-K'awil, the son of the Mutul king sacrificed by Dos Pilas, finally exacted vengeance from his hated enemies. He went to war against Kalak'mul and captured his rival king, Yich'ak-K'ak' (also known as Jaguar Paw). He sacrificed his enemy thirteen days later, and began a forty-year period in which he and his son regained much of the lost glory of their kingdom.[26] During this same period, battles also raged in Chiapas and along the Usumacinta River between states allied to one or the other of these great combatants.

Thus, we see that k'atun 8 Ahaw saw the defeat of major kingdoms, the exile of rulers and nobles, and finally, the deaths of kings from both Tikal and Kalak'-mul. Both sides suffered devastating defeats and enjoyed moments of victory. These wars would have produced highly trained soldiers and refugee populations who could have migrated in exactly the way described in the Chilam Balams and the central Mexican chronicles for this period. We suggest that these migrations began in k'atun 8 Ahaw, but as we shall see, they continued through the next several k'atuns as the wars in the south persisted and even intensified. We also suspect that most of the refugees/migrants were nobles, because the accounts say that the migrants went without their wives so that they married local women during their migrations. This fact may account for the change in emphasis from fathers to mothers and grandmothers in the parentage statements at Chich'en Itza. Marriage to women from Yukatekan lineages may have given the foreign Itza local legitimacy.

At least some of these migrants called themselves Itza before they left their homes. We have a text on a looted pot that names its owner as a *yune Itza ahaw*, "the child of the Itza lord." Later texts from Motul de San José proclaimed their protagonists to be *K'ul Itza Ahaw*, "Holy Itza Lord." All these texts are from the north shore of Lake Peten Itza,[27] where people calling themselves Itza still live today. Although the *Itza Ahaw* title also occurs at Chich'en Itza, the earliest examples come from Peten. Apparently the Itza had long lived in central Peten. During k'atun 8 Ahaw, some of them moved north to establish new kingdoms, while others apparently never left their homeland.[28]

The Books of Chilam Balam say their migrations took over eighty years, and that they settled at various places along the way, including perhaps Xkalumk'in,[29] where they married local women. Perhaps these migrants included refugees from Teotihuacan, who had also been forced into exile by the destruction of their own kingdom at about the same time. Moreover, the Olmeca-Xicalanca, who were taking Maya imagery into the central Mexican area, very likely began their migrations from the Gulf Coast at about the same time. They may have been kinsmen or allies of the people moving north into Yukatan.

Other refugee groups migrated north through *Siyankan Bak'halal* ("Born of Heaven, Surrounded by Reeds," the Maya name for southern Quintana Roo). Various groups arrived in the north at different times, but when they got there, they formed alliances with older kingdoms like Tz'ibilchaltun (Ichkantiho) and Itzamal. The Chilam Balam of Chumayel describes an assembly at Ichkantiho where the Itza formed an alliance in the k'atun that ended on 9.18.0.0.0 11 Ahaw.[30] They conquered yet other kingdoms and replaced the old lineages with the newly arrived ones. These many groups, both new and old, became known in Yukatekan history as the Itza.

A general chronology[31] of events gleaned from the inscriptions and the Chilam Balams is as follows:

> K'atun 8 Ahaw (672–692) included the discovery[32] of Chich'en Itza and
> the beginning of the migrations to the north from Nonowal and
> Siyankan Bak'halal.
> K'atun 4 Ahaw (711–731) was the time of the Great and Little Descents.
> The Itza brought the Pawahaekuh as their gods and they ruled for thir-
> teen k'atuns.
> K'atun 2 Ahaw (731–751) was when Ah-Kuy-Tok'-Tutul-Xiw and his
> people established themselves at Uxmal.
> K'atun 11 Ahaw (771–791) included the founding ceremonies of the Itza
> alliance at Ichkantiho (Tz'ibilchaltun).

K'atun 5 Ahaw (830–849) saw the first dated monuments erected at Chich'en Itza. A second group of Tutul Xiw arrived at Uxmal.

K'atun 3 Ahaw (849–869) included the dedication of the Great Ballcourt.

K'atun 1 Ahaw (869–889) was the period into which most of the Chich'en dates fall.

K'atun 12 Ahaw (889–909) saw the dedication of the ballcourt and Nunnery Quadrangle at Uxmal. The latest monuments at Uxmal and Chich'en record the end of this k'atun. It is also the latest date at Tonina in the south.

K'atun 8 Ahaw (928–948) was the k'atun in which Chich'en Itza was abandoned by the Itza, who established Chak'anputun and ruled for thirteen k'atuns. Chak'anputun may have been a province west of Lake Peten Itza.

K'atun 10 Ahaw (1165–1185) saw the first dated monument at Mayapan.

K'atun 8 Ahaw (1185–1204) was the k'atun of the Hunak-Kel action against Chak-Xib-Chak of Chich'en Itza; the Itza returned from Chak'anputun, but were forced to retreat to Tan-Muluk-Xok near Lake Peten Itza. They returned north forty years later.

K'atun 4 Ahaw (1244–1263) included an attack against Mayapan by the Itza and their allies, the lords of Itzamal.

K'atun 13 Ahaw (1263–1303) was the k'atun in which the Itza forced an alliance upon Mayapan and became known as Maya.

K'atun 8 Ahaw (1441–1461) saw the final abandonment of Mayapan.

K'atun 4 Ahaw (1480–1500) was the k'atun of the first European voyages to the Caribbean.

K'atun 11 Ahaw (1539–1559) saw the final conquest of Yukatan and the establishment of Christianity.

When the Itza first migrated to Chich'en Itza, one of their initial tasks was to create the supernatural charter for their political power. To accomplish this, they embarked on one of the most ambitious and creative building and sculptural programs in Mesoamerican history. They built Snake Mountain, the Primordial Sea, and the Council House, and next to them, the crack that opened into the space and time of Creation. That crack in the earth—the Great Ballcourt—held a critically important array of founding imagery. It may even represent the founding of the Itza alliance at Ichkantiho as an act of Creation.

THE CITY

The Itza divided the sacred center of their capital into at least two precincts and surrounded them with demarcation walls (Fig. 6.1). The northern precinct, the

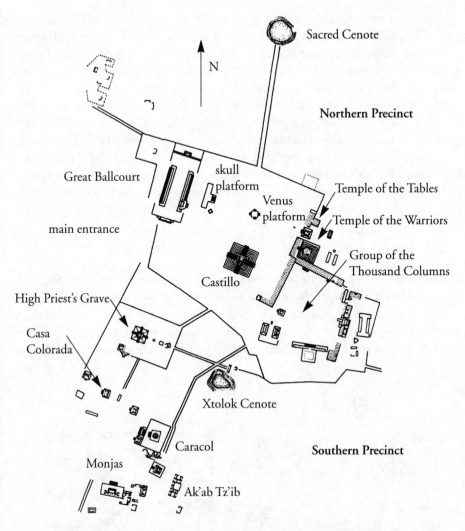

N

Sacred Cenote

Northern Precinct

Great Ballcourt

skull platform

Venus platform

Temple of the Tables

Temple of the Warriors

main entrance

Castillo

Group of the Thousand Columns

High Priest's Grave

Casa Colorada

Xtolok Cenote

Southern Precinct

Caracol

Monjas

Ak'ab Tz'ib

Fig. 6.1. A map of the central core of Chich'en Itza and its precincts.

larger of the two precincts,[33] pivots on the Castillo, a huge radial pyramid with four stairways rising to a temple on its summit. Famous for the light-and-shadow serpents that appear on the equinoxes, the pyramid represents Snake Mountain,[34] the place of origin established at the beginning of the world at the legendary "Place of Reeds." To the east of this great pyramid sits the Temple of the Warriors, where the council met to run the Itza kingdom. Next to it on the north is the Temple of the Tables, and the Group of the Thousand Columns is to the south. A small Venus platform lies north of the Castillo on the way to the causeway, or *sak beh* ("white road"), that leads to the Sacred Cenote, where the Itza threw offerings into the dark waters that lie sixty feet below.[35] This principal group is completed by the Great Ballcourt and the Platform of the Skulls, which sit to the west of the Castillo across from the Temple of the Warriors.

The southern precinct repeats all these components, albeit in smaller scale. The High Priest's Grave with intertwined serpents carved into its balustrades corresponds to the Castillo[36] and its light-and-shadow snakes. In both structures, these snakes are the *kuxan sum,* or "living cord," that connected the Itza lords to the heavens. This group also has a Venus platform, a second platform with tombs inside, and a causeway leading to a temple beside another cenote, called Xtolok. An early ballcourt lies under the Casa Colorada, and farther to the south are the council houses called the Monjas and the Ak'ab Tz'ib. The Caracol is a special-function building that does not have its analog in the northern precinct. Both the earliest and latest dates at Chich'en occur in this southern precinct, so that it played an important role throughout the site's history.

THE BALLCOURT

The Great Ballcourt in the northern zone is our focus in this chapter (Fig. 6.2). Besides being the largest ballcourt yet discovered in Mesoamerica, it is also the most complex in its sculptural program. In fact, we are still learning about its nuances and discovering new meaning in its programming.[37] The playing alley of the Great Ballcourt lies between two large parallel buildings, with low, shallow

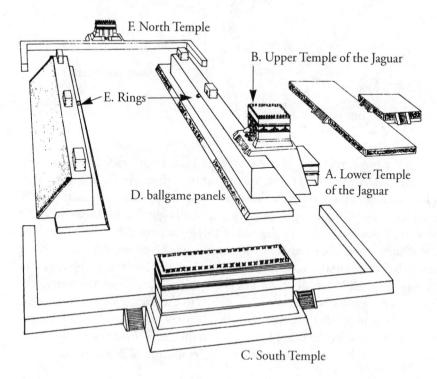

**Fig. 6.2.
The Great Ballcourt.**

benches and towering vertical walls (Fig. 6.3a). Although the cross-section of this playing alley appears to be very different from the ballcourts found in the cities to the south, the components—that is, an angled bench and vertical wall—are the same. It is the proportions between these components that is so different, because no other ballcourt has such high vertical walls in proportion to the benches.

There are other differences. The two sets of three relief panels on the benches replace the three floor markers usually found in other Maya ballcourts. And here huge rings mounted in the center of both the vertical walls (Fig. 6.3d) replace the six bench markers of the southern ballcourts, like that of Copan. Yet with all these differences, the ballcourt of Chich'en Itza is profoundly Maya in its definition.

The ancient glyph (Fig. 6.4) for the ballgame was *pitz,* while the glyph for the ballcourt showed a cross-section of the playing alley. The stepped shape of the ballcourt glyph reflects its definition as the crack in the top of the Creation Mountain. In the Popol Vuh of the K'iche' Maya, *hom,* "crevice,"[38] is the word for "ballcourt." As a crevice in the surface of the earth, the ballcourt gives human beings access to the Otherworld, where the gods and the ancestors live. For the Maya, to play the ballgame was to bring back the moment when the Third Creation ended and the Fourth one began.

At Chich'en Itza, this *hom,* or "crevice," in the earth has a wall enclosing the playing field so that the ballgames could not be viewed by large audiences (Fig. 6.3b). The games played there were not sport, but deadly serious affairs involving the charter of the state and communication with the Otherworld. The sculptures and paintings housed in the several buildings of the ballcourt tell us about its meaning.

The Lower Temple of the Jaguar sits at the plaza level below the Upper Temple of the Jaguar (Fig. 6.3e). Together, the imagery associated with these buildings records two critical moments in the city's history—what happened to the ancestors of the Itza at the moment of Creation and the founding of their city, and what happened during the wars of conquest that gave the Itza their right to rule. To complete the ends of the ballcourt, a little temple with seven doorways sits above the southern boundary wall, balanced by a three-doored temple on the northern end. Called the South and the North Temples, these two buildings carry relief murals that apply Creation imagery to the two critical domains of statecraft—the sacred art of warfare and sacrifice, and the role of the ballgame in the passage of authority from generation to generation through rites of accession.

We have several descriptions of the Aztec and Maya ballgames played at the time of the conquest, but none of the chroniclers of that period wrote down the rules or how the game was scored.[39] Ballgame images show players flinging themselves into the air or onto the floor to strike the ball with their hips or forearms (Fig. 6.5). Since no picture shows them touching the ball with their hands or feet, we deduce that the solid rubber ball could not be caught or kicked. The ball was a little larger than a basketball and must have packed quite a wallop

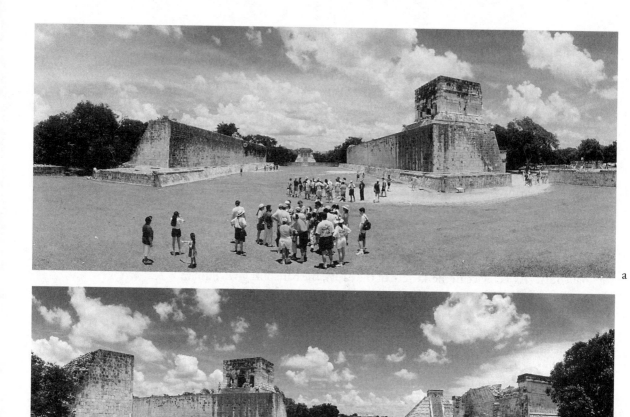

a

b

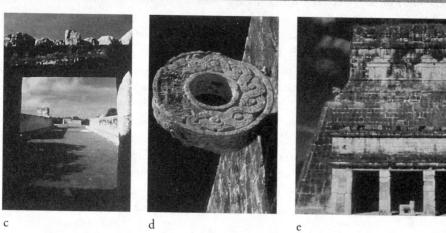

Fig. 6.3.
A photo-
graphic
medley of
the Great
Ballcourt.

c

d

e

pitzah
"he played ball"

Ah Pitzlawal
"ballplayer"

ballcourt

section of the
Chich'en ballcourt

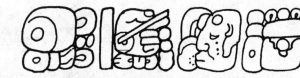

names of the Copan Ballcourt as *Eb*, stair

utiy hom, pitz ti Wak-Ballcourt; "it happened at the
chasm, he played ball at the Six-Ballcourt"

when it hit. To protect themselves, players wore U-shaped belts called "yokes." These objects were made of wood or stone over thick padding to protect the hips and ribs against blows from the ball (Fig. 6.6). They also wore heavy leather skirts and wound padding around their forearms, presumably to enable them to slam or block the ball with their forearms. Since players wore a single knee pad, we deduce that they usually went down on the same knee during play. The players of Chich'en also wore a special shoe on the same side as the knee pad, and they carried a handstone, perhaps for returning the ball in play.[40] Unlike their counterparts in the southern lowlands, they wore a long carved object jutting out from the front of their belts. Archaeologists call this object a "palma."

Fig. 6.4. Glyphs associated with the ballgame.

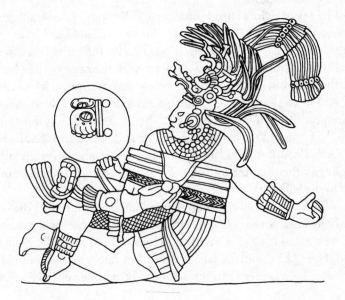

Fig. 6.5. A ballplayer flinging himself under the ball so that it will bounce off his yoke.

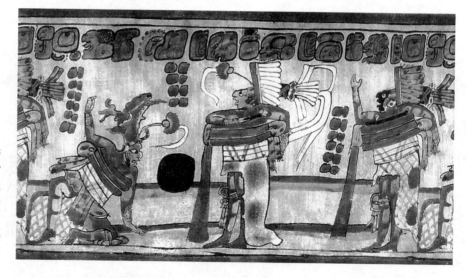

Fig. 6.6. Ballplayers wearing heavy leather skirts and wooden belts called "yokes" to protect themselves from the heavy rubber ball.

THE MYTH AND MEANING OF THE BALLGAME

Many modern myths have grown up about the ballgame. The most popular says that the Maya sacrificed the winners so as to give a perfect gift to the gods. There is no evidence for this interpretation in any of the ancient or historical sources. In fact, our best information about the ballgame comes from the Popol Vuh of the K'iche', a seventeenth-century transcription of a Creation myth that appeared in the archaeological record by 400 B.C. The story recounts the activities of two sets of twins at the end of the third in a series of four creations. We live in the Fourth Creation.

The older set of twins, Hun-Hunahpu and Wuqub-Hunahpu,[41] correspond to the Maize Gods of the Classic period, who were called Hun-Nal or Hun-Nal-Ye ("One-Maize-Ear" or "One-Maize-Seed"). In the story, they were great ballplayers who disturbed the Lords of Death with the noise of their ballplaying. Xibalba, the Place of Fear and Awe, lies below the ballcourt in Maya cosmology. The irritated lords summoned the miscreants and required them to answer for their disrespect through a series of trials. The Maize Gods lost their confrontation with the Lords of Death, who killed them and buried their bodies below the floor of the ballcourt at the Place of Sacrifice in Xibalba. To warn anyone else who might risk their ire, the lords hung the head of Hun-Hunahpu in a gourd tree next to the ballcourt.

Eventually, Xkik', the lovely daughter of a Xibalba lord, sought the skull, who spoke and convinced her to hold out her hand. It spat into her hand and she became pregnant with a second set of twins named Hunahpu and Xbalanke, or, in the Classic period, Hun-Ahaw and Yax-Balam. Her angry father ordered her killed when he found out she was pregnant, but with the help of her owl executioners, she escaped and fled to the Middleworld. The grandmother of the children in her womb gave her shelter and eventually her sons, the Hero Twins, were born.

The adventures of her sons as they grew up explain how the world came to be as it is. In time, a rat helped the Twins find their fathers' ballgame equipment and they began playing with the skills and joy of their forebears. The Xibalbans, angry again at the noise, summoned the younger Twins to answer for their misbehavior, but this time the Twins turned the tables on the Lords of Xibalba. As the story progresses, the Twins faced the Xibalbans in a series of scoreless ballgames, followed each night by an encounter in one of the perilous houses of the Death Lords. Each night they tricked the Xibalbans and survived the traps that had been laid for them, thus humiliating the Lords of Xibalba. We will not recount all of these confrontations. Suffice it to say that they found out that the frustrated Xibalbans were going to kill them anyway, so they arranged for a death that would let them come back.

When the Xibalbans brought the Twins to a fiery oven, they knew the time had come. They jumped into the fire, and then the victorious Xibalbans ground their bones into powder and threw it into the nearby river. Five days later they emerged, first as fish-men and then as youthful humans, to begin their campaign to defeat the Xibalbans by disguising themselves as miraculous dancers and performers. Eventually the Twins tricked the Lords of Death into submitting to sacrifice by dismemberment, but the Twins did not revive them and thus did they defeat death. They went to the ballcourt and dug up their forebears.

Once revived, the Maize Gods went on to oversee the Fourth Creation. This part of the story was not included in the Popol Vuh, but we have been able to reconstruct it from Classic-period texts and imagery.[42] After being reborn from a snake, the Maize Gods grew into maturity. To bring them fully to life, beautiful women tended them by helping them to dress and painting their bodies. Revived, the Maize Gods with their attendant dwarves woke up three old gods who were to play crucial roles in the creation of the world. Because we have not been able to decipher their ancient names, today we call them the Paddler Gods and God L. The Paddler Gods carried the Maize Gods in a great canoe that corresponded to the Milky Way. Across the sky they paddled until they arrived at the place of Creation in the constellation we call Orion. The Maya saw the belt of Orion as a huge Cosmic Turtle. The god Chak cracked open the turtle's back with a great lightning stone. Watered and nurtured by the Hero Twins, the Maize Gods grew from the crack, which also happens to be the ballcourt (Fig. 6.7). Standing in this crack, they stretched out two serpents, who formed the path of the sun through the ecliptic.[43]

Then the old gods who were their helpers set up the first hearth in the cosmos. Located below the Cosmic Turtle, the hearth became a triangle of stars in Orion—Alnitak, Saiph, and Rigel. The Paddler Gods, who had brought the Maize Gods to the Cosmic Turtle, set up the first stone of the hearth—the

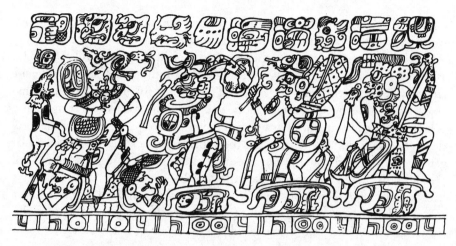

Fig. 6.7. The two Paddler Gods stand in canoes on the right. Chak holds up the lightning stone he used to crack open the Cosmic Turtle. The reborn Maize God stands in the turtle crack holding a seed sack as he prepares to direct the gods who will generate the Fourth Creation and the human beings who populate it.

Jaguar Throne Stone—at a place called *Na-Ho-Kan*, "First-Five-Sky." God L sat on this throne once it was set up. Another god set up the second stone—a snake throne stone—at *Kab-Kun*, "Earth-Seat." Itzamna, the first sorcerer of Creation, set up the third stone—Shark Throne Stone. This hearth is the place where the first fire was drilled, and just as a hearth centers a Maya house, so this heavenly hearth centered the cosmos.

Five hundred and forty-two days after the hearth was laid, the Maize Gods completed the second action needed to organize the cosmos. On the other side of the sky, where Scorpius lies across the Milky Way, they raised the tree at the center of the world. Called the *Wakah-Kan*, "Raised-up Sky," this tree was both a giant ceiba tree and the Milky Way as it arches across the sky from south to north. As they raised this tree, the Maize Gods laid out the four sides and corners of the world to create a "north house." This house pivoted on the north pole of the sky (which was a dark hole without a north star during the Classic period) and was a metaphor for the cosmos itself.

Because the reborn Maize Gods could not name all their parts, they were not allowed to return to the human world in their original form. They stayed in the ballcourt, where all human beings must go to worship them. We know them in their form as the sacred maize plant.

When the Maize Gods and their helpers finished their work, their mother and father, who were the grandparents of the Hero Twins, molded the first generation of humanity from maize dough. The K'iche' call these grandparents Xpiakok and Xmuqane. For the Maya of Yukatan, they were Pawahtun, the old god who holds up the corners of the sky, and Chak-Chel, "Great Rainbow," who was the old Moon Goddess. In both traditions, the old goddess is the midwife of Creation, and the old god is her husband-helper.[44] The mother of the Hero Twins and wife of the Maize Gods was the young Moon Goddess, named Ixik and Sak Ixik.[45] All of the great Maya lineages descended from these primordial ancestors.

The myth of Creation gives us critical information about the meaning of the ballgame. It was the arena in which the Maya confronted death, disease, and war. The Maize Gods lost the ballgame and died for it. Yet even in death, they miraculously engendered their sons, who returned to resurrect them in the great Maya miracle of mutual reproduction. The fathers begat the sons, who in turn reengendered the fathers. Both sets of Twins confronted the Lords of Death in the ballgame, which was a symbolic form of warfare. The Hero Twins used the dance to defeat Death, and it was in the ballcourt that they resurrected their dead forebears. It was also in the ballcourt that the Maize Gods stayed after the successful Fourth Creation and the engendering of humanity. It is there that human beings must go to worship the Maize Gods.

The ballgame was the metaphor for life and death, the arena in which players worked out fate and confronted chance. It was sometimes played for the joy of the sport, as with the Twins before the Xibalbans summoned them. The ballgame was also a metaphor for war, in which great states and heroes strove for victory against enemies. But most of all, the Hero Twins played the ballgame as a necessary forerunner to Creation and the making of humanity. The ballcourt truly was a crevice leading into the Otherworld. When the Maya played their game, they remade Creation again and again.

A—THE LOWER TEMPLE OF THE JAGUAR

This little temple sits outside the ballcourt so that audiences standing in the main plaza could see its interior and the rituals that took place there (Fig. 6.8). Artists carved shallow relief sculptures into its walls inside and out, covering the building with polychrome scenes (Fig. 6.9). These relief images depict the moment of Creation when the world and the charter of Itza authority were formed by the gods and the first ancestors.

Fig. 6.8. A: The elevation, plan, and section of the Lower Temple of the Jaguar.

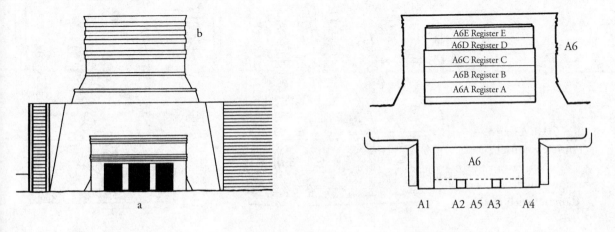

The Outer Facade: A1, A4—The End Walls

The north and south wall panels depict two Pawahtuns, the old gods who held up the sky (Fig. 6.10). Since the Chilam Balam of Chumayel says that Pawahaekuh were the lords of the Itza on 4 Ahaw, the day of Creation,[46] we think they were the patron gods of the Itza state. The south one wears a giant turtle around his middle as he stands among square-nosed serpents representing the sacred aura of the cosmos. Waterlilies with fish decorate his headdress, and a cut-shell pendant hangs from his neck. Both gods hold a rattle in one hand as they dance beside an offering plate with round objects, perhaps tamales, resting inside. The thin frame surrounding the scene has the eyebrow and nostril elements of a serpent head attached to it, suggesting that these gods stand inside the mouths of great Vision Serpents. They are the patron gods of the Itza attending the moment of Creation.

Both of them stand on a register filled with a curious feathered beastie combining the head of a snake with bird legs and feathers. The face of an emerging warrior fills the mouth of the creature, who is neither snake nor bird. We are looking into the mouth of a befeathered snake who has front legs. This creature of the imagi-

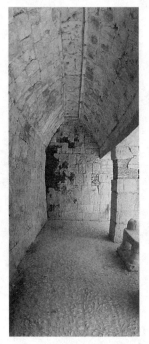

Fig. 6.9. The interior of the Lower Temple of the Jaguar.

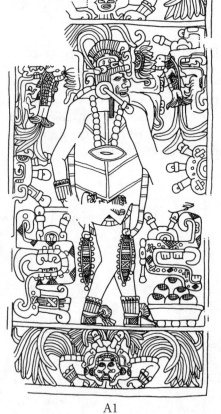

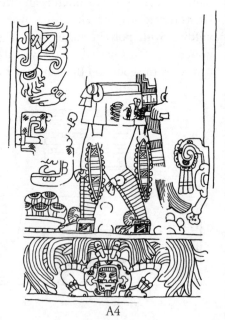

A1

A4

Fig. 6.10. A1 and A4: These two outer piers depict Pawahtuns bringing offerings and dancing with rattles.

nation first appeared in the imagery of Copan, far to the south of Chich'en Itza, during the sixth century.[47] This legged snake also appears in the murals of Cacaxtla, at Tula, and eventually it became the *xiuhcoatl*, or "fire serpent," of the Aztecs.

A2, A3, AND A5—THE SQUARE COLUMNS AND JAGUAR THRONE

While the world-bearing Pawahtuns dance on the outside piers, the inner columns represent Creation itself (Fig. 6.11). Because of missing pieces, archaeologists could not restore any of them completely, but by combining all four sides, we can know what the Maya meant to represent. The south (A2) column depicts four Pawahtuns, each wearing a different kind of shell or kilt. On the south side of the column, the Pawahtun wears a turtle shell, on the east a knobby conch shell, on the north a snail shell, and on the west a plain kilt.

The north column (A3) depicts his female opposite, but in two versions. The front and back planes (east and west) of the column display a bare-breasted goddess wearing a net skirt that identifies her as Sak Ixik, the Moon Goddess and wife of the Maize God.[48] On the left and right sides (south and north), a skull-headed goddess stands wearing a skirt marked with concentric disks and crossed bones. She is Goddess O, known as *Chak-Chel*, or "Great Rainbow," who was the goddess of childbirth and the midwife of Creation. The Mams or Pawahtuns on the other column represented her husband, who became the helper of the midwife in his old age.

We think these two old gods—Pawahtun and Chak-Chel—are the parents of the Maize God and grandparents of the Hero Twins. If we are right, they represent the same generation as Xmuqane and Xpiakok of the Popol Vuh. While their son, Hun-Nal-Ye (Hun-Hunahpu in the Popol Vuh), may have generated the order of the Fourth Creation, they formed human beings from a mixture of maize dough and water. These columns depict the midwife and her helper as they enable the rebirth of their son so that he can initiate the Fourth Creation.

The contexts represented on all eight sides are the same. The gods stand on personified mountain monsters with plant stalks emerging from their eyes. The stalks become waterlily pads on which fish nibble and around which waterbirds and turtles walk. This combination of waterlily, fish, and birds marks the primordial swamp or sea in which the mountain sits. No reeds are here, but this is the way the Maya always represented the swamps in which the reeds grow. The cracks in the top of the mountains mark them as cleft mountains in a tradition that descended from the Olmec. Moreover, snakes emerge from the clefts to undulate their way upward behind the old gods. They rise up to the bottom of the upper register, where their mouths gape open to emit the image in the upper register.

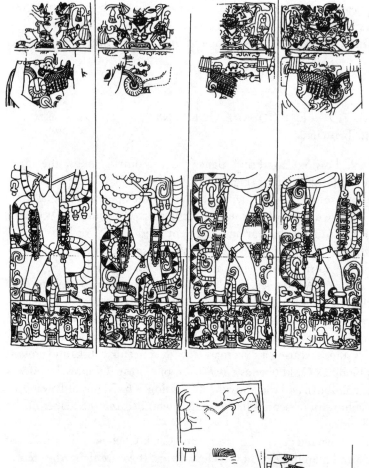

A2

A3

Fig. 6.11. A2 and A3:
The inner columns
depict four Pawahtuns
(A2) and Chak-Chel,
the midwife, and
Sak Ixik, the wife of
the Maize God (A3).
They stand on Snake
Mountain and sustain
the rebirth of the
Maize God from the
Cosmic Turtle.

The snake is a metaphor that operates on many different levels. It marks the lower image as Snake Mountain, a metaphor that referred to the Mountain of Sustenance as early as the Late Preclassic period. The Castillo and the High Priest's Grave with their serpent balustrades are magnificent manifestations of Snake Mountain. The snake in the mountain also represents the conduit from the supernatural world into the human world—it is a kind of Vision Serpent. At the same time, the serpent symbolizes the birth canal, so that the image in the upper register is being born from the snake. Even today, the Maya of Santiago Atitlan in Guatemala say that a rainbow serpent connects the infant to its mother.

The snakes' mouths open to emit images of the Maize God's resurrection from the Cosmic Turtle that Chak cracked open with his lightning stone. In each scene, a reborn Maize God rises from the turtle cleft and stretches out his arms to grasp squash vines growing from the heads of gods who are themselves emerging from the ends of the turtle shell. Farmers plant maize, squash, and bean seeds together in their *milpa,* or cornfields. The squash spreads out along the ground to preserve moisture, while the beans climb the stalk of maize. Here both maize and squash come into the world at the moment of First Father's rebirth in the company of his parents, who stand on Snake Mountain.

Between the columns sits a jaguar throne (A5), the first stone of the Cosmic Hearth that the gods set up below the Cosmic Turtle (Fig. 6.12). According to the Creation myth, the Paddler Gods set up this Jaguar Throne Stone at a place called *Na-Ho-Kan,* "First-Five-Sky."[49] By putting this jaguar throne between the midwife of Creation and her helper, the Itza declared Chich'en Itza to be the

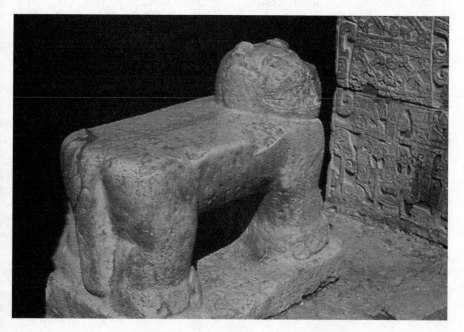

Fig. 6.12. A5: The Jaguar Throne Stone that was set up at *Na-Ho-Kan* on the day of Creation.

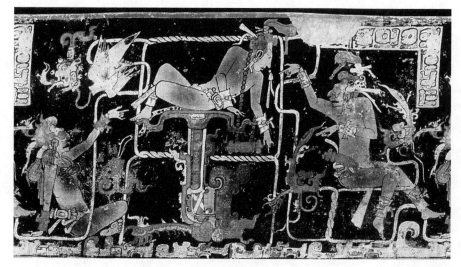

Fig. 6.13. A pot that shows the birth of a god at a place called *Na-Ho-Kan Witz Xaman,* "House Five Sky Mountain North."

location of the first stone of Creation and Itza power to have come into being at the beginning of Creation. No wonder the Lower Temple of the Jaguar opens out onto the largest public space in the city.

A6—THE INNER MURALS

We are lucky to have an extraordinary ceramic masterpiece (Fig. 6.13) that shows us how the Maya conceived of the place they called *Na-Ho-Kan.*[50] Located in the north sky, *Na-Ho-Kan* is a place of darkness because the sun had not yet appeared. Entwined serpents representing the *kuxan sum,* "the living cord," or umbilicus that ties together all of Creation undulate through the dark space as young deities recline on the mountain symbols in the position of transition from one status to another. Here the text says the event is birth, but the same reclining posture on the sarcophagus at Palenque signals death. In *Na-Ho-Kan,* it is both at the same time, for "to die" in one world is to be born into the other.

The same entwined serpents, the *kuxan sum,* flow through the mural on the inside of the Lower Temple, creating registers in which the Itza ancestors stand (Fig. 6.14). They are the *Ah Puh,* or "Toltecs"—the inventors of civilized life—standing at the moment of Creation in the place where the first throne stone was set up. The Chilam Balam of Chumayel also describes the founding of the Itza alliance by the heads of all the participating lineages at a city called *Ichkansiho.*[51] This is a reference to Tz'ibilchaltun, whose original name was Ichkantiho, "In the Sky at Five" (Fig. 6.15). According to the story, the founding lords, who came from all the groups, lineages, and families who formed the Itza, measured the land, and swept it clean. We think the inner mural of the Lower Temple of

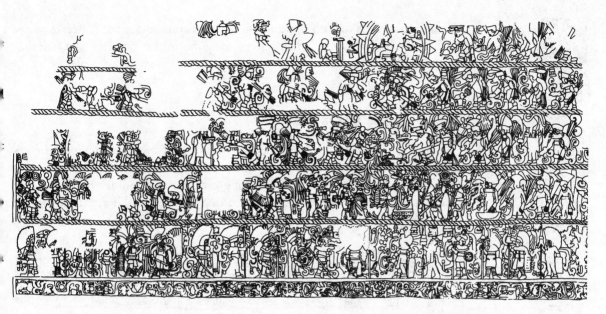

south wall   west wall

north wall   east wall

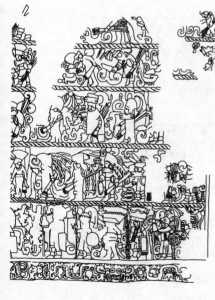

the entwined snakes
that separate the
registers of the mural

Fig. 6.14. A6:
The mural carved on
the interior walls of
the Lower Temple of
the Jaguar. The scene
shows the Itza ances-
tors at the time of
Creation and the

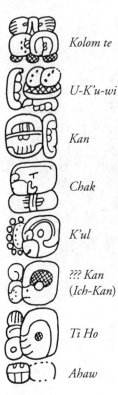

Kolom te

U-K'u-wi

Kan

Chak

K'ul

*??? Kan
(Ich-Kan)*

Ti Ho

Ahaw

Fig. 6.15. Text from Tz'ibilchaltun Stela 19 naming a lord as "Holy *Ich Kan Ti Ho* [In Heaven at Five] Lord." The founding assembly of Itza lords took place at Ichkantiho.

the Jaguar refers to both these occasions: the Creation event at *Na-Ho-Kan* and the founding events at Ichkantiho. The figures in the mural are the founding ancestors of the Itza.

A6—Basal Register

The artists affirmed the cosmic setting by filling the lower register with the Primordial Sea, represented as five great waterlily plants (Fig. 6.16). The two outer ones have fish nibbling waterlilies that grow from a personified mountain. The next inner pair have human figures cavorting among waterlilies emerging from a strange birdlike head, and the center one has the Maize God and waterlilies

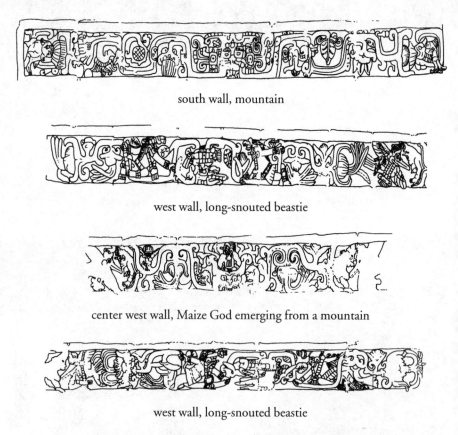

south wall, mountain

west wall, long-snouted beastie

center west wall, Maize God emerging from a mountain

west wall, long-snouted beastie

north wall, mountain

Fig. 6.16. The basal register showing waterlilies emerging from various sources.

coming forth from a mountain. Gods emerge from the end blossoms of the waterlily to play with hovering birds. Once again, the imagery asserts the context of Creation for the scenes above.

A6A: REGISTER A

The names of many of the figures in this mural appear next to their heads, although these name signs are not traditional Maya glyphs (Fig. 6.14). In fact, they are more like name signs used at Cacaxtla, El Tajín, Xochicalco, and Tula. They represent names as pictographs that could be read equally well in any language and by illiterate people. The utility of this kind of pictograph system to communicate in any language may explain why it occurs at so many sites throughout Mesoamerica exactly at this crucial time. The Itza, like their counterparts elsewhere, wanted everyone in Mesoamerica, Maya speakers and non-Maya speakers alike, to know who their founding ancestors were.[52]

All of the ancestral figures stand amid great flowery scrolls that may signal two things—that they are speaking,[53] and that great power emanates from their persons. The twenty-four people in Register A walk toward the center axis wearing what are, for the most part, traditional Maya costumes. Many of them wear masks, so that they either represent gods or they are humans in the guise of gods. Or just as likely, they are people parading after they had transformed into their *way*, or "spiritual companions." All twenty-four figures wear tied cloths around their lower legs.[54] As the two lines converge, the center figures look up toward the scene above them in the second register.

A6B—REGISTER B

The surviving figures in the second register parade toward the center carrying a variety of weapons: spearthrowers and clusters of lances, clubs, knives, and spears. Many wear mirrors on the backs and fronts of their belts in the form traditionally associated with the Toltecs.[55] Several of them wear moon-shaped nose ornaments, while others have "butterfly" pectorals. And as with the lower row of people, name signs float near their heads.

The central figures (Fig. 6.17) in this register are the critical ones because they performed a ritual that brought the Feathered Serpent into the service of the community. Let's look at the figures that flank this snake first. On the left of the snake scene stand two figures. The left one has long bejeweled hair tied by an *itz* headband made of jade. He carries a sacrificial knife and a large flapped bag as he follows a blowgun-wielding man wearing a back mirror. This second figure wears an elaborate turban with a snake tied to its front.

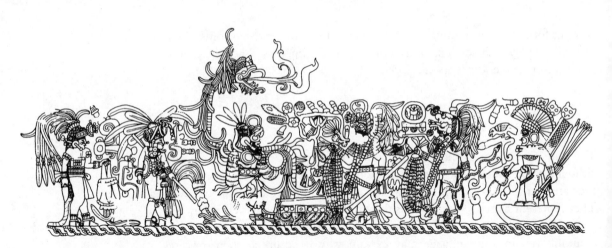

Fig. 6.17. A6B: Detail from Register B showing the arrival of the Feathered Serpent.

On the right, three figures march toward the central scene. The rightmost warrior stands in an object that looks like a huge bowl or a canoe. In front of him strides a pot-bellied old man, who may be either a Pawahtun or an Itzamna.[56] He and the figure in front of him wear knee-length jade necklaces, Maya hip cloths, and flower sprigs float in front of their faces. These vines may be the yellow-flowered *kokom* vine used to identify the Kokom[57] founders. Between them floats 6 Knot,[58] a day sign written in the system used at Xochicalco and Monte Alban. The rear man has a rattlesnake staff in his left hand, while his partner carries something that may be a blowgun. Both of them hold out large objects that may be canopies for palanquins[59] as they step toward a large opened bag lying on the ground. It has triangular flaps and a netlike pattern woven into the material.

The figure in front of this bag is the most important one in the scene. He wears the arm-padding of a ballplayer and a yoke around his waist. Curving rays of power spring from his body as he engages in the ritual. Most important, he carries a gold mirror in his hand that he may have taken from the bag. These mirrors were critically important to political office at Chich'en Itza. The Itza placed one inside the bench in the Temple of the Chak Mol and one on top of the jaguar throne that they sealed inside the Castillo-sub. Sacred objects since Olmec times, mirrors opened portals into the Otherworld through which ancestors and gods materialized themselves. They gave rulers the special vision of prophecy.[60]

Not only is this mirror-wielding person a ballplayer, but he also wears the personified wings of the *Itzam-Ye* bird around his mouth and rings around his eyes (Fig. 6.18). Objects exactly like these were dredged up from the great cenote. These golden face ornaments mark him as an Itzam, a sorcerer who penetrates the portal to the Otherworld with his mirror and in his role as ballplayer.

From behind this sorcerer ballplayer, a great feathered rattlesnake rises upward, crossing into the register above. "Feathered Serpent," or *K'uk'ulkan,* was the name of the famous hero/god of Yukatek myth. Here K'uk'ulkan is not a man, but the great rearing Vision Serpent he had always been for the Maya.[61]

Thus, this central figure wields a mirror that is an instrument to penetrate into the reality of the supernatural world. The result of his action was to materialize the serpent that was the conduit between worlds. Through this action, the ancestral ruler of Chich'en attained the capacity to call the Feathered Serpent and to communicate with the sacred world for his people.

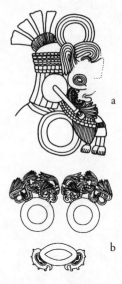

A6C—REGISTER C

The figures in the third register march toward the Feathered Serpent's head as it crosses the ground line at their feet (Fig. 6.19). Twenty of the figures survive—nine on the right and portions of eleven on the left. They bow from the waist as they near the serpent's head. Most of them are dressed in the "Toltec" mode, wearing belts and carrying shields, spearthrowers, and darts. Some wear cylindrical headdresses made from a mosaic of something like shell. The "pillbox" headdresses are the Chich'en versions of the drummajor headdress that was associated with warfare and the Tlaloc-Venus complex in the southern kingdoms. Many of the other figures in this register wear "butterfly" symbols on their chests and their headdresses. Person 17 wears eye-ring pieces and a mouth bar that resemble the ornaments worn at Copan by the founder of that lineage.[62] This fellow and his companions at Chich'en are also the founders of the Itza alliance.

Some of the processional figures are not warriors. A bent old man, perhaps a priest, strides along sixth to the left of the rising serpent head. He may represent a priest because he carries an offering bowl, as does the fourth man in front of him. That one also wields a snake-lashed bag along with a handful of spears. All of these people wear mosaic backshields, but the four people at the head of the line wear special headdresses composed of multiple racks of feathers over their

Fig. 6.18. Detail of Register D showing the mirror-wielding main character (a) wearing serpent-eye ornaments and wing-mouth ornaments. Identical gold objects (b) were recovered from the Sacred Cenote.

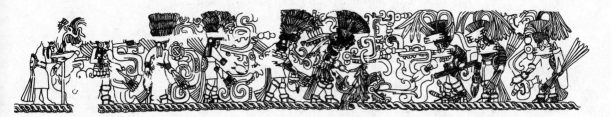

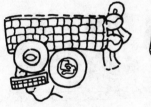

Fig. 6.19. A6C: Detail from Register C showing a serpent-skirted warrior with breasts honoring the Feathered Serpent. The heads (*below*) are details from another figure in this register and from a Copan incensario. Both heads wear eye rings (*ch'ok*) and a mouth ornament with teeth (*ko*).

drummajor-cotinga headdresses. This kind of warrior bonnet resembles head-dresses worn in battle scenes at Bonampak' and Yaxchilan. The kilts they wear also differ from those of the other warriors in this procession.

The man at the head of these four officials is the most important. He wears a mosaic headdress with a *yaxun,* "cotinga," attached, but the front surface rises into a triangular peak. This headdress was worn by Aztec emperors[63] and even today marks the K'iche' image of the king in the effigy known as the *Ah Itz.* This is the earliest-known example of this headdress in Mesoamerican history, so that the Aztec crown may well have its roots here.

But there is more. This figure also wears a skirt made of snakes and he has a woman's breasts. Linnea Wren[64] identified this odd cross-sexed person as the prototype of the Aztec *Cihuacoatl,* "Woman-Serpent," who was the war leader of Tenochtitlan and the second in command to the *Tlatoani,* or "speaker." The image also predicts *Coatlicue,* "Serpent-Skirt," who was the mother of Huitzilopochtli, the war god and patron of the Aztecs. In their founding myth, Coatlicue gave birth to Huitzilopochtli at Snake Mountain near Tollan.[65]

Interestingly, the image of a "serpent skirt" has important significance in Yukatek Maya quite apart from any of its meanings in the Aztec sources. *Kan* is "snake," "four," and "sky," so that the same icon could stand for any of those meanings. There were two words for skirt—*pik,* "skirt," and *puh,* "lap of a skirt" or "to carry in a skirt." *Pik* also meant "eight thousand," and it was used in some glyphic texts for "cycle bundle," so that *kan pik* could be "snake, four, or sky bundle." *Puh* was also the word for "cattail reed," so that *kan puh* could be the metaphor for "four tulans." The important thing is that "serpent skirt" was loaded in meaning for the Maya without external reference.

This register brings people wearing the symbolism of war and kingship into contact with the great Feathered Serpent that was generated in the register below. Here the founding ancestors participate in linking Chich'en Itza to its supernatural source of power in the Otherworld.

Fig. 6.20. A6D: Detail from Register D depicting the arrival of the Mosaic War Serpent.

A6D—REGISTER D

The fourth register is the first one to circle the entire room because it lies above the height of the doors (Figs. 6.14, 6.20). The procession that it features begins

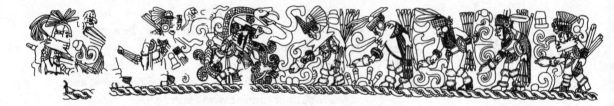

over the central door with a pair of back-to-back figures. Thirteen figures on each side dance around this register to meet in the center of the western, interior wall. The twenty-six dancers all wear the garb of "Toltec" warriors with back mirrors, spearthrowers, and lances. Many of them bend over in the posture of the dance.

The two leaders meet in the center above the Feathered Serpent scenes below. The man on the right wears the pointed headdress of rulers, but he bows toward the man in front of him, who carries weapons as he dances among the folds of a huge Mosaic Serpent. The Maya of the southern kingdoms and Teotihuacan used this serpent as an emblem of war.[66] Since this entire scene takes place at the moment of Creation in the place of *Na-Ho-Kan,* where the Jaguar Throne Stone was placed, we are seeing the great ancestral heroes and lineage founders of the Itza receiving their symbols and rituals of the state at the moment of Creation. This great War Serpent[67] documents the Itza right of conquest.

A6E—REGISTER E

In this register, yet another procession of warrior figures converge on a huge sun-mirror cartouche (Fig. 6.21). Inside, an ancestral figure with the square-nosed serpent in front of his face sits on the jaguar throne that the Paddler Gods set up at *Na-Ho-Kan.* Here is the ancestor who documents the Itza role as inheritors of the jaguar throne—the first stone laid in the Cosmic Hearth. And this ancestor wears the headband called *Sak Hunal,* the crown of Maya kings for over a thousand years before the artists of Chich'en carved this scene.

The cartouche around this glorious ancestor represents both the sun and a mirror like the ones worn by warriors and placed as offerings in the bench of the Temple of the Chak Mol and on the jaguar throne inside the Castillo-sub.[68] Just as important, these mosaic mirrors have square-nosed serpents in their corners like the ancestor-cartouches so prominent in the cities of the south. The Maya regularly marked these cartouches both as mirrors and as the sun, but they also showed their ancestors emerging from the center of the sun-mirrors to communicate with their descendants. Moreover, the kings of Tikal regularly wore them on the back of their belts,[69] as did the warriors of Teotihuacan. Here, the sun-mirror emits the first occupant of the jaguar throne—the original ancestor modeled from maize by the hands of Chak-Chel herself.[70]

Fig. 6.21. A6E: Detail from Register E depicting the sun-mirror cartouche and the occupant of the jaguar throne.

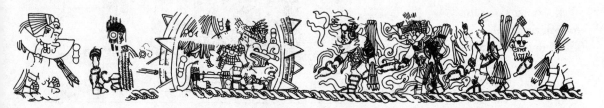

SUMMARY

The entire processional scene carved into the walls of the Lower Temple of the Jaguar documents the empowerment of the Itza at the moment of Creation. At the same time, it equates this narrative of Creation with the assembly of lords who met at Ichkantiho (Tz'ibilchaltun) to found the Itza alliance. At eye level, the first lord of the Itza draws out the Feathered Serpent, which was the conduit to ancestral time and space. By controlling it through ritual, the Itza bound the forces of Creation to their will. The War Serpent gave them the charter for making war and dominating their lands through the right of conquest. The sun-mirror portal documented their descent from the first human beings created by Chak-Chel and Pawahtun. The entire composition declared for all to see that the Itza descended from the *Ah Puh*, "People of the Reeds," who invented civilized life and the arts of war. Their right to conquest, their right to rule, and their identity as Itza were part of the fabric woven together by the midwife of Creation and her child, the Maize God, during the first moments of Creation.

Fig. 6.22. B: Reconstruction drawing of the Upper Temple of the Jaguar. The upper medallions represent "spear-shield" symbols of war, the middle register shows feathered serpents, and the lower band alternates shields and jaguars. Feathered serpents surround the base of the building and stand as columns in the middle of the door. Warriors taking blood from their genitals stand on both sides of the door, while other warrior images guard the inner sanctum. An offering table with fifteen figures supporting its carved top once sat in front of the door.

B—THE UPPER TEMPLE OF THE JAGUAR

This temple partners the Lower Temple we have just examined in a very special way (Fig. 6.22). The imagery on the outside depicts feathered serpents entwining around

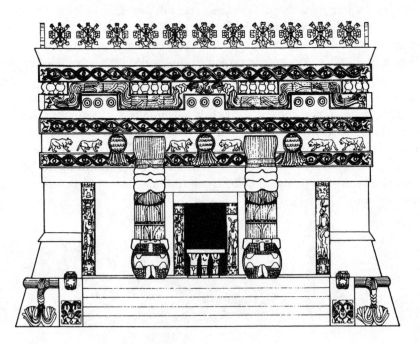

flowers, with jaguars prancing among shields. Parapet sculptures combining crossed spears and shields lined the upper edge of the roof. Called the *tok'-pakal*, "flint-shield," by the Maya, this emblem was a symbol of war. This great war temple and its pair, the Lower Temple of the Jaguar, replicate the imagery associated with the temple inside the Castillo. It, too, had prancing jaguars and shields on the entablature along with the twisted cords of the "sky umbilicus." The jaguar throne sitting between the columns of the Lower Temple of the Jaguar has its counterpart inside the Castillo-sub in the famous red jaguar throne found there by archaeologists. And a mosaic mirror lay on its seat, surmounted by three jade beads laid out in the form of the Cosmic Hearth. This is the mirror used to materialize the Feathered Serpent inside the Lower Temple. Thus, we think the combination of the Upper and Lower Temples of the Jaguar in the Great Ballcourt replaced the first Castillo when the Itza rebuilt the center of their capitol.

Feathered serpents crawl along the edge of the substructure of the Upper Temple and a great legged serpent stares out from the balustrades rising to the interior. Similar serpents frame the stairway rising up from the courtyard below. Huge descending feathered serpents (B1) serve as columns of the temple (Fig. 6.23). Like all the other descending serpents in the city, they represent the *kuxan sum*, the umbilicus cord that connected the Itza rulers to the heavenly source of their authority. Today, legends abound in Yukatan saying that this cord was cut by the Spaniards. The blood ran out and separated the Maya from their divine source of authority. Many believe that this cord lies coiled under the Great Ballcourt, waiting for the Maya to achieve sovereignty again. They say that when a Maya king once again sits on his throne, the umbilicus will unfold through a cavern leading to the great cenote, where it will rise and reattach the Maya to the *Sak Beh,* the Milky Way.

Fig. 6.23. B1: The Upper Temple of the Jaguar overlooks the playing alley.

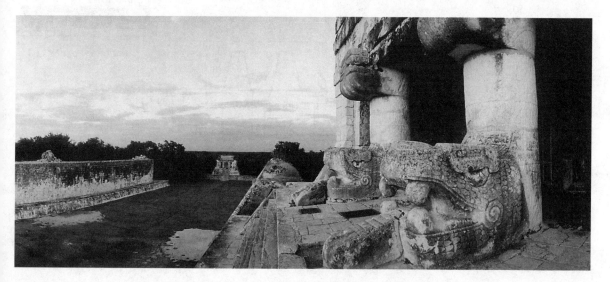

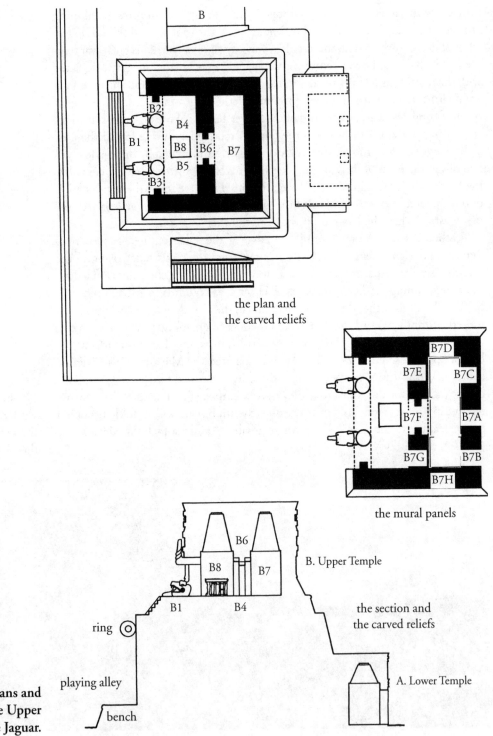

the plan and
the carved reliefs

the mural panels

B. Upper Temple

the section and
the carved reliefs

A. Lower Temple

ring

playing alley

bench

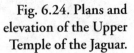

Fig. 6.24. Plans and
elevation of the Upper
Temple of the Jaguar.

The temple has two chambers—an outer one behind the serpent columns and an inner one (Fig. 6.24). The outset jambs leading into both of these chambers have figures carved onto their surfaces (B2, B3, B4, B5). The inner doorjambs had five figures wrapping around each side, although some of these and some of the outer ones have suffered erosion over the centuries.

THE DOORJAMBS

In each panel, a warrior figure stands between upper and lower registers that depict a strange creature wearing a flower headdress. We think the headdress refers to the nectar of flowers, *itz* in Yukatek and other Maya languages. Headdresses similar or identical to these were worn by kings, lords, and high-ranking women in the southern lowlands, although these headdresses often had three blossoms instead of one.[71] Hummingbirds could be shown hovering in front of the blossoms as they drank the nectar. *Itz* was also the word for "sorcerer" and very likely identifies all of these figures as Itza. Interestingly, similar headdresses occur on Teotihuacan figurines, especially female ones, after A.D. 450, although the contexts are not clear. At Chich'en, the head in these registers combines human features with a jaguar's teeth. We do not know what they were intended to represent.

Between these registers, Itza lords stand inside a thin framing band marked with jewels and flowers to identify the context as one filled with *k'ulel*, the sacredness that permeates the cosmos. They wear the garb of warriors and carry weapons consisting of spearthrowers, darts, fending sticks,[72] and bags. All wear sandals, knee bands, and defensive wrappings on their left arms. All have their genitals exposed and many have knots tied around their penises. These men are involved in bloodletting rites—perhaps in association with the making of war or with the commemoration of the ancestral history contained in this building. Let's look at how the individual figures differ from one another.

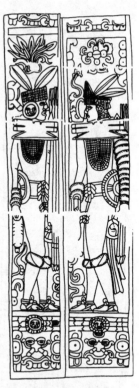

Fig. 6.25. B2: Foldout of two of the three panels of the outer doorjamb on the north side.

B2—THE NORTH OUTER JAMBS

The three figures on the north jamb (two are illustrated in Fig. 6.25) wear bib collars consisting of small cylindrical beads, probably made of jade. They all have "butterfly" pectorals on their chests and they wear drummajor headdresses with huge feathers attached to the tops. The center figure has the peaked form of this mosaic headdress, like the man who confronts the war serpent in Register D of the Lower Temple. The two outer figures have large round earflares with a human face carved in their centers, while the middle person wears a rectangular ear panel displaying a Tlaloc head surmounted by a snake head. Iconic signs name all three figures. The first name consists of a large plant with long flowers,

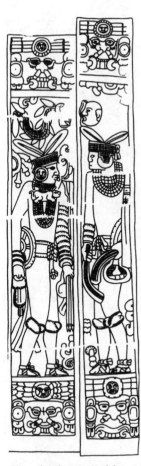

Fig. 6.26. B3: Foldout of two of the three panels of the outer doorjamb on the south side.

while the middle name is a four-part flower blossom. The third name sign depicting the top view of a frog also occurs with Person A7 in the Lower Temple. If these are personal names, then we have the same person appearing in both scenes, but if these are lineage names, as Cynthia Kristen-Graham has suggested, then we have members of the same lineage acting in both contexts.

B3—THE SOUTH OUTER JAMBS

The warriors on the south outer jambs carry bags as well as their other weapons, and Person 3 has two fending sticks instead of lances (Fig. 6.26). For their name signs, the inner person has a jaguar, the middle one has a mosaic plant (or perhaps a snake), and the outer one has a human head, The inner and middle warriors wear jaguar pectorals hanging from their collars.[73] A Chak Mol figure found in the ballcourt, and now in the museum at Tz'ibilchaltun, also wears this jaguar pectoral (Fig. 6.40).

B4-B5—THE INNER DOORJAMBS

The inner doors have five figures stepping around their inset forms, giving ten panels in total, although the name signs of three pairs of these people repeat (Fig. 6.27, Fig. 6.28). Persons 1 and 6 are Flower-Flint; Persons 2 and 9 are Snake; and Persons 5 and 10 have two feathers (each with the phonetic value *o*). These may represent duplicated portraits of the same people, or different people who were members of the same lineage. The remaining four figures have different names, with Person 4 repeating the same rodent name sign as two people in Register E of the Lower Temple. Once again, either the same people or members of the same lineage were depicted in both the Upper and Lower Temples.

We also have variations in the necklaces, including bib collars, "butterfly" pectorals, flint knives, and another jaguar pendant. Earflares include both the round forms and a type with bars thrust through the lobes. The scrolls in front of their mouths show at least six of these fellows singing or speaking as they participate in this bloodletting ritual.

B6—THE WOODEN LINTEL

The wooden lintel spanning the inner door is original and still has relief visible on all three sides (Fig. 6.29). The sculptors carved essentially the same image on each surface, although part of the underside rests on the doorjambs. The ancestor of the jaguar throne sits inside his sun/mirror/ancestor cartouche. He wears the *Sak*

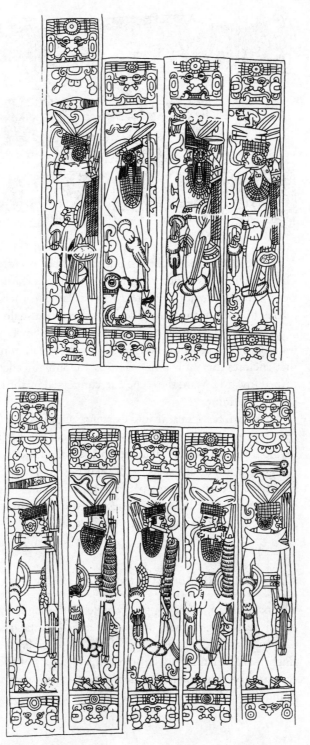

Fig. 6.27. B4: Foldout of four of the five panels of the inner doorjamb on the north side.

Fig. 6.28. B5: Foldout of the inner doorjamb on the south side.

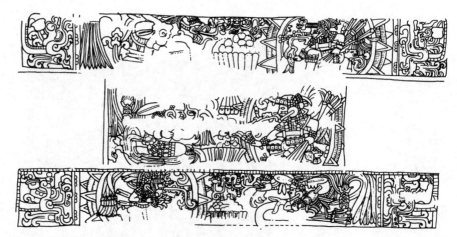

Fig. 6.29. B6: The
wooden lintel over the
door to the inner sanc-
tum of the Upper
Temple of the Jaguar
showing the ancestral
ruler on a jaguar
throne with a com-
panion lord entwined
in a feathered serpent.

Hunal headband, bar nose ornament, and bar pectoral typical of Maya rulers. Opposite him sits another figure entwined in a feathered serpent. This person wears the drummajor headdress with its large feathers, while he has a net skirt made of beads on the underside. This skirt was usually worn by the Maize God.

In the space between them sits an offering bowl with tamales. Above them waterlilies emerge from the eyes of a strange head hung from the serpent frame that encloses the entire scene. This is a Double-headed Serpent with each head turned inward toward the scene and connected by the body that forms the upper part of the frame.

These two beings came into existence at *Na-Ho-Kan,* where the gods ordered the cosmos, stretched out the sky umbilicus, and connected the Itza to their divine source of power. Here they protect the inner sanctum of the temple and charge this important space with their power. The warriors outside have taken blood from their penises, perhaps to materialize these beings and to act as guardians for what lies inside. These are the two principal figures depicted in the *Na-Ho-Kan* procession in the Lower Temple.

B7—THE MURAL PAINTING

The back room of the Upper Temple of the Jaguar was covered with a set of murals recording the wars of conquest that gave the Itza their right to rule. These paintings are badly damaged now and impossible to see, but an extraordinary English artist named Adela Breton made copies of them in the late nineteenth century. Today her paintings are the best way to study the imagery of these great founding wars.

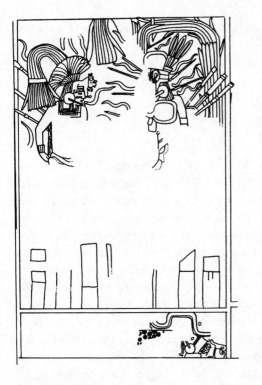

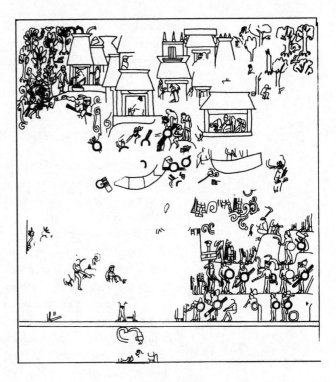

B7A—East Wall, Central Panel

This central panel (Fig. 6.30) faces the door and thus received the most light, especially during the sunset hours around August 13, the day of Creation when the Maize God was reborn, the first hearth was laid, and the crack in the back of the Cosmic Turtle was opened. The middle door of the Upper Temple of the Jaguar faces 285 degrees,[74] the position of the sun at sunset on that day. This means that on the day of Creation, and for several days on either side of it, the light of the setting sun illuminated this panel.

On the right of the panel in the Upper Temple is the mirror-wielding actor who is in the Lower Temple. The feathered serpent arches above him as he wears his mirrors on his chest and helmet, and the yellow color tells us they are gold disks like those dredged from the cenote. The gold feathered serpents of his eye ornaments are visible, so that we assume he also wore the mouth ornament. He holds lances as he sits or stands on top of a scaffold structure.

The scaffold opposite him supports the figure who sits in the sun-mirror in the Lower Temple. Here we find out that his hair is yellow, a sign the Aztecs used to mark the Sun God. This identification is also possible here, but the imagery has more affinities with the Maya Maize Gods and their sons the Hero Twins. The yellow hair may just as well refer to corn silk. Be he Sun God or Maize God, he wears elaborate jade jewelry made in the traditional Maya forms and a *Sak*

Fig. 6.30. B7A: The central panel of the east wall shows the mirror-wielding lord with his feathered serpent facing a companion.

Fig. 6.31. B7B: The southeast panel shows the prelude to battle.

Hunal, the god of the royal headband, tied to the front of his head. He is the first occupant of the jaguar throne and founding ancestor of the Itza. Below the two ancestral figures lies a fragmentary figure wearing a jade shirt. Here almost all the details have been lost, but we shall see this figure again over the west door.

B7B—The Southeast Panel

The narrative sequence[75] appears to begin in this panel because it is the only one that does not show active combat (Fig. 6.31). The scene was already badly damaged when the drawing was made, but we can see a town amid a forest at the top. Animals of various types fill the forest as the townspeople go about their business. The hilly landscape in this scene suggests that it does not represent the area around Chich'en Itza. It could represent a town in the Puuk region, but since there are canoes in the scene, it is more likely someplace in the southern lowlands.

On the left edge of the town walk two warriors, one wearing a Venus sign and the other wearing a drummajor helmet with three feathers above. They appear to be moving into the town, but not in battle. The area below the canoes also shows many warriors, but none of them are engaged in battle. They carry weapons and banners around small thatched houses and more hills. This entire scene seems to show a peaceful town before the battles of conquest begin. Whether these are the Itza before their migrations or the people the Itza conquered, we do not know, but the tropical forest and the hills suggest this scene depicts a location to the south.

B7C—The Northeast Panel

This panel begins the battle sequence (Fig. 6.32). The surviving parts show one group defending the summits of red hills against another group of attackers. The leaders of the aggressors flank the scene, with one emerging from a white Vision Serpent on the left. Of the one on the right, only fragments of a green Feathered Serpent survive.

Once again we cannot know for sure where these red hills were, but the likely candidate is the Puuk hills in Yukatan to the west of Chich'en Itza. If so, this scene may represent an Itza attack against one of the Puuk states, perhaps in concert with the Tutul Xiw lords of Uxmal.[76]

B7D—The North Panel

In this scene, the battle intensifies and takes on supernatural properties (Fig. 6.33). The sun-mirror hangs above the center of the battle, although its ancestral

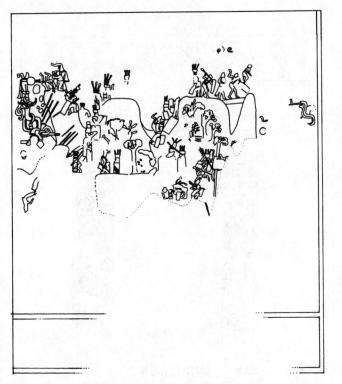

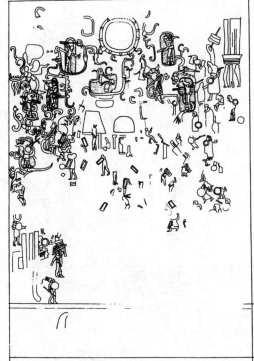

Fig. 6.32. B7C: The northeast panel (*top left*) shows a battle among red hills.

Fig. 6.33. B7D: The north panel shows a battle among a town of thatched-roof buildings.

figure has been totally destroyed. To the left, a warrior floats in the sky,[77] while other supernatural fighters emerge from portals surrounded by Vision Serpents of various types. Below them a mighty battle rages among the houses of a town. Some warriors wave giant banners as their fellows clash around them. One army carries blue-bordered square shields, while their opponents wield red-bordered round ones. Naked prisoners enter from the upper right, controlled by leaders of the round-shield fighters. Presumably the round-shield people are the attackers.

B7E—THE NORTHWEST PANEL

This scene (Fig. 6.34) shows an attack against a town fortified by a low red wall[78] much like those surrounding various precincts at Chich'en, the center of Ek' Balam, Uxmal, and Mayapan. They did not work very well, because the blue-painted attackers have penetrated into the town and are taking captives. The sun-mirror cartouche floats to the left of the scene, complete with the corner serpents used with the ancestor cartouches in the southern kingdoms. To its left floats a Venus warrior, anticipating a similar pair in the battle scene on the south wall. The lower part of the scene depicts a large open field where the victors line up naked captives who will soon meet their fate.

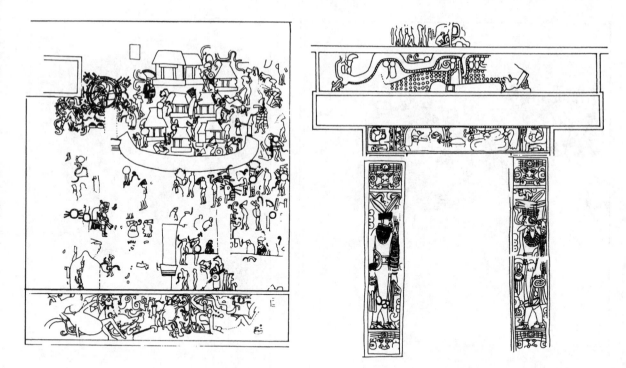

B7F—The West Central Panel and Door

Fig. 6.34. B7E:
The northwest panel
(*top left*) shows a bat-
tle at a walled town.

Fig. 6.35. B7F:
The west central
panel shows the
sacrificed Maize God
and the analogous
human sacrifice.

The imagery around and above the west door counterpoints the focal panel on the east wall (Fig. 6.35). The door itself is framed by the images of standing warriors that we discussed in B4 and B5. The wooden lintel (B6) above the door depicts the Sun-Mirror and the Feathered-Serpent ancestors flanking a waterlily monster and a bowl of tamales. The same beings fill the east panel opposite the door.

Above these ancestral figures lies the jade-clothed figure whose fragmentary remains also filled the lower register of the east panel across the room. On this side, we can see it is a reclining figure who has a pair of snakes emerging from the center of his belly. He is the sacrificed Maize God,[79] whose death and resurrection led to the Fourth Creation in which we live. On the eastern wall, he lies under the feet of the primordial ancestors, while he reclines above them over the west doorway.

Above the image of divine sacrifice sits the depiction of its analog in the human world. Immediately above the cleft in the Maize God's belly, a black-painted priest cuts open a victim's belly to remove his heart in the analog of the Maize God's death. Four assistants hold the victim's feet while a great Feathered Serpent rears up behind the priest. The snake has the same energy streamers as the mirror-wielding ancestor who first materialized it at *Na-Ho-Kan*. Other participants in the ritual stand to the right of the sacrifice, while to the left, warriors bring bound captives toward a large cluster of battle standards. In the scene

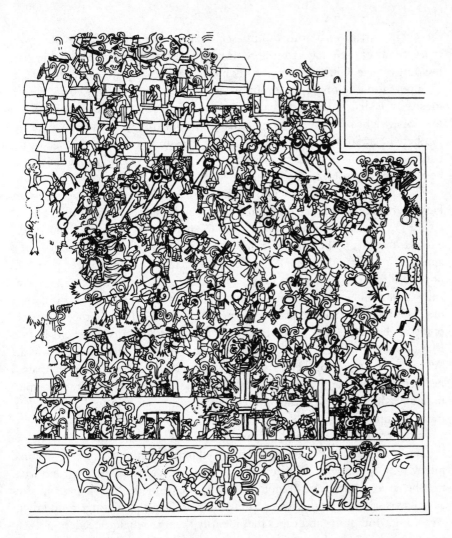

Fig. 6.36. B7G: The southwest panel shows a battle in front of a town.

above the sacrifice, we see a set of warriors converging on the Feathered Serpents. Above this stately procession, other warriors cavort either in dance or in battle.

B7G—THE SOUTHWEST PANEL

This extremely complicated scene (Fig. 6.36) depicts a battle showing clusters of warriors running toward one another with their spearthrowers cocked. Lances fly through the air in a confused tangle of engagement. At the top, supernatural warriors materialize above a town composed of *xanil na,* "thatched houses." Women and men sit in houses or walk among them with a few warriors who appear to be defenders. At the very bottom of the scene, other people, mostly dressed in warrior garb or that of priests, sit around or within houses of various types. Many of them have conical roofs in contrast to the forms of the domestic buildings above. Clusters of men flank braziers and engage in banner rituals.

Supernatural actors appear in this scene in profusion. The Sun-Mirror Ancestor sits immediately above the banners of the lower scene and above the town in the upper right corner. A serpent warrior without the energy streamers of the Feathered-Serpent Ancestor cavorts among trees in the center left edge of the battle scene, while another similar figure sits in the lower right-hand corner as he tends a brazier or offering bowl.

The Feathered-Serpent Ancestor with his energy streamers also appears twice. He materializes with his snake from a red portal in the center right of the battle scene. He carries a shield with half-moon shapes like those depicted in the entablatures of this building. Behind him the Mosaic-Serpent Ancestor, who appeared in Register D of the Lower Temple, emerges from another red portal. In both contexts, the serpent has scrolls appended to its body, but here the snake's color is white, suggesting that its identification as a "cloud serpent" is the correct one.[80] Feather and cloud serpents entwine as the sky umbilicus on the balustrades of the High Priest's Grave, so that the pairing is one that occurs elsewhere. In fact, Maya artists associated Vision Serpents of various types, including the Mosaic War Serpent of the southern kingdoms, with cloud imagery. Here the paired Feathered Serpent and Cloud Serpent enter the battle as if they are the supernatural leaders of the attacking hordes. They confirm supernatural participation in Itza conquest.

In the bottom of the scene, the other Feathered-Serpent Ancestor sits below the sun-mirror symbol in a position that well may pair him with it. He sits on a pillow, gesturing toward a cluster of battle banners, a bowl of offering, and what may be either a bundle or his gold mirror. Battle banners of all shapes and sizes as well as small huts fill this lower band. Some of the people sitting around them wear long white skirts and capes that identify them as religious leaders and secondary nobles.[81] These are the leaders of the army and its religious officials, who are involved in rituals either before or after the battle.

The lowest register again confirms the supernatural character of these events. As on the north side of the door, two Pawahtuns, the patron gods of the Itza, sit on either side of a Vision Serpent, holding up the scene of battle. An ancestor emerges from the serpent's open mouth, as waterlily stems and flowers meander through the background space.

B7H—THE SOUTH PANEL

The last image also depicts an assault against a town, but this time, the attackers use scaffolds and climb logs to get at the defenders (Fig. 6.37). The town build-

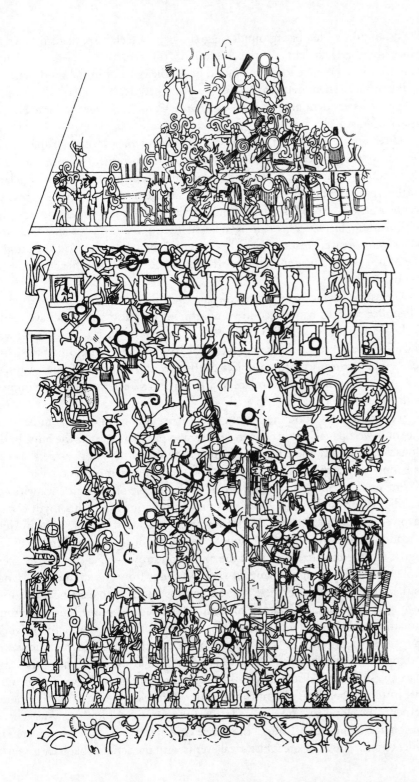

Fig. 6.37. B7H: The south panel shows a battle with scaffolds and battle banners.

ings stand on a blue background, suggesting the attack took place near water. Since there are no lakes in the interior of Yukatan, this is clearly not near Chich'en Itza. Possible locations would be on the coast or in the south, but one of the primary enemies opposing the Itza was Koba. It has two large lakes in the center of its residential and ceremonial area. Perhaps this scene represents an attack against Koba.

Three supernatural warriors float over the town, and other supernatural beings dot the landscape. On the left side, a feathered-serpent warrior and a red-snake warrior emerge from red portals, presumably as patrons for the attackers. In the upper right corner below the village sits the Sun-Mirror Ancestor with a Venus warrior next to him. The Venus warrior sits in a red serpent ornamented with feather clusters. This pairing suggests that our sun-mirror and feathered-snake warriors were associated with Venus and the sun as the twin offspring of the Maize Gods. The panel to the left of this one holds the other image of the Venus warrior.

The scaffolds also have feathered-snake warriors in their top compartments. The taller scaffold had a second compartment that also seems to have held a snake-warrior, but it is mostly eroded now. The last of the feathered-snake warriors sits on a throne in front of a hut in the band along the bottom of the battle scene. He gestures toward an object on the ground in front of him. A flower ornament hangs in front of his face, marking the red background as one imbued with sacred power.

Secondary lords sit on the ground or on benches in front of other huts. As on the southwest panel, battle banners of several types stand next to the huts. In the Bonampak' murals, these kinds of banners go into battle, but they were also set in banner stones that the Maya placed in front of their temples and palaces.

The myth of Snake Mountain provided the people of Mesoamerica with the paradigms for establishing kingdoms and conducting war. This myth always involved a migration that led the people into new lands, which they take by right of conquest and the will of the gods. The murals of the Upper Temple of the Jaguar recorded the Itza version of the migration story—which, as we have seen, probably related the movements of various groups from the southern lowlands to the north. Once there, these migrant groups joined with existing kingdoms, such as Ichkantiho and Itzamal, to form a new confederation. This new group took the name the migrants had brought with them from the southern lowlands: they called themselves the Itza. The murals document these Itza migrations and the conquests that they saw as legitimizing their right to rule.[82] The murals also place the supernatural actors from the Creation scenes of the Lower Temple into this historical context. The mirror-wielding lord who conjured the Feathered Serpent, the cloud-serpent war leader, and the sun-mirror lord punctuate these great battle scenes. The death of the Maize God appears twice in the sequence in order to associate these great historical events with the actions that were essential precursors to Creation itself. The death of the Maize God as shown in these murals also generated the archetype for death by sacrifice.

B8—THE ATLANTEAN ALTAR

Augustus Le Plongeon, an eccentric early explorer, photographed an altar in the shape of a square table mounted on fifteen Atlantean figures set in three rows of five.[83] Fortunately, the English artist Adela Breton recorded all of the legs and the carved tabletop in watercolor drawings in 1902. Shortly after her visit to the site, archaeologists moved the legs to Mexico City. Today some of them can be seen in the Museum of Anthropology.

This table sat in the outer chamber in front of the door that leads into the inner sanctum (Fig. 6.38). Priests probably used it to hold braziers and food offerings for the ceremonies that took place in the temple. The top of the table depicted warrior-ballplayers entwined with a Feathered and Mosaic Serpent.

The table legs represent fifteen men wearing elaborate costume (Fig. 6.39). Almost all of them wear "pillbox" or "drummajor" headdresses, although the detail in material and design varies from figure to figure. Persons 1 and 10 have peaks on their headdresses, while Person 7 wears one made of beautiful white feathers. Person 6 has large rings mounted on his hat, and Person 8 wears only a headband, with his hair tied up in a scalp lock with feathers attached. They all wear large round ear ornaments and different kinds of nose and face jewelry. The pectorals vary also with bibs of several types, including a jaguar, "butterfly" plaques, a mirror, crossed bands of cloth, and complex assemblages of bars. They also wear a variety of belts, hip cloths, knee ornaments, and sandals. Finally,

Fig. 6.38. B8: The Atlantean altar in front of the door leading into the inner room of the Upper Temple of the Jaguar, and the image on the top of the table.

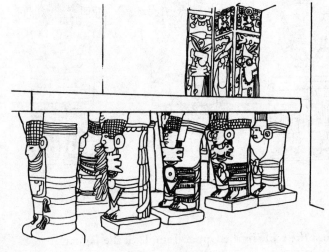
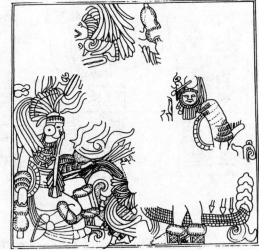

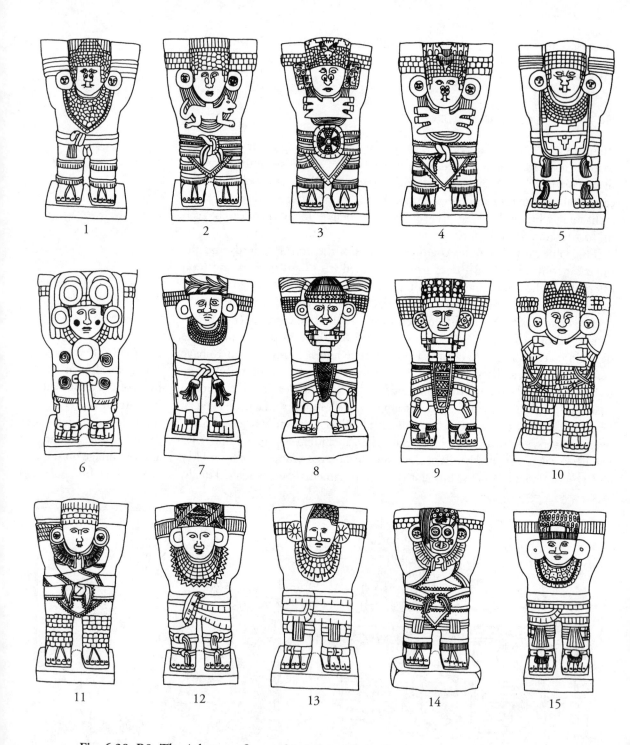

Fig. 6.39. B8: The Atlantean figures from the table in the Upper Temple of the Jaguar.

fourteen of them wear capes made of long flowing feathers, while the cape of one consists of richly patterned cloth. The Maya painted each sculpture with naturalistic color reflecting the materials used in the costume.

We do not know the meanings of these different face and body decorations, but we have the distinct impression we are looking at uniforms. Mesoamerican history describes the ritual of nose piercing and the awarding of nose ornaments as the signs of particular ranks and offices. Moreover, headdresses and other items of clothing clearly show rank and ritual context in Maya art from the Late Preclassic period and after. We suspect these fifteen figures represent a set of specific offices and ritual functions in the Itza state. In fact, the Maya artists of many sites personified parts of buildings as people holding up the roof. They called this kind of Atlantean image a *bakab*. Most *bakab* images from the southern lowlands represented the old god Pawahtun, but the word *bakab* also means "representative" and "agent," as well as "Atlantean." The Itza apparently used the meanings of "representative" to enlarge this category to include the office-holders who were part of the council that ruled their kingdom.[84]

C—THE SOUTH TEMPLE

This colonnaded building merges with the south boundary wall of the playing field, but the two stairs leading up to it are outside the ballcourt (Fig. 6.40). The single interior room was once vaulted, and six square columns and seven door-

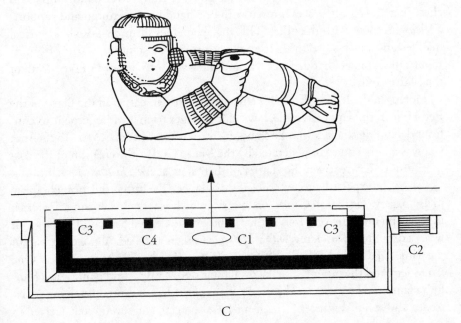

Fig. 6.40. C: The South Temple and its relief panels; C1: the Chak Mol from the South Building.

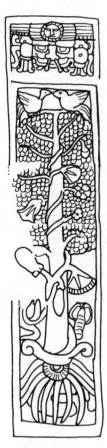

Fig. 6.41. C2: A balustrade from the South Temple.

ways formed its northern wall. We do not know the function of the building, but long, single-roomed buildings with nine doorways occupy the southern side of twin-pyramid complexes at Tikal. We suspect the South Temple may reflect that earlier tradition.

C1—This Chak Mol figure apparently sat in the center of the south building looking out between the piers onto the ballcourt.[85] The statue represents a ballplayer lying on his hip, with his legs drawn up toward his body. His upper body rises on an elbow as he holds a cup in both hands at his waist. He wears a band around his long hair and the three black-tipped feathers of a warrior on the top of his head. His left arm and right forearm have the wrapped padding that was worn by both soldiers and ballplayers. The small jaguar on his neck collar identifies him with several of the figures on the doorjambs and Leg 2 of the table that once sat in the front chamber of of the Upper Temple of the Jaguar. This Chak Mol may represent an office-holder of particular importance to the ballgame and a ritual in which he makes or receives an offering.

C2—Only the balustrades of the east stairs have been restored, but we can deduce that the west stairs had identical features. The eastern balustrades depict the World Tree with a vine climbing up the trunk into its branches (Fig. 6.41). The upper register contains the same flower-headed *itza* symbol that we saw on the doorjambs of the Upper Temple. Mounting the stairs to the South Temple is analogous to climbing the Tree at the center of the world.

C3—The inside surface of the two end walls are carved with a critically important image relating to war. The jade-skirted Maize God who lies in sacrificial death in the Upper Temple of the Jaguar sits with his knees drawn up to his chest (Fig. 6.42). He braces himself with one hand on the ground and supports a Vision Serpent with the other. This snake emerges from his nose like a visual manifestation of his breath. It rises upward to emit a standing warrior from its mouth in an image that declares war and the warrior to be born of the breath of the Maize God.

Moreover, the Itza depicted this emergent warrior in battle. In the Battle of the Red Hills in the Upper Temple, a warrior emerges from a white serpent to confront defending soldiers who pitch boulders down on their attackers. To the Itza, war was a holy endeavor generated by the Maize God at the creation of the cosmos, just as they received the charter of their state at *Na-Ho-Kan* (Ichkantiho).

C4—Of the partially reconstructed carved piers, the fifth is the most complete in its imagery (Fig. 6.43). Carved on four sides, each pier depicts warriors with back mirrors and butterfly pectorals as they stand on the Legged Serpent. Each warrior wears a drummajor headdress with three large feathers attached. Above the hats float the names of each individual, although only two of the names have survived. One is a rodent and the other is a snake over a star sign. This second name reads Kan-Ek', a famous name associated with the kings of the Itza of central Peten in the sixteenth and seventeenth centuries. Kan-Ek' also occurs on several stela erected in

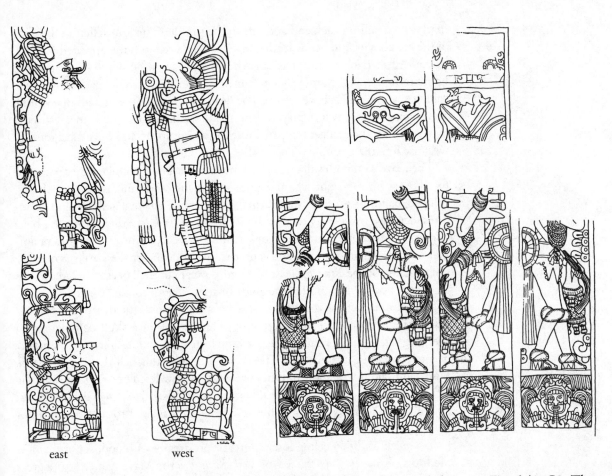

east   west

central Peten during the tenth century, including one of Wat'ul's stelae at Seibal. The presence of Kan-Ek', "Serpent-Star," here in Chich'en strengthens the connection between the Itza of Chich'en Itza and their cousins to the south.

Each figure strides forward with one of his hands on his shoulder as he holds a fending stick and a bag in the other. This bag is the same as the one that lies open next to the Feathered Serpent and the Mirror-wielding Lord in the Lower Temple of the Jaguar. Here a warrior carries the bag that the Mirror Lord used in conjuring up the Feathered Serpent at the time of Creation. The sacred objects used and received at Creation now function as part of the political symbolism of Chich'en's ballcourt.

D—THE BENCH PANELS

Instead of using three round floor markers, the Itza set pairs of reliefs on the benches of their ballcourt corresponding to the positions of the traditional

Fig. 6.42. C3: The panels on the end walls of the South Temple (*top left*). Both depict a warrior emerging from a Vision Serpent that materializes the breath of the Maize God.

Fig. 6.43. C4: A foldout of pier 5 in the South Temple. The second figure is Kan-Ek'.

markers—a pair on each end and one in the middle. The four reliefs at the ends of the benches unfold below feathered serpents carved into the upper edge of the bench. All six panels repeat basically the same scene, although details vary from figure to figure. For example, some panels have eleven players in addition to the captains, while others have twelve. The headdresses and other details of costume also change from player to player, although the variation conforms to a restricted pattern. Since the east central panel is the most complete and the easiest to read, we'll use it as the example (Fig. 6.44).

The players on both sides wear back mirrors with long feathers, knee pads and foot covers on the right leg, and knee ornaments and sandals on the left leg. Fringed padding protects their arms, while their personal jewelry and headdresses change from individual to individual. The *hachas* in their protective belts also vary individually, and they hold hand stones carved into the effigies of animals. As they march toward the center scene, vine and snake scrolls symbolize their singing or speaking. At least two figures wear cut shell pectorals and one has a crescent nose ornament like the gold crescents that decorated shields.

The central scene is the critical one, because it shows the decapitation sacrifice at the heart of ballgame mythology. The image of a skull complete with speaking scrolls and a head fringe marking him as a *way*, or "spirit companion," decorates the huge center ball. The Popol Vuh gave this ball the name "White Flint" and said it was made of flint covered with powdered bone. To the left, the victorious player wears an *itz* headband around his jade-spangled hair. In his right hand, he wields the large flint knife that he has used to sever the head of his opponent.

The neck of the kneeling loser spurts seven streams of blood, six of them in the form of snakes. "Six snake," or *Wak-Kan*, was the Maya name for the great Tree at the center of the world. The Maize God raised this tree as the north-south Milky Way after his resurrection in the Cosmic Hearth of Orion. The seventh and central spurt represents this tree, but in the form of a squash vine like those held by the emerging Maize Gods in the Lower Temple of the Jaguar. Here, blossoms, buds, and the mature fruit hang from the vine, materialized through the death of the Maize-God ballplayer.

E—THE BALLCOURT RINGS

Feathered serpents entwine their way around the ballcourt rings, turning the rings into portals penetrating into the Otherworld (Fig. 6.45). Human eyes look out from between the bodies, so that the rings become "seeing" instruments like mirrors and battle banners. A ring found outside the ballcourt shows these feathered serpents swimming through the fish of the Primordial Sea in an image that evokes the Temple of the Feathered Serpent at Teotihuacan and the Platform of

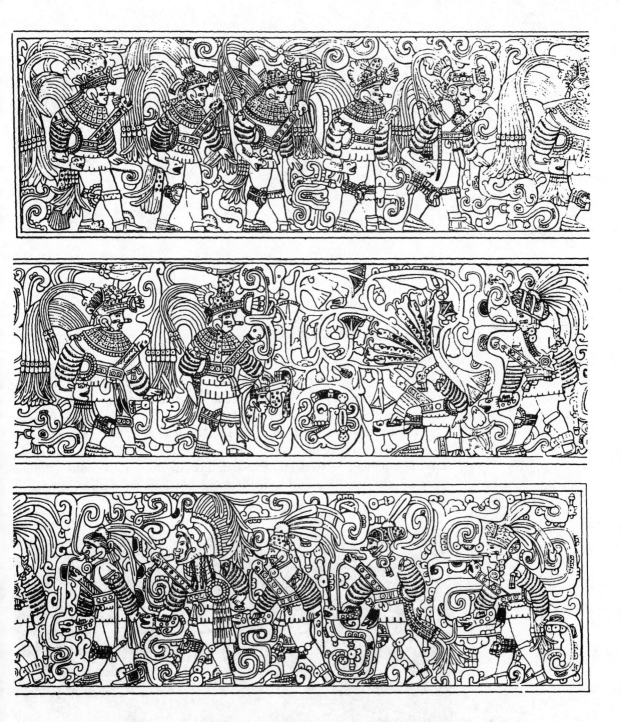

Fig. 6.44. D: The east central panel of the ballcourt, showing the sacrifice of the loser and the eruption of the World Vine from his bleeding neck.

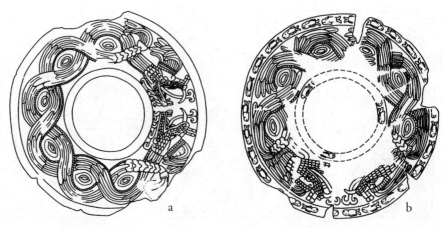

Fig. 6.45. E: The ballcourt rings show entwined feathered serpents with eyes to see into the Otherworld; (a) west ring, (b) back side ring.

a

b

Venus at Chich'en. The player who got the ball through one of these rings sent it into the Otherworld.

F—The North Temple

This little temple sits above the containing wall on the north end of the playing field (Fig. 6.46). As with the South Temple, the balustrades of the stairs (F1) that lead up to the temple both from the containing wall and from the tiny courtyard behind depict the vine-entwined World Tree (Fig. 6.47). Butterflies and birds cavort among the stems and branches. The North Temple, like the South Temple, sits at the center of the cosmos at the crack in the back of the Cosmic Turtle and the Mountain of Creation. Two round columns break the front wall into three doorways leading into a single-chambered interior. Intricately detailed reliefs cover all of the walls from floor to capstone.

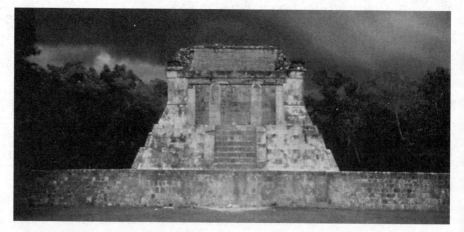

Fig. 6.46. F: The North Temple of the Great Ballcourt.

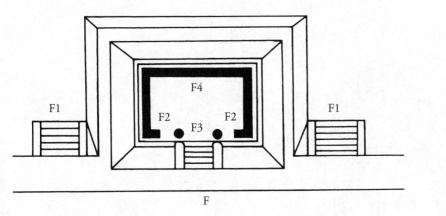

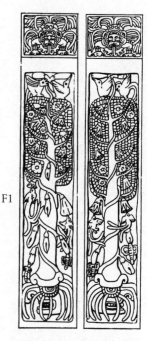

Fig. 6.47. Plan of the North Temple and (F1) the balustrades used with all the stairways.

F2—THE DOORJAMBS

The jambs of the two outer doors (Fig. 6.48) depict warriors, with the same person apparently repeated on the east and west jambs. Although they are not dressed as ballplayers, they do wear the same headdress as some of the ballplayers in the six ballgame panels. All of them grip long staffs that appear to be blowguns, so that they may be hunters more than warriors. They stand on a lower register filled with the same long-toothed head used with the warrior figures of the Upper Temple of the Jaguar. Instead of the *itz* headband, however, this North Temple version has long bejeweled hair tied on top of its head. This hairstyle appears on the ballplayers also, and was favored by warriors, perhaps to taunt those who hoped to capture them. Perhaps these heads represent trophies from ballgame sacrifices.

F3—THE ROUND COLUMNS

The two columns[86] pull together much of the iconography from other ballcourt buildings (Fig. 6.49). The lower register depicts two jade-shirted Maize Gods lying down head to head. They lean back on one elbow, while holding up a serpent body with their free hand. The serpent emerges from their torsos as a symbolic reference to the umbilical cord and to intestines from sacrificial rites. The serpent bodies terminate in heads pierced by flint knives. These reclining Maize Gods and those on the walls of the South Temple have their heads and knees raised in a position recalling the famous Chak Mol figures. The context here identifies this posture with the sacrifice of the Maize God in the ballgame, so that the Chak Mol figures must also represent sacrificial victims who replaced the Maize God in public ritual.[87]

The scene above includes the same squash vine that emerges from the necks of the sacrificed ballplayers, from the ends of the Maize God's turtle carapace,

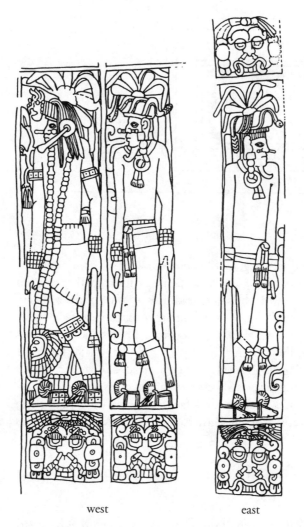

Fig. 6.48. F2: The reliefs from the doorjambs of the North Temple. Each door had three panels, but several of them are now very eroded.

west   east

and that entwines the World Trees of the North and South Temple balustrades. Here the vine issues from a personified root mass and twists in lattice fashion around a column. At the top, the two vines interlace to surround the column. This is the squash vine brought into juxtaposition with the forms of the human-made city. These columns join the imagery of Creation and Origins to the living space constructed by the Itza in their capital.

On both columns, two figures stand between the vine lattices, one holding a blowgun and the other a head-down rattlesnake. Both wear beaded necklaces that fall to their knees. The blowgunner wears a *Sak Hunal* headband and a cluster of feathers on the crown of his head. The snake-spear person wears a fan of feathers and has the glyph "Five Knot" in front of his face. Since each figure wears the same headdress, and since "Five Knot" also occurs with the same figure

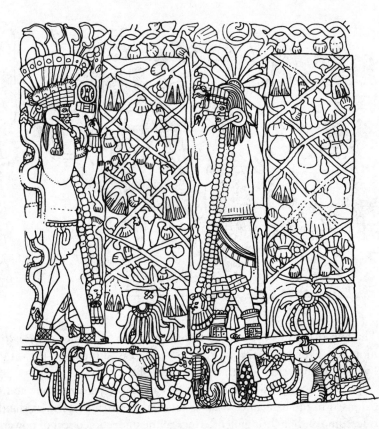

Fig. 6.49. F3:
The west column in
the doorway of the
North Temple.

on both columns, we think only two people are depicted. The second of the two carries a "reptile eye" glyph on both columns.

The Five-Knot[88] name recalls the Six-Knot person from Register B of the Lower Temple of the Jaguar (Fig. 6.50). There, too, we have two persons wearing knee-length necklaces, with one carrying a blowgun and pellet bag while the other wields a rattlesnake staff. In fact, these are the same person, even though the number in his name glyph varies. In the Lower Temple, these two persons carry large bags to the Mirror-wielding Lord who conjured the Feathered Serpent. Here, these two assistants stand between the squash-vine lattices. Perhaps the bags they bring to the Mirror Lord in the Lower Temple contain the seeds of the squash and maize associated with the rebirth of the Maize God.

F4—THE INNER MURAL

The walls of the inner chamber document the accession rituals of Chich'en Itza in the context of the ballgame (Fig. 6.51).[89] The main scene of accession was carved on the north wall of the chamber immediately opposite the central door.

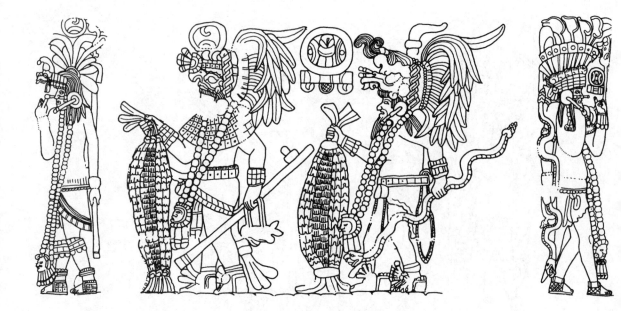

Fig. 6.50. The figures
from the columns of
the North Temple
(outside figures) and
from Register C of the
Lower Temple of the
Jaguar (inside figures).

The lowest register depicts the sacrificed Maize God once again with the flint-mouthed serpents emerging from his belly. Pawahtuns, the patron gods of the Itza, sit among waterlilies that fill the rest of the register.

Just above the Maize God's belly sits an empty jaguar throne and the rubber ball used in the ballgame. Warriors and other ritual performers stand on either side, some of them bringing offerings to the unoccupied seat of power. They sing toward the throne.

The middle register of the scene depicts the council lords of Chich'en Itza flanking a central pair of figures. The principal lord wears the jade shirt of the Maize God as he takes the primary office of the city. The great Feathered Serpent that we saw in the Lower Temple of the Jaguar rears up in front of him aided by a squatting lord or priest. The upper register brings the city's warriors parading toward two central images hovering above the jade-shirted lord. One is the Sun-Mirror Ancestor seated on the jaguar throne and the other is the Mosaic Serpent of War. Both these beings came into existence at *Na-Ho-Kan* in the first moments of Creation. Now they hover above the accession scene to vest their supernatural power in the lords who rule the city and fulfill the role of the Maize God.

This great accession scene flows out to both side walls in imagery that links the political power of the city to the ballgame. The lower left corner depicts bird dancers wearing beaked masks, wings, and tail feathers. Exactly this kind of figure served as Atlantean legs for the bench from the High Priest's Grave, and such bird dancers appear in sacrifice scenes on the gold disks from the cenote.[90] In the North Temple, the dance moves onto the west wall, where one of the dancers kneels next to a tree with a dog and offering plate nearby. Next to them dance three other people, one dressed in a dog costume known as *Sak-Ox-Ok,* "White-Three-Dog." Other scenes on the west wall depict both birds and bird dancers, and in the upper center a person carries a large ball toward a bird impersonator. Finally, at the very summit of the wall, a turban-dressed lord addresses a tree with a bat hovering on its trunk. We do not understand all of the scenes, but presume that they detail preparatory rituals and dances for both the ballgame and the rites of accession.

The narrative sequence apparently moves to the two registers above the north wall. We do not understand them all, but they include in the upper register from left to right: a penis perforation ceremony using one of the phallic stones that are known from several Yukatekan sites; a ritual with dogs; a nose-piercing ceremony[91]; and several rituals involving houses, a bundled corpse, and a tree. The lower of the two registers includes a ritual with birds and a water tank; a vomit ritual; a steam bath rite; and a series of interactions with trees and houses. Blow-gunners kneel and aim at the birds in the trees. This blowgun scene evokes an episode in the Popol Vuh myth of Creation.

The narrative continues onto the east wall with scenes from the ballgame. At the top, snake ribbons of blood spurt from the decapitated ballplayer. Below him are other scenes with groups of figures, trees, and, in the lower right corner, a ritual with a corpse.

G—PUTTING CHICH'EN ITZA AND ITS GREAT BALLCOURT IN CONTEXT

Like some of the other buildings we have visited in this book, our feelings about Chich'en Itza and its Great Ballcourt have changed over the years. When we first visited the site, Chich'en was full of Toltecs—warlike invaders from a foreign land who had forced the gentle Maya into the ways of war and imperial politics. Over the years, the continuing decipherment of the ancient histories changed the image of the Classic Maya from peaceful corn farmers into people who engaged in power politics and conducted war with the best of them. Most of the "Toltec" traits that earlier scholars had identified at Chich'en appeared in the art of the southern Maya kingdoms by A.D. 400. As we learned more about the history and imagery of the Classic period, we realized that we did not have to evoke foreign invaders to explain what we were seeing on the walls of Chich'en Itza. We could see that the people of Chich'en were deliberately appropriating style and images from other areas of Mesoamerica, but the way they used those appropriated images was purely Maya. The artists of Chich'en Itza, like those of Seibal, engaged in a bravura performance of innovation and subtle variation on the ancient themes of Creation and Origins that had shaped Maya art for a thousand years.

Using architecture and imagery, these artists combined narratives from Maya Creation with the origin myths associated with Snake Mountain, where gods were born and war began, and with the "Place of Reeds," where human beings first invented civilized life. The Castillo with its serpent balustrades and columns was Snake Mountain. The Sacred Cenote penetrated through the surface of the earth to the water of the Primordial Sea. Cattail reeds grew around the edges of the cenote. The ballcourt was the crack in Sustenance Mountain through which the Itza contacted the forces of the Otherworld. Creation was the subject of the Lower Temple of the Jaguar. The Itza combined Creation imagery with the founding of their confederation and the charter of royal power received by their ancestors—who were the inhabitants of the Place of Reeds—*Tollan* in Nahuatl and *Puh* in Maya.

The Upper Temple of the Jaguar documents auto-sacrificial rites by the leaders of the Itza, and the wars of conquest that gave them the right to rule. The South Temple depicts the founding lineages, including Kan-Ek', carrying bags associated with the conjuring of the Feathered Serpent. The side walls attest that war came from the jade-shirted Maize God.

The panels in the alley of the ballcourt document the death of the Maize God as a ballplayer during the Third Creation. His death led to the birth of the Hero

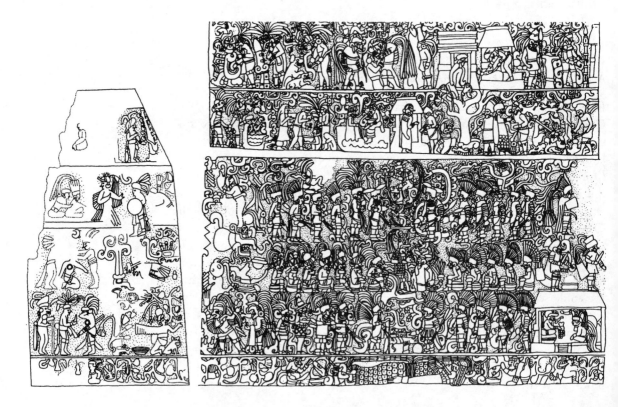

Twins, the defeat of the denizens of Xibalba, the resurrection of the Maize God, the inception of the Fourth Creation, the generation of humanity, and finally the establishment of the Itza state. The orderly transfer of authority within that state is the subject of the North Temple and its imagery. These extraordinary narratives of the Great Ballcourt lie at the heart of everything that was Itza.

However, these programs of authority also deliberately reached out beyond the Maya world to embrace the rest of Mesoamerica and to create a truly cosmopolitan style. The Itza used day signs from Xochicalco and chose to name the participants in the narrative scenes within the Great Ballcourt with pictorial signs that can be read in any language. They brought in gold from Central America, obsidian from all over western Mesoamerica, and turquoise from the American Southwest. They collected jade from all over the southern lowlands to throw as offerings into the Sacred Cenote. By combining the old, the new, and the appropriated, the Itza generated a new way of expressing the charter of governance that made sense in the languages of all Mesoamerica, not just those of the Maya.

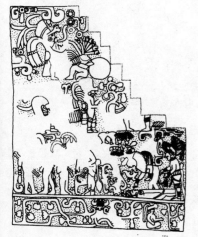

Fig. 6.51. F4: The mural in the North Temple, showing the accession of the Itza ruler framed by the activities of the ballgame and the office of ruler.

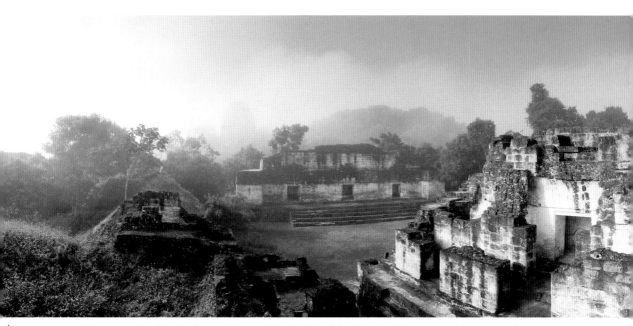

1   Early morning in the Central Acropolis at Tikal with Maler's Palace across the courtyard.

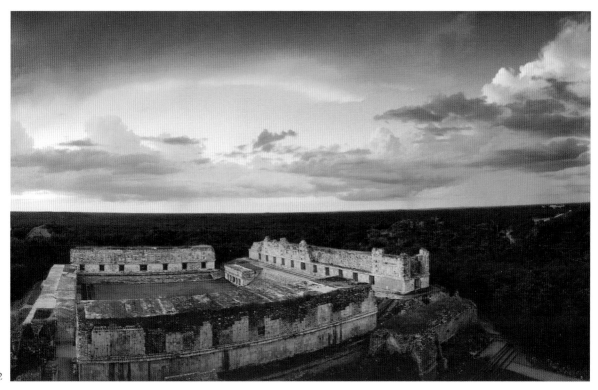

Sunset at Uxmal looking across the Nunnery Quadrangle.

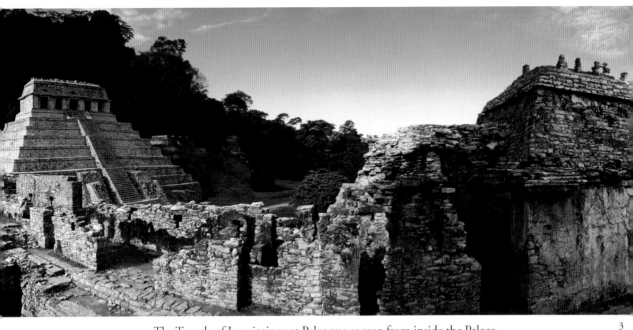

The Temple of Inscriptions at Palenque as seen from inside the Palace.

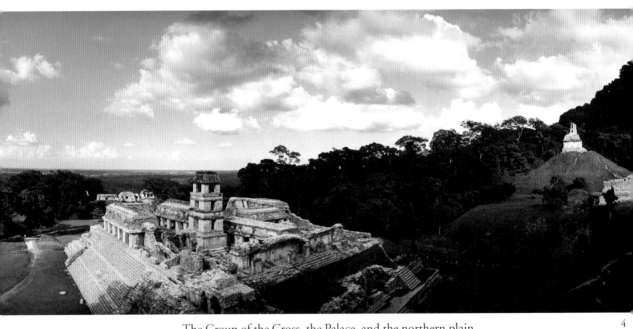

The Group of the Cross, the Palace, and the northern plain
at Palenque as seen from the Temple of Inscriptions.

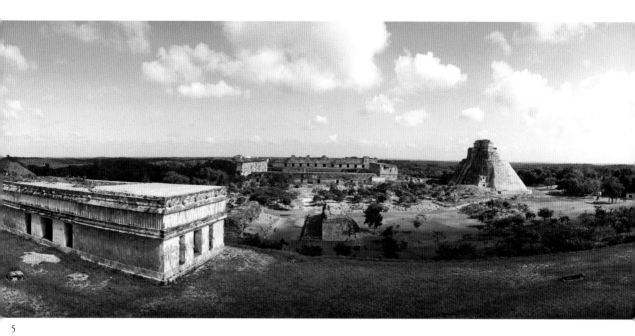

5

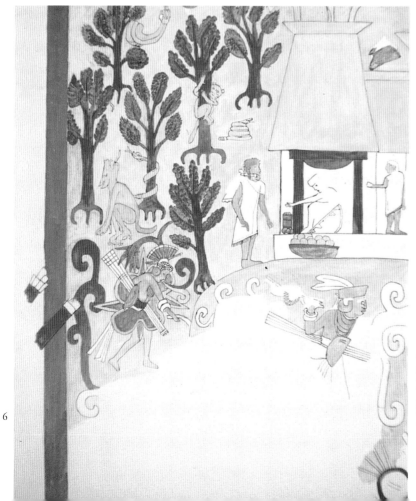

6

The House of the Turtles,
the ballcourt, the Nunnery
Quadrangle, and the Pyramid
of the Magician at Uxmal.

Animals in the forest, houses,
and a star warrior from Adela
Breton's watercolor of the southeast
panel in the Upper Temple of the
Jaguar at Chich'en Itza.

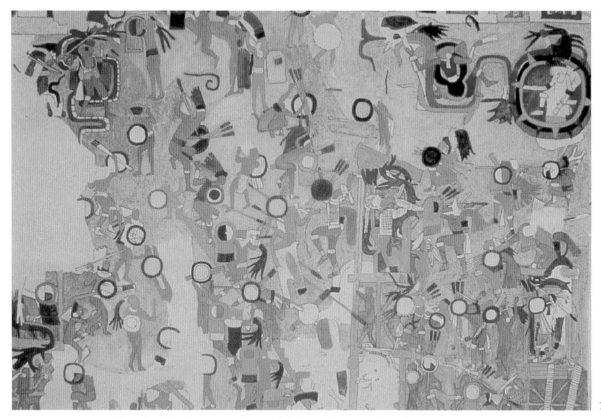

Detail of the battle scene from Adela Breton's watercolor of the south panel
in the Upper Temple of the Jaguar at Chich'en Itza.

7

The head of a Pawahtun from Temple 11 at Copan.

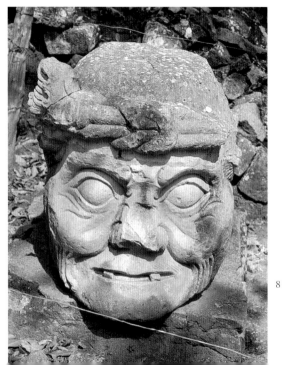

8

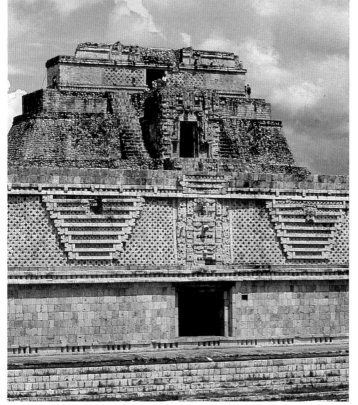

The East Building of the Nunnery Quadrangle with the Pyramid of the Magician behind it at Uxmal.

Warriors and court officials bringing tribute to a noble.

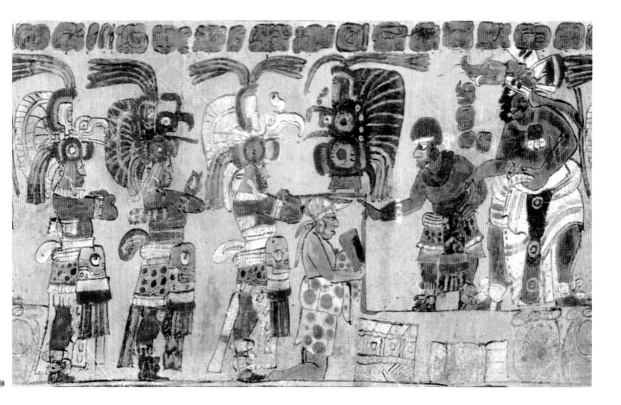

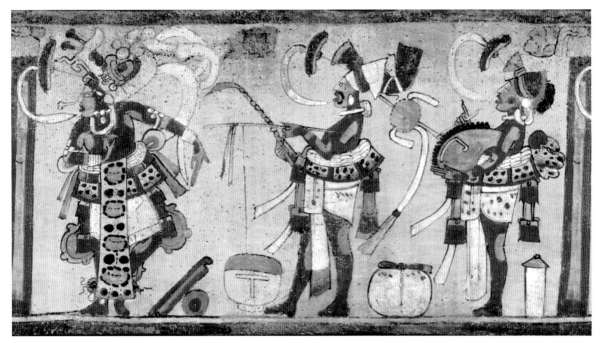

Dance with drums, string instrument, and conch trumpet.

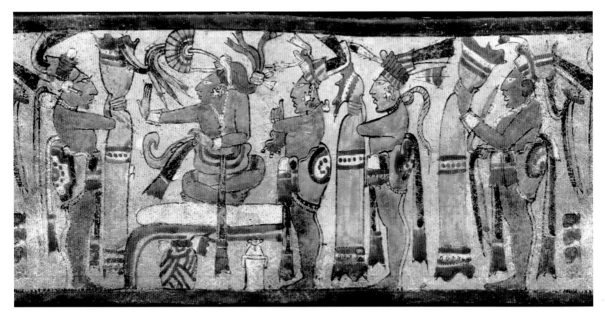

Court scene with officials presenting cloth.

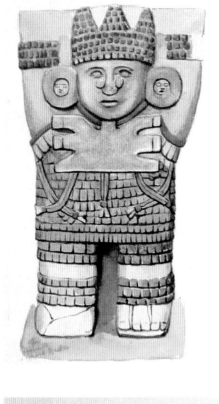
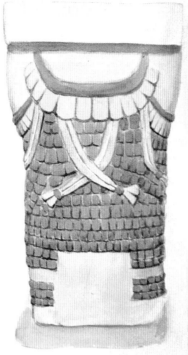

Adela Breton's paintings of Atlantean figure 10 from the table inside the Upper Temple of the Jaguar at Chich'en Itza.

Adela Breton's paintings of Atlantean figure 2 from the table inside the Upper Temple of the Jaguar at Chich'en Itza.

3

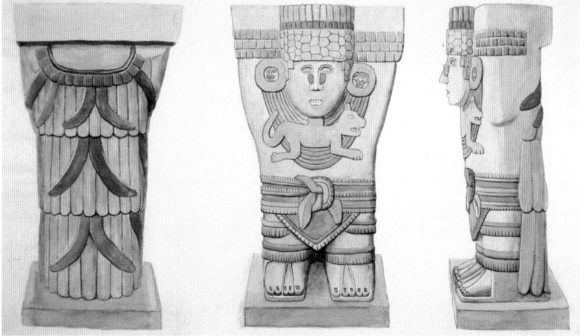

4

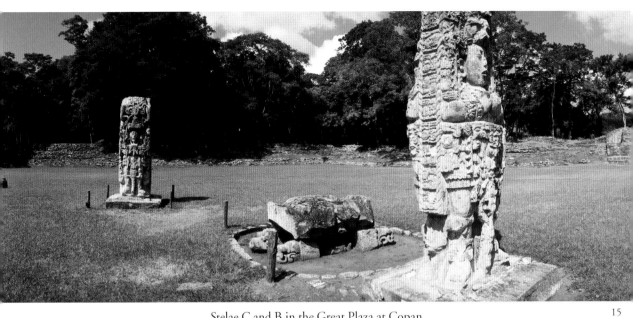

Stelae C and B in the Great Plaza at Copan. 15

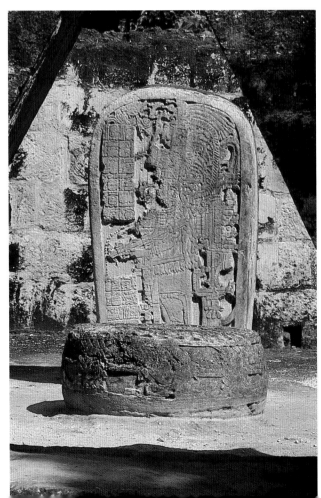

Tikal Stela 22 inside its walled enclosure.
Altar 10 is in front of the stela. 16

CHAPTER 7

Uxmal: The Nunnery Quadrangle of Chan-Chak-K'ak'nal-Ahaw

Uxmal is the most famous and best known of the cities that grace the region of Yukatan known as the Puuk, the Yukatek Maya word for "hills." On their northern edge, these hills rise dramatically several hundred feet above the limestone shelf of Yukatan. A low forest carpets the rolling landscape of this hill country, where the seasons make for vivid contrasts in color. During the wet season (June through December), the forest is a lush green, while in the dry season it is the color of bone. This region was settled late in Maya history, largely because it has almost no surface water. The ancient Maya built cisterns, called *chultun,* to collect rain water when they lived in these ruined cities. Even today, villages are few and far between, leaving the land mostly to the old ruined cities. When approached through this forested landscape, Uxmal appears without warning, gleaming like a jewel among the green hills, red soil, and white limestone outcrops of the surrounding area. The mosaic facades of Uxmal's famous architecture play with the light and shadow of the tropical sun in ways that have won the admiration of visitors from around the world.

Traditionally, scholars have translated the word *uxmal* as "three times," supposedly referring to its having been "thrice built."[1] On a 1557 map of the province of Mani, the name Uxmal appears with a rectangle that most likely represents the Nunnery Quadrangle (Fig. 7.1). Diego Lopez de Cogolludo, a seventeenth-century Spanish chronicler, named some of its buildings, including the Nunnery, so that Uxmal has figured prominently in European ideas about the Maya from the very beginning of contact between the two worlds. Archaeologists date Uxmal and the Puuk region to the Terminal Classic period, roughly A.D. 800–1000. This was a period of great change in Mesoamerica, when most of the cities of the lowland forests to the south were in decline or abandoned.

A wall surrounded the central part of the city, including all of the major buildings and mounds now visible at the site (Fig. 7.2). The wall may have been defensive, but it also served to separate the sacred and royal zone of the city from

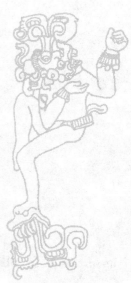

Fig. 7.1. Uxmal on the
1557 map from Mani.

the surrounding residential areas. The sacred precinct includes platforms, buildings, courtyards, and plazas combined into interrelated groups with different
functions and ritual associations. At the same time, the builders integrated these
discrete groups into a greater whole by means of vistas, lines of sight, controlled
access, imagery, and the repetition of pattern and design.

THE HISTORY OF THE TUTUL XIW AND THE BUILDING OF UXMAL

Scholars have always seen Uxmal as the apogee of Puuk-style art and architecture
and of Maya accomplishment in northern Yukatan. According to the traditional
interpretation of Yukatek history, Uxmal and its neighboring cities existed
between A.D. 700 and 1000, and an aggressive group of "Toltec-Maya" from
Chich'en Itza attacked and destroyed the peaceful Maya states of Puuk. As we
have seen, many archaeologists and epigraphers now question this scenario. New
interpretations of the ceramics of Yukatan as well as radiocarbon dates support
the idea that Chich'en was contemporary with Uxmal and other sites in the
Puuk region.

In addition, the Books of Chilam Balam give us information on the later

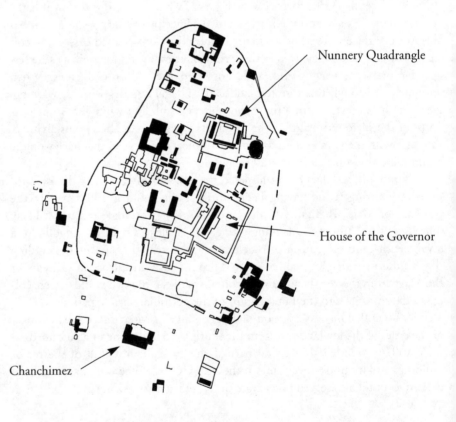

Nunnery Quadrangle

House of the Governor

Chanchimez

Fig. 7.2. Uxmal and
its surrounding wall.

rulers of Uxmal as well as on the Itza of Chich'en. According to these chronicles,[2] the migrations of the Itza and the Tutul Xiw, who were the rulers of Uxmal, to northern Yukatan began in k'atun 8 Ahaw (672–692). A group of the Tutul Xiw led by Ah-Kuy-Tok'-Tutul-Xiw established themselves at Uxmal and reigned from k'atun 2 Ahaw (9.16.0.0.0, or 751) through k'atun 10 Ahaw (10.5.0.0.0, or 928). Interestingly, archaeologists[3] now place the beginning of the Puuk polities to the middle of the eighth century.

Ah-Kuy-Tok' means "he of the owl-flint." The combination of an owl with a shield and *atlatl* spears occurs in association with the Tikal-Waxaktun war as a title and symbol of warfare. It served the same function at Teotihuacan. Later Maya inscriptions and images converted this combination to a flint blade, *tok'*, over a shield, *pakal*, to form the Maya symbol of war, *tok'-pakal*. Moreover, *ah kuy* or *kuy* means "warrior" in the Telchaquillo dialect of Yukatek.[4] Ah-Kuy-Tok'-Tutul-Xiw apparently was a warrior and perhaps a conqueror.

Forty years later in k'atun 11 Ahaw, ending on 9.18.0.0.0, the Itza organized a founding assembly at Ichkantiho, the Classic-period name for Tz'ibilchaltun.[5] Among the group there were lords from Mutul (the Classic-period name for Tikal), Chich'en Itza, Tz'ibilchaltun, Itzamal, a place called Chable, and other unidentified places. The chronicle also says that "the Xiw might have been there also." While this text seems less than sure, the inscriptions at Uxmal are clear. The Hieroglyphic Step from the Chanchimez Group at Uxmal refers to the famous K'ak'upakal of Chich'en Itza. The stones in this step are out of order; nevertheless, we can recognize his name and a title sequence, *bate ch'ak hol*, that is common in names at Chich'en.[6] Although the context is unclear, the text names the contemporary ruler of Chich'en in an Uxmal inscription. We think the rulers of Uxmal were allies of the Itza.

The Chilam Balams chronicle another event in which the Tutul Xiw, the group traditionally identified as the rulers of Uxmal, left a place called *Nonowal ti Chik'in Suywa*, usually identified with Tabasco and the lower drainage of the Usumacinta. Their leaders were Holon-Chan-Tepew, who was probably their king, and Ah-Mek'at-Tutul-Xiw, who may have been one of his chiefs.[7] The Tutul Xiw people[8] migrated for eighty-one years until 9.16.1.0.0, when they reached a region called *Chaknabiton*. We suspect this was the region around Xkalumk'in in central Campeche. They reigned there for ninety-nine years, and then they moved to Uxmal. That places their arrival at Uxmal in the k'atun-ending on 10.1.0.0.0, or A.D. 849. We presume they joined with their cousins who had arrived at Uxmal a hundred years earlier.

To judge from his architecture and inscriptions, Chan-Chak-K'ak'nal-Ahaw must have been one of the most successful of the Uxmal rulers. On Stelae 11 and 14, he is portrayed in a war costume that has affinities to those worn by warrior kings in the murals of Bonampak', the relief narratives of Chich'en Itza, and very late monuments from central Peten, especially at Jimbal and Ucanal. The key to this imagery may be at Mulchik, a site near Uxmal, where murals depict warriors wearing the same costumes attacking and conquering people who were subsequently sacrificed by hanging or stoning. Because there are glyphic texts in the murals, they must be from the Classic period. In fact, Walters and Kowalski[9] have proposed that they record a battle perhaps led by Chan-Chak-K'ak'nal-Ahaw himself as part of his establishment of a regional state headed by Uxmal.

Chan-Chak-K'ak'nal-Ahaw was one of the greatest patrons of architecture in Maya history. Three of the most important buildings at Uxmal have been attributed to his reign—the House of the Governor, the Ballcourt, and the Nunnery Quadrangle. Archaeologists, architects, and tourists all agree that these buildings represent the most refined and beautiful expressions of Maya architecture ever built.

THE NUNNERY QUADRANGLE

The central complex at Uxmal includes the Nunnery Quadrangle (Fig. 7.3), the Court of the Birds (Fig. 7.4), the Pyramid of the Magician (known locally as the *Adivino*) (Fig. 7.5), and the Ballcourt. Today the modern tourist path leads past the northern side of the *Adivino* toward a back entrance to the Quadrangle. However, the formal entrance lies in its southern building. To reach that entrance, visitors must skirt the south side of the *Adivino* and its associated court. Heading toward the ballcourt, they parallel the platform base of the Quadrangle until arriving at the formal stairway on the south side that leads to the interior. The builders marked this ceremonial entrance with a towering corbeled arch that funneled elaborate processions into the courtyard (Fig. 7.6). It acts as a huge frame

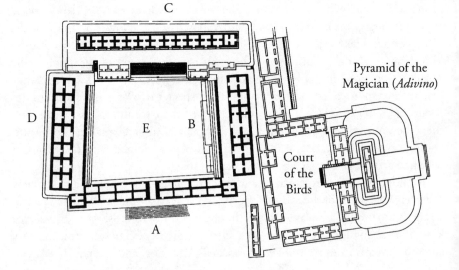

Fig. 7.3. Map of the Nunnery Quadrangle with the Court of the Birds, the Pyramid of the Magician. Today visitors can enter the Quadrangle from the northeast corner, the southeast corner, or through the ceremonial entrance in the middle of the South Building.

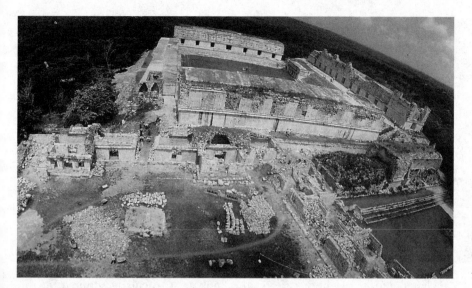

Fig. 7.4. The Nunnery Quadrangle with the Court of the Birds in the foreground.

focusing on the North Building of the Quadrangle from the outside looking in, and on the House of the Governor from the inside looking out.

The four buildings of the Quadrangle (Fig. 7.7) stand on different levels and vary in form and design. Yet all blend harmoniously into a whole, forming one of the most beautiful architectural complexes ever produced. The South Building with its nine doorways stands at the lowest level of the four. The East Building with its five doorways has a low platform raising it to an intermediate level, quite a bit lower than the imposing North Building with its eleven doorways. Two small buildings sitting on the court floor flank the massive stairway that leads from the court up to the North Building. The West Building stands at the same level as the East Building, and has seven doorways.

Fig. 7.5. The East Building with the Pyramid of the Magician in the distance.

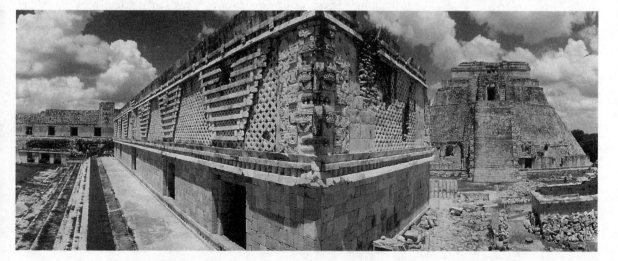

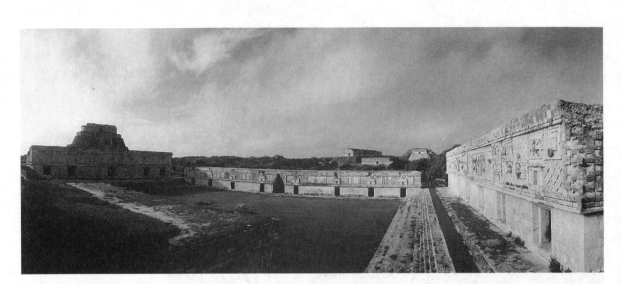

Fig. 7.6. A view over the South Building toward the House of the Governor.

Uxmal and its neighbor cities in the Puuk are particularly admired for the beauty of their architecture (Fig. 7.8). The hallmark of the Puuk architectural style is the richly ornamented mosaic stonework that commonly surrounds the upper facades or entablatures of the structures. Builders assembled these mosaics using stones carved in low relief to create complex compositions of images and patterns. The bright tropical sun playing on these facades creates symphonies of light and shadow that have inspired modern architects like Frank Lloyd Wright. For the ancient Maya, these extraordinary sculptural passages were not just decoration; they transformed the buildings into sacred spaces that were the habitations of gods, supernatural beings of all sorts, ancestors, and kings. They also identified and labeled the buildings so that from afar people could understand their function in both the political and spiritual life of the city.

The Quadrangle is especially noted for the way Chan-Chak-K'ak'nal-Ahaw integrated its levels and building lines. This coordination of scale and architectural detailing included not only the internal views, but also the vista over the South Building toward the House of the Governor and the House of the Turtles, and over the East Building toward the Pyramid of the Magician.

A—THE SOUTH BUILDING

The ceremonial entrance to the Quadrangle bifurcates the South Building, placing four doors and their attendant mosaic imagery on each side of the arch (Fig. 7.9). There are eight doors on each side of the building, each leading to a single room. Builders added small, double-roomed annexes to both ends of the principal structure at some later time.

Exactly the same imagery graces both the north and south facades of the build-

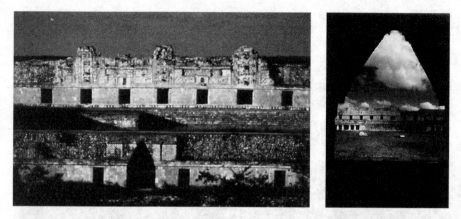

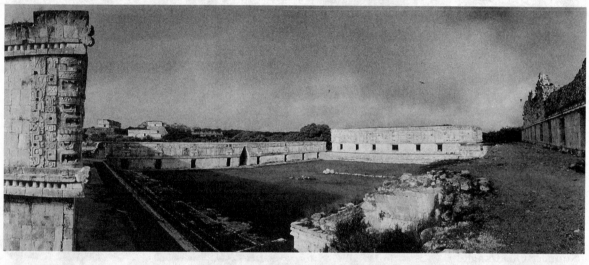

Fig. 7.7. A medley of photographs showing different views of the Nunnery Quadrangle.

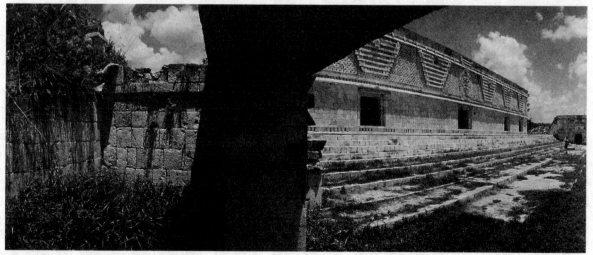

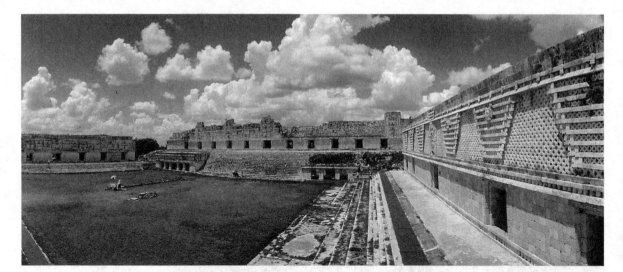

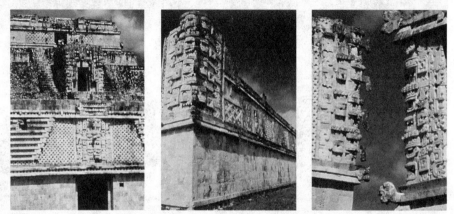

Fig. 7.8. A medley of
photographs of the
Nunnery Quadrangle.

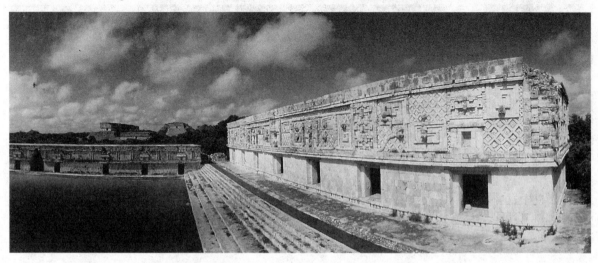

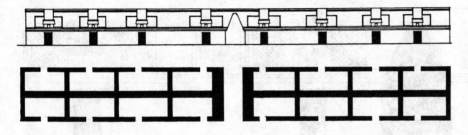

Fig. 7.9. A: Elevation and plan of the South Building.

ing. Medial and upper moldings divide the walls into three zones, the lowermost of which is plain. The upper molding carries at regular intervals small flower designs that read as *itz* (Fig. 7.10).[10] In Yukatek, *itz* refers to substances like nectar, tree sap, candle wax, morning dew, and other sacred liquids. *Itz* also means "to make magic," so that this building is a house where magic was made. In ancient Maya parlance, this makes the South Building an *Itzam Nah,* a "Conjuring House."

The entablature has a mosaic sculpture over each of the eight doors that flank the central arch (Fig. 7.11). Each of these sculptures (Figs. 7.12a, c) consists of a thatched-roof house called a *xanil nah* by the modern Maya (Fig. 7.12d). The depiction of the thatch shows some of its strands blown by the wind. The house sits amidst a lattice pattern. We have seen exactly this pattern on modern *xanil nah* that serve as commercial and religious buildings throughout Yukatan (Fig. 7.12b). The pattern results from overlapping poles placed on the diagonal. In the relief of the sculptural lattice, one line overlaps the other, just as it does in the modern pattern. If the lattice had the same meaning for the ancient Maya as it does now, it marks this building as one of special function.

Each house in front of the lattices has a zoomorphic monster head on top of the roof, just like a roofcomb in temple architecture. The features of the face are anonymous, but maize foliation grows from the top of the head. The maize reminds us of Palenque, Copan, and Tikal, where texts mention houses called *Na Te'-K'an,* "First Tree-Precious." At Palenque and Copan, the actual houses survive[11] and show us that the maize tree represents the reborn Maize God and the place where the gods formed the first human beings from maize dough. We think the maize houses on the South Building convey the same meaning. The South Building represents the house where the first people were made, and where their descendants remember First Father in his guise as a maize plant.

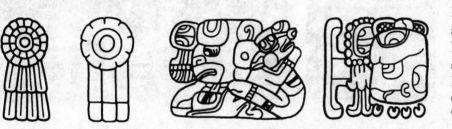

Fig. 7.10. Two *itz* signs (*left*) from the Nunnery Quadrangle and the deity name Itzamna from Quirigua Stela C and Tikal Stela 26.

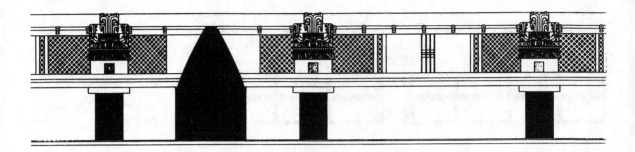

B—THE EAST BUILDING

Fig. 7.11. A: Elevation of part of the South Building and the grand entrance to the Quadrangle.

The East Building sits on a platform that is level with the medial molding of the South Building (Fig. 7.7). By using this device, the builders allowed lines along the platform and base of the East Building to recede into the medial molding of the South Building, thus integrating the two buildings into a visual whole. A stairway running along the entire front of the building rises from the court to the front facade with its five doorways. The central door leads to a complex of six rooms, while the outer doors open into double-chambered compartments (Fig.

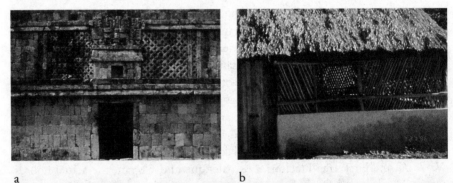

a

b

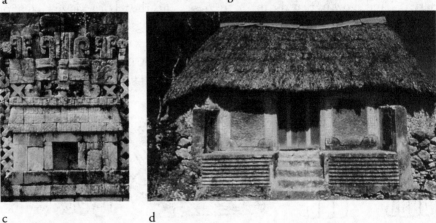

Fig. 7.12. A: (a) Detail of the mosaic design on the South Building; (b) crossed lathing on a modern building in Yukatan; (c) detail of the house motif; (d) a modern *xanil nah* from Valladolid, Yukatan.

c

d

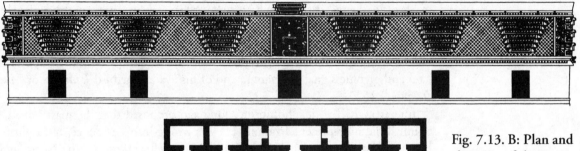

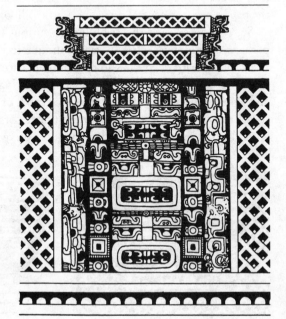

Fig. 7.13. B: Plan and elevation of the East Building.

7.13). There is no access from the back, so that this structure, unlike the South Building, faces exclusively into the court.

All the moldings include repeating cylinders in their design, while the medial and upper moldings have three-dimensional serpent heads on their corners.[12] The upper molding has *itz* flowers at regular intervals, marking it as an *Itzam Nah,* "House of Magic," just like the South Building.

The entire front entablature carries a lattice pattern interrupted by stacks of masks at the corners and over the central door. Each of these stacks consists of three heads, all wearing a flower headband (Fig. 7.14). Historically, these masks have always been identified as Chaks because of the long muzzles. However, the Chak of the codices is not known for his long nose, and these masks have none

Fig. 7.14. The central mask stack of the East Building with the name of the building sitting above the top mask.

of his other characteristics, such as shell earflares. To us, these masks depict the great bird who stood on the top of the World Tree. Almost all his images sport a huge angled beak that appears to be the forerunner of the long nose of these masks. Moreover, the flower headbands are *itz* symbols, the most important icon and glyphic signal of Itzamna and of his avatar, the bird *Itzam-Ye* or *Mut Itzamna*.[13]

Interestingly, J. Eric Thompson[14] long ago proposed that the masks on the South Building represent Itzamna. He was wrong in his evidence, but right in his idea. These masks on the East Building as well as those on the North and West Buildings are, in fact, images of Itzamna in his form as the bird. Their presence further marks this compound as an *Itzam Nah,* or "House of Sorcery," where kings and nobles called forth ancestors and gods from the Otherworld.

One of the most enigmatic images in the Nunnery Quadrangle is the stacks of double-headed serpents that form V-shaped designs above the outer doors (Fig. 7.15). Perhaps the most interesting suggestion concerning the identification of this design came from Viollet-le-Duc, a nineteenth-century French architect who wrote commentaries for Désiré Charnay's photographs.[15] He suggested that the pattern represents wood cribbing. We would like to go further and suggest that the design represents a corn crib for storing dry maize. In fact, the Yukatek of today call this kind of crib a *kan che',* or "snake wood." Each of the elements in the stack has a snake head on both ends. It is a *kan che'.* This idea seems particularly appropriate to the iconography of the neighboring South Building, which shows growing corn. The building itself may have been named for this crib, because a smaller version of it consisting of three levels surmounts the masks over the central door like a little billboard.

Superimposed over the cribbing are curious motifs that resemble masks or perhaps shields (Fig. 7.16). They are unique to this building. A central mosaic face or mask with deep eye and mouth holes surmounts a scaled or mosaic base. Over the face is a headdresslike device consisting of concentric bands of shells and jewels, cropped feathers, and twisted cords or feathers. Elements resembling spearthrower darts protrude from the upper corners. An odd device decorated with knots covers the nose and a "tongue" emerges from the mouth hole. If the

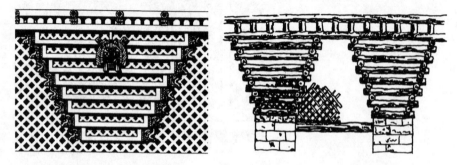

Fig. 7.15. Viollet-le-Duc's architectural reconstruction compared to the *kan che'* on the East Building.

corner devices are indeed spearthrower darts, then the central image may represent a shield, possibly as a symbol of war—the arrow-shield—known to have been used by the Maya and other Mesoamerican peoples.[16]

The ends and rear of the East Building carry different and less detailed sculptural arrays. All four corners have *Itzam-Ye* masks, and the intervening entablatures alternate plain walls with lattice panels. The *itz* flowers continue around the upper molding, so that the building is recognizable as an *Itzam Nah* from all directions.

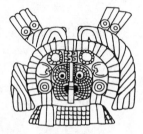

Fig. 7.16. This represents a mosaic mask with crossed javelins behind it.

C—THE NORTH BUILDING

The North Building rests on the highest platform in the Quadrangle, arranged so that it stands on the level of the medial moldings of both the East and West Buildings. A grand stairway (Fig. 7.8 top), flanked by two colonnaded buildings, rises from the court up to the North Building. The dark openings of eleven doorways punctuate the front facade, and an additional door penetrates each end of the building, to give thirteen doors in all. Each door leads to a double-chambered room. Nine towering stacks of masks divide the entablature of the front facade into compositional zones (Fig. 7.17). Different individual symbols and images grace background patterns consisting of flower lattices and "cloud" scrolls (Fig. 7.18).

The flower lattice consists of crossed diagonal members with recessed centers and zigzag edges. Flowers lie in the diamond shapes formed by the diagonals. We think this lattice replicates a kind of flower-laden scaffolding once used in Maya ritual. But more important, sixteenth-century Yukatek dictionaries gloss *nikte'il nah* (literally "flower house") as "an assembly house," and say that it is the same as a *popol-nah* (literally "mat house"), "a community house, where they assemble to deal with the affairs of state, and to teach dancing for community festivals."[17]

Fig. 7.17. C: The west half of the North Building.

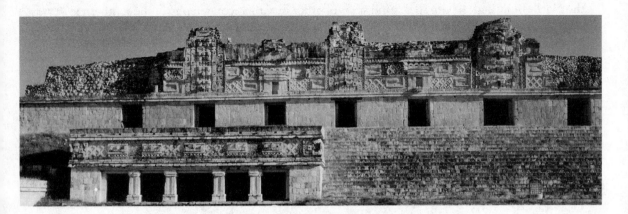

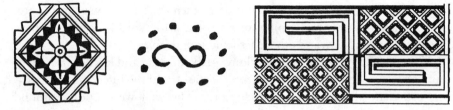

The presence of the flower lattice on this building marks it as a flower house, and thus tells us that it was used for council meetings, and for dancing in public festivals. The elevated level and the presence of a stela on the stairs suggest that the king and his nobles would have stood in front of the North Building to oversee rituals in the court below.

Alternating with the flower lattice are squared, S-shaped scrolls. These scrolls have glyphic counterparts in a sign that reads *muyal,* "cloud."[18] Therefore, the entablature tells us that not only is this building a flower house, but it presents its imagery as if it were among the clouds. Snake heads project from the upper molding all around the North Building at regular intervals. In Yukatek, the word for "snake," *kan,* is a near homophone with "sky," *ka'an.* The hieroglyphs and the iconography of the Classic period demonstrate that the ancient Maya freely used one form for the other as a play on words. We think that the same is true here, and that the snake heads mark the upper zone of the building as "sky." Combined with the cloud symbols, the snakes give us a "cloudy sky."

A house sits over doors 3 and 5, counting from the left (west) corner of the front facade. Although no houses survive on the eastern half of the entablature, we can reconstruct two, by the rule of symmetry,[19] over doors 7 and 9 (Fig. 7.19). The best preserved house is the one over door 3. The roof pattern again indicates that the thatch is wind-blown (Fig. 7.20). Three double-headed serpents adorn the roof. The lowest set occurs without a body, so that the heads protrude directly from the thatch. The middle pair of heads has a body consisting of a staff decorated with diamond shapes and knots. This pattern occurs with spears and staffs of office in earlier iconography in the southern lowlands.

Fig. 7.19. C: Elevation and plan of the North Building.

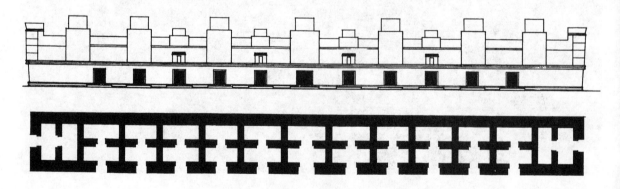

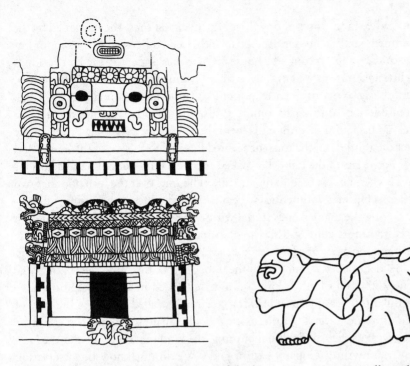

Fig. 7.20. The snake house and upper masks on the North Building. The goggle-eyed mask on the top reads *ch'ok,* "sprout" or "young person," while the house shows conjuring snakes emerging from the roof.

Fig. 7.21. The jaguar throne at the base of the house image. Rather than being a double-headed jaguar, this image shows two jaguars with entwined tails.

Two serpents emerge from the top of the house in an image recalling the rearing Vision Serpents at Yaxchilan and elsewhere. These serpents appear to mark the thatched-roof house as a place where vision rituals took place. By extension, these little houses mark the entire North Building in the same way. It was a *kan-nah,* a "sky house" or a "serpent house." Interestingly, Maya artists often depicted their visions floating in clouds, sometimes clouds of incense, sometimes the clouds of the sky: these are the *muyal* of the entablature.

Under the door of the little house image sits a jaguar throne (Fig. 7.21), but unlike most Maya jaguar thrones, this one does not have a single body with two heads. Instead, two jaguars sit back-to-back with their tails entwined. Their presence indicates that the king was a central figure in the rituals enacted here. We assume that similar jaguar thrones, although now missing, were originally under the other three houses.

A mask head sits above the houses, separated from them by the upper molding. The nineteenth-century artist Frederick Catherwood showed the complete mask over the fifth door. Today no mask survives in a complete condition, but parts of the various examples can be combined to reconstruct the original form. It represents a standard zoomorphic creature, but his head is made of flowers, once again identifying him as *Itzam-Ye* and the house as an *Itzam Nah.*

This *Itzam Nah* mask had yet another mask above him. Early drawings of the surviving details and our own observations have identified large ringed eyes that read *ch'ok,* "sprout" or "young person," in the glyphs. Teeth fill the oval mouth below in a sign read *ko* in the inscriptions. Together they spell *ch'ok,* the term used by the Maya for members of a lineage. At Copan and several other sites, the word for lineage was *ch'ok-te-nah,* "sprout-tree-house." These masks identify the North Building as a lineage house as well as a place where conjuring was done, so that one of its functions was as a shrine center, not unlike Toh-Chak-Ich'ak's Palace at Tikal.

The builders of the North Building distributed other images among the flower/cloud background, although few of these have survived (Fig. 7.22). In the zone over the third door, the torso of a seated figure is to the left of the house, and a bound captive sits to the right. The naked captive has his hands bound across his chest and his genitals exposed to his enemies. The zone over the fifth door has two holes where sculptures with tenons were once set. They are now missing, but perhaps lie among the many stones stored within the rooms of the North Building.

The easternmost zone still has two sculptures attached, one of a kneeling drummer and the other of a fat quetzal. Seler[20] published a drawing of another figure that he identified as coming from the upper part of the cloud sign in the same zone (Fig. 7.23). This figure represents a male dressed in a cape holding a large torch. Similar torches appear in burning ceremonies called *puluy*[21] in the texts of Chich'en Itza and several southern sites. Such burning ceremonies could be associated with warfare, agricultural burning, the kindling of new fires at the New Year, and the myth of Copan's patron gods. We do not know the association intended here, but in the eastern annex we found another figure with the same kind of cloak and carrying his own torch bundle. Sticks perforate the skin down his arm in an act of self-sacrifice. Another example now in the Museum at Tz'i-bilchaltun shows that all of them were naked and had perforated their penises as well. Blood was the most sacred substance that Maya could give in offerings to their gods and ancestors. They chose parts of the body that bleed freely and that had special symbolic import. For men that was their penises, and for both men and women, their tongues. Bloodletting rituals of this sort also involved trance states in which people could talk to their ancestors and their gods.

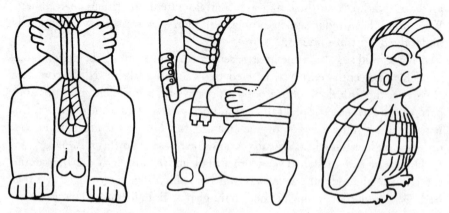

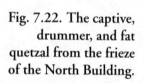

Fig. 7.22. The captive, drummer, and fat quetzal from the frieze of the North Building.

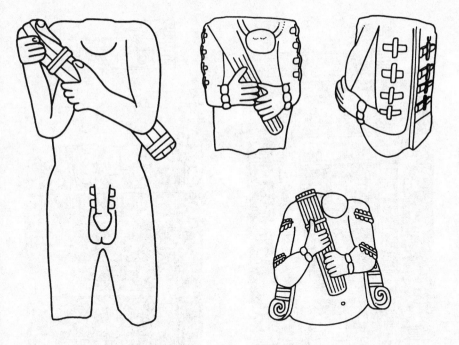

Fig. 7.23. Nude figures holding torches and engaged in blood-letting sacrifice. The larger figure to the left now resides in the museum at Tz'ibilchaltun.

C1—THE MASKS

The front of the North Building had seven mask stacks across its entablature as well as additional stacks on its corners (Fig. 7.24). Of these only four of the interior stacks and the eastern corner stack survive. Nevertheless, we can determine a pattern in the surviving sample. Each mask has the image of a Tlaloc sitting on top. The Tlaloc mask consists of eye rings mounted above a nose bar and a curving upper lip containing a mouth full of teeth. Bands interlock to form a "bar-and-trapeze" sign that appears at Chich'en Itza on a special bundle associated with Venus signs and war implements. Although this symbol is usually associated with the "Toltecs," its presence in Maya imagery goes back to the Early Classic period. It first appeared in association with the Tikal-Waxaktun war that culminated in A.D. 378. For the Maya, the Tlaloc mask and the bar-and-trapeze sign signaled a special kind of war associated with Venus and territorial conquest, and it especially evoked the great city of Teotihuacan. Remember that the Classic Maya called Teotihuacan *Puh,* the "Place of Reeds," or *Tollan* in the language of the Aztecs.[22] The presence of the Tlaloc images here refers to the ancient war complex, but it also served to declare Uxmal to be a "Place of Reeds."

Below the Tlaloc images are four stacked masks. Their generic features include eyes with plates above and below them, muzzles (many of them now broken) protruding from their faces, and wide mouths set with fangs. The details, however, vary greatly among these components. Some eyebrows are curled, some have dots,

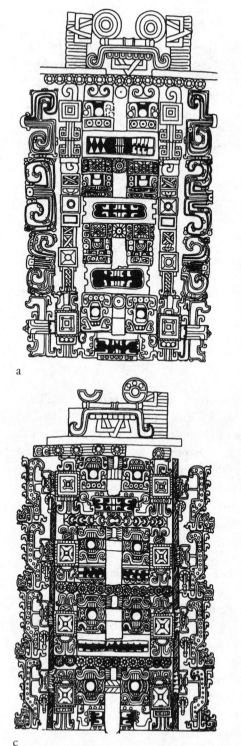

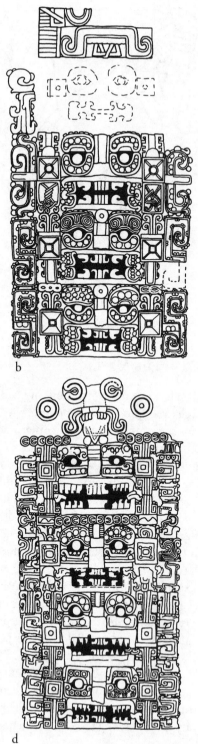

Fig. 7.24. C1: The masks from the North Building. (a) The westernmost mask with corn foliation in the outer frame; (b) mask with cloud signs in its outer frame (its pair on the eastern end does not survive); (c) mask with serpent heads in its outer frame sits over the center door; (d) mask with foliation in its outer frame sits above the easternmost door.

and others have crossed bones. Details of the eyes and cheeks also vary, as do the shape and variety of teeth. Ear ornaments representing flowers and appended foliation flank each head, with the same variety of detail as the other components. We do not know if these variations were simply decorative or whether they carried subtle meanings that are now lost.

For us, the most significant features of the masks are their forehead ornaments and the vertical bands that frame them. All of the masks in the central stack have flower headbands and a tightly tied bundle of fibers sitting over their muzzles. Most of the masks in the outer stacks lack the flower headbands, but carry instead a single flower above the muzzle. Although there is significant variation in these masks, almost all of them carry flower ornaments on their foreheads that identify them as *Itzam-Ye.* They reinforce the Nunnery Quadrangle as a place of sorcery and magic.

The most interesting contrasts occur in the framing bands flanking the masks. The central masks are flanked by stacked snake heads with the twisted cords of the *kuxan sum,* or the sky umbilicus that connected Maya leaders to their sacred source of power. S-shaped cloud scrolls frame the masks adjacent to the central stack. Foliation scrolls surround the remaining masks. This places the serpent umbilicus in the center, flanked by clouds in the sky, and surrounded by foliation (maize?) of the earth. This detailing incorporates the most important domains in Maya life.

C2—THE BACK

The back of the North Building is very different in design from the front facade (Fig. 7.25). The corners have the expected stacks of masks adjacent to a half cloud scroll above a flower lattice panel. The remaining entablature contains

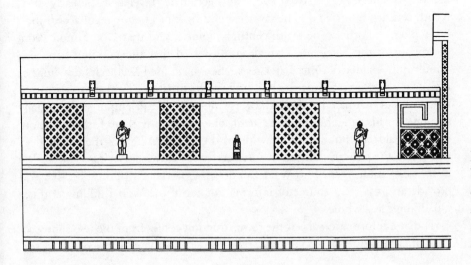

Fig. 7.25. C2: The back of the west end of the North Building, showing the placement of the captives and War Serpents.

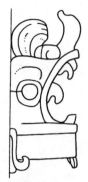

**Fig. 7.26.
The feathered War
Serpent from the rear
of the North Building.**

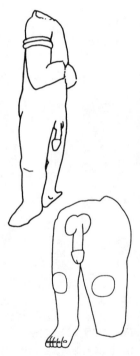

**Fig. 7.27.
Bound, naked captives
from the rear facade of
the North Building.**

alternating plain walls and lattice panels without flowers. The fifteen plain panels display human figures alternating with snake heads (Fig. 7.26). The snakes have "feather fans" attached, identifying them as the Maya War Serpent known as Waxaklahun-Ubah-Kan.[23] This particular snake is part of the Tlaloc-Venus complex of symbols that occurs on the front of this building.

The human figures in the entablature reinforce the war associations of this snake. They stand naked with their upper arms bound by ropes (Fig. 7.27). Their genitalia hang free in the mode of public humiliation practiced by the ancient Maya. These men are captives.

Unfortunately, the lintels over the end doors collapsed, leaving no detail of the entablatures on the ends of the North Building between the corner masks. A crack near the northwest corner of this building reveals an earlier construction, including not only the wall but also the medial molding.[24] The outer facades visible today are a veneer that encases the earlier building.

D—THE WEST BUILDING

The West Building rests on a platform at the same level as the East Building, so that its medial molding aligns with the basal platform of the North Building (Fig. 7.28). A stairway runs along the entire width of the structure, which has seven doors leading into double-chambered rooms. The back wall has collapsed, but it is clear that there were never any doors on the back or sides of this building.

The upper front facade of the West Building was originally decorated with a spectacular entablature running between stacked corner masks. Unfortunately, most of this entablature fell before the era of modern photography, so that only two small sections were photographed in situ at the end of the last century. Jean-Frédéric Waldeck, a self-styled count and eccentric traveler of the early nineteenth century, reported that he saw the building intact before it collapsed. John L. Stephens, another nineteenth-century explorer, said that Don Simon Peón, the owner of the Hacienda Uxmal, also asserted that the building had been standing in Waldeck's time. Later researchers have used Waldeck's drawings as the most reliable record of the building. Unfortunately, Waldeck has a mixed reputation. His unaltered field drawings of sites like Palenque are unusually accurate for his time, but he had a habit of embellishing them for publication. In fact, Waldeck's published[25] drawing of the northern half of the facade does not match the pattern that can be inferred from the two surviving sections. We must use caution, then, with Waldeck's drawings and descriptions, but they still provide an important source of information about the West Building and the Quadrangle as a whole.

The best information about the reconstruction comes from the two short sections of entablature that never collapsed (Fig. 7.29). These included a short sec-

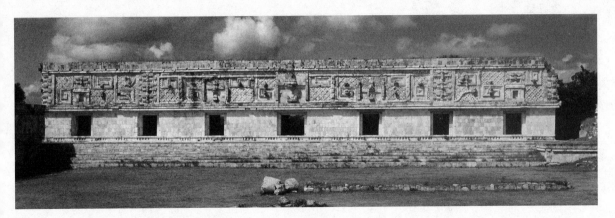

Fig. 7.28. D:
The West Building.

tion between doors 2 and 3, and a longer section over door 6. These sections appear in Catherwood's drawings from the first half of the nineteenth century as well as in Maler's photographs from the end of the century. If we assume that the facade was bilaterally symmetrical, we can use these two sections to confirm the detail of about one-third of the present restoration. Beginning in the 1930s, Mexican archaeologists used a similar strategy along with the positions of fallen sculpture as the basis for their restoration work. Although they may have gone further in the restoration than is customary today, the accuracy of the restoration is generally quite good, with ample evidence underlying the choices they made.[26]

D1—THE ENTABLATURE

The medial and upper moldings of the West Building terminate at the corners in snake heads (Fig. 7.30). In addition, the upper molding has a few surviving examples of the *itz,* "flower," signs, indicating that originally they were distributed along the entire length of the building. The basal molding carries clusters of four cylinders alternating with plain zones. The corner masks are all reconstructed, but their detail is consistent with the surviving mask stack over door 6, and all of their components were found collapsed below the corners. As with the East and North Buildings, the masks have flower headbands, but in all examples, snakes emerge from both sides of the flower (Fig. 7.31). The lower two snakes in

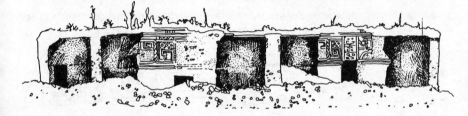

Fig. 7.29. D:
Sketch of the West
Building as it was in
the nineteenth century
before restoration.

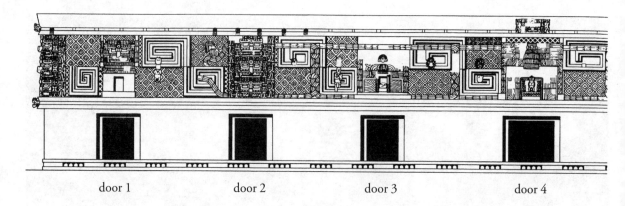

door 1   door 2   door 3   door 4

Fig. 7.30. D1:
The frieze on
the entablature of
the West Building.

each mask stack have diamondback patterns, while the upper snake on the southeast corner has a feathered body.

The background of the frieze was a series of flower-lattice panels interlocked with *muyal,* "cloud," scrolls. As with the North Building, this combination of symbols marks this building as a community house and a cloud house. The distribution of these cloud and flower-lattice panels across the facade can be deduced from the portions that never fell.

The areas at each end of the frieze (over doors 1 and 7) have been restored. The zones immediately adjacent to the corner mask stacks have flower lattices and cloud scrolls reduced to half of the normal shape. A house with a mask on top sits directly over the doors. The masks as reconstructed have feather frames on both sides, and they wear headbands combining a flower with a feathered serpent (Fig. 7.32). Assuming the restoration is reasonably accurate,[27] these images depict "Sorcery Houses," or *Itzam Nah.*

The adjacent zones (between doors 1 and 2 and between doors 6 and 7) contain cloud scrolls and flower-lattice panels. In both areas, a three-dimensional human figure overlaps the outer sides of the cloud scroll (Fig. 7.33). A Mexican archaeologist, Mañuel Cirerol, found the southern sculpture in the rubble under that section of the frieze. He also reconstructed a jaguar head above the figure as though it were his headdress. Both figures stand naked, with rows of short sticks penetrating the skin on their thighs and penises.

The other halves of these zones contain the heads and tails of feathered rattlesnakes that entwine across the entire facade. Each scholar who has reconstructed this facade has proposed a different solution to the snake patterns. Waldeck reconstructed the snakes intertwining at the ends and centers of every *muyal,* "cloud," scroll. However, there are not enough entwined body elements

Fig. 7.31. A flower-
serpent headband
from the corner masks
of the West Building.

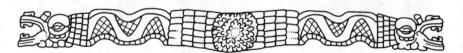

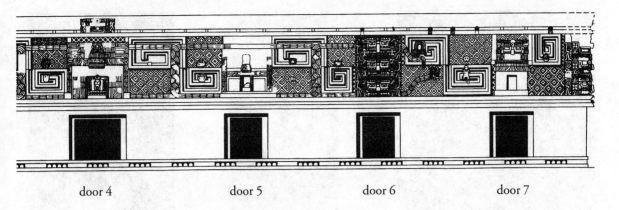

door 4   door 5   door 6   door 7

to enable such a reconstruction. Frans Blom, on the other hand, reconstructed four feathered serpents, two on each half of the front facade, with only one inter-twining section between them. However, there are too many intertwining segments and too few heads and tails for this reconstruction. Stephens reported that in his day the heads and tails of these snakes on the southern end were in place. Therefore, we can confirm that there was a head and a tail of snakes on both the northern and the southern ends of the facade in the mid-nineteenth century. Given the number of intertwined segments, we believe that the reconstruction of these feathered serpents on the facade today is essentially correct.

Stacks of three masks rise over doors 2 and 6, and while those of door 2 have been reconstructed, their counterparts over door 6 are original. The masks have headbands with multiple flowers mounted over feathers that once again mark these creatures as *Itzam-Ye* birds. The earflare assemblages are also flowers, and the frames on both sides of the masks consist of serpent heads with feather fans and protruding bifurcated tongues. They are shown in profile view and are stacked four high.

The zone between doors 2 and 3 and much of the corresponding zone between doors 5 and 6 never collapsed. Both are filled with a *muyal*, "cloud," scroll and lattice-flower panels. The entwined bodies of the serpents form a column in the middle of both zones.

The south end also has a standing human figure wearing a loincloth and a feathered cape (Fig. 7.33f–g). The figure holds a thick staff diagonally across his body. He wears a mask that appears to represent a bird who may well be our old friend *Itzam-Ye*. In the flower lattice above him, the builders tenoned another stone that probably depicted his headdress. This sculpture has a rosette and some sort of open-mouthed animal head with a jeweled headband. A battered equivalent of this figure survives in the north end of the frieze.

The zone between doors 3 and 5 is entirely reconstructed. It includes the expected *muyal* scrolls and lattice-flower panels, as well as two vertical sections of entwined serpent bodies. As presently reconstructed, the panels directly over the

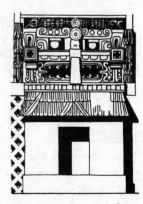

Fig. 7.32. Image of an *Itzam Nah*, "conjuring house," on the entablature of the West Building.

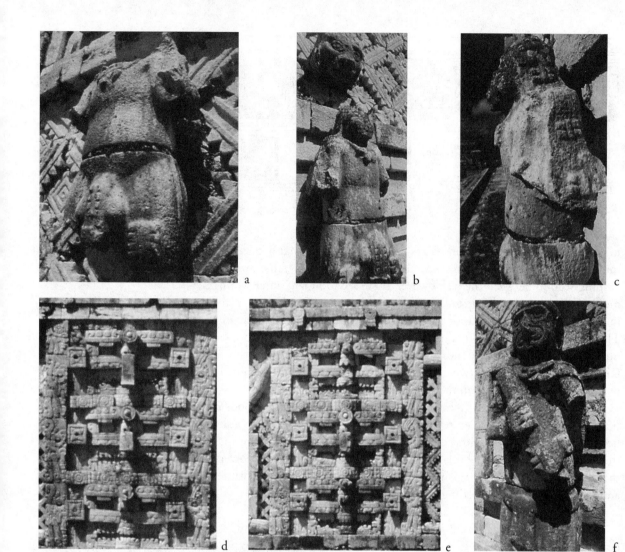

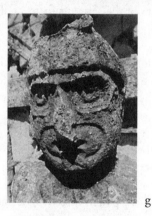

Fig. 7.33. Men engaged
in auto-sacrifice (a) from
the south end and (b–c)
from the north end. The
masks from the south
end (d) are reconstructed,
but the north set (e)
is original. A lord
holding a scepter (f–g)
survives on the southern
side of the frieze.

doors 3 and 5 represent some kind of feathered structure. Early photographs confirm the presence of feather framing on the left of the south panel (Fig. 7.33f). These unusual objects are, we believe, palanquins. Maya artists at Tikal and elsewhere depicted such litters as the conveyances of lords and the patron gods of the kingdom. Enemies could capture these palanquins in war, and apparently the Maya considered them to hold enormous supernatural power.[28] The depiction of this palanquin shows kneeling legs inside the structure, and a round umbrellalike form that may have provided shade to the lord. The feathers covering the palanquin transmitted the wealth and power of its owner. On the top of the palanquin, archaeologists have reconstructed a head with flowing hair and large earflares. Although we are not sure this is the correct position, one of Cirerol's photographs from 1938 shows this head on the ground in front of this zone of the facade.

Other details are much better preserved on the south end than on the north side. For example, a small sculpture of a torso in a rosette was tenoned into the cloud scroll next to the palanquin. This image represents the birth of a god from a flower (Figs. 7.34b–c). There are several beautiful figurines that show just such an emergence from a flower. Moreover, modern Lakandon myth holds that the gods were born from plumeria flowers, and among the modern Kaqchikel and K'iche' of Guatemala the word for placenta is *kotzij* or "flower." Thus we have a

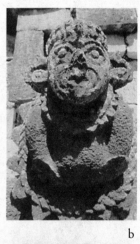

a

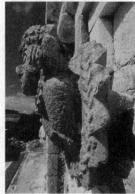

b

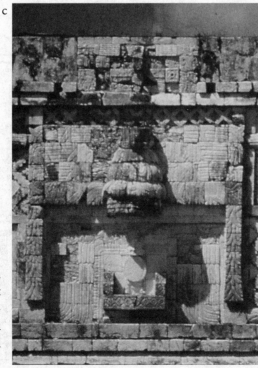

c

Fig. 7.34. Sculptures from the south frieze of the West Building showing (a) a palanquin with the crossed legs of a lord inside, and (b–c) an old god emerging from a flower.

statue that may relate to a moment in Creation or depict the materialization of a god or ancestor through the vision rite.

We think that he is a Pawahtun, one of the gods who held up the corners of the Earth. Archaeologists placed the image of another Pawahtun next to the flower-man. Standing in front of a spiderweb (Fig. 7.35a), this Pawahtun also appears at Chich'en Itza, where it served as one of the patron gods of the Itza.[29]

The largest and most ornate palanquin (Fig. 7.35c) sits over the central door on the pivotal axis of the composition. It has a large cylindrical canopy adorned with feathers and with a headband surrounding its summit. The sides and interior of the palanquin are also covered with feathers. The base of the palanquin has the shape of a box. The front edge carries patterns that resemble weaving, while the sides and underside are sprinkled with flowers and petal motifs. Even today, Maya cover the *andas* on which they carry saints with flowers, mirrors, and precious weavings. In the center of the palanquin, the archaeologists placed a relief image of Pawahtun wearing a turtle shell. His round belly here is the underside of the turtle carapace (Fig. 7.35b). Since there was a Pawahtun for each of the four directions and the center, this facade presents images of all five. This fellow must be the Pawahtun of the center.

Above the palanquin, the archaeologists reconstructed a zoomorphic mask wearing a flower-serpent headband. Its ornate earflares have open-mouthed serpents on either side from which human faces emerge. The Maya used this image of ances-

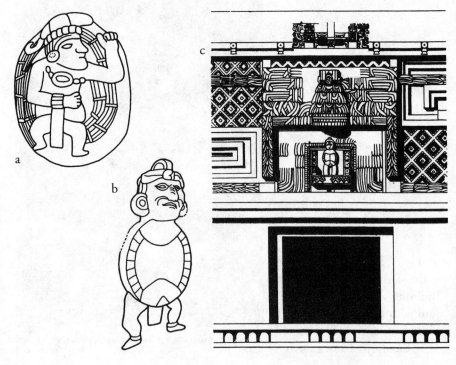

Fig. 7.35.
The small medallion (a) is located to the left of the main Pawahtun (b). The main Pawahtun is shown in a palanquin (c): he was the patron god of the Itza.

tors emerging from the mouths of serpents as a metaphor for birth and communication with the Otherworld. Once again, if the reconstruction is close to the original, this mask names the building as an *Itzam Nah* for conjuring ancestors.

The snake head and tail to the right of the mask stack over door 6 (Fig. 7.36) are original, like the masks. The head that goes with the tail once graced the opposite end of the frieze, as this head goes with the tail on the other end. The intertwined positions of these two feathered snakes evoke the twisting form of the umbilicus and the breeding behavior of snakes. The northern snake rears up from the medial molding as he emerges from behind the mask stack. A human figure (perhaps an ancestor) emerges from its gaping mouth (Figs. 7.37a–b). This emerging head wears a mask representing a shark, known to the Maya as *xok*. The serpent's head once again has a feather fan above its head and a mosaic panel behind it, marking this snake as the War Serpent.[30] The tail of the serpent clearly carries rattles. In the curve of the tail sits a feather-covered, globular object that has a huge arch of feathers emerging from the top (Fig. 7.37c). At first glance this seems to be a unique object in Maya imagery, but the feather arch is the key to its identification. At Palenque, accession scenes depict a drum-shaped mosaic headdress with exactly the same arch of feathers (Fig. 7.37d). Moreover, this "drummajor" headdress appears on warriors from Early Classic times on. The Uxmal headdress is a later version of the Palenque example and its Early Classic prototypes.

What we have on this facade, then, are two war serpents carrying headdresses

Fig. 7.36. The mask stack with the serpent tail and head in the zone over door 6.

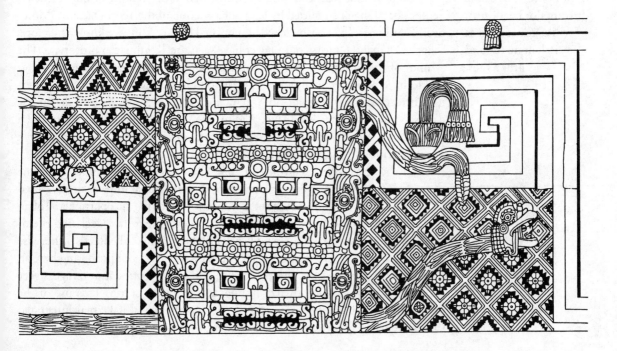

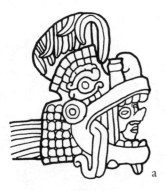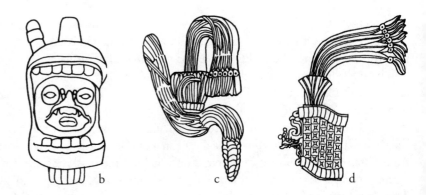

a　　　　　b　　　　　c　　　　　d

Fig. 7.37. Details
(a–b) of the entwined
serpents that criss
cross the entablature
of the West Building.
The masked head
emerging from the
serpent's mouth may
be an ancestor. The
feathered headdress
sitting on the tail (c) is
Uxmal's version of the
drummajor headdress,
like those used at
Palenque (d) and
other sites.

on their tails. There is only one other image of this combination in all of Mesoamerica: the Temple of the Feathered Serpent at Teotihuacan, where feathered serpents carry mosaic headdresses on their tails (Fig. 7.38a).[31] The Teotihuacan headdress has a drum shape, round eye pieces mounted on its upper cylinder, and a royal nose ornament inside the mouth of the creature that constitutes the base of the headdress. The Great Goddess of Teotihuacan, who personifies the World Tree, wears this nose ornament as one of her diagnostic features. The king of Teotihuacan also wore it because he embodied this goddess in his person.[32] The Feathered Serpent carries the insignia of royal authority—this headdress, eye rings, and nose ornament—out of the Primordial Sea to bring them to the rulers of Teotihuacan.

At the time the West Building was constructed, the Temple of the Feathered Serpent had long been buried by later construction of the Teotihuacanos. Moreover, Teotihuacan had been sacked and burned by A.D. 700. We know, therefore, that the Uxmal sculptors could never have seen the Teotihuacan prototype. The symbol of the Feathered War Serpent carrying the headdress of warrior kings had to have been a general symbol understood by all the peoples of Mesoamerica. In fact, the War Serpent on Yaxchilan Lintel 25 emits the founder of the dynasty from its upper head (Fig. 7.38b). He wears a balloon headdress and a Tlaloc mask. Exactly this headdress and mask emerge from the lower head in a Maya rendition of the Teotihuacan idea.

Since the Maya called Teotihuacan *Puh,* "Place of Reeds," we know it was one of the principal Tollans of the Classic period. The Uxmal lords may have used the War Serpent–headdress symbol as a means of evoking this particular Tollan as the source of their legitimacy and power. They were in fact declaring themselves to be descendants of the people of *Puh,* the people of the Reeds, otherwise known as "Toltecs." We want to make it clear that we are not proposing here an invasion of foreigners from central Mexico, although Teotihuacan refugees very likely came to Yukatan with Itza immigrants from the south. This use of the Teotihuacan tradition was a strategy by which the lords of Uxmal integrated themselves into the Mesoamerican system of royal charter. Other Maya king-

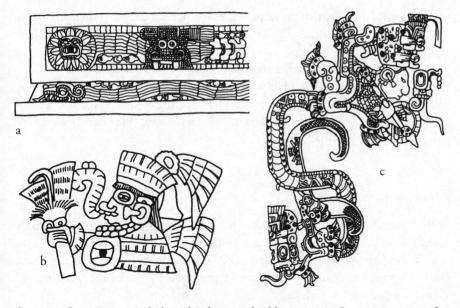

a

b

c

Fig. 7.38. The feathered serpent from the Temple of the Feathered Serpent at Teotihuacan (a) carries a mosaic headdress on its tail. This headdress has the eye rings and nose ornament of Teotihuacan, both of which were symbols of power carried by an Early Classic from Tikal (b). The rearing Vision Serpent from Yaxchilan Lintel 25 (c) emits the founder from one mouth and the Tlaloc war helmet from the other. The feather fans on this snake also occur on the Uxmal snake.

doms, such as Copan, Tikal, and Palenque, had been using the same strategy for hundreds of years before the Nunnery Quadrangle was built.

E—THE COURT

Today the remnants of a small building sit near the center of the Nunnery court. It had walls on three sides, with its open side facing the West Building. This kind of C-shaped building is found at Terminal Classic and Early Postclassic settlements throughout the Maya lowlands. It was probably added to the Nunnery Quadrangle very late in its life, or perhaps after Uxmal was abandoned as a major center.

Alberto Ruz discovered the remains of a narrow *sak beh,* or "road," leading from the center of the court to the great entry arch in the South Building. A low altar mound sat on its eastern edge. The shattered sculpture of a jaguar (Fig. 7.39) lay near this altar, and a very large column shaft stood a short distance away.[33] This combination of altar, jaguar, and column also occurs in front of the House of the Governor, which was built by the same king. The column represents the World Tree, called the *Wakah-Kan* by the Maya of the southern lowlands. A sixteenth-century Yukatek dictionary[34] describes *Waklom-Chaan* as idols from Ichkansiho, the precursor to the colonial city of Mérida.

In Classic Maya Creation mythology,[35] the Maize God directed a set of gods to put the universe in order on August 13, 3114 B.C., by setting up the Cosmic Hearth in Orion. The jaguar altar represents the first stone set in that hearth—the Jaguar Throne Stone. Later, on February 5, the Maize God raised the axis, called the *Wakah-Kan,* that corresponds in the natural world to the Milky Way in its north-south orientation. The analog of that tree is the column shaft near the jaguar. This combination of symbols centers the world in the Nunnery Court. The later *sak beh* leads from the entrance to this center point. Interestingly, Le Plongeon photographed a pile of sculptures that had been hidden away in the South Building for a visit by Empress Carlota.[36] Among them is a giant phallus stone (Fig. 7.39). It may well have been set up in the court or in one of the buildings of the Quadrangle.

F—THE INSCRIPTIONS

Artists placed a number of painted and carved inscriptions in the Nunnery Quadrangle that identify its builder as the king Chan-Chak-K'ak'nal-Ahaw, who is also known in the literature as Lord Chak.[37] Chan-Chak-K'ak'nal-Ahaw commissioned the Nunnery Quadrangle and shaped most of the final stage of Uxmal that people see today.

F1—THE CAPSTONE FROM THE EAST BUILDING

The artist painted this inscription on the capstone in the northwest room of the East Building (Fig. 7.40a). The date reads 5 Imix 17 K'ank'in in tun 18 of k'atun 12 Ahaw, which falls on 10.3.17.12.1, or October 2, 906. The verb reads *k'alah*[38] *u nen k'awil* in the upper band of glyphs and *k'alah . . .* in the lower band. The first phrase is a standard dedication expression meaning "they finished the mirror-statue." Since *k'awil* can refer to statues, it may refer to an effigy god of some sort. The second expression records "the finishing" of an unknown some-

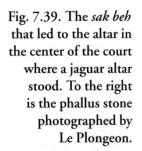

Fig. 7.39. The *sak beh* that led to the altar in the center of the court where a jaguar altar stood. To the right is the phallus stone photographed by Le Plongeon.

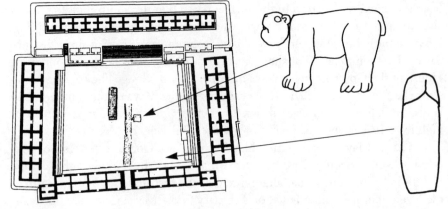

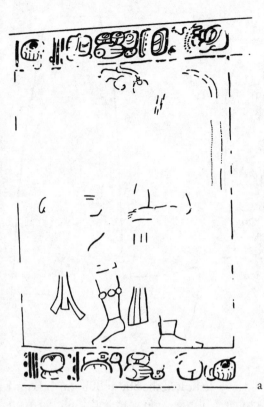

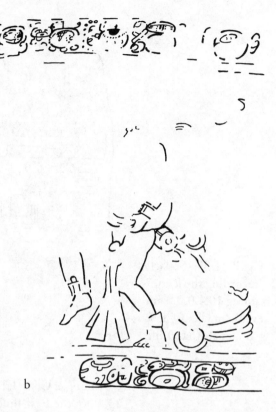

a   b

thing else. This ceremony probably involved the display of an effigy statue or a divination mirror during the dedication ritual for the East Building.

F2—THE CAPSTONE FROM BUILDING Y

The small building in the northeast corner of the court also has a painted capstone (Fig. 7.40b). It records a date, 4 Eb 5 Keh, that falls on 10.3.18.9.12 or August 9, 907. The rest of the text reads *t'ab*[39] *u tzib* . . . *Chan-Chak-K'ak'nal-Ahaw*, "the writing of Chan-Chak-K'ak'nal-Ahaw was raised." This inscription then confirms that Chan-Chak-K'ak'nal-Ahaw dedicated this building on August 9, 907, about a year after the inauguration of the East Building.

F3—THE CAPSTONE FROM THE SOUTH BUILDING

A third date in very battered condition was found in the South Building that is best reconstructed as 10.3.17.3.19 12 Kawak 16 Xul, or April 23, 906. Together, these dates give us a building sequence for three of the buildings in the Nunnery

Fig. 7.40. F1 and F2: (a) Capstone 1 from the northwest chamber of the East Building, and (b) Capstone 2 from Building Y.

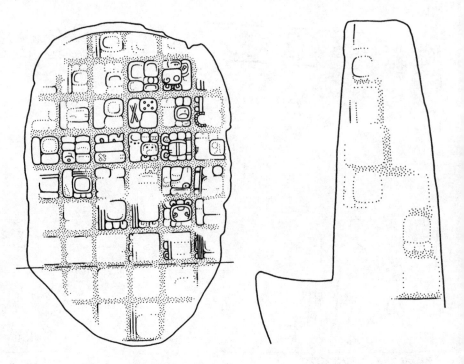

Quadrangle. Chan-Chak-K'ak'nal-Ahaw dedicated the South Building on April 23, 906, the East Building on October 2 of the same year, and Building Y on August 9 of the following year.

F4—STELA 17

This seat-shaped stela stands in the middle of the north stairway (Fig. 7.41). Unfortunately, the surface is very badly eroded, so that we have not been able to identify any names or dates. However, the front of the stela twice records 12 Ahaw as the current k'atun in which the recorded actions occurred. 12 Ahaw ended on 10.4.0.0.0, or January 20, 909, so that all the events must have taken place sometime in the twenty years before this date. It appears that the stela once recorded biographical information about its protagonist in the tradition of inscriptions from the southern lowlands, because the glyph at E2 is *siyah,* "he was born." Moreover, we can see the *k'ak'nal-ahaw* part of his name at C4-D4. The rest of Chan-Chak-K'ak'nal-Ahaw's name must have been in the blocks above, although we have no idea about the date or nature of the event. The birth clause may refer to an heir.

G—The Nunnery Quadrangle, One of the Architectural Legacies of Chan-Chak-K'ak'nal-Ahaw

Like tourists over the last century, we have always found Uxmal to be a gorgeous site. We first saw it under the gentler sun of December, when the colors intensify in the softer light and the shadowed reliefs that grace the buildings are at their sharpest resolution. The limestone sings against the deep blue of the sky and the green of the rain-soaked forest. We have always loved Uxmal for its breathtaking beauty, but the reconstruction of its political context that we offer here gives it a different kind of personality. When we walk into the Nunnery Quadrangle, we can now contemplate Chan-Chak-K'ak'nal-Ahaw and the symbolism he incorporated into the beautifully proportioned buildings. In the South and East Buildings, he mainly concerned himself with themes of maize and the Creation of the world. In the North and West Buildings, he featured the images of war, capture, and sacrifice. Chan-Chak-K'ak'nal-Ahaw presented this imagery in the visual language of Tlaloc-Venus war, the complex that first appeared in the Maya symbolic repertoire with the Tikal-Waxaktun war in A.D. 378. But he also evoked the other great tradition of the Classic period, when he rendered the great Feathered Serpent of war and vision rites in the style of the Temple of the Feathered Serpent at Teotihuacan, the great destroyed Tollan of the west.[40] Truly Chan-Chak-K'ak'nal-Ahaw was one of the greatest Maya of his day, and it is only fitting that his name can now be attached to the Nunnery Quadrangle and the other buildings of his architectural legacy.

CHAPTER 8

Iximche': The Capital of the Kaqchikel Maya

The mountainous highlands of Guatemala are very different from the hot, wet lowlands. Punctuated by towering volcanoes (Fig. 8.1) that occasionally cough up clouds of ash, the rugged landscape contrasts mountains and valleys drained by rivers that mostly run north toward the Caribbean or the Gulf of Mexico. "Mountain-valley" is the word for the "world" among many of the Maya people who farm the mountainsides and the fertile valleys that lie between them. Great crater lakes provide breathtaking beauty among the pine forests that still cling to the upper slopes. Locked in an eternal spring that rarely changes from a comfortable 72 degrees, the highlands of Guatemala are among the most beautiful places on earth.

Maya people have populated this country for millennia, growing corn for themselves and today raising vegetables for the North American market. The richly patterned, brilliantly colored traditional dress that they wear as they go about their lives contrasts sharply with the greens and ochers of the landscape. Weaving is a way of life here; it provides the bright cloth so in demand by the tourists who come to enjoy the country and the climate. In many regions, Maya men still wear their traditional, handmade clothes, but Maya women everywhere in Guatemala wear the indigenous blouses called *po't* in Maya and *huipil* in Spanish, and skirts called *uq* or *corte,* made of meters of cloth wrapped around and held in place by tightly cinched belts (Fig. 8.2). Although many women can no longer afford expensive handmade textiles, they cling to their *uq* and their *po't* as markers of their Maya identity.

West of Antigua and Guatemala City lies Kaqchikel country. Today the principal Kaqchikel center is Chimaltenango, a bustling town clouded by fumes from the converted school buses that constitute Guatemala's principal transportation system. The main highway passes through Chimaltenango on its way west to the mountains around Lake Atitlan, a crater lake that has become a favorite place for tourists and wealthy Guatemalans from the city. Halfway between Chimalte-

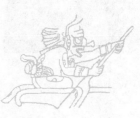

THE CODE OF KINGS   291

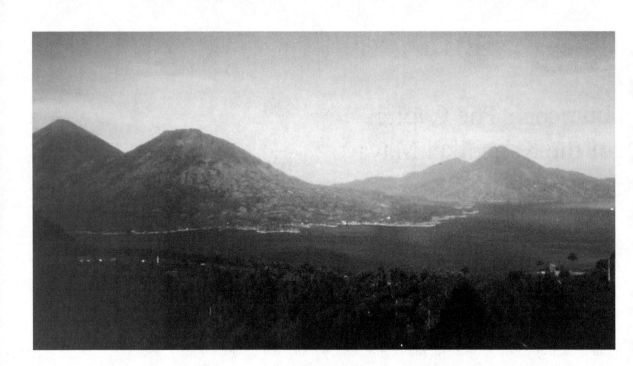

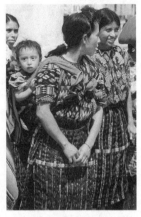

Fig. 8.1.
The volcanoes over-
looking Lake Atitlan.
The view is from the
Kaqchikel side toward
Tzutuhil territory.

Fig. 8.2. K'iche'
women wearing their
po't and *uq.*

nango and the lake lies Iximche', the last capital of the independent nation of the Kaqchikel, and the first capital of the Spanish invaders. The Spaniards called the town Guatemala, after the Aztec word *Quauhtemallan,* or "Forested Land," an apt description even today. The Aztecs may simply have translated the word *K'iche',* "many trees," the name of the dominant people of the region. The Aztec name for the dominant K'iche' people became the name of the modern nation of Guatemala.

THE HISTORY OF THE KAQCHIKELS AND THE BUILDING OF IXIMCHE'

After the Spanish invasion, the Kaqchikels recorded their history in a book called the *Annals of the Kaqchikels.* Using the new alphabet of their conquerors, but writing in the Kaqchikel language, they told the story of their origins, their history, and their tragic encounter with the Spaniards and its aftermath. The *Annals* are but one of many postconquest documents[1] written by the Maya of the Guatemalan highlands to document their history in the face of Spanish domination. These documents register a detailed record of the century before the appearance of the Spanish. These chronicles had their roots in a tradition of history and political symbolism that was already two thousand years old when Columbus first touched the Americas.

The Kaqchikels are part of a larger group called the K'iche'an peoples by modern researchers. The founding stories of the various peoples in the highlands record that they were led by great ancestral heroes from a place called *Tulan*. The K'iche' called their place of origin *Tulan-Suywa, Wuqub'-Pek, Wuqub'-Siwan,* "Tulan-Suywa, Seven Caves, Seven Ravines,"[2] echoing the origin place, *Chicomoztoc,* "Seven Caves," that figured prominently in Aztec myths. The Kaqchikels wrote of four Tulans and said they came from the western one, led by the great lords Q'aq'awitz and Saqtekauh. There at the western Tulan, the Kaqchikels and other K'iche'an peoples received their patron gods, their badges of office, their thrones, their bundles, and the other insignia from which they derived magic power and their political authority. The Kaqchikels also received their staffs (*chamey*) made from red trees (*kaqa che'*), from which came their name.

After leaving their Tulan, the Kaqchikels described traveling across water to reach *Suywa,* which was located somewhere in the Gulf Coast region of Tabasco or Veracruz. There they encountered peoples they called the *Nonowalkat* and *Tepew-Oloman*.[3] The Kaqchikels fought the Nonowalkat, but both the K'iche' and Kaqchikels said they were brothers to the *Tepew-Oloman,* who "stayed there in the east." These Oloman may have been the Olmeca-Xicalanca who conquered Cholula in the eighth century, built Cacaxtla as their capital, and perhaps were at Xochicalco as well.[4] It is clear from these many accounts that *Nonowalkat, Tepew-Oloman,* and *Tulan-Suywa* were the same places and people that are mentioned in the Books of Chilam Balam.[5] The Tutul Xiw said that they came from *Nonowal,* West *Suywa,* while the Kaqchikels said they came from the Tulan located in the direction of the setting sun. The *Nonowalkat* they fought after crossing the water may have been the inhabitants of *Nonowal.* In central Mexican documents, *Nonoalco* was a term for the southern Gulf Coast region of Tabasco, while *Anahuac Xicalango* was an Aztec name for the same region. Both *Nonowal* and *Tlapallan,* "the Place of Red and Black" (where the central Mexican documents say some of the Toltecs went to live), are general Aztec terms for the Maya area.

Our problem is to correlate these descriptions of a legendary past to archaeological and linguistic evidence. That the K'iche' had contact with Terminal Classic peoples from the Maya lowlands has been confirmed at Seibal. The K'iche' version of the migrations from *Tulan-Suywa* related that their progenitors arrived at a place called *Hakawitz,* where they set up their first government. *Hakawitz* was also the god given to the K'iche' progenitor, Mahucutah, founder of the *Ahaw* clan. We have found the name *Hakawitz* in the inscriptions of Seibal.[6] When the ruler Ah-Bolon-Abta Wat'ul-Chatel built his great stelae program to commemorate the end of the first k'atun of the tenth bak'tun, he recorded a visitor named *K'ul Puh Ahaw Hakawitzil.* The first three words call him a "holy lord" from "Cattail Reed," or *Tulan,* while the final word gives his name as *Hakawitzil.*

Hakawitz has no meaning in K'iche', but in Cholan it means "Beginning Mountain." We do not know which Tulan the Seibal scribe meant, nor can we prove for certain that this Hakawitzil is the Hakawitz of K'iche' legend, but we think the two are related. For the K'iche', Hakawitz is a god and a legendary place, but the K'iche' have turned history into myth on at least one other occasion. Tekun-Uman, the leader who led the K'iche' army against the Spanish and who died at the hands of Alvarado, is today the principal *Mundo,* or "earth god," in many highland communities. Our problem is to connect the legend of Hakawitz to a historical reality, and we think it can be done.

After the Kaqchikels and their K'iche'an brethren left Nonowal and Suywa, they traveled to many places, sometimes to fight, sometimes to settle and take wives, and then moved on.[7] So long were these migrations that the K'iche' noted a change in their language: "The speech of B'alam K'itze, B'alam Aq'ab', Mahukatah, Ik'i B'alam is different! Oh! We have given up our speech! What have we done? We are lost. How were we deceived? We had only one speech when we arrived there in Tulan; we were created and educated in the same way." Were they noting language diversification that had taken place among their various groups? If so, they were describing events that took place over centuries of history.

When the ancestors of the Kaqchikels moved east from their homeland to the region where they would make their homes, they found a people they called the *Chol Amaq',* the "Chol nation," who spoke a different language. These Chol speakers may supply a vital clue about the chronology involved in this history. From Late Preclassic times on, Cholan was spoken in the southern half of the lowlands, from Palenque all the way to Copan. What were Cholan speakers doing in the highlands of Guatemala? There may be an answer at Kaminaljuyu, the ancient city on the outskirts of Guatemala City, where the inscriptions from the Late Preclassic period appear to be written in a Cholan language.[8] Recent excavations there[9] have shown that the lake supplying water to the city dried up around A.D. 200. Apparently the Cholan-speaking people left around this time, and over the next century or so, a new people migrated into the central highlands to merge with and partially replace the old population. From the household pottery they brought with them, archaeologists have identified these new people as K'iche'ans.[10]

The arrival of the K'iche'ans in the central highlands at this early date has significant ramifications for the interpretation of the myth of Tulan. Between A.D. 350 and 500, a new enclave with buildings that used the style of the distant city of Teotihuacan was built at the edge of Kaminaljuyu. The people living in this enclave buried their dead in elaborate, richly furnished tombs, using pottery made in the local tradition mixed with others that mimicked contemporary styles in the Maya lowlands and at Teotihuacan.

Since their discovery fifty years ago, Temples A and B, as they are called, have stimulated furious debate over the identity of their inhabitants and what their role was in the Maya region. While we cannot supply answers for these difficult questions, the very presence of such strong influence from Teotihuacan among these K'iche'an inhabitants of the Guatemalan highlands may be enough. We know now that the Maya of the period identified Teotihuacan as *Puh*, "Place of Reeds." In fact, the ancient K'iche'an word for "lord," *Ahpu*, may simply mean "He of Cattail Reeds."[11] If the K'iche'ans of the Early Classic period were allied with the Teotihuacanos, or perhaps were their trading partners, then the legend of Tulan and the transfer of symbols and objects to the founding ancestors is likely to be a description of events of the fourth, fifth, and sixth centuries. Thus, both archaeological and linguistic evidence support the presence of the K'iche'an people in highland Guatemala at least as early as 1000 B.C. and their movement into the central highlands around A.D. 300. They could well have been allies with Teotihuacan as well as with lowland Maya kingdoms, who traded for highland material like obsidian. The founding myths may reflect their long-term interaction with the political and economic powers of the Classic period and perhaps their position as a place of refuge when those great kingdoms collapsed between A.D. 700 and 1000.[12]

The *Annals of the Kaqchikels* continue with an account of the Postclassic history that led to the founding of Iximche'. Still allied with the K'iche' and under the leadership of their own leader, Q'aq'awitz, "Fire-Mountain," the Kaqchikels arrived in the land of the Tz'utuhil without wives or families. After Q'aq'awitz entered the waters of Lake Atitlan and transformed himself into a feathered serpent, the intimidated Tz'utuhil ceded half of the lake and its surrounding land to the Kaqchikels.

For many years, the Kaqchikels served the K'iche', helping one of their most famous kings, Q'uq'kumatz, "Quetzal-Serpent," to found a new capital at *Q'umarkah (Utatlan)*, "Ancient or Rotting Reeds." This place was a re-creation of the ancient "Place of Reeds" and therefore a new *Tulan*. The K'iche' placed their patron gods in its temples and proceeded to subjugate the surrounding area through conquest and diplomacy. The Kaqchikels were their willing soldiers in this endeavor. Like Topiltzin-Quetzalcoatl, his Toltec counterpart, Q'uq'kumatz was a great diviner and sorcerer who could transform himself into a jaguar, an eagle, a snake, or a pool of clotted blood. Q'uq'kumatz conquered lands as far away as the Soconusco region in the Pacific lowlands of modern Chiapas.

Q'uq'kumatz's heir was born in the midst of one of his wars. Named K'iq'ab', "Many Hands," this youngster would eventually outdo his father and become the greatest of all K'iche' kings. His fame began when his father died in battle trying to avenge the death of his daughter and son-in-law at the hands of a rival king. Two years later K'iq'ab' gathered his armies and attacked the town that had killed his father. He avenged Q'uq'kumatz, burned the offending town to the ground, enslaved the surviving lords, and brought his father's bones back to Q'umarkah.

After consolidating his power, K'iq'ab' embarked on an empire-building campaign of grand scale. When K'iq'ab' and his soldiers were done, the K'iche' empire stretched from the upper Usumacinta watershed in the east to near the Isthmus of Tehuantepec in the west. It extended into Alta Verapaz at its northern limit and to the Pacific Ocean in the south, incorporating over 26,000 square miles and a million people.[13]

The Kaqchikel rulers Hun-Toh ("One Toh") and Wuqu-Batz' ("Seven Batz'") served K'iq'ab' throughout these wars, conquering thirty-six towns for the glory of the K'iche' king. Their service led K'iq'ab' to elevate them to royal status, giving them the titles *Ahpo Sotz'il* and *Ahpo Xahil*,[14] and vesting them with the power to rule (*ahawrem*).

K'iq'ab' organized his new conquests by setting up military outposts throughout the region and establishing tribute obligations for the conquered peoples. He sacrificed captives at Q'umarkah, but at the same time he assimilated the conquered elites into his own political hierarchy. He might have enjoyed continued success in stabilizing his empire, except for the acts of two of his sons. Jealous of their father's power and growing wealth, they conspired with other dissatisfied lords, and staged a successful revolt in which they humiliated K'iq'ab' in a public ceremony and seriously damaged his authority. The disruption gave heart to the conquered towns to resist K'iche' domination and the empire began to fall apart. K'iq'ab' never forgave his sons and remained a bitter man for the rest of his life.

The Kaqchikel rebellion started shortly after this disastrous event. According to Kaqchikel accounts, it began when a K'iche' soldier tried by force to take the bread that a Kaqchikel woman was trying to sell in the market at Q'umarkah. She resisted and drove him off with a stick. The Kaqchikels demanded that the soldier be hanged, while jealous K'iche' lords decided to humiliate the Kaqchikels, who they thought had taken all the glory in K'iq'ab's wars. They demanded that the woman be handed over for punishment, and when Hun-Toh and Wuqu-Batz' refused, they called a council and, against K'iq'ab's wishes, condemned the Kaqchikel kings to death.

When K'iq'ab' could not stop his lords, he warned his endangered Kaqchikel friends and advised them to take their people away from Q'umarkah to a place where they could build their own kingdom. On the day 13 Iq', the Kaqchikel kings Hun-Toh, Wuqu-Batz', Chuluk, and Xitamal-Keh led their people away from Q'umarkah. The Kaqchikel scribes did not anchor this date to a particular year, but most scholars have placed the establishment of Iximche', the new capital, sometime between 1470 and 1485.

K'iq'ab' did one more thing for his Kaqchikel soldiers—he prevented his lords from making war on the Kaqchikels for as long as he lived. His loyalty gave the Kaqchikels time to build their city, prepare its defenses, and begin to set up their own tribute empire—primarily with people who wanted protection from the K'iche'.

In time, the first two independent Kaqchikel kings died. Hun-Toh was replaced by his son Lahuh-Ah ("10 Ah"), who died in 1488, and was succeeded in turn by Kablahuh-Tihax ("12 Tihax"). Wuqu-Batz's son, Oxlahuh-Tz'i' ("13

Tz'i'"), lived through the reigns of two corulers. He was a particularly successful king who consolidated Kaqchikel power by leading a series of attacks against nearby K'iche' towns. The war with the K'iche' culminated on the day 10 Tz'i' around the year 1491, when Oxlahuh-Tz'i' and his coruler, Kablahuh-Tihax, captured the K'iche' kings, Tepepul and Itzayul, and their god Tohil. They sacrificed the kings and other captured lords, including the *K'alel Achi* and the *Ahpop Achi* (who were the son and grandson of the king), the *Ah Xit* ("Jade Carver"), the *Ah Puwak* ("Metalsmith"), the *Ah Tz'ib'* ("Scribe"), and the *Ah K'ot* ("Engraver"), as well as high-ranking soldiers. Afterward, the K'iche' were forced to pay tribute to their former vassals.

Soon after the defeat of the K'iche', the Kaqchikels faced a rebellion from some of their own clans, the Akahals and the Tukuches. Oxlahuh-Tz'i' and Kablahuh-Tihax won the dispute decisively and the day of their victory, 11 Ah (May 20, 1493),[15] became the anchor date for all subsequent Kaqchikel history.

Oxlahuh-T'zi' continued to lead the Kaqchikels in consolidating their power and weakening the K'iche's until he died on 3 Ahmak (July 23, 1508), to be replaced by his son Hun-Iq' ("1 Iq'"). His companion king, Kablahuh-Tihax, died shortly thereafter, on February 4, 1509, to be replaced by his son Lahuh-Noh ("10 Noh").

The wars with the K'iche' continued through the next eleven years, but the Kaqchikels suffered from nature as well. There was a locust plague in 1513, a bad fire that swept through Iximche' in 1514, and in 1519 a devastating plague that did not end until 1521. It was likely the first appearance of smallpox, which had ravaged Yukatan a few years earlier. Motecuhzoma, the emperor of the Aztecs, sent emissaries to the K'iche' and Kaqchikels in 1510 and again in 1512. The second messenger, named Witz'itz'il, warned the Maya against the Spanish, who were then appearing along the coast of Yukatan and Veracruz. Later, after the fall of Tenochtitlan, the Kaqchikels apparently sent an embassy to Cortés, offering to ally themselves with this new force that had conquered the Aztecs.[16]

When Alvarado finally came to Guatemala in 1524, he found people weary from two decades of continuous warfare and decimated by the first plagues of European diseases. He and his army confronted the K'iche' first, defeating them in the battle of Xelahuh on February 22, 1524. On March 9, he burned the defiant K'iche' kings at the stake and destroyed their capital, Q'umarkah.

The Kaqchikels welcomed the invaders into their capital and even provided troops for them to use against their old K'iche' enemies and the nearby Tz'utuhil. The Spaniards entered Iximche' (Fig. 8.3) on 1 Hunahpu, or April 14, 1524, and were welcomed by the Kaqchikel chiefs.[17] After a short stay, Alvarado continued his campaign across the Guatemalan highlands, returning triumphantly to Iximche' on July 23, 1524. Four days later, on 1 Q'at, or July 27, 1524, Alvarado declared the Kaqchikel city to be *Santiago de los Caballeros de Guatemala*. This happened in the twenty-ninth year after the revolt.[18]

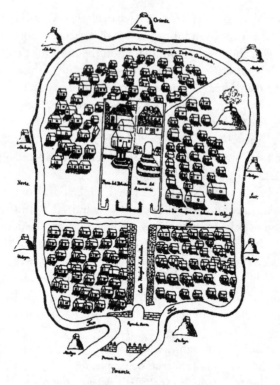

Fig. 8.3.
A seventeenth-century
map of Iximche'.

The illusion of friendship between the Kaqchikels and the Spanish ended quickly when Alvarado began demanding gold in tribute. At the instigation of a priest, the outraged Kaqchikels abandoned their capital on 7 Ahmak (August 28, 1524) and retreated to the hills and forests, expecting their gods to destroy the Spaniards. The destruction never came, and the Spaniards began their war against the Kaqchikels ten days later, on 4 Kamey, or September 7, 1524. Two years later on February 9, 1526, another 4 Kamey, a group of Spanish deserters set fire to Iximche' as they made their escape from Alvarado.[19] Later that year, Bernal Díaz reported returning to Iximche' and spending the night "in the site of the old city of Guatemala where once lived the caciques called Sinakan and Saqachul." He said that the rooms and houses were still in good shape, but this is the last known description of Iximche' as a habitable city.

The rebellious Kaqchikels did no better against the Spaniards than did the K'iche' and the other highland peoples. The rebels managed to hold out for another four years, but on 7 Ahmak, May 9, 1530, the kings of the two principal lineages came out of the forest. On the following day, many other chiefs, their families, and a large number of people joined them as they surrendered to Alvarado at Panchoy, the Kaqchikel name for the new capital that the Spaniards had built to replace the destroyed one at Iximche'. Today called Cuidad Vieja ("Old City"), it was located southwest of the present-day town called Antigua.

The Kaqchikel resistance was over. The Spaniards established the new town of *Tecpan Guatemala*[20] near Iximche'. Some of the surviving people from Iximche' were moved there, and others went to Solola and other towns on the shores of Lake Atitlan. Alvarado waited ten years, and then he hanged the *Ahpo Sotz'il* Kahi-Imox on May 28, 1540. During the following year, he had other Kaqchikel lords hanged, but he did not long outlast them, for he died on July 4, 1541. The Maya gods seemed to have taken a small taste of vengeance for the Spanish destruction of Iximche', Q'umarkah, and other Maya cities. On 2 Tihax, or September 10, 1541, after three days of torrential rain, the side of the volcano called Hunahpu by the Maya and Agua by the Spaniards broke loose in a huge mud slide and destroyed the Spanish town. For the third time, the capital was moved, this time to the site of modern-day Antigua.

THE CITY OF IXIMCHE'

Today the approach to Iximche' passes through Tecpan Guatemala, the town that replaced the burned, pre-invasion city. The road leads past the church and the central square of Tecpan, and then winds out of town toward the ruins of the ancient capital. The museum and the area where visitors park, have picnics, and play soccer once held the houses of the townspeople. The palaces of the kings and the temples of the gods sit beyond this area on a plateau surrounded by a deep barranca (Fig. 8.4). The first kings chose this location with the hostility of the K'iche', the Tz'utuhil, and other highland groups in mind. After all, they had honed their skills as soldiers while they served K'iq'ab' in conquering an empire; they knew what to expect if the K'iche' came against them. But Hun-Toh and Wuqu-Batz' had more on their minds than just a fortified site, because like Maya kings throughout the centuries, they needed a sacred center that materialized the supernatural charter of their political power. The symbolism they built into their new capital drew upon 1,500 years of Maya thought about the nature of power, authority, and the ideological charter that underlay both.

George Guillemin,[21] the Swiss-Guatemalan archaeologist who excavated Iximche', associated the old city's arrangement with the organization of Tecpan as seen in the Spanish documents describing its founding in 1540. The four barrios of Tecpan, which are today called Asunción, San Antonio, Patakabah, and Poroma, were then called *Naveahpop, Rucanahpop, Ispansay,* and *Poroma'.* These four names are Spanish renditions of *Nab'ey Ahpo* ("First Lord"), *Rukab' Ahpo* ("Second Lord"), and the family names *Xpantsay* and *Poroma'.*

Kai-Noh and Kai-Batz', the sons of Q'aq'awitz, who had led the Kaqchikels out of Tulan, received the titles *Ahpo Xahil* and *Ahpo K'amahay Xahil.* The Sotz'ils were one of the original clans that left Tulan. In recognition of their service to the K'iche', the leaders of these two clans became the *Ahpo Sotz'il* and

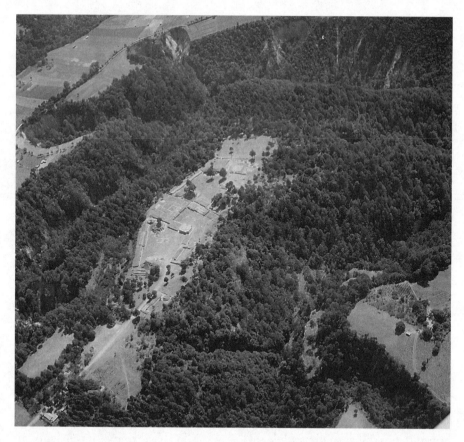

Fig. 8.4. Aerial photograph of Iximche' showing the deep barranca that surrounds the site on three sides.

Ahpo Xahil. In theory, the two groups were supposed to be equal, but the *Ahpo Sotz'il* was the *nab'ey al,* "firstborn child," and the *Ahpo Xahil* was the *chipil al,* "last-born child."[22]

The *Ahpo Sotz'il* at the time of the establishment of Iximche' was Wuqu-Batz', while the *Ahpo Xahil* was Hun-Toh. Chuluk and Xitamal-Keh held two other titles called *K'alel Achi* ("principal person") and *Ahuchan* ("speaker"). The new city had a palace, a court, and temples (Fig. 8.5) for each of these four lords, with the size and complexity of each area depending on the prestige of the office of its lord.

A—Plazas A and B

Guillemin proposed that these two plazas constituted a single complex (Fig. 8.6), serving as the ritual center for the Sotz'il clan and the residence of the *Ahpo Sotz'il.* The road leading through the rampart that once guarded the inner precinct of Iximche' passes through unexcavated mounds until it reaches Plaza

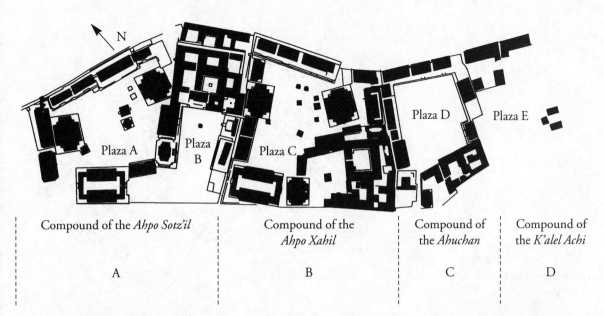

| Compound of the *Ahpo Sotz'il* | Compound of the *Ahpo Xahil* | Compound of the *Ahuchan* | Compound of the *K'alel Achi* |
| A | B | C | D |

A. Temple 2 lies on the western side of the plaza facing the position of the rising sun on the summer solstice. Built from adobe finished in plaster, the pyramidal base had sides with high *talud-tablero* forms broken by stepped-back corners. Two of the three stages[23] of this temple are visible in the consolidated remnants (Fig. 8.7). The innermost phase, not visible today, should be the work of Wuqu-Batz', the middle one of Oxlahuh-Tz'i', and the final one a commission of Hun-Iq'. The Kaqchikels placed a turtle in an offering under the floor on the central axis of the temple. Turtles played a critical role in the rebirth of the Maize God during the Classic period. Perhaps this mythology was shared by the Kaqchikels.

The remnants of the adobe temple on top of the pyramid belonged to the second phase, commissioned by Oxlahuh-Tz'i'. It had three doors entering into a long chamber lined with a bench (Fig. 8.8). The builders set a round fire pit into the floor behind the central doorway, and a wide block altar sits in front of the same doorway, perhaps for use in sacrificial rituals or for placing censers in ceremonies conducted in front of and inside the temple. A small chamber, also lined with benches, extended out from the rear of the temple. This may be the inner sanctum where the *Ahpo Sotz'il* placed the gods given to his clan at Tulan.

Incised drawings decorated the outside walls of the temple as well as the piers that separated the entry doors (Fig. 8.9). Artists[24] first engraved the drawing with a sharp instrument into a finished surface of fine clay. Then they painted color between the lines—red, yellow, and blue were still visible when the drawings were discovered. Ten figures graced the front, with others on the rear facade.

The Kaqchikel artists used what scholars call the Mixteca-Puebla style in these drawings. Starting around A.D. 900, the style developed at Cholula and in the Mixtec area and spread throughout Mesoamerica. The painters of the Mix-

Fig. 8.5. Map of Iximche' with the compounds of the ruling lineages.

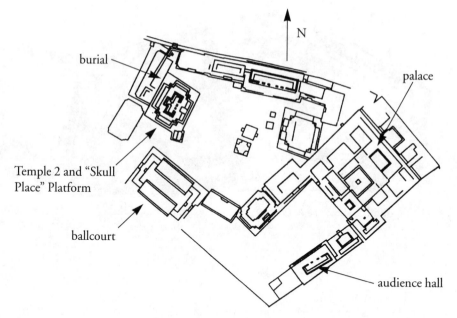

N

burial

palace

Temple 2 and "Skull Place" Platform

ballcourt

audience hall

Fig. 8.6. A: Plazas A and B, the ritual space, palace, and ballcourt of the *Ahpo Sotz'il*.

Fig. 8.7. A view of Plaza A with the ball-court on the left, Temple 2 in the center, and two altars on the right.

tec and central Mexican codices used this style for depicting both deities and historical narratives. These Iximche' images could be either, but the presence of so many figures around the temple suggests that they represented a Kaqchikel ritual in progress. One of the figures has very long perforators piercing his tongue. The composition had a double row of disks above a lower register with vertical strips, with the figures placed on this striped background.

A low platform sits on the floor on the south corner of Temple 2. A few rem-

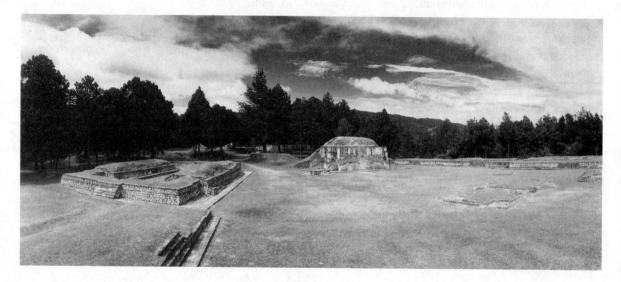

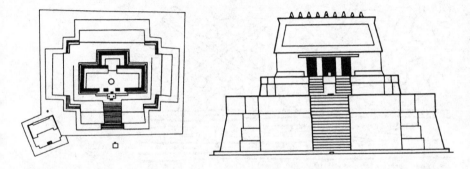

Fig. 8.8. Plan of
Temple 2 with the
"Skull Place" platform,
Itzompan, next to
it. Reconstructed
elevation of the phase
associated with
Oxlahuh-Tz'i.

nants of the paintings that once graced this platform can still be seen on the inner side, although it is very hard to read them today. The drawing made at the time of their discovery shows a skull and crossed bones sitting above two bands, one with chevrons and one with an unknown pattern (Fig. 8.10). Chevrons signaled war for the Mixtec, and were used by the Maya pottery painters of Chama to mark their local pottery. We do not know how the Kaqchikels of the fifteenth century defined it, but Guillemin, who excavated it, suggested this platform might represent an *itzompan,* or "skull place."[25] In the Aztec myth of Tulan, an *itzompan* located in the ballcourt at the base of Snake Mountain generated waters to the fields where the Aztecs grew crops, while they learned the arts of civilized life. If the Kaqchikels were building a new Tulan, setting a "skull place" at the base of the pyramid-mountain fits the paradigm.

On Temple 3 across the court (Fig. 8.11), archaeologists found the fragments of over a dozen clay censers scattered across its surface, exactly as the Kaqchikels left them when they abandoned their capital to the Spanish. Modeled in three-dimensional splendor (Fig. 8.12), one represented an old god emerging from a serpent mouth and two others show the same god standing on the front side of the censer. Could this bulbous-nosed effigy represent one of the Kaqchikel patron gods, B'elehe-Toh or Hun-Tihax?

Plaza A has long, single-galleried buildings closing its northern side. The arti-

Fig. 8.9. Drawings
from the walls of
Temple 2. These figures were not adjacent
to each other.

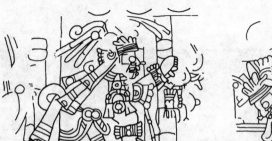
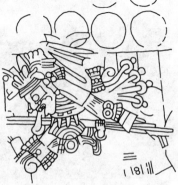
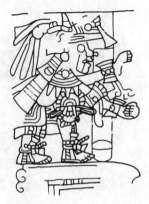

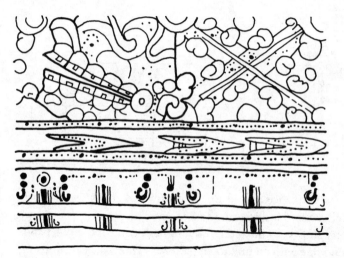

Fig. 8.10. Fragment of the mural on the platform next to Temple 2.

facts found in them suggest that they served as ceremonial houses rather than as family residences.[26] Two low platforms in front of Temple 3 served as altars or perhaps as dance platforms.

A ballcourt (Fig. 8.13) closes the south side of Plaza A, adding the last component necessary to create a sacred space in the Maya mode. For the Kaqchikels and K'iche', the word for "ballcourt" was *hom*. Today this word means "grave" because graves, like ballcourts, are portals leading to *Xibalba,* the K'iche' name for the Otherworld. Like the Itza at Chich'en Itza, the people of highland Guatemala used the story of the Third Creation, the death and resurrection of the Maize Gods by the Hero Twins, and the drama of their harrowing of hell as the center of their religious and political life. The ballcourt was the arena in which this great drama played out its consequences. This ballcourt and the plaza

Fig. 8.11. A: View of Plaza A, looking toward Temple 3 and the palace of the *Ahpo Sotz'il.*

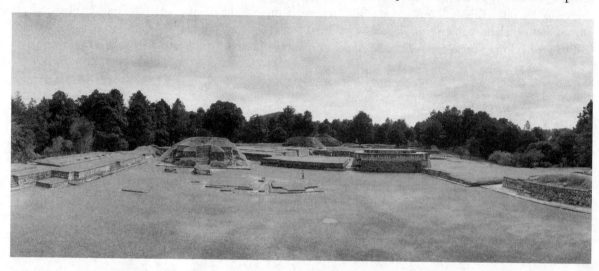

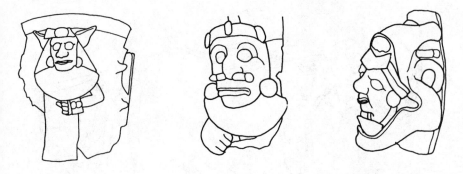

Fig. 8.12. Fragments of the censers found in the rubble of Temple 3.

adjacent to it must have hosted many great dance-dramas in which the myth was replayed for large audiences of lords and townspeople.

Wuqu-Batz' thus built a sacred space with all of the components we have seen at other Maya sites. He constructed pyramid-mountains to hold the patron gods B'elehe-Toh and Hun-Tihax, whom the Kaqchikels had received at Tulan. At the foot of the pyramid-mountain he located the "skull-place," and next to it the ballcourt. In the legend of Tulan, this pyramid-mountain is where the patron god was born. The ballcourt gave rise to the waters of the earth and provided a place where human beings learned to live in a civilized way. For the Maya, the mountain held the seeds of corn used to make the flesh of human beings, and the ballcourt was where the Maize God stayed after his resurrection so that humanity could worship him. This courtyard sanctified authority by repeating patterns that were two thousand years old before the Kaqchikels laid the first stone of their new capital.

Fig. 8.13. The ball-court in the compound of the *Ahpo Sotz'il.*

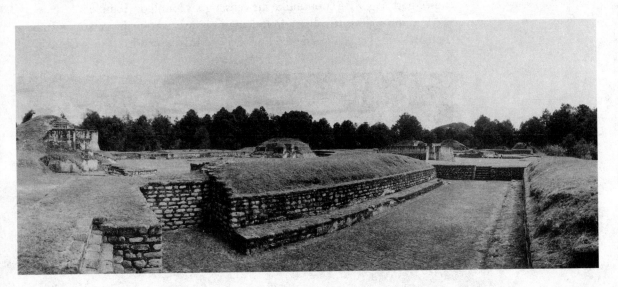

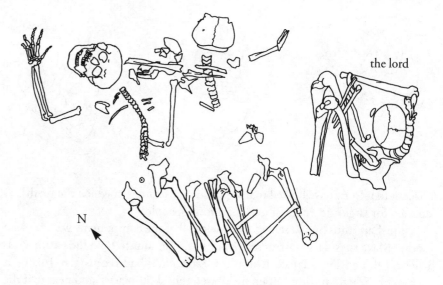

Fig. 8.14.
Tomb E-27-A.
The three skeletons on
the left are the sacrificial offering, while the
lord sits in the right
corner of the grave.

A1—THE BURIAL OF A LORD

The richest tomb (Fig. 8.14) yet discovered at Iximche' lay in Building 27 behind Temple 2. Having died in battle by a blow to the forehead, the lord went into his grave accompanied by three attendants, lying face down in positions that often identify sacrificial victims.[27] The lord sat under his companions, wearing a gold headband with a turquoise and jade mosaic and an extraordinary necklace consisting of ten gold jaguar heads and forty gold beads (Fig. 8.15). He had a moon-shaped, copper nose ornament like those shown at Chich'en Itza, as well as several jade beads. One of them was carved into the image of a bulbous-nosed god (Fig. 8.16) not unlike the censer gods found on Temple 3.

The most unusual object found in the grave was an bracelet cut from a human skull (Fig. 8.17). Incised lines depict birds suspended from a cloud band

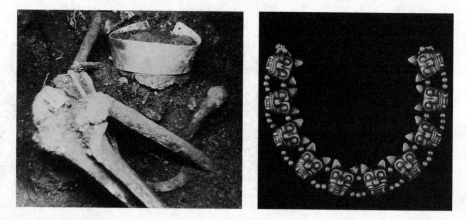

Fig. 8.15. The gold
headband in situ and
the gold jaguar necklace of the dead lord
in Tomb E-27-A.

with eyes attached to the bottom. In the central Mexican and Mixtec tradition such eyes represent "stars," but in the Maya symbol system collars with disembodied eyes signal *wayob,* "spirit companions." We do not know which was intended here, but this bracelet was likely made from the skull of a revered ancestor or perhaps an enemy taken in battle.

The gold headband and extraordinary jaguar necklace are signs of the prestige and noble status of the dead man. Jorge Guillemin,[28] who excavated the tomb, identified this man as a noble rather than a king, because he had a copper nose ornament. Guillemin believed a king would have had a gold one. Moreover, none of Iximche's kings died in battle, as this man apparently did. Combining the archaeological evidence with accounts of Iximche's history, Guillemin suggested that he was either Chopena-Tz'i'kin Uka or Chopena-Tohin, both brothers of Oxlahuh-Tz'i', and both of whom did die in battle.

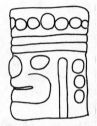

**Fig. 8.16.
A carved jade bead
from the tomb.**

A2—THE PALACE

Moving past the ballcourt into Plaza B leads into the palace of the *Ahpo Sotz'il.* A large court with a central altar (Fig. 8.18) provided a formal audience space for the residence on its northeast side. The palace with its small patios and buildings has three construction phases built one on top of the other. The lowest level corresponds to Wuqu-Batz', the intermediate one to Oxlahuh-Tz'i', and the final one to Hun-Iq'. The earliest palace had long, single-galleried buildings surrounding a court with an altar in the center (Fig. 8.19). This form recalls the

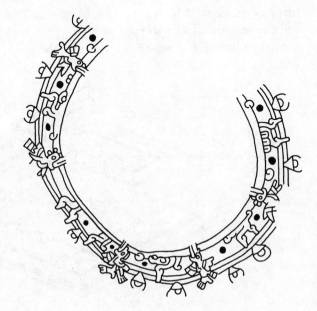

**Fig. 8.17. The human
bone bracelet showing
birds, eyes, and clouds
hanging from the sky.**

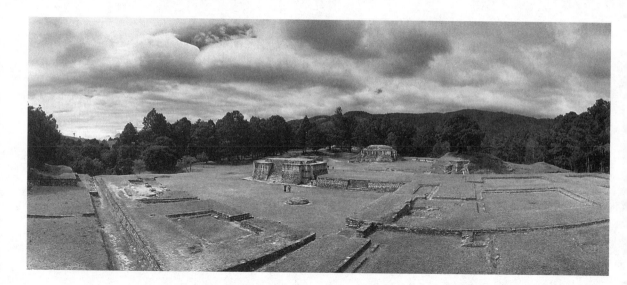

Fig. 8.18. A2:
View of the palace
of the *Ahpo Sotz'il*
and its forecourt.

plans of apartment compounds at Teotihuacan and Early Classic compounds like Group 6C-16 at Tikal, so that the Kaqchikels were drawing on ancient traditions to create the king's residence. Later versions of the palace broke the large central space into several small patios, presumably because the king's family grew larger with each generation.

The southwestern side of the audience court has low platforms, perhaps used in dancing or other rituals, while the southeastern side has a building (Fig. 8.20) with benches around three of the interior walls and fire pits at each end. Buildings with C-shaped benches like this have a long tradition in Maya architecture. Many can be found in both the residential zones and the sacred precinct at Copan, and they are particularly associated with Terminal Classic occupations in Peten and northern Yukatan. The *Ahpo Sotz'il* very probably held court and received tribute

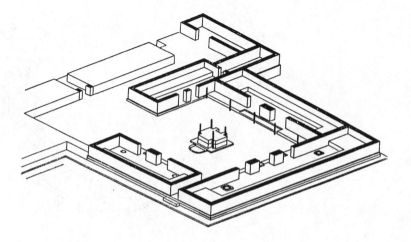

Fig. 8.19.
Reconstruction of
the first *Sotz'il* palace
built at Iximche'.

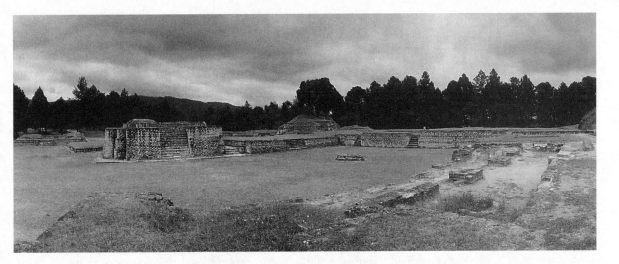

from vassal groups in this building. Perhaps Kahi-Imox sat on these benches to speak with Alvarado in the days after the Spaniards entered Iximche'.

B—PLAZA C

A wall separated Plazas A and B from Plaza C, which held the ritual zone and palace for the *Ahpo Xahil,* who was a coruler and "youngest child" of the two sovereigns of Iximche'. Like the *Ahpo Sotz'il,* he required a full sanctification of his space. The *Xahil* used the same pattern—two temples facing each other across a wide plaza dotted with low altars (Fig. 8.21). The western temple (Fig. 8.22) had

Fig. 8.20. View of the forecourt of the *Ahpo Sotz'il's* palace, with the audience house on the right.

Fig. 8.21. B: View of Plaza C, with the forecourt of the palace on the right and the eastern temple in the center.

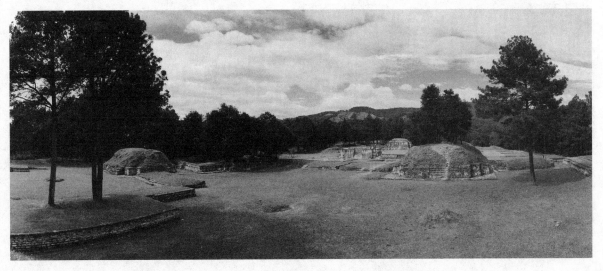

a small platform attached to its southeastern corner. In Plaza A, the analogous platform has skulls and crossed bones: this one had forty-eight severed heads under the court floor just to its west. We can't help but wonder if these people are not the K'iche' kings, Tepepul and Itzayul, and captured members of their court. At least eleven of these sacrifices were decapitated and two of them were women, perhaps taken as captives along with their men after the Kaqchikel victory.[29]

Single-galleried buildings closed in the northern side (Fig. 8.22), while the ballcourt sat in the southwestern corner of the plaza. The *Ahpo Xahil* placed his palace in the southeastern third of the plaza, but the form was essentially the same. Built on an east-west axis, the large entry court with its central altar occupied the western half of the palace. The main section of the palace had its entry on the eastern side of this audience court. Once again, the builders enclosed a small patio by arranging three buildings in a U-shape. These buildings had benches around three walls and fire pits to counter the cold highland weather. The smaller rooms and tiny courts that crowd this palace area were full of domestic debris.

Alvarado and his Spanish soldiers may have lived in this palace. Guillemin found evidence of a massive fire followed immediately by the collapse of the adobe walls. On February 9, 1526, Spanish deserters started a fire to cover their escape. Since Bernal Díaz saw complete buildings several years later, we presume the fire's spread was confined to the Spanish residence and nearby buildings. This historical tragedy preserved far more archaeological information about the final moments of the *Xahil* palace than we have from its *Sotz'il* counterpart. When the walls and roof collapsed, they encased the artifacts of everyday life, and apparently no one went back to clean up the mess.

Fig. 8.22. B: View of Plaza C, with the forecourt of the palace on the left, the ballcourt in the center, and the western temple on the right.

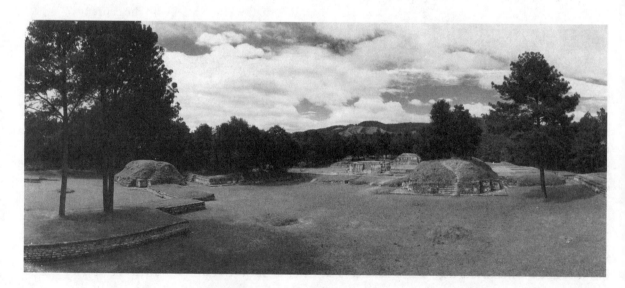

C—Plazas D, E, and F

Beyond the palace and the temples of the *Ahpo Xahil* lies another large plaza, with a much smaller palace built on its southern side. The archaeologists only cleared this area enough to map it, so that we do not know much about its archaeology. No equivalents of the east and west temples appear in the maps, although relatively high mounds surround the plaza. The small southern palace had three interior courtyards, with the westernmost of these courts having a cruciform altar in the center. Although smaller, this palace has the same features as the larger residences of the *Ahpo Sotz'il* and the *Ahpo Xahil*.

Further to the east under the trees lie other plazas and palace constructions that Guillemin did not include in his published maps. Designating these areas Plazas E and F, he speculated that these eastern areas held the court and palace of yet another high lord. There were two titles that qualified for such prestigious residences: the *Ahuchan*, "speaker" (Plaza D), and the *K'alel Achi*, "principal person" (Plazas E and F).

IXIMCHE' TODAY

Iximche' remained a sacred place to the Kaqchikels even after the Spanish destroyed it and forced its people into exile. Today its importance grows because the Kaqchikel community has once again centered their ceremonial life and identity in its plazas, pyramid-mountains, and ballcourts. We think the best way to describe this aspect of Iximche' is from the viewpoint of our own personal experiences. Linda Schele's first visit happened in the summer of 1990 at the invitation of a Kaqchikel family from Tecpan.

This magical trip took place at the conclusion of a week-long workshop that she and Nikolai Grube, a German epigrapher, had given to forty Maya from all over Guatemala. These people, many of them university students and community leaders, had studied the story of the Yaxchilan king Bird-Jaguar (Yaxun-Balam), in order to experience for themselves how the dry facts and dates in the inscriptions become history through discussion, analysis, and study. The workshop had gone so well that Nora England, the linguist who had organized it, asked José Obispo Rodríguez (Pakal-Balam), one of the Kaqchikel participants, if he thought that maybe Linda and Nikolai should see Iximche'. The answer was self-evident and so it was arranged—on Sunday everyone would go to Iximche'. Since neither Linda nor Nikolai had ever been there, it was to become a special day indeed. Linda remembers it this way:

Nora England borrowed a van to drive us up the long winding climb out of Antigua to Chimaltenango, where the backroad joins the highway that crosses the highlands. Driving west along the winding road, we passed through pine-forested mountains checkerboarded by carefully kept cornfields, until we finally turned onto the smaller road that leads into Tecpan. We parked in front of Pakal's house, and Nora knocked on the door. Greeting us with a huge smile, Pakal led us into the living room, where he had been giving a Kaqchikel lesson to the children of the family.

Pakal and Nora introduced us to everyone present—his father, Don Rodrigo, who speaks only Kaqchikel and still wears the traditional men's *atz'iaq* ("clothing") of his town; his mother, Doña Juana, an astute businesswoman who runs the family store in the front of the house; his wife, Ix-Ah; his daughter, his sister and brother-in-law and their two sons, and various cousins and neighbors who were there for the lesson.

Nora was like a member of the family and soon joined the women in the back part of the house, leaving Linda, Nikolai, and his friend Mareike Sattler in the living room. The children were curious about their strange guests, and the adults were polite, moving in and out of the room to make sure we were all right; but, as in all such situations, we felt terribly awkward. Pakal, smiling in excitement, brought his father into the living room and asked us how to write *pakal* in glyphs. There was a white dryboard in the room, so Nikolai and I, each of us with a marker, began to write everyone's Maya names in glyphs. Don Rodrigo watched in polite fascination, as the rest of them laboriously copied the glyphs, writing the phonetic values carefully beside each sign. Warned not to erase anything from the rapidly filling board, we drew for an hour, discovering during the process that the best artists in the room were Pakal's seven- and nine-year-old nephews, Sinakan and Ahkiku.

Having thus filled the waiting time while Pakal's mother, sister, wife, and Nora prepared a huge picnic lunch, our time as scribes ended, and we filed out through the house courtyard to the waiting van. I felt my eyes widen as I realized just how many people expected to fit in that poor little van. Ten adults—four of them Gringo-size—and enough children to bring our total number to twenty-one. At that time, the road from Tecpan to Iximche' was more like a washboard than a highway, a fact that delighted the children, drew suppressed groans and occasional giggles from the adults, and protests from the sorely tested springs of the van. We arrived, parked on the grass among the cars of Sunday visitors from Guatemala City and Chimaltenango, and gratefully pried ourselves out of the tightly packed van. Under Doña Juana's direction, we removed the bulging baskets and bundles from the back of the van and carried them to the spot under a clump of pine trees that she had selected for our picnic. She spread out a large cloth and began arranging our lunch where the houses of Iximche's townspeople had once stood. Satisfied that she had everything, she shooed us away to go see the ruins while she directed the preparation of our lunch (Fig. 8.23).

We left, the children and Pakal's father and cousins in tow, to make our way through the old ramparts that had once guarded the entry into the area where

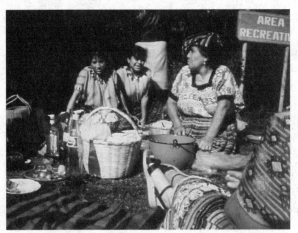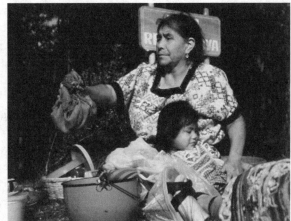

Fig. 8.23. Doña Juana
prepares the picnic
in the parking area
at Iximche'.

the Kaqchikel kings lived and ruled their people. We were an unusual group of people—Mayas, Gringos, and Germans—led by the enthusiastic boys who had become would-be scribes earlier that day. Pakal stayed near his father to translate our Spanish into Kaqchikel, for Don Rodrigo had loved Iximche' in a special way all his life. He had come there in times of sadness and joy to touch in some quiet way what it had once been for his people—to feel the power of history, even the wordless history around him. Pakal and his sister had named their children for some of the last Kaqchikel princes who had ruled there, and although the family was very much a part of the modern world, they also nurtured strong ties to their cultural past—and Iximche' is the pivot of that sense of identity.

For me, seeing the ruins for the first time unfolded as an experience of wonder. I had heard about Iximche' for twenty years, but my work and my interests had always kept me in the lowlands. I had never read about the archaeology of the site and thus had no idea about what to expect. We wandered through the entrance into the first large court and, although it did not have quite the quadrangular shape I expected, it rang true to all I knew about the ancient Maya. I could see the expected pyramids with temples on top and a plaza surrounded by building platforms. Pakal's cousin led us to the small platform next to Temple 2, where we could examine the remnants of the paintings around its base. Nikolai, Nora, Mareike, and I knelt on the plaster floor and worried out the imagery until we found the skull and bones and bits and pieces of the borders of the painting.

Satisfied we had found all we would see in the pitiful remnant of a once-complicated mural, we continued on to the nearby ballcourt. At first, it looked like another mound, but when we climbed the side, I saw the I-shape of the ballcourt before me. The playing field was a lot smaller than Chich'en Itza's, but it clearly had a related shape and function. It was even enclosed like the Chich'en ballcourt. I climbed down the stairs onto the playing floor, telling Pakal about the imagery at Copan and how the Popol Vuh myth was played out on a court just like this. He translated for his father (Fig. 8.24), who listened with rapt attention. Pakal later told me that in all the years his father had come to Iximche', no one had ever told him about the archaeology or how its buildings were so like those of the ancients. As I turned around and saw Pakal explaining to his father and cousin what we had said, I suddenly realized what a special privilege it was to be there with them that day. Together we were participating in a touching of worlds, on a momentary path that crossed boundaries, both between cultural realities and across time.

I led the climb out of the other end of the ballcourt and proceeded into Plaza B, where the palace of the *Ahpo Sotz'il* lay. In the middle of the court, I turned to Nikolai, who had just deciphered the glyph for "dance" that summer, and said, "This is where they danced."

"Yes," he agreed as we strolled across the plaza to its northern side and, upon climbing the platform, saw the remnants of the palace for the first time. Ah-ha, I thought to myself—here was the palace of the Kaqchikel king. We investigated its many rooms—demarcated now only by wall stubs—and then we ambled around to the east and found the long, single-roomed building with a wide bench around all its interior walls. I became terribly excited, shouting to Pakal that there was a building exactly like it at Copan. Pakal, Don Rodrigo, and the rest joined us as our imaginations ignited. To our right was the palace where the king and his family had lived, and in front of us were the courts where the Kaqchikels had danced and engaged in the great pageants that gave life meaning. We speculated about where the musicians would have been and how dancers and shamans would have paraded into the court, and we were all certain that the king and his highest councillors would have sat through the pageants and conducted the affairs of state where we sat.

Fig. 8.24. Pakal translates for his father, Don Rodrigo, in the ballcourt at Iximche'.

Exhilarated with the beauty of the place and the excitement of discovery, we crossed a deep gully and the remnants of a wall I later learned was the boundary between the two halves of the town. We crossed this boundary and entered a third great court. Spreading out across the open platforms and down onto the

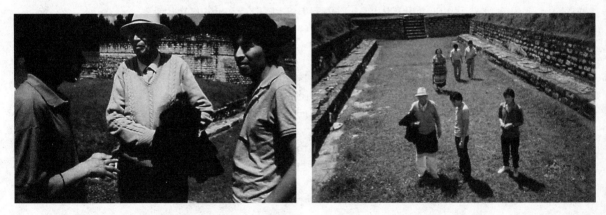

grassy plaza floor, we all explored on our own. I crossed a large platform and saw another ballcourt on the southern side of the court. Surprised that there would be two ballcourts so close to each other in space, size, and style, I walked across the plaza and climbed the side mound so I could look down into the playing field. Why are there two? I thought to myself, and I scrambled through the trees growing atop the grass-covered mound. The boys raced me through the low branches as my own excitement and fascination ignited their curiosity. Nora shouted at me to wait for Don Rodrigo and Pakal, for the seventy-four-year-old man could not move through the ruins as easily as the rest of us.

I slowed down but I could not wait. Climbing down the end of the ballcourt, I crossed the narrow gap to the next mound, climbed up, and found another palace more complex than the last one unfold before my eyes. Not only were there two ballcourts, there were two palaces, and beyond them another court-yard. Four courts, two palaces, and two ballcourts, I thought to myself. What's going on? Everything looked Maya, but why was everything duplicated?

My confusion brought me to the halt that Nora's words had not managed to achieve. I waited for Pakal to catch up and asked him how many lineages the Kaqchikels had. I expected him to tell me four, but I found my confusion renewed when he replied, "Two—the *Sotz'il* and the *Xahil*." I still couldn't explain why there were four courts, but now the two palaces, the two ballcourts, and the clear division of the city into halves made sense. One palace, one ball-court, and one plaza belonged to each lineage.

With Pakal's words, Iximche' made sense for me for the first time. Each lin-eage had built its own sacred space, complete with pyramid-mountains and dance platforms surrounding a "court," with the portal to the Otherworld in the nearby ballcourt. The Classic-period imagery of war and conquest was not read-ily visible, but according to the *Annals,* the Kaqchikels considered that their political charter descended from Tulan and that they were the warriors who helped K'iq'ab' make an empire, and then successfully defended themselves against their former overlords. Life among the highland Maya in the centuries before the conquest was as fraught with war as was their predecessors' lives dur-ing the Classic period. Like the Maya at Chich'en Itza and elsewhere, they also associated war, conquest, and the sacrifice of captives with the ballcourt, for the cache of severed heads in Plaza C lay between the pyramid-mountain and the ballcourt. For the Itza of Chich'en and the Kaqchikels of Iximche', the ballcourt was the portal into the Otherworld where the sacred contest of the Hero Twins was duplicated and sacrificial messengers were sent to the world of ancestors and the gods.

For Don Rodrigo and his family, Iximche' has always played a role in their lives. Pakal has worked with other Kaqchikel scholars transcribing the *Annals of the Kaqchikels* into modern orthography and translating it into Spanish for themselves. He teaches the children in his family how to write and count in the ancient ways. Sinakan not only learned to write his name in glyphs, but he now signs his school papers and his drawings with his glyphic signature. And Pakal's family is not alone.

Kaqchikels all over the highlands of Guatemala return to the sacred ground at Iximche' in ever-increasing numbers. They come as individuals, as families, as huge crowds of people uniting in the celebration of their past and their identity today as Kaqchikels and as Maya. They bring no captives or offerings of precious jade and obsidian, and the ballgame they play outside the rampart is *futbol* (soccer in the English-speaking world), not the game of their ancestors. They burn incense and candles, bring flowers and sacred maize, as they dance, pray, and sing to honor their ancestors. On special days, like Waxaqib' B'atz', "8 B'atz'," thousands of Kaqchikels converge on Iximche' to participate in the initiation of new Daykeepers, the *Ah Q'ihab'*.

Peter Mathews met just such a crowd when he first saw Iximche' in January of 1996. He describes his experience this way:

When I first went to Iximche', there were cars parked most of the way from the town to the entry gate of the site. It was the day of Epiphany, and it was clear to me and my companions that a lot of people were visiting Iximche'. Upon our arrival we saw just how many. The place was packed with Kaqchikel families. There were picnics everywhere, both outside around the parking area and inside among the plazas. The noise was incredible. Children were playing soccer in the ballcourts, periodically being shooed out in a lighthearted way by adults. Children squealed in exuberant play. Smiling adults strolled about, filling the plazas with conversation. "Tropical" and marimba music sang out from boom boxes carried by small groups of laughing teenagers. In more secluded corners, *Ah Q'ihab'* chanted prayers at makeshift altars.

I was awestruck by what I saw around me. I had been to many other Maya sites, but never to one full of Maya. My first impression was that I was experiencing what a Maya site must have been like when it was alive. On that day, Iximche' *was* alive. The thousands of Maya there were not focused on one single ceremony, but I felt an electric charge in the air that mixed the joy of a family outing with a reverence for Iximche'.

I glanced at my companions and saw mixed emotions on their faces. Should we be intruding here? We had been to other Maya sites and had usually had them to ourselves. Now we were in a place where there were thousands of other people. What's more, they weren't tourists, as at Copan. Virtually everyone else at Iximche' on that day was Kaqchikel. As we crossed the gap from *Ahpo Sotz'il*'s palace to the buildings beyond, a young Kaqchikel in a group ahead of us turned casually to lend a hand to help us across. He was smiling. At that moment, I think we all stopped feeling like intruders.

To us, what Peter saw at Iximche' is something new. We have both been to Maya sites that were full of people, but in every case, the people were as much strangers as we were—whether Ladinos, Gringos, Europeans, or Asians. At Iximche' the crowd was Kaqchikel. They had gone to their sacred ancestral place with the same respect and emotion that people have when they go to such places around the world. It is not strange that Kaqchikels should feel such emotion and attachment to their old capital. That has never changed. The change is in the fact that they have taken back its sovereignty after almost five hundred years.

For the last thirty years, millions of pilgrims from all over the world have come to the land of the Maya to witness the works of their hands and to see the roots of their civilization. Today, Maya people have joined these pilgrims, but their connections with these sacred places are more than curiosity—knowing their own past and understanding what their ancestors built has become a means of resistance against the fate of being strangers in their own land.

Concordance
of Maya Personal Names

The list below contains all of the personal names of the kings and nobles mentioned in this book, along with other names that they have been called in the literature. The variations in these names result from the ongoing process of deciphering Maya hieroglyphs, by which readings continue to be refined and emended, and the use of the unified alphabet as the orthography in this book.

Name(s) Used in This Book	*Also Known as*	*Brief Descriptions*
TIKAL		
Yax-Moch-Xok	Yax-Ch'akte-Xok	the founder of Tikal's dynasty (ruled ca. A.D. 220)
Foliated-Jaguar	Scroll-Jaguar	(ruled ca. 292)
Toh-Chak-Ich'ak	Great-Jaguar-Paw	(ruled ca. 317–378); died of wounds from war with Waxaktun
K'ak'-Sih	Smoking-Frog, Smoke-Frog	conquered Waxaktun in 378; (ruled at Waxaktun until ca. 396)
Yax-Ain I	Curl-Snout	tenth king (ruled ca. 379–420)
Siyan-Kan-K'awil, Sian-Kan-K'awil	Stormy-Sky	eleventh king (ruled 426–ca. 456)
K'an-Ak	Kan-Boar	twelfth king (ruled 458–480)

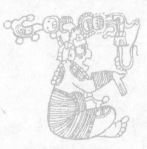

Name(s) Used in This Book	Also Known as	Brief Descriptions
Double-Bird		twenty-first king (ruled ?537–ca. 562)
Animal-Skull	Animal Head	twenty-second king (ruled ca. 593–?628)
Nun-Bak-Chak, Nu-Bak-Chak	Shield-Skull	(ruled ca. 633–679); killed after a series of wars against Kalak'mul and Dos Pilas
Hasaw-Kan-K'awil I	Ruler A Hasaw-Chan-K'awil	son of Nun-Bak-Chak; twenty-sixth king (ruled 682–734)
Yik'in-Kan-K'awil	Ruler B	twenty-seventh king (ruled 734–750)
Yax-Ain II	Ruler C	twenty-ninth king (ruled 768–ca. 790)
Hasaw-Kan-K'awil II		last known king of Tikal (ruled ca. 869–879)

PALENQUE

Name(s) Used in This Book	Also Known as	Brief Descriptions
K'uk'-Balam	Quetzal, Kuk I, Bahlum-K'uk' I	the founder of Palenque's dynasty (ruled A.D. 431–?435)
Casper	11 Rabbit	second ruler (435–?487)
Butz'ah-Sak-Chik	Manik, Sak-Chik	third ruler (487–?501)
Akul-Anab I	Cauac-Uinal I, Chaacal I, Chaac I	fourth ruler (501–524)
K'an-Hok'-Chitam I	Kan-Xul I, Hok	fifth ruler (529–565)
Akul-Anab II	Cauac-Uinal II, Chaac(al) II	sixth ruler (565–570)
Kan-Balam I	Bahlum, Chan-Bahlum I	seventh ruler (572–583)
Lady Olnal	Lady Ik, Lady Kan-Ik, Lady K'anal-Ik'al	ninth ruler (583–604)
Ah-Ne-Ol-Mat	Aahc-Kan, Ah K'an, Ac-Kan	tenth ruler (605–612)
Hanab-Pakal	Pacal I	never ruled (died 612)

Name(s) Used in This Book	Also Known as	Brief Descriptions
Lady Sak-K'uk'	Lady Zac-Kuk	mother of Hanab-Pakal "the Great" (died 640)
K'an-Mo'-Balam	Kan-Bahlum-Mo'o, Bahlum-Mo'o	father of Hanab-Pakal "the Great" (died 643)
Hanab-Pakal, Pakal	Lady 8 Flower, Subject A, Sun-Shield, Pacal ("the Great"), Lord Shield-Pacal	the greatest king of Palenque (ruled 615–683)
Lady Tz'ak-Ahaw	Lady Ahpo-Hel	wife of Hanab-Pakal
Chak-Kan, Yuk-Sahal, Mut		architects or overseers in the building of the Temple of Inscriptions
Kan-Balam II	Chan-Bahlum	son and successor of Hanab-Pakal (ruled 684–702)
K'an-Hok'-Chitam II	Subject B, Hok', Xul, K'an-Hok-Xul	younger son of Hanab-Pakal (ruled 702–ca. 711)

COPAN

Yax-K'uk'-Mo'	K'inich Yax-K'uk'-Mo'	the founder of the Copan dynasty (ruled A.D. 426–ca. 437)
Popol-K'inich	Mat Head	second king (rule began around 437)
Balam-Nan	Waterlily-Jaguar	seventh king
Butz'-Chan	Smoke-Snake, Smoke-Sky	eleventh king (ruled 578–628)
K'ak'-Nab-K'awil	Smoke-Imix-God K, Smoke-Jaguar	twelfth king (ruled 628–695)
Waxaklahun-Ubah-K'awil, Waxaklahun-Ubah	18 Rabbit, 18 Jog	thirteenth king (ruled 695–738)
Smoke-Monkey		fourteenth king (ruled 738–749)
Smoke-Shell	Smoke-Squirrel, Smoke-Caracol	fifteenth king (ruled 749–763)

Name(s) Used in This Book	Also Known as	Brief Descriptions
Yax-Pasah	Yax-Pac, Yax-Pas, Sun-at-Horizon, New Dawn, Madrugada	sixteenth king (ruled 763–820)
(Nu-)Yahaw-Kan-Ah-Bak		subordinate lord late or personal god of Yax-Pasah
U-Kit-Tok'	U Cit Tok'	last king, tried to start a new dynasty (ruled 822–ca. 830)

SEIBAL

Yich'ak-Balam	Jaguar Paw-Jaguar	king of Seibal, conquered by Dos Pilas, A.D. 735
Ah-Bolon-Abta Wat'ul-Chatel, Wat'ul		king of Seibal (ruled ca. A.D. 830–849)

CHICH'EN ITZA

K'ak'upakal	Kakupacal	ruler of Chich'en Itza
Ah-Holtun-Balam		a founding lord of the Itza Confederacy
Hun-Pik-Tok'	Hun-Pic-Tok	the conqueror of Itzamal
Zamma	?Itzamna	the first priest of Chich'en Itza

UXMAL

Ah-Kuy-Tok'-Tutul-Xiw		leader of the group who established themselves at Uxmal
Chan-Chak-K'ak'nal-Ahaw	Lord Chak	ruler of Uxmal and builder of the Nunnery Quadrangle

Name(s) Used in This Book	*Also Known as*	*Brief Descriptions*
Iximche'		
K'iq'ab'	Qikab	greatest of the K'iche' kings
Hun-Toh	One Rain	Kaqchikel *Ahpo Sotz'il*
Wuqu-Batz'	Seven Monkey	Kaqchikel *Ahpo Xahil*
Chuluk	Chuluc	Kaqchikel leader
Xitamal-Keh	Xitamal Queh	Kaqchikel leader
Lahuh-Ah	Ten Reed	son and successor of Hun-Toh
Oxlahuh-Tz'i'	Thirteen Dog	son and successor of Wuqu-Batz'
Kablahuh-Tihax	Twelve Flint	successor of Lahuh-Ah
Hun-Iq'	One Wind	son and successor of Oxlahuh-Tz'i'
Lahuh-Noh	Ten Earth	son and successor of Kablahuh-Tihax
Tekun-Uman	Tecun Uman	K'iche' war leader against the Spaniards
Other Sites		
Yahaw-te (K'inich)	Lord Muluc	king of Caracol (ruled A.D. 553–599)
Balah-Kan-K'awil	Flint-Sky-God K	king of Dos Pilas (ruled 625–698)
Lady Wak-Kan-Ahaw	Lady 6-Sky	princess of Dos Pilas (daughter of Balah-Kan-K'awil); reestablished Naranjo dynasty, A.D. 682
Yich'ak-K'ak'	Jaguar Paw-Smoke, Jaguar Paw	king of Kalak'mul (ruled 686–695); captured by Tikal A.D. 695
K'ak'-Tiliw	Smoking-Squirrel, Cuc	king of Naranjo (ruled A.D. 693–ca. 720)

Name(s) Used in This Book	Also Known as	Brief Descriptions
Itzam-Balam	Shield-Jaguar	king of Yaxchilan (ruled A.D. 681–742)
K'ak'-Tiliw	Two-legged Sky, Cauac-Sky	king of Quirigua (ruled A.D. 724–785)
Yax-May-Kan-Chak		king of Naranjo; captured by Tikal, A.D. 744
Yaxun-Balam	Bird-Jaguar (IV)	king of Yaxchilan; son of Itzam-Balam (ruled A.D. 752–768)

Key to Pronunciation and Orthography

In Maya studies, spelling has always been a problem. Early Spanish chroniclers and friars had to cope with consonants and vowels that did not exist in their own language. Each order developed different conventions, so that many different systems were used in the colonial-period documents. Modern scholars have continued to add their own orthographies to the resulting hodgepodge, so that the same word appears in many different spellings, causing confusion among scholars and interested readers alike. For example, the word for "lord" can appear as *ahaw, ahau, ajau,* or *axaw,* depending on which orthography is used. Having to cope with all these different ways of spelling is often the first problem to be faced by interested readers and scholars alike.

The Maya communities of Guatemala have addressed this problem by adopting a uniform alphabet with which to write all of their languages. In 1989, the Ministry of Culture and Sports of Guatemala adopted this alphabet and published *Acerca de los alfabetos para escribir los idiomas Maya de Guatemala* by Margarita López Raquec as the official government documentation of the new alphabet and the history of its development.

We have used this alphabet throughout this book to write Maya words, with one exception. We have used *h* instead of *j,* because *j* is very often mispronounced by English speakers. We have applied the alphabet uniformly, including to the names of people and places, both ancient and modern, that occur in any of the thirty-three Maya languages. In this orthography, words now look the way they sound. *Cimi* is *Kimi* and *Ceh* is *Keh,* although some of the spelling will seem strange. *Dzibilchaltun* becomes *Tz'ibilchaltun* and *Uaxactun* becomes *Waxaktun.* We have retained traditional spellings when names derive from Nahuatl or Spanish, so that Olmec, Toltec, Aztec, and Zinacantan remain the same.

The traditional orthography of Yukatek corresponds to this new uniform alphabet as follows:

a=a   (pronounced like the *a* in f*a*ther)
b=b
c=k   (pronounced like the English *k*)
e=e   (pronounced like the *e* in s*e*t)
h=h   (pronounced like the English *h*)

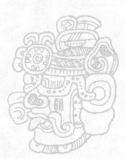

i=i   (pronounced like the *ee* in s*ee*)
j=j   (pronounced like a hard *h* sound, as with the Spanish *j*)
k=k' (pronounced like a *k*, but with the glottis closed)
l=l
m=m
n=n
o=o   (pronounced like the *o* in h*o*ld)
p=p
pp=p' (this is a glottalized *p*, pronounced with the glottis closed)
q=q   (this postvelar *k* is pronounced deep in the throat and has no equivalent in a European language; neither is it present in the lowland languages)
q=q' (glottalized version of the same consonant)
s=s
t=t
th=t' (this is a glottalized *t*, pronounced with the glottis closed)
tz=tz (this is another consonant that does not exist in English or Spanish)
dz=tz' (to the confusion of both native and nonnative speakers, the old Yukatek orthography had *dz* for the glottalized form of this consonant)
u=u   (pronounced like the *oo* in z*oo*)
u=w   (in consonantal use; for example, many traditional spellings, such as *ahaw* or *Uaxactun,* have a *u* in the place of the consonant *w*)
x=x   (this is equivalent to the English *sh*)
y=y
z=s

The plural in Yukatek and several other languages is *-ob*. We have used this plural with Maya words in order to escape problems of using English pluralizing suffixes with Maya nouns. We use Maya as both noun and adjective, and reserve Maya to refer to the languages spoken by the Maya peoples.

Notes

CHAPTER 1: PYRAMID-MOUNTAINS AND PLAZA-SEAS

1. We used numbers at Copan to avoid confusion because most of the stelae are designated with letters.
2. The reconstruction of this history has been one of the great intellectual adventures of the late twentieth century. Heinrich Berlin (1959) and Tatiana Proskouriakoff (1960, 1961, 1963–1964) laid the foundation by identifying emblem glyphs (titles that include the name of the kingdom) and proving that the contents of the inscriptions were historical. Proskouriakoff especially identified events and names at many different sites that set the precedent for later studies. Thomas Barthel (1968) first began to apply their work toward understanding larger political structures. His observations on emblem glyphs prefigured Joyce Marcus's (1973, 1976) work in trying to combine historical studies with reconstructing the political structure of the Classic period. Many scholars contributed to the reconstruction of the histories of individual sites, but it was Schele and Freidel (1990) who first published a wider chronicle of Maya history, joining it to contemplation of social organization and intersite warfare. Building from this long accumulation of historical information and debate about political and social structure, Simon Martin and Nikolai Grube (n.d.) have proposed that the states of the Classic-period southern lowlands organized themselves into two great competing hegemonies led by Tikal and Kalak'mul. Although no overall central state mechanism ever dominated the region, the rulers of many kingdoms acknowledged subordinate status to one or the other of these two states. Loyalties often shifted and wars were fought on a more or less continuous basis between subordinate members of these hegemonies. More rarely, the principal states engaged in direct warfare. The result was volatile, shifting political ground for everyone. A later analysis of these wars and their outcomes can be found in the workbooks for the 1994 and 1995 Workshops on Maya Hieroglyphic Writing at the University of Texas, Austin (Schele and Grube 1994, Grube and Schele 1995).
3. Schele and Freidel (1990) discussed the economics of tribute in the contexts of the wars of the fifth- and sixth-century Peten kingdoms. Excavations of sites involved in these wars (Chase 1991, Demarest 1993) have shown that winners benefited enormously, probably through tribute extractions, while losers suffered both economically and physically. Roys (1957) has discussed the predatory tribute extant in the

northern lowlands just prior to the arrival of the Spanish. Maya documents from the highlands of Guatemala, such as the Popol Vuh and the *Annals of the Kaqchiqels,* describe the tribute system of the K'iche' empire during the fifteenth century. The use of tribute extraction was a fundamental economic mechanism in the Mexica (Aztec) empire (Hassig 1985: 103–109; Berdan and Anawalt 1992: 55–79).

4. David Freidel (Schele and Freidel 1990: 92–93) discussed the use of commodities as currencies in Mesoamerica and Maya markets. We draw much of our information on the economy from his thoughts as expressed in *A Forest of Kings.*

5. Mary Helms (1993) discusses the importance of attaining goods from far-distant places to the prestige of chiefs and kings in various parts of the world.

6. Peter and Linda met each other for the first time at this 1973 conference, which had been organized by Merle Greene Robertson, an artist and researcher who spent over a decade documenting the architecture and sculpture of Palenque. At the time, we were both unknown and just beginning our love affairs with the Maya, but that conference occurred at one of those pregnant moments in time when new ways of understanding something are ready to be born.

   The moment had been made pregnant by the work of many people. Principal among these were Alberto Ruz, who had led a major project of excavation at Palenque beginning in 1948. He had found a tomb deep under the Temple of the Inscriptions in 1952, the same year that Yuri Knorozov published a paper showing how the ancient Maya writing system worked phonetically. "History" took a bit longer, but in 1960, Tatiana Proskouriakoff demonstrated that the contents of Maya inscriptions primarily concerned historical events of rulers and lords. Heinrich Berlin, who had made his own contributions to the "historical hypothesis," had applied these new ideas to Palenque's inscriptions and identified the names of four rulers, whom he called A, B, C, and D, on the Tablet of the 96 Glyphs. George Kubler had added one more ruler, whom he called Snake-Jaguar.

   The "historical hypothesis," as it is called, was presented in a series of pivotal papers by Proskouriakoff (1960, 1961, 1961a, 1963–64) in which she identified historical rulers at Piedras Negras and other sites, as well as identifying women in the inscriptions and presenting the first coherent analysis of Yaxchilan's dynastic history. Berlin (1958, 1959) was the first person to identify historical portraits of rulers and he found emblem glyphs, which turned out to be titles identifying people as "holy lords of particular kingdoms." His contribution (Berlin 1968) included the identifications of four rulers at Palenque, including the famous Hanab-Pakal. Others followed their lead in historical interpretations, including David Kelley (1962), who proposed a dynastic history for Quirigua, and George Kubler (1972), who amplified Berlin's dynastic identifications for Palenque.

7. The First Round Table was held in December 1973. In March 1974, Elizabeth Benson, then the director of the Precolumbian Studies Center of Dumbarton Oaks, invited us to a mini-conference that led to another critical breakthrough. She assembled a team consisting of Mathews and Schele along with David Kelley, Floyd Lounsbury, and Merle Robertson. This team returned to Dumbarton Oaks to work on the inscriptions of Palenque during the next six years. Many of the interpretations and techniques of decipherment grew out of these meetings.

8. Stuart and Houston (1994) published much of the pioneering work on identifying

place names and how they work. Grube and Schele (1991) added *tzuk,* the term for "province," to the decipherments of glyphs referring to place and geographic organization.

9. Robert Wauchope's (1938) classic study remains the major comparative source on modern Maya houses. Many modern ethnographies also discuss the house, its meanings and symbolism, rituals of dedication, and methods of construction.

10. We believe that lineage structures provided the basis of labor organization because of descriptions of Maya communities at the time of the conquest and in modern ethnographies. Moreover, archaeological interpretations associated with residential groups at Copan, Tikal, Palenque, and elsewhere have concluded that these compounds housed lineage groups (e.g., Fash 1983; Fash et al., 1992; Haviland 1977, 1981, 1985; Rands and Rands 1961; Sanders 1986–present). Epigraphers have identified titles and statements of subordination that can be used to plot affiliations and relationships of status (e.g., Houston and Mathews 1985; Martin and Grube n.d., 1995; Mathews and Justeson 1984: 212–213; Schele 1990; Schele and Freidel 1990: 262–305; Stuart n.d.; Villela 1993a). Other decipherments have identified glyphs recording parentage (Schele, Mathews, and Lounsbury n.d.; Jones 1977) and other kin relationships (Stuart 1989) between various individuals. This epigraphic evidence in particular points toward kinship as a fundamental principal of Maya social, political, and economic organization.

11. We are basing our interpretations on the compounds that have been excavated and reconstructed at Copan, Tikal, and Palenque, as well as on our personal observations of living arrangements in modern Yukatan, Peten, and the highlands of Guatemala and Chiapas.

12. Archaeologists usually associated this kind of clay platform with southern Guatemalan influence, but their appearance in Kahal Pech suggests they were in wide use in the lowlands as well as the highlands. They are very difficult to detect archaeologically and may well have been missed in past excavations.

13. Elliot Abrams (1994) ascertained the relative cost of plaster in comparison to other materials in experiments at Copan. Not only is the making of plaster labor intensive, but it also requires a lot of trees. Wood was also used in cook fires, so that reserving plaster for the most critical uses may have been a necessity as the forest areas near sites were cut down.

14. Barbara Fash has led the effort at Copan to reassemble the mosaic sculptures and understand how the architectural sculpture worked. Her work in this regard has been truly remarkable and recovered lost conceptions of Copan architecture. See her reconstruction drawings in W. Fash (1991), Fash and Fash (1994), and Andrews and B. Fash (1992), and reconstruction of facades in the sculpture museum at Copan.

15. Flora Clancy (1994) and Peter Harrison (1994) have proposed a system of spatial geometry used in the art of Tikal. Their system was based on a series of angular relationships. While accepting their observed data as relevant, we are less confident in their reconstructions of how these proportions were generated. In 1993, Christopher Powell, an MA student at the University of Texas, solved the problem of "how" by showing that Maya geometry used a cord to measure geometric shapes and to determine proportional relationships. Moreover, he found that the system is still widely used throughout the Maya area, and that it played a crucial role in the ancient

story of Creation. For us, the final proof came when Powell described red lines that Fernando Lopez of ECAP (the Early Copan Acropolis Project of the University of Pennsylvania, headed by Robert Sharer) had discovered on the temple floors in the tunnels under the Acropolis at Copan. He had found the "smoking gun" showing how the master builders laid out the plans of their buildings, and how they had used exactly the geometry he had detected. The same red lines have been reported at Tikal. We consider the system Powell has elucidated to provide profound insights into the way the ancient Maya detected and generated symmetry in their world.

16. This translation is adapted from one by Allen Christenson. Tedlock (1985: 244) included the following passage in his commentary section on the Popol Vuh:

> Andrés Xiloh understood this to be four sticks or poles driven in the ground at the four corners. . . . The measuring in this passage is done according to a unit still in use among the Quiché, the *4aam* or "cord" (a length of rope). Don Andrés was familiar with the phraseology used here. . . . He explained that the "folded" measurement is done with the cord folded back upon itself to half its length, and that the "stretched" measurement is done with the cord pulled out to its full length. . . . He observed that the P.V. describes the measuring out of the sky and earth as if a cornfield were being laid out for cultivation.

Powell has confirmed a similar use of a measuring cord all over the Maya-speaking area, although the customary use of it varies from community to community. Cord measuring is also a critical part of land-establishment rituals in the Mixtec Vindobonensis codex and in the Yukatekan Book of Chilam Balam of Chumayel.

17. Jon McGee (personal communication, 1994) told us that Old Chank'in, the famous leader of the Lakandon Maya, told him that the fat area of the Milky Way around Scorpius is the "roots of a tree."

18. In our telling of this story, we are following a study of the art of El Tajín by Rex Koontz (1994). He determined that the myth of Snake Mountain and the birth of patron gods related directly to the symbolism of El Tajín. The versions of the myth we tell here come from Tezozomoc (1975, 1975a), Sahagun (1961, 1978), and Matos (1988).

19. This version was told by Alvarado Tezozomoc (1975a), but we also consulted with Tezozomoc (1975).

20. This myth is recorded in Book 10 of Sahagun's (1961) account of the Aztecs.

21. See the notes to the chapter on Chich'en Itza for a fuller discussion of the history of this debate.

22. Stuart (n.d.a) presented his arguments at the 1994 Conference on Copan at the School of American Research in Santa Fe.

23. Enrique Florescano (1994: 199–206) discussed Tollan as the capital of the ideal Mesoamerican kingdom. Using Maya, Zapotec, and Nahuatl texts, he showed that "Tula" referred to the capital in any kingdom, instead of to one location, such as Tula in Hidalgo. David Carrasco (1982: 4) said that

> Quetzalcoatl and Tollan were religious symbols in the sense that they revealed and were utilized to demonstrate sacred modes of being in pre-Columbian society. Their sacrality derived from their capacity to participate in powers that transcended the pragmatic realms of textures, spaces, and beings, or what Mircea Eliade calls celestial

archetypes. Put simply, Tollan was a symbol of sacred space and Quetzalcoatl was a symbol of sacred authority. . . .Tollan expressed and gave sacred prestige to the effective organization of space associated with ceremonial cities while Quetzalcoatl was the standard for the vital relationship between kingship and divinity.

Carrasco (1982: 107) also stated that "as the evidence shows, there are 'other' Tollans and 'other' Quetzalcoatls, but there is always Tollan and Quetzalcoatl," and he argued that Teotihuacan was one of the Tollans of Mesoamerica. His discussion of these central myths is particularly useful.

24. On Structure E-VII-sub at Waxaktun, snake heads decorate the lowest level, maize-mountain monsters sit on the middle level, and the latch-beaked *Itzam-Ye* bird decorates the balustrades of the stairs leading up to the temple. Waxaktun Group H, a Late Preclassic compound, depicts a plant-sprouting mountain resting in the Primordial Sea. Above it sits the image of a second pyramid-mountain penetrated side to side by a Vision Serpent, in the earliest known image of a Snake Mountain.

Kathryn Reese-Taylor informs us that the base of Acropolis 6C at Cerros has mountain monsters with snakes emerging from their mouths. A huge banner stone sits at the base of the stairs leading to the summit of the Acropolis, and a large ballcourt lies nearby. The entire area is surrounded by channeled water and raised fields. This Acropolis, like both of the buildings at Waxaktun, represents Snake Mountain and the Place of Reeds, two hundred or more years before the core buildings at Teotihuacan were built.

25. See Ortiz and Rodríguez (1994: 76) for a description of the Olmec wooden statues and rubber balls found in the peatbog at El Manatí. Reilly (1994) discussed this identification in his study of the imagery associated with shamanism at La Venta.

26. Frans Blom (Blom and LaFarge 1926: Fig. 21) published a photograph of this sculpture and described how he found it. The egg from the island and the statue from the volcano are now in the Regional Museum of Anthropology in Xalapa, Veracruz.

27. Barbara Fash (personal communication, 1992) suggested that the Maya of Copan considered the water draining out of the Acropolis to be sacred because it came from Creation places. We think she has a good idea here, because channeling water through sacred centers was a very ancient practice. Almost every Olmec site known has canals to channel water around and through its sacred center. To be sure, Maya aqueducts had a functional purpose of draining courts and roofs, but the Maya were very good at combining functional and sacred purposes in the same objects.

28. Eduard Seler (1908) first associated the long-nosed mask with Chak based on the images of Chak in the Dresden Codex. Few people have challenged that identification, although Michael Coe and others have argued that it is the muzzle, not the nose, that was long. We began to rethink this identification many years ago, when it became apparent that many gods had long muzzles. Moreover, Chak of Classic-period imagery has a short muzzle. Other identifications, such as the mountain monsters at Copan, showed that the "long-nosed" category included more than one god, and that long-muzzled blank heads could be attached to almost any object to show that it was alive and imbued with power. See a discussion of the personification of objects in Schele and M. Miller (1986: 43–44).

29. Many scholars contributed to the decipherment of dedication texts, beginning with

Michael Coe's (1973) identification of the Primary Standard Sequence of glyphs on pottery. During the two decades after he pointed out the repetitive pattern in this text, other scholars, led principally by Nikolai Grube (1990, 1991), Barbara MacLeod (1990, 1990a; MacLeod and Reents-Budet 1994), and David Stuart (1989a), figured out that the text recorded the dedication of the pot, the type of vessel it was (Houston and Stuart 1989a), what it was meant to contain, its owner, and sometimes its artist. Stuart (in much earlier research on Copan texts), Schele (1990), Freidel and Schele (1989), and Krochock (1991) applied the information from Primary Standard Sequence to texts concerning buildings, stelae, and other art objects. Research in this area continues, not only in decipherment, but also in commensurating the archaeological record with the inscriptions.

30. David Stuart (1986; personal communication, 1992) first identified the words for "scribe" (*ah tz'ib*), "sage" (*itz'at*), "scribbler" (*ah bik'*), and "sculptor" (although Nikolai Grube discovered its reading as *ah ux* [personal communication, 1994]).

CHAPTER 2: TIKAL

1. The upright stone slabs that the Maya used to portray their kings and record their history are called stelae (singular—stela), after the Greek word for tombstone. The early explorers who first published drawings and photographs of these monuments designated them with numbers or letters in the order of their discovery. Our dates for these monuments come from the dates the Maya carved on them to give a chronological framework to the history they recorded.

2. The name consists of the *yax* sign prefixed to a cage made of tied sticks in front of a shark head. Following an earlier suggestion by Lounsbury and Coe (1968), Schele (1986, 1992) used *moch* as the reading of the cage glyph and named this founder Yax-Moch-Xok. However, Nikolai Grube (personal communication, 1993) noted a context in which the cage is written *ch'akte*, a Yukatek word for "cage." This new reading gives an alternative reading of Yax-Ch'akte-Xok for the founder's name.

3. David Stuart (personal communication, 1992) used phonetic complements on various examples of the Tikal/Dos Pilas emblem glyph to read the main sign as *mu-tu* or *mu-tu-la*. Although no single example has all three complements together, there are enough examples to deduce that these were the correct spellings of the sign. In Yukatek, *mut* means "rumor, news, tidings, bird, a bun or knot of plaited hair, a padded ring." In the Cholan languages, *mut* is the general word for "bird." At Tikal and Dos Pilas, *mut* was written as a knot of plaited hair seen from the rear of the head. At Palenque, it appears as a bird head. Several examples at Tikal included *yax*, "first," or "green," so that the lords of Mutul marked their kingdom as the "First Mutul."

4. There is an example on Stela 26 written *natal mutul*, another way of saying "First Mutul." One example on Stela 5 combines the tied hair with a head variant of the *way*, "nawal," "sorcerer" glyph. Two of the early stelae at Tikal depict the king as a *way*, or "sorcerer," a usage that connects directly to the meaning of *mut* as "prognostication."

5. There have been two major campaigns: one directed by the University of Pennsylvania during the late fifties and sixties, and extensive excavations by Guatemalan archaeologists during the 1980s.

6. David Stuart (personal communication, 1993) circulated a letter to epigraphers proposing that the split in the sky sign of this king's name reads *siyan,* "born." Phonetic spellings of the name support his proposal in this and other contexts. This king's name, Sian-Kan-K'awil, meant something like "Heaven-born Embodiment" or "Heaven-born Sustenance."

7. Stela 31 records that he ended the k'atun on 8.14.0.0.0 and 8.17.0.0.0. Since each k'atun is twenty years of 360 days long, he reigned for a minimum of sixty years. Other scholars, such as Jones (1991), have speculated that there were two early rulers named Toh-Chak-Ich'ak. This earlier conclusion was based primarily on assuming that the Leiden Plaque was looted from Tikal and therefore recorded the seating of the Tikal ruler after the 8.14.0.0.0 k'atun-ending. However, subsequent analyses of these early texts have found no inscriptional evidence to support the Tikal provenience for the Leiden Plaque. If it does not record the seating of another Tikal ruler, then the two Toh-Chak-Ich'aks recorded on Stela 31 with k'atuns 8.14 and 8.17 are likely the same person.

8. Peter Mathews (1985) first identified this interaction between Tikal and Waxaktun, proposing that it resulted either from a war or marriage alliance. Schele and Freidel (1990: 130–164) argued for war and interpreted this conflict as a seminal event in Tikal's history. If the conflict was protracted, as we suspect, then the absence of monuments between Stela 29 and this battle may have been the result of unrecorded defeats suffered by Tikal. Victors often smashed monuments as a way of destroying the history of the defeated.

9. Peter Mathews (1985) first published evidence of this war, while Schele and Freidel (1990: 130–165) discussed the contexts and political implications of the texts associated with this history. For example, the victors erected a memorial monument, Stela 5, at Waxaktun, showing the conqueror K'ak'-Sih (also known as Smoking-Frog) striding with his weapons. In their original analysis of this war, they (Schele and Freidel 1990: 148–149) proposed that Toh-Chak-Ich'ak let blood in honor of the victory, but subsequent decipherments have changed this interpretation. Two verbs record his actions: *yah,* "he was wounded or hurt in some part of his body," and *och ha,* "he entered the water." Epigraphers led by David Stuart identified the second verb as a metaphor for "death." Thus, we know that Toh-Chak-Ich'ak was wounded and that he died. While interpretations of some of the glyphs have been refined and details of the story adjusted (Schele and Grube 1994; Schele, Fahsen, and Grube 1992; Fahsen and Schele 1991), this conquest event remained one of the most celebrated in Mutul history.

10. Schele and Freidel (1990: 156) tentatively identified Yax-Ain as the son of Toh-Chak-Ich'ak, based on the distribution of an owl war-title as the name of his father. At the time, no direct statement of parentage was known. Subsequently, this identification has been supported by another look at the texts in Burial 10. Coggins (1976: 140–176) identified the occupant of Burial 10 as Yax-Ain, who is apparently named on pots in the burial as "the child of the ninth successor." Toh-Chak-Ich'ak carries the ninth successor title on a pot found in his palace and on pots from Burial 22, which has been identified as his tomb. He has been reconstructed as the ninth successor based on the text of yet another pot. Recent study of the badly eroded Stela 2 has identified a passage that may be a direct parentage statement, but the

condition of the stela makes a firm conclusion impossible. There is growing evidence supporting the proposal that Yax-Ain was the son of Toh-Chak-Ich'ak.

11. The history of research in this area is long and complicated. Heinrich Berlin (1958) discovered the first piece of the puzzle by identifying emblem glyphs, special titles we now know to name particular people as lords of a specific kingdom. Thomas Barthel (1968) suggested that four of these emblem glyphs named regional capitals, an idea that was developed further by Joyce Marcus (1973, 1976) in her studies of the political structure of the Classic period. Peter Mathews (1985) plotted out the dates and interactions of the Early Classic kingdoms in the central Peten and first identified the early Waxaktun-Tikal interaction. Finally, excavations at Caracol revealed that it had defeated Tikal in the early sixth century (Houston 1987).

    In dealing with the aftermath of the Caracol defeat of Tikal, Schele and Freidel (1990) presented evidence that Caracol acted in concert with Kalak'mul, which had built an alliance network surrounding Tikal that led to its defeat. Simon Martin and Nikolai Grube (n.d., 1995, Grube 1993, Schele and Grube 1994) developed a detailed analysis of these two hegemonies, their structures, and their history of rivalry and war. Their work has demonstrated the existence of large political structures in these hegemonies and the use of war as an instrument of policy by both sides.

12. We do not have archaeological or inscriptional evidence from the period leading up to the victory over Waxaktun, but the examples of other wars may give hints of what happened. Major wars like this were often conducted over the years, with both sides achieving victories and suffering defeats. Inscriptions document this kind of reversal of fortune for the Tikal-Caracol war, the Tikal–Dos Pilas war, and the Palenque-Kalak'mul war. One reason for the absence of major monuments from Toh-Chak-Ich'ak's reign may be that they were destroyed or badly damaged during an earlier Waxaktun victory, but without further evidence, these speculations must remain tentative.

13. We relied heavily on Peter Harrison for our dating and attribution of buildings to particular rulers. His dissertation (Harrison 1970) details his study of the function of the component buildings. Clemency Coggins's (1976) dissertation on the pottery and other artifacts found in the University of Pennsylvania is one of the few available sources concerning the dating of the pottery found in the excavations. And the most recent evaluations of building sequences of the East Court appear in Jones (1991, 1996). Our most crucial information has come directly from Peter Harrison, who read early versions of this chapter and provided detailed information to correct our reconstructions.

14. Christopher Jones (1991, 1996) described these changes and renovations in detail. We base our chronology and sequence of events on his interpretations.

15. We base our description of the architectural history on Jones (1991, 1996) and Coggins (1976). Full archaeological detail of the excavation of Burial 195 and nearby structures is now available in W. Coe (1990), and Jones (1996) documents similar information on the East Court and its various stages.

16. Houston et al. (n.d.) suggested this kinship relationship based on a parentage statement at Dos Pilas. Although the name of the father is damaged, we think their identification is very probably correct. This makes the Dos Pilas line a cadet segment of the Tikal dynasty, at least at the beginning. The son soon switched loyalty and

joined the Kalak'mul hegemony. Houston et al. (n.d.) have also identified the name of the Burial 195 king on an Altar de Sacrificios stela dating 9.9.15.0.0 (A.D. 628).

17. Archaeologists George Guillemin and Rudi Larios designated this tomb as Burial 195. They found it under Temple 5D-32, a building on the platform in front of the North Acropolis. They found the tomb full of silt. Seeing cavities in the silt, they injected them with plaster and recovered casts of wood and gourd objects that had rotted long ago. The rich contents of this tomb included several painted and carved texts that recorded the name of the twenty-second king of the dynasty.

18. There were two intervening rulers of which we know nothing—not even their glyphic names. However, the maximum amount of time for both their reigns could not have exceeded the span between 9.9.15.0.0 +5 years and 9.11.0.0.0. One of them could be interred in Burial 23, if Temple 33-1st was the commission of Nun-Bak-Chak. However, evidence from the construction technology of Temple 33-1st and associations of particular episodes within its construction sequence suggests it was the work of Hasaw-Kan-K'awil. If this is the correct attribution, then Burial 23 may have held Nun-Bak-Chak.

19. This history was first placed in a larger regional context by Schele and Freidel (1990: 165–216), but their interpretation was premature by a matter of months. In the summer of 1991, the Dos Pilas Regional Project excavated a stairwell at Dos Pilas that recorded the capture and death of the king of Tikal at the hands of the Dos Pilas lord. Stephen Houston and colleagues (Houston 1993; Houston et al., n.d.) from the Dos Pilas project made the first analyses of this remarkable text. Martin and Grube (n.d.) and Schele and Grube (1994) took these interpretations and placed them in the far wider historical context of the Kalak'mul/Tikal wars that dominated the central Peten during the Late Classic period. We also note that Clemency Coggins (1976) in her analysis of the artifacts of Tikal got remarkably close to some of this history before the major texts and complementary evidence were available. Houston (1987, 1989) also first identified the Caracol victory over Tikal.

20. W. Coe (1990: 841–846) described both episodes in great detail, and using radiocarbon evidence, ceramic analysis, and inscriptional contexts, he dated the second of these episodes to a period between 9.11.0.0.0 and 9.12.0.0.0. This period falls into the reign of Nun-Bak-Chak, but the timing is close enough to Hasaw-Kan-K'awil's reign to have been his work also. Moreover, Coe (1990: 844–845) emphasized the innovativeness of Temple 33-1st in terms of its engineering and related it to Temples 1 and 2, which according to him completed the program begun in Temple 33-1st. Coe also tentatively supported Jones's idea that Burial 24 was that of Nun-Bak-Chak. This evidence points toward Hasaw-Kan-K'awil as the builder of all of them, but the hieroglyphic information from the ballcourt favors Nun-Bak-Chak as its builder.

History may help a little here. Nun-Bak-Chak was driven out of Tikal in 657 and did not return until sometime before 672. He was then killed within five years. Thus, the years immediately around 657 (9.11.4.5.14) and after 677 (9.12.5.10.1) were not likely times for major building projects. If Nun-Bak-Chak was the builder, Temple 33-1st was most likely built between his return from exile and the second war with Dos Pilas/Kalak'mul.

However, if Coe (1990: 846) is right in following suggestions by Jones that Burial 24 held Nun-Bak-Chak, then there is a historical problem. Nun-Bak-Chak was killed in sacrifice at Dos Pilas and presumably buried there. To be in Burial 24, his bones would have to have been retrieved by his son through negotiation or war in an act that foreshadowed the K'iche' king K'iq'ab's retrieval of his slain father's bones from an enemy (see chapter eight). If Hasaw-Kan-K'awil was responsible, then the most likely timing is in the years preceding his defeat of Kalak'mul in 695 (9.13.3.7.18), as posited by Schele and Freidel (1990: 195–212).

21. Coggins (1976) identified Burial 22 as that of Jaguar-Paw, or Toh-Chak-Ich'ak. Her reasoning is still persuasive today, especially in light of the looting of this tomb in the final days of Tikal's history. This tomb was under Temple 26-1st on the central axis of the North Acropolis. Other tombs on this axis included Burial 85, the probable tomb of the founder, and Burial 48, which held Sian-Kan-K'awil.

22. Some of the fire evidence may come from a sacking event.

23. Jones (1996: 84) connected the laying of the floor that covered the old twin-pyramid complex to the construction episode associated with Burial 195, the tomb of Animal-Skull. However, he said that the masonry techniques used in the ballcourt and Structure 5D-43 were like those used in Temple 33-1st and the episode associated with Burials 23 and 24. Coggins (1976: 418) dated Structure 5D-43 to the early Imix phase, or around 9.13.0.0.0, placing it in Hasaw-Kan-K'awil's reign. While less sure, Jones conceded that the ballcourt and 5D-43 could be the work of Hasaw-Kan-K'awil.

24. See Jones (1996) for descriptions and drawings of the ballcourt and its glyphic panel. The western panels included an emblem glyph in final position, a period-ending glyph reading *yatah,* another glyph reading *yitah,* "companion," and a variant of the *k'inich* title. None of the known examples of Nun-Bak-Chak's or Hasaw-Kan-K'awil's names have the *k'inich* title. However, a later ruler named Nun-Bak-Chak has it among his titles, so that it could well have been part of the earlier ruler's appellative string.

25. This text has a distance number of which one k'atun and fifteen tuns survives. The distance number precedes *utiy Hun Ahaw,* "it happened after 1 Ahaw." If this 1 Ahaw date is 9.10.0.0.0, as Jones (1996: 2) suggested, the distance number leads to a date within a tun of 9.11.15.0.0. This text could, of course, represent a retrospective chronicle of events, but if the text recorded events in the life of the builder of the ballcourt, it identifies Nun-Bak-Chak as the builder.

26. Jones (1996: 32–35) described the sequence of construction phases in this building and specifically associated its *talud-tablero* style with El Tajín and Xochicalco. Moreover, following John Carlson (1991), he connected the imagery on the substructure with Cacaxtla imagery of war and sacrifice. His analysis here seems particularly cogent because this exact time saw the rise of Cacaxtla and Xochicalco and the destruction of Teotihuacan.

    Tikal's use of symbolism and imagery shared with Teotihuacan and other central Mexican sites began much earlier with the victory monuments from the Tikal-Waxaktun war. When Stela 31 was originally discovered, many researchers, led principally by Clemency Coggins (1976, 1979), proposed that Teotihuacanos through an intermediary at Kaminaljuyu took over or very heavily influenced Tikal in the years after A.D. 378. This issue has been hotly debated in the last decades with Schele

(1986), Schele and Freidel (1990: 130–165), Freidel, Schele, and Parker (1993: 293–337), and Laporte (1988) challenging the interpretations that require political and economic domination of the central Peten by Teotihuacanos. Schele and Freidel (1990) associated the appearance of Teotihuacan-like iconography with the Tikal-Waxaktun war that ended in A.D. 378, proposing that Tikal had made some special alliance or association with Teotihuacan and in the process appropriated this complex of images. John Carlson (1991) focused on Cacaxtla and studied this imagery throughout Mesoamerica. Warren Barbour (personal communication, 1995) associated the same body of iconography with Teotihuacan royalty, an interpretation that parallels some of Schele's (1995) own suggestions. Barbour also said that the figurines bearing this imagery complex are late, dating from A.D. 450 onward. That the complex is earlier at Teotihuacan is clear, because it occurs in the burials and iconography of the Temple of the Feathered Serpent, which was built around A.D. 225. Nevertheless, the Teotihuacanos seem to have been developing an expression of this iconography in portable form just as it appears with such prominence in the Maya zone. In our view, its spread throughout Mesoamerica does not signal the domination of Teotihuacan politically or militarily, but rather the growth of a system of affiliations through trade, religion, and perhaps alliance.

27. The style of this little *talud-tablero* temple and its ballcourt may reflect momentous historical events that took place far away from Tikal. Tikal's victory over Waxaktun corresponded to the appearance of Teotihuacan style and symbolism in the central Peten zone. While we do not know the precise mechanism of Tikal's interaction with Teotihuacan, the three generations of kings after that victory flaunted Teotihuacan-style images and symbols. We suspect Tikal and Teotihuacan had a successful and probably profitable alliance after 378. However, between A.D. 650 and 700, an unidentified enemy sacked and burned Teotihuacan, forever destroying its political and economic power. Xochicalco and Cacaxtla grew into prominence as Teotihuacan declined. They may even have contributed to the fiery end of the great metropolis. Tikal may have been responding to those distant events, because this temple, which was also built between 650 and 700, has more affinities with Xochicalco than with Teotihuacan. Perhaps the king who commissioned it was looking for new alliances in response to the political upheavals in central Mexico.

28. Remember that Temple 1 and its ballcourt did not exist at this time. There was an unobstructed view from this ballcourt to Temple 33-2nd.

29. David Stuart (n.d.a) determined that the Maya name for Teotihuacan was *puh*, the Maya word for "cattail reed," documented in Yukatek and Tzotzil. This identification has provided another connection that informs us about Maya intention in appropriating Teotihuacan royal and war imagery. Cattail reeds mark Tollan, the mythical place of origin central to state mythology in Mesoamerica for over 1,500 years. The Maya had Tollan-related imagery at Late Preclassic sites like Waxaktun and Cerros, so that we know the concept of the Place of Reeds is older than Teotihuacan. However, the Maya of Tikal and other kingdoms very deliberately adopted Teotihuacan imagery beginning in A.D. 378. This signals an intensified contact with the great capital to the west, but it also suggests that Teotihuacan's definition of this concept was becoming widely accepted throughout Mesoamerica. The Maya may have adopted it as a way of declaring that their ruling dynasties were also descended

from the original inventors of civilized life, of the arts and war, and of the institutions of the state. Who the original "Reed People" were is still a matter of passionate debate. Some believe they were the Teotihuacanos, but we suspect the original inhabitants of the Place of Reeds—Toltecs to the Postclassic peoples and *Ah Puh* to the Maya—were the Olmec. Yet for our discussion here the resolution of this dilemma is not required. The "Teotihuacan" set of symbolism functioned to identify and link together royal dynasties all over Mesoamerica as descendants of the *Ah Puh,* "People of the Place of Reeds." See the chapter on the Great Ballcourt of Chich'en Itza for a discussion of the Toltecs in the Terminal Classic period.

30. The graffiti of Tikal were drawn, photographed, and published by the University of Pennsylvania project (Trik and Kampen 1983).

31. Peter Harrison, who excavated the Central Acropolis, kindly read early versions of this chapter and provided this information to us. He has provided photographs and detailed information for which we are grateful. He suspects that Hasaw-Kan-K'awil ripped out the original stair and replaced it with a new one, complete with a new cache. This means the third stairway was probably placed by his son, Yik'in-Kan-K'awil (Ruler B).

32. William Coe (1967: 70) described this cache and its context. Peter Harrison provided us with further detail and, in fact, he is the first one who identified 5D-46 as Toh-Chak-Ich'ak's Palace, based on Schele's reading of the text on the pot in the cache.

33. There are several problematic interpretations in this reading that require some elaboration. Nikolai Grube (Grube and Schele 1995) tentatively assigned a reading of *t'ab* for the step verb, following a substitution pattern pointed out to him by Elizabeth Wagner. *T'ab* is Yukatek for "to climb up or ascend something." In sixteenth-century Tzotzil (Laughlin 1988) it means "to burnish or polish." Here it may refer to the finishing of the building or to the ascent of the king during its dedication rituals.

Nikolai Grube (1995) also read the *ah-k'ul-na* title as *ah k'ul hun,* based on substitutions in which the word *hun,* "book," was fully spelled out. He proposed that the *ah-k'ul-na* version was read as *ah k'ul un,* with the soft *h* absorbed by phonetic processes documented in Maya languages. His reading leaves open the possibility that the house was named *yotot k'ul un,* "the house of the holy books." We think this is a less likely possibility because of the *li* suffix attached to the glyph. *Li* may be marking the possessive form of *na,* or it may use the Cholan affix that marks a noun as being a part of a larger whole. This palace was part of a larger conglomerate of buildings.

We also read the Six-Sky title as *Wak-Kan-Ak* based on a substitution set in the Early Classic lintels of Yaxchilan. The reading is tentative because of the wide variation in this title at Tikal.

34. Peter Harrison (personal communication, 1996) attributes this renovation work to Yik'in-Kan-K'awil based on stratigraphy and historical context. He also assigns the building of 5D-141 on the north side of Toh-Chak-Ich'ak's Palace to Hasaw-Kan-K'awil.

35. See Schele and Miller (1986: 175–209) and Freidel and Schele (1993: 175–230) for a detailed description of the vision rites of the Classic period. Also see McAnany (1995) for an anthropological approach to archaeological data concerning the question of ancestor worship.

36. In our original study, we had badly misidentified the patron of these renovations. Peter Harrison (in a letter dated April 23, 1996) provided us with the proper attribution and details of the stratigraphy. His excavations identified Structures 51, 49, 53, and 55 as a single construction episode that was started after the building of the stairway to the second story of Structure 52, a building identified glyphically as a commission of Yik'in-Kan-K'awil. He said, "I ascribed this grand alteration of Court 6 to Yax-Ain (Ruler C), because he was the last great master builder who fits the stratigraphic sequence." He offered Structures 54, 48, and 122 as possible commissions by Hasaw-Kan-K'awil.

37. Nikolai Grube (1992) first identified the glyph for dance and discussed how the Maya named their dances. He recognized the central importance that dance held in Maya life. Freidel, Schele, and Parker (1993: 257–292) and Matthew Looper (1991) also discussed the role of dance in Creation mythology.

38. Houston and Stuart (1989) and Nikolai Grube (n.d.) independently recognized the glyph for *way*. Grube and Nahm (1994) inventoried the *wayob* that appear on pots and discussed their significance. Work into use of trance states by many people all over the world show that the experience includes near death, visual and auditory effects, and other phenomenon that make transformation a "real" experience to the person undergoing trance. When the rituals include many participants, the effect can involve many people. See Johannes Wilbert (1987) and David Lewis-Williams (1986) for a discussion of trance experience, shamanism, and art imagery.

39. Peter Harrison presented these data on the last days of Tikal and the Central Acropolis at the 1995 Symposium of the Texas Meetings.

40. The patron god on the Lintel 2 palanquin was the Mosaic War Serpent named Waxaklahun-Ubah-Kan. An effigy battle banner found in Group 6C-16 at Tikal records the taking of the same god in the victory against Waxaktun. Thus, Hasaw-Kan-K'awil may have been linking these two great victories through the imagery on these lintels.

41. This building is named after a nineteenth-century photographer who used it as his camp while exploring the ruins.

42. We had considered an earlier date until a conversation with Peter Harrison in 1995. He pointed out that Maler's Palace is later than Structure 5D-52, which is dated by its wooden lintel to 9.15.10.0.0 and the reign of Ruler B, Yik'in-Kan-K'awil. Given this stratigraphy, Maler's Palace and its court was a commission of Yax-Ain. He ends up having been a major builder in the Central Acropolis.

43. Clemency Coggins (1976: 502–512) quoted a letter by Proskouriakoff, who first pointed out that the costume worn by these lords connected them to the western sites of Yaxchilan and Bonampak'.

44. Mathews and Justeson (1984) first identified this title, although they suggested a reading of *kahal* for it. Several epigraphers, led by Stuart and Grube, later corrected the reading to *sahal,* meaning something like "he who is timid or fearful," presumably of the king. David Stuart (n.d.) built upon Mathews's identification and circulated a paper on its distribution in the Maya inscriptions. This title is received through accession rites and could be held occasionally by people, both men and women, who were of the *ahaw* rank. *Sahalob* had various responsibilities within the court, such as "keeper of the royal crown," "war leader," and "keeper of fire." They also ruled provinces and towns within the greater kingdom. No evidence has been

found in other inscriptions for the presence of *sahalob* at Tikal, but subordinate ranks were rarely depicted there. Thus, these robed figures could represent visitors from the western zones or local lords.

45. William Coe (1990: 518–521, Fig. 168B) documented four pits set in a square in front of the stairs leading up to Structure 33-2nd. He suggested that stelae had once been set in these pits, but the arrangement in a square is not a likely pattern for stelae. Freidel and Suhler (1995) identified these pits as the site of a scaffold structure. We agree with their analysis. See Karl Taube (1988a) for a full discussion of scaffolds in Maya imagery.

46. Peter Harrison has spent years thinking about how they accomplished their aim. Each successive king who built a new palace in the Central Acropolis used Toh-Chak-Ich'ak's Palace as the pivot for a geometry controlling the placement of new buildings. As they added their own residences to the complex, the Central Acropolis grew into the administrative heart of the kingdom and of the royal lineage that ruled it. See Harrison (1994) for a full description of his ideas concerning the internal geometry detectable in the Central Acropolis.

CHAPTER 3: PALENQUE

1. The name of the city itself was *Lakam Ha,* but *Bak,* the name of the kingdom, could mean "bone," "seed," or "heron." The people of Bak may have intended all three meanings in the symbolism of their city.

2. Alberto Ruz (1973: 229–240) documented this transformation. When he removed the remnants of these great buttressing walls, the entire substructure slumped (Ruz 1973: Fig. 24) and had to be reconstructed.

3. These locations appear on offering plates and inside the entries to the Otherworld (Freidel, Schele, and Parker 1993: 268–270). On the Tablet of the Cross, Pakal stands on the Nine-God Place after his death, and the founder of Copan was associated with this pair of places in the earliest buildings of the Acropolis. See George Kubler (1977) for a study of the distributions and contexts of these two glyphs.

4. We used the surviving data from the lunar series and the 819-day count to reconstruct two possibilities for the initial series date: 9.12.16.12.6 and 9.12.18.2.17. A distance number of 12.3.0 leads from this date to a now-missing date earlier or later than the initial series—we cannot tell which. We believe the later of the two initial series alternatives is the more likely reading, because that date is only fifty-nine days before Kan-Balam dedicated the Group of the Cross. We chose to subtract the distance number because we feel the text connects two dedication events—one in Pakal's lifetime and the final sanctification of his burial structure. If the scribes intended the other alternatives, the dates would be December 10, 688, and December 13, 676.

5. All time periods in the Maya Long-Count calendar ended on the day *ahaw.* Since there were thirteen possible numbers that could go with *ahaw,* the same number repeated every thirteen tuns. Thus, a name of day of a k'atun-ending, such as 8 Ahaw, repeats thirteen tuns later.

6. Another attack by Kalak'mul occurs in the text on the Hieroglyphic Stairway of House C.

7. Connecting a calendar-round date to a tun-ending, especially ones corresponding to a k'atun or its subdivisions, fixes it into an enormously long cycle. As Thompson (1950: 184) observed, a date, such as "6 Ahau 13 Muan, the end of 14 katuns, cannot recur with the same numbered k'atun for 949 bak'tuns, or 375,000 years. Any calendar-round date noted as a k'atun-ending without the specification of the number cannot recur as the ending day of any k'atun for 949 k'atuns, or 19,000 years." Any calendar-round date linked to a specified period-ending date must be moved into the future or past by those lengths of time if they are to be moved in the Long Count. Obviously, this temporal structure fixes the position of dates without the possibility of doubt—after all, the whole of written human history, much less Maya history, is less than 19,000 years.

8. The date 13.0.0.0.0 4 Ahaw 3 K'ank'in will occur on Sunday, December 23, 2012. Many people have asserted that the ancient Maya defined this date as the end of the world, but Hanab-Pakal wrote about dates and events long after that date. The world-ending myth is a modern "prophecy" that has no basis in the ancient Maya texts. In fact, only one text, Tortuguero Monument 6, recorded the 2012 date at all. Unfortunately, erosion has badly destroyed the verb in the relevant passage. The protagonist was a god named Bolon-Yokte, but there is no evidence of a destruction-creation cycle like that associated with the famous era date—13.0.0.0.0 4 Ahaw 8 Kumk'u.

9. Nikolai Grube (personal communication, 1995) suggested a reading of this glyph as *e-te,* and pointed out that *eht* appears in modern Chol as a word for "image" or "likeness." He suggested that this "nine images" refers to the nine stucco figures in the tomb. We like his idea and point out that Pakal also used nine k'atun-endings to frame the history he recorded in the inscriptions of this temple.

10. These books record myths of Creation, histories of various types, and long passages called the k'atun prophecies. These prophecies are in fact the histories of what happened during long sequences of k'atuns beginning with 9.13.0.0.0 8 Ahaw 8 Wo and continuing until well after the conquest of Yukatan by the Spaniards.

11. We draw our descriptions of the excavations and sequence of events from Albert Ruz's (1973) monograph describing and interpreting his work in the Temple of Inscriptions.

12. See Ruz (1973: 548–552) for a detailed description of these excavations.

13. See Freidel, Schele, and Parker (1993) for a full description of Creation.

14. Several people have come to this same conclusion independently. Dorie Reents identified the imagery of Pakal falling as the Maize God in MacDuff Everton's book *The Modern Maya* (1991: 25). Enrique Florescano (1994: 98) came to the same conclusion, as have other scholars.

15. There are only two known examples of a king transformed into K'awil: Pakal as he falls has the ax through his forehead, and on Copan Stela 11, the dead king Yax-Pasah has the ax penetrating his forehead as he stands in the portal of the Otherworld. The Ceremonial Bar that he holds has white flowers in place of the serpent heads. Both of these images depict kings in death.

16. The reading for this phrase is still under debate, although the meaning is clear. The verb has two proposed readings: Stuart suggested a value of *pat,* "formed" or "made," while we prefer a reading of *k'al,* "closed." The second part of the verbal glyph reads *buy,* a word glossed in Chol as "smooth" or "planed" in reference to the lid. The phrase is either "formed the lid" or "closed the lid."

The next two glyphs also have two proposed readings. MacLeod (personal communication, 1993) has suggested that the word for the sarcophagus box is *u kuch tunil,* "his carrier" or "his bench stone." Alfonso Lacadena (personal communication, 1995) argued instead that its name is *yamay tunil,* "his cornered stone" or "his table stone." Since both readings have rich bodies of supporting evidence and mean approximately the same thing, we cannot decide between them at the present time.

The last glyph in the phrase reads *nal,* the word for "ear of corn" and a name of the Maize God. Since the text names him as the possessor of the stone, the name must refer both to the god and to Hanab-Pakal as the god.

17. Hanab-Pakal was born on 9.8.9.13.0 (March 26, 603), and he died on 9.12.11.5.18 (August 31, 683).

18. A text on the Hieroglyphic Stairs at Tamarindito records *itz'at winik* as a term for the nobility.

19. Heinrich Berlin (1958) figured out the relationship of the names to the figures soon after the tomb was opened.

20. Until recently, we knew nothing about this earlier Hanab-Pakal, but the Mexican archaeologist Arnoldo Gonzalez supervised excavations in Group IV at Palenque that discovered a limestone head with a long inscription including the names of several important *sahalob.* Two of these *sahalob* tied on their headbands under the authority of Hanab-Pakal, so that we know now that he held administrative authority, even though he never ruled.

21. *Choh* has a wealth of meanings that might fit the context here. In sixteenth-century Tzotzil (Laughlin 1988: 191) *chojol* is "blood relationship" and "genealogy," while in Chorti, *choh* is "thick growth" and *choh te'* means "jungle." In Yukatek, *choh* is "dripping and flowing water."

22. Boot, Looper, and Wagner (1996) proposed this reading based on the identification of the flower as *k'a.* The glyphic name of this mountain consists of the number five, *ho,* prefixed to the flower to spell *hok',* a verb meaning "to come out or leave." They demonstrated that this particular designation applies to the mountains where people were buried and to houses in which they acceded. The Maya apparently thought of both activities as "leaving" or "coming out."

23. See *The Mysterious Maya* (Stuart and Stuart 1977: 195).

24. Since we first published our analysis of the history of Palenque and the life of Hanab-Pakal in 1974, there has been controversy over his dates and his age at death. The first estimate was published by the physical anthropologists Davalos and Romano (1955: 107), based on observations and studies made in the 1952 season, soon after the tomb was opened. Romano reconfirmed his findings in a report to Alberto Ruz in 1975. A second estimate came from an unpublished report by biologists Balcorta and Villalobos that was cited in an article by Ruz (1977: 293). In 1989, Romano (1989: 1419–1422) published for the first time the process that he and Davalos had used in their first examination and how they came to their conclusions. The principal evidence cited for age was Ruz's reading of the dates on the sarcophagus and commentary on the condition of the teeth. He reiterated his earlier conclusions as to the age and declared that no other interpretation was possible. Fashlicht (1971) supported the aging of the teeth as middle-aged because of the relative lack of wear.

For our part, we have always maintained that the arithmetic involved in analyzing the inscriptional dates of Hanab-Pakal is incontrovertible, whether or not our proposed interpretations of specific events are overturned. To prevent ambiguity, Palenque's scribes tied Hanab-Pakal's birth, accession, and death dates to the Long Count and to named k'atun-endings that recur only once every 375,000 years. And as we discussed above, they also tied his birth and accession dates to the end of the first piktun, which will occur in A.D. 4772. Thus, if his dates are to be changed, they must move at least 375,000 years into the past or future.

As Schele (1992) put it:

> The last argument against the chronology is that in some way the epigraphers do not understand what the Maya intended to say—that, for example, two people are being named as one person, that the history is a fabrication, or that some special way of dealing with time was being used. Concerning these possibilities, I can only say that each of those propositions requires that all of the inscriptional data that use the same calendrics or historical glyphs must be thrown out with the Palenque data, including all knowledge about the Maya and the Mesoamerican calendar in precolumbian, colonial, and modern contexts. This includes the entirety of Tatiana Proskouriakoff's "historic hypothesis" and all of the histories that have been published for all Maya sites. Palenque's history and the readings of the inscriptions associated with Pakal, in fact, lie at the heart of a matrix of knowledge that involves all we think we know about the Maya calendar and history. We cannot selectively decide to disbelieve the inconvenient part of this matrix without tossing it all out the window.

This debate has usually been couched as a conflict between "scientific" and "non-scientific" research methodology. Some have asserted that our interpretations of the inscriptions are simply wrong, while others have declared that even if they are correct, they must yield to the "scientific" interpretation of the bones. This alternative considers the inscriptional histories as nothing but propaganda to be discarded as misleading or downright lies. We think that the debate should be reframed as a challenge to the techniques employed to age ancient populations and the way resulting interpretations can be used.

Recent evaluations of the debate on Pakal's age make the following points. Javier Urcid (1993), an anthropologist who has worked with the skeletal repatriation program of the Smithsonian Institution, criticized the technique attributed to the biologists Balcorta and Villalobos because no experimental data has ever been published by which other scientists could evaluate the method. Hammond and Molleson (1994), a team composed of an experienced field archaeologist and a physical anthropologist who worked in the Spitalfields project in London, dismissed the method as too subjective. Both these reviews assert that the age estimates that have been published cannot be evaluated because no data or criteria of evaluation were included in the reports.

Both reviews also discussed the validity and reliability of the best aging techniques available today for use with ancient populations. The primary problems they described include the absence of comparative data from control groups that have known ages documented by nonphysical anthropological methods, such as written records. In Urcid's assessment, many of the aging methods available are not able to detect advanced age. Hammond and Molleson point out that new studies suggest that people who survive to advanced age in any population naturally have "young bones" compared to their contemporaries. Aged survivors with "young bones" will look younger than they actually were, and their skulls will retain open cranial sutures and more of their teeth. These survivors do not age as rapidly as the other members of the same population, so they might look younger to physical anthropologists assessing their age from skeletal remains. Moreover, the statistical methods used to estimate age inevitably underrepresent the extremes, so that ages of the very young and the very old tend to get skewed toward the mean.

The Fastlicht (1971) observation of moderate tooth wear for Pakal represents the clearest set of evidence supporting the age as estimated from the remains. Frank and Julie Saul (personal communication, 1996) have told us that they agree with this assessment. However, Allen Christenson (personal communication, 1996), a dentist with extensive forensic experience in the Smithsonian collections, has told us that "wear is not a factor in elite dentition as they likely had a diet with more boiled *atole* which caused little wear. Individuals with inlays [elites] often have little or no wear. The more accurate test is radiographic examination of incisal pulp chambers." Urcid pointed out that the "amount of dental wear varies greatly among populations and even individuals within the same populations, because of differences in diet, occlusion, or use of teeth as tools."

Hammond and Molleson, the authors of one of these evaluations, concluded, "We should not dismiss the epigraphic evidence for Pakal's proclaimed age at death in favor of any anthropological age determination, even were Pakal's remains able on reexamination to yield more data than were held to be relevant four decades ago."

25. See Ruz (1973: 198 and Figs. 220–221) for his discussion of this object.
26. Magdiel Castillo first pointed out this affinity in a seminar at the University of Texas.
27. This is our translation of Ruz (1973: 207–208). Also see Ruz (1968 and 1973: 206–208) for his commentary on the use of red paint on precolumbian bones.
28. This information comes from Rebecca Storey's (n.d.) study of the bones of Copan.
29. Grube and Schele (1993) analyzed the texts involving the staining of bones with red paint and the cutting of bones. The use of bone relics and red paint in tombs is widely distributed in Maya and Mesoamerican archaeology, but it has only been recently discovered in Maya inscriptions.
30. Sedat and Sharer (1994) describe a reentry stairway and corridor built into an early tomb in the Acropolis at Copan. Reentry tombs are also known at Caracol and reentry events are abundantly documented at Tikal.
31. Other examples of this rare Vision Serpent tell us more about what it meant to the designers of the tomb. On Pier C of House D, the Maize God wears the jeweled leaf on his ear as a way of signifying that the *Tz'at Nakan* rides in his hand as he dances with a woman dressed as First Mother. See Freidel, Schele, and Parker (1993: 276–286) for a more detailed discussion of this dance and the symbolism associated with the Maize God and resurrection. This image recounts part of the Creation myth. The jeweled leaf also occurs in the corners of the quatrefoil cartouches holding the inscription on the outer piers of the Temple of the Sun. The message in these *ol* portals describes the arrival of the patron gods of Palenque into the *pib na,* "underground house," inside the Cross Group temples. Thus, they can be conceived as the view down the gullet of the *Tz'at Nakan.* The *Tz'at Nakan* also appears on Copan Stela 7, but the context is unclear.

32. This combination reappears on Lintel 3 of Tikal Temple 4, which portrays Yik'in-Kan-K'awil (Ruler B) on a palanquin. The text says he is impersonating God A and the serpent that arches over his head may be a later version of the *Tz'at Nakan.* The base of the palanquin juxtaposes God A with Maize Gods emerging from a mountain in the analog of the image on the offering plate.

CHAPTER 4: COPAN

1. He is also known to modern readers as 18-Jog and 18-Rabbit. David Kelley (1962) first identified his name glyph and discussed the history of his reign. Stephen Houston and David Stuart have recently suggested that his name means "Eighteen Images of K'awil," and that the name of the War Serpent means "Eighteen Images of the Snake" as a reference to the Pyramid of the Feathered Serpent at Teotihuacan, where the terraces on each side of the stairway have eighteen feathered serpents. They have also interpreted the verb *u bah,* which appears frequently in Copan's inscriptions, as "his self," "his spirit," and "his likeness." We think these suggestions are good ones and provide productive interpretations.

2. Matthew Looper (1991a) first read the emblem glyph phonetically and proposed it corresponded to the word for Motmot, a colorful, long-tailed tropical bird. As he pointed out, there are several variants of the emblem glyph spelling, including *xuk, xukpi,* and *xukup. Xuk* is also "corner." As David Sedat (personal communication, 1991) pointed out to us, Copan is in the corner of the Maya area, and *xuk* can also mean "summit." Furthermore, in the Popol Vuh, the gods set up the *kan xuk kan tzuk,* "four corners, four partitions," as the first act of Creation. *Pi* is the glyph used for cycles of times, such as the bak'tun and the k'atun, and for a special type of sacred bundle used in ritual. Thus, Copan's name could refer to the Motmot bird, to its identification as the corner of the Maya world, and as the place of the corner bundle.

3. William Fash (1991) has published the most detailed recounting of the archaeological history yet available. Also see Schele and Freidel (1990: 306–346) for a discussion of the reign of the last king, Yax-Pasah.

4. Under the direction of Robert Sharer and the University of Pennsylvania ECAP (East Court Archaeological Project), archaeologists have been excavating tunnels through the various levels of the Acropolis. In the southern areas deep under Temple 16, teams led by David Sedat have found extraordinary buildings richly decorated with stucco sculpture. Inscriptions and imagery associated with the buildings identify them as the works of the founder and his first son. The building containing the tomb of the founder is *talud-tablero,* while the subsequent buildings have apron moldings characteristic of Tikal architecture. Other details of iconography also derived directly from the Late Preclassic traditions of central Peten. Moreover, the pottery found associated with one of these early tombs includes vessels that archaeologists have identified as imports from Kaminaljuyu, central Peten, and central Mexico.

5. David Stuart (n.d.a) deciphered the Maya name for Teotihuacan as *Puh* using much of the material from Copan. The final stages of Temple 26 and Temple 11 especially emphasize this iconography. As Schele (1989; Schele and Freidel 1990: 130–164; Freidel, Schele, and Parker 1993) has pointed out, this iconography is often associ-

ated with founders as well as with conquest-warfare. See chapter seven for a more detailed discussion of Tollan and the concepts of *Ah Puh*.

6. Scholars long ago recognized that Pusilha and Quirigua had the same emblem glyph (reading *tzuk*, "partition"). The evidence for interaction with Copan comes from Pusilha Stela D, which directly mentions K'ak'-Nab-K'awil, Holy Tzuk Lord. Stela 1 also has a very similar name in an *u kabi* expression of agency. Lords at Nimli Punit used the Ek' Xuk title, which also appears in Quirigua names. They are also used in the Copan turban.

7. David Stuart (n.d.a) came to this conclusion based on his investigation of the floors around and under the altar at the base of the Hieroglyphic Stairs.

8. Maudslay (1889–1902, I:20 and I:Plate 27) described this offering and published a drawing of some of its contents. The little shell figurines match closely those found in a cache in the buildings called Motmot and Margarita. Both these buildings have been attributed to the second ruler of Copan, nicknamed Popol K'inich. This cache was probably placed by him or his father, Yax-K'uk'-Mo'. Interestingly, Stela 35 was also found inside this pyramid. We suspect this stela depicted one of these two rulers.

9. Elizabeth Newsome (1991) first made this observation. Her study of these stelae also associated them with Creation mythology and with passages in the Books of Chilam Balam referring to the setting up of stones.

10. Spinden (1913:Table 1) used stylistic analysis and the deciphered dates then available to propose a developmental sequence that spanned close to seventy years.

11. Contrary to the general impression about Maya sculpture, a tradition of volumetric sculpture always coexisted with that of shallow relief. However, since the media was modeled plaster sculpture used in architecture, only a fragmentary and very badly damaged sample has survived. Perhaps the best way to appreciate Maya volumetric art is in the hundreds of clay figurines and incensarios that have survived. The remarkable accomplishment of the Copan sculptors is that they were able to achieve the plasticity of modeled plaster and clay in their monumental stone sculptures. This development came about because of the nature of the volcanic tuff available to the Copan sculptors. It was amenable to a volumetric approach, where most of the limestone available at other Maya sites was not. The only other site that elaborated an equivalent volumetric tradition was Tonina, although the stelae there are much smaller in scale.

12. This crocodile tree was first created on Middle Preclassic Olmec celts and in the imagery of Izapa during the Late Preclassic period. It also appears on several Early Classic Maya objects. This particular tree also occurs in Popol Vuh imagery as the tree in which Wuqub-Kaqix sat. The Maya apparently connected this tree to the Milky Way by associating the head with the clefted area above Scorpius. They saw this cleft as the mouth of a crocodile as well as the path to Xibalba (Freidel, Schele, and Parker 1993: 89–91).

13. Floyd Lounsbury (1981, 1982) first proved that the Maya paid attention to the Eveningstar. Using Palenque's records of the 9.11.0.0.0 k'atun-ending, he identified the god of the Eveningstar as a jawless skeletal god, and confirmed that it also occurs in the Grolier Codex and on Tikal Stela 16.

14. Elizabeth Newsome (1991) first pointed out this connection and suggested that the combined altar and west stela face represent Creation-rebirth imagery.

15. We are not entirely sure who is being born from the Cosmic Turtle. It could be Wax-

aklahun-Ubah-K'awil dressed for the west, or perhaps an ancestor, most likely his father, whose resurrection corresponded to this day.

16. David Stuart (letter circulated to epigraphers in 1993) confirmed this reading through a set of examples carrying phonetic complements. The full spelling is on Stela A. *Lakam* means "big," but it is also the word for "banner."

17. This interpretation has been developed by Nikolai Grube (personal communication, 1996). By associating the name of the patron gods with scenes on pottery, he was able to identify a series of narratives describing events in the myth. These scenes include Kan-Te-Ahaw burning this Bearded Jaguar God; Kan-Te-Ahaw dropping a bound rock on the same god; and a series of scenes in which Chak and a Death God throw a Baby Jaguar God into a mountain. Grube identified one particularly important pot showing the Baby Jaguar God scene combined with a Pax Tree and Deer Snake belching up an old god who may be Wuk-Sip. The tail of the snake turns into the other patron god of Copan—Bolon-K'awil. In turn the old god who emerges from the snake seduces a voluptuous young woman. Additional scenes include the death of the old god, mummy bundles holding the Pax God and Chak, and the young woman with a deer.

   That this mythic narrative played an important role in Copan's imagery is clear. A huge sculpture of a giant stingray spine from the East Court shows the tumbling Baby Jaguar and an Early Classic stela fragment records its name. The full details of this myth are still under study by Grube and others, but it has already begun to inform several themes in Copan's sculpture.

18. The text on the back of Naranjo Stela 35 uses the verb *puluy,* "it burned," as in the pottery scene. The name of the person who burned is eroded, but enough remains to identify it as the same Baby Jaguar that was the patron of Tikal's early dynasty. This Baby Jaguar gets thrown into a mountain by Chak and a Death God, so that he is often shown tumbling down a mountain. Naranjo goes on to say that it happened at *Na-Ho-Kan,* the place where the first stone throne of the Cosmic Hearth was set up by the gods. *U kabi,* "they oversaw it," follows, thus naming the agent as *Kan-Te-Ahaw Kan-Te-Ch'ok,* the patron god of Copan. Finally, the last three glyphs include the same bent throne glyph that appears on Stela 4.

   The name of the Baby Jaguar includes the title *Ek' Hun,* "Black Headdress." This title also occurs in the name of the Bearded Jaguar God on Tikal Temple 4, Lintel 3, but there his personal name is *K'in-Hix Ek' Hun,* "Sun-Jaguar Black Headdress." Thus, we know that this god can appear in the form of a baby and an adult and that it can personify the sun and Venus.

19. We included two new readings in our transcription that have been proposed by other epigraphers. For the mirror sign with the *ba* rodent head, Nikolai Grube (personal communication, 1995) has suggested *winba,* a Maya word for "image" or "statue." It would be used here to specify that Stela 4 is a portrait image of Waxaklahun-Ubah-K'awil. This glyph is followed by another, *k'uy nik,* that Kristaan Villela (1993) has identified as a term for "ceiba flower."

20. Strömsvik (1941) cited Dieseldorff's (1930) report on the excavation of this cruciform vault. Although the contents included only one bivalve shell, the two ancient sculptures were powerful caches indeed.

21. Schele and Grube (1987) proposed a reading for this text as the birth of the eleventh

king, but the date is problematic. It is 6, 7, or 8 Kimi 19 Wo. They chose 9.6.9.4.6 7 Kimi 19 Wo because of biological contingencies, thus giving Butz'-Chan an age of 3.5.12.3, or almost sixty-five years, at the time of his death.

22. The interpretation of this stela has long been the subject of controversy. The skirt he wears led us to identify the person as a woman, until we realized that no female names appear in the inscription. Waxaklahun-Ubah-K'awil was clearly the protagonist, but we thought he was wearing the guise of a woman because of the associated bloodletting symbolism. In time, we realized that skirts could be worn by males as well as females, and that the net skirt shown on this monument signaled First Father, who was the Maize God, and First Mother, who was the Moon Goddess. Humans wearing the net skirt symbolize one of these divine parents.

23. We recounted these events in chapter one in our discussion of the myths of Creation and Origin.

24. Such lip-to-lip caches consist of two large plates, one inverted over the other as the lid. The Maya used this particular kind of cache vessel to contain dedication offerings from Late Preclassic times onward. They contained many different offerings, including severed heads, stingray spines, obsidian and flint blades, thorns, shells, jade, red pigment, and the remains of bundling material. Although Copan's rulers favored other kinds of cache vessels shaped more like buckets or large vases, the sculptors may still be referring to the much more widely used plate containers.

25. The stingray spine is the lancet. The shell receives the blood, but it is also the materialization of *k'ulel,* the life force that permeates the cosmos in the Maya view. Finally, epigraphers have shown that the crossed-bands sign with its cartouche substitute for other *way* glyphs. *Way* is not only the word for spirit companion, but it also means "to dream" and "to transform" into one's *way.*

26. *Makom* or *macom* is glossed as "mora" in Tzotzil and Chol. *Mora* can refer to blackberry vines, but in eastern Guatemala and Honduras, the *mora* tree is the gourd tree.

27. The other possibility is that the bones were taken during burial rites a century earlier and were later used in ancestral rituals. In discussing these texts, Schele and Grube (1992) pointed out that Waxaklahun-Ubah-K'awil took advantage of many astronomical coincidences in planning this monument and festival. Venus appeared in Sagittarius, on a maximum elongation of the Morningstar for his father's accession, on one of the dates on Stela 3, and for the 9.14.0.0.0 date on Stela C. On the Stela H day, the sun was in the same position in Sagittarius as Venus on those other dates. Stela 3 also recalls an ancestral conjuring of Butz'-Chan, so that Waxaklahun-Ubah-K'awil wove a tapestry of associations between his stelae and those of his father.

28. Moreover, the date of the Stela A erection also fits into the pattern because K'ak-Nab-K'awil's accession and his own recall of Butz'-Chan on Stela 3 fell on February 8 and February 7 of their respective years. 9.14.19.8.0 fell on February 3, 731. All three events were timed to fall within range of the second day of Creation, and K'ak'-Nab-K'awil's accession and his conjuring event fell on days when Venus was at maximum elongation as the Morningstar.

29. The contents of this cache and the analysis of the style and metal of these legs were reported in Strömsvik (1941).

30. The Palace Tablet at Palenque depicts the king K'an-Hok'-Chitam wearing a similar headdress for his accession. Shield-Jaguar of Yaxchilan wears it in his posthumous

portrait on a ballcourt marker. The earliest example occurs on a stela from Abah Takalik, which shows a being wearing this headdress as he stands under a skyband. His cheek is marked with the *k'in*, "sun," sign.

Another important example comes from a looted pot showing a scene in which a male and female god sit on thrones. Both wear moon signs on their backs and the male had a throne composed of a skyband supported by Pawahtuns. He wears the same mat headdress as Waxaklahun-Ubah-K'awil, and he carries the same paper-decorated spear and a shield. He is a male moon god who appears in the lunar series of the Maya calendar. The Maya divided the lunar year into three groups of six lunations. They used a glyph designated Glyph C by Morley (1916) to record how many lunations had been completed by the day in question. The glyph includes a number, a hand reading *k'al*, "closed" or "ended," and a head representing the moon. Each group of six lunations had its own head, including the head of the Young Moon Goddess, a skull, and this male moon god (Schele, Grube, and Fahsen 1992). Interestingly, Dennis Tedlock says that the full moon is male and is called Xbalanke by the K'iche'. The moon was full on the night that Waxaklahun-Ubah-K'awil dedicated Stela A. Today the K'eq'chi use *Xbalanke* as a term for the sun, so that we have even in postconquest times a dual identity for one of the Popol Vuh Hero Twins. If this equation holds for the Classic period, then this headdress may have been associated with both the sun and the full moon as well as with Kan-Te-Ahaw.

31. Barthel (1968: 185–187) first analyzed the distribution of references to foreign emblem glyphs and suggested large political or ritual structures were reflected in these cross-references. Joyce Marcus (1973, 1976) built upon his work and suggested a subordination scheme headed by four main capitals. Peter Mathews (1985, 1986) took issue with many of Marcus's interpretations. He showed patterns not only of emblem glyph distribution, but also of war and marriage between sites. Major excavations between 1986 and 1995 uncovered additional monuments that opened up a new interpretation using elements from all of the earlier studies. Martin and Grube (1995; n.d.) have used recent decipherments to show two major hegemonies that centered on Tikal and Kalak'mul during the Classic period. Most southern lowland sites were affiliated with one or the other of these great centers at one time or another during the Classic period.

32. This glyph has given us trouble because of the various possibilities for its reading. The triangle of dots in the center of the main sign may make it the "dotted kan" sign that has the value *tzi*. However, Altar S, also erected on 9.15.0.0.0 by Waxaklahun-Ubah-K'awil, has a variant of this glyph reading *u mi yol u kan kun. Yol*, "his portal" or "the heart of," refers, among other things, to the cleft in the mountain and the Cosmic Turtle. Since it is clearly parallel to Stela B, we have taken the reading on that stela to be *mi ol. Mi* is used as the negative or "no" in Long Counts and distance numbers. We do not know how to interpret it here, except perhaps as the proper name of the *ol*.

33. This name also appears on Stela F, which shows Waxaklahun-Ubah-K'awil as a Jaguar God wearing the same shell beard as he does on this monument.

34. The verb is a conflation of *u bah*, "his image" or "his self," and the number tree that reads *an*, based on phonetic complements attached to the sign. The scribe abbreviated the number tree to the number seven drawn in front of the rodent's ear. *An* has

several meanings, depending on the Maya language. In Yukatek, it means "to exist," while in sixteenth-century Tzotzil, it is glossed as "to kindle or burn coals," "to hew and carve," and "to hurt oneself causing blood to flow." Here the phrase mostly refers to Waxaklahun-Ubah-K'awil's portrayal as the "carved image" of the lord of Macaw Mountain. Both the stela and the king materialize this image.

35. Although these place names have been the subject of study for some time (Kubler 1977), we still have not been able to decipher the component glyphs of the "Nine-God Place." These locations occur in pairs at several different sites, but most important are their appearance on the tops of lip-to-lip cache vessels. In that and other contexts, these glyphs occur inside of the quatrefoil symbol read as *ol,* "portal." They record locations that are found when people cross that portal. At Tonina, the "Seven-Black-Yellow Place" was in the ballcourt, which was another kind of portal.

36. The date falls on 8.7.17.14.4 3 K'an 12 K'ank'in (March 18, 197). Werner Nahm (personal communication, 1992) associated the particular *wayob* that climb the Hauberg snake with the constellations that flank the Wakah-Kan. These are Capricorn, Sagittarius, Libra, and Virgo, which the Maya saw, respectively, as a jaguar, a rattlesnake, a shark, and Chak. We have been unable to make similar associations with the *wayob* on Stela D, although they are also four in number.

37. Both of the monuments associating the Nine and Seven Places with Yax-K'uk'-Mo' were commissioned after his death.

38. Matthew Looper (1995) discovered the reference to Kalak'mul and proposed the interpretation of events we give here. The Quirigua defeat of Copan has always puzzled Mayanists, because it was a small site compared to Copan by any calculation. How did such a small subsidiary site defeat a much larger one? Looper's new interpretation places this conflict in the larger pattern of the Kalak'mul-Tikal discord. Copan shows affinities with Tikal during the time of the dynasty founding. We assume that it was always affiliated with Tikal.

39. "Four *Witik*" also occurs on Altar L, and as far as we know, there are no references to "Three *Witik*" after 9.18.10.0.0, the date of Altar G. This pattern suggests that this phrase referred to some attribute of Copan's political organization that changed late in Yax-Pasah's reign.

40. The original assessment was based on an interpretation of Altar U, but the glyph we had possibly taken to be "child of father" turns out to be *u bah an,* "the carved image of." The glyphs following this verb are not the names of the father, as we thought, but rather the names of the old gods carved on the corners of the altar. Moreover, David Stuart (personal communication, 1997) has suggested that Nu-Yahaw-Kan-Ah-Bak may also have been a personal god of Yax-Pasah, rather than a brother.

41. In her own study of the Great Plaza, Elizabeth Newsome (1991) associated these stelae with descriptions of Creation and the organization of human space in the Chilam Balam of Chumayel. She related the stelae to World Trees and the stones set up by the gods at Creation. Her work has exploited a rich association of connections and interpretations that inform these great stelae in different ways.

CHAPTER 5: SEIBAL

1. Unfortunately we still do not know the phonetic value of this sign. One example of the three-stone sign in the Seibal inscriptions has a *mi* suffix, while another has *tzi*. Neither phonetic complement has led to a reading. The Cholan and Yukatek languages use *yokib*, "foot or foundation things," for hearth stones. Freidel, Schele, and Parker (1993) called the Cosmic Hearth *Yax-Ox-Tunal* as a literal reading of the glyph. In time, a new reading based on phonetic complementation may eventually be found.

2. The Peabody Museum, Harvard University, conducted a major excavation program at Seibal from 1964–1968. The program focused primarily on stratigraphy and settlement in an attempt to understand the overall archaeological history of the site. The project published its results in a five-volume set of reports (Willey 1975–1990).

3. Research into this regional history began with Mathews's (1976) study of Dos Pilas Stela 8. Shortly thereafter a number of scholars prepared histories of the interactions in the region, including Johnson (n.d.), Houston and Mathews (1985), Mathews and Willey (1991), Schele and Freidel (1993), Houston (1993), and Schele and Grube (1994). Excavations at Caracol directed by Arlen and Diane Chase found a text recording the defeat of Tikal by Caracol (Houston 1987, 1989). Grube (1993) subsequently refined the history of Caracol and placed it in a pan-Maya context. The Vanderbilt University project under Arthur Demarest discovered a new stairway at Dos Pilas (Demarest et al., 1993) recording that Tikal's king, Shield-Skull, had been captured and sacrificed at Dos Pilas. Finally, Houston (Houston et al., n.d.) identified Dos Pilas Ruler 1 as the son of the twenty-second ruler of Tikal and recognized the name of the same Tikal king at Altar de Sacrificios (Houston et al., n.d.). Martin and Grube (n.d., 1995) built upon this body of information and interpretation in their studies of the larger political structures of the Classic period.

4. Paul Matthews (1994) first realized that these texts implied the destruction of public inscriptions with their record of history.

5. *Abta* is the sixteenth-century Tzotzil and Tzeltal word for "work," perhaps meaning that this lord had nine specific areas of responsibility in his "work" as king. This title with a number prefix is characteristic of royal names from the Dos Pilas/Aguateca polity as well as with this later revival group. Since Wat'ul came from Ucanal, traditionally a member of the Kalak'mul hegemony, he may have carried the title because of his continuing affiliation with that political sphere, or because he was reestablishing the old Dos Pilas/Aguateca authority.

6. Archaeological and epigraphic data also contradict the idea that the new lords of Seibal were Mexicanized foreigners. The major arguments for the "foreignness" of these new elites have been that they brought "fine paste" pottery wares with them and that they did not deform their heads like earlier Maya lords. Subsequent investigations have shown that this kind of pottery appeared all over the Maya area during the Terminal Classic period, so that it is now taken as a diagnostic feature of this period and thus cannot be used to assert foreignness at any one site.

   The burials from this period also cry out the basic Maya-ness of Seibal's new people. Skull deformation, the hallmark of Classic-period Maya elites, appears for the first time at Seibal during this era. Ironically, Proskouriakoff pointed to their lack of undeformed foreheads as a sign of their foreignness. The burials tell us that the people used specific Maya ethnic traits regardless of how they represented themselves on the monuments.

7. Ledyard Smith (1982: 30–32) described the methods used for the reconstruction process. When they began clearing Temple A-3, the archaeologists found that the entablature on all sides had fallen outward and down the platform. The stucco had shattered into thousands of pieces, but many of them still adhered to their stone armatures and mounting stones. They carefully plotted where the fragments had fallen and began putting some of the pieces back together on site. Even at Seibal, they realized that the frieze "represented life or mythical scenes of men, animals, and deities in ornamented frames and with accompanying hieroglyphics and other embellishments." Proskouriakoff, with the help of other artists, used this information to prepare reconstructions of the scenes.

8. Jessica Christy (1995) documented the relationship between period-ending rituals of the Classic period and Creation mythology. Karl Taube (1988) discussed this destruction/creation aspect of New Year ceremonies. In various modern Maya communities, destruction/creation cycles are expressed through public ritual. The Chamulas destroy the world and give command to the monkeys of the Third Creation in their Festival of Games (Gossen 1986). In the middle of the festival, they bring the Sun-Christ back to life in a world-making event. When the Lakandon remake their god pots every twenty years or so, jaguars destroy the world so that it must be re-created with the new god pots (McGee 1990).

9. Heinrich Berlin (1963) first identified GI in his study of the Palenque Triad of Gods. K'awil was his GII, and GIII was a version of the Bearded Jaguar God. At Palenque, he was also called *Yahaw-K'in* and *Yahaw-K'ak'*, "Lord of Sun" and "Lord of Fire." At Palenque, GI was also called *Hun-Nal-Ye* and was a version of the Maize God. Seibal used two of these gods, GI and GII, as its patrons.

10. *Kan-Ek'* can be written in several ways, because the words for "four," "snake," and "sky" (*kan*) were the same in Maya, as were the words for "star" and "black" (*ek'*). The version of the name at Seibal is written with "four" prefixed to the phonetic spelling, *e-k'e* (Nikolai Grube, personal communication, 1993). On a stela from Motul de San José, a site on the northern shore of Lake Peten Itza in Guatemala, it is written "four black" (Nikolai Grube, personal communication, 1994) and at Chich'en Itza it is written once as "snake-star" and once as "sky-star" (Eric Boot, personal communication, 1995). No matter how it is written, it is the same name and it shows that this distinctive Itza name existed widely during the Terminal Classic period wherever tradition or the inscriptions say the Itza were. Furthermore, the title *Itza Ahaw* occurs both at Motul de San José and Chich'en Itza.

11. This verb appears to read *pet-ta*. *Pet* is the word for "round things," such as spindle whorls, in most Maya languages. As a verb, *pet* means "to make things round," while in Tzotzil it is the verb used to describe the circular dancing around the water drums in the Festival of Games at Chamula. In the Palenque story of Creation, *pethi* is the action of the gods in turning the constellations around the north axis of the sky. Period-ending rituals throughout Maya history have involved circumambulation through the four directions. This may be the action recorded in this text.

12. Actually Venus returns to the same station in near approximation every three k'atuns. Hanab-Pakal of Palenque recorded this same god in association with

9.9.0.0.0 in the Temple of Inscriptions. He also recorded a Venus elongation with 9.12.0.0.0 (Closs 1979). A Venus association also occurs on Copan Stela B, dated at 9.15.0.0.0. Although Venus had moved away from the elongation by 9.18.0.0.0 and 10.1.0.0.0, the Maya continued to anticipate Venus associations with these particular k'atun-endings.

13. In the name of Bird-Jaguar of Yaxchilan, the "bird" is a *yaxun,* so that his name reads Yaxun-Balam.

14. The moon sign here has a single dot in its center, a sign that normally records the number twenty, *k'al.* The phonetic sign *ha* usually has three dots in the same location to distinguish it from *k'al.* However, in Terminal Classic texts, this distinction began to break down, so that both signs were used to write either *k'al* or *ha.* Given that this is a nonnumerical context, we think *ha* is the intended value. Martin and Grube (Schele and Grube 1994: 17a–18) used substitution patterns to show that the second sign, a cartouche with a tailed dot, has the phonetic value of *ka.* The second half of the glyph is a *witz,* "mountain," sign merged with the beak and mouth of a bird, identified by Grube and Nahm (personal communication, 1993) as phonetic *tzi.* And the last sign is phonetic *li.* Combined, they give the reading *ha-ka-witz-tzi-li* or *hakawitzil.*

15. *Hak* is the Chorti word for "beginning," while *witz* is "mountain" in the lowland Maya languages and in the inscriptions.

16. In discussing Hakawitz, Tedlock (1985: 340) said: "*Uitz* is Cholan for 'mountain' (K.) and the rest is of uncertain derivation. Patron deity of the Lord Quiché lineage, carried by Mahucutah from Tulan Zuyua and eventually placed 'above a great red river' on a mountain that then took the name Hacauitz. The Lord Quichés were there when the first dawn came, and the same mountain was the site of the first Quiché citadel, built by Jaguar Quitze, Jaguar Night, Mahucutah, and True Jaguar and abandoned after their deaths. Hacauitz was also the name of the temple that housed the god Hacauitz in the citadel of Rotten Cane, with its back marking the south side of the main plaza."

   If the *Hakawitzil, K'ul Puh Ahaw* at Seibal is related to the Hakawitz of this founding myth, then we have evidence of K'iche' ties to the Terminal Classic history in central Peten and the Pasión region. The process that led to the transformation of a historical person into a patron god has been repeated by the K'iche'. Their war captain, Tekun-Uman, died at the hands of Alvarado during the conquest. Today some K'iche' have Tekun as their principal *mundo* and they worship him in the cave under Ancient Reed, their old capital. "Ancient Reed," or *Qumar-Kaj,* may be another metaphor for the "Place of Reeds."

17. At Copan, the text of the southeast panel of Temple 11 specifically says that *K'awil* is the "*way* of his foot." The snake foot is the Vision Serpent.

CHAPTER 6: CHICH'EN ITZA

1. David Stuart circulated his ideas about three founding brothers of Chich'en Itza in a letter dated 1987. He identified a glyph reading *yitah* that stands between the names of important nobles as "sibling." Dieter Dütting (personal communication, 1989) had noticed the same glyph and read it as "companion." Schele and Freidel (1990)

used Stuart's ideas to identify the government of Chich'en Itza as a *multepal*, "joined reign," a council form of governance that is known to have been in force also at Mayapan, a later kingdom in Yukatan. Building on these ideas, Nikolai Grube (1994) identified *multepal* governments at Xkalumk'in and several other northern sites by the early eighth century. Additional work on the *yitah* glyph by Barbara MacLeod, Stephen Houston, Nikolai Grube, and Hector Escobedo suggested that Dütting's idea of "companion" is more likely than the "sibling" reading, but it is also very clear from the inscriptions at Chich'en Itza and other sites that brothers as well as unrelated nobles could fall into the category of "companion." In fact, *yitah* can appear with kinship statements identifying the people involved as brothers of the king. However, *yitah* is more likely a title of special rank, rather than one limited to a kinship relationship.

2. The Books of Chilam Balam are prophetic histories kept by scribes in the various towns of Yukatan from the time of the conquest until today. Although written in the Latin alphabet, the sections with the k'atun histories have the syntactical pattern and "feel" of the inscriptional histories familiar to all epigraphers. We think many parts were simply transcribed from preconquest histories. Today most of these histories reside in libraries in the United States and elsewhere, but books like the Chilam Balams are still kept by scribes among the Cruzob Maya, the descendants of the people who fought the Caste Wars of the nineteenth and early twentieth centuries.

3. David Kelley (1968) first recognized this name in the inscriptions of Chich'en Itza. His discovery was crucial in deciphering the name of the famous Pakal of Palenque.

4. The Chilam Balam of Chumayel names Ah-Holtun-Balam as one of the founding lords of the Itza confederacy. *Ah-Holtun-Balam, Peten, Itzamal Ahaw* appears among the lords named on a disk from the Caracol at Chich'en.

5. David Stuart first identified Hun-Pik-Tok' on the Halak'al lintel and circulated his discovery in a letter to several epigraphers. The man in the Chich'en inscriptions may well be the same person.

6. The famous Yukatek scholar Alfredo Barrera Vásquez (1980: 272) first suggested that *Itz-a* meant "water wizard." Glyphically, the title *Itza Ahaw* first appeared in the ninth century on a monument at Motul de San José, a site on the northern shore of Lake Peten Itza in Guatemala, and in an even earlier text on a looted pot said to be from the same region. Nikolai Grube has suggested that *itza* was the original name of Lake Peten Itza and that the people around the lake were called *itza* from at least the Early Classic period onward. We think he is right and suggest that the Itza of Yukatan brought this name with them in their migrations to the north. Thus, the *itza* name came from the south and went north, where it appeared in inscriptions from the Caracol at Chich'en Itza by the late ninth century.

7. Erik Boot (1994) identified the collocation *yabnal* in the names of several lords at Chich'en. As an alternative, the Spanish epigrapher José Miguel García Campillo pointed to several toponyms spelled *wak-ab-li*, "Six Years" or "Six Grandchildren." He also pointed out that the original texts of the Chilam Balams use the number six as well as seven, but that translators have regularized the references to "seven."

   Boot (personal communication, 1996) has found several more *yabnal* collocations and an *Ah Habnal*. *Yab* is "abundance" in Yukatek, but *abil* is not. Instead, *abil* is "maternal grandchildren." Several researchers have pointed out that the few parentage statements at Chich'en Itza record the relationships of rulers to their mothers and grandmothers, but not to their fathers. This emphasis on the descent from the mother to the exclusion of the father is very rare in Maya inscriptions. Perhaps it results from the practice of incoming elites taking local wives so that their descendants' claims to authority through kinship were more important on the mother's side than the father's. The focus on mothers and grandmothers may be reflected in this toponym.

One of the associations with maternal grandparents is with a lineage called the *Sabakna*. According to the Chilam Balam of Chumayel, they were founding members of the Itza confederation. Erik Boot identified *Sabak Ahaw* in the texts of the Monjas at Chich'en Itza. Moreover, Matthew Looper (1995) has also found *Sabakna Ahaw* in the titles of Quirigua and Copan. The title also appears in the name of the sixteenth ruler of Tikal. This lineage name, like the Itza title, may have originated in the south and migrated to the north during the Terminal Classic period.

Erik Boot disagreed with our assessment of the *abil/yabnal* reading and offered the following alternative in a letter dated May 1996:

> I have suggested "place of abundance" and "place of bushy reeds/shrubs," the Maya conceptualization of Tollan. I now base this on the following: in discussing the toponym *wuk yabnal/wak habnal*, Roys (1933: 133, note 7) mentions the fact that *abnal* is a patronym. Later he states (Roys 1940: 42) that *abnal* is a modern form of *haban*, and he defines the meaning of *haban* as "a bush or large herb," a "definition inferred from plant-name compounds, such as *ic-aban, kik-aban, kutz-aban*, and *tok-aban*, in most of which the element, *-aban*, appears to designate a large herbaceous plant or shrub" (Roys 1940: 42, note 75). To this, I think, plant-name compounds can be added which contain *habin* or *haba*. In Tzeltal, *habnal/habnel* means "big leaves" (Terry Kaufman, personal communication, 1994), which can be compared to the Yukatek entries. The root as such seems to be *(h)ab*, which is also the root for *(h)abnal*.
>
> You have suggested it to mean "years" or "(maternal) grandchildren" in the chapter on Chich'en Itza: I would say that stretches the argument, but it could be possible. I rather think that a good case can be presented that the original name of Chich'en was *wak habnal/wuk yabnal*, referring to a "place of bushy reeds/shrubs," a Tollan. So the Maya referred to a "Tollan" in more than one way: *pu* (as referring to Teotihuacan), *bak'halal* (when settled at Siyan Kan), *(h)abnal* (referring to Chich'en Itza)."

8. J. Eric Thompson (1937) showed that Chich'en scribes anchored calendar round dates by recording the particular tun in which they occurred within a named k'atun. For example, the date on Lintel 1 of the Temple of Four Lintels reads "9 Lamat day 11 Yax in tun thirteen of One Ahaw." This corresponds to 10.2.12.1.8 in the Long-Count system and July 9, 881, in the modern system. Such dates do not repeat for cycles of over 17,000 years.

At the 1995 "Symposium on the Terminal Classic Period" at the Texas Meetings, Ruth Krochock argued that the date in the Temple of the Hieroglyphic Jambs should be read as 10.0.2.7.13 9 Ben 1 Sak (August 4, 837). Her new reading makes this date the earliest in the city's written history. The latest date, 10.4.0.0.0, is found in texts associated with the Caracol and with the area of the Casa Colorada.

9. Two early travelers played crucial roles in planting the "Toltec" idea in modern

interpretations. John Stephens, who was among the first to publish images of Chich'en Itza, associated what he saw to newly discovered Aztec images, although at the time, no one knew how to date Chich'en in relationship to the Aztecs. The French explorer Désiré Charnay went further. Using European and indigenous documents written soon after the conquest, he assembled the legend of the Toltec-Maya on both the Mexican and Maya sides. But most important, he went to Tula, Hidalgo, before he went to Chich'en and, thus, could compare the two directly. He was also the first person to use the myth of Quetzalcoatl and the fall of Tollan as an explanation for the stylistic resemblance of the two sites.

Not only did Charnay (1887: 366–367) use the indigenous documents to support his arguments, but he juxtaposed images from Chich'en with Aztec representations to show that the style and imagery are the same. His most powerful comparison was between a Chacmol that Le Plongeon had found under the Platform of Venus at Chich'en and one that had been recently found in Tlaxcala. He presumed that the Chich'en version derived from the highland Mexican one, although at the time, the chronology of Mesoamerican archaeology still was only vaguely known. In 1887, an English translation of his interpretations was published in the United States and the legend became a powerful force in subsequent interpretations.

The great ethnohistorian Alfred Tozzer published the most elaborate discussion of this interpretation. He based his arguments largely on imagery and symbols that occur both in the "Toltec-Maya" art at Chich'en and the art from the site of Tula in the state of Hidalgo and of the later Aztecs. He assumed, as many others have, that since these Toltec elements were not found in earlier Maya art, they could only have come from an invasion like those recorded in the k'atun histories.

David Carrasco's analysis of the Quetzalcoatl myth provides one of the most thought-provoking studies of the role these fundamental constructs played in Mesoamerican history. Florescano (1995) has also studied the myth of Quetzalcoatl and its history in various Mesoamerican cultural traditions. Susan Gillespie's (1989: 134–155) study of the mythology of Aztec rulership also examined the various manifestations of the myth in their political contexts. Nigel Davies's (1977) assessment of the "Toltec" myth provides a thorough review of the documentation, although his solutions are different from those of Carrasco and Gillespie. These sources provide good reviews of the debates over chronology and interpretation that have raged in the field since the end of the nineteenth century.

10. In 1898, Eduard Seler, a famous German scholar, published excerpts from all of the available chronicles. His presentation was more systematic than Charnay's had been, and he included a detailed analysis of the imagery of Chich'en Itza, using the drawings published by Maudslay. Tozzer (1940: 20–26) discussed not only Landa's information, but also material from related chronicles. The next contribution of major public import came in 1946 from Morley, who published a detailed analysis of the k'atun histories in his widely read book, *The Ancient Maya*. This book is central to the history of the Toltec hypothesis because it continued to be published in updated form as Morley and Brainerd (1956) and then as Morley, Brainerd, and Sharer (1983). Later editions softened the Toltec interpretation, but the presentation of the Yukatekan histories as Morley summarized them were retained in each subsequent edition.

Alfredo Barrera Vásquez, the highly respected Maya-speaking scholar from Yukatan, cooperated with Morley in an important comparative study of the k'atun histories in the Chilam Balams. They (Barrera and Morley 1949) laid out the migrations documented in those sources and attempted to assign European dates to all the primary events.

11. Many prominent scholars still support this interpretation. Among them are David Kelley, Michael Coe, Karl Taube, and Mexican archaeologists working at Chich'en in recent years. However, from the very beginning there were scholars who challenged the Toltec invasion hypothesis. Tozzer acknowledged David Kelley's contribution to his own great work on the Toltecs at Chich'en, although Kelley himself has never published his ideas in his own words. One of the few sources for his opinions consists of his reviews of other scholars' work (Kelley 1984, 1985, 1987).

12. Brinton (1882, 1885) published translations of the k'atun histories from a set of Chilam Balams as well as the *Annals of the Kaqchikels* from highland Guatemala. These documents, along with the Popol Vuh, constitute the core of the postconquest histories. Brinton's notes and commentaries demonstrate his thorough command of Spanish sources as well as the indigenous ones. Here is what Brinton (1982: 112–113) said about Tula in his introduction to the k'atun histories:

> It is, in fact, nowhere in terrestrial geography that we need look for the site of the Tula of Quetzalcoatl, nor at any time in human history did the Tolteca ply their skillful hands, nor Tezcatlipoca spread his snares to destroy them. All this is but a mythical conception of the daily struggle of light and darkness, and those writers who seek in the Toltecs the ancestors or instructors of any nation whatsoever, make the once common error of mistaking myth for history, fancy for fact. Therefore, any notion that Yukatan was civilized by the Toltecs after their dispersion, or owes anything to them, as so many, and I might say almost all recent writers have maintained, is to me an absurdity.

George Kubler and the Mexican archaeologist Roman Piña Chan challenged the Toltec interpretation on different grounds. In 1962, George Kubler (1962, 1984: 77, 288–290) argued that the formative stages for the "Toltec" style are to be found at Chich'en and not at Tula. He suggested that Tula "may have been the stylistic outpost of Chich'en rather than the reverse." Most important, he pointed out that the fusion of forms and images from central Mexican sources, i.e., Teotihuacan, with Maya means of representation goes back to at least A.D. 375 at Kaminaljuyu, and as we now know, in central Peten. Roman Piña Chan (1980) also argued that Chich'en Itza predated Tula, Hidalgo. Marvin Cohodas (1978) also completed an extensive study of the Great Ballcourt and argued for a much earlier chronology.

Richard Diehl's (1983) book represents the most recent exegesis on the archaeological and historical interpretations of Tula, Hidalgo. Archaeological evidence points to the beginning of Tula before A.D. 700, when it was settled by immigrants perhaps from several areas of Mesoamerica, including the Basin of Mexico and the Gulf Coast. Tula experienced a major population expansion between A.D. 800 and 950, when Tula Chico was the major ceremonial area. He dated the Tollan phase of the city to A.D. 950–1150, based primarily on comparisons with the ceramics of the Valley of Mexico and on ethnohistorical information. Although the four radiocarbon dates from the Tollan phase fell between A.D. 900 and 1000, he placed Tula

Grande and most of the "Toltec"-style art and architecture in the later period. The problem with Tula's chronology is that it, like that of Chich'en, has been profoundly influenced by historical reconstructions made before the decipherment of the Maya writing system. If the Tollan phase at Tula really fell in the later period, then Tula, Hidalgo, postdated the period in which most or all of Chich'en's public architecture was erected. In this interpretation, Tula would have to be a copy of Chich'en rather than the reverse.

Augusto Molina (1982) pointed out that the reconstruction of Temple B at Tula was affected by its presumed relationship to Chich'en. He identified details that were made to resemble the Temple of the Warriors at Chich'en with little or no evidence to back them up. In 1995, Diehl (personal communication) told us that while the general chronology of Tula is reasonably accurate, there is no reliable evidence that can be used to place Temple B in that framework. Until further excavations are done at Tula to answer this question, the relative chronology of Tula Temple B and Chich'en Itza remains open.

Other researchers have added further observations to the growing challenge. E. Wyllys Andrews V (1979) used archaeological evidence (especially C14 dates) from Yukatan to date the majority of Chich'en's construction to the Terminal Classic period, while Joseph Ball (1979) supported Andrews's conclusions based on ceramic distribution. Charles Lincoln (1986, 1990) found additional evidence to show that the buildings in the Toltec-Maya style could not be distinguished chronologically or ceramically from those in the Maya style. More recently, Huchim, Toscano, and Perazo (1995) have found Sotuta pottery (the type associated with Chich'en Itza) in sealed contexts in the Nunnery Quadrangle and the Court of the Birds at Uxmal. In addition, Kurjack, Maldonado, and Robertson (1991) reported Sotuta ceramics in the Uxmal ballcourt. The inscriptions in these buildings date them to between A.D. 904 and 909. This growing body of evidence places the majority of Chich'en's buildings in the Terminal Classic period.

The sharing of imagery in the art of Chich'en Itza, Tula, and the later Aztecs has always been the strongest evidence of the Toltec contribution to Chich'en Itza. Alfred Tozzer (1957) made this kind of comparison the heart of his own argument. Karl Taube (1994a) has continued in this tradition in several papers.

This visual, stylistic, and inscriptional evidence for the identification of the Toltecs has also been challenged. The great epigrapher Tatiana Proskouriakoff (1970) pointed out that Maya hieroglyphic texts appeared in "Toltec" art. Linnea Wren (1991) followed up on this evidence by dating a text in the Great Ballcourt to the Terminal Classic period.

Mary Miller demonstrated that the Chak Mol (a name made up by Le Plongeon), previously assumed to be Toltec in origin, derived from earlier Maya images of captives bound for sacrifice. Peter Schmidt's excavations in the Group of the Thousand Columns confirmed Miller's insight. He discovered a new Chak Mol that lies on its side, naked with its arms bound like a captive. These Chak Mols symbolize sacrificed captives sent to the Otherworld as messengers for their captors. The use of columns, which has been associated with Toltec-style architecture, is found at sites in southern Quintana Roo, such as Tz'ibanche, during the Early Classic period. Mary Miller (personal communication, 1995) also pointed out to us that the stelae of Tula have affinities with earlier stelae at the Maya site of Piedras Negras. In fact, the stela form was rarely used in central Mexico, so that Tula's use of the form may be because of Maya influence.

Images with Maya affinities also appear at Cacaxtla and Xochicalco during the Terminal Classic period. Moreover, historical narratives in architectural murals proliferate at Cacaxtla and El Tajín during the same period. There is no precedent for such narrative sculpture in the early art of central Mexico, while it is the rule in Maya art of the same period.

Furthermore, much of the warrior imagery that has been identified as Toltec has as many precedents in Classic Maya art as it does in central Mexico. In fact, the Toltec-Maya warriors wear much of the same costuming and imagery as the Tlaloc-Venus warriors of earlier Maya art. "Toltec" imagery, for example, appears four hundred years earlier on the monuments celebrating the victory of Tikal over Waxaktun in A.D. 378. See Virginia Miller's (1989) analysis of the star warrior for an example of how a figure shown frequently in Maya art and infrequently in central Mexican imagery has been interpreted as Toltec.

The other evidence often cited to support Chich'en's later dating is the presence of gold offerings in the cenote and the use of turquoise at Chich'en. Gold does not represent a problem. Strömsvik (1941) reported the discovery of the gold legs of a figurine in the cache of Stela H at Copan. The dedication date of this monument, 9.14.19.8.0 (A.D. 731), dates the import of gold from lower Central America into the Maya region as early as the first half of the eighth century. Gold was also found in Terminal Classic and Early Postclassic contexts at Quirigua.

Coggins and Shane (1984) date the gold disks related to the Upper and Lower Temples of the Jaguar to the ninth century. These artifacts also include imports from lower Central America. In fact, Sharer (1994: 719) says that the gold and copper alloys found at Chich'en came from Colombia, lower Central America, Guatemala, Chiapas, Oaxaca, and the Valley of Mexico. The other artifacts dredged from the cenote come from equally distant sources. Braswell (1995) has shown that the obsidian of Chich'en Itza came from sources all over Mexico—including the sources in central Mexico as well as the major Puebla and Veracruz mines. A much smaller percentage came from the highland sources of Guatemala, but this may be because the Kalak'mul-Koba alliance cut Chich'en off from the southern sources. Chich'en also imported turquoise from distant sources in the American Southwest, although they probably got it through intermediaries.

One thing is sure—that Chich'en Itza had wider and more distant trading relationships than any other Mesoamerican site up to the ninth century. The breadth of these trading connections puts Chich'en into a special category for Maya sites. We feel it emphasizes the internationalization that went on during the Terminal Classic period. The turquoise may have arrived through intermediaries, but the gold in the cenote suggests that Chich'en may have acted as the main supplier of metal art for Mesoamerica between 800 and 1000.

Finally, we are recognizing major affinities between Chich'en Itza and Terminal Classic sites like Cacaxtla and Xochicalco. Chich'en scribes used dates written in the calendar used by those sites in the contexts of founding narratives. Ethnohistorical documents identify Cacaxtla with the Olmeca-Xicalanca, a people said to have come from the Gulf Coast, the same area known as *Nonowal*. Both the Itza and the Olmeca-Xicalanca claimed the same place of origin, suggesting that they were ethnically and politically related. The Olmeca-Xicalanca may have been trading allies with the Itza and provided the conduit by which Maya symbolism and style spread to western Mesoamerica and Teotihuacan symbolism spread to eastern Mesoamerica. Debra Nagao (1989) analyzed the affinities between these various sites in a particularly useful way.

13. Archaeologists working in northern Yukatan have been finding evidence (especially Carbon-14 dates and reevaluation of ceramic chronologies) that "New Chich'en" dates to an earlier period than previously suspected. Archaeologists associated the Maya phase with a type of ceramics called Cehpech, while they connected the "Toltec" phase to another type called Sotuta. Charles Lincoln (1986, 1990) summarized the historical debates over the chronology of Chich'en Itza and argued for a "total overlap model" in which Sotuta and Cehpech were contemporary. He tested his reinterpretation with excavations in the outlying areas of Chich'en. Recent excavations at Uxmal have provided strong supporting evidence by finding Sotuta ceramics in caches of Puuk-style buildings like the ballcourt (Kurjack, Maldonado, and Robertson 1991), the Nunnery Quadrangle, and the Courtyard of the Birds (Huchim, Toscano, and Peraza 1995). Furthermore, Andrews V (1979) compiled all the radiocarbon dates associated with Sotuta and found that none of them fall later than A.D. 1000. Ringle, Bey, and Peraza (1991: 2) use ceramics and radiocarbon dates to argue that "there is no solid evidence—indeed there is evidence to the contrary—that Chichen was a vigorous center much later than A.D. 1000." We agree with their analysis, which builds upon earlier studies by Andrews V (1979) and Ball (1979). Recent surveys and excavations on the causeways of Chich'en Itza have yielded radiocarbon dates of around A.D. 900 (Rafael Cobos, personal communication, 1996). These data place Sotuta within the Terminal Classic and very early Postclassic periods and support the dating of all major buildings at Chich'en to this period.

14. Linnea Wren and Ruth Krochock (Wren 1991) deciphered the dedication date of the ballcourt, while Wren noted that the earliness of the date disputes the Toltec association with the ballcourt. Wren et al. (1992) also pointed out that this date is near the nadir position of the sun, which placed the three stones of the Cosmic Hearth at zenith position in the sky at midnight. The Itza linked their ballcourt to the time of Creation by this means. See Freidel et al. (1993: 492) for a discussion of the astronomy. Proskouriakoff (1970) also noted Maya-style inscriptions with "Toltec-Maya" figures at Chich'en, so that the overlap between the two styles has been recognized for a long time.

15. Suhler and Freidel (1994) argued that the main buildings in the sacred precinct at Chich'en were deliberately destroyed by people who left Mayapan ceramics as part of their ritual "killing" deposits. If they are right in their interpretation, there was a major destruction (or termination) episode around A.D. 1100. However, Mary Miller (personal communication, 1995) points out that Landa's description of Chich'en suggests that it still served as a ritual center, although not a population center, at the time of the conquest. Her observations suggest that Chich'en remained a vital center of ritual performance and political charter long after its role as a capital was over. Moreover, the termination rituals associated with Mayapan

ceramics do not require that Chich'en was still an active center when the destruction occurred, especially if the Mayapan lords considered that they had to terminate the old capital as part of the ritual to establish their city as the replacement capital.

16. *Tollan* and other locations associated with many different origin myths also occur in Maya chronicles. The Popol Vuh of the K'iche' Maya located this place of origin at "*Tulan Suywa,* Seven Caves, Seven Ravines" and said that their ancestors had traveled to the east across water when they left on their migrations. Many scholars have pointed out that "Seven Caves," or *Chicomoztoc* for the Aztecs, was a widespread and ancient description of a mythical place of origin. The Kaqchikels had four Tulans, each associated with a world direction. They also spoke about *Suywa, Tapku Oliman,* and a group called the *Nonowalkat.* The Yukateks said that the Tutul Xiw, rulers of Uxmal, came from *Nonowal,* to the west of *Suywa. Nonowal,* "place of broken language," has been identified as the Aztec word for the provinces that became Tabasco and Campeche, and in a more general context, it referred to the Maya region as a whole. Tozzer (1941: 23, note 128) quoted Torquemada as saying it referred to "the lands of Onohualco, which are near the sea and those which we call Yukatan, Tabasco, and Campeche, since all these provinces were called by these natives [the Aztecs] in their heathendom, Onohualco." Most of the Maya sources point toward the Veracruz-Tabasco coast as the location of *Nonowal.*

17. See a full discussion of this complex of imagery in Schele and Freidel (1990) and Freidel, Schele, and Parker (1993). Researchers long ago recognized that this imagery came from Teotihuacan, but the mechanisms of the diffusion and its meaning to the history of Mesoamerica are still under debate. By studying where this complex of imagery appears, we have determined that it was closely related to conquest warfare and ancestry among the Maya. Andrea Stone (1989) has suggested that the Maya used the complex to signal foreignness or association of royal authority with distant places. This complex of iconography includes the goggle-eyed deity called Tlaloc by the later Aztecs, owls, a war serpent called Waxaklahun-Ubah-Kan, spearthrowers, and warfare timed by Venus and Jupiter stations. Stuart (n.d.a) further associated the *puh* sign with the "reptile-eye" design from Teotihuacan, and suggested that the "reptile eye" represented cattail reeds for other traditions in Mesoamerica. Reptile-eye glyphs are also prominent at Cacaxtla and Xochicalco.

18. And one could just as well talk about Mayanized Mexicans, because places like Cacaxtla and Xochicalco in the Mexican highlands show equally strong influence from the Maya lowlands at the same time as the "Toltec" imagery appeared at Chich'en. Many scholars now identify the people of Cacaxtla as Olmeca-Xicalanca, a group that conquered Cholula in the seventh century and established their capital at Cacaxtla. We think that the Olmeca-Xicalanca were also at Xochicalco. The writing system seems to be the same one used at Cacaxtla, and both sites used the same political symbolism (see Berlo [1989] for a comparison). The Olmeca-Xicalanca may also have been the Tapku Oliman of the Kaqchikel accounts of their Terminal Classic history. Moreover, the people of Cacaxtla represented the Maya deity "God L" as their god of merchants, and much of their public imagery merged Maya style and symbolism with imagery from Teotihuacan and a calendar system that shares features with that of the Zapotec. The Olmeca-Xicalanca were important carriers of central Mexican religious and political imagery to the Maya area, and Maya imagery into central Mexico.

We suspect that the Olmeca-Xicalanca may have been trading partners with the Itza of Chich'en Itza, and perhaps were related to each other through kinship ties. Xicalanco was a place on the Gulf Coast of Tabasco, very near the region called Nonowal, that was claimed by one branch of the Itza people as their place of origin. Certainly such a connection helps explain how the Itza got obsidian from all of the sources in western Mesoamerica and turquoise from the U.S. Southwest. The Itza also may have traded for gold and transformed it into a prestige material that could carry political and religious information.

19. There is another intriguing idea that may account for some of the "Toltec" imagery. Most archaeologists now date the violent sacking of Teotihuacan to between A.D. 650 and 700. The Chilam Balams record that the migrations leading to the founding of Chich'en Itza began with the k'atun-ending in 692. These migrations may well have included Teotihuacan elites who had fled the destruction of their kingdom. If Teotihuacan was a principal "Place of Reeds," then the "Toltecs" may have come to Yukatan not as conquerors, but as refugees looking for a home. The other possible conduit was the Olmeca-Xicalanca, who were moving into the central highlands of Mexico starting around A.D. 650. David Freidel (1986) anticipated these ideas in his discussion of cartel groups among Classic and Terminal Classic peoples of Mesoamerica.

20. Tozzer (1957: 22) cites Lizana and Cogolludo as the source of the Zamma name for the first priest.

21. See Tozzer (1957: 22) for the Zamma reference and Roys (1967: 75–76) for the passage that called Chich'en the place of Itzam.

22. J. Eric Thompson (1970) put forward the Putun as the invaders in his discussion of Maya history. Kowalski (1989) has recently compared and evaluated all of the known evidence and interpretation concerning the Itza in light of the Putun hypothesis.

23. Anthony Andrews (1978) has found Sotuta ceramics along the northern and western coasts of Yukatan, especially around an island called Isla Cerritos. His work points toward a northern entry from the sea and gradual penetration south toward the territory controlled by the Maya of Koba in the west and the Puuk kingdoms to the east. The Itza established their capital at the juncture of these different political spheres and began a campaign of conquest that has been documented in detail at Yaxuna by David Freidel and his colleagues. William Ringle and his colleagues (Ringle, Bey, and Pereza 1991), working at Ek' Balam, point out the geographical and temporal restrictions of Sotuta ceramics and its rarity at their site. In fact, Ringle (personal communication, 1995) told us that he does not see Sotuta as a foreign ware nor does he see any evidence of an intrusion in the ceramic history.

24. Nikolai Grube (personal communication, 1995) has confirmed that the Koba inscription also uses the same verb, *huli,* "she arrived." However, the section that recorded the name of the person who arrived is too eroded to read.

25. This child, who was born on 9.12.15.13.7 (January 6, A.D. 688), is also known as Smoking-Squirrel in the literature.

26. See chapter two for a discussion of these events.

27. Nikolai Grube (personal communication, 1995) first noted the title at Motul de San José. He suggested that the original name of the lake was *itz ha,* "enchanted water,"

and that the people of the region called themselves Itza. Erik Boot (personal communication, 1995) found the same title in texts from the Caracol at Chich'en Itza.

28. Tikal's ancient name was Mutul, and the k'atun histories say the Itza came, at least in part, from Mutulpul, which Roys took to refer to Motul. We think Motul is simply a corruption of Mutul. Other place names in the migration story echo the names of Classic-period kingdoms. Because Siyankan occurs with Bak'halal, it surely refers to southern Quintana Roo near Lake Bak'halar, but the original names of Yaxchilan and Waxaktun were also *Siyankan. Ak'e* may refer to the modern Ak'e of Yukatan, but Bonampak's ancient name was also *Ak'e.* The names Chak'an, Chak'anputun, and Tan Xuluk Mul can be associated with provinces around Lake Peten Itza. We suspect these and many other names in the Chilam Balams will connect to the Classic-period political landscape as more decipherments are made.

Moreover, Teotihuacanos may have been among the refugees moving into the north. That great city had been destroyed sometime between A.D. 650 and 700. The *Mercado* at Chich'en has a floor plan that closely resembles the apartment arrangements at Teotihuacan, although the Chich'en example was constructed following local practices (that is, using thatched roofing) and at a much larger scale.

Several of the Books of Chilam Balam speak of *noh emal, tz'e emal,* "the Great Descent, the Little Descent," by which the Itza came down to the region of Chich'en. Barrera and Morley (1949) argued that the Great Descent came out of Chiapas and the Usumacinta drainage, up the west coast of Yukatan to Uxmal, Ichkansiho (now known as Tz'ibilchaltun), and finally Chich'en Itza. They brought the Little Descent out from central Peten into northern Belize and up the eastern coast of Yukatan to Koba and eventually Chich'en. In light of the new information from the Classic inscriptions, we think they were right in their assessment, although Koba was probably allied with Kalak'mul, while the Itza came out of Tikal's allied kingdoms. The Itza were originally around Lake Peten Itza and associated with Mutul during the Classic period. The emigrés from that region apparently took that name with them in their migrations north.

29. Nikolai Grube conducted a 1995 seminar on the inscriptions of Yukatan. He and his students concluded that the inscriptions of Xkalumk'in began around 9.14.0.0.0 (A.D. 652), include Cholan spellings, and refer to a group of *sahalob* who formed an early *multepal* alliance. *Sahal* was a principal subordinate title used along the Usumacinta and in Chiapas during the Classic period, but it is not characteristic of other regions. Grube proposes that these people were Chol-speaking refugee elites from the southern wars who set up interim kingdoms between 9.14. and 10.0. They shut down about twenty years before dated inscriptions show up at Uxmal. We suspect these are the people of the "Great Descent" who became the Tutul Xiw of Yukatekan legend.

30. Here is the description of the founding of the Itza state from the Chilam Balam of Chumayel adapted from Roys (1967: 73–74):

> Then the rulers began founding this country. There was the Ah K'in of Palonkab. There was the Ah K'in of Mutupul (Mutul), its name; also the Ah K'in of Palonkab, Ah May; also the Ah K'in of Mutul, Ah Kanul Wayom Ch'ich', who spoke brokenly; also He of Chable, He of Ichkansiho, Holtun-Balam, his son. Chak'an received the

cotinga. Then finally all their rulers were seated. These rulers were the companions, the speakers of the rulers of the 11 Ahaw tun, its cargo name. Then they founded the territory (land); then they founded the country (earth-houses). Then they settled at Ichkansiho. Then they of Holtun-Ak'e descended; then they of Sabakna descended. And then the rulers were seated, all together. Also He of Sabakna was the origin of the Na people. And then they gathered themselves at Ichkansiho where the jaguar mat was during the reign of Holtun-Balam at his cenote, during the reign of Pochek'-Ix-Tz'oy. He was the first of the men of Kopo. Tutul Xiw might have been there also. The Chakte lord, Chakte is the land their rulers won in conquest.

This passage goes on with descriptions of rituals that founded the nation by setting the four corners and sweeping the land. But there are important points to make here. *Mutul* was the old name of Tikal. Roys translated *yaxum* as "quetzal," but the decipherment of Bird-Jaguar's name at Yaxchilan is *yaxun,* or "cotinga." This gorgeous blue bird appears on the helmets of Chich'en's warriors, where it is usually identified by its Aztec name, *xiuh tototl.* However, the *yaxun* is a very ancient symbol in Maya imagery and it appears in the Dresden Codex and the Books of Chilam Balam under its Maya name as a bird of omen. In this passage, it was given to *Chak'an,* which is recorded both as the province around Tz'ibilchaltun and as a province west of Lake Peten Itza in Guatemala. *Ak'e* is the name of a site in Yukatan, but it was also the name of Bonampak'. And finally, *chakte* was the title of the high king of Tikal and war leaders at many other Maya sites. The "west chakte" title went with the Tlaloc-Venus complex—the prototype of the "Toltec" imagery at Chich'en Itza. Roys translated the Chakte passage as "Chacte was the ruler, Chacte was the land where their rulers arrived," but the passage uses the verb *chuk,* which is glossed as "to win conquering." Roys (Tozzer 1941: note 172) apparently also thought that some of the Itza came from the Peten. He quoted the Kalk'ini Chronicle as saying that some of the people came from Peten Itza. Ah Kanul, who is associated with Mutul in the Chumayel passage, is one who is supposed to have come from there. Kan-K'awil is a name sequence that shows up repeatedly is the name phrases of Tikal's late kings. The *Ah Kanul* of the Chilam Balam may refer to someone of this family.

The location called Ichkansiho closely matches a location recorded on Tz'ibilchaltun Stela 19 as *k'ul ?? kan ti ho ahaw.* Since the pre-European names for Mérida were *Ichkansiho* and *Tiho,* we feel that we can identify Tz'ibilchaltun as Ichkantiho and the site of the assemblage described in the Chumayel.

31. The chronology of the migrations also begins to make sense in light of the inscriptions. The histories of the k'atuns in the Books of Chilam Balam are told in twenty-year cycles called k'atuns. The names of these k'atuns come from the days on which they ended, but since there are thirteen numbers that can appear with the Ahaw name, any named k'atun repeats every 260 years. The k'atun contains 7,200 days, so that for every k'atun, the number of the Ahaw name reduces by two in a regular sequence: 8 Ahaw, 6 Ahaw, 4 Ahaw, 2 Ahaw, 13 Ahaw, 11 Ahaw, 9 Ahaw, 7 Ahaw, 5 Ahaw, 3 Ahaw, 1 Ahaw, 12 Ahaw, 10 Ahaw. The sequence then begins again after encompassing a full 260 tuns, or 13 k'atuns. This pattern of repetition has caused the problem. Which 260-year cycle is the correct one for the named events?

The answer has been there since J. Eric Thompson (1950) figured out that the scribes of Chich'en Itza anchored their dates by noting the tun and k'atun in which they occurred. A typical date notation was "9 Lamat the day on the 11th of Yax in tun 13 of 1 Ahaw [k'atun]." This date would repeat every 18.16.19.5.0, or 7,431 years. That cycle of repetition is clearly outside of Chich'en Itza's history. This system locks all of the known dates from Chich'en Itza to a span between A.D. 832 and 909. Thus, the "discovery of Chich'en Itza" mentioned in the Books of Chilam Balam must have occurred in the 8 Ahaw k'atun immediately before these dates. That places the discovery in the k'atun spanning the years A.D. 672 and 692.

This placement of the 8 Ahaw k'atun is further supported by the notations of time durations of the various migrations recorded in the Chilam Balams. For example, we are told that the Tutul Xiw traveled for eighty years and then they settled and ruled in a place called Chaknabiton for ninety-nine years. Then they migrated again and came to Uxmal. That places their first stop around 771 and their arrival at Uxmal in the k'atun-ending in 889. The first date fits well with the chronology of Xkalumk'in and its region, while the second falls just before the dates associated with Lord Chak at Uxmal.

These k'atun histories have recently received detailed attention from other scholars, including A. Chase (1986), Lincoln (1986, 1990, 1994), Edmonson (1982, 1986), and Ball (1986). Also see Tozzer (1941: notes 123, 159). Because of its comparison of archaeological, ethnohistorical, and epigraphic data, we found William Ringle's (1990) study particularly useful, especially for his analysis of the lineage names.

By correlating the events recorded in the Chilam Balams with the history in the inscriptions, we get the following chronology:

In k'atun 8 Ahaw (ending on 9.13.0.0.0: A.D. 692)
> Dos Pilas and Kalak'mul captured and sacrificed the king of Tikal; the Dos Pilas king sent his daughter to Naranjo to restore the fallen dynasty there. She gave birth to a son.
> Teotihuacan was burned and destroyed during the fifty-year period ending on this date.
> The Tutul Xiw led by Chan Tepew left their home called Tulipan Chiconah T'an in Nonowal, west of Suywa. They journeyed for four k'atuns.
> Chich'en Itza was discovered. The province of Siyankan Bak'halal was discovered.

In k'atun 6 Ahaw (9.14.0.0.0: A.D. 711)
> The Naranjo child became king at age five and a year of war followed. At its end, Naranjo captured a Tikal noble named Sian-K'awil.
> Tikal's king captured and sacrificed the king of Kalak'mul; Chich'en was discovered.

In k'atun 4 Ahaw (9.15.0.0.0: A.D. 731)
> Naranjo attacked Ucanal and Yaxha; Tonina attacked Palenque and killed its king.
> The Great Descent and the Little Descent occurred. The Itza arrived at Chich'en Itza and ruled for thirteen k'atuns. The migrations occurred in four divisions originating from different locations.

In k'atun 2 Ahaw (9.16.0.0.0: A.D. 751)
> Tikal attacked Naranjo and killed its king; Tikal attacked El Peru and captured its palanquin gods; Dos Pilas conquered Seibal; Quirigua captured and sacrificed the king of Copan; Palenque captured lords from Piedras Negras.

Inscriptions appear at Xkalumk'in and nearby.

Ah-Kuy-Tok' established himself at Uxmal.

In k'atun 13 Ahaw (9.17.0.0.0: A.D. 771)

Yaxchilan and Piedras Negras were in battle separately and as allies; Tamarindito destroyed Dos Pilas and broke up the regional hegemony.

9.16.1.0.0 Ah-Mek'at-Tutul-Xiw arrived at Chaknabiton and he stayed for ninety-nine years.

The mats were set in order at Siyankan Bak'halal ("Born of Heaven, Surrounded by Reeds"); the Itza reigned for sixty years and then went to Chich'en Itza.

In k'atun 11 Ahaw (9.18.0.0.0: A.D. 790)

Ixkun attacked Iwin; Itzan attacked Lakamtun; Yaxchilan made a series of captures with the Laxtunich lords; Bonampak' with Yaxchilan's help attacked Sak Tz'i; Piedras Negras made a series of captures.

An assembly of Mutul, Itza, Tutul Xiw, and other lords was held in Ichkansiho (Tz'i-bilchaltun); the assembly founded the country and the state. They came to Wuk-Yabnal (Yabnal in the inscriptions of Chich'en Itza). They began to take tribute.

In k'atun 9 Ahaw (9.19.0.0.0: A.D. 810)

Piedras Negras and La Mar waged war against Pomona; Bonampak' made war; Yax-chilan made captures on two separate occasions; Aguateca made a capture; Naranjo attacked Yaxha; Caracol attacked Bitol; Aguateca was destroyed.

In k'atun 7 Ahaw (10.0.0.0.0: A.D. 830)

Caracol made war in its region in cooperation with Ucanal; Ucanal sent lords to reestablish the state at Seibal.

In k'atun 5 Ahaw (10.1.0.0.0: A.D. 849)

Chich'en Itza (CI) 10.0.2.7.13 The Temple of the Hieroglyphic Jambs dedicated.

CI 10.0.12.8.0 The High Priest's Grave dedicated.

In k'atun 3 Ahaw (10.2.0.0.0: A.D. 869)

CI 10.1.15.3.6 The Great Ballcourt dedicated.

In k'atun 1 Ahaw (10.3.0.0.0: A.D. 889)

CI 10.2.0.1.9 Fire ceremonies for K'ak'upakal, Yax-Uku?-K'awil, and Hun-Pik-Tok in the Casa Colorada.

CI 10.2.0.11.8 The Halak'al Lintel mentions Hun-Pik-Tok'.

CI 10.2.3.12.1, 10.2.4.8.4 K'akupakal does a fire ritual (Yula lintels).

CI 10.2.8.10.4 The Temple of Owls capstone dedicated.

CI 10.2.9.1.9 The Temple of the Initial Series dedicated.

CI 10.2.10.11.17 The Monjas lintels dedicated.

CI 10.2.12.1.8 Members of the Multepal dedicate the Temple of the Four Lintels.

CI 10.2.12.13.1 Monjas capstones dedicated.

CI 10.2.13.15.11 A capture depicted at K'abah.

Last dates at Tikal, Waxaktun, Seibal, Ixlu, and other Peten sites.

In k'atun 12 Ahaw (10.4.0.0.0: A.D. 909)

Lord Chak dedicated the Ballcourt and the Nunnery Quadrangle at Uxmal; last date at Tonina; last date at Uxmal.

CI Last dates at Chich'en Itza (found in the Caracol).

In k'atun 10 Ahaw (10.5.0.0.0: A.D. 928)

10.4.1.0.0 Itzimte Stela 6, latest dated monument.

In k'atun 8 Ahaw (10.6.0.0.0: A.D. 948)

Chich'en Itza was abandoned and the Itza established Chak'anputun, which they ruled for thirteen k'atuns.

Chak'anputun is usually associated with Champoton in Campeche, but there is a region called Chak'an that was part of the Itza hegemony around Lake Peten Itza. Could Chak'anputun have been Chak'an Peten? Another place of exile called Tan Xuluk Mul was mentioned by Avendaño as being a short distance west of Lake Peten Itza (Tozzer 1941: 34). When consulted on this issue in 1995, Grant Jones agreed that our idea is a good possibility.

In k'atun 10 Ahaw (10.18.0.0.0: A.D. 1185)

Stela 1 of Mayapan celebrated 10 Ahaw.

In k'atun 8 Ahaw (10.19.0.0.0: A.D. 1204)

The Itza left Chak'anputun.

10.18.10.0.0 (A.D. 1194) The Hunak-Kel incident where Chak-Xib-Chak was forced out of Chich'en Itza.

Mayapan attacked Ulil of Itzamal and forced his people into exile.

In k'atun 4 Ahaw (11.1.0.0.0: A.D. 1244)

The Itza, in concert with the men of Ulil of Itzamal, attacked Mayapan.

Stela 4 of Mayapan celebrated 4 Ahaw.

In k'atun 2 Ahaw (11.2.0.0.0: A.D. 1263)

Stela 13 of Mayapan celebrated 2 Ahaw.

In k'atun 13 Ahaw (11.3.0.0.0: A.D. 1283)

The Itza established themselves at Mayapan and became known as Maya.

In k'atun 11 Ahaw (11.4.0.0.0: A.D. 1303)

11.3.3.0.0 Strangers from the mountains who had occupied Mayapan left.

In k'atun 1 Ahaw (11.9.0.0.0: A.D. 1401)

Tankah Mayapan was abandoned and the Tutul Xiw left Mayapan.

In k'atun 8 Ahaw (11.12.0.0.0: A.D. 1461)

Mayapan was finally abandoned and the Maya were scattered throughout the region.

In k'atun 4 Ahaw (11.14.0.0.0: A.D. 1500)

Columbus's voyages brought Europeans to the New World and the first epidemics were introduced into Yukatan from the Caribbean.

In k'atun 2 Ahaw (11.16.0.0.0: A.D. 1520)

Guerrero and Aguilar were shipwrecked in Yukatan; smallpox swept through Yukatan. Cortés landed at Cozumel on his way to his conquest of the Aztecs.

In k'atun 11 Ahaw (11.17.0.0.0: A.D. 1559)

10.16.1.0.0 The Spaniards conquered Yukatan and Christianity was introduced.

These historical accounts suggest that the Itza were not a single group, but rather an alliance made of people from both the northern and southern lowlands. Some of them were local, while others were apparently Itza-speaking people from central and northeastern Peten. Still others, including the legendary K'ak'upakal himself, were *u nun*, "those who speak brokenly." Evidence suggests they were Cholan speakers from the Usumacinta drainage. All of these groups appear to have assembled in Ichkantiho (Tz'ibilchaltun) to found their government.

Tz'ibilchaltun's stelae date from exactly this period, and the House of the Seven

Dolls has iconography consistent with foundation places. E. Wyllys Andrews V (Andrews and Andrews 1980) dated the House of the Seven Dolls to the period between 9.13.0.0.0 and 9.15.0.0.0. He (Andrews V 1974) compared it to the tower and surrounding palace at Palenque. We now know that the Palace at Palenque is a *Popol Nah,* or Council House. He pointed out its affinity to Group E structures from Late Preclassic and Early Classic Peten architecture (Andrews and Andrews 1980). The radial design of the House of the Seven Dolls, in turn, anticipated the Castillo at Chich'en, but more important, the interior tower surely presaged the Caracol. The E-group arrangement and the radial pyramid used at Tz'ibilchaltun are ancient Maya forms deeply involved in foundation and dynastic symbolism. Their presence at Tz'ibilchaltun suggests the builders of the House of the Seven Dolls knew ancient Peten forms and used them to establish a new charter of power in the north.

Moreover, as Clemency Coggins (1983: 36–63) observed, the House of the Seven Dolls includes imagery of the sea and it had *talud-tablero* forms on its lowest terrace. The entablature frieze represented the Primordial Sea with four Chak gods on the corners of the building. The tower may represent the central axis of the world or the mountain rising from the Sea of Creation. It is a "Split-Mountain, Bitter Water" place of Creation like that described in the Popol Vuh and perhaps Snake Mountain at the Place of Reeds. The House of the Seven Dolls is a place of Creation and Foundation.

The Chilam Balam of Chumayel says that this founding ceremony included the measuring and sweeping of the land. The listed participants include people from several different historical episodes, but even so, the family names mentioned are still widespread in Yukatan. The founding seems to have resulted in a confederacy that included the rulers of Ichkantiho, Uxmal, Itzamal, and Chich'en Itza. Their greatest enemies appear to have been the kingdom of Koba and its allies. If Koba was linked to Kalak'mul and its hegemony, while Chich'en was founded by Itza from the Tikal region and the Chiapas zone, then the Itza wars may have been a continuation of the southern "star-wars."

32. The word used in this passage is *chiktahal,* which means "to find something that one is looking for." The Itza set about finding a place where they could found their new state.

33. This zone was built at least twice, but the first version apparently did not include a ballcourt. In fact, the iconography of the Lower and Upper Temples of the Jaguar occurs in the Castillo-sub, as shields, jaguars, and entwined serpents. The famous red jaguar with its mirror has its analog in the jaguar throne of the Lower Temple of the Jaguar and the Chak Mol corresponds to the ballplayer Chak Mol that was found in the South Building (Linnea Wren, personal communication, 1997). This Chak Mol now rests in the Museum at Tz'ibilchaltun. We suspect the second construction phase split the iconography of the Castillo into two units and put it in the ballcourt.

34. Snake Mountain is particularly associated with the Aztec founding legends as a place where the Aztecs stopped during their migrations. Located at Tollan, Nahuatl for "Place of Cattail Reeds," Coatepec was the place where the Aztecs' patron god Huitzilopochtli was born. He brought the banners and war serpent with him into the world. The Templo Mayor at the Aztec capital of Tenochtitlan was the human-made replica of Snake Mountain. The Aztecs called upon an ancient tradition of placing ser-

pent heads at the bottom of balustrades to mark a temple as Snake Mountain. This device is known at Teotihuacan, but it came to artistic maturity in the architecture of Chich'en Itza. But the idea of Snake Mountain is far older than either Teotihuacan or Chich'en Itza. It is found on the main building in Group H at Waxaktun and at Cerros between 100 B.C. and A.D. 100. In these very early examples, the snake penetrates an image of a pyramid-mountain from side to side or emerges from the mouth of the mountain monster. The snakes at Chich'en Itza very likely also represent the idea of the *kuxan sum,* the "living cord," that connected rulers to the sky. Snake Mountain as a place of origin is a very ancient concept in Mesoamerican mythology.

35. Nikolai Grube identified phrases in the inscriptions of the Monjas that call this water in the Sacred Cenote the *Sak Nab,* or "Pure Sea." The inscriptions speak of "looking into" or "conjuring from" the *Sak Nab.* Sak is "white" or "pure," while *nab* is "lake" or "sea."

36. Recent excavations by Peter Schmidt have revealed extraordinary images of *Itzam-Ye,* the great bird that sits atop the World Tree, all over the upper three terraces and the temple atop this pyramid. On the terraces, fruit, maize, beans, jewels, and all the *utz,* or good things, of the cosmos float around the birds as if the bounty of the universe pops into existence in their presence.

    Annabeth Headrick (1991) first proposed the equivalency of the High Priest's Grave to the Castillo and suggested that it was the prototype of the larger group. Peter Schmidt's excavations certainly confirmed her idea about the relationship between the two groups, although he does not agree with her about the chronological relationships. In conversations with him in the summer of 1994, he told us that he feels the style of the carvings associated with the High Priest's Grave are far more mature and developed than those he has excavated in the Group of the Thousand Columns. In our judgment, the sculptures of the bird *Itzam-Ye* that we saw are far closer to the sculptural traditions of the Classic period than to those in the Principal Group. We believe that Headrick's initial assessment is the more likely, and that the High Priest's Grave should be dated to 10.0.12.9.0 2 Ahaw 18 Mol (June 16, 842).

37. We have worked extensively with the Chich'en group at the Texas Meetings. This group has been working on the inscriptional history and iconographic meaning of Chich'en's sculpture since 1990. Led by Ruth Krochock, this group has included many people, with the core being Linnea Wren, Erik Boot, Lynn Foster, and Peter Keeler. We have benefited from long-term consultation with them, and many of the ideas and insights we present here grew out of their work. David Freidel and Linda Schele also wrote on Chich'en Itza in both *A Forest of Kings* and *Maya Cosmos.* These interpretations also grow out of that collaboration. We would like also to acknowledge the generous cooperation of Peter Schmidt, who not only showed us his excavations, but also shared his thoughts with us. And finally, Logan Wagner provided us with drawings and measurements he made with teams of students from the University of Texas and Earthwatch, while working on his own project on Maya architecture of the precolumbian and colonial periods.

38. Several people made this connection with the crevice independently. It appears prominently in Schele and Freidel (1991) and Freidel, Schele, and Parker (1993: chapter 8). Gutierrez (1993) has also discussed this concept in relationship to Yaxchilan's ballcourt.

39. There have been several recent publications on the Mesoamerican ballgame that have contributed greatly to our understanding. See Leyenaar (1978) for a very interesting description of a similar game still being played in Mexico. Several important conferences have been published in Wilcox and Scarborough (1991), van Bussel, van Dongen, and Leyenaar (1991), and Uriate (1992). Also see the chapter on the ballgame in Freidel, Schele, and Parker (1993).

40. At Teotihuacan, players used a stick to hit a smaller ball. Merle Robertson (1991) has pointed out similar sticks in the imagery of Seibal and suggested this version of the game was also played at Chich'en Itza.

41. These are calendar names combining the numbers one and seven with the name of the twentieth day, which is Hunahpu or Ahpu in K'iche' and other highland languages. One of the sons of this pair was named Hunahpu. *Ahpu* has generally been translated "He, the Blowgunner," but while the word for "blowgun" is *pub'* in these languages, none of the early documents use a *b'* in the spelling of these names. David Stuart (personal communication, 1994) suggested that *ahpu* may be, instead, *Ah Puh,* "He of Cattail Reeds," as a means of declaring these great heroes and the K'iche' lords to be from the place of origin.

42. See Freidel, Schele, and Parker (1993) for a detailed study of how the Classic-period story of Creation was conceived and represented in art and architecture. That ancient story was the forebear of the seventeenth-century Popol Vuh myth.

43. This path is also represented as cords as well as entwined serpents. Both of these symbolize an umbilicus. Often a white flower representing the human soul is attached to the cord or snake. Matthew Looper (1996) has found a text at Quirigua that records the disposition of these white flower cords on the Creation day.

44. See Karl Taube's (1994) seminal study of this goddess as the postmenopausal midwife who enables birth. Her helper is the Mam or Pawahtun, the old god who holds up the corners of the world and gives each newborn infant its spirit soul companion.

45. Following Lounsbury's demonstration of the *na* value for the female head, most epigraphers have read this glyph as *na,* "mother" or "lady," while rejecting the earlier suggestions of *ix, ixik,* or *ixok.* Recently, epigraphers like Nikolai Grube (personal communication, 1995) and Garcia Campillo (1994) have used the appearance of *ki* phonetic complements, especially in the Dresden Codex, to revive the older reading. We are not particularly happy with assigning more than one value to this glyph, but the phonetic complementation seems to support both the *na* and *ixik* values. This evidence suggests that the name of the young Moon Goddess was Ixik or Sak Ixik.

46. See Barrera and Morley (1949: 46–47) for a discussion of this passage.

47. The earliest known example in Mesoamerican art of the serpent with legs occurs on the roofcomb of a temple at Copan called Rosalila by Ricardo Agurcia, its excavator. Commissioned by the tenth ruler, Rosalila depicted legged serpents arching over a mountain and a young god stretching his arms outward. Legged serpents also appear on Altars G and O, during the reign of Yax-Pasah during the eighth century. See chapter five.

48. In Classic-period iconography, both the Maize God and the Moon Goddess wear this net skirt. Males and females in these roles wore the same skirt, although males wore it in hip- and knee-length forms. Women wore skirts that fell to the top of their sandals.

49. *Na* can also be "structure," "mother," and "lady." The name may pun on all these meanings.

50. The text identifies the depicted location as *Na-Ho-Kan Witz Xaman,* "First-Five-Sky Mountain North."

51. The Chilam Balam of Chumayel names the place of the founding as *Ichkansiho,* which is generally translated as "heaven-born." However, Stela 19 at Tz'ibilchaltun records *?? kan ti ho,* which we suspect was *Ich kan ti ho,* "In the sky at five." We suggest this was the Yukatekan version of *Na-Ho-Kan.* See note 30 for a more detailed description of this assembly.

52. Cynthia Kristen-Graham (1989) has suggested that these signs are not personal names, but refer instead to the family or lineage names of the participants. This alternative would fit our interpretation of this mural as the creation of the world and the founding assembly.

53. *Kan* is the Yukatek word for "snake," "a herbaceous vine," and "to chat, hold a conversation." This homophony identifies these volutes as "speech" and explains why these flowery volutes sometimes have serpent features.

54. These leggings look very much like those worn by the losing lord in the sacrifice scene at Cacaxtla. Many scholars have commented on the "Maya-ness" of the losers in this scene. However, if the slaughter scene represents sacrifice after a founding war, then the winners may be the Olmeca-Xicalanca and the losers the old people of the region who were conquered. Interestingly, the leader of the losing side wears a woman's garment. In Teotihuacan political symbolism, the king embodied the World Tree in the form of the Great Goddess (Schele 1996). It may be that the Olmeca-Xicalanca artists of Cacaxtla represented this older form of royal symbolism by showing the ruler of the "old people" with female attributes.

55. At Teotihuacan, dozens of warriors wearing these mosaic belt mirrors were sacrificed and buried in long trenches on all four sides of the Temple of the Feathered Serpent. This particular temple was a unique structure at Teotihuacan, and it remained a model of later architecture in Mesoamerica, much like the Parthenon and Pantheon function in the Western world.

56. The Chich'en Group from the Texas Meetings suggested that these two figures are Pawahtuns, but they are wearing *Itz* headdresses, so that they may be Itzamnas. The ethnohistorical sources support both identifications. Lizana said that the first priest of Chich'en Itza was Zamma (Itzamna), while the k'atun histories of the Chumayel say that the first rulers were named Pawahaekuhs. These figures may be either one.

57. The Kokoms were one of the ruling families of Chich'en. They are recorded both in the k'atun histories and in the inscriptions at Chich'en. Kristen-Graham (1989) first made this identification of the vine as *kokom.*

58. John Justeson (personal communication, 1995) first suggested to us that this is the knot day sign in the Zapotec system. The knot day sign is also found at Xochicalco, which used the same writing system as Cacaxtla. If both sites were Olmeca-Xicalanca centers, the presence of the 6 Knot day sign at Chich'en Itza may signal profound interactions between the Itza and the Olmeca-Xicalanca. Both were said to come from the Gulf Coast of Tabasco and Campeche.

59. Objects almost identical to these appear in a palace scene where it is called a *yub,* the Yukatek word for "bed curtains" and a "canopy." This object is wound around a pole

in the pottery scene, but we know of no other image in Maya art that is so close in form to this Chich'en object.

60. Schele (Schele and J. Miller 1982) discussed the meaning and function of mirrors in Maya art (although the readings proposed in this monograph are incorrect). See Taube (1992) for a discussion of the meaning of mirrors at Teotihuacan and throughout Mesoamerica.

61. Starting in the Early Classic period, feathered serpents appear with some frequency in Maya art, but they were usually associated with vision scenes or with images of the Sun God or Maize God holding the ecliptic. Feathered serpents appear frequently in the art of Copan, especially in the art of Yax-Pasah, and a huge one arches over Ruler B on Lintel 3 of Tikal Temple 4.

Perhaps the most intriguing example of *K'uk'ulkan,* "Feathered-Serpent," comes from a polychrome pot excavated at Waxaktun. The pot has a Long Count of 7.5.0.0.0 combined with the calendar round and moon age for 8.17.19.10.0 8 Ahaw 13 K'ank'in (January 29, 396). The scene shows a ruler with two attendants facing a pair of ornately dressed figures wearing large backracks. The one in front has a feathered serpent in his backrack, while the name in front of his face reads *K'uk-Kan Sahal.* However, the scribe uses "sky" for *kan,* rather than "snake." The other figure has a Venus serpent head and may be named Hun Ahaw. These two figures may represent Hero-Twin impersonators engaged in a ritual with the king. Most important, this pot provides an Early Classic example of a being called *K'uk'(ul)kan* in the southern lowlands. Thus, we can say with some certainty that K'ukulkan and the Feathered Serpent is far older in Maya imagery than in Chich'en Itza.

See Taube (1992a) for his discussion of feathered serpents and mirrors at Teotihuacan.

62. This figure occurs on a large incensario lid. It is one of twelve found outside a tomb in Structure 10L-26 at Copan. William Fash (personal communication, 1992) and most of the other researchers at Copan take the presence of the eye rings and mouthpiece to identify that particular portrait as that of Yax-K'uk'-Mo'. The mouthpiece at Copan has the image of teeth on it. Schele (1992) suggested that the eye pieces read *ch'ok* and that the mouth ornament is *ko* to mark the wearer as *ch'ok.* This title was used for members of a lineage who were not its head, but it could also apply directly to founders.

63. Karl Taube (1994a: 239) pointed out this association. According to him, the Aztecs called this crown *xiuhhuizolli* and made it from turquoise. He pointed toward other mosaic objects, including backshields and butterfly pectorals, that were made of turquoise. In fact, in the Maya lowlands, turquoise has been found only at Chich'en Itza in any quantity, although Mary Miller (personal communication, 1995) has taken the blue color of some jewelry in the Bonampak' murals to signal turquoise.

Several scholars have used turquoise as evidence that "Toltec-Chich'en" is later than the "Maya" side, but the growing evidence from both inscriptional and archaeological data challenges these older presumptions. The import of turquoise from the north as well as gold from the south appears to have begun much earlier than has been previously thought. Gold was found in the dedication cache of Stela H at Copan, dated at A.D. 731. And researchers working in the Southwest now date the earliest appearance of turquoise in Mesoamerica at A.D. 480.

The *cotinga* was a sacred bird known as the *xiuh tototl* to the Aztecs. Its presence here has been taken as a signal of Toltec influence by Taube and others. However, the cotinga was known as the *yaxun* among the Maya and appears in Maya iconography by the Early Classic period. It was a bird of omen and was often paired with the quetzal. A look at its natural history and range is enlightening. It lives in the canopy of lowland tropical forests, while the quetzal occupy highland cloud forests. The ranges of the two birds are complementary, but they are not found in the Mexican highlands at all. In other words, both birds are found in the Maya region and have a long history of meaning there. They are not native to central Mexico and had to be imported from the Maya zone by the Aztecs.

64. Linnea Wren made these identifications in her presentation at the 1995 College Art Association meetings and at the Symposium of the XIXth Texas Meetings on Maya Hieroglyphic Writing.

65. The Maya also associated snakes with Chak-Chel, the old midwife who oversaw Creation. Mary Ciaramella (1994) discussed the snake associations with various goddesses and connected them with weaving. The Tzutuhil Maya of Santiago Atitlan say that the turban headdress worn by married women is a "rainbow" serpent. Rainbow serpents also connect babies to their mothers before birth. Cihuacoatl of the Aztec was also a goddess of midwifery, who exhorted women to be like warriors when they expelled the baby from their wombs. See M. Miller and Taube (1993: 61) for a description of this goddess.

We do not know if the Maya associated Chak-Chel with warfare, but women could conjure lineage founders from the War Serpent to participate in important war and accession rituals. Yaxchilan Lintel 25 depicts Lady K'abal-Xok conjuring up the founder of Itzam-Balam's lineage on the day of his accession. The serpent who carried the apparition was the War Serpent called Waxaklahun-Ubah-Kan.

While this role likely contributed to the war/woman associations at Chich'en, another likely source was Teotihuacan. We know of no serpent-skirted images of warriors or rulers from Teotihuacan, but the ruler there personified (Schele 1996) a female deity known as the Great Goddess, whom Taube (1983) identified as Spider Woman. If this association holds true, then the idea of a king in female guise may have been adapted from Teotihuacan religio-political symbolism. Perhaps the Maya combined their traditions with those of Teotihuacan refugees to create a ruling warrior with a serpent skirt and the breasts of a woman. The Aztecs later split this complex symbol to get the male speaker, who wore the turquoise crown, and the male war-leader called Woman-Serpent.

66. Taube (1992a) identified this creature as the headdress carried on the tail of the feathered serpent on the Temple of the Feathered Serpent at Teotihuacan. Built around A.D. 150, this building featured symbolism that spread throughout Mesoamerica in subsequent centuries, and became far more prominent in Maya imagery than it ever was at Teotihuacan. In Maya contexts, this Mosaic Monster sometimes has the features of a jaguar and sometimes of a serpent, and was one of the primary symbols of the Tlaloc-Venus complex associated with Maya warfare from A.D. 378 onward. See Schele and Freidel (1990: 130–215) and Freidel, Schele, and Parker (1993: 293–336) for a detailed discussion of this kind of warfare.

67. Arthur Miller (1977) called this figure Captain Serpent and the one above it Cap-

tain Sundisk. He suggested they represent historical people who led the migrations of the Itza to Chich'en. Schele and Freidel (1990: 371–373) proposed a more generic function as legendary ancestors. We now think that Miller's arguments have merit, but we associate the figures with the kind of founding ancestors recorded in the Popol Vuh and the *Annals of the Kaqchikels*. Both sources named particular ancestors who received objects and titular gods at Tulan. The founding scenes in the Lower Temple of the Jaguar appear to record Itza ancestors receiving objects that empowered their reign at Creation. The Itza framed their founding in the symbolism of Tulan.

68. See Taube (1992) for a discussion of these mirrors at Teotihuacan and other Mesoamerican iconography. Schele and Freidel (1990: 393–395) argued that the placement of these mirrors within or on the throne vested power into the office rather than into the individual who held it.

69. Even when the Maya displaced the sun-mirror imagery to other locations in the composition, such as at Yaxchilan, kings wore the name of the father on the back of their belts. The Maize God as First Father appears in this location on the north panel of the Temple of the Foliated Cross at Palenque.

70. In the parallel origin story of the Popol Vuh, the first four human beings modeled by Xmuqane were the founding ancestors of all the tribes of the highlands. We think the occupant of the jaguar throne materializes the same concept for the Itza.

71. We checked the entire corpus for examples of this flower headdress and found several examples that clearly depict the feather background of the cylinder. See Tikal Stela 16 and Yaxchilan Lintel 58 for particularly telling examples. Single-flower headdresses also occur, especially at Piedras Negras, where both kings and their wives (Stelae 1 and 3) wear this kind of flower-feather turban. The most important example appears on a looted lintel from the Piedras Negras region that shows Piedras Negras Ruler 2 with a sublord from Kalak'mul. This sublord wears exactly this same kind of headdress. However, we have found similar headdresses on Teotihuacan figurines published by Seler (1915: Fig. 54). Most important, we think Yax-Ain, the king of Tikal portrayed on the side of Stela 31, wears a very early version of this headdress, with the flower blossom rolled out so that the viewer could discern what it was.

72. These may represent throwing sticks for offense rather than fending sticks for defense.

73. Taube (1994a: 239) associated these jaguar collars with the turquoise *xolocozcatl* pectorals shown in Aztec sources. However, this type of pectoral has not been documented for any earlier tradition in central Mexico. Their earliest occurrences are at Chich'en Itza.

74. Logan Wagner measured the ballcourt with a plane-table and an alidade and found that the front wall of the Upper Temple has an orientation of 15 degrees east of north. This places the perpendicular (the direction the building faces) at 285 degrees. Aveni (1980: 312) gives 17 degrees 24 minutes as the orientation of the Great Ballcourt and 16 degrees 6 minutes for the Temple of the Jaguar, but he did not say which wall had this latter orientation.

75. The three published interpretations of these paintings by Marvin Cohodas (1978), Arthur Miller (1977), and Coggins and Shane (1984) begin their narrative sequence with this panel also. Cohodas first argued that the position of the sun-mirror cartouche marked the position of the sun, so that we begin with dawn in this panel,

move to morning in the northeast, noon in the north, afternoon in the northwest, sunset in the southwest, and night in the south. Coggins and Shane (1984: 157–165) accepted his pattern, but added the five-day journey leading to the heliacal rising of Venus. We will not emphasize this sequencing because of our belief that these images record the Itza wars that chartered their right to rule. Thus, we do not see Toltecs from Central Mexico so much as the wars of the southern kingdoms leading to the establishment of Chich'en Itza. There may be astronomical sequencing here, but we are not sure how it works.

76. Walters and Kowalski (n.d.) presented an analysis of the battle scenes from the site of Mulchic near Uxmal. They suggested that these battles may represent the establishment of a regional state in the Puuk region late in the tenth century. We think this interpretation is correct and that the scenes represent a battle by the Tutul Xiw and their Itza allies against a neighboring site. The Book of Chilam Balam of Chumayel places the Tutul Xiw at the Itza founding assembly, so that Uxmal was an ally rather than an enemy. The Chich'en mural may depict an episode in the same war.

77. Similar floating figures appear on the gold disks from the cenote and on the late stelae of Ucanal, Ixlu, and Jimbal from the southern lowlands. All these floaters carry spearthrowers and javelins, and the examples from the southern lowlands materialize in dotted scrolls that symbolize clouds. Chich'en's artists represented the same idea with a blue field representing the sky.

78. Coggins and Shane (1984: 162) pointed out the presence of this wall and associated it with another one depicted in wall murals in the Monjas. Uxmal and Ek' Balam have a wall like it, as do the various precincts of Chich'en. Moreover, walls with log palisades have been found throughout Dos Pilas and Aguateca, where there is no doubt about their function as defensive walls. In the north, such walls may have served both as demarcation and defensive walls.

79. Coggins and Shane (1984: 164) identified this prone figure as an earth goddess, while Taube (1994a: 214–216) associated her with the Aztec deity Tlaltecuhtli, whose body was sundered to create the earth. However, in Maya cosmology, the deity whose death leads to the creation of the world is not a goddess, but rather the Maize God. Images of this god show him stretching out serpents symbolizing the sky umbilicus and the ecliptic. Moreover, in the Paris Codex New Year pages, this umbilicus is clearly shown to be the intestines of the sacrificed Maize God. Freidel, Schele, and Parker (1993: 381, 492) also associated this image with the Maya version of Creation. At El Tajín (Koontz 1994), the intestines of a sacrificial victim become maize and lead to the erection of the World Tree.

80. Kelley (1982) identified this Mosaic Serpent fellow as Mixcoatl, "Cloud Serpent," of Toltec myth. Coggins and Shane (1984) followed his interpretation, but cloud serpents, like feathered serpents, have a long history with the Maya, including examples from the Early Classic period. They are related to the cloud volutes that were used on Tikal stelae from the Early Classic period on to show the media in which visions of ancestors arrived. These cloud scrolls could be appended or float around Vision Serpents and Cosmic Monsters (as in Copan Temple 22). At Chich'en Itza, artists connected the cloud motif with the Mosaic Serpent, whose white color apparently signaled his substance as either shell or cloud.

81. At Bonampak' and Yaxchilan, white robes and necklaces of large spondylus shells are the characteristic garb of the secondary nobles known as *sahalob*. This *sahal* title occurs primarily in Chiapas and along the Usumacinta, but as Nikolai Grube (1994) has noted, it also occurs at Xkalumk'in, exactly along the route that the Tutul Xiw migrations would have taken if they originated in the Tabasco-Chiapas area. The white-robed figures may represent the equivalent of the *sahal* rank in Itza society.

Coggins and Shane (1984: 165) suggested that the people in the bottom zone of this and the south panel represent Toltec officers sitting on campaign stools. This general idea may be correct, but we believe the people shown in these murals are Itza rather than invaders from central Mexico.

82. We were inspired in many of these interpretations by the work of Rex Koontz (1994) on El Tajín, a site in northern Veracruz that used these same myths as the basis of its political symbolism. Koontz identified the War of Heaven in the Mixtec codices as another example. He has coined the concept of "paradigmatic war" to describe the use of these myths to create political charter.

83. The photographs that appeared in Le Plongeon's (1896) *Queen M'oo and the Egyptian Sphinx* were later reproduced by Seler (1908) in his study of Chich'en Itza. The English painter Adela Breton's paintings appear in Romandía de Cantú and Piña Chan (1993) and Giles and Stewart (1989). Adela Breton has documented the discovery of this table and its removal to Mexico City in 1903 (Giles and Stewart 1989: 48–51).

84. George Kubler (1982) first made the connection between the concept of *bakab* and Atlantean figures of all sorts. We follow him in this identification.

85. This unusual statue sat in the basement of the Regional Museum in Mérida. It was recently put on exhibition in the Museum at Tz'ibilchaltun, where we were able to examine it in detail. The published data we were able to find only identifies this statue as coming from the ballcourt, but doesn't say exactly where it was found. Linnea Wren (personal communication, 1997) informed us that she had information from Peter Schmidt, who once headed the museum in Mérida, that museum records on the statue have a provenience locating it in the South Temple. We cannot confirm this information from our own knowledge, but we thought that even a tentative placement of this object was important to the understanding of the Great Ballcourt.

The unusual posture of this Chak Mol was unique until the recent excavations in the Court of the Thousand Columns. The team working with Peter Schmidt found another reclining Chak Mol in one of the buildings there, but that one represented a naked captive lying in the same general posture.

86. Round columns have been taken as another "Toltec" feature borrowed from central Mexico. However, recent excavations in southern Quintana Roo at sites like Tz'ibanche and Kohunlich have found doorway columns used in Early Classic architecture. That region is the legendary Siyankan Bak'halal from whence some of the Itza came.

87. Mary Miller (1985) proposed exactly this interpretation in her study of the Chak Mol. She connected them to the captive figures often shown on the base of stelae or their associated altars. Her interpretation has been confirmed by a recently discovered Chak Mol from the Group of the Thousand Columns that shows a naked bound captive lying with his hips twisted to the side. She also recalled Alberto Ruz's comment on the resemblance of the image of Pakal on the sarcophagus at Palenque

to the Chak Mol and asserted that this image could also be connected with sacrifice. We agree, because Pakal falls as the Maize God who will be sacrificed in the Xibalba ballcourt. In fact, Magdiel Castillo, in a seminar at the University of Texas, pointed out that the floor plan of the Palenque tomb has the I-shape of a ballcourt. If these connections are correctly identified, then the Great Ballcourt connects captive sacrifice to the great Creation myth in which the Maize God died. To kill captives in the ballcourt replayed this great central myth at the heart of Maya life.

88. This day sign is shared by Xochicalco. Since these two figures clearly participate in the founding and sanctification of political authority at Chich'en Itza, we wonder if their presence may not signal a fundamental association with the Olmeca-Xicalanca at Xochicalco and Cacaxtla.

89. Linnea Wren (1991; Wren and Schmidt 1991) first connected the iconography of the North Temple to accession rituals, especially as they were described in late Aztec sources. Freidel, Schele, and Parker (1993: 381–384) followed her analysis and locked the general iconography of the ballcourt to Maya traditions in the southern lowlands.

90. These bird dancers have a very ancient pedigree in Mesoamerican imagery. The Olmec-style painting at Oxtotitlan presents a bird dancer seated on a personified bench, while Altar 4 of La Venta, a similar kind of bench, depicts an Olmec lord wearing a bird mask headdress seated inside a cave niche. Bird impersonators are also a major theme in the art of Izapa and Kaminaljuyu, and bird imagery plays a central role in Preclassic and Early Classic imagery from central Peten, especially in the great mask programs. Many of these birds are the supernatural bird *Itzam-Ye* or *Mut Itzamna,* a symbol of the art of the sorcerer and the capacity to communicate with the Otherworld. The Chich'en examples fall within this domain also.

91. Villela and Koontz (1994) first identified the central scene in the upper register as a nose-piercing ceremony. They compared the Chich'en example to the Mixtec codices, where the nose-piercing ritual was essential to the legitimization of rulers. Although we have no direct evidence of a parallel Maya ritual from earlier written sources, Maya lords wore nose ornaments from the earliest times. We surmise that the Maya had an analogous ritual, although they did not apparently think of it as essential political information until Chich'en Itza.

CHAPTER 7: UXMAL

1. See Jeff Kowalski's (1987: 17–24) study of the House of the Governor for a detailed history of research on Uxmal. The map of Mani appears in Roys (1943).

2. The Books of Chilam Balam were written by Yukatek Maya scribes using the Latin alphabet to write in their own language. These books contain historical chronicles that go back into the eighth century, although these accounts have become as much legend as history. We used the comparative analysis of these various histories by Barrera and Morley (1949). Although we use a different chronology based on information from the Classic-period inscriptions (Schele, Grube, and Boot, n.d.), we find their command of the k'atun histories and their interpretation of the associated events to be the most insightful of the published sources. See chapter six for a discussion of the Itza history recorded in these books.

3. See E. Wyllys Andrews V (1979) for a summary of the relevant archaeological data on the early phases of Uxmal and the Puuk region. After reviewing the published information on the Puuk, he placed its beginnings in the middle of the eighth century.

4. See Grube and Schele (1994: 14) for this entry and a wider discussion of the association of owls with warfare.

5. This incident is recorded in the Chilam Balam of Chumayel as the founding of Mayapan. Eric Boot (personal communication, 1994) identified one of the names in this passage, Sabakna, in the inscription of the Monjas at Chich'en Itza. Schele (Schele, Grube, and Boot, n.d.) discovered another participant's name, Ah-Holtun-Balam, on the disk from the Caracol at Chich'en. Thus, it is apparent that this founding assembly concerned the establishment of an Itza confederation that included at minimum Chich'en Itza, Tz'ibilchaltun, Itzamal, Chable, and Uxmal. One line in this passage records that "the Xiw might also have been there."

6. Nikolai Grube (1994: 331–335) deciphered these titles and analyzed their distribution in the inscriptions of Chich'en Itza. We note that K'ak'upakal's name on Lintel 4 of the Monjas includes *k'ak'nal ahaw,* the same title that appears in Chan-Chak's name at Uxmal. Since this is a rare title, it further strengthens the proposed ties between the two leaders.

7. Barrera and Morley (1949: 27 [fn. 9] and 29 [fn. 18]) discussed the etymologies of these names. They suggested that *Holon-Chan-Tepew* is a Cholan-derived name meaning "Head Snake Ruler." *Holon* is the agentive for the word *hol,* "head." *Chan* is the Cholan term for "snake," but it is also a family name in Yukatan. *Tepew* is a Yukatek word for "to reign." The snake heads tenoned into Uxmal's buildings may be metaphorical expressions of this title. *Ah-Mek'at* is a Yukatek title meaning "chief" or "ruler." This title could be another way of referring to Holon-Chan-Tepew or to a chief in charge of a segment of the community of the Tutul Xiw.

8. We have considered two ways of explaining these migrations. Wars of major consequence erupted in central Peten and Chiapas between 650 and 700. More than one kingdom was sacked and at least two major kings, Nun-Bak-Chak of Tikal and Yich'ak-K'ak' of Kalak'mul, were captured and sacrificed. These wars may well have resulted in refugee elites who migrated northward in the wake of these wars. See the chapters on Tikal and Chich'en Itza for a more detailed description of the wars and their consequences.

   The other possibility is that these wars created a class of highly trained and experienced soldiers who set out on their own in the wake of these Peten wars. If this alternative is the correct one, then they may have been part of the Olmeca-Xicalanca migrations into central Mexico as well as the Tutul Xiw migrations into northern Yukatan. This scenario would also account for the strength of Chich'en's connections with the Mexican highlands.

9. Walters and Kowalski (n.d.) presented this interpretation at a 1995 conference in Palenque. Their arguments were finely detailed and convincing in their presentation.

10. Seler (1917: 35) first made the suggestion that these designs represent flowers or jewels, although he did not identify them with the word *itz.* Floyd Lounsbury first associated the word *itz* with the design in the name of Itzamna in the Dresden Codex. Freidel, Schele, and Parker (1993: 210–213, 410–412) linked Seler's flower identification with Lounsbury's *itz* reading by showing that *itz* refers to the nectar in the flower.

11. Temple 11 at Copan and the Temple of the Foliated Cross at Palenque include *Na Tè'-K'an* in their proper names (Freidel, Schele, and Parker 1993: 53–57). At Tikal, Stela 31 records this name as a location, but we have no idea where it was in the city. At Copan, zoomorphic Maize Gods appear on the west side of Stela C and as the headdress on Stela H. Thus, the zoomorphic version at Uxmal has precedents in the southern lowlands.

12. Maler (Herrmann 1992: 257–259) shows the snake on the medial molding, but the upper corners had already been damaged by his time and so we cannot confirm the original presence of the upper snakes from his photographs.

13. Freidel, Schele, and Parker (1993: 70–71) identified this as the name of the bird that stands on top of the World Tree. He is the Classic-period archetype of the bird called Vuqub-Kaqix in the Popol Vuh. David Stuart (in a letter to Schele dated November 14, 1994) also identified names for it at Xkalumk'in in the form of *Mut Itzamna,* or "Bird Itzamna." Karl Taube (1992b: 40) had earlier identified this bird as the *way,* or animal form, of Itzamna, the god who was the first sorcerer of the present Creation. This bird was especially prominent at Late Preclassic sites such as Izapa and Kaminaljuyu, and Richard Hansen (personal communication, 1992) has found a huge plaster image of the bird rendered on the terrace of a building at Nak'be, an early Late Preclassic site (ca. 300 B.C.) in northern Peten.

14. Thompson (1943) argued the identification of the masks on the South Building as Itzamna to counter Seler's (1990) earlier suggestion that they represented the feathered serpent, Quetzalcoatl.

15. These commentaries of Viollet-le-Duc were published in Charnay and Viollet-le-Duc (1862–1863).

16. Jeff Kowalski (1994: 108–110) discussed the various identifications of this image, especially agreeing with Taube's (1992b: 37) association with the Teotihuacan headdress and War Serpent.

17. The concept of the community house has long been included in the work of ethnographers. Barbara Fash (Fash et al., 1992) first identified the archetype of the *popol-nah* at Copan in Temple 22a. Her work has led to the recognition of community houses at other Maya sites, so that we are now confident that the institution of the council of nobles and the community house is an ancient and widespread concept among the Maya. Stephen Houston (personal communication, 1992) pointed out that the Cordemex dictionary (Barrera Vásquez 1980: 570) says that a "flower house" (*nikte'il-nah)* is the same as a "mat house" (*popil-nah* or *popol-nah*).

18. The *muyal* reading was discovered independently by Houston and Stuart (personal communication, 1993) and by Stone (1995: 177). This sign is often accompanied by phonetic complementation, including the prefix *mu-* and the suffixes *-ya* and *-yal.*

19. Mesoamerican artists from the Olmec period on produced designs that featured bilateral ("mirror-image") symmetry. Thus, when parts of a design are missing, they can often be reconstructed by simply repeating the surviving sections.

20. Seler (1917: 60, Taf. 16) was quite specific about this location, perhaps because a Maler photograph shows the sculpture sitting on the platform immediately below the cloud scroll. He described the figure as a flute player.

21. David Stuart and Nikolai Grube have worked independently on these burning rituals. They worked together to identify several of the glyphic expressions for this rit-

ual, while Stuart first connected images of the ritual from monuments to those on pots. Both have investigated the role of burning in warfare, and such burning rituals are important in the texts of K'ak'upakal at Chich'en Itza. Some rituals involved the burning of captured towns, material goods, and sometimes people. Others included the kindling of "new fire" and the reenactment of mythical events involving fire.

22. The Itza of Chich'en Itza also used this imagery to mark their capital as a "Place of Reeds," as did many other sites in the Maya area. See chapter six for a discussion of *Puh* imagery at Chich'en Itza.

23. Freidel, Schele, and Parker (1993: 308–312) discussed the function of this serpent creature as the symbol of war and ancestral origins. Schele (1990) first identified the Maya name of the beastie on Stela 6 from Copan, while Taube (1992a) surveyed the War Serpent in the larger framework of Mesoamerica.

24. Frans Blom's measured drawings of the North Building include detailed evidence of the inner structure. In his restoration work on the North Building, Ruz (1957) also detailed this inner structure in drawings and photographs.

25. Waldeck's (1838) published drawing, which Totten (1926) reproduced in his study of Maya architecture, reconstructed the entablature with the entwined serpents across the entire front. Waldeck's placement of the figural sculptures within the background patterns was clearly improvised. Even if Waldeck did see the facade intact, he misdrew it. Photographs of the surviving portions of the facade taken later in the century differ from his drawings. Moreover, a comparison of his drawing with the archaeologically recovered sculptures from the facade show his reconstruction to be impossible. Thus, his drawing cannot be taken as an accurate rendition of what was there.

26. Jeff Kowalski allowed us to see copies of the reports submitted by the various archaeologists to the Instituto Nacional de Antropología e Historia of Mexico. It is clear from the photographs of the rubble below the facades that the walls had collapsed and were not subsequently disturbed. Whole mask assemblages had collapsed in integral groups that could be easily discerned and rearranged. The archaeologists could therefore surmise into which part of the facade sculptures belonged, although not necessarily their exact positions. Using logic, comparison with surviving facade sections, and assuming bilateral symmetry, they reconstructed the pattern. As far as we can tell from the photographs and descriptions in their reports, they had good reason for each of their decisions concerning the patterns and arrangement of the elements. Manuel Cirerol and Alberto Ruz were especially clear in describing the techniques they used to reason out the pattern of the sections they restored. Cirerol did much of the work on the West Building, while Ruz restored the largest sections of the North Building. The accuracy of their reconstructions is especially important for our own analysis of the iconography of these facades, especially of the West Building. We accept the basic pattern as they restored it.

27. This section and its complement on the opposite end were the last segments to be put in place. Peniche (Report T160, No. 4 of the INAH archives) surmised that the remaining stones not used in previous restoration had images of thatch roofing and a monster head. He reasoned that they composed the picture of a hut with a god image above just as on the South Building. We have no information about where he found the parts of the monster head, but his deduction of a thatch-roofed house seems reasonable. After he completed this restoration, Peniche reported that there

were still a few sculptured stones left over from the rubble under the north end of the West Building. He maintained that they were in a different style, and that they probably had fallen from the North Building. The techniques used by the Mexican archaeologists are quite similar to those used at Copan today to detect the original pattern of fallen facades. Although they did not detail their work in the same way, and although today archaeologists prefer not to restore facades unless the proof of their original pattern is close to absolute, the restoration work of the Mexican archaeologists on the Nunnery Quadrangle is excellent for its time.

28. See Freidel, Schele, and Parker (1993: 310–317) for a discussion of palanquins and their usage during the Classic period.

29. We have already discussed the appearance of the Itza ruler K'ak'upakal in Uxmal's inscriptions. This identification of the Itza at Uxmal is supported by the appearance of Sotuta pots, the ceramic style characteristic of Chich'en Itza, in sealed contexts in Uxmal's Ballcourt, the Nunnery Quadrangle, and the Court of the Birds. Moreover, the most recent archaeology at Uxmal has reconstructed the south side of the Court of the Birds as a colonnaded hall in the style of the Court of a Thousand Columns at Chich'en. The most recent archaeological evidence emerging from Uxmal supports an intimate association between its rulers, especially Chan-Chak-K'ak'nal-Ahaw and the Itza lords of Chich'en.

30. Karl Taube (1992a) discussed this war serpent throughout Mesoamerican art. Its most important and perhaps earliest example is on the Temple of the Feathered Serpent at Teotihuacan. However, feathered serpents have much greater longevity in Mesoamerican art because they appear in Olmec art at La Venta.

31. The first person to identify this image as a headdress was Mark Parsons (1985). Karl Taube (1992a) came to the same conclusion independently. This kind of headdress with the ring attachments on its upper zone appears in Maya art associated with captives, administrators, and kings. A man wearing such a headdress, carrying a bundle of *atlatl* darts, and wearing cuffs made of bivalve shells has been found in a grave in the early levels of the Copan Acropolis (Sharer 1995). This costume closely resembles that worn by the man on the sides of Tikal Stela 31. Thus, this headdress with its ring designs had wide distribution in Mesoamerica as a mark of authority from very early times.

32. This is a revolutionary interpretation that some scholars will find unlikely. However, Schele (1995) has proposed that the Great Goddess was the personification of the World Tree at Teotihuacan. As with other Mesoamerican peoples, we believe that the ruler of Teotihuacan considered himself to be the embodiment of this tree, and he wore the symbols to prove it. This nose ornament is the principal symbol of the Great Goddess and therefore of the tree.

33. Erosa discussed this jaguar in his 1943 report to the Instituto Nacional de Antropología e Historia. Jeff Kowalski (1994: 111) interpreted this column as the World Tree, called the *Yax Cheel Kab* by the Itza of the central Peten in the seventeenth century. He found the fragments of the jaguar in the northeastern room of the South Building and proposed that it had once been mounted on the altar in the center of the court, a suggestion confirmed by Erosa's report. Kowalski further associated the combination of altar, jaguar, and column shaft with the same assemblage in front of the House of the Governor. He proposed cosmological and political significance for this combination of symbols.

34. Roys (1952: 143) assembled the references to Mérida found in the early sources of the colonial period. Among these, he mentioned an entry in the Vienna dictionary on page 129r for *Uaclom-Chaan* as "idols that the ancients had at the site of Mérida." This name seems to be borrowing from *Wakah-Kan,* the ancient Cholan name of the tree at the center of the world. Therefore, both the *Yax-Cheel-Kab* and *Wakah-Kan* names for the World Tree were extant in northern Yukatan at the time of the conquest.

35. Freidel, Schele, and Parker (1993: 59–122) discuss this Creation mythology and its imagery in great detail.

36. Le Plongeon (Desmond 1988) described this event and photographed himself with a pile of sculptures he retrieved from inside a room on the eastern end of the South Building.

37. Jeff Kowalski (1985; 1987: 33–38, 68–74; 1991: 85) first identified this ruler and discussed his appearances in the inscriptions of Uxmal. He associated Lord Chak with the House of the Governor, the Ballcourt, and the Nunnery Quadrangle. Stuart and Houston (1994: 23) deciphered the *k'ak'nal ahaw* portion of his name, while Nikolai Grube (personal communication, 1992) read the *chan* part of the name. Unfortunately, the first glyph in this name has not yet been deciphered. His name meant something like "Little Chak Fire-Place Lord."

38. This verb, which consists of a hand with extended fingers, has long eluded decipherment, even though it was widely used in period-ending, dedication, and accession expressions. In November 1995, Werner Nahm, a German epigrapher, pointed out a phonetic substitution for this verb in the Monjas lintels at Chich'en Itza demonstrating its value as *k'alah.* We understand that David Stuart has also made this identification. The hand apparently has the phonetic value of *k'a, k'al,* and sometimes *k'ab,* "hand." *K'a* is a Cholti word meaning "to end or terminate," while *k'ah* means "to know, to make known, and to commemorate" in Yukatek. Finally, *k'al,* which is the value used in accession contexts, means "to close." Apparently it referred to closing or tying the royal headband around the head of the king when he acceded to his office. The hand could also be used as a simple phonetic sign with the value *k'a.*

39. Nikolai Grube and Elizabeth Wagner (Grube and Schele 1995: 197) observed a substitution pattern for this dedication verb suggesting that it reads *t'ab.* In Chorti, *t'ab* means "to ascend, climb up, or lift up," a meaning that fits many contexts in which this verb refers to some action done with temples. In sixteenth-century Tzotzil, *t'ab* means "to burnish or polish," so that this meaning is appropriate in contexts referring to dedication or finishing action. Since the scribes of Chich'en also used this verb to describe an action in relationship to their capstone paintings, the best interpretation seems to be the idea of "lifting up" the writing or capstone.

40. Jeff Kowalski (1994, 1994a) came to very similar conclusions in his extensive studies of the Nunnery Quadrangle and other buildings in Uxmal. Specifically, he argued for the cosmic connection of the maize symbolism of the East and South Buildings and the center arrangement of the jaguar throne and column. He also interpreted the Tlaloc symbolism on the North Building as an evocation of ancestral legitimization through Teotihuacan and "Toltec" affiliation in ways very close to our conclusions.

CHAPTER 8: IXIMCHE'

1. See Recinos (1984) for a translation of these important documents. *El Titulo de Totonicapán* (Carmack and Mondloch 1983) and the Popol Vuh (Tedlock 1985) also recorded the K'iche' version of many of the same events.
2. Robert Carmack's (1968) study of Toltec influences in highland Guatemala summarizes this data in particularly salient ways.
3. We follow Villacorta's (1934: 193, 196) transcription of this name. Brinton (1885: 81–83) and Recinos and Goetz (1953) transcribed this same name as *tapcu oloman*. We take this difference to reflect a paleographic problem. Since *tapcu* has no meaning known to us, and *tepew* does, we will use Villacorta's interpretation here.
4. In 1942, Jiménez-Moreno (1995: 82–86) identified the Olmeca-Xicalanca and the Olmeca-Uixtotix as Nahualized Mazateco-Popoluca speakers who were closely linked with the Toltecs of Tula. In 1943, Armillas (1995) identified Cacaxtla as the capital of the Olmeca-Xicalanca in the highlands based on ethnohistorical sources. Excavations at Cacaxtla in the last two decades have proven Armillas correct, but the amazing murals uncovered there suggest another identity for the Olmeca-Xicalanca. In these paintings, Maya deities, narrative painting styles, images of rulers, and other features are fused with traditional symbols and representations from Teotihuacan. Since the writing system, the primary political charter, and strong affiliations with the Maya area are common to both sites, we suggest that Xochicalco and Cacaxtla were both Olmeca-Xicalanca sites. The *Historia Tolteca-Chichimeca* says that the Olmeca-Xicalanca conquered Cholula in the eighth century and were thrown out by the Nahua-speaking Chichimecs in the twelfth century.

   Other sources associate the Olmeca-Xicalanca with the region called *Nonowal* and with a group of displaced Toltecs called the *Nonowalca*. We suspect they were one and the same and that the original Olmeca-Xicalanca were Chontal-Maya–speaking traders who allied themselves with other language groups on the Veracruz Coast. Both ethnohistorical and archaeological evidence suggests that these groups moved into the central Mexican highlands during the eighth century. They may have played a role in the demise of Teotihuacan.

   Coming from the region called *Nonowal,* the Olmeca-Xicalanca were traders who worshiped the Maya deity known as God L as their special patron. After the excavation of a Cacaxtla mural showing God L with a merchant's pack, many scholars identified this god with merchants. Grube and Schele (1994) identified him with *Ek' Chuwah* based on his appearance with a scorpion tail in the Madrid Codex and his association with canoes and merchant packs in the Dresden Codex. Ethnohistorical sources in Yukatan identify *Ek' Chuwah* as the god of merchants, but *Ek' Chuwah* is also a term for "scorpion." The Olmeca-Xicalanca gave this Maya god a highland name—4 Dog.

   The Olmeca-Xicalanca were important players in the legend of Tulan as it passed into the Postclassic period. They appear to have had profound economic and political affiliations with Chich'en Itza and the Maya kingdoms of the southern lowlands, like Seibal. These trading people were the conduit by which Teotihuacan symbolism came to Chich'en Itza in such force and by which Maya symbolism came to profoundly affect Cacaxtla, Xochicalco, and other central Mexican cultures of the Terminal Classic period.

5. Our sources on these myths of origins include our own research into the histories of the Chilam Balams, Nigel Davies's (1977) work on the Toltec legends in central Mexico, and Robert Carmack's (1968) seminal analysis of Toltec influence in highland Guatemala. We have also used a study by Allen Christenson that puts these various sources together. Of particular interest to us is Carmack's (1968: 68) suggestion that *Wuqub'-Siwan,* "Seven Ravines," may be related to the original name of Chich'en Itza—*Wuk Abnal,* which Roys (1962: 42) interpreted as "Seven Bushy Places." Like many other scholars, Carmack recognized that *Wuqub'-Pek* recalls *Chicomoztoc,* "Seven Caves," the Aztec place of origin.

6. See the chapter on Seibal for a detailed description of this text and the K'iche' history associated with the name.

7. Nacxit, a legendary character also found in the histories of the Books of Chilam Balam, appeared in the migrations as a great lord of Tulan. Many scholars have associated him with Topiltzin-Quetzalcoatl, the main character in the famous story of the fall of Tula when he was expelled from Tulan. The association with Tula, Hidalgo, seems unlikely now, but perhaps this legend refers to an earlier Tulan, called *Puh* by the Maya—the great city of Teotihuacan.

8. Recent research by Federico Fahsen (1996) on the writing system of Kaminaljuyu has identified the most likely language as Cholan. He identified glyphs for *winal, hunal* ("headband" and the name of the Maize God), and several other signs that prefigure glyphs in the Classic-period writing system.

9. These archaeological investigations have been conducted by Juan Antonio Valdés and Marion Hatch. They have targeted remnants of a huge canal system that supplied water to the fields at one end of the lake. Not only have they documented the drying up of the lake and the adjustment of the canals to changing water levels, but their work has detected a population replacement that corresponded to the loss of the lake. The earlier people used Usulatan ceramics, erected stone monuments, and had a writing system. According to Hatch's (1996) analysis of the ceramic complexes involved, the Late Preclassic people left the valley of Guatemala, moving toward the northeast down the Motagua Valley. This displacement is remarkably well timed to participate in the Early Classic developments at Copan, which has strong pottery affiliations to the highland traditions. In the century after its abandonment, a new people moved into Kaminaljuyu and the nearby region. Hatch (1996) says that the entire ceramic repertoire, especially the domestic wares, was entirely replaced by new types with affinities to the northwest. Since this new pottery has affinities with subsequent pottery traditions in the highlands, she has identified the incoming people as the ancestors of the K'iche'an groups that occupy the highlands today. Kaminaljuyu Temples A and B, which have been associated with Teotihuacan, belong to this second K'iche'an period of occupation.

Geoffrey Braswell (1996) has informed us that he has documented a related sequence of events in the region of San Martín Jilotepeque and that he agrees with Hatch's historical reconstruction. He wrote us that the San Martín Jilotepeque region was abandoned in the Late Preclassic and resettled during the Early Classic. He pointed out that there are no continuous occupations from this time in the valley of Guatemala, but that he has been able to trace a continuity between Early Classic and Early Postclassic ceramics, architecture, and sculpture at the ethnohistorically known site of Chuisac, a Kaqchikel (Xpantzay) town. His belief is that "the origin of the modern Kaqchikel speakers can be traced to a K'iche'an migration (probably from Quiché or Quetzaltenango) about A.D. 250."

10. Marion Hatch (1996) said that the ceramic tradition, especially in the domestic wares used by women to cook and keep house, completely changed at this juncture. The old pottery has affinities with the traditions in El Salvador and Copan, while the new one came to the central highlands from the northwest. Because that new tradition developed into the highland traditions of the Classic and Postclassic periods, she now believes that this juncture represents the immigration of the K'iche'an peoples into the central highlands of Guatemala.

11. David Stuart (personal communication, 1994) made this suggestion and we suspect he is correct. Other etymologies suppose that the term derives from *Ah Pub'*, "He, the Blowgunner," but to my knowledge none of the day names or personal names from the ethnohistorical sources include the *b*. *Ah Puh* makes perfect sense as an ancient title from lords who claim an origin in Tulan.

12. If this chronology is the correct one, then the references to *Nonowal* and *Tepew Oloman* may refer to a later interaction with lowland peoples at the time Teotihuacan collapsed (A.D. 600–700) and the centuries thereafter. The Olmeca-Xicalanca would have played their role in these histories between A.D. 600 and 1000. The collapse of the lowland kingdoms in the ninth and tenth centuries would also have produced refugee elites that may have brought lowland symbols and histories into the highlands. But more to the point, if the central highlands were occupied by K'iche'an peoples as early as the third and fourth centuries, they would have been players in Classic-period history. Certainly, the histories of the Popol Vuh and the *Annals of the Kaqchikels* suggest that the K'iche'an peoples knew of and were involved in the sweeping events at the end of the Classic period and that they traced much of their political charter to their interactions with the great powers of the time.

    Furthermore, Kaufman (1974), using linguistic evidence combined with archaeological data, placed the migration of the K'iche'an peoples into the modern departments of Quiché, Chimaltenango, and Totonicapán at around 600 B.C., with Greater K'iche'an differentiated into Poqom, Uspantek, and K'iche'an proper around 200 B.C. He also postulated that the Late Preclassic inhabitants of Kaminaljuyu spoke Poqom. He made his proposals over twenty years ago based on archaeological interpretations available at the time. Nevertheless, his reconstruction is remarkably close to the interpretation we offer based on new archaeological investigations in the central highlands. The timing of the diversification would perhaps be the same, but the movement of K'iche'ans into the valley of Guatemala and Chimaltenango would be later, during the third and fourth centuries.

13. K'iq'ab' attacked to the east, conquering the Rabinal and the Poqomchi along the Chixoy drainage and the people around Sacatepequez. Then he turned his soldiers south to take Pokoh and the Pipil town at Cotzumalguapa. Moving onward to the west, they took Retalhuleu, Xetulul, and drove west into the Socunusco, taking territories in the lowlands until they came up against Aztec armies expanding from central Mexico into the area of modern Chiapas. Then K'iq'ab' turned toward the Mam, driving them out of their capital at Zaculeu. Villacorta (1938) described the size and population of the resulting empire.

14. *Sotz'il* and *Xahil* were names for the principal lineages of the Kaqchikel rulers. *Sotz'il* is "bat," while *xahil* is "dancer." The bats worn by the men of Solola on their jackets today have their origin in the ancient lineage names. *Ahpo* and *Ahpo K'amahay* were titles the Kaqchikels received at Tulan. *K'amahay* referred to officials of the court in charge of tribute (Recinos and Goetz 1953: 52).

15. Recinos (1980: 89) calculated this date to be May 18, but this requires a 584281 correlation. He (Recinos 1980: 27) based his dating on a letter that Alvarado sent to Cortés saying that he left Utatlan (Q'umarkah) for Iximche' on April 11, 1524. In another letter, Alvarado said he arrived two days later. Recinos calculated his arrival to have occurred on April 12, 1524, and cited Gómara's *Historia General de las Indias* (1552) as confirming evidence. The *Annals of the Kaqchikels* says that Alvarado arrived on 1 Hunahpu. The problem is that in the 584283 correlation, 1 Hunahpu fell on April 14, 1524. Recinos apparently took the Spanish records to be the primary evidence, and thus placed all of the Kaqchikel dates two days earlier, requiring a 584281 correlation. When Federico Fahsen and Schele searched the *Annals* for pairs of dates in which the Kaqchikel scribes had recorded a date in both the European and Kaqchikel systems, they found them all to be consistent with the 584283 correlation. It seems to us that Recinos put too much faith in the vague Spanish records, and too little in the precise and consistent chronology recorded by the Kaqchikel. We think Alvarado left Q'umarkah on April 11, traveled for two days to arrive outside Iximche' on April 13, but that he did not formally enter the Kaqchikel capital until the following day—April 14, or 1 Hunahpu. We have recalculated all the Kaqchikel dates to be consistent with the 584283 correlation.

16. Recinos (Recinos and Goetz 1953: 18) pointed to a letter from Cortés to Charles V that described this contact.

17. The map in Figure 8.3 is from Fuentes y Guzman as published in Maudslay 1889–1902, vol. 2: pl. 73.

18. The Kaqchikels used years of 400 days, not the 360-day cycle used in the lowland Long-Count and k'atun prophecies.

19. The story in the *Annals of the Cakchiquels* blamed Alvarado for the destruction, but Spanish records (Guillemin 1977: 238; Recinos 1952: 21–22) show that sixteen soldiers had rebelled when they were ordered to go with Cortés to Honduras. They set the city on fire, kidnapped a priest, took valuable objects from the temples, and as they escaped through the countryside, sacked peaceful towns along the way.

20. *Tecpan* is the Nahuatl word for "house" or "palace." The name is thus "palace of the forested land."

21. See Guillemin (1977) for his arguments concerning the organization of Iximche'. He correlated Kaqchikel, Spanish, and archaeological data to present an interpretation of Iximche's plans that seems well founded to us. We accept his assignments as he presented them.

22. Holders of the *Ahpo Sotz'il* title included Kai-Noh, Wuqu-Batz' (who broke away from the K'iche'), Oxlahuh-Tz'i', his son Hun-Iq', and finally Kahi-Imox, who ruled when Alvarado came. The *Ahpo Xahil* included Kai-Batz', Hun-Toh, Lahuh-Ah, Kab'lahuh-Tihax, and Lahuh-Noh.

23. Guillemin (1965: 27) reported three stages of construction, with the innermost reached by tunneling. This inner temple would have been the work of Wuqu-Batz',

the second phase of Oxlahuh-Tz'i', and the third of Hun-Iq'. The last king, Kahi-Imox, reigned during the disaster of the conquest and probably did not have the time to commission his own buildings. Guillemin also reported that material used in the final phase was taken to build houses in Tecpan.

24. Guillemin (1965: 28) described these images and the technique used to make them, and included drawings of the best preserved of them in his description of Temple 2.

25. Guillemin (1969: 27) suggested that this platform and the one at the southwest corner of Temple 4 represent *tzompantli* in the Kaqchikel mode. The *tzompantli*, or "skull racks" was usually located near ballcourts, as at Chich'en Itza. In the myth of Tollan, a "skull place" located in the ballcourt was the source of water and fertility. Stephen Whittington informed us that there was a deposit of two skulls in a pit in the plaza floor next to the "skull place."

26. Guillemin (1977: 232) used the artifact assemblage he found to propose that these were houses used in rituals and not for family residences.

27. Stephen Whittington et al. (1996) has studied these bones and photographs of the tomb. The bones of the companions have been studied, although the labeling on much of the material has been lost. He provided information concerning their positions, suggesting that one of them may have been decapitated.

28. See Guillemin (1961) for a full description of the grave and his discussion of the identity of the dead man.

29. Whittington et al. (1996) reported these gender identifications in their study of the bones from Iximche'. They also found that seven of the people were between fifteen and twenty-one when they died.

References

Abrams, Elliot Marc
  1994   *How the Maya Built Their World: Energetics and Ancient Architecture.* Austin: University of Texas Press.
Andrews, Anthony P.
  1978   Puertos costeros del Postclásico Temprano en el norte de Yucatán. *Estudios de Cultura Maya* 11: 75–93. México: Universidad Nacional Autónoma de México.
Andrews V, and E. Wyllys
  1974   Some Architectural Similarities Between Dzibilchaltun and Palenque. *Primera Mesa Redonda de Palenque, Part II,* ed. by Merle Greene Robertson: 137–147. Pebble Beach, CA: Robert Louis Stevenson School.
  1979   Some Comments on Puuc Architecture of the Northern Yucatan Peninsula. *The Puuc: New Perspectives,* ed. by Lawrence Mills: 1–17. Pella, IA: Central College.
Andrews V, E. Wyllys, and Barbara Fash
  1992   Continuity and Change in a Royal Maya Residential Complex at Copan. *Ancient Mesoamerica* 3: 63–68.
Armillas, Pedro
  1995   Los olmeca-xicalancas y los sitios arqueológicos del suroeste de Tlaxcala. *Antología de Cacaxtla,* Vol. 1, ed. by Angel García Cook and Beatriz Leonor Merino Carrión: 110–119. México: Instituto Nacional de Antropología e Historia. A reprint of a 1943 article.
Aveni, Anthony
  1980   *Skywatchers of Ancient Mexico.* Austin: University of Texas Press.
Ball, Joseph
  1979   Ceramics, Culture History, and the Puuc Tradition: Some Alternative Possibilities. *The Puuc: New Perspectives,* ed. by Lawrence Mills: 18–35. Pella, IA: Central College.
  1986   Campeche, the Itzá, and the Postclassic: A Study in Ethnohistorical Archaeology. In *Late Lowland Maya Civilization, Classic to Postclassic,* ed. by Jeremy A. Sabloff and E. Wyllys Andrews V: 379–408. A School of American Research Book. Albuquerque: University of New Mexico Press.
Barrera Vásquez, Alfredo
  1980   *Diccionario Maya Cordemex, Maya-Español, Español-Maya.* Mérida: Ediciones Cordemex.

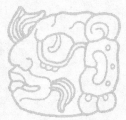

Barrera Vásquez, Alfredo, and Sylvanus G. Morley

1949   The Maya Chronicles. *Contribution to American Anthropology and History,* Vol. 10, No. 48: 1–85. Washington, D.C.: Carnegie Institution of Washington.

Barthel, Thomas

1968   El complejo "emblema." *Estudios de Cultura Maya* 7: 159–193. México: Universidad Nacional Autónoma de México.

Berdan, Frances, and Patricia Anawalt

1992   *The Codex Mendoza,* Vol. 1. Berkeley, CA: University of California Press.

Berlin, Heinrich

1958   El glifo "emblema" en las inscripciones mayas. *Journal de la Société des Américanistes,* n.s., 47: 111–119. Paris.

1959   Glifos nominales en el sarcófago de Palenque. *Humanidades* 2(10):1–8. Guatemala: Universidad de San Carlos de Guatemala.

1963   The Palenque Triad. *Journal de la Société des Américanistes,* n.s., 52: 91–99. Paris.

1968   The Tablet of the 96 Glyphs at Palenque, Chiapas, Mexico. *Archaeological Studies in Middle America,* Middle American Research Institute, Publication 26: 135–149. New Orleans: Tulane University.

Berlo, Janet Catherine

1989   Early Writing in Central Mexico: In Tlilli, In Tlapalli Before A.D. 1000. *Mesoamerica After the Decline of Teotihuacan—A.D. 700–900,* ed. by Richard Deihl and Janet Catherine Berlo: 153–172. Washington, D.C.: Dumbarton Oaks.

Blom, Frans, and Oliver Lafarge

1926   *Tribes and Temples,* Vol. 1. New Orleans: Tulane University.

Boot, Erik, Matthew Looper, and Elisabeth Wagner

1996   A New *k'a* Syllable: T627a/538/583. *Texas Notes on Precolumbian Art, Writing, and Culture,* No. 77. The Center for the History and Art of Ancient American Culture, Art Department. Austin: University of Texas.

Braswell, Geoffrey

1995   Obsidian Sources at Chichén Itzá. Paper presented at the III Conferencia de Mayista, Chetumal, Quintana Roo.

1996   A Maya Obsidian Source: The Geoarchaeology, Settlement History, and Ancient Economy of San Martín Jilotepeque, Guatemala. Ph.D. dissertation, Department of Anthropology. New Orleans: Tulane University.

Brinton, Daniel

1882   *The Maya Chronicles.* Brinton's Library of Aboriginal American Literature 1. Reprinted in 1969 by AMS Press, Inc., New York.

1885   *The Annals of the Cakchiquels.* Brinton's Library of Aboriginal American Literature, No. 6. Reprinted in 1969 by AMS Press, Inc., New York.

Carlson, John

1991   Venus-regulated Warfare and Ritual Sacrifice in Mesoamerica: Teotihuacan and the Cacaxtla "Star Wars" Connection. Final draft of a paper presented at the Third "Oxford" International Conference on Archaeoastronomy, St. Andrews, Scotland, September 10–14, 1990.

Carmack, Robert M.

1968   Toltec Influence on the Postclassic Culture History of Highland Guatemala.

Archaeological Studies in Middle America, Middle American Research Institute, Publication 26: 50–92. New Orleans: Tulane University.

Carmack, Robert M., and James L. Mondloch
  1983   El Titulo de Totonicapan. México: Universidad Nacional Autónoma de México.

Carrasco, David
  1982   Quetzalcoatl and the Irony of Empire. Chicago: University of Chicago Press.

Charnay, Désiré
  1887   The Ancient Cities of the New World Being Voyages and Explorations in Mexico and Central America, trans. by J. Gonino and Helen S. Conant. New York: Harper and Brothers.

Charnay, Désiré, and M. Viollet-le-Duc
  1862–1863   Cités et ruines américaines: Mitla, Palenqué, Izamal, Chichen-Itza, Uxmal; recueillies el photographiées par Désiré Charnay; avec un texte par M. Viollet-le-Duc. Paris: Gide (etc.)

Chase, Arlen
  1986   Time Depth or Vacuum: The 11.3.0.0.0 Correlation and the Lowland Maya Postclassic. In Late Lowland Maya Civilization, Classic to Postclassic, ed. by Jeremy A. Sabloff and E. Wyllys Andrews V: 99–140. A School of American Research Book. Albuquerque: University of New Mexico Press.
  1991   Cycles of Time: Caracol and the Maya Realm. Sixth Palenque Round Table, ed. by Virginia M. Fields; gen. ed., Merle Greene Robertson, 1986, Vol. 8: 32–42. Norman: University of Oklahoma Press.

Christenson, Allen
  n.d.   Prehistory of Quichean Peoples. Unpublished manuscript provided by the author.

Christy, Jessica Joyce
  1995   Maya Period Ending Ceremonies: Restarting Time and Rebuilding the Cosmos to Assure Survival of the Maya World. Ph.D. dissertation. Austin: University of Texas.

Ciaramella, Mary A.
  1994   The Lady with the Snake Headdress. Seventh Palenque Round Table, ed. by Virginia M. Fields; gen. ed., Merle Greene Robertson, 1989: 201–209. San Francisco: The Pre-Columbian Art Research Institute.

Clancy, Flora
  1994   Spatial Geometry and Logic in the Ancient Maya Mind, Part I: Monuments. Seventh Palenque Round Table, ed. by Virginia M. Fields; gen. ed., Merle Greene Robertson, 1989: 237–242. San Francisco: The Pre-Columbian Art Research Institute.

Closs, Michael
  1979   Venus in the Maya World: Glyphs, Gods and Associated Phenomena. Tercera Mesa Redonda de Palenque, ed. by Merle Greene Robertson and Donnan Call Jeffers, Vol. 4: 147–172. Palenque: The Pre-Columbian Art Research Center.

Coe, Michael D.
  1973   The Maya Scribe and His World. New York: The Grolier Club.
  1977   Supernatural Patrons of Maya Scribes and Artists. Social Process in Maya Pre-

history. Studies in Honour of Sir Eric Thompson, ed. by Norman Hammond: 327–349. London: Academic Press.

Coe, William R.

1967   *Tikal: A Handbook of Ancient Maya Ruins.* The University Museum. Philadelphia: University of Pennsylvania.

1990   *Excavations in the Great Plaza, North Terrace and North Acropolis of Tikal.* Six volumes. Tikal Report No. 14. The University Museum. Philadelphia: University of Pennsylvania.

Coggins, Clemency C.

1976   *Painting and Drawing Styles at Tikal: An Historical and Iconographic Reconstruction.* Ann Arbor, MI: University Microfilms.

1979   Teotihuacan at Tikal in the Early Classic Period. *Actes du XLIIe Congrès International de Américanistes,* Vol. 8: 252–269. Paris.

1983   The Stucco Decoration and Architectural Assemblage of Structure 1-sub, Dzibilchaltun, Yucatan, México. *Archaeological Studies in Middle America,* Middle American Research Institute, Publication 49. New Orleans: Tulane University.

Coggins, Clemency C., and Orrin C. Shane III

1984   *Cenote of Sacrifice: Maya Treasures from the Sacred Well of Chichén Itzá.* Austin: University of Texas Press.

Cohodas, Marvin

1978   *The Great Ballcourt at Chichén Itzá, Yucatan, Mexico.* Outstanding Dissertations in the Fine Arts. Garland, NY.

Dávalos H., Eusebio, and Arturo Romano

1955   Estudio Preliminar de los restos osteológicos encontrados en la tomb del Temple de las Inscripciones, Palenque. Appendix to *Exploraciones arqueológicas en Palenque: 1952. Anales del Instituto Nacional de Antropología e Historia* 6: 107–110. México: Instituto Nacional de Antropología e Historia.

Davies, Nigel

1977   *The Toltecs Until the Fall of Tula.* Norman: University of Oklahoma Press.

Demarest, Arthur A.

1993   The Violent Saga of a Maya Kingdom, *National Geographic* 183, No. 2: 94–111.

Demarest, Arthur A., and Stephen Houston

1990   Proyecto Arqueológico Regional Petexbatun: informe preliminar no. 2, segunda temporada. Nashville: Vanderbilt University.

Desmond, Lawrence Gustave

1988   *A Dream of Maya: Augustus and Alice Le Plongeon in Nineteenth-Century Yucatan.* Albuquerque: University of New Mexico Press.

Dieseldorff, Erwin P.

1930   Kunst und Religion der Mayavölker im alten und heutigen Mittelamerika II. Die Copaner Denkmäler. *Zeitschrift für Ethnologie* 62: 1–44.

Edmonson, Munro S.

1982   *The Ancient Future of the Itza, the Book of Chilam Balam of Tizimin.* Austin: University of Texas Press.

1986   *Heaven Born Mérida and Its Destiny: The Book of Chilam Balam of Chumayel.* Austin: University of Texas Press.

Erosa Peniche, José A.

1943 Zona Arqueológica de Uxmal: Cuadrángulo de Monjas, Edificio Poniente. Unpublished report in the Archives of the Instituto Nacional de Antropología e Historia de México, T160, No. 4.

Everton, MacDuff

1991 *The Modern Maya: A Culture in Transition.* Albuquerque: University of New Mexico Press.

Fahsen, Federico

1996 The Early Writing System of Kaminaljuyu. Paper presented at the 1996 Symposium "Paradigms of Power: Genesis and Foundation in Mesoamerica" of the Texas Maya Meetings. Austin: University of Texas.

Fahsen, Federico, and Linda Schele

1991 Curl-Snout Under Scrutiny, Again. *Texas Notes on Precolumbian Art, Writing, and Culture,* No. 13. The Center for the History and Art of Ancient American Culture, Art Department. Austin: University of Texas.

Fash, Barbara, and William Fash

1994 Temple 20 and the House of Bats. *Seventh Palenque Round Table,* ed. by Virginia M. Fields; gen. ed., Merle Greene Robertson, 1989: 61–69. San Francisco: The Pre-Columbian Art Research Institute.

Fash, Barbara, William Fash, Sheree Lane, Rudy Larios, Linda Schele, and David Stuart

1992 Classic Maya Community Houses and Political Evolution: Investigations of Copan Structure 22A. Paper submitted to the *Journal of Field Archaeology,* September 1989.

Fash, William

1983 Deducing Social Organization from Classic Maya Settlement Patterns: A Case Study from the Copan Valley. In *Civilization in the Ancient Americas: Essays in Honor of Gordon R. Willey,* ed. by Richard M. Leventhal and Alan L. Kolata: 261–288. Albuquerque: University of New Mexico Press; and Cambridge, MA: Peabody Museum of Archaeology and Ethnology, Harvard University.

1991 *Scribes, Warriors, and Kings: The City of Copan and the Ancient Maya.* London: Thames and Hudson.

Fastlicht, Samuel

1971 *La odontología en el México prehispánico.* México: Ediciones Mexicanas.

Florescano, Enrique

1994 *Memoria Mexicana.* México: Fondo de Cultural Económica.

1995 *El mito de Quetzalcóatl.* México: Fondo de Cultura Económico.

Freidel, David A.

1981 The Political Economics of Residential Dispersion Among the Lowland Maya. In *Lowland Maya Settlement Patterns,* ed. by W. Ashmore: 371–382. A School of American Research Book. Albuquerque: University of New Mexico Press.

1986 Terminal Classic Lowland Maya: Successes, Failures, and Aftermaths. In *Late Lowland Maya Civilization, Classic to Postclassic,* ed. by Jeremy A. Sabloff and E. Wyllys Andrews V: 409–430. A School of American Research Book. Albuquerque: University of New Mexico Press.

Freidel, David A., and Linda Schele

1989 Dead Kings and Living Temples: Dedication and Termination Rituals

Among the Ancient Maya. In *Artifacts and Symbols of Maya Culture and the Language of Writing in the Mayan Region,* ed. by D. Rice and W. Hanks: 233–243. Salt Lake City: University of Utah Press.

Freidel, David A., Linda Schele, and Joy Parker

1993   *Maya Cosmos: Three Thousand Years on the Shaman's Path.* New York: William Morrow and Co.

Freidel, David A., and Vernon L. Scarborough

1982   Subsistence, Trade and Development of the Coastal Maya. In *Maya Agriculture: Essays in Honor of Dennis E. Puleston,* ed. by K. V. Flannery: 131–155. New York: Academic Press.

García Campillo, José Miguel

1994   Antroponimía y Toponimía en las Inscripciones Mayas Clásicas de Yucatán. Ph.D. dissertation, Universidad Complutense de Madrid.

Giles, Sue, and Jennifer Stewart, eds.

1989   *The Art of Ruins: Adela Breton and the Temples of Mexico.* Bristol: City of Bristol Museum and Art Gallery.

Gillespie, Susan D.

1989   *The Aztec Kings: The Construction of Rulership in Mexican History.* Tuscon: The University of Arizona Press.

Gossen, Gary

1986   The Chamula Festival of Games: Native Macroanalysis and Social Commentary in a Maya Carnival. In *Symbol and Meaning Beyond the Closed Community: Essays in Mesoamerican Ideas,* ed. by Gary Gossen: 227–254. Institute for Mesoamerican Studies. Albany: SUNY Albany.

Grube, Nikolai

1992   Classic Maya Dance: Evidence from Hieroglyphs and Iconography. *Ancient Mesoamerica* 3: 201–218.

1993   Epigraphic Research at Caracol, Belize. An unpublished manuscript circulated by the author.

1994   Hieroglyphic Sources for the History of Northwest Yucatan. *Hidden Among the Hills, Maya Archaeology of the Northwest Yucatan Peninsula. Acta Mesoamericana 7,* ed. by Hanns J. Prem: 316–358. Bonn: Verlag Von Flemming.

n.d.   Commentary on the *way* glyph. Letter dated November 17, 1989, with notes written on September 10, 1989, sent to the authors and other epigraphers.

Grube, Nikolai, and Werner Nahm, eds.

1994   A Census of Xibalba: A Complete Inventory of *Way* Characters on Maya Ceramics. *The Maya Vase Book,* by Justin Kerr, 4: 686–714. New York: Kerr and Associates.

Grube, Nikolai, and Linda Schele

1991   *Tzuk* in the Classic Maya Inscriptions. *Texas Notes on Precolumbian Art, Writing, and Culture,* No. 15. The Center for the History and Art of Ancient American Culture, Art Department. Austin: University of Texas.

1993   Naranjo Altar 1 and Rituals of Death and Burials. *Texas Notes on Precolumbian Art, Writing, and Culture,* No. 54. The Center for the History and Art of Ancient American Culture, Art Department. Austin: University of Texas.

1994   Kuy, the Owl of Omen and War. *Mexicon* 16(1): 10–17.

1995   *The Workbook for the XIXth Maya Hieroglyphic Workshop at Texas, with Commentaries on the Last Two Hundred Years of Maya History.* Department of Art. Austin: University of Texas.

Guillemin, George
1965   Iximche 1964. *Antropología e Historia de Guatemala* 17: 41–42.

Gutierrez, Mary Ellen
1993   Ballcourts: The Chasms of Creation. *Texas Notes on Precolumbian Art, Writing, and Culture,* No. 53. The Center for the History and Art of Ancient American Culture, Art Department. Austin: University of Texas.

Hammond, Norman, and T. Molleson
1994   Huguenot weavers and Maya kings: anthropological assessment versus documentary record of age at death. *Mexicon* 16: 75–77.

Harrison, Peter D.
1970   The Central Acropolis, Tikal, Guatemala: A Preliminary Study of the Functions of Its Structural Components During the Late Classic Period. Ph.D. dissertation, University of Pennsylvania. Ann Arbor, MI: University Microfilms.
1994   Spatial Geometry and Logic in the Ancient Maya Mind, Part I: Architecture. *Seventh Palenque Round Table,* ed. by Virginia M. Fields; gen. ed., Merle Greene Robertson, 1989: 243–252. San Francisco: The Pre-Columbian Art Research Institute.

Hassig, Ross
1985   *Trade, Tribute, and Transportation.* Norman: University of Oklahoma Press.

Hatch, Marion P.
1996   Population replacements at Kaminaljuyu. Paper presented at the 1996 Symposium "Paradigms of Power: Genesis and Foundation in Mesoamerica" of the Texas Maya Meetings, University of Texas.

Haviland, William A.
1977   Dynastic Genealogies from Tikal, Guatemala: Implications for Descent and Political Organization. *American Antiquity* 42: 61–67.
1981   Dower Houses and Minor Centers at Tikal, Guatemala: An Investigation into the Identification of Valid Units of Settlement Hierarchies. In *Lowland Maya Settlement Patterns,* ed. by Wendy Ashmore: 89–117. School of American Research Advanced Seminar Series. Albuquerque: University of New Mexico Press.
1985   *Excavations in Small Residential Groups of Tikal: Groups 4F-1 and 4F-2.* Tikal Reports No. 19. The University Museum, Philadelphia: University of Pennsylvania.

Headrick, Annabeth
1991   The Chicomoztoc of Chichen Itza. Master's thesis. Austin: University of Texas.

Helms, Mary
1993   *Craft and the Kingly Ideal: Art, Trade, and Power.* Austin: University of Texas Press.

Herrmann, Andreas
1992   *Auf den Spuren der Maya. Eine Fotodokumentation von Teobert Maler (1842–1917).* Graz, Austria: Akademische Druck-u. Verlagsanstalt.

Houston, Stephen D.

1987   Notes on Caracol Epigraphy and Its Significance. In *Investigations at the Classic Maya City of Caracol, Belize: 1985–1987. Pre-Columbian Art Research Institute, Monograph 3.* San Francisco: The Pre-Columbian Art Research Institute.

1989   Caracol "Altar 21." Appendix to "Cycles of Time: Caracol in the Maya Realm," by Arlen F. Chase. In *Sixth Palenque Round Table, 1986,* Vol. 7, ed. by Merle Greene Robertson: 32–42. Norman: University of Oklahoma Press.

1993   *Hieroglyphs and History at Dos Pilas: Dynastic Politics of the Classic Maya.* Austin: University of Texas Press.

Houston, Stephen D. and Peter Mathews

1985   The Dynastic Sequence of Dos Pilas, Guatemala. *Pre-Columbian Research Institute, Monograph 1.* San Francisco: The Pre-Columbian Art Research Institute.

Houston, Stephen D., and David Stuart

1989   The *Way* Glyph: Evidence for "Co-essences" Among the Classic Maya. *Research Reports on Ancient Maya Writing* 30. Washington, D.C.: Center for Maya Research.

1989a   Folk Classification of Classic Maya Pottery. *American Anthropologist* 91: 720–726.

Houston, Stephen D., Stacey Symonds, David Stuart, and Arthur Demarest

n.d.   A Civil War of the Late Classic Period: Evidence from Hieroglyphic Stairway 4. Recent Finds at Dos Pilas, Guatemala III. Unpublished paper circulated by the authors.

Huchim Herrera, José, Lourdes Toscano Hernández, and Carlos Peraza L.

1995   Proyecto Uxmal, Reporte de la temporada 1994. Paper presented at the III Conferencia de Mayista, Chetumal, Quintana Roo.

Jiménez Moreno, Wigberto

1995   El enigma de los olmecas. *Antología de Cacaxtla,* Vol. 1, ed. by Angel García Cook and Beatriz Leonor Merino Carrión: 73–109. México: Instituto Nacional de Antropología e Historia. Reprint of a 1943 article.

Johnston, Kevin

n.d.   Maya Dynastic Territorial Expansion: Glyphic Evidence from Classic Centers of the Pasion River, Guatemala. Paper presented at the Quinta Mesa Redonda de Palenque, Palenque, Chiapas, June 1983.

Jones, Christopher

1977   Inauguration Dates of Three Late Classic Rulers of Tikal, Guatemala. *American Antiquity* 42: 28–60.

1991   Patterns of Growth at Tikal. In *Classic Maya Political History: Archaeological and Hieroglyphic Evidence,* ed. by T. P. Culbert: 102–127. A School of American Research Book. Cambridge, MA: Cambridge University Press.

1996   *Excavations in the East Plaza of Tikal.* Tikal Report No. 16. The University Museum. Philadelphia: University of Pennsylvania.

Kelley, David

1962   Glyphic Evidence for a Dynastic Sequence at Quirigua, Guatemala. *American Antiquity* 27: 323–335.

1968   Kakupacal and the Itzás. *Estudios de Cultura Maya* 7: 255–268. México: Universidad Nacional Autónoma de México.

1982   Notes on Puuc Inscriptions and History. In *The Puuc: New Perspectives: Papers Presented at the Puuc Symposium, Central College, May 1977, Supplement,* ed. by Lawrence Mills. Pella, IA: Central College.

1984   The Toltec Empire in Yucatan. *The Quarterly Review of Archaeology* 5: 12.

1985   Late Classic Yucatecan Architecture. *The Quarterly Review of Archaeology* 6: 4.

1987   Imperial Tula. *The Quarterly Review of Archaeology* 7: 14–17.

Koontz, Rex

1994   The Iconography of El Tajín, Veracruz, Mexico. Ph.D. dissertation. Austin: University of Texas.

Kowalski, Jeff Karl

1985   An Historical Interpretation of the Inscriptions of Uxmal. In *Fourth Palenque Round Table, 1980,* Vol. 6, ed. by Merle Greene Robertson and Elizabeth P. Benson: 235–248. San Francisco: The Pre-Columbian Art Research Institute.

1987   *The House of the Governor: A Maya Palace at Uxmal, Yucatán, México.* Norman: University of Oklahoma Press.

1989   Who Am I Among the Itzá?: Links Between Northern Yucatán and the Western Maya Lowlands and Highlands. In *Mesoamerica After the Decline of Teotihuacán* A.D. *700–900,* ed. by Richard Diehl and Janet Berlo: 173–186. Washington, D.C.: Dumbarton Oaks.

1991   The Ballcourt at Uxmal, Yucatán, Mexico: A Summary of Its Chronological Placement and Mythic Significance. In *The Mesoamerican Ballgame,* ed. by Gerard W. van Bussel, Paul L. F. van Dongen, and Ted J. J. Leyenaar: 81–90. Leiden, The Netherlands: Rijksmuseum voor Volkenkende.

1994   The Puuc as Seen from Uxmal. In *Hidden Among the Hills, Maya Archaeology of the Northwest Yucatan Peninsula,* ed. by Hanns J. Prem: 93–120. Möckmühl, Germany: Verlag Von Flemming.

1994a   Los Mascarones de Tláloc del Cuadrángulo de las Monjas, Usmal: Formas Teotihuacanos Como Símbolos "Toltecas." *Memorias del Primer Congreso Internacional de Mayistas.* México: Universidad Nacional Autónoma de México.

Kristen-Graham, Cynthia

1989   Art, Rulership and the Mesoamerican Body Politic at Tula and Chichén Itzá. Ph.D. dissertation. Los Angeles: University of California.

Krochock, Ruth

1991   Dedication Ceremonies at Chichén Itzá: The Glyphic Evidence. *Sixth Palenque Round Table,* ed. by Virginia M. Fields; gen. ed., Merle Greene Robertson, 1986: 43–50. Norman: University of Oklahoma Press.

Kubler, George

1962   Chichén Itzá y Tula. *Estudios de Cultura Maya I:* 47–80.

1972   The Paired Attendants of the Temple Tablets at Palenque. *Religion en Mesoamerica, XII Mesa Redonda,* ed. by Jaime Litvak King and Noemi Castillo Tejero: 317–329. México: Sociedad Méxicana de Antropología.

1977   Aspects of Classic Maya Rulership on Two Inscribed Vessels. *Studies in Pre-Columbian Art and Archaeology 18.* Washington, D.C.: Dumbarton Oaks.

1982   Serpent and Atlantean Columns: Symbols of Maya-Toltec Polity. *Journal of the Society of Architectural Historians 41* (2): 93–115.

1984   *The Art and Architecture of Ancient America: The Mexican, Maya and Andean Peoples,* 3d ed. Harmondsworth, UK: Penguin Books.

Kurjack, Edward, Ruben Maldonado C., and Merle Greene Robertson
1991   Ballcourts of the Northern Maya Lowlands. In *The Mesoamerican Ballgame,* ed. by Vernon Scarborough and David R. Wilcox: 145–160. Tuscon: University of Arizona Press.

Laporte Molina, Juan Pedro
1988   Alternativas del Clásico Temprano en la relación Tikal-Teotihuacán: Grupo 6C-XVI, Tikal, Petén, Guatemala. Tésis en Antropología, Universidad Nacional Autónoma de México.

Laughlin, Robert M.
1988   The Great Tzotzil Dictionary of Santo Domingo Zinacantán. *Smithsonian Contributions to Anthropology 31.* Washington, D.C.: Smithsonian Institution Press.

Le Plongeon, Augustus
1896   *Queen M'oo and the Egyptian Sphinx.* New York: privately printed.

Lewis-Williams, J. D.
1986   Beyond Style and Portrait: A Comparison of Tanzanian and Southern African Rock Art. In *Contemporary Studies of the Khoisan,* ed. by R. Vossen and K. Keuthmann: 93–139. Hamburg, Germany: Helmut Buske Verlag.

Leyenaar, Ted J. J.
1978   *Ulama: The Perpetuation in México of the Pre-Spanish Ball Game Ullamaliztli.* Leiden, The Netherlands: Rijksmuseum voor Volkenkunde.

Lincoln, Charles E.
1986   The Chronology of Chichén Itzá: A Review of the Literature. In *Late Lowland Maya Civilization: Classic to Postclassic,* ed. by Jeremy A. Sabloff and E. Wyllys Andrews V: 141–196. A School of American Research Book. Albuquerque: University of New Mexico Press.
1990   *Ethnicity and Social Organization at Chichén Itzá, Yucatán, México.* Ph.D. dissertation. Ann Arbor, MI: University Microfilms International.
1994   Structural and Philological Evidence for Divine Kingship at Chichén Itzá, Yucatán, México. *Hidden Among the Hills, Maya Archaeology of the Northwest Yucatan, Peninsula. Acta Mesoamericana 7,* ed. by Hanns J. Prem: 164–196. Bonn: Verlag Von Flemming.

Looper, Matthew
1991   The Dances of the Classic Maya Deities *Chak* and *Hun Nal Ye.* Master's thesis, Art Department. Austin: University of Texas.
1991a   The Name of Copan and of a Dance at Yaxchilan. *Copan Note 95.* Copan Acropolis Archaeological Project and the Instituto Hondureño de Antropología. Copan, Honduras.
1995   The Political Strategies of Butz'-Tilwi at Quirigua. Ph.D. dissertation. Austin: University of Texas.
1996   *The Workbook of the XXth Workshop on Maya Hieroglyphic Writing, with commentary on the Inscriptions of Quirigua and Copan.* Austin: University of Texas.

Lounsbury, Floyd G., and Michael D. Coe
1968   Linguistic and Ethnographic Data Pertinent to the "Cage" Glyph of Dresden

36c. *Estudios de Cultura Maya* 7: 269–284. México: Universidad Nacional Autónoma de México.

MacLeod, Barbara

1990 Deciphering the Primary Standard Sequence. Ph.D. dissertation. Austin: University of Texas.

1990a The God N\Step Set in the Primary Standard Sequence. In *The Maya Vase Book,* by Justin Kerr, 2: 331–347. New York: Kerr and Associates.

MacLeod, Barbara, and Dorie Reents-Budets

1994 The Art of Calligraphy: Image and Meaning. *Painting the Maya Universe:* 106–163. Chapel Hill, NC: Duke University Press.

Marcus, Joyce

1973 Territorial Organization of the Lowland Maya. *Science* 180: 911–916.

1976 *Emblem and State in the Classic Maya Lowlands: An Epigraphic Approach to Territorial Organization.* Washington, D.C.: Dumbarton Oaks.

Martin, Simon, and Nikolai Grube

1995 Maya Superstates. *Archaeology 48* 6: 41–43.

n.d. Evidence for Macro-Political Organization Amongst Classic Maya Lowland States. Paper circulated to archaeologists and epigraphers in 1994 and 1995.

Mathews, Peter

1976 The Inscription on the Back of Stela 8, Dos Pilas, Guatemala. Paper prepared for a seminar at Yale University. Copy provided by author.

1985 Maya Early Classic Monuments and Inscriptions. In *A Consideration of the Early Classic Period in the Maya Lowlands,* ed. by Gordon R. Willey and Peter Mathews: 5–54. Institute for Mesoamerican Studies. Albany, NY: SUNY Albany.

Mathews, Peter, and John S. Justeson

1984 Patterns of Sign Substitution in Mayan Hieroglyphic Writing: "The Affix Cluster." In *Phoneticism in Mayan Hieroglyphic Writing,* ed. by John S. Justeson and Lyle Campbell: 212–213. Institute for Mesoamerican Studies. Albany, NY: SUNY Albany.

Mathews, Peter, and Linda Schele

1974 Lords of Palenque—The Glyphic Evidence. *Primera Mesa Redonda de Palenque, Part I,* ed. by Merle Greene Robertson: 63–76. Pebble Beach, CA: Robert Louis Stevenson School.

Mathews, Peter, and Gordon Willey

1991 Prehistoric Polities in the Pasion Region: Hieroglyphic Texts and Their Archaeological Settings. In *Classic Maya Political History: Hieroglyphic and Archaeological Evidence,* ed. by T. P. Culbert: 30–71. Cambridge, MA: Cambridge University Press.

Matos Moctezuma, Eduardo

1987 Symbolism of the Templo Mayor. *The Aztec Temple Mayor,* ed. by Elizabeth Hill Boone: 185–210. Washington, D.C.: Dumbarton Oaks.

Matthews, Paul

1994 Ch'akah U Tz'ibal: The Axing of History at Seibal. *Texas Notes on Precolumbian Art, Writing, and Culture,* No. 65. The Center for the History and Art of Ancient American Culture, Art Department. Austin: University of Texas.

Maudslay, Alfred P.

    1889–1902   *Biologia Centrali-Americana: Archaeology.* 4 volumes. London: R. H. Porter and Dulau and Co.

McAnany, Patricia

    1995   *Living with the Ancestors. Kinship and Kingship in Ancient Maya Society.* Austin: University of Texas Press.

McGee, R. Jon

    1990   *Life, Ritual, and Religion Among the Lacandon Maya.* Belmont, CA: Wadsworth Publishing Co.

Miller, Arthur G.

    1977   Captains of the Itzá: Unpublished Mural Evidence from Chichén Itzá. In *Social Process in Maya Prehistory: Studies in Honour of Sir Eric Thompson,* ed. by Norman Hammond: 197–225. London: Academic Press.

Miller, Mary E.

    1985   A Re-examination of Mesoamerican Chacmool. *The Art Bulletin* LXVII: 7–17.

Miller, Mary E., and Karl Taube

    1993   *The Gods and Symbols of Ancient Mexico and the Maya.* London: Thames and Hudson.

Molina Montes, Agusto

    1982   Archaeological Buildings: Restoration or Misrepresentation? In *Falsification and Misreconstructions of Pre-Columbian Art,* ed. by Elizabeth Boone: 125–141. Washington, D.C.: Dumbarton Oaks.

Morley, Sylvanus Griswold

    1916   The Supplementary Series in the Maya Inscriptions. *Holmes Anniversary Volume:* 366–396. Washington, D.C.: privately printed.

    1946   *The Ancient Maya.* Stanford, CA: Stanford University Press.

Morley, Sylvanus Griswold, and George W. Brainerd

    1956   *The Ancient Maya.* Stanford, CA: Stanford University Press.

    1983   *The Ancient Maya,* 4th ed., rev. by Robert J. Sharer. Stanford, CA: Stanford University Press.

Nagao, Debra

    1989   Public Proclamation in the Art of Cacaxtla and Xochicalco. *Mesoamerica After the Decline of Teotihuacan—A.D. 700–900,* ed. by Richard Deihl and Janet Catherine Berlo: 83–103. Washington, D.C.: Dumbarton Oaks.

Newsome, Elizabeth

    1991   The Trees of Paradise and Pillars of the World: Vision Quest and Creation in the Stelae Cycle of 18-Rabbit-God K, Copan, Honduras. Ph.D. dissertation, Art Department. Austin: University of Texas.

Ortíz, Ponciano, and Maria del Carmen Rodríguez

    1994   Los espacios sagrados olmecas: El Manatí, un caso especial. *Los Olmecas en Mesoamérica,* ed. by John Clark: 69-92. México: Citibank.

Parsons, Mark

    1985   Three Thematic Complexes in the Art of Teotihuacán. Paper prepared at the University of Texas. Copy in possession of author.

Piña Chan, Roman

    1980   *Chichén Itzá, la cuidad de los brujos de agua.* Mexico City.

Proskouriakoff, Tatiana

1960   Historical Implications of a Pattern of Dates at Piedras Negras, Guatemala. *American Antiquity* 25: 454–475.

1961   Lords of the Maya Realm. *Expedition* 4(1): 14–21.

1961a   Portraits of Women in Maya Art. *Essays in Pre-Columbian Art and Archaeology*, ed. by Samuel K. Lothrop et al.: 81–99. Cambridge, MA: Harvard University Press.

1963–1964   Historical Data in the Inscriptions of Yaxchilán, Parts I and II. *Estudios de Cultura Maya* 3: 149–167 and 4: 177–201. México: Universidad Nacional Autónoma de México.

1970   On Two Inscriptions at Chichén Itzá. In *Monographs and Papers in Maya Archaeology, Papers of the Peabody Museum of Archaeology and Ethnology*, Vol. 67, ed. by William R. Ballard, Jr.: 459–467. Cambridge, MA: Harvard University.

Rands, Barbara C., and Robert L. Rands

1961   Excavations of a Cemetery at Palenque. *Estudios de Cultura Maya* 1: 87–106. México: Universidad Nacional Autónoma de México.

Recinos, Adrián

1952   *Pedro de Alvarado, conquistador de México y Guatemala*. México: Fondo de Cultura Económica.

1980   *Memoria de Solola. Anales de los Cakchiqueles. Titulo de los Señores de Totonicapan*. Guatemala: Biblioteca Centroamericana de las Ciencias Sociales.

1984   *Crónicas Indígenas de Guatemala*. Guatemala: Academia de Geografía e Historia de Guatemala.

Recinos, Adrián, and Delia Goetz

1953   *The Annals of the Cakchiquels*. Norman: University of Oklahoma Press.

Reilly, Kent

1994   Visions of Another World: Art, Shamanism, and Political Power in Middle Formative Mesoamerica. Ph.D. dissertation, Institute of Latin American Studies. Austin: University of Texas.

Ringle, William

1990   Who Was Who in Ninth-Century Chichén Itzá. *Ancient Mesoamerica* 1: 233–243.

Ringle, William, George Bey, and Carlos Peraza

1991   An Itza Empire in Northern Yucatan?: A Neighboring View. Unpublished manuscript provided by the author.

Robertson, Merle Greene

1991   The Ballgame at Chichén Itzá: An Integrating Device of the Polity in the Post-Classic. In *The Mesoamerican Ballgame,* ed. by Gerard W. van Bussel, Paul L. F. van Dongen, and Ted J. J. Leyenaar: 91–109. Leiden, The Netherlands: Rijksmuseum voor Volkenkunde.

Romandía de Cantú, Graciela, and Román Piña Chan

1993   *Adela Breton, una artista Británica en México (1894—1908),* ed. by Mario de la Torre. México: Smurfit Cartón y Papel de México.

Romano Pacheco, Arturo

1989   El entierro del templo de las inscripciones en Palenque. *Memorias del Segundo Coloquio Internacional de Mayistas* 2: 1413–1474. México: Universidad Nacional Autónoma de México.

Roys, Ralph L.

1943   The Land Treaty of Mani. *The Indian Background of Colonial Yucatan.* Carnegie Institution of Washington, Publication 548: 175–185. Washington, D.C.: Carnegie Institution of Washington.

1952   Conquest Sites and the Subsequent Destruction of Maya Architecture in the Interior of Northern Yucatan. *Contributions to American Anthropology and History,* Vol. 11, No. 54: 129–182. Washington, D.C.: Carnegie Institution of Washington.

1957   *The Political Geography of the Yucatan Maya.* Carnegie Institution of Washington, Publication 613. Washington, D.C.: Carnegie Institution of Washington.

1962   Literary Sources for the History of Mayapán. In *Mayapán, Yucatan, Mexico* by H.E.D. Pollock, R. L. Roys, T. Proskouriakoff, and A. L. Smith. Carnegie Institution of Washington, Publication 619. Washington, D.C.: Carnegie Institution of Washington.

1967   *The Book of Chilam Balam of Chumayel.* Norman: University of Oklahoma Press.

Ruz Lhuillier, Alberto

1957   Trabajos de Restauración en Uxmal de 1956. Report to the Instituto Nacional de Antropología e Historia T162, No. 2.

1968   *Costumbres Funerarias de los Antiguos Mayas.* México: Universidad Nacional Autónoma de México.

1973   *El Templo de las Inscripciones.* Instituto Nacional de Antropología e Historia, Colección Científica, Arqueología 7. México.

1977   Gerontocracy at Palenque? In *Social Process in Maya Prehistory, Studies in Honour of Sir Eric Thompson,* ed. by Norman Hammond: 287–296. New York: Academic Press.

Sahagun, Fray Bernardino de

1961   *Florentine Codex: General History of the Things of New Spain. Book 10: The People.* Trans. and ed. by Arthur Anderson and Charles Dibble. Santa Fe: School of American Research.

1978   *Florentine Codex: General History of the Things of New Spain. Book 3: The Origin of the Gods.* Trans. and ed. by Arthur Anderson and Charles Dibble. Santa Fe: School of American Research.

Sanders, William T.

1986–present   *Excavaciones en el area urbana de Copan.* Tegucigalpa: Secretaria de Cultura y Turismo, Instituto Hondureño de Antropología e Historia.

Schele, Linda

1986   The Founders of Lineages at Copan and Other Maya Sites. *Copan Note 8.* Copan Mosaics Project and the Instituto Hondureño de Antropología e Historia. Copan, Honduras.

1989   The Inscription on Altar Q. *Copan Note 66.* Copan Mosaics Project and the Instituto Hondureño de Antropología. Copan, Honduras.

1990   Further Comments on Stela 6. *Copan Note 73.* Copan Mosaics Project and the Instituto Hondureño de Antropología. Copan, Honduras.

1992   The Founders of Lineages at Copan and Other Maya Sites. *Ancient Mesoamerica* 3: 135–145.

1996   The Olmec Mountain and Tree of Creation in Mesoamerican Cosmology. In *The Olmec World: Ritual and Rulership*: 105–117. The Art Museum, Princeton University, in association with Harry N. Abrams. Inc.

n.d.   The Tlaloc Heresy: Cultural Interaction and Social History. Paper given at "Maya Art and Civilization: The New Dynamics," a symposium sponsored by the Kimbell Art Museum, Fort Worth, TX, May 1986.

Schele, Linda, Federico Fahsen, and Nikolai Grube

1992   El Zapote and the Dynasty of Tikal. *Texas Notes on Precolumbian Art, Writing, and Culture,* No. 34. The Center for the History and Art of Ancient American Culture, Art Department. Austin: University of Texas.

Schele, Linda, and David Freidel

1990   *A Forest of Kings: Untold Stories of the Ancient Maya.* New York: William Morrow and Co.

1991   The Courts of Creation: Ballcourts, Ballgames, and Portals to the Maya Otherworld. In *The Mesoamerican Ballgame,* ed. by David Wilcox and Vernon Scarborough: 289–317. Tucson: University of Arizona Press.

Schele, Linda, and Nikolai Grube

1987   The Birth Monument of Butz'-Chaan. *Copan Note 22.* Copan Mosaics Project and the Instituto Hondureño de Antropología e Historia. Copan, Honduras.

1992   Venus, the Great Plaza, and Recalling the Dead. *Copan Note 108.* Copan Acropolis Archaeological Project and the Instituto Hondureño de Antropología. Copan, Honduras.

1994   The Workbook for the XVIIIth Maya Hieroglyphic Workshop at Texas, with Commentaries on the Tlaloc-Venus Wars from 378 A.D. to 730 A.D. Palenque. Department of Art. Austin: University of Texas.

Schele, Linda, Nikolai Grube, and Erik Boot

n.d.   Some Suggestions on the K'atun Prophecies in the Books of Chilam Balam in Light of Classic-period History. A manuscript in preparation.

Schele, Linda, Nikolai Grube, and Federico Fahsen

1992   The Lunar Series in Classic Maya Inscriptions: New Observations and Interpretations. *Texas Notes on Precolumbian Art, Writing, and Culture,* No. 29. The Center for the History and Art of Ancient American Culture, Art Department. Austin: University of Texas.

Schele, Linda, Peter Mathews, and Floyd Lounsbury

n.d.   Parentage Expressions from Classic Maya Inscriptions. Manuscript dated 1983.

Schele, Linda, and Mary Ellen Miller

1986   *The Blood of Kings: Dynasty and Ritual in Maya Art.* New York: George Braziller, Inc., in association with the Kimbell Art Museum, Fort Worth, TX.

Schele, Linda, and Jeffrey H. Miller

1983   The Mirror, the Rabbit, and the Bundle: "Accession" Expressions from the Classic Maya Inscriptions. *Studies in Pre-Columbian Art and Archaeology 25.* Washington, D.C.: Dumbarton Oaks.

Sedat, David, and Robert Sharer

1994   The Xukpi Stone: A Newly Discovered Early Classic Inscription from the Copan Acropolis. Part 1: The Archaeology. *Copan Note 113.* Copan Acropolis

Archaeological Project and the Instituto Hondureño de Antropología. Copan, Honduras.

Seler, Eduard

1908   Die Ruinen von Chich'en Itza in Yucatan. *XVIth International Congress of Americanists*: 151–239, Vienna.

1915   Die Teotihuacan-Kultur des Hochlands von México. *Weitere Beiträge sur Alterthumskunde der Maya-Länder.*

1917   Die Ruinen von Uxmal. Abhandlungen der Königlich Preußischen Akademie der Wissenschaften, Philosophisch-Historische Klasse, 3. Berlin.

1990   Quetzalcoatl-Kukulcan in Yucatan (originally published in 1898), *Collected Works in Mesoamerican Linguistics and Archaeology*, trans. by Charles Bowditch, ed. by Frank Comparato, Vol. 1: 198–218. Culver City, CA: Labyrinthos.

Sharer, Robert

1995   The Beginning and the End of the Copan Dynasty. Paper presented at "War Serpents and Flint Shields: Collapse and Survival of the Lowland Maya," the Second Annual UCLA Maya Weekend. Los Angeles, CA.

Smith, Ledyard

1982   Excavations at Seibal, Department of Petén, Guatemala: Major Architecture and Caches. *Memoirs of the Peabody Museum of Archaeology and Ethnology, Harvard University*, Vol. 15. Cambridge, MA: Harvard University.

Spinden, Herbert J.

1913   A Study of Maya Art, Its Subject Matter and Historical Development. *Memoirs of the Peabody Museum of American Archaeology and Ethnology, Harvard University*, Vol. 6. Cambridge, MA: Harvard University.

Stone, Andrea

1989   Disconnection, Foreign Insignia, and Political Expansion: Teotihuacan and the Warrior Stelae of Piedras Negras. *Mesoamerica After the Decline of Teotihuacan—A.D. 700–900*, ed. by Richard Deihl and Janet Catherine Berlo: 153–172. Washington, D.C.: Dumbarton Oaks.

1995   *Images from the Underworld: Nah Tunich and the Tradition of Maya Cave Painting.* Austin: University of Texas Press.

Storey, Rebecca

n.d.   Health and Life Style (Before and After Death) Among the Copan Elite. Paper presented at the School of American Research seminar on "Copan: Rise and Fall of a Classic Maya Kingdom," November 1994.

Strömsvik, Gustav

1941   Sub-stela Caches and Stela Foundations at Copan and Quirigua. *Contributions to American Anthropology and History*, Vol. 7, No. 37: 63–96. Washington, D.C.: Carnegie Institution of Washington.

Stuart, David

1986   The Classic Maya Social Structure: Titles, Rank, and Professions as Seen from the Inscriptions. Paper presented at "Maya Art and Civilization: The New Dynamics," a symposium sponsored by the Kimbell Art Museum, Fort Worth, TX, May 1986.

1989   Kinship Terms in Mayan Inscriptions. Paper prepared for "The Language of Maya Hieroglyphs," a conference held at the University of California at Santa Barbara, February 1989.

1989a   Hieroglyphs on Maya Vessels. *The Maya Vase Book,* by Justin Kerr, 1: 149–161. New York: Kerr and Associates.

n.d.   Epigraphic Evidence of Political Organization in the Usumacinta Drainage. Unpublished manuscript dated 1984.

n.d.a   The Texts of Temple 26: The Presentation of History at a Maya Dynastic Shrine. Paper presented at the School of American Research seminar "Copan: The Rise and Fall of a Classic Maya Kingdom," October 1994.

Stuart, David, and Stephen Houston

1994   Classic Maya Place Names. *Studies in Pre-Columbian Art and Archaeology 33.* Washington, D.C.: Dumbarton Oaks.

Stuart, George E., and Gene S. Stuart

1977   *The Mysterious Maya.* Washington, D.C.: National Geographic Society.

Suhler, Charles, and David Freidel

1994   Conquest and Termination at Yaxuna and Other Yucatecan Sites. Lecture presented at the 1994 Symposium of the Texas Maya Meetings. Austin: University of Texas.

n.d.   Termination Rituals: Implications for Maya War. Paper presented at the Primera Mesa Redonda de Palenque, Nueva Epoca, Palenque, Chiapas, September 1995.

Taube, Karl

1983   The Teotihuacan Spider Woman. *Journal of Latin American Lore* 9: 107–189.

1988   The Ancient Yucatec New Year Festival: The Liminal Period in Maya Ritual and Cosmology. Ph.D. dissertation. New Haven: Yale University.

1988a   A Study of Classic Maya Scaffold Sacrifice. In *Maya Iconography,* ed. by Elizabeth Benson and Gillett Griffin: 331–351. Princeton: Princeton University Press.

1992   The Iconography of Mirrors at Classic Teotihuacan. In *Art, Polity, and the City of Teotihuacan,* ed. by Janelt Catherine Berlo: 169–204. Washington, D.C.: Dumbarton Oaks.

1992a   The Temple of Quetzalcoatl and the Cult of Sacred War at Teotihuacan. *Res* 22: 53–87.

1992b   The Major Gods of Ancient Yucatan: Schellhas Revisited. *Studies in Pre-Columbian Art and Archaeology.* Washington, D.C.: Dumbarton Oaks.

1994   The Birth Vase: Natal Imagery in Ancient Maya Myth and Ritual. *The Maya Vase Book* by Justin Kerr, 4: 650–685. New York: Kerr and Associates.

1994a   The Iconography of Toltec Period Chichen Itza. *Hidden Among the Hills: Maya Archaeology of the Northwest Yucatan Peninsula,* ed. by Hanns J. Prem: 212–246. Möckmühl, Germany: Verlag von Flemming.

Tedlock, Dennis

1985   *Popol Vuh: The Definitive Edition of the Mayan Book of the Dawn of Life and the Glories of God and Kings.* New York: Simon & Schuster.

Tezozomoc, Alvarado

1975   *Crónica Mexicayotl.* México: Universidad Nacional Autónoma de México, Instituto de Investigaciones Históricas.

1975a   *Cronica Méxicana.* México: Porrua.

Thompson, J. Eric

1937   A New Method of Deciphering Yucatecan Dates with Special Reference to

Chichén Itzá. *Contributions to American Archaeology,* Vol. 4, No. 22: 177–197. Carnegie Institution of Washington Publication 483. Washington, D.C.: Carnegie Institution of Washington.

1943 Las Llamadas "Fachadas de Quetzalcoatl." *Vigesimoseptimo Congreso Internacional de Americanistas.* México: Secretaria de Educacion Publica.

1950 *Maya Hieroglyphic Writing: An Introduction.* Carnegie Institution of Washington, Publication 589. Washington, D.C.: Carnegie Institution of Washington.

1970 *Maya History and Religion.* Norman: University of Oklahoma Press.

Totten, George

1926 *Maya Architecture.* Washington, D.C.

Tozzer, Alfred M.

1941 Landa's Relación de las Cosas de Yucatan: A Translation. *Papers of the Peabody Museum of American Archaeology and Ethnology,* Vol. 18. Cambridge, MA: Harvard University. Reprinted with permission of the original publishers by Kraus Reprint Corporation, New York, 1966.

1957 Chichén Itzá and Its Cenote of Sacrifice: A Comparative Study of Contemporaneous Maya and Toltec. *Memoirs of the Peabody Museum of Archaeology and Ethnology,* Vols. 11 and 12. Cambridge, MA: Harvard University.

Trik, Helen, and Michael E. Kampen

1983 *The Graffiti of Tikal.* Tikal Report No. 31. The University Museum. Philadelphia: University of Pennsylvania.

Urcid, Javier

1993 Bones and Epigraphy: The Accurate Versus the Fictitious? *Texas Notes on Precolumbian Art, Writing, and Culture,* No. 42. The Center for the History and Art of Ancient American Culture, Art Department. Austin: University of Texas.

Uriate, María Teresa (ed.)

1992 *El Juego de Pelota en Mesoamérica: raíces y supervivencia.* México: siglo veintiuno editores.

van Bussel, Gerard W., Paul L. F. van Dongen, and Ted J. J. Leyenaar (eds.)

1991 *The Mesoamerican Ballgame.* Leiden, The Netherlands: Rijksmuseum voor Volkenkende.

Vienna Dictionary

1972 *Bocabulario de Mayathan: Das Worterbuch de yukatekische Mayasprache.* Bibliotheca Linguistical Americana 1. Graz: Akademische Druck- u.Verlagsanstalt,

Villacorta C., J. A.

1934 *Memorial de Tecpan-Atitlan (Anales de los Cakchiqueles).* Guatemala City: La Tipografia Nacional.

1938 *Prehistoria e historia antigua de Guatemala.* Guatemala: Sociedad de Geografía e Historia de Guatemala.

Villela, Khristaan D.

1993 Ceiba Flower Titles of Copan. *Copan Note 109.* Copan Acropolis Archaeological Project and the Instituto Hondureño de Antropología. Copan, Honduras.

1993a The Classic Maya Secondary Tier: Power and Prestige at Three Polities. Master's thesis. Austin: University of Texas.

Villela, Khristaan D., and Rex Koontz

1993 A Nose Piercing Ceremony in the North Temple of the Great Ballcourt at

Chichén Itzá. *Texas Notes on Precolumbian Art, Writing, and Culture,* No. 41. The Center for the History and Art of Ancient American Culture, Art Department. Austin: University of Texas.

Waldeck, Jean-Frédéric Maximilien

1838   *Voyage pittoresque et archéologique dans la province d'Yucatan (Amerique Centrale),* pendant les années, 1834 et 1836.

Walters, Rachel, and Jeffrey Kowalski

n.d.   Paper presented at the Primera Mesa Redonda de Palenque, Nueva Epoca, Palenque, Chiapas, September 1995.

Wauchope, Robert

1938   *Modern Maya Houses: A Study of Their Significance.* Carnegie Institution of Washington, Publication 502. Washington, D.C.: Carnegie Institution of Washington.

Whittington, Stephen, and David Reed

n.d.   Evidence of Diet and Health in the Skeletons of Iximché. A manuscript submitted to *Estudios Kaqchikeles:* In memoriam *William R. Swezey,* May 1994.

Wilbert, Johannes

1987   *Tobacco and Shamanism in South America.* New Haven: Yale University Press.

Wilcox, David, and Vernon Scarborough (eds.)

1991   *The Mesoamerican Ballgame.* Tucson: University of Arizona Press.

Willey, Gordon R. (gen. ed.)

1975–1990   Excavations at Seibal, Department of Peten, Guatemala. *Memoirs of the Peabody Museum of Archaeology and Ethnology, Harvard University,* Vols. 14–17. Cambridge, MA: Harvard University.

Wren, Linnea

1991   The Great Ballcourt Stone at Chichén Itzá. *Sixth Palenque Round Table,* ed. by Virginia M. Fields; gen. ed., Merle Greene Robertson, 1986: 51–59. Norman: University of Oklahoma Press.

Wren, Linnea, Ruth Krochock, Erik Boot, Lynn Foster, Peter Keeler, Rex Koontz, Walter Wakefield

1992   Maya Creation and Recreation: The Great Ballcourt at Chichén Itzá. A manuscript prepared after the 1992 Advanced Seminar of the Texas Meetings on Maya Hieroglyphic Writing.

Wren, Linnea, and Peter Schmidt

1991   Elite Interaction During the Terminal Classic Period of the Northern Maya Lowlands: Evidence from the Reliefs of the North Temple of the Great Ballcourt at Chichén Itzá. In *Classic Maya Political History: Archaeological and Hieroglyphic Evidence,* ed. by T. P. Culbert: 199–225. A School of American Research Book. Cambridge, MA: Cambridge University Press.

Glossary of Gods and Supernaturals

Baby Jaguar appears frequently in scenes where Chak in the company of a death god throws him down a mountain into the Otherworld. The Baby Jaguar becomes the Bearded Jaguar God when he grows up. The Baby Jaguar most often appears with the body of an infantile human, although he may also be represented as an adult, fully zoomorphic jaguar. In both aspects, he can wear a scarf and his human aspect sometimes wears a cruller. He was a patron god for Early Classic Tikal and Caracol, and the people of Copan included him in the myth of their patron gods Kan-Te-Ahaw and Bolon-K'awil.

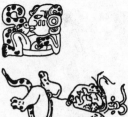

Bearded Jaguar God, also known as GIII of the Palenque Triad and the Jaguar God of the Underworld, is an anthropomorphic god who wears a jaguar ear, a twisted cord called a cruller under his eyes, and a beard with *lakam* signs. On Tikal Temple 4, Lintel 3, he carries the name *K'in-Hix Ek'-Hun* ("Sun-Jaguar, Black Headband"), while in the text of Copan Stela F, he is *Hun-Kanal Tzuk-Ahaw* ("One-Heaven, Bearded-Lord"). Palenque texts record his birth and an array of names, including *Ahaw K'in* ("Lord Sun"), *Yahaw-K'ak'* ("Lord of Fire"), *K'inich-Tah-Way* ("Sun-faced-Torch-Macaw"), and *K'in-tan-Bolay* ("Sun-centered Jaguar"). This cruller-eyed Jaguar God can personify both the sun and Venus depending on the ritual context. He is one of the patron gods of Palenque, Tikal, and Naranjo, and he played a major role in the story of Copan's patron gods. One of his most frequent appearances is as an isolated head worn on a belt, carried in the arm, or surmounted on shields carried by kings and nobles.

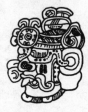

Bicephalic Serpent Bar, see Serpent Bar.

Blood is represented by a bifurcated scroll, sometimes with plain contours and sometimes with a beaded outline representing the blood itself. To mark the scroll as blood rather than smoke or mist, the Maya attached a number of signs representing precious materials: *k'an* "yellow," *yax* "blue-green," *chak* "red," shell, jade jewelry like beads and earflares, obsidian, mirrors of various sorts, "zero" signs, and bones. The symbol of blood is the same as *k'ul* or *ch'ulel,* the symbol of the "soul-force" that imbues all sacred things. See *k'ul.*

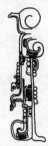

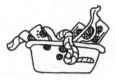

Bloodletting Bowl, called a *lak,* was a flat, shallow plate with angled sides. As the principal offering bowl, it opened an *ol,* "portal," that allowed the Vision Serpent to arrive from the Otherworld and the World Tree to grow. In bloodletting scenes, the bowl usually holds bloodied paper, lancets of various sorts, and rope to pull through perforations. See Quadripartite Monster.

Bolon-K'awil, "Nine-K'awil," was one of the patron gods of Copan. This k'awil materialized on the tail of a snake held by a beautiful young goddess. An old deer god emerged from the serpent in episodes of the myth surrounding these patron gods.

Celestial Bird, see *Itzam-Ye.*

Ceremonial Bar, see Serpent Bar.

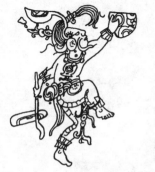

Chak was the god of lightning and could appear in many different aspects, including: *Chak-Xib-Chak* ("Red-Young-Chak"), *Kan-Yoat-Chak* ("Sky-Erect Penis-Chak"), and *Ek'-Wayeb-Chak* ("Black-Nawal-Chak"), among others. Chak is distinguished by a shell diadem, a shell earflare, and usually by a zoomorphic visage. He frequently wields an ax or a quatrefoil lightning-stone in the shape of an *ol* "portal." Chak also cracked open the Cosmic Turtle with lightning so that the Maize God could be reborn. Kings frequently portrayed themselves in the guise of Chak or wore him behind their legs suspended on a chain. Chak was also a title that could be carried by lords and by other gods.

Cosmic Hearth, see Hearth.

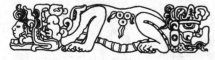

Cosmic Monster, also known as the Celestial Monster and the Bicephalic Monster, is a dragonlike beastie with a crocodilian head marked by deer ears. The body has legs, usually terminating in deer hooves, and with joints in the form of water scrolls. Its body can have several forms, including a crocodile marked with "kawak" signs, a skyband, and lazy-S cloud scrolls. At Yaxchilan, the monster has two crocodile heads, but usually the rear head is a Quadripartite God. Venus signs often mark the front head, while the rear Quadripartite head has an offering plate with a *k'in* sign. This plate holds an *ol* portal through which Vision Serpents arrive and the World Tree emerges. The Cosmic Monster personified the Milky Way in its east-west configuration. See the World Tree and Quadripartite Monster.

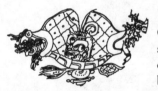

Cosmic Turtle, also known as the Turtle of Creation, had two heads, one a turtle or saurian type and the other representing personified waterlilies, or k'awil. Chak cracked open his carapace so that the Maize God could be reborn. He often has a *k'an* sign on his back where the portal cracked open.

Death God (God A) appears as an animated skeleton, with the bloated belly characteristic of parasitic disease or a decaying corpse. There appear to have been many versions of this god, differentiated by slight variations in their anatomy, the objects they carried, and their actions. These variations may represent different aspects of the same god, or just as likely, different Lords of Death named for various diseases or actions. God A, for example, is an anthropomorphic death god who usually has a black band across its eyes.

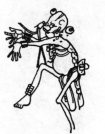

Double-headed Serpent Bar, see Serpent Bar.

Earth is represented by bands marked with *kab* signs from the glyph meaning "earth." These bands may be split to represent clefts from which trees grow or ancestors emerge. In some representations, earth bands may also represent the concept of territory or domain.

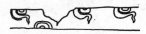

Flint-shield, or *tok'-pakal,* combines a flint lance blade or an eccentric flint with a shield made from a flayed human face. It is an object transferred from ancestor to king in the accession rites at Palenque. In war, the capture or throwing down of the flint-shield signaled defeat.

GI is an anthropomorphic god distinguished by a fish barbel on his cheek, a shell earflare, and serpent markings on his body. He wears the Quadripartite Monster as his headdress and was both the father of and the firstborn god in the Palenque Triad. As the father, he was one of the avatars of the Maize God, so that one of his names was Hun-Nal-Ye. See Maize God and Palenque Triad.

Hearth, also the Cosmic Hearth, was a cooking facility made from three large stones arranged in a triangle. Pots sat on top of the rocks, while wood was fed into the fire between them. The Maize Gods directed other gods in setting up the first hearth in the constellation of Orion as the stars of Alnitak, Saiph, and Rigel. The three stones of this hearth consisted of a Jaguar Throne Stone set up by the Paddler Gods at *Na-Ho-Kan;* a Snake Throne Stone set up by an unknown god at *Kab-Kah;* and a Shark or Water Throne Stone set up by Itzamna. The Maya called this hearth place *Yax-Ox-Tunil* and it was located at *K'a-Kan,* "Closed or Lying-down Sky."

Hun-Nal, Hun-Nal-Ye, see Maize God.

Ichkantiho, "In Heaven at Five," was the ancient name for Tz'ibilchaltun and Mérida. It was the location of the founding assembly of the Itza confederation and the counterpart of *Na-Ho-Kan* in the Yukatekan tradition. Later sources called it *Ichkansiho.*

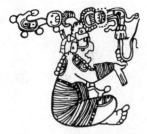

Itzamna was an old god with large square eyes, a hooked nose, a toothless mouth, and a headband embossed with a beaded flower. This flower reads *itz,* the word for "magic" and substances that ooze, such as milk, sap, candle wax, honey, dew, sweat, etc. These are magic substances used by shamans to contact and manipulate the Otherworld. This old god was the first and most powerful sorcerer in this Creation. He set up the water-ocean throne stone in the Cosmic Hearth. *Itzam Nah* was also the name of a "conjuring" or "sorcery" house. To mark structures as *Itzam Nah,* the Maya put images of the *Itzam-Ye* bird into the decoration. See Hearth and *Itzam-Ye.*

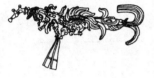

Itzam-Ye, also known as *Mut Itzamna,* the Serpent Bird, and the Principal Bird Deity, has a long tail, personified wings, and the head of a zoomorphic monster. Often it appears with a round object and woven ribbon held in its mouth, a trifoil pectoral around its neck, and a cut-shell ornament attached to a jade headband. It was the nawal of Itzamna, the first sorcerer of Creation. Most commonly it sat atop the World Tree, astride the body of the Cosmic Monster, or it decorated conjuring buildings. It was a prominent god by 300 B.C. in both the Maya highlands and lowlands, where it marked buildings as *Itzam Nah,* "sorcery house," or dove into scenes of rulers engaged in conjuring rituals. See Itzamna.

Jester God was the personification of the royal headband, called *Hunal* or *Sak Hunal,* "Headband" or "White Headband." The Maya inherited him from the Olmec, who defined him as personified maize or the World Tree. The Maya generalized him into the royal headdress and he became the special marker of *ahaw,* "lord." Putting a *Sak Hunal* headband on a human or animal head in the glyphs converted that sign to *ahaw.* The Jester God sometimes has fish fins on his face.

Kan-*Te*-Kan, "Four-*Te*-Sky," was one of the patron gods of Copan. He is an anthropomorphic deity marked by parallel slashes on his arms and legs. Pottery scenes show him dropping a bound rock on the Bearded Jaguar God and then burning him.

***Kawak* Signs** consist of a triangular arrangement of disks in groups of three, five, or more, combined with a dotted semicircle nearby. These signs derive from the day sign *kawak,* but in the iconography they mark things made of stone and the *Witz* Monster. In zoomorphic form and with a wavy contour, *kawak* signs also mark Eccentric Flint. See *Witz* Monster.

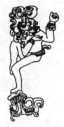

K'awil, also known as God K, the Manikin Scepter, and the Flare God, personifies the concept of sacred statue and the spirit that occupies the statue. There were several different forms of k'awil that personified different aspects and supernaturals. This deity is distinguished by having a cigar, a torch holder, or an ax blade penetrating a mirror in his forehead. His face has zoomorphic features, but his body is often shown as an infantile human with one leg transformed into a serpent. One text at Copan says that this serpent foot is his nawal, and he is often recorded as the nawal of Vision Serpents. As the second-born god of the Palenque Triad, he was Nen-K'awil, the spirit of the divination mirror. With the number nine, he was Bolon-K'awil, a patron god of Copan. See Vision Serpent.

K'ul or **k'u** or **k'ulel** appears as dotted or plain scrolls marked with flowers, obsidian, shells, jade, mirrors, and *yax, k'an,* and *chak* signs. Glyphically, *k'ul* can mean "god," but also the indestructible "soul" that imbues all living things and all sacred places and objects. In the Cholan languages, the term was *ch'ul* or *ch'ulel.* Human *k'ulel* resides in blood, so that giving blood in sacrifice was to offer "soul-force." *Wayob* or nawals shared the *k'ulel* of their human counterparts. The Maya placed *k'ulel* in their buildings and objects during dedication rituals. See Blood and *Way.*

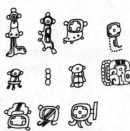

Legged Serpents were a form of Vision Serpents that developed at Copan in the sixth century. Distinguished by legs attached to the front of their bodies, these serpents often carried feathers. While Chich'en versions resemble Serpent Birds, they are simply the front, head-on view of the Copan serpent. The Jaguar-Snake at Cacaxtla also derives from this special serpent, as do others at Tula.

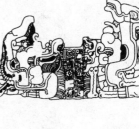

Maize God, also named *Hun-Nal* ("One Ear of Maize"), *Hun-Nal-Ye* ("One Grain of Maize"), and *Wak-Kan-Ahaw* ("Raised-up Sky Lord"), was First Father and the overseer of Creation. The Maya had at least three Maize Gods, all pictured as beautiful young men with maize foliation growing from their heads. After being called to Xibalba, the Maize God was killed by the Lords of Death and buried in the ballcourt in Xibalba. His sons, the Hero Twins, resurrected him and brought him back to life so that he could generate the Fourth Creation.

Maw of the Otherworld, see *Sak-Bak-Nakan.*

Mexican Year Sign is a trapezoidal configuration of bands that represents a bundle. The Maya associated it with the Tlaloc-Venus sacrifice complex and with imagery connected with *Puh,* or Tollan. Its name comes from the function of a similar sign to mark year dates in central Mexican codices. See Tlaloc.

Moon Goddess in her Classic-period form has a moon sign attached to her head or body, depending on the context. Her head glyph functions as the numeral one and as phonetic *na.* Since *na* was also the word for "noblewoman," the head of the Moon Goddess precedes female names, distinguishing them from the names of male nobles. There were two versions of the Moon Goddess: a young one who was the mother of the gods and wife of the Maize God (her name was probably *Sak Ixik* and *Na Huntan*) and the Old Moon Goddess, Chak-Chel, who was the grandmother of the Hero Twins and midwife of Creation.

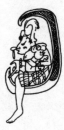

Mountain Monster, see *Witz* Monster.

Mut Itzamna, see *Itzam-Ye.*

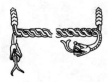 **Na-Ho-Kan,** "House-Five-Sky," was the location where the Paddler Gods set up the Jaguar Throne Stone of the Cosmic Hearth. Its distinctive feature was intertwined snakes representing the sky umbilicus.

Nawal, see *Way.*

 Ol or **hol,** "portal," "door," or "hole," was the Maya name of the quatrefoil portal into the Otherworld. It was also the name of the crack in the Cosmic Turtle's back.

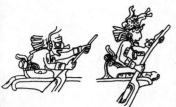 **Paddler Gods** are named from their appearance on four bones from the burial chamber of Hasaw-Kan-K'awil of Tikal. In these incised scenes, two old gods paddle the Maize God in a canoe to the place of Creation, where he will direct the construction of the Cosmic Hearth. Both gods have aged features with the Old Stingray God, distinguished by squinty eyes and a stingray spine piercing the septum of his hooked nose. He sometimes wears the helmet of a fish monster called *xok.* His aged twin wears a jaguar pelt on his chin, a jaguar ear, and sometimes a jaguar helmet. The Paddlers appear with special frequency in period-ending rites, where they are born from the king's blood offering. From glyphic contexts, we know the Old Stingray Spine Paddler was the sun and the Jaguar Paddler was darkness, so that they also represent the fundamental opposition of day and night.

  Palenque Triad is composed of three gods most fully described in the inscriptions and imagery of Palenque, where they are asserted to be the direct ancestors of the dynasty. Sired by the mother and father of the gods who had survived from the previous creation, they were born only eighteen days apart. They were the patron gods of Palenque, but individually they also could serve as the patrons of other kingdoms. GI (an abbreviation for God I) was a fish-finned god named *Hun-Nal-Ye;* GII was *Nen-K'awil* and GIII was the Bearded Jaguar God, called *K'inich Tah Way, Ahaw K'in,* and *Yahaw-K'ak'.*

Partition, see *Tzuk.*

Patron Gods were the titular gods of each site. Palenque had a triad of gods, including Hun-Nal-Ye, Nen-K'awil, and Ahaw K'in. Tikal featured the Baby Jaguar and the Bearded Jaguar God, while Copan had Kan-*Te*-Kan and Bolon-K'awil. According to later ethnohistorical sources, the patron gods of the K'iche' and the Kaqchikels were given to them at *Tulan*. The Maya kept these gods in sacred locations called *Pib Nah* and *Kun*. They could be captured in battle and destroyed as a way of dissolving the supernatural protection of enemies.

Pawahtuns (also known as God N) are the four old gods who hold up the world and corresponded to the grandfather of the Hero Twins and helper of the Old Moon Goddess. Their features are aged with snaggle teeth, small human eyes, and a wrinkled visage. They often wear net headdresses in combination with *kawak*, or "stone" markings, on their bodies as spellings of their name, *pawa* ("net") + *tun* ("stone"). Characteristically they wear a cut-shell pectoral or their bodies emerge from a conch shell or turtle carapace. Some versions wear waterlilies in addition to the net headband. They were the patron gods of the Itza.

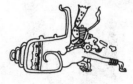

Principal Bird Deity, see *Itzam-Ye*.

Puh, "Cattail Reed," was the Maya name for Teotihuacan and other cities that represented themselves as places of Origin. Inhabitants of the "Place of Reeds" were the *Ah Puh*. See Tollan.

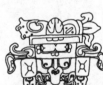

Quadripartite Monster personifies an offering plate and censer stand. An *ol* portal in the plate provides a conduit for Vision Serpents and the World Tree. The plate also carries a three-part symbol consisting of a stingray spine, a spondylus shell, and a crossbands device. The stingray spine is the lancet that draws blood; the spondylus shell symbolizes *k'ulel*; and the crossbands read either *nun* or *way*. *Nun* is "to speak strangely (as in a trance)" and "to be an intermediary." *Way* is "to dream" and "to transform into a nawal."

Royal Belt consists of a heavy waistband that carried three jade heads designating the owner as an *ahaw*. Typically, these heads surmount a mat sign (or an equivalent symbol of royal status) and three celts made of polished jade or flint. A chain hung from the sides of the belt to drape across the back of the wearer's legs, where the *Kan-Yoat-Chak* hung from the chain. This dangling version of Chak cracked open the Cosmic Turtle so that the Maize God could be reborn.

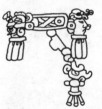

Sak-Bak-Nakan, also known as White-Bone-Snake and the Maw of the Otherworld, was the personified opening to the Otherworld. This bony serpent marks the corners of ancestral sun mirrors and spearheads emerge from its gullet. On the Palenque sarcophagus it appears as a split representation of two profiles joined at the lower jaw. This snake represents the point of transition between the natural world and the Otherworld of Xibalba.

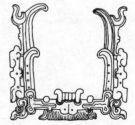

Sak Hunal, see Jester God.

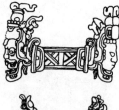

Serpent Bar, also known as the Bicephalic Serpent Bar, the Double-headed Serpent Bar, and the Ceremonial Bar, is a scepter carried in the arms against the chest of the ruler. Maya rulers usually held the bar in the crook of their arms with the palms of their hands turned outward, although more rarely they held it on a diagonal. Its original function in the Late Preclassic period was to symbolize "sky," based on the homophony in Maya languages between *kan,* "sky," and *kan,* "snake." The Bar also symbolized the "sky umbilicus" that connected kings to their sources of supernatural power and the ecliptic path across the sky. Gods and ancestors materialized in the open mouths of the serpents, and at Copan these supernaturals manifested in the form of eccentric flints.

Serpent Bird, see *Itzam-Ye* and Legged Serpent.

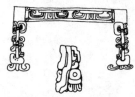

Skyband consists of a narrow band divided into segments by bars. Each segment contains a glyph for the sun, the moon, a planet, or some other celestial object.

Sky Umbilicus was realized as intertwined snakes or serpent frames. Often these snakes have square snouts that can also personify the stamens of flowers. White flowers, written *sak nik,* often merge with these snakes or with the twisted cords that can replace them. Late Preclassic versions of the serpent frame often have *sak* signs fused with the nose as a partial signal of the *sak nikal,* which was both the flower of the ceiba tree and a symbol for the human soul.

Sun God can appear in several different versions, but typically he appears as a Roman-nosed human head with square eyes and squintlike pupils in the inner corners. The four-petaled flower *k'in* marks the head as the image of the sun.

Throne Stone, see Hearth.

Tlaloc, a symbol of war and bloodletting, consists of a jawless head with blood scrolls emerging from its mouth and large circles around its eyes. It is associated with spear-throwers and javelins, and with a flexible, rectangular shield. Often, Tlaloc-warriors wore a full bodysuit made from a jaguar pelt, and a *kuy* owl often occurs with the imagery. *Ah kuy* meant "soldier." Many contemporaneous Mesoamerican societies, including Teotihuacan, used this symbolic complex. It not only signaled war and conquest, but also identified places and lineages with the concept of *Tollan.* This complex is nicknamed after the Aztec Rain God, who is portrayed with similar iconography.

Tok'-pakal, see Flint-shield.

Tollan or **Tulan,** "Place of Cattail Reeds," was the central Mexican name for the origin place where patron gods were born. It consisted of Snake Mountain surrounded by a swamp full of cattail reeds. Nearby was a ballcourt with a skull place, *Itzompan,* from which the sweet waters of the earth emerged. The first inhabitants of Tollan, the "Toltecs," were great artists, poets, builders, and warriors. See *Puh.*

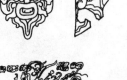

Tzuk, or "partition," appeared in the form of a variant God C. This symbol occurred on the trunks of World Trees to mark them as partition devices. Since *tzuk* also meant "belly," it appeared on the belly of the *Itzam-Ye* bird at Kaminaljuyu.

Vision Serpents were rearing snakes that embodied the conduit between human beings and the supernatural world. Some had feathers lining their body and others had their bodies partially flayed. *Sak nik,* "white flower," both in the form of foliated *ahaw* signs and a personified form, decorate the tails of many serpents. See Serpent Bar.

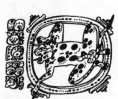

Wakah-Kan, see World Tree.

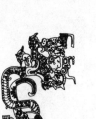

Way or nawal is the name for the animal and spirit companions who shared the souls of human beings. Great sorcerers and kings could transform into their *wayob.* The glyph can also mean "to dream" and "to transform into one's animal-spirit companion."

Waxaklahun-Ubah-Kan was the war serpent associated with Tlaloc-Venus warfare. This serpent wears feather fans as its distinguishing feature. On Yaxchilan Lintel 25, it is double-headed and emits the founder of the dynasty from its upper head. A Tlaloc headdress comes out of the lower head in an image evoking the feathered war serpent of Teotihuacan.

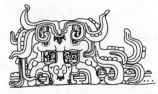

Witz Monster is the symbol of the living mountain. It is depicted as a four-legged zoomorphic creature marked with the distinctive signs of the *kawak* and "stone." To distinguish the *Witz* Monster from the zoomorph representing "stone," the Maya represented the mountain with eyelids and with a stepped cleft in the center of its forehead. The *Witz* Monster was often placed on temples to transform them into sacred, living mountains. The mouth of the *Witz* Monster often gapes open as the entry into the mountain or a cave. See *Kawak* Signs.

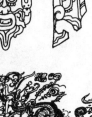

World Tree is the central axis of the world. Called the *Wakah-Kan* ("Six Sky" or "Raised-up Sky") in the glyphs, it appears in the form of a cross with a *tzuk,* "partition," sign on its trunk and *sak nik,* "white flowers," on its branches. Often a Double-headed Serpent wraps through its branches and the Celestial Bird perches on its summit. The tree can

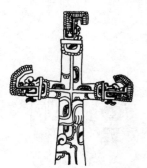

have the single trunk of the ceiba tree or it can have multiple trunks resulting from the Maya practice of harvesting the branches of living trees for wood. The tree grows out of an *ol,* or "portal," in an offering plate or in the mouth of the *Sak-Bak-Nakan* on the southern horizon. It symbolized the Milky Way in its north-south orientation. The king personified the World Tree in his flesh.

Index

Abrams, Elliot, 329n. 13
Aguateca, 177, 178, 185
Agurcia, Ricardo, 370n. 47
Ah-Bolon-Abta Wat'ul-Chatel
  (Wat'ul), 179, 195–96, 293,
  322
  depicted on Stela 8, 190–93
  depicted on Stela 9, 187–90
  depicted on Stela 10, 184–88
  depicted on Stela 11, 179, 182–84
  depicted on Stela 21, 193–95
  as Maize God, 188
  temple built by, 179–82
Ah-Holtun-Balam, 197, 322
ah kuy (warrior), 259
Ah-Kuy-Tok'-Tutul-Xiw, 203, 259,
  322
Ah-Mek'at-Tutul-Xiw, 259
Ah-Ne-Ol-Mat (Aahc-Kan; Ah K'an;
  Ac-Kan), 105, 119, 120, 130,
  320
Ahpo Sotz'il, 296, 299–300, 315
  palace of, 307–9, 311, 314, 315
Ahpo Xahil, 296, 299–300, 315
  palace of, 309, 310, 311, 315
Ahpu, 295
Ah Puh, 40, 134, 201, 218, 226, 284,
  338n. 29, 370n. 41
Akul-Anab I (Cauac-Uinal I; Chaacal
  I; Chaac I), 104, 105, 117,
  119–20, 128, 130, 320
Akul-Anab II (Cauac-Uinal II; Chaa-
  cal II; Chaac II), 105, 117,
  130, 320
altars, 145, 150, 152–54, 156, 168
  Atlantean, 241–43
  jaguar, 285

snake, 170–73
turtle, 144, 145–46
Alvarado, Pedro de, 297, 298, 299,
  309, 310, 386nn. 15, 19
Anahuac Xicalango, 293
ancestors, 40, 282–83
  bones of, 156–58
  psychoduct and, 109, 119, 130–31
  rituals and, 80, 84
  shrines and, 78–79
  trees and, 122–23, 127
Ancient Maya, The (Morley), 356n.
  10
Andrews, Anthony, 362n. 23
Andrews, E. Wyllys, V, 358n. 12,
  368n. 31
Animal-Skull (Animal Head), 69, 70,
  177, 320, 336n. 23
Annals of the Kaqchikels, 292, 295,
  315, 328n. 3, 357n. 12, 385n.
  12, 386nn. 15, 19
Antigua, 298, 299
aqueducts, 95, 331n. 27
architecture, 23–36
  access and movement controlled
    in, 29
  as backdrop for drama and ritual,
    23, 26, 27, 29, 30, 40, 42
  builders and specialists in, 27–29
  construction techniques and styles
    in, 30–34
  corbeled vaults, 26, 31–32, 33
  courtyards, 17, 23, 26, 29
  C-shaped benches in, 308–9
  dedication of buildings and their
    proper names, 26, 48–50
  E-group complexes, 180, 368n. 31

houses, *see* house
informative facades in, 31
plans and layouts in, 31
plazas, *see* plazas
pyramids, *see* pyramid
roofcombs, 33–34
roofs, 31–32, 33, 34
rubble-core buildings, 30, 31
rulers' patronage and, 34, 260
site and building planning and
  construction in, 27–29
spanning of interior space in,
  31–33
stone and masonry buildings, 26,
  27, 30–31
symbolism in, *see* symbolism
symmetry in, 34–36, 270
see also sculpture
Armillas, Pedro, 383n. 4
artists and craftsmen, 27–29, 39, 82,
  171–72
Atlantean Altar, 241–43
Awakatek, 79
Aztecs, 37–38, 200, 224, 292, 293,
  297, 356n. 9, 361n. 16, 368n.
  34, 373n. 65

Baby Jaguar, 147, 148, 149, 150, 152,
  162, 409
Bak, 95
bakab, 243
bak'tuns, 52, 168
Balah-Kan-K'awil (Flint-Sky-God K),
  69, 70, 177, 202, 323
Balam-Nan (Waterlily-Jaguar), 138,
  139, 321
Ball, Joseph, 358n. 12

past and future linked to birth and accession of, 106–7

tomb of, *see* Hanab-Pakal, Tomb of

Hanab-Pakal, Tomb of, 95–132
  ancestors on sides of sarcophagus in, 119–25
  coffin in, 125–28
  discovery of, 109–10
  downward passage in, 108–9
  inscription panels in temple of, 104–8
  psychoduct in, 109, 119, 130–31
  pyramidal base of, 97–98
  sarcophagus in, 110–25, 130, 131, 132
  sarcophagus imagery in, 110–17
  sarcophagus lid in, 110–19
  sarcophagus text in, 117–19
  temple of, 98–108
  temple balustrades of, 101
  temple interior of, 101–4
  temple piers of, 99–100
  wall figures in, 128–30
Hansen, Richard, 379n. 13
Harrison, Peter, 84, 88, 93–94, 329n. 15, 334n. 13, 338nn. 31, 32, 34, 339n. 36
Harvard University, 351n. 2
Hasaw-Kan-K'awil I (Ruler A; Hasaw-Chan-K'awil), 33, 70, 78, 80, 86, 91, 144, 202, 320, 336nn. 23, 24, 338n. 31
  palace of, 85–86
Hasaw-Kan-K'awil II, 320
Hatch, Marion, 384n. 9, 385n. 10
Hauberg Stela, 168
headband, 306, 307
head deformation, 187, 351n. 6
headdresses, 158, 224
  black, 152, 347n. 18
  drummajor, 283–84
  flower, 229
Headrick, Annabeth, 369n. 36
hearth, 17, 26, 175
Hearth, Cosmic, 26, 37, 44, 116, 148, 168, 175, 182, 211–12, 217, 227, 246, 285, 411
  throne stones of, 37, 44, 148, 154, 212, 217, 218, 225, 285, 360n. 14
Helms, Mary, 328n. 5
heron-GI, 185

Hero Twins, 36, 116, 117, 143, 144, 148, 211, 212, 213, 215, 233, 254–55, 304, 315, 349n. 30
Hidalgo, Tula in, 39, 198, 199, 200, 215, 356n. 9, 384n. 7
hieroglyphic writing systems, *see* writing
history(ies), 51–61
  chronology of events, 52–61
  Classic period, *see* Classic period
  of Copan, 134, 170–71
  of Kaqchikel Maya, 292–99, 315, 328n. 3, 357n. 12, 385n. 12, 386nn. 15, 19
  k'atun, 104–8, 117–19, 198, 201–2, 203–4, 357n. 12, 363n. 28, 364–67n. 31
  of Palenque, in Hanab-Pakal's Tomb, 104–6, 117–19
  periods of, 16, 51
  Postclassic period, 16, 20, 51, 59–61, 295, 360n. 13
  Preclassic period, 16–18, 51, 52–53, 294
  of Seibal, 176–79, 195–96
  of Tikal, 65–66, 67–70
  writing of, 13, 18; *see also* writing
Holon-Chan-Tepew, 259
Honduras, 15, 133
house(s), 17, 25–26, 33
  cloud, 278
  community, 44, 269–70, 278
  dedications of, 48
  flower, 44, 269–70
  maize, 265
  Na-Te'-K'an, 265
  in residential compounds, 26, 29
  sky or serpent, 271
  sorcery (Itzam Nah), 47, 83–84, 85, 114, 265, 267, 268, 269, 271, 278, 283
  stela in form of, 136
  thatched, 25–26, 33, 34, 43, 136, 265, 270–71
  words for, 43
House of the Seven Dolls, 367–68n. 31
Houston, Stephen, 328n. 8, 335n. 19, 345n. 1, 379n. 17
huipil, 125, 291
Huitzilopochtli, 37, 38, 224, 368n. 34

Hun-Ahaw, 36, 116, 210
Hunahpu, 210
Hun-Hunahpu (Hun-Nal-Ye), 210, 215
Hun-Iq' (1 Iq; One Wind), 297, 301, 307, 323
Hun-Kanal-Tzuk-Ahaw, 191
Hun-Pik-Tok' (Hun-Pic-Tok), 197, 322
Hun-Tihax, 305
Hun-Toh (One Toh; One Rain), 296, 299, 300, 323

Ichkantiho (Ichkansiho; Tz'ibilchaltun), 203, 218–20, 226, 244, 259, 285, 411
Inscriptions, Temple of the (temple of Hanab-Pakal's Tomb), 98–108
  balustrades of, 101
  inscription panels of, 104–8
  interior of, 101–4
  passage in, 108–9
  piers of, 99–100
itz, 229, 265, 267, 268, 269, 277
Itza, 20, 63, 187, 198, 200, 201–4, 207, 259, 315
  artistic styles and images combined by, 253–55
  migrations of, 20, 202–3, 240, 259, 284, 363n. 28
  murals depicting wars of, 232–41
  patron gods of, 203, 214, 252, 282
  see also Chich'en Itza
Itzamal, 197, 203, 259
Itzam-Balam (Shield-Jaguar), 185, 324
Itzamk'anak, 20
Itzamna, 37, 46, 114, 201, 212, 268, 412
Itzam Nah (Sorcery House), 47, 83–84, 85, 114, 265, 267, 268, 269, 271, 278, 283
Itzam-Ye (Itzam-Kah; Mut Itzamna), 46–47, 114, 143, 155, 201, 268, 269, 271, 275, 279, 369n. 36, 412
itz'at (sages), 77, 89, 104, 119
Itzayul, 297, 310
itzompan (skull place), 37, 303, 305
Ixik, 212
Iximche', 292, 297, 299–317
  ballcourts at, 304–5, 310, 313–15

Lahuh-Ah (10 Ah; Ten Reed), 296, 323

Lahuh-Noh (Ten Earth), 323

Lakam Ha (Big Water), 23, 95

Lakamtun, 190

Lake Atitlan, 291–92, 295, 299

Lake Catemaco, 39–40

Lake Peten Itza, 203, 354n. 6

Landa, Diego de, 197, 198, 199, 201

landscape, 15–16

Larios, Rudi, 335n. 17

La Venta, 39

Le Plongeon, Augustus, 241, 286, 356n. 9, 358n. 12

Lincoln, Charles, 358n. 12

lineages, 24, 200, 230, 272, 371n. 52
building construction and, 28

logographs, 22

Long Count, 52, 355n. 8

long-nosed god, 46, 47

Looper, Matthew, 345n. 2, 350n. 38, 355n. 7, 370n. 43

Lopez, Fernando, 330n. 15

Lopez de Cogolludo, Diego, 257

lords (nobles), 19, 23, 24–25, 89
building projects and, 28
Hanab-Pakal and, 111
itz'at (sages), 89, 104, 119
names of, 319–24

Lords of Death, 36, 116, 144, 154, 156, 210, 211, 213

Lounsbury, Floyd, 328n. 7, 346n. 13, 370n. 45, 378n. 10

lunations, 349n. 30

Macaw Mountain, 163

McGee, Jon, 330n. 17

MacLeod, Barbara, 332n. 29, 342n. 16

Mahucutah, 192, 293

maize, 212, 265
cribs for drying of, 268
houses, 265
tree, 265

Maize God(s), 36–37, 73, 78, 104, 116, 127, 132, 144, 145, 154–56, 158, 162, 210–13, 215, 217, 226, 232, 233, 236, 240–41, 244, 246, 249, 251, 252, 254–55, 265, 285–86, 301, 304, 305, 344n. 31, 345n. 32, 413

Ah-Bolon-Abta Wat'ul-Chatel as, 188

Hanab-Pakal as, 115–17, 127, 132, 377n. 87

Waxaklahun-Ubah-K'awil as, 154, 158

Maler, Teobert, 175, 277, 379nn. 12, 20

Maler's Palace, 86–93

Marcus, Joyce, 327n. 2, 334n. 11, 349n. 31

markets, fairs, and festivals, 18–19, 23, 29, 269–70

Martin, Simon, 327n. 2, 334n. 11, 335n. 19, 349n. 31, 353n. 14

masks, 82–83, 267–69, 271–72, 273–75, 277–78, 279, 282–83

Mathews, Peter, 21, 316, 328n. 7, 333nn. 8, 9, 334n. 11, 349n. 31, 351n. 3

mat house (popol nah), 44, 269–70

Matthews, Paul, 351n. 4

Maudslay, Alfred, 135, 356n. 10

Maya, 13–20
architecture of, see architecture
calendars of, 18–19, 52, 349n. 30, 335n. 8
cities of, see cities and towns
history of, see history
kingdoms of, 23
landscape of, 15–16
myths of, see myths
politics and economics of, 18, 19–20, 23, 170, 253; see also war
writing of, see writing

Mayapan, 20, 43, 204, 354n. 1, 378n. 5

merchants, 19

Mesoamerica, 14–15
historical periods of, see history

Mexican year sign, 413

Mexico, 14, 15, 20

migrations, 20, 202–3, 240, 259, 284, 293, 294, 362n. 19, 363n. 28, 365n. 31, 368n. 34

Milky Way (Sak Beh; White Road), 37, 114, 115, 143, 144, 156, 185, 205, 211, 212, 227, 246, 286

Miller, Arthur, 373–74n. 67

Miller, Mary, 358n. 12, 360n. 15, 372n. 63, 376–77n. 87

mirrors, 222–23, 225, 227

Mixtecs, 200, 301–2, 303

Molina, Augusto, 358n. 12

Molleson, T., 343n. 24

monsters:
Cosmic, 185, 188, 410
mountain, 43, 143, 150, 155, 163, 417
Quadripartite, 415

moon, 349n. 30

Moon Goddess, 168, 212, 215, 413

Morley, Sylvanus Griswold, 356n. 10, 378n. 7

Morris, Chip, 125

mosaics, 30, 31, 199, 262, 268

Mosaic War Serpent, 225, 226, 238, 252, 339n. 40
see also Waxaklahun-Ubah-Kan

Motecuhzoma, 297

Motul de San José, 187

mountain(s), 43, 73, 147–48
caves in, 43
Macaw, 163
monsters, 43, 143, 150, 155, 163, 417
pyramid, 17–18, 24, 29, 39, 43, 303, 305, 315
Snake, 37–40, 43, 70, 73, 74, 180, 204, 205, 217, 224, 240, 254, 303, 368n. 34
Sustenance (Yax-Hal-Witz; First True Mountain), 43, 127, 207, 217, 248, 254
terraces and, 95
ways of writing, 22

Mulchik, 260

murals, 259, 260, 359n. 12
at Chich'en Itza, 232–41

Mut, 111, 321

Mut Itzamna (Itzam-Ye), 46–47, 114, 143, 155, 201, 268, 269, 271, 275, 279, 369n. 36, 412

Mutul (at Dos Pilas), 177

Mutul (Ixlu), 187

Mutul (Tikal), see Tikal

Mysterious Maya, The (Stuart and Stuart), 125

myths, 30, 36–40, 73, 147–48
ballgames and, 36, 37, 38, 73, 116, 144, 207, 210–13, 246, 303, 304, 315
Place of Cattail Reeds in, see Place of Cattail Reeds
see also Creation mythology

politics, 18, 23, 170, 253
   see also war
pop (mat), 136
Popol-K'inich (Mat Head), 166–67, 321, 346n. 8
popol nah (mat house), 44, 269–70
Popol Vuh (The Community Book), 36, 116, 152, 192, 207, 210, 211, 215, 246, 253, 328n. 3, 345n. 2, 346n. 12, 357n. 12, 361n. 16, 370n. 42, 385n. 12
popul (mat), 23–24
portals (*ol*), 45, 50, 146, 166, 193, 222, 246–48, 304, 315, 414
   represented on Hanab-Pakal's sarcophagus, 113
Postclassic period, 16, 20, 51, 295, 360n. 13
   chronology of events in, 59–61
po't, 291
potbelly figures, 154
pottery, 82, 83–84, 88–91, 92–93, 122–23, 135, 294, 303, 351n. 6, 358n. 12, 360n. 15, 362n. 23, 372n. 61, 384n. 9
Powell, Christopher, 35, 329n. 15, 330n. 16
Preclassic period, 16–18, 51
   chronology of events in, 52–53
   Early, 52
   Late, 53, 294
   Middle, 52
pronunciation, key to, 325–26
Proskouriakoff, Tatiana, 134, 178, 180, 327n. 2, 328n. 6, 351n. 6, 358n. 12, 360n. 14
provinces (*tzuk*), 23, 24
psychoduct, 109, 119, 130–31
Puh, 39, 40, 74, 134, 180, 192–93, 200–201, 273, 284, 295, 415
   see also Place of Cattail Reeds
puluy (burning ceremonies), 272
Pusilha, 134
Putun, 201
Puuk, 34, 199, 257, 259
   architectural style of, 262
   see also Uxmal
pyramid(s), 17–18, 24, 26, 29, 39
   Castillo, 205, 206, 217, 225, 227, 254, 368n. 31
   caves and, 43
   at Copan, 135–36

of Feathered Serpent, 39, 284, 289, 337n. 26, 345n. 1, 371n. 55, 373n. 66
Hanab-Pakal's Tomb, 97–98
at Iximche', 301
of Magician (*Adivino*), 260, 262
mountain, 17–18, 24, 29, 39, 43, 303, 305, 315
radial, 40–42, 135–36, 179–82, 205, 368n. 31
temple at Seibal, 179–82
twin-pyramid complexes, 42, 67, 71, 180

Q'aq'awitz (Fire-Mountain), 295, 299
Quadripartite Badge, 113
Quadripartite Monster, 415
quatrefoil, 45, 193
quetzal (*k'uk*), 192
Quetzalcoatl, 198–99, 330n. 23, 356n. 9, 379n. 14, 384n. 7
quincunx, 27
Quintana Roo, 31, 33, 71, 203, 358n. 12, 363n. 28, 376n. 86
Quirigua, 134, 165, 166, 170–71, 328n. 6
Q'umarkah (Utatlan), 295, 296, 297, 299
Q'uq'kumatz (Quetzal-Serpent), 295

rainbow serpent, 131, 217, 373n. 65
rainwater, 46
Recinos, Adrián, 386n. 15
Reese-Taylor, Kathryn, 331n. 24
Reilly, Kent, 39
rituals, 26, 29, 253
   ancestral, 80, 84
   bloodletting, 78, 155, 158, 165–66, 229, 230, 232, 272, 410
   buildings as backdrop for, 23, 26, 27, 29, 30, 40, 42
   burning, 272
   period-ending, 179, 182, 185, 191, 352n. 8
   sacrificial, 84, 93, 241, 246, 249, 253, 272, 310, 315
   scattering of drops, 185
   scenes depicting, 81–82, 91, 92–93
   trance, 78, 83–84, 166, 167, 171, 272
   see also dance

Robertson, Merle Greene, 328n. 7, 370n. 40
Rodrigo, Don, 312, 313, 314, 315
roofcombs, 33–34
roofs, 31–32, 33, 34
Rosalila, 34, 48, 172, 370n. 47
royal belt, 415
Roys, Ralph L., 327n. 3, 363–64n. 30, 382n. 34
Ruz, Alberto, 95, 108–10, 127, 128, 285, 328n. 6, 340n. 2, 342n. 24, 376–77n. 87, 380n. 26

Sabakna lineage, 355n. 7
sacrifice, 84, 93, 241, 246, 249, 253, 272, 310, 315
   decapitation, 246, 253, 310, 315
sages (*itz'at*), 89, 104
sahalob, 89, 342n. 20, 363n. 29, 376n. 81
Sak-Bak-Nakan (White Bone Snake), 45, 113, 114, 115, 415
Sak Beh (Milky Way; White Road), 37, 114, 115, 143, 144, 156, 185, 205, 211, 212, 227, 246, 286
sak beh (white road), 23, 136, 176, 285, 286
Sak Hunal (Jester God), 115, 142, 145, 182, 184, 225, 412
Sak Ixik, 212, 215
Sak-K'uk', Lady (Lady Zac-Kuk), 95, 105–6, 119, 122, 321
sak nah (white house), 44
sarcophagus of Hanab-Pakal, 110–25, 130, 131, 132
   ancestors on sides of, 119–25
   coffin in, 125–28
   imagery on lid of, 110–17
   inscriptions on lid of, 117–19
   lid of, 110–19
Sattler, Mareike, 312, 313
scaffolds, 93, 269
Schele, Linda, 21, 93–94, 131–32, 311–17, 327n. 2, 328n. 7, 329n. 8, 332n. 29, 333nn. 8, 9, 10, 334n. 11, 335n. 19, 337n. 26, 343n. 24, 347n. 21, 348n. 27, 353n. 1, 369n. 37, 372n. 62, 381n. 32, 386n. 15
Schmidt, Peter, 358n. 12, 369nn. 36, 37, 376n. 85

ILLUSTRATION AND PHOTOGRAPH CREDITS

Drawings by George Andrews: Figs. 1.8 (1a, 1b, 4); 3.4 (architectural drawing), 3.5, 3.6 (architectural elevation); 7.3, 7.11, 7.13 (center masks), 7.14–15 (left), 7.18 (right), 7.32, 7.35 (c), 7.39 (left)

Drawings by Lin Crocker-Deletaille: Fig. 1.24 (top row)

Drawings by Ann Dowd: Figs. 4.17, 4.22, 4.27 (front view), 4.29, 4.31–32, 4.34 (left)

Drawings by Barbara Fash: Figs. 1.23 (second row, left); 4.9, 4.16, 4.20, 4.23

Drawing by M. A. Fernandez: Fig. 6.47 (right)

Drawings by Dora Garzón: Figs. 8.5, 8.6 (after George Guillemin)

Drawing by Virginia Greene from *The Ceramics of Tikal: Vessels from the Burials, Caches, and Problematic Deposits*. The University Museum. Philadelphia: University of Pennsylvania, 1983 (fig. 68A): Fig. 2.31

Drawing by Nikolai Grube: Fig. 3.27

Drawings by Matthew Looper: Figs. 6.25–28

Drawings by Peter Mathews: Figs. 1.1, 1.4, 1.20; 3.7; 4.14, 4.21, 4.24, 4.30, 4.35; 5.1, 5.5, 5.8–9, 5.11, 5.13–15, 5.17–19, 5.21–22; 6.18, 6.45 (after rubbings by Merle Greene Robertson); 6.47 (left); 7.10, 7.16, 7.21–23, 7.26–27, 7.30–31, 7.35 (a–b), 7.41–42

Drawings by Garrett Minear: Figs. 6.8, 6.24, 6.40 (architectural drawing)

Drawings by John Montgomery: 2.29 (c); 6.44

Drawings by Kathryn Reese-Taylor: Figs. 2.6; 6.1 (after Kilmartin), 6.2 (after Marquina), 6.22 (after Marquina)

Drawings by Merle Greene Robertson: Figs. 3.16, 3.25–26, 3.31

Drawings by Linda Schele: Figs. 1.5, 1.7, 1.8 (1c, 2, 3), 1.9–11, 1.13–17, 1.19, 1.22–23 (except second row, left), 1.24 (bottom row), 1.25; 2.3, 2.7 (glyph drawing after a drawing by William Coe from *Excavations in the East Plaza of Tikal,* Tikal Report No. 16 by Christopher Jones. The University Museum. Philadelphia: University of Pennsylvania, 1996 [figs. 15L, 15C]), 2.9 (right), 2.11–12, 2.18, 2.20, 2.24–25, 2.26 (detail), 2.29 (a–b); 3.4 (map, adapted from David Byland), 3.10–13, 3.17–24, 3.28–30, 3.33–34; 4.1–2, 4.4, 4.5 (west), 4.7, 4.11–13, 4.15, 4.18–19, 4.25–26, 4.27 (side views), 4.28, 4.34 (right), 4.36, 4.38–39; 5.7 (stuccos after slides provided by Gordon Willey), 5.12; 6.4–5, 6.7, 6.10–11, 6.14–15, 6.17, 6.19–21, 6.29, 6.30–34 (after paintings by Adela Breton), 6.35 (after a painting by Adela Breton and rubbings by Merle Greene Robertson), 6.36–37 (after paintings by Adela Breton), 6.38 (after a painting by Adela Breton and rubbings by Merle Greene Robertson), 6.40 (sculpture), 6.41–43 (after a painting by Adela Breton and rubbings by Merle Greene Robertson), 6.49–50, 6.51 (center panel); 7.20, 7.29 (after Charnay photograph), 7.37–38, 7.39 (right), 7.40 (after photograph by Jeff Kowalski); 8.9–10 (after George Guillemin), 8.12 (after George Guillemin), 8.14 (after George Guillemin), 8.16–17 (after photographs by George Guillemin); all glossary drawings

Drawings by Linda Schele and Peter Mathews: Figs. 1.2, 1.21; 2.2,

2.10; 3.6 (piers), 3.9; 4.33; 5.10, 5.16 (a); 6.39 (after a painting by Adela Breton); 7.18 (flower lattice and "cloud" glyph)

Drawings by Mark Van Stone: Figs. 1.18; 5.3, 5.16 (b); 6.16, 6.48; 7.24, 7.36

Drawings by David Stuart: Fig. 4.5

Drawings by Helen Trik from *The Graffiti of Tikal,* Tikal Report No. 31 by Helen Trik and Michael E. Kampen. The University Museum. Philadelphia: University of Pennsylvania, 1983 (figs. 47, 48, 71, 72, 73): Figs. 2.13, 2.22, 2.34

Drawings by Logan Wagner: Figs. 4.3; 7.9, 7.19

Drawings by Linnea Wren: Fig. 6.51 (outer panels)

Drawings by Nestor Zabala: 1.12; 2.7 (architectural drawing), 2.9 (architectural drawing), 2.26 (architectural drawing); 7.2 (after INAH map of Uxmal), 7.13

Drawings by Nestor Zabala and Dora Garzón: Figs. 5.2, 5.7 (plan and perspective); 7.25; 8.8 (after George Guillemin reconstruction); 8.19 (after George Guillemin)

Drawings by Nestor Zabala and Kathryn Reese-Taylor: Figs. 2.5

All Chapter 6 sculptural drawings by Looper, Mathews, and Schele that are not after Breton are after rubbings by Merle Greene Robertson.

Drawings inked by Matthew Looper: Figs. 4.5, 4.26 (bottom), 4.27–28, 4.36

Drawings inked by Mark Van Stone: Figs. 3.10–13, 3.27; 4.9 (north), 4.16, 4.20, 4.23, 4.26 (top)

Photograph by Daniel Chauche: Fig. 8.15 (right, courtesy of the Fundación G&T, Guatemala)

Photographs by MacDuff Everton: Figs. 2.1, 2.8, 2.15, 2.16 (upper), 2.17 (right), 2.19, 2.21, 2.27–28, 2.30; 3.2–3, 3.8, 3.14–15; 4.6; 5.4, 5.6, 5.20; 6.3, 6.9, 6.12, 6.23, 6.46; 7.4–8, 7.12, 7.17, 7.28, 7.33–34; 8.7, 8.11, 8.13, 8.18, 8.20–22

Photographs by William Ferguson: Figs. 2.4, 2.14; 3.1; 8.4 (courtesy of William Ferguson and the Department of Art and Art History, University of Texas at Austin)

Photographs by George Guillemin: Fig. 2.20 (courtesy of CIRMA, Guatemala); 8.15 (left, courtesy of CIRMA, Guatemala)

Photograph by Peter Harrison: Fig. 2.17 (left)

Photograph by Helene Jorgenson: Fig. 3.34

Photographs by Justin Kerr: Figs. 2.16 (lower), 2.23, 2.32–33, 2.35–36; 6.6, 6.13

Photograph by Bonnie Mayer: Fig. 8.2

Photographs by Linda Schele: Figs. 1.6; 3.32; 4.8, 4.10, 4.13, 4.15, 4.37; 8.1, 8.23–24

Courtesy of the Instituto Hondureño de Antrpologíía e Historia: Figs 4.5, 4.9, 4.16–17, 4.20, 4.22–23, 4.26–29, 4.31–32, 4.34 (left), 4.36, 4.38–39